ABSTRACTS OF WILLS

RECORDED 1752 THROUGH 1800
in

ORANGE COUNTY, NORTH CAROLINA

WILL BOOKS A B and C

PLUS 20 PAGES IN BOOK D


and


202 EARLY MARRIAGES NOT SHOWN

in the

ORANGE COUNTY MARRIAGE BONDS


Compiled by

Ruth Herndon Shields, Chairman
Genealogical Records Committee
Davie Poplar Chapter, NSDAR
Chapel Hill, North Carolina

# ABSTRACTS OF WILLS RECORDED IN ORANGE COUNTY, NORTH CAROLINA

## 1752-1800

*and*

*(202 Marriages Not Shown in the Orange County Marriage Bonds)*

*and*

# ABSTRACTS OF WILLS RECORDED IN ORANGE COUNTY, NORTH CAROLINA

## 1800-1850

By
Ruth Herndon Shields

Two volumes in one

CLEARFIELD

Reprinted for
Clearfield Company, Inc. by
Genealogical Publishing Co., Inc.
Baltimore, Maryland
1991, 1997, 2002


Originally published: Volume I, 1957
(Third Impression, 1966)
Volume II, 1966
Reprinted: Genealogical Publishing Co., Inc.
Baltimore, 1972, 1979
Library of Congress Catalogue Card Number 72-000078
International Standard Book Number 0-8063-0504-5
*Made in the United States of America*

## A FEW FACTS ABOUT ORANGE COUNTY

Orange County was formed in 1752 largely from Granville, partly from Bladen and Johnston.

From Orange were taken:

All of Chatham in 1771.     The bill for the formation of
Part of Guilford in 1771.   Chatham, Guilford and Wake was
All of Wake in 1771       passed at the 1770-1771 Assembly.
All of Caswell in 1777.
All of Person, which was formed from Caswell in 1791.
All of Alamance in 1849.
Part of Durham in 1881.

                                   partly
Randolph and Rockingham Counties were formed/from that part of Guilford which was taken from Orange.

– – – – –

Please read the note following A-184, and one following A225.

– – – – –

## FOREWORD

This book was begun in 1955 as a project of the Genealogical Records Committee of Davie Poplar Chapter, NSDAR, of which I was a member. Memory Alldredge Lester was then Chairman of the Committee, and Edna Allen Lane was Regent of the Chapter. The work was continued in 1956.

Knowing how valuable such a record would be to the many thousands of descendants of Orange County residents now scattered over the United States, I undertook to complete and publish this volume. In this I have been greatly helped by our former Regent, Mrs. Lane.

In the INDEX TO WILLS in the Courthouse at Hillsboro, only the testator, and the legatees are indexed. Many other persons are mentioned in the wills, deeds, and powers-of-attorney recorded in the Will Books. Many children are mentioned who had already received their part of estates, and thus were not legatees. Executors, neighbors, and others are mentioned, and each will has two or more witnesses who sre not indexed in Hillsboro. All such persons are indexed in this book.

This book has been a labor of love, and it is the sincere wish of the Committee that it will prove of value to future genealogists.
                     Ruth Herndon Shields, Chairman

Memory Alldredge Lester (Mrs. Robert M.), Chapter Regent
Edna Allan Lane (Mrs. B.B.), Past Regent

THESE ORIGINAL PAPERS ARE PRESERVED IN THE ARCHIVES IN RALEIGH,
BUT ARE NOT RECORDED IN HILLSBORO.

Will of THOMAS BOWLS of Orange Co., N.C.    Recorded 1789

wife: Elizabeth Bowls

sons    Thomas Bowls & William Bowls receive "land on N. Fork of
        Little River, 220 acres, bought from John Embry.

son: John Bowls            granddau: Sarah Clark

daus: Elizabeth Murdak, Sarah Bowls

Executors: sons Thomas and William Bowls
Witnesses: Jane x Davis, James Latta, Jr.
- - -

"September 24th 1782. The subscriber having business to travel to
the Westward & over the Mountains & thru the uncertainty of life
& and the precarious Traveling at this critical time doth assign
all his Right Title & Claim to her the deed of his land to
Eliz'a Lemon the Relict of Henry Lemon deceas'd in Security for
a certain sum of money that he the subscriber owes her. In
witness whereunto he hath set his hand the day & year above
written.
                    (Signature very bad)

Signed in presence of            James ? Gideaon ? "
Philip Jackson            (Indexed in Archives as I. Gideon.)
Elizabeth Williams
- - -

Will of WILLIAM HANNAH of Orange Co., N.C.    Date of probate
                                              not known.
wife; Sarah Hannah        Date of will: 12 October 1785

son: David Wiley Hannah, under age.

daus: Mary and Sarah

Executors: wife Sarah, and son David Wiley Hannah.
Witnesses: Robert Gray, Jane Mordak.

Note on back of will " Sarah Hannah qualified"(as Executrix).
- - - - -

Will of William Hooper. Dated 24 April 1788 Date of probate
                                            not known.

wife: Anne

daughter Elizabeth, under age

sons: Thomas, William , both under age.
                              - continued -

Pages 1,2,3 and 4 indexed on page 5

Original wills in Archives, but not recorded in Hillsboro.

Will of WILLIAM HOOPER continued -

This will is 12 pages long, devises a number of slaves, and several parcels of land, eight lots in Hillsboro, some property in Charlotte, N.C., etc.

Executors: wife Anne, and sons William and Thomas,
        James Hogg, and Jesse Benton.

Friends to advise executors: Samuel Johnston, Archibald Maclaine, Alfred Moore, James Iredell, and John Huske.

Witnesses: McDonald Hogg, Walter Alves, Helen Hogg.

-----

This is a paper attempting to free a slave, not a will, though it is endorsed on the back "Martha Nial's will". The spelling is confusing, in the body of the instrument it is spelled Nail, the signature is MARTHA x NIAL, the paper is indexed in the Archives as NEIL !

"I, Martha Nail, widow of Robert Nail late of Orange County, N.C." .... frees her slave Lucy and her issue"if the law allows it".... her son-in;law is to attempt to handle the matter if the instrument itself is not sufficient. Lucy is to be no part of her estate in any future will she (Martha) makes.

son-in-law: Daniel Cloud.
                                signed: Martha x Nial
Witnesses: Jonathan Lindly
           Thomas Lindly
Dated 29 (month not clear) 1797, date of probate not shown.

- - -

Will of WILLIAM PHILLIPS of Orange County, N.C. Dated 9 May 1794

wife: Elizabeth

son Joel
son David "tract where he now lives" (100 acres)
son William "tract where he now lives " bounded by Trousdell..
    on Haw River.

daus: Susannah and Pheby and Elizabeth

"My four daughters by my first wife" Mary, Lucy, Hannah, Sarah.

Executors: wife Elizabeth, sons David and Joel
Witnesses: William Rainey, Mary Simmons.

Note on back of will: "Widow and Joel Phillips qualified".

- - -

Pages 1,2,3 and 4 indexed on 5

Original will in Archives, but not recorded in Hillsborough.

Will of SUSANA RAY of Orange County, N.C.  Dated 11 Oct 1794,
daughter: Mary Ray
date of probate not
on will

Mother is to raise Mary Ray and "school her". If Mary dies,
estate is to go to testator's brothers and sisters (names not
stated). Mother is to have use of estate to care for Mary.

Executors: "Two brothers-in-law William Ray and Joseph Buckner ?
(or Brecken ?)"
Witnesses: Jno. Baker, Agnes (x) Few ? Margaret Baker.
Note on back of will "Executors qualified".
- - -

Will of WILLIAM RAY of Orange County, N.C. Dated 11 March 1794,
wife: Martha
date of probate not
on will

sons: Robert, John, William, James      (Testator has sold land
to John Homes, son of
daus: Christian, Elizabeth, Isabell    Robert Homes.)

Executors: wife, and Benjamin Rainey.
Witnesses: William Rainey, Mary (x) Rainey, James Stockedd.

Probate of the two wills below in the Court Minutes for Orange
County, N.C., but the wills are not in GRIMES or in the will
books in Hillsborough.

Court of July 1754. "On motion of Richard Parker the last will
and testament of SAMUEL HARLAN and the codicil annexed thereto
was proved in open court by the oath of James Vassey (?) and
affirmation of Valentine Hollingsworth, Quaker. Elizabeth Harlan widow of the deceased and Aaron Harland, Executors thereof,
qualified as such ..."

Court of July 1754.  The will of JOSEPH HARDIN deceased was
proved by the oath of Benjamin Martin. Elizabeth Harlan, widow,
appeared and qualified as Executrix.

Also available ABSTRACTS OF ORANGE COUNTY, N. C. WILLS 1800-1850.
Price $6.50.
and
ABSTRACTS OF THE MINUTES OF THE COURT OF PLEAS AND QUARTER
SESSIONS OF ORANGE COUNTY, N.C. 1752-1766 - completely indexed.

abstracted by Ruth Herndon Shields, published April 1966

The MINUTES 1752-1766 cover the first fourteen years of county
records, two large volumes with a total of 1045 pages.

Pages 1, 2, 3 and 4 are indexed on page 5

4

Five abstracts of Orange County wills from "GRIMES".

J. Bryan Grimes' wonderful book NORTH CAROLINA ABSTRACTS of
WILLS 1690-1760 lists just seven wills for Orange County.Of
these seven only two are now on record in the will books in
Hillsborough, and the originals have been lost. They are the
wills of MICHAEL ELLETT (Grimes says ELIOT), and JOSEPH WADE.

Grimes, page 124 Will of JAMES FORASTER. Dated 5 Sept 1755,
                                            proved Dec 1755
sons: William and James, land on Eno River
sons: Benjamin and Thomas,"my plantation"
son-in-law: John Manning, land on Eno River
Executrix: wife Ann. Witnesses: Pat McCulloch, Hugh Wood.
The Clerk of Court was James Watson.
No mention of the probate of this will is in the Court Minutes.

Grimes, page 358 Will of JOHN STANFIELD. Dated 4 Aug 1755,
                                            proved Sept 1755
wife: Hannah
sons: John (land on Haw River), Thomas (land known as the
      Meeting House Tract), Samuel ("plantation whereon I now
      live"). Thomas and Samuel also get land near the Rich
                                                       Hills.
Executors: John Jones, Joseph Maddox.
Witnesses: Thos. Lindley, Hugh Laughlin, Thos. Lowe.
(probate of this will not in Court Minutes but items about the
estate in Minutes for June 1759 and March 1760)
- - -

Grimes, page 395 Will of HENRY WEBB. Dated 10 Jan 1756,
                                         proved March 1759
sons: Wentworth and John.

Executrix: wife Elizabeth Webb. Witnesses: George Laws,
Witnesses: George Laws, Elias Downs.
(Probate of this will in Minutes for March 1759.)
- - -

Grimes, page 171 Will of JAMES HOPKINS. Dated 8 Feb 1759,
                  of St Mathews Parish   proved March Court 1759.
"Children" mentioned but not named.      (Probate is in Minutes)

Executors: William Hopkins,William Phillips, John Hopkins.
Witnesses: Allicksander Ferguson,John Dobbins,David Smith.
- - -

Grimes, page 246 Will of ROBERT MELTON. Dated 24 April 1759,
                                           proved Nov 1759
sons: James, Nathaniel
      Nathan, Isesum, Ancel
Executor: son Nathan Melton.
Witnesses: James Sellers, Mary Stratton. Clerk: James Watson.
( Probate of this will is in Court Minutes for June 1759, by
"oath of Richard Parker one of the witnesses" (he was an attorney). Mary Stratton and James Sellers were summoned to appear
at next court as witnesses.)
- - -                           Pages 1, 2, 3 & 4 indexed on 5

— — — — — — — — — — — — —

Note by R.H.S.  A woman's name
indexed thus - Mary (..) Smith -
means that she is married, and
that I do not know her maiden
name.

— — — — — — — — — — — — —

The will of SARAH COTTON of
Northampton County is among the
Orange County, N.C. wills in
the State Archives. It appears
to be a copy, and was probably
used in a suit concerning an
estate settlement. Since it is
not an Orange County will I did
not abstract it. R.H.S.

— — —

ABSTRACTS OF ORANGE COUNTY, N.C. WILL BOOKS A, B and C.


A-1 Will of MICHAEL ELLETT. Dated 5 Oct 1756, proved 10 Dec 1756.

Sole heir: Wm Phillips, no relationship stated.
"A saddle & 4 shillings to be demanded of Joseph Bugg...
7 shillings, etc to be demanded of David Phillips ...
1 pound 10 shillings to be demanded of James Lindsey ...
3 shillings 4 pence to be demanded of Samuel Mains."

Executor: Wm. Phillips.
Witnesses: Wm. Offill, James Hopkins, Wm. Hopkins.
– – –

A-2 Will of CHARLES FOSHEE.    see A-62 for same will.
                        Dated 23 Nov 1757, proved Dec 1757.
wife: Susanna
sons: William and Charles Foshee, get land.
After wife's death - everything else to be divided among
"my children".
Executors: Joseph Foshee, and wife Susannah.
Witnesses: Wm (x) Marsh, Elmore or Elmon (x) George.
– – –

A-3 Will of JONATHAN FINCHER. Dated 20 March 1757,
                                    proved May 1757.
wife: name not stated, ten shillings.
sons: "eldest son" name not stated, but called Joshua in Codicil.
      Jonathan, Richard, Joseph, Benjamin (he is to be bound to
daughters: Mary, Hannah                  Joseph Mattox).

No Executors named.
Witnesses: Benj. Cate, Charles Jonas, (Margaret (x) Whitehead.
– – –

A-5 Will of DUNCAN BOHANNON   Dated 1760

wife: Susannah.              sons: John, Benjamin, Richard

daus: Frankey Boyd, Mary Bohannon
granddaughter: Betty Bohannon

son Benjamin "one survey of land at the mouth of Second creek
of New Hope joining land formerly John Rhodes" ..."

Executors: sons Benjamin and Richard, and John Brantley.
Witnesses: Hannah Brantley, Jos. Fuller, Jos. Brantley.

A-7 Will of JOSHUA HADLEY. Dated 20 Sept 1760, proved Nov 1760.

wife: Patience
sons: Joseph, Joshua, Thomas, Simon
      Benjamin gets "land on James River in Virginia"
daus: Ruth Marshel, Mary Piggott, Sarah Ford,
      Hannah, Deborah, Katherine ? or Hatherner ?
                                        - continued -

8

Book A, page 7 Will of Joshua Hadley continued-

Executors: wife Patience, son Joshua
Witnesses: Simon Di....., Wm. Holmes, Francis Dorset.

- - -

A-9 Will of AARON VAN HOOK. Dated 10 May 1760, proved
Aug 1760.
wife: Katherine

sons: Lawrence, David.

Executors: wife, and sons Lawrence and David.
Witnesses: Lidia Van Hook, Bridget Van Hook, Thos. Morgan.

- - -

A-11  Will of MARY ANN CURRIE. Dated 20 Sept 1759, proved
Nov 1759.
sons: John, James.        daus: Margaret, Mary.

Executors: sons John and James
Witnesses: Edward Nash

- - -

A-12  Will of HENRY MAYNOR. Dated 3 March 1760, proved
March 1760.
"loving wife", name not stated.

daus: Rachel, Mary, Elizabeth, Susanna, Betty

Executors: friends Anthony Champess, and John Marshal.
Witnesses: Charles Davis, John Pike, William Marshall.

- - -

A-13  Will of JAMES ALSTON. Dated 28 Feb 1760, proved
2 May 1760.
wife: Christian        sons: John, James

daus; Mary, Charity, Sarah      brother: Joseph Jphn Alston

"... that Warham Glenn make my son John a deed for land
where Warham Glenn and Ann Downs lived .."
he mentions "John Woods line" ...! Josiah Sumner to pay "

"son John land on Neuse River and 2 lots in Newbern ...
land in Chowan Co. on Bird's Creek where my father lived ...
son James land in Halifax and Granville counties"

Executors: sons John and James
Witnesses: Warham Glenn, James Alston, James Boyd,
- - -        Thos. Hines

A-17 Will of MARY SHEPHEARD, Widow.   Dated 5 May 1761,
                                                            proved Aug 1761
son: Jacob Slater
daughters: Mary Whitehead, Mary Dennis
granddaughter: Mary Dennis

"to Isaac Dennis .. to children of John Dennis & John Slater"

Executors: John Dennis, John Slater.
Witnesses: Isaac Jackson, Samuel Maury, Samuel Jackson.

– – –

A-16 Will of RICHARD BRACEWELL, BRASWELL or BRANWELL.
                                  Dated Aug 1761, proved Aug 1761
wife: Joyce
daus: Mary, Tabitha
sons: Valentine Jacob, Richard William

He devises land on S side of Haw River bought of H. Mackneel.

Executors: wife,"loving friend Hector Mackneel, brother Henry."
Witnesses: Thomas Tucker, Henry Bracewell, John Records.

– – –

A-19 Will of THOMAS BERRY. Dated 10 April 1761, proved May 1761

wife:Elizabeth          son-in-law: James Morrow

sons: James, Thomas, Benjamin
daus: Elizabeth, Margaret Morrow, Nancy
grandchildren: William & Jane Berry children of Wm Berry dec'd.

No executor named. Witnesses: Paul Harmon, Wm. McMath.

– – –

A-23 Will of JOHN BOOKER. Dated 18 Aug 1761, proved Nov 1761.

wife: Patience    dau: Patience    son: James

No executor named.
Witnesses: Wm. Brevard, Susannah Brown, Mary Richards.

– – –

A-25 Will of ADAM MASON. Dated 4 Aug 1763, proved Nov 1763.

sons: Anthony. Francis, Tobias, Jacob
daughters: Elizabeth, Anne Phillipina
Executors: sons Tobias and Jacob.
Witnesses: Francis Nash, Ralph McNair, Phillip Jackson.

– – –

A-27  Will of JOHN BONNEY. Dated 10 April 1761, proved
                                              May 1761.
"loving wife", name not stated.

sons: Richard, Simon, Daniel, John, William.

Executors: wife,"with help of my son John".
Witness: William Clark

- - -

A-27  Will of JAMES COLLINS. Dated 4 Dec 1762, proved
                                              May 1763.
wife: Elizabeth (writing not clear)

sons: James (oldest), John

No executor named.        Witness: Elizabeth ..(?)

- - -

A-27  Will of JOHN COLLINS. Dated 4 Nov 1762, proved
                                              Nov 1762.
brother: "all mother left me to go to my brother William
         Collins"

sister: Catherine

Executor: brother-in-law Enos Ellmore
Witnesses: Lawrence Thompson, Thos. Thompson, Enos Ellmore.

- - -

A-29  Will of TIMOTHY TERRELL. Dated 1 Feb 1763, proved
                                              Feb 1763.
wife mentioned, name not stated.

sons: Solomon, Micajah, Nimrod (under age), Simon (minor),
      Daniel, Richard, Aron, Moses (under age).

daus: Jemima, Ruth, Millie, Mary, Betty, Cuzziah,

Executors: wife, and John Pills (?).

Witnesses: Abraham Teague, Jos McLester, Moses Teague.

- - -

A-31  Will of WILLIAM BROWN. Dated  18 Feb 1764, proved
                                              May 1764.
heirs, relationship not stated:
Margaret Ray, Wm. Brown McClintock,
Janette and David Alsoms

No Executor named.
Witnesses: Geo. Johnston, John Kornegay, Thos. Holygam (?).

- - -

A-32   Will of WILLIAM FORBIS. Dated 28 Nov 1763,
                                        proved Feb 1764
wife: Margaret

sons: William, Hugh, George.
      After 3 years George is to be bound to a trade.

"other 6 young children...."

Executors: Andrew Finley, William Willis.
Witnesses: John Willis, James Mathews, Martha Willis,
           Thomas Willis, Hugh Willis.
"Approved: Margaret Forbis, John Forbis, Thomas Morgan,
           Rachel Forbis, Arthur Forbis.

— — —

A-34 Will of JOEL BROOKS. Dated 26 Aug 1764, proved Sept 1764

wife: Mary                    son: John

Executor: brother James
Witnesses: Wm. Brown, Charles Stout, Joseph Kyes.
This will was very hard to read, but the Court Minutes give
the names of the witnesses in the probate of the will.
This BROOKS family is given in the BROOKS genealogy by
Mrs. Ida Brooks Kellam.

— — —

A-36 Will of WILLIAM (x) LOUNG (LONG) Dated 6 April 1764,
                                        proved May 1764
wife: Catrin

sons: "oldest son George", & "youngest son" name not stated.

Executors: Charles Johnson, David Craig.
Witnesses: Mary Mitchell, John Craig.
The handwriting of the Clerk is extremely hard to read, it
looks beautiful, but the elaborate capital letters are much
like one another. OLDS has this name as SAWNEY, and I read
it as YOUNG, but the Court Minutes prove that LONG is correct.

— — —

A-37 Will of DANIEL NORRIS. Dated 27 May 1760, proved
                                        Aug 1765
wife: Mathews          son-in-law: Thomas Beale

No relationship stated to: Evan Jones, Elizabeth Hart.

Executors: wife Mathews, and son-in-law Thomas Beale.
Witnesses: John Thompson, Peter Bornal, Mary Jones.

— — —

Book A, page 39  Will of HUGH LAUGHLIN. Dated 24 Feb 1765,
                                        Proved 26 Feb 1765.
wife: Mary            brother: William Laughlin

daus: Elizabeth, Mary, Rebecca, Charrity, Joannah, Susanna.

Testator owns a Mill.      No witnesses. No Executors.

Proved 26 Feb 1765 by the oath of John Laughlin.

- - -

A-45  Will of JOHN (x) THOMAS. Dated 24 April 1765, proved
                                                    May 1766.
wife: Elizabeth            daughter Mary

sons: eldest son John, James

he says "my three children"      No Executor named.

Witnesses: Henry Ledbetter, John (x) Hamlett, Ann (x) Hamlett

- - -

A-42  Will of JAMES ROONEY (or RONEY), of St. Matthew's
      Parish, Orange Co., N.C. Dated 2 Aug 1765, proved
                                        2nd Tuesday, Nov 1765.
sons: Benjamin, Thomas

daus: Elizabeth, Ann.    He says "my four children".

Sole Executor: John Sample
Witnesses: James McCarley, Mary Sample, John Bul....

- - -

A-44  Will of ANDREW CALDWELL. Dated 26 March 1765,
                                  proved 2nd Tuesday, May 1766.
wife: Jannet

sons: Samuel, William.
daus: Mary, Elizabeth.      "my four children"

Executors: wife Jannet, and James Freeland.
Witnesses: Alex'r Mebane, Jno. Sample, A..... Sanford.

- - -

A-45  Will of CHARLES (x) SINKLER. Dated 5 June 1766
                                  Proved 2nd Tues. Aug 1766.
wife: Ann              dau: Catherine
son: Charles

"All my children, being seven in number".

Executors: wife and "well beloved friend John Buchanon of
            Augusta Co., Va." to settle affairs in Augusta
            Co., Va., and wife and "my trusty friend Amoss
            Evans to settle affairs in this province."
(His land in Augusta Co., Va. was on South Fork of Hototin
River, called Indian River.)        -continued-

A-45. Witnesses: Joseph McLester, Amoss Evans, James Harvey.
- - -

A-48  Will of THOMAS MELER or MILES, Dated 14 March 1766
                or MILLS.              Proved 2nd Tues. May'66.
wife: Hannah

sons: Aquilla, Moses, Abraham, John, Thomas, Peter, Jacob.

daus: Hannah Slade, Pottiet ,            No Executor named.

Witnesses: Lewis Bartow, Isaac (x) Robuck,Joseph Peterson.
- - -

A-49  Will of HUGH (x) SINON. Dated 1 June 1766, proved
                                              Nov 1766.
He seems to be a bachelor, no relationships to heirs given.

Thomas Lindsey, Jr. 525 acres on Pine Hill Creek.
William Welsh, 125 acres, same location.
"Thomas Lindsey, Sr. and his wife Ruth should have my slave
Sarah".
William Lindsey, son of James Lindsey, Daniel McCavoy,
Owen Dowd (?), Samuel Stuart.

"If my brothers or brothers-in-law come in from Ireland"
they are to receive some property.

Executors: "my friends Samuel Stuart, William Lindsey".
Witnesses: Michael (X) Wufner (?), Thomas Lindsey, Sr.
- - -

A-52  Will of William Asten. Dated 16 Nov 1766, proved
                                              Feb 1767.
wife: Mary

sons-in-law: Peter Downey, Archibald McLeroy

grandsons: William Asten Downey, Thomas Stinky (?) McLeroy,
           William McBride

Executors: wife, and Archibald McLeroy and George Finley.
Witnesses: David Fulton, Andrew Dark, Henry Cowden.
- - -

A-53  Will of WILLIAM COX. Dated 20 Jan 1767, proved 2nd Tues
                                              Feb 1767.
sons: Harmon Cox, land on east side of Deep River
      William Cox, land on west side of Deep River
      John Cox, land lying on the Mill Creek adjoining Wm.
                                              McFarson's
      Solomon Cox, land "on Little Brush Creek where Benja-
      min William's formerly lived"
      Thomas Cox gets the mill.  He says "my five sons".

-continued-

A-53 Will of WILLIAM COX continued

daus:   "Rebecca Dixon in Pennsylvania, 4 shillings"
        "Mary Lindley wife to James Lindley"
        "Martha Terrell wife to William Terrell"
        "Marjory Nicholas wife to Isaac Nicholas"
        "Catherine Hunt wife to Elizor Hunt"

Executors: "My trusty and well beloved son and cousin,
          William Cox and Isaac Cox."
Witnesses: John Cox, William Moffitt (?), John Allen.

— — —

A-56 Will of JOHN (x) FIELDS. Dated 16 Nov 1766, proved
                                    Feb 1767
wife: name not stated

son John one-half of estate
son Roger other half of estate

Abeneasar Starnes and Ann Starnes his wife and Roger Murphy
"should have the care of the child" - the oldest to live
with the Starnes - the younger to live with Roger Murphy,Sr.
If Murphy Sr should die, he is to live with Roger Murphy,Jr.

Witnesses: William Ward, James Morgan, Roger Murphy, Jr,
          Rachel (x) Fields.

— — —

A-57 Will of ISAAC HOLDING. Dated 13 Jan 1767, proved
                                    Feb 1767
wife: Sarah        father: Thomas Holding

"well beloved brother John Douglass..."
"loving brother Thomas Holding ..."
"beloved brother John Kelly ..."

sons: Thomas Holding, Isaac Holding

If sons die without issue land goes to Margaret Douglas,
daughter of John Douglas, Ann Holderness daughter of John
Holderness, Fanny Wood daughter of John Wood, John Holderness son of Thomas Holderness, Sr, and Thomas Kelly son of
John Kelly.

Executors: John Douglas and Sarah Holding.
Witnesses: John McVinchey, Benjamin Fincher,
          Richard Fincher.

— — —

A-59 Will of JOSEPH AKIN. Dated 4 Jan 1766, proved Feb 1767

sons: Thomas, Joseph Akin.

daus: Mary Akin, Suillah ?, Sarah, "my three daughters"

"Joseph Ostin - 370 acres of land lying on the head of San-
dy River in Hallyfax CO. in Va. which he bought of me."
                                             - continued -

A-59 Will of JOSEPH AKIN continued -

"George Jefferson - 600 acres on Lick Fork of Moore's Creek in Orange County, N.C. which he bought of me."

Executor: "Thomas Asgah living in Hallyfax County in Va."
Witnesses: Alex (x) Montgomery, John (x) Luis, Sam Barton.

- - -

A-62 Will of CHARLES FOSHEE.    Dated 23 Nov 1757,
                                proved, 2nd time, Feb 1759.
wife: Susannah

"... my two sons" William Foshee and Charles Foshee get land

After wife's death everything else is to be sold and "divided among all my children."

Executors: Susannah Foshee, Joseph Foshee.
Witnesses: William (x) Marsh, Elmon or Elmore George.

Note by R.H.S. Evidently there were two copies of this will. Neither copy was ever signed. Susabbah proved the will in Dec 1757, and qualified as Executrix. Joseph Foshe proved the will again in Feb 1759, and renounced his right as Executor. He began a suit against Susannah, accusing her of wasting the estate, but dropped it. Susannah died in 1761, and Joseph Foshee was appointed Administrator of her estate and of Charles'. She seems to have been Charles' second wife, as Joseph Foshee was appointed Guardian to the orphan daughter of Charles and Christian Foshee. There are several items about these two estates in the Orange County Court Minutes. I have abstracted and published these Court Minutes for the years 1752 through 1766--see page 5.

- - -

A-60 Will of ALEXANDER STUART or STEWART   Dated 18 Aug 1764,
                                           proved Feb 1767
wife: Elizabeth

eldest son: Robert, under age
youngest son: John, under age

daughter: Abigal Stuart

Executors: William Piggott, Jeremiah Piggott.
Witnesses: John Pike, Samuel Pike.

- - -

A-63 Will of SAMUEL (x) LEHMAN. Dated 18 Oct 1766,
                                proved May 1767
wife: Priscilla

son: Gorabebel? Lehman

Executrix: wife Priscilla.
Witnesses: Wm (x) Barker, Lewis (x) Barker, Chris. Woodward.

- - -

A-64 Will of ADAM ROGER. Dated --, proved May 1767

Wife, her name not stated, is pregnant...."child that my
     wife is with now ..."

daughter: Mary

"brother John's children, William and John .."

"Guardian over this my estate brother Hugh Roger and
Robert Rea."

Executors: brother Hugh Roger and Irabel or Isabel Roger.
Witnesses: John Patton, Elinore Rogers.
(Proved by John Patton and Eleanor Rogers.)

— — —

A- 66 Will of THOMAS CATE. Dated 5 Nov 1765, proved May
                                                    1767
wife: Elizabeth

son: Richard "plantation whereon I now live"

daughter Sarah      "daughters" mentioned

granddaughter Ann " daughter of my son Thomas .."

Executors: sons Thomas and Joseph.
Witnesses: William Smith, Eliza beth (x) Cate.

— — —

A-67 Will of JOSEPH WADE. Dated 3 Jan 1757, proved Aug
                                                    1767
wife: Sarah

sons: John, James

daus: Mary Strawther, Susannah Hart, Elizabeth Talley,
     Lucy Powell, Sarah Fountain

grandson: Joseph Strawther

Executors: "son Joseph Wade and my son-in-law Joseph Powel".
Witnesses: William Bradford (GRIMES says this is Burford),
     Samuel Burton.

— — —

A-68  **Will** of DAVID HALLIBURTON. Dated 3 Jan 1767, proved
Aug 1767.
Wife, name not stated, is pregnant.

Sons: Thomas, David, John, William, all under 21 years.

"son Charles which is now a cripple" to be educated.

Executors: wife, and George Moore.
Witnesses: John (x) Adams, Thomas (x) Beach (?),
Susannah Adams.

— — —

A-70  Will of  **WALTER**(x) THEDFORD. Dated 13 August 1767,
proved Nov 1767.
wife: Rebecca

sons: Josias (eldest), William (land on Stony Creek).

dau: Deborah

son-in-law: William Williams.

Executors: wife Rebecca, and eldest son Josias.
Witnesses: Abigal Bracken, John Baker.

— — —

A-72  Will of WILLIAM BASKETT. Dated 17 July 1767, proved
Nov 1767.
Wife: Ruth Baskett

"my three daughters Mary, Elizabeth and Ruth, as they marry
or arrive to the age of twenty years"

sons: Thomas, William.

Executors: "trusty and beloved friends William White and
John Baskett".
Witnesses: Jane (x) Dael (?), Dianah (x) Collingsworth.

— — —

A- 74  Will of SOLOMON DEBOW. Dated 1 Sept 1767, proved
Nov 1767.
wife: Hannah

Sons: John, tract of land lying on Winn's Creek.
Frederick, land on Cain Creek and land on Hyco Creek.
Benjamin (now under 21)
-continued-

A-74   Will of SOLOMON DEBOW continued-

daus: Hannah, Jane (unmarried)
"daughters Ann, Mary, Sarah and Elizabeth to have reasonable schooling" etc.

Executors: wife Hannah, and son John Debow.
Witnesses: John Pearson, Rachel (x) Gold, L.?. V.Hook.

- - -

A-76   Will of Michael Holt. Dated 31 June 1765, proved
                                                        Nov 1767.
wife: Elizabeth             son: Peter

"my children" name and number not stated.

Executors: "my dear son Michael Holt, Junior, and
           Nicholas Holt, Junior."
Witnesses: John Butler, William Carlisle.

- - -

A-77   Will of WILLIAM (x) SERJANT, SENIOR.

Dated 11 Feb 1768, proved April 1768.

wife: Sarah                 son-in-law: Joseph Gold

sons: Joseph, Thomas, James, Stephen

dau: Elizabeth "100 acres which I purchased of Thos. Bailey".

Executors: Sons Stephen Bryant and Joseph Gold".
Witnesses: John Lea, Sarah Serjant.

- - -

A-79   Will of FREDERICK (x) NALL. Dated 7 March 1768,
                                        proved April 1768.
Wife: Martelenor Nall

Executrix: wife
Witnesses: John Watson, John Campbell, Peter Wolf,
           .. ?.. Bavin.

- - -

A-80   Will of CHARLES (x) MURROW. Dated 16 Dec 1767,
                                        proved April 1768.
cousin: Robert Barnhill, one half of estate.

"well beloved brother Adam Murrow" other half of estate if
he comes to America.

Executor: cousin Robert Barnhill.
Witnesses: James Humphill, Thomas Humphill, John Hood (?).

- - -

A-81  Will of ALEXANDER MONTGOMERY. Dated 27 July 1767
                                     proved April 1768.
wife; name not stated

son: Alexander Montgomery

son-in-law: Robert Barnett in Amhurst Co., Va. "my planta-
            tion that lyeth in Rockfish settlement".

son: William Montgomery 5 shillings.

"rest of my children namely John, Elizabeth, and my daughters Ann and Mary ... one shilling sterling".

Sole Executrix: "well beloved wife".
Witnesses: William Robinson, Charles Crawford, Wm. Maxwell.
- - -

A-83  Will of JAMES (x) HAYGOOD. Dated 20 Feb 1768,
                                 proved 29 July 1768.
Wife: name not given

sons: George, Benjamin, James, William.

dau: Rebecca.

Executors: wife, and William Partin.
Witnesses: Philip Gee, George (x) Haygood, William (x) Partin.
- - -

A-84  Will of JOHN (x) McCALLISTER. Dated 11 July 1768
                                    proved July 1768.
wife: Rosannah

sons: James, Joseph

unmarried daus: Sarah, Mary, Martha, Margaret McCallister.
married daus: Margaret Patent? I .?.., Elizabeth.

Executors: brother James McCallister,
           son-in-law Andrew Patent? or Poteat ?
Witnesses: Henry Petillo, Cairns Tinnin, Margaret (x) Tinnin.
- - -

A-86  Will of PETER (x) POOR. Dated 31 May 1768, proved
                                          Oct. 1768.
wife: Elizabeth

son: Peter Poor (under age)

daus: Mary Ann, Ann Phillipinia, Eva Catarina, Elizabeth,
      "my four daughters", (all under age).

Guardians: John Oliver, George Fogleman.
Executrix: wife.
Witnesses: Josias Mogar, Joseph Bogs, Anthony ...?...
- - -

A-89  Will of ISAAC (x) GREASON. Dated 10 Sept 1768,
                              proved Oct 1768.
wife: Margaret

sons: Nicholas, Jacob "land on west of Beaver Creek", John.

daus: Margaret Loew, Unitie Lionburger.

Sole Executor: son Nicholas Greason.
Witnesses: George Fogleman, John Oliver.

— — —

A-92  Will of JOHN McCOY, of St. Mathew's Parish, Orange Co.

Dated 4 April 1767, proved October 1768.

Wife, name not stated.

"oldest son Francis", daughter Elizabeth, "younger children".

Guardian: "well beloved friend, Robert Rea".
Executor: W. McCoy.
Witnesses: John Armstrong, Matthew J. Cobey (?).

— — —

A-93  Will of WILLIAM BORING. Proved 11 October 1768.

On his death bed William Boring orally left to Charles and
Joseph Boring, brothers, a slave, etc.

John Currie and James Culbertson swore to the above before
William Lee, Justice of the Peace, on June 20 1768.

— — —

A-94  Will of JOHN McCOMB. Dated --, proved April 1769.

wife: Rachel                wife's sons: John, William

"my son Jesse"

daus: Mary, Jane, Darcas, Harrow (?),
      Sarah, Margaret, Elizabeth

Executors: John McComb, Rachel McComb, Mary McComb,
           Jane McComb, Jesse McComb, Darcas McComb.
Overseer of Executors: James Allison.
Witnesses: John Smith, Elizabeth Smith.

— — —

A-95  Will of OWEN THOMAS. Dated 17 March 1769,
                                   proved April 1769.
wife: Mary

"six small children: Hester, Joana, Lewis, Jonathan,
John, Elizabeth".                -continued-

A-95 Will of OWEN THOMAS continued-

brother James Thomas "as long as he lives with them" (the children).

sons: William, James, George, Michal.

daus: Mary Hard (or Hart), Ann Wilks.

Executors: John Gray, Thomas Cate son of Robert.
Witnesses: John Baskett, Frederick Williams.

— — —

26 Dec 1768
A-97  Will of JOHN RECORD. Dated /  , proved April 1769.

wife: Comfort          dau: Mary Record

sons: David, John,  Sion

Executors: wife Comfort, and Joseph Brantley Idison.
Witnesses: James Brantley, Wm. Brantley.

— — —

A-99  Will of THOMAS PETTEY. Dated 26 Aug 1766,
                                    proved July 1769.
wife: Mary          dau: Martha Pettey

sons: Thomas, land on George Herndon's line
      Reubin, John. All the sons seem to be under age.

Friend Robert Marsh to care for children if wife dies
before children come of age.

"youngest children, Thomas and Martha".

Executors: Robert Marsh, James Younger.
Witnesses: James Stewart, Robert Carlile.

— — —

A-101  Will of WILLIAM WALKER. Dated  24 March 1769,
                                    proved July 1769.
"beloved wife"

sons: James, John, William, Abraham, Alexander.

Testator mentions money received in Pennsylvania.

Executors: John Robertson, John Corry.
Witnesses: John Corry, Jr., Shasana (x) Corry.

— — —

A-102  Will of SAMUEL REED. Dated 4 Sept 1765, proved
                                    July 1769.
wife: Mary

"Samuel Stewart now living with me".. to him at the age of 21...

Elizabeth Jones ... to be of age at 18          -continued-

A-102  Will of SAMUEL REED continued-

Executors: wife Mary, and Thomas Lindley, Sr.
Witnesses: Wm. Lindley, John Maroon.

— — —

A-105  Will of JOHN GEER. Dated 12 Aug 1769, proved Jan 1770.

beloved wife, name not stated

sons: David, Frederick, William, John.

daus: Mimma, Tabitha, Mary Burnett, Siny (?), Sarah.

son-in-law: James Roper.

Witnesses: Jacob Garrard, Jr, Michael Dent.

— — —

A-106  Will of ROBERT DONALDSON. Dated 20 March 1770,
                              proved April 1770.
wife: Hannah

sons: Thomas (married), Robert

daus: Margaret, wife of William Ray
      "Undutiful daughter Mary 2 shillings"
    " Hannah, Elizabeth, Jean, Ritteren (?), Sarah and
      Robert, I allow equal shares."
Executors: wife Hannah, & Wm. Ray. Overseer: Thomas Donaldson.
Witnesses: Honor Nicks, Elizabeth Thomas, Thomas Douglass.

— — —

A-107  Will of SAMUEL YARBOROUGH. Dated 5 Nov 1769,
                                  proved April 1770.
wife: Sarah

sons: William, "land in Amelia Co., Va. whereon his grand-
      father lived lying between Cold and Nottoway ... like-
      wise land on Tarr River adjoining Robert Bumpas..."

      Samuel, John, both are under 21 years of age.

daus: Elizabeth Yarborough, Sarah Yarborough, Lewcey Yar-
      borough, all under 18 years of age.

Executors: wife Sarah, Wm. Yarborough, John Bumpass.
Witnesses: Abraham Womack, Jr., Isaac Johnston, James Evans.

— — —

A-109  Will of ROBERT MOTHEREL. Dated 8 Jan 1769,
                                proved April 1770.
wife: name not stated

sons: John, Samuel, Joseph, Robert "100 acres each when
      they come of age".
                              -continued-

A-109 Will of ROBERT MOTHEREL contiued-

Executors: wife, and David Mitchell
Witnesses: James Culbertson, Jr., John Carson, David Porter.

— — —

A-111  Will of WILLIAM PEGGOTT. Dated 9 Feb, proved
                                        April 1770.
wife: Sarah

sons: eldest son John, youngest son William "all land bought
      of Richard Henderson on middle fork of Rocky River ..
      adjoining Thos Ransom's line" ...

      "second son Samuel"; "third son Jeremiah".

"six daughters, Abigail, Marjory, Sarah, Marah, Elizabeth,
Rachel."

Executors: Jeremiah and Benjamin Peggott.
Witnesses: Henry Underwood, Thos. Molborough, Simeon Adamson.

This will is signed William Piggotte.

— — —

A-112  Will of JAMES TALBERT. Dated  5 Oct 1769,
                                    proved April 1770.
wife: Mary

"My father and mother to live where they are now without
being disturbed."

sons: oldest son John to be bound to his uncle Joseph to
      learn tailor's trade at age of fifteen.

      sons Benjamin and Loran (?) to be bound to him when
      fifteen till they are twenty-one years of age.

daughter mentioned but name not stated," 3 sons and 1 dau."

Executors: "loving brothers Abraham Miles and George Sea".
Witnesses: Thomas McNeil, George See. (Possibly Lee)

— — —

A-114  Will of JOSEPH DIXSON. Dated 5 Dec 1769,
                                proved April 1770.
wife: Mary

sons: Nathan, Stephen
dau: Anne Bailey wife of Caleb
sons: Solomon land on Terrell's Creek on waters of Haw River
      adjoining John Lambral's land.
      Jesse land bought of John May.
      Eli land bought of Howil Brown, adjoining Geo. Dixson.
      Samuel and Joseph to enter into full possession of
      their land when they reach 21 years of age.
                    -continued-

24

A-114  Will of JOSEPH DIXSON continued-

Executrix: wife Mary.
Witnesses: William Moffitt, Joab Brooks, Jr., Solomon Cox.
- - -

A-116  Will of JAMES McGOWN. Dated Nov 1769, proved
                                        April 1770.
Wife: name not stated

sons: James, William

daus: Mary, Susannah, Ettar.

Executor: George Tate.      Witness: Robert Mebane.
- - -

A- 117  Will of ALEXANDER LARKIN. Dated 19 August 1772
                          proved - no date given.
Wife: Mary

sons: Thomas, William.

daus: Mary and her husband Mordecai Moor
      Margaret, Sarah,
      Elizabeth Boring.

Executors: wife, and son Thomas.
Witnesses: John Tinnin, Jane Tinnin, William Anderson.
- - -

A-119  Will of JOHN MILES. Dated 6 May 1769, no probate date

Wife: Mary

sons: Charles, Thomas, John, youngest son William.

Executors: Charles Smith, Christopher Smith.
Witness: Charley Smith.

A-121  Will of ROBERT SMITH, of St. Mathew's Parish.

Dated 20 June 1772, no probate date.

Wife: Mary        sons: John, Andrew, Robert

daus: Elizabeth, Mary, Isabel.

Executors: Joseph McCaffrity, and son William.
Witnesses: John Walker, Robert Chassen (?).
- - -

A-122  Will of JOSEPH ALLEN. Dated --

Wife: Sarah        daus: Elizabeth, Sarah

-continued-

A-122 Will of JOSEPH ALLEN continued-

sons:John, William, Daniel, George, Joshua.

"other children, Solomon, Samuel, Elisha, Joseph".

Executors: sons William and Daniel, and friend Wm. Clark.
Witnesses: Daniel Allen, William Allen, Joshua Allen,
           George Allen, William Clark.

— — —

A-124  Will of EDMUND HARDIN. Dated 20 August 1769,
                                    no probate date.
Wife: Mary

"Estate to be divided between wife and 3 children and
unborn child".

Executors: wife Mary, and Thomas Cate.
Witnesses: John Baskett, Jonathan Hardin, Moses Rice.

— — —

A-125  Will of HOSEA TAPLEY. Hatdded 21 March 1770.

Affidavit: "This day came Victory Rankin and made oath that
she was at Hosea Tapley's Jr. before he died and he said
land to go to sons John Pryor Tapley and Hosea Tapley. One
part to go to another son if his wife have one".

Witness: John Pryor.     Affidavit made 22 March 1770.

— — —

A-125  Will of JOSEPH GEORGE. Dated 14 Feb 1770, proved --

Wife: Ellenor

sons: Ambrose, Daniel Pegg, William, Isaac, James, Jesse.

daus: Mary Hinsford, Cathrine Riddle, Peggy George.

Executors: sons Ambrose and James, and wife Ellenor.
Witnesses: James Younger, John Page, Jr.

— — —

A-127  Will of JOHN PENDEXTER. Dated 23 Oct 1772, proved --

Wife: Elizabeth

sons: William, John, Lionel (?), Chapman, Thomas, Francis.

Executors: James McCann, John Hart        *
Witnesses: Abraham Whittiker, Nelly Ruby, Elizabeth Tate.

— — —   * Witness is Nelly Reily, not Ruby.
          All three witnesses signed with a "mark", x.

A-128  Will of GEORGE BOWER. Dated 15 July 1770, proved --

Wife: Margaret

"sons as they come of age" name and number not stated
"daughters as they come of age" name and number not stated

Executrix: wife Margaret
Witnesses: Edward Turner, James Browning, Hugh Finley.

- - -

A-129  Will of WILLIAM BLACKWOOD. Dated 8 Oct. 1772, proved -

Wife: Elizabeth     sons: James, John, William

daus: Martha, Mary, Jennet, Elizabeth, Ann.

Executors: son William, daughter Margaret.
Witnesses: Alex. Mebane, William Tate, Mary Sample.

- - -

A-131  Will of NATHANIEL WALTON. Dated 31 July 1771, proved -

Wife: Mary        "Peter, only son now living"

daus: Mary, Jemima, Keziah.

Executors: wife Mary, and son Peter.
William Durbin, John Reeves, Lancelot Johnston.

Codicil dated 4 August 1771.

- - -

A-135 Will of JOHN BASKETT. Dated 26 Feb. 1771, proved --

Wife: Ann                brother: James

sons:William, Thomas (under age).

Executors: friends Thomas Cate and James Baskett.
Witnesses: John Cate, Elizabeth Cate.

- - -

A-137. Will of JOHN MORDAUGH. Dated 8 July 1771, proved --

Wife: Elizabeth

sons: James "plantation bought of Enos Elliman"
      David, John

daus: Catrin, Agness, Janet, Elizabeth.

Executors: wife Elizabeth, and son James Sr.
Witnesses: Wm. Rutherford, John Mordaugh.

- - -

A-140  Will of ANDREW HARRISON. Dated 16 May 1773,
                                        proved May 1774.
Wife: Jane

sons: Ninian, youngest son Andrew.
      "William and Thomas 1 shilling, already having received
      their part".

daus: Milley Moore,  Elizabeth Harrison, Anne Ware, Molly, Jane.

Executors: Wm. Harrison, Thomas Harrison, John Ware, Wm. Moore.
Witnesses: Robert Payne, Charles Burton.
- - -

A-143  Will of PRISCILLA (x) BURTON.  Dated 22 May 17--,
                                        proved May 1774.
son: Robert Burton

granddaughters Sarah Burton, daughter of Robert, Judah Coleman.

dau: Priscilla Burton, daughter of Robert Burton.

Executor: son Robert Burton.
Witnesses: Abram Perkins, Thomas Dudley, Charles Burton.
- - -

A-144  Will of GEORGE TATE.  Dated Feb 1774, proved May 1774.

sons: George Tate, James Tate                wife

daus: Kitturah (oldest), Akness, Mary, Elizabeth, Litia, Janet,
      Margaret, "my seven daughters". All seem to be minors.

Sole Executrix: wife.
Witnesses: William Tate, Hugh Willson, James Smith.
- - -

A-146  Will of NATHANIEL HARRIS of the Parish of St Mathews.

Dated June 1773, proved May 1774.

Wife: Ellender

sons: Nathaniel, Archer, Edward, Charles Harris

daus: Unity Callahan, Lenora Burks

granddaughter: Mary Harris.

Executor: Edward Harris.
Witnesses: Wortham Glenn, Ann Glenn, Mildred Woods.

Note: OLDS' ABSTRACTS OF N. C. WILLS lists the above will
      as NATHANIEL HARRISON, but HARRIS is correct.
- - -

A-147 Will of ALEXANDER ROBBINSON or ROBERTSON   23 April 1774,
will proved May 1774

sisters:. Esthy Robeson
          Ellenor Ceasey wife of John Ceasey
nephews: James Ceasey, David Ceasey
brother-in-law: John Ceasey

Executors: Hugh McAden, William Powell.
Witnesses: Hugh McAden, Wm Powell, William Maxwell.

— — —

A-148 Will of SAMUEL UNDERWOOD. Dated March 1773, proved
                                                May 1774.
wife: Anna

sons: Henry, Alex, Samuel, Benjamin, James

daus: Mary Cloud eldest, Anne
      "Jane, Ruth, Sarah, Elizabeth, four youngest"

Executors: wife Anna, son Alexander.
Witnesses: John Marshall, William Ward, Jacob Marshall.

— — —

A-150 Will of HENRY SEARS. Dated 8 Nov 1768, proved May 1774.
                                                         *
wife: Rose                sons: John, Edward, Harry, Barbey
                                    (Henry Sears' wife wa
daughters: Sally, Nancy and Sears        Rosannah Barbee)

Executors: wife Rose, and John Barbee, Jr.
Witnesses: Mark Morgan, Benjamin Hart, Wm (x) Barbee.

— — —

A-152 Will of BURGES HARRILSON. Dated 9 May 1772, proved --

wife: Elizabeth, gets "her maintanance"

son: Ezekiel "plantation I purchased of Wm. Chambers, Sr"
son: Elijah, 20 shillings

dau:"Elishaba Harrilson the wife of Elkanah Harrilson, plan-
     tation whereon he now lives"

dau: Drusilla Harrilson
dau: Jemima Harrilson land in Henrico Co., Va."on Stoney Run
     which I purchased of James Allen (?)"

grandson:"I. Harrilson, the oldest son of Elijah Harrilson,
          land I purchased of my brother Paul Harrilson, lying
          on Stony (or Storey's) Creek"

Executors: Ezekiel Harrilson, Elkanah Harrilson.
Witnesses: Joe Johnson, William Stone, John (x) Harrilson.

— — —

A-154 Will of WILLIAM REA of Little River, Parish of Saint Matthew. Dated 16 October 1769, proved May 1774.

wife: Catherine "money that is now in Joseph Allison and Patrick Rutherford's hands", etc

son: William          grandson: David Rea.

sons-in-law: Michael Robbinson, John Mordah, James Mordah, Patrick Rutherford.

After wife's death, Joseph Allison is to have a slave.

Executors: Joseph Allison, William Rea.
Witnesses: Robert Willson, James Rea,Jr, Samuel Sample.
- - -

A-156 Will of ISAAC ALLEN. Dated 24 Nov 1773 ?, proved
                                          Jan 1772 ?
wife: Mary

"My children" names and number not stated.

Executrix: Mary Allen.  Witnesses: John Rainey, Wm. Rainey.
- - -

A-158 Will of ALEX RUSSELL. Dated 10 Dec 1771, proved Jan
                                              1772
wife: Jane          sons: James, Alex

daughters: Margaret, Elenor, Elizabeth, Jane

friends: Eli McDaniel and wife.

Executors: "friends William Rogers and James Neville, guardians to see the same duly executed."
Witnesses: William Hannah, Nathaniel Lyon, Josiah Blaik.
- - -

A-160 Will of JOHN PRYOR. Dated 28 Sept 1771, proved Jan 1772.

wife: Margaret

son: Robert "tract in Granville County, 640 acres"
sons: John Henry Pryor, Abner

daus:Elizabeth Flournoy, Rhoda Stone, Leah Perkins, Mildred Womack, Lucy Tapley, Rachel Pope, Dorothy Pyror, Martha "when she comes of age"

grandchildren: John Pryor son of Green Pryor
               Betty Green Pryor
grandson: John Pryor Smith "tract I purchased of Hosea Tapley"

Executors: son-in-law William Stone, wife Margaret, son-in-law David Womack.
Witnesses: Burgis Harralson, Joseph Hicks, Peter Rogers.
- - -

A-164 Will of DAVID PINKERTON,"yoeman" of St. Matthew's Parish.
Dated 27 Feb 1764, proved Jan /
wife: Margaret                                                    1772

sons: John, William, David
daughters Martha and Mary, both under 18 years of age

step-daughter Agnes Trickey ? 5 shillings.

Executors: wife Margaret, son John.
Witnesses: George Miller, James Latta.

- - -

A-166 Will of JOSEPH BARNETT. Dated 18 April 1771, proved
Jan 1773.
wife: Rachel is pregnant -"child wife is with" ..

son: Samuel        daughters: Mary and Sarah Barnett.

Witnesses: John Barnett, Wm Miles, Thomas Barnett.

- - -

A-168 Will of HENRY LEA. Dated 14 Dec 1774, proved Aug 1774.

wife: Elizabeth "all parts of my estate given to me by her
parents"...

daughter, Frances, is under age.

Executors: friends James Lea "my brother in law",
Ann McNiel, Sr.
Witnesses; James Roberts, Thomas McNeill, John Lea.

A-169 Will of THOMAS DOBBINS. Dated 31 July 1774, proved
Aug 1774
wife: Rachel
sons: Hugh -440 acres, John, 2nd son, 432 acres,
Thomas, youngest son, plantation. The lands lie on
Country Line Creek and Reedy Fork of Hico Creek.
daus: Margaret, Elizabeth Dobbin.
"My two little daughters Rachel and Nancy"

Executors: wife Rachel, son Hugh, friend Archibald Murphy.
Execs are to make a deed to Daniel Hall for "land he bought
of my cousin Thomas Dobbins."
Witnesses: William Zachary, John Connor.

A-172 Will of JACOB BISHIND (BASON) Dated 11 Oct 1773,
proved Aug 1774
wife: Catherine
daughter: Hannah        son: Jacob.

Executors: wife Catherine, son John.
Witnesses: David Rainey, Jane Attcut (?).

- - -

A-174  Will of ISAAC WRITE of St. Mathew's Parish.

Dated 26 May 1772, proved Aug 1774.    Wife: Mary

sons: Zacharias and Isaac, both under age.

"Rest of my estate to be equally divided amongst all my
children: Providence, Zacarias, Mary and Isaac Write."

Executrix: wife Mary.
Witnesses: Bridger Haynie, Benjamin Ingram, Abraham Miles.
- - -

A-176  Will of JOHN PIKE. Dated 30 March 1771, proved
                                            Aug 1774.
Wife: Abigail

sons: John, Samuel, Nathan (youngest)

"My six daughters: Sarah Piggott, Anne Hughes, Susannah Lee,
Elizabeth Stuart, Ruth Winner, Rachel Williams."

Executors: wife Abigail, son John.
Witnesses: Thomas Hill, Priscilla Pike, Obediah R..?..
- - -

A-177  Will of THOMAS CRABTREE. Dated 11 April 1774,
                                    proved Aug 1774.
Wife: Elizabeth

sons: William, John, James, Thomas

daughter: Mary

Executrix: wife Elizabeth.
Overseers of Will: friends Thomas Barton, John Connor.
Witnesses: Thomas Barton, John Connor, Elizabeth Connor.
- - -

A-179  Will of STEPHEN NORTON. Dated 3 July 1773,
                                    proved Aug 1774.
Wife: Jane

sons: John, William, Richard.

daus: Anne Norton, Margaret Norton, Elizabeth Norton.

Executors: Abam. Armstead, John Armstrong.
Witnesses: Wm. Bailey Smith, John Middlebrooks,
           Richard Boggass.
- - -

A-181 Will of JONATHAN WEST. Dated 1 June 1774,
                                        proved Nov 1774.
Wife: Elenor

cousin: Jonathan West.

Sole Executrix: wife Elenor.
Witnesses: Josiah Black, James Tinnen.

— — —

A-182 Will of JOHN GRAY. Dated 19 Feb 1775, proved May /
                                                        1775
To Colonel Thomas Hart, land on Seven Mile Creek,
beginning date 25 March 1752 from Lord Granville.

Executors: Col. Thomas Hart, Maj. David Hart,
           Nathaniel Hart.
Witnesses: John Riley, James Weeks, Henry Hastings.

— — —

A-184 Will of JOSEPH SUTTON. Dated 20 March 1775, proved -

Estate to Daniel Hughes, oldest son of Gabriel Hughes, for
love and good will.

Executor: Gabriel Hughes. He is to keep estate in hand
          until Daniel arrives at 21 years of age.
Witnesses: Shrewood Parish, James Dickings,
           Sherwood James.

— — —

NOTE by Ruth Herndon Shields.

    In reading this book you will no doubt notice the con-
fusing dates given for the probate of the wills and other
papers. We have copied the dates as given in the books.
The books appear to have been copied from older books, or
rebound, and the dates are badly confused.

    For instance the wills probated at the November 1800
term of Court, precede the wills recorded at the Court of
August 1800.

    This book is intended solely as a guide to what is in
the WILL BOOKS in Hillsborough. In citing these wills as
proof it is advisable to get the full text of the will.
Unless I have stated that the will is preserved in the
State Archives, the original has been lost, and a copy can
only be obtained from the Clerk of Court in Hillsborough.
If the original is in Raleigh, a photostat or Xerox copy
can be ordered from The Historical Commission, Raleigh, N.C.

    Spelling of proper names in some of the wills was not
uniform. Sometimes a name was spelled three different ways
in the same will. In other cases the writing was so poor
the name could only be guessed. Look for every variation
of the name you are seeking.

A-185 Will of JOHN BURGESS. Dated 27 Feb 1775,
proved May 1775.
Wife: Elizabeth McConkey

After wife's death property to Lidy Breeze, Susannah Stone, Benjamin Williams. No relationship stated.

Executrix: wife Elizabeth.
Witnesses: Thomas Palmer, Edward Roberts.

— — —

A- 187 Will of JOHN BORING. Dated 6 Jan 1775,
proved May 1775.
Wife; Elizabeth

daughters: Ribecca, Nicy, Mary.

Executors: wife Elizabeth, James Boren (Boring).
Witnesses: James Currie, James Borin, Ann Green.

— — —

A-188 Will of JOSEPH BORRIN. Dated 11 Jan 1775,
proved May 1775.
Wife: Susannah

sons: James, William, Isaac, Joseph Jr, David (under age)

..."to be paid by oldest brother John when David comes of age."

relationship not stated: "john Borrin to have ..."

daughters: Susan, Becky, Phebe, Sara

cousin: Patty Clarke.

Executors: Charles Stephens, James Currie.
Witnesses: James Culberson, James Currie.

— — —

A-189 "ill of JOHN CAMPBELL, tailor. Dated 22 Feb 1761,
proved May 1775.
Wife: Margaret

sons-in-law: John Ferguson, Andrew Ferguson.

sons: Robert, David,
Joseph land adjoining James Stewart's line.

Testator owns land in Albemarle County, Virginia.

Witnesses: Samuel Bell, Thomas Dobbins.
Executors: wife Margaret and son-in-law John Ferguson.

— — —

34

A-191  Will of JOSEPH (or JONES?) PARKER. Dated 21 Oct 1771,
                                       proved May 1775.
Wife: Rebecca

Children, named in this order:
Richard, Stephen, David, Powell, Francis, Abner, Winny,
Sally, Betty.  "My son Richard to come of age at 21".

Executors: Thomas Person, Edward Bumpass.
Witnesses: Robert Bumpass, William Fowler,
           Grace Fowler, Joanna Person.
- - -

A-194  Will of CHRISTOPHER MIER. Dated 17 August 1775,
                                 proved Nov 1775.
Wife mentioned but name not stated.

"Eldest son George"

He seems to have other sons and daughters, but no names
are given.

Executors: Adam I..?... , Jacob Grissom.
Witnesses: George Fogleman, George Cortner (?), Doolin Law.
- - -

A-194  Will of GEORGE G. GIBSON. Dated 5 Nov 1775,
                                 proved May 1775.
Wife: Mary

Sons mentioned, but number and names not stated.

Daughters mentioned, but number and names not stated.

Executors: Sherw'd Parrish, Thomas Gibson Liner.
Witnesses: Sherw'd Parrish, Joel (x) Gibson,
           Lucreasy (x) Collons.
- - -

A-196  Will of MOSES FARLEY. Dated 25 March 1776,
                             proved May 1776.
Wife: Sarah

son: Josiah.    dau: Elizabeth.    brother: John James Farley.

Executors: John James Farley, William Price.
Witnesses: George Vincent, David Penyman, Henry Burton.
- - -

A-197  Will of JAMES SANDERS, SENIOR.  Dated 28 Feb 1776,
                                       proved May 1776.
Wife mentioned, name not given.

sons: James Sanders, Richard, William.

A-197 Will of JAMES SANDERS, SR. continued -

daus: Sarah wife of William Trigg, Cassandra,
      Susannah wife of Robert Terry,
      Fanny wife of William Sanders the Elder.

grandson: Jeremiah Terry, son of daughter Susannah.

granddaughter: "Casandra's oldest daughter"...

Executors: son James, Richard Sanders, William Trigg.
Witnesses: Andrew Haddock, James Sanders, Robin Terry.
- - -

A-199 Will of ALEXANDER (x) COHARON (?). Dated 28 Oct 1775,
                                        proved May 1776.
Wife: Easter , unborn child

sons: eldest son John "land purchased of Barnabas Grims"
      second son James "plantation purchased of Richard /
      Alexander, Samuel                          Parsons"

daus: eldest Minny wife of Joseph Guy,
      Jean, Easter, Esibal.

Executors: wife Easter, son John.
Witnesses: Ezicaia (x) Witt, John Moor.
- - -

A-200 Will of ARTHUR (x) STEPHENS. Dated 2 March 1776,
                                   proved May 1776.
"Three sons" mentioned, but names not given.

daughters: oldest Sarah, second Leviner,
           third Elizabeth.

Executors: Joshua Johnston, Joel Johnston,
           John McCane, Abraham Stephens.
- - -

A-201 Will of WILLIAM (x) BUMPASS. Dated 10 March 1776,
                                   proved May 1776.
Wife: Mary

father: Robert Bumpass.

Executors: Gabriel Davey, Mary Bumpass, Edward Bumpass.
Witnesses: Isaia Vanhook, Wm. Yarborough, James Davis.
- - -

A-202 Will of JAMES WATSON. Dated 5 Dec 1776, proved Aug 1777.

son: James
daughter: Helen Reed wife of William Reed

grandsons: James Reed, Robert Reed, William Reed,
          Watson Reed, James Watson.

granddaughters: ....?... Reed, Helen Watson,
               Rebecca Watson, ...?.. Watson.

Executors: son James Watson, William Johnston,
          James Morris, Nathaniel Rochester.
No witnesses. Will proved by William Courtney.

— — —

A-203 Will of LODOWICK CLAPP. Dated 25 July 1768,
                                    proved Feb 1778.
Wife mentioned but name not stated.

sons: John, others mentioned but names & number not stated.

Daughters mentioned but names & number not stated.

Executrix: wife.
Witnesses: John Graves, Lodowick (x) Swing, George Cortner.

— — —

A-205 Will of ROBERT HOLLOWAY. Dated 9 Nov 1776,
                                    proved Nov 1778.
Wife: Martha, his third wife.

sons: oldest Samuel, Stephen.

daus: Elizabeth Horner, Brigett, Mary Readen.

"Remainder of children of the body of Martha, my third wife
... namely: Priscilla, Susannah, Ann, Stephen, Rachell, Ruth,
Jane, Litici (?)."

Executrix: wife Martha.
Witnesses: Joseph Baker, Mary Baker, John Baker.

— — —

A-206 Will of ANDREW McBRIDE. Dated 1 Oct 1778,
                                    proved Feb 1779.
Wife: Jane

Executrix: wife Jane.
Witnesses: John Steel, William Morrow.

— — —

A-207 Will of WILLIAM FORREST. Dated 8 Aug 1777,
                              proved Aug 1778.
Wife: Lovina

sons: Shadrack, Gresham, Joel, William, Jesse.


Executors: Edward Gresham, Archer (Gresham ?),
           wife Lovina (this name may be Louisa).
Witnesses: Edward Gresham, Jr, Isaac Forrest.
— — —

A-207 Will of MARTIN LAY. Dated 15 July 1777,
                          proved May 1779.
Wife: Catherreney

sons: Henry, George          daughter: Mary.

Executors: Jacob Allbright, George Lay.
Witnesses: Henry Garhurt, Isaac (x) Sharp.
— — —

A-208 Will of JACOB CAIN. Dated 6 Aug 1779, proved - 1779.

Wife: Joanna is pregnant, unborn child mentioned.

Executors: wife Joanna, Jacob Allen.
Witnesses: James Fen (?), Wm. (x) Leathers, Wm. Johnston.
          W (?)
— — —

A-209 Will of ROBERT ABERCROMBY. Dated 31 May 1779,
                                 proved Aug 1779.
sons: Charles, Robert.
daughter: Jenny Mebane.

Executors: sons Charles and Robert.
Witnesses: William Saxon, James (x) Desern.
           Enoch Liner (or Lewis ?).

— — —

A-210 Will of GEORGE (x) HILL. Dated 24 Jan 1779,
                               proved Feb 1780.
Wife mentioned, name not stated.

son: Henry

"After wife's marriage estate to be "equally divided
amongst every one of my children." (Names and number not
stated.)

Executors: wife, James Wood, Joseph Wood.
Witnesses: Thomas Guin, Mealy (x) ..?.., James Wood.
— — —

A-211 Will of MELCHI (x) DANIEL. Dated 23 Jan 1779,
          or McDANIEL              proved Feb 1780.
Wife: Marget

"Remaining children" .. names and number not stated,
(others may have died or married and left home ?).

Executors: Lewis Kirk, Richard Cate.
Witness: Benjamin (x) McCool (?).

− − −

A-212 Bill of Sale from TIMOTHY CAIN to JAMES CAIN, for
negroes. Dated 20 Feb 1781, proved August 1781.
Witnesses: Jno. Kelley, Jno. Cabe.

− − −

A-212 Bill of Sale from TIMOTHY CAIN to MARY CAIN.
Dated 20 Feb 1781, proved August 1781.
Witnesses: Jno. Kelley, Jno. Cabe.

− − −

The following wills dated 1800 and earlier, are preserved
in the Archives in Raleigh, N.C. Proved 1801 or later.

| TESTATOR | DATE OF WILL | BOOK |
|---|---|---|
| Bird, James | 1793 | D-155 |
| Brewer, Katy | 1800 | D-30 |
| Curry, James, Sr. | 1800 | D-137 |
| Deley, William | 1794 | D-105 |
| Dunnagan, Sherwood | 1800 | D-22 |
| Freeman, William | 1800 | D-43 |
| Gant, John | 1800 | D-30 |
| Guthrie, James | 1800 | D-40 |
| Harvey, Isaac | 1800 | D-63 |
| Kell, John | 1800 | D-28 |
| McCracken, Jeremiah | 1794 | D-66 |
| Moore, John | 1800 | D-27 |
| Clendenin, William | 1790 | D-25 |
| Newlin, John, Sr. | 1799 | D-162 |
| Forest, Benjamin | 1800 | D-21 |
| Rainey, David | 1800 | D-68 |
| Rice, Jesse | 1798 | D-111 |
| Robertson, John | 1800 | D-46 |
| Smith, Adam | 1798 | D-59 |
| Stalcop; John | 1800 | D-125 |
| Tenning, Elizabeth | 1800 | D-53 |

− − − − −

A-213 Bill of Sale from JAMES FRAZER to Thomas Hart for
    twelve slaves. Dated 18 Nov 1780, proved Nov 1780.
                            Witness: Jesse Benton.

– – –

A-214 Power of Attorney from THOMAS HART to "trusty friends
    James Hogg and Jesse Benton."    Dated 19 Nov 1780,
    Witness: Susannah Miller.         proved Nov 1780.

– – –

A-215  Will in Archives. Dated 10 Oct 1777, proved Nov 1780.

THOMAS CAPPES (indexed in Archives as CAPPER)

"dear and only daughter Nancy"

Executors: wife Ann, "trusty friends Tapley Patterson and
            James Trice, Jr."
Witnesses: Jos. Harwood, Eliz. Trice, John (x) Davis.

– – –

A-217  Will in Archives. Dated 31 March 1779, proved Aug
                                                    1781.
MICHAEL SYNNOTT

Servant Mary Humphreys gets "land on Gooseberry Mountain"
as long as she "lives single" unmarried.

Nephew Richard Synnott of St Catherine's Parish in Wapping,
London- land "on Crooked Run, the Waters of Eno River."

He mentions bond on wearing apparel & books from Thomas
Barefield, Arthur Brown & Benjamin Cotton (bond & inventory
in the care of Dr. Thomas Burke.)

Executor: William Johnston.
Witnesses: R'd Bennehan, Mich'l (x) McGee.

– – –

A-220 Will in Archives. Dated 21 June 1780, proved Aug 1781.

THOMAS LAPSLIE                      wife: Charity

son: Thomas Lapslie gets land "on waters of Back Creek" ...
    and "tract he now lives on .. Dodson's Cabin ..."

daus: Elizabeth and Charity, both minors.
sons: David and James, both minors.

Executors: wife Charity, son Thomas, friend Wm. Anderson.
Witnesses: Francis Wilkinson, David Anderson,
– – –        Robert Anderson.

40

A-223  Will in Archives. Dated 15 Aug 1779, proved Aug 1781.

JAMES TRICE            wife: Sarah

"... my father and his wife should live with my wife ..."

nephew: Charles Trice "son of Edward Trice my brother"

brother: John Trice "my stallion"

relationship not given: James Trice and Joseph Trice.

Loney Hunter "Ŀ 50 and my watch, etc, for building a
            Meeting house."

Executors: brother Edward Trice, Robert Campbell.
Witnesses: Robert Campbell, Abraham Massey, Richard Leigh.
— — —

A-225  Will in Archives. Dated 24 Sept 1781, proved Nov 1781.

JOSEPH YOUNG                    father: John Young

Wife mentioned, name  not stated, is pregnant ? he says "if
my wife is now with child ..."

son: John.

Executors: wife, and friend Robert Agnew.
Witnesses: Wm. Galbreath, R. Galbreath.
— — —

A-226  Will in Archives.  Dated 25 Nov 1780, proved Aug 1781.

THOMAS CLARK (Yeoman)

wife: Susanna "that legacy that William Clark deceased
       Father to Susannah Clark did bequeath to me at his
       decease."

daus: Sarah Clark, Mary Clark, Catherine Clark.

sons: Thomas, William and Abner (youngest, a minor) Clark.

He mentions "land situated on Broad River, S.C."

Executors: James Carson, James Carr, Jr.
Witnesses: Wm. Strain, John Ray, Wm. Williams.
— — —

A-229  Will in Archives.  Dated 24 Nov 1780, proved Aug 1781.

WILLIAM WILSON                 wife: Mary      dau: Mary

sons: Samuel and Gregory.
                                                      tree
Executors: "trusty friends" Richard Holman & Thomas Round-/
Witnesses: John Wilson, James Wilson, Susanna (x) Farmer.
— — —

A-231  Will in Archives. Dated 2 April 1781, proved Aug 1781.

GEORGE WAGGONER                    wife: Mary

daus: Elizabeth and Ann (both minors)

father: Henry Waggoner "land adjoining his line and Robert
        McCaul's line".

Executors: Mary Waggoner, Robert Berry.
Witnesses: Step. Smyth, George Clower, James Waggoner.

- - -

A-233  Will in Archives. Dated 10 Feb 1781, proved Nov 1781.

JOHN TAPLEY PATTERSON              wife: Sarah

son: Mann Patterson land on Capper's Branch of New Hope

only daughter: Milly (Amelia)

son: Page Patterson "plantation I bought of John Whatly and
               tract I bought of William Whatly."

Executors: wife, and "only and well beloved brother Mark
          Patterson."
Witnesses: Jos. Barbee, John Patterson, Baxter Boling.

- - -

A-235  Will in Archives.  Dated 21 June 1781, proved Nov 1781.

HUGH CAINE              daughter: Ann Caine "all her mother's
                        and sisters' wearing apparel" etc.
son: William

sons: Hugh, James, Allan "land and plantation whereon I at
               present reside"

cousin: Elizabeth McKinley.

called nephews - "John Caine son of my son William"
                 "James Caine another child of my son William"
called nieces: "Ann Caine another child of my son William"
               "Fanny and Margaret twins of my son William".

Executors: sons William and Hugh Caine.
Witnesses: Moses Leathers, Wm. Johnston.

- - -

A-237  Will in Archives.  Dated 15 Sept 1781, proved May 1782.

PETER (x) NOE        wife: Hannah, all estate

sons: John, Joseph, 5 shillings each.

daus: Kathereana Rightenhous, Susannah Ridge, 5 shillings each,
      Elizabeth Coons, Elizabeth Ragen, 5 shillings each.

Executrix: wife. Witnesses: Jno. Armstrong, Anne (x) Armstrong.

- - -

A-239   Bill of Sale (in State Archives) dated 20 April 1781,
        proved Feb Court 1782, from CHARLES WHITE to Alexander
Carnes, for negroes. Witnesses: William Clark, Wm. Williams.

— — —

A-240   Will in Archives. .Dated 20 March 1775, proved Feb 1782.

JOHN LUTTRELL        wife Susanna - unborn child or children -

Three brothers Thomas, Hugh and William Luttrell.

"Lands purchased by Richard Henderson & Co. of the Cherokee
Indians on the waters of the Mississippi".

No executor named.
Witnesses: Jesse Benton, Thomas Farrar, Nath'l Henderson.

— — —

A-241   Will in Archives.   Dated 27 June 1781, proved Feb 1782.

ISAAC (x) SHARP           wife: Philipina - unborn child

two oldest sons: John and Bostian

children: Peter, Christian, Elizabeth and Philipina, minors.

Executors: "beloved friends Nicholas Gibbs & John Albright."
Witnesses: Samuel Suther or Luther, Jacob Albright.

— — —

A-243   Will in Archives.   Dated 3 March 1779, proved Feb 1782.

WILLIAM CLARK           wife: Mary

son: William - land from place he is now living on "south end
             of tract adjoining Peter Waltons"

son: James - land adjoining Samuel Allis ? or Allen

son: John          daughters: Susannah, Hannah.

Executors: sons James and William Clark.
Witnesses: Nath'l Rochestor, John Allison.

— — —

A-245   Power of Attorney from JOHN RUTLEDGE, Esq, of Charles-
        ton, S.C. to Col. William Blount of North Carolina,
to collect debt owed to Rutledge by John Cruden, Esq. late of
North Carolina.   Dated 3 May 1784, proved May 1784.

Witnesses: John Rutledge, Jr., Samuel Gruben ?.

— — —

A-247  Will in Archives.  Dated 9 June 1781, proved Aug 1782.

WILLIAM CARRIGAN (signed WILLIAM KARGIN)

wife: name not stated

four children, John, Joseph, Elie, Mary

"bond ... to be paid by Robert Nelson."

Executors: Robert Nelson, Robert Burnside.
Witnesses: Brice Collins, John Carrigan.

— — —

A-248  Will in Archives.  Dated 25 March 1781, proved Aug 1782

JOHN MORDAK of the Parish of Saint Mathews

wife: Mary is pregnant     unborn child

son: Robert, a minor.

Executors: Robert Gray, Mary Mordak.
Witnesses: James Mordak, Margaret (x) Griffin.

— — —

A-249  Will dated 25 Sept 1780, proved August 1782.

JAMES MULLINS or MULLON     Only legatee, James Ross.

Witnesses: Richard Clayton, James (x) Kanady,
           Margaret (x) Wilson.

— — —

A-250  Will in Archives.  Dated 8 Sept 1780, proved Aug 1782.

MOSES (x) GWINN, Planter, of Parish of Saint Mathews
"very sick and weak"

wife: Elizabeth

daus: Jane, Mary, Elizabeth

son: Moses "plantation he now lives on" and "horse I got
          from my brother Joseph", etc

Executors: James Mordah, Elizabeth Gwynn.
Witnesses: James Mordah, Elizabeth Mordah.

— — —

A-252  Will in Archives.  Dated 15 March 1780, proved Aug 1782.

THOMAS LINDLEY                  wife: Ruth Lindley
"far advanced in years"

son: William, 200 cares     son: Jonathan, remainder of land

- continued -

44

Will of THOMAS LINDLEY continued

dau: Katherine White Ⱡ 20

"All my other children to wit, Thomas Lindley, Ruth Hadley,
William Lindley, John Lindley, Elinor Marriss, Deborah Newlin,
Ⱡ 20 each".

"Thomas Lindley, son of James Lindley, dec'd" Ⱡ 10

grandson: Thomas Lindley (a minor) son of Thomas Lindley Ⱡ 10
"         Thomas Lindley (a minor) "    "  William Lindley Ⱡ 10

To "friends of Spring Meeting two acres of land whereon the
Meeting House now stands."

Executors: sons William and Jonathan Lindley.
Witnesses: Zacharias Dicks, John Carter, John Newlin.
- - -

A-255  Will in Archives. Dated 22 July, proved Aug 1782.

JOHN KING                        wife: Hannah

son: Thomas - land "beginning at a beach on Bolings Creek
               Nathaniel King's corner .. Ready branch .. to
               Charles King's line ... to Joshua Eason's line.."

son: William - land "joining land of Thomas Lloyd, Jr"

daus: Nancy, Elizabeth, Obedience, Hannah, Rebecca , all are
      under age except Nancy

son: Thomas King (a minor).

Executors: wife Hannah, son William.
Witnesses: John Hogan, Thos. Lloyd, Jr, Nathaniel King.
- - -

A-257  Will in Archives. Dated 20 April 1781,proved Aug 1782.

AMOS (x) THOMSON or THOMPSON         wife: Martha

son: Littlebury Thomson

brother: Charles Thomson "all my Land in Donwoody County, Va."

Executors: Lewis Kirk, Richard Cate, brother Charles Thomson,
           Jesse Roper.
Witnesses: Hen. Hancock, Robert Peebles, Buckner (x) Floyd,
           Benjamin Tarver.
- - -

Footnotes to will of JOHN CHRISTMAS, on following page.

The will was proved by "James Pickhart and Wm. Richards."

Ann Peealer Christmas marriage bond to Nathaniel McLemore
was dated 22 August 1786.

A-259  Will in Archives. Dated 1 July 1783, proved  Nov 1783.

JOHN DEBOW, Minister of the Gospel.          wife: Liney

son: Solomon (a minor) "tract of land lying on waters of Eno"
son: Stephen (a minor)

Guardian, in case of wife's death, Mr. Lake.

"To Liney Lake at her sixteenth year" ...

"to John De Hodge L for his education ... "

Executors: Liney Debow, Mr. Jacob Lake.
Witnesses: William Tate, John (x) Hodge, Joel Rice, Jos. Baker.
— — —

A-261 Will in Archives. Dated 12 Oct 1782, prpved Nov 1783.

EDWARD CARRIGAN          wife: Margaret is pregnant -
Wife's father is living.          "unborn child"

brothers: John and James

brother in law: John Paul.

Executors: brothers John and James.
Witnesses: John Carragan, James Carragan.
— — —

A-262 Will in Archives. Dated 19 Jan 1783, proved Nov 1783.

JOHN (x) RICE          wife: Catrin          dau: Hannah

"Son-in-law Jesse Towel and daughter Hannah" ...

grandsons: John Towel, Henry Towel

Executors: son-in-law Jesse Towel, nephew John Murry.
Witnesses: James Thomson, John Marduk, Prudence Marduk.
— — —

A-264 Will in Archives. Dated 11 Aug 1783, proved Nov 1783.

JOHN CHRISTMAS (planter)  daus: Mary, Elizabeth, Heneritta

wife: Mary "plantation where I now live, with all land on S
          side of Cane Creek & below Mockasson branch"
dau: Ann Pickat ? or Peeler ?
sons: Thomas, John, William, Nathaniel
son: Richard - land on N side of Cane Creek - near mouth of
          Richland Branch with the land where Thomas
          Mason formerly lived.
young sons, all minors, Robert, James and Charles.
grandson Henry Christmas, son of John, dec'd, land in Warren
   County adjoining land formerly Charles Allen's"

Executors: wife Mary, sons Richard and Robert.
Witnesses: Richard Christmas, Wm. Richards, James J. Pickat.

A-268 Will in Archives. Dated 30 July 1780, proved Nov 1783.

HUGH MORROW of Cane Creek                    wife: Sarah

children: James ( a minor), Mary

Exeos: wife Sarah, friend and neighbor John Murdock.

Witnesses: John Jenkinson, Richard Laughlin, Margaret Harper.

— — —

A-270  Will in Archives. Dated 6 March 1776, proved Nov 1782.

WILLIAM RIGGS                         wife: Mary

sons: George, Thomas and James (minors), Henry, Samuel, John

daus: Ann, Jane (a minor), Mary "Barnaba Grymes' wife".

Executors: wife Mary and son George.
Witnesses: John Latta, George Riggs.

— — —

A-272 Will in Archives (indexed there as BERRY).
       Dated 28 Sept 1782, proved Nov 1782

MICHEL BURY death bed will, witnessed by Samuel Ector and
                                        John Daley.
His accounts to be settled and residue given to John Dunnevin.

— — —

A-273  Will in Archives. Dated 17 Oct 1782, proved Nov 1782.

MATHEW SCOBY                          wife: Jenit

Eldest son: David Scoby                son: Robert
Eldest daughter: Margaret Tait
He speaks of "the girls"...
Guardians: Robert Burnsides and Jno. Patton.

Executors: wife Jenit, and David Scoby.
Witness: Robert Burnsides, Jr.

— — —

A-275  Will in Archives. Dated 2 April 1783, proved May 1783.

BENJAMIN BLAKE (planter)         wife, name not stated

son: Benjamin Blake

daus: Martha Cain, Sarah Braswell, Rebecca Mason? or iLSSEY?
       Penelope Blake, Ann Blake, Bethana Blake, all minors.

grandchildren: Penelope, Mary, Ann, Obedience, Hardy Philips,
               children of Thomas Philips.
               Sarah and Absalom Cane, children of Elisha Cane.
Trustee: "trusty friend, my near neighbor, Edward Trice".
Sole Executor: son Jones Blake.
Witnesses: Enoch Lewis, James Trice, William Trice.

— — —

Book A, page 277. Bill of Sale, dated 28 Aug 1782. Rec'd
of RALPH WILLIAMS .. for a negro man, formerly the property
of Thomas W. Knight or Parker.
John Ramsey          Comms. of Confiscated Property for
John Montgomery      the County of Chatham, N.C.
Zach. Harmon

    "Transfer of right and property of above ... negro man
Africa unto William Courtney ... this 28th day of Aug. 1782"

Witnesses: John Ramsey                    RALPH WILLIAMS
           Zach. Harmon
           John Montgomery      Proved in Orange Court
                                August 1782

— — —

A-277  JOHN SEARS of North Carolina paid ... by John Booth
of the said Province .. 100 pounds ... for all my Right of
my father's Estate ... after my mother's death of both land
and negroes and everything else ..." Dated 27 August 1781
                                      Proved August 1782
          signed: JOHN SEARS

Witnesses: John Partin, John Boothe, Junior

— — —

A-278 DEED OF GIFT , dated          recorded August 1783

From SUKEY CASSELBURY to dau. Gilley, dau. Mary, dau. Rosy,
dau. Elizabeth, dau. Ruth, dau. Dise, son Solomon, son David,
granddaughter Patsy , "the third part of the Estate of Paul
Casselbury Deceased. This Deed of Gift made to keep any person or persons from taking of any of this Estate for any
debts or demands contracted by Anson Brown & Anson Brown
shall deliver up all the estate to Paul Casselbury children
or their guardians at his wife's death"

Witnesses: Thomas Roberts        Susanah (x) Casslbury
           Joseph Casslbury      Anson Brown

— — —

A-279  Will in Archives. Dated 13 August 1781, proved
                                          August 1783.
EDWARD GANT              wife: Elizabeth

sons: John, Thomas
                        "land joining Luis Simmons"
daus: Cary, Sarah ("Sary")

Executors: brother John Gant,and wife Elizabeth.

Witnesses: William Rainey, Mary (x) Rainey

— — —

48

Book A, page 280. Will in Archives. Dated 4 Sept 1779
Proved May 1783
WILLIAM SMITH      Wife: Mary Smith gets "Mansion House".

sons: Samuel, Robert, William, Cunningham, Jonathan
daus: Marget, Ann
"to my son Samuel my large Bible & my walnut chest"...

Executors: Thomas Tilford, wife Mary Smith, son Samuel.
Witnesses: John Robertson, James (x) Warnock,
_ _ _      George Hamilton.

A-283  Will in Archives. Dated 14 Nov 1783, proved April '84

THOMAS BURKE          wife: J ..?..          (Burke owes Robert
                                             Little a balance
dau: Mary (under 21 years of age)            on a plantation.
                                             Little has given
Executors: Willie Jones, James Hogg.         a note to William
Witnesses: Jno. Williams, Alfred Moore.      Wylie.)
_ _ _

A-286  Will in Archives. Dated 17 May 1770, proved May 1784.

THOMAS BREAZIER          wife: Hannah

sons Thomas, John and Aquilla get 1 shilling each

"2youngest sons James and Samuel my land and plantation"

daus: Elizabeth Jones,    Sarah Pyle, Hanah Teague

"youngest daughters Mary Cassa Jean and Rachel" (no punctuation). "Until they marry or come of age"

Executors: John Pyle , Sen'r, William Cox
Witnesses: William Paine, Mary Paine, H.. Black, Wm. Cox.
_ _ _

A-288  Will in Archives. Dated 7 Feb 1784, proved May 1784.

RICHARD LEAK

dau: Elizabeth Terry, wife of James Terry

grandchildren: Richard Leak Terry, John Terry and others

dau: Mary Moore

"to Richard Leak Moore one negor now in the care of my
daughter Mary Moore"    John Moor, relationship not stated.

daus: Jean Harley, Susannah Campble

Richard Campble...
                         -continued-

A-288 Will of Richard Leak continued-

grandson: Walter Slatter (Slaughter ?)

"my grandson Walter Slatter's son Richard Slatter"

Testator has land in Richmond County upon P D (Pee Dee River

Executor: Walter Slatter.
Witnesses: Charles Clindenin, George Webb, John Pugh.

— — —

A-290 An agreement between Hannah King and William King,
both of Orange County, Executors of the last will and testament of JOHN KING deceased of the one part and John King,
Baxter King, Charles King, Nathaniel King, William Blackwood
Richard Morris, Anne King and Elizabeth King as well on be-
half of themselves or for Obedience King, Thomas King, Hannah King and Rebecca King minors all legatees of the aforesaid ... John King, Deceased. Jesse Buckner one of the
legatees and the guardian of Thomas, Obedience, and Rebecca
King, minors.   After the death of Hannah King .. "to be
equally divided amongst her children".

Witnesses: John Hogan, William (x) Partin
                                        Proved May 1784
Dated 12 June 1783

(John King's will is recorded on page 255, Book A.)
— — —
A-292 There is another item concerning the Estate of John
King, which names the same persons as those above.


— — —

Note by Ruth Herndon Shields.

        Many of these signatures are given thus : John x Smith.
Such a signature means that the person did not actually sign,
but made "his mark". Not every person who signed a will or
other paper with an x was illiterate. Many of these are death
bed wills, others were made by old infirm, possibly blind,
persons. In all the wills I personally abstracted I have
copied "the mark" wherever used, as a matter of accuracy.
But in checking the work of some of my helpers, I found
that they did not make a note of it. Many, many of the witnesses signed with a mark, especially the women.

        In every case where the original has survived, and is
preserved in the State Archives in Raleigh, I have noted
that fact. Photostats of these original wills can be obtained
from the Archives. For those wills which have been lost,
write to the Clerk of Court, Hillsboro, N.C.

50

Book A, page 293. This will is in N. C. Archives.

JOHN (x) TROUSDALE of Orange County, "Taylor"

wife : Elizabeth

Dated 3 August 1779
Proved  February 1784

sons : William
       James

daus : Margaret
       Mary

Executors : sons William and John.

Witnesses : James Wilkins, Jno. T. Sharp, Wm. Phillips

— — —

Book A, page 294.  Will in N.C. Archives.

ANDREW McBROOM

Dated 1 December 1783
Proved February 1784

wife : Mary

sons : Andrew
       William

"my three daughters" , Jane, Rebecca and Mary.

John McCaleb (no relationship stated) is to live with wife.

Executors : "trusty friends Andrew McBroom and
                        John Armstrong ".

Witnesses : Jno. Armstrong, John Allison.

— — —

Book A, page 295   Will in Archives

JAMES McCANLIS

Dated 28 December 1783
Proved February 1784

wife : Jane

" amongst my children, to wit : John Cammons, Robert Lindsey,
  Elizabeth John, James, David & William McCanlis."

Executors : wife Jane, son David.

Witnesses : Jno. Armstrong
            Thomas Jordan
            Anne (x) Armstrong.

Book A, page 296 ,Will in Archives, indexed as BREESE.

THOMAS (x) BRUCE                    Dated 1 June 1783
                                    Proved February 1784
wife : Martha

sons : Richard
       John
       Robert
       William

dau : Jannet Robeson

no relationship stated, possibly grandchildren :
"James Bruce & his sister Martha"
"William's son Thomas Bruce"
"Martha Robison & Rachel Robison".

Executors : wife Martha and son John·

Witnesses : Joseph Allison, John Berks.

— — —

Book A, page 298    Will in Archives

PHILIP DOSSETT                      Dated 7 December 1783
                                    Proved  February 1784
wife : Selah Dossett

daus : Seney
       Susannah

son : William

Executors : Benjamin Forrest
            Stephen Forrest·

Witnesses : Jacob Allen , Blaton Wood
            Joseph (x) Townsend.

— — —

Book A, page 300    Will in Archives

WILLIAM (x) EDWARDS,"son of John Edwards, Senior "

wife mentioned, name not stated    Dated  24 January 1784
                                   Proved February 1784
" all my sons .". .

Executors : Benjamin Davis , Sackfield Brewer.

Witnesses : Benjamin Lacy
            John Durham
— — —        John Edwards ·

52

Book A , page 301    DEED OF GIFT

STEPHEN KIRK to his son Jesse Kirk, two negroes.

Dated  22 October 1783, proved November 1784.

Witnesses : Wm. Kirk,  Lewis Kirk,  Jesse (x) Brown.

— — —

Book A, page 301  DEED OF GIFT

STEPHEN KIRK  to his son Thomas Kirk, both of Orange County,
one negro girl.

Dated 22 October 1783, proved November 1784.

Witnesses : Wm. Kirk , Lewis Kirk , Jesse (x) Brown.

— — —

Book A , page 304  POWER OF ATTORNEY

HADAWICK (x) DAVIS, spinster, to John Latta, both of Orange,

to sell lands in Orange and Mecklenberg counties.

Dated  4 July 1782, proved August 1784.

Witnesses : John Davis,  Robert Davis.

— — —

Book A , page 306

INVENTORY of Sundries sold by James Elliott, Administrator

to BENJAMIN NICHOLSON, deceased.  August 1784

— — —                                              — — —

Book A , page 30 7              Dated 5 July 1784
                               Recorded  August 1784
INVENTORY of goods and chattels of FRANCIS BARTLETT deceased

sold at public auction by Joseph Woody, Administrator.

Purchasers were : Joseph Woody , John Thompson, James Partin,
Henry Paris, Caleb Williams, Rachel Phinney, Joseph Norman,
Thomas Bradshaw, Samuel McMullen, Thomas Whitehead, Henry
O'Daniel, Mary Pennel, Margaret McMullin, Mary Taylor,
John Winnery, Robert Winnery, Samuel Stuart, John Morton,
John Steel, Moses Payce, Catren Whitehead, William Paris,
Wm. Barekley, Elie McDaniel, John Payne, Molton Mubanks (?),
James Roach.
— — —

Book A, page 309  BILL OF SALE

BOOTH PERRY of Granville Co., N.C. sells to Bernard Major of
Dinwiddie Co., Va., his right in three negroes " now in the
possession of Agnes Perry widow and relict of Peter Perry
late of Dinwiddie Co., Va. "

Dated 17 June 1763, proved August 1784.

Witnesses : John Duke, John Bowie, Mary Bowie.

— — —

(This original paper is in the Archives.)
Book A, page 310  DEED OF GIFT from

SARAH MORGAN to son Hardy Morgan, both of Orange Co., N.C.,
four negroes ... money ... stock ... household furnishings.

Dated  15 January 1780, proved August 1784.

Witnesses : Claud Bailey, Thomas Bailey.

— — —

Book A, page 311      Will in Archives

WILLIAM LINDLEY          Dated 22 September 1784
                         Proved  November 1784
wife : MARY

son  Thomas (under 21) gets plantation testator now lives on,
                with the mill.

" 2 daughters, namely Ruth and Mary " (under 18)

son Samuel (under 21) " plantation formerly owned by
                Reubin Hollingsworth "
son William (under 21) "plantation that John Lindley formerly
                owned."

brothers : Jonathan,  Thomas
        John Lindley "plantation joining James Newlin's."

relationship not stated : "Susannah Maris and her brother
William  Maris " (both under age).

Executors : brothers Thomas and Jonathan Lindley.

Witnesses : Joshua Hadley, Henry Holloday, Mary (x) Holloday.
— — —

54

Book A, page 314        Will in Archives

ROBERT (x) SCOTT " of Orange Co., N.C., being now in
                     Culpeper Co., Va. "

Dated 5 September 1780 , proved in Orange Co., N.C. Nov. 1784
                     by Rawley Corbin

Proved in Culpeper Co., Va. 20 Nov 1780 by William Roberts.

wife : Mary Scott

"my beloved children , Jesse Scott, William Scott,
Vaughan Scott, Molley Scott, John Scott, Henry Scott,
Richard Scott".

Executors : wife Mary,
            Fhannon (?) Viscrarser (?).

Witnesses : Rawley Corbin,
            Wm. Roberts.

— — —


Book A, page 315   QUIT CLAIM DEED from

HARDY MORGAN to Sarah Morgan, both of Orange Co., N.C.

Dated 15 September 1784, proved November 1784.

Witnesses : Benjamin Yeargin,  John Morgan
            Joseph Harwood,     John Owen.

— — —


Book A, page 316  Bill of Sale from WILLIAM HOOPER, SR. to

  his daughter Elizabeth, for a slave.

  Dated 25 Sept 1784, proved the same day.

  Witness: John Hogg.

  — — —

  A-316  Bill of Sale from WILLIAM HOOPER, SR. to his son

  Thomas Hogg Hooper, for a slave.

  Dated 25 Sept 1784, proved the same day.

  Witness: John Hogg.

  — — —

Book A, page 319     Will in Archives

JOHN (x) HALL            Dated 20 December 1784
wife : Jean Hall        Proved  February 1785

dau : Rebecca

"remainder of my children, viz : William Hall, Robert Hall,
Mary Hall, Sarah Hall, John Hall, Thomas Hall & Rachel Hall".

"father-in-law William Deal to live on plantation where he
now lives for 1 shilling rent ".

Executors : "Thomas Rountree and William Rountree, both
            of Orange County. "

Witnesses : William Buchannon   , Wm. McKie.

— — —

Book A, page 320     Will in Archives

MORDECAI (x) GWINN      No date
wife : Elizabeth        Proved  February 1785

"my three sons, John, Alexander and James " (all under age).

son : Edward

daus : Margaret
       Mary
       Jane
       Sarah
       Elizabeth.

grandsons : John Gwinn and Mordecai Gwinn.

Executors : wife, and son Edward.

Witnesses : Thomas (x) Moore , William Gwinn.

— — —

Book A, page 321     Will in Archives

ABEL (x) POCOCK       Dated  25 October 1784
wife : Temperance Pocock   Proved February  1785

dau : Nancy Pocock (under age )

(continued _
     next page⁻ )

56

Will of Abel Pocock, continued

son : James Pocock.

Executors : John Butler, Henry Bunch.

Witnesses : John Butler , Henry Bunch
Betsy (x) Rebe Horn.

- - -

Book A, page 323     Will in Archives

GEORGE FOGLEMAN                Dated   18 March 1785
                              Proved   May 1785
wife : Catherine

sons : Henry, George, John, Peter

dau : Eve (unmarried)

"my daughters when they left me", names & number not stated.

Executors : Malachi Fogleman,   Adam Starr.

Witnesses : Adam Smith,   Peter Hume (?).

- - -

Book A, page 325     Will in Archives

THOMAS TELFORD                 Dated   20 October 1784
                              Proved   May 1785
wife : Elizabeth

sons : Robert, Hugh, Thomas, all under age.
        William and Samuel, under 17 years

daus : Rosannah and Elizabeth

Telford land is bounded by James Warnock, Samuel Smith and
Cunningham Smith.

Executors : wife Elizabeth,
            "sons Robert Telford and Hugh Telford".

Witnesses : David Macklin,
            James Moore,
            James Macklin.

Book A, page 329      Will in Archives

WILLIAM (x) CRAIGE          Dated 11 January 1785
                           Proved    August 1785
wife : Abigail Craige

step-daughter : Elinor Black

daus : Joanna McMullin
       Abigail Pasmore (Parmore ?)
       Bathsheba Craton
       Ruth Simmons
       Mary Sheart.

relationship not stated : Rebecca Freeman.

Sole Executor : "my friend Samuel Freeman."

Witnesses : James Thompson   , Jacob Manhill?

— — —

Book A, page 330      Will in Archives

WILLIAM (x) WATSON         Dated  15 December  1785
                         Proved   August 1785
wife Ellenor Watson.

Executors : Thomas Barbee, Job Farmer.

Witnesses : David Drishall, John Green, Job Farmer.

— — —

Book A, page 330      Will not in Archives

HENRY (x) WAGGONER         Dated 1 July 1784
                         Proved  May 1785
wife : Ketriana

sons : John Waggoner, Henry Waggoner, Jacob Waggoner,
      all under age , get " tract of land adjoining John
      Brown, Alexander Torrentine and others" .

son : Stephen Smith

daus : Susannah Smith
       Elizabeth Johns
       Mary Waggoner   , Judith Waggoner
       Ketrin Waggoner, Uli Waggoner

granddaughters : "my son George Waggoner's children Mary
               and Agnes Waggoner"

Executors : wife Ketrin, son Stephen Smith.

Witnesses : John Hall, William Buchanon, William Hannah.

58
Book A, page 333    Will in Archives. Dated 1780

WILLIAM JOHNSTON of Orange Co., N.C., Merchant, "only son
and heir of Robert Johnston late of Harthwood (?) in the
Parish of Lochmabin and Shire of Annandale in Scotland,
deceased by Isabell his then wife."

mother : Isabell Johnston

"to the children of Catherine Gardner deceased late wife of
Mr. Edward Gardner of the City of Lincoln in the Kingdon of
Great Britain."

"my cousin Mary Robson, wife of Henry Robson, now or late
of the County of Cumberland near Carlisle in the Kingdom of
Great Britain, sister to the said Catherine Gardner. "

Mary Harrison widow of James Harrison dec'd, near the town
of  South        in the Shire of Lincoln in G. Britain.

"Elizabeth Robinson widow of Jno Robinson Esq. dec'd , late
of City of Lincoln."

"Robert Read now of Lincoln"

"John Dixon Esq. of Lochmaben in shire of Annandale"

£ 100 to Seminary of learning.

William Johnston's  deceased wife and children are buried
at his plantation at Little River in Orange Co., N.C.


Trustees for the estate of "beloved daughter and only child
Amelia Johnston ( a minor) are : Edward Stabler, Esq. of
Petersburg, Va., Samuel Johnston, Esq. of Edenton, N.C.,
James Hogg, Thomas Hart, Jno. Kinchen, Richard Bennehan.

"Mrs. Ann Hamilton, late of the City of Lincoln, widow of
Hamilton Hamilton late of town of Kingston upon Hull in the
shire of York... daughter of Wm. Alderman Fow. "

"Mrs. Mildred Fenton wife of Thos. Fenton near the town of
Leeds in the shire of York .. dau. of Jno. and Elizabeth
Robinson."

" to Robert Burnett of the Parish of  Morshall (?)  and County
of Withdall (Millsdale ?) in Scotland, brother to my said
mother."

- continued on next page -

Will of WILLIAM JOHNSTON continued

"Mrs. Jane Craik of Moorshall Parish,sister to my said mother"

"my friend James Gibson of Kelton in the Shire of Galloway in Scotland"

Executors: friends James Hogg, Thomas Hart, John Kinchen,
Richard Bennehan.          No witnesses.

─ ─ ─

A-337   Will in Archives. Dated 26 Aug 1785, proved Nov 1785.

JAMES (x) HARRIS               wife: Hannah

daus: Mary Harris, Elizabeth Harris, Sarah Harris,
Susannah Harris, "Martha Hargrove wife of Henry Hargrove"

sons: Richmond, James, John, "lands and plantation on Flat
River and Eno".

Executors: son Richard, friends Edward Harris and Richard
Bennehan.
Witnesses: Susannah (x)Glen, Wm (x) Pettigrew, Harris Pettigrew.

─ ─ ─

A-339   Will in Archives. Dated 28 Sept 1784, proved Nov 1785.

WILLIAM (x) FOSSETT, farmer    "sick and very weak"

wife: Margrete whole estate during her lifetime.

son: William -"the place he now lives on" - "Ł 20 more than
any of the rest "
daughter: Elenor ? (OLDS has this daughter as Eliza).

No executor named.
Witnesses: David Fossett, Richard Fossett, Jno. Umstead.

─ ─ ─

A-340   Bond between William McCauley, Chairman of the County
Court of Orange County, N.C. and Matthew McCauley for
apprenticeship of THOMAS KEE (10 years old) as a blacksmith.

Dated 3 March 1785.   Witness: J. Benton, C.C.

─ ─ ─

A-341   Bond between Jno. Ray, Chairman of Orange County, N.C.
County Court and Roswell Huntington. Dated 3 March 1785.

FRANCIS NASH (13 years old) is apprenticed to Roswell Huntington, silver and gold smith.

Signatures to Indenture: Archer Grisham, Roswell Huntington.
Witness: J. Benton, C.C.

─ ─ ─

A-342 Bond between Wm. McCauley, Chairman of Orange County,
N.C. County Court, and John Steel, Sr. March 3, 1785.

BETSY COOK is apprenticed to "learn the art of a spinster".

Signatures to Indenture: Wm. McCauley, Jno. Steel.
Witness: J. Benton, C.C.

— — —

A-343 Deed of Gift from JOHN STEEL, SR to John Steel, Jr
for wagon and gears, cattle, etc, etc.

Witnesses: Thomas Howard, Samuel Steel.

— — —

A-345 Power of Attorney from JOHN EVANS of Philadelphia, Pa.
to JOHN LATTA, of Orange County, N.C. "trusty and
esteemed friend", to collect from "John Kelly trader late of
said county" and "William Jackson, trader of Hillsboro"....

Dated 13 Jan 1786, proved Feb 1786.
Witnesses: William Gregson, Thos. Latta.

— — —

A-347 same as A-342 above - BETSY COOK apprenticed.

— — —

A-348 Deed from JAMES ARMSTRONG, Planter, to grandson
THOMAS ARMSTRONG, of Lincoln County, Va. for one negro.

Dated 3 May 1786, proved May 1786.
Witnesses: Jacob Lake, Mary Lake.

— — —

A-349 Power of Attorney from JOHN TRICE to EDWARD TRICE, SR
to execute deed of conveyance to Thomas Gwinn for
land joining land of Edward Grisham, Sr & Edward Grisham, Jr.

Dated 7 Nov 1784, proved Feb 1785.
Witnesses: Thomas May, Thomas Lay, Robert Abercrombie.

— — —

A-350 Deed from JOHN MAY to "JAMES DESERN my son-in-law"
for land on Elibees Creek ... joining lands of John
Baker, John Vickers and ..... Grisham. "for love and
affection..."

Dated 14 Feb 1785, proved Feb 1785.
Witnesses: Henry Bunch, George Grisham.

— — —

A-351  DEED for negroes and other chattels from

SAMUEL MAY to son Southerland and daughters Molly and Sally.

The negroes were willed to him or to his wife Izzabel by
Thomas Stephens late of Virginia after the decease of Mary
Stephens the widow and relict of the said Thomas Stephens,
dec'd.      Dated 26 May 1785, proved May 1785.

Witness: Jacob Richards.

- - -

A-352  DEED (Improvements and Rite of Entry) from
PENELOPE DIXON to Joseph Buckingham.

Witnesses: Benjamin Piggott        Dated 3 May 1784
           Drury (x) Hunnycutt     Proved  Feb 1785.

- - -

A-353 DEED for negroes from ATHANISIUS ROBISON to

granddaughter Sarah Lindsay, son Nathaniel Robison,
daughter Mary Lindsay.

Witnesses: Eli McDaniel          Dated 25 May 1785
           John Murry            Proved  May 1785.

- - -

A-354 DEED to plantation from GEORGE HORNER to
son James Horner.

Witnesses: Thomas Hunter         Dated 17 Feb 1785
           George Horner, Jr.    Proved  May 1785

- - -

A-355 Will in Archives. Dated 31 March 1783, proved Feb 1785.

JOHN McCOLLOCH              wife: Mary

sons: Robert, James, John.

Executors: John Armstrong, William Brayns.
Witnesses: Robert Idan (?), Sarah (x) Locklin, John Armstrong.

- - -

A-356 BOND (for Sheriff). Archibald Latta, Wm. Mebane,
Alexander Mebane, Jr., Wm. McCauley, Matthew McCauley,
Anthony Sharp, William Bell.
                        Archibald Lytle, Commissioner
Witness: A.Tatom
Dated 1 March 1785.

- - -

A-357 Will in Archives. Dated 9 Sept 1785, proved Feb 1786 ?

JOHN VAUGHAN                 wife: Catron.

Executors: wife and James Walker.
Witnesses: James Vaughan, Thomas (x) King.

62

A-358  Will in Archives. Dated 25 Dec. 1785, proved Feb 1786

WILLIAM NELSON          wife: Ann

daus: Rachel, Rebeca, Ruth, Elinor, Hannah.

son: Samuel.

Executors: wife Ann, William Adams.
Witnesses: John Allen, Samuel Stout, Joseph Stout.
- - -

A-359  MEMORANDUM OF WILL. Recorded Feb 1786 ? Not dated.

JINNET TATE

sons: James, George

daus: Margaret, Elizabeth, Keturo, Polly, Agnes,
      Jinnet (a minor), Lettice (she gets a black mare "I
                  had of Andrew Mitchell")
"The sum betwixt Samuel Nelson and me I leave betwixt his
own two daughters to be divided equally betwixt them and
one to his son David the overplus I paid to John Mitchell
above his wife's dower I leave to his daughter Jinnet."

Bequests made to Andrew Mitchell's oldest son, and to "my
daughter Polly".
Samuel Nelson is requested to take Jinnet and Margaret
to raise.

Executors: son James Tate, Samuel Nelson.
Witnesses: Thomas Mulhollan, Jas. Mebane, Edward Willson.
- - -

A-361  Will in Archives. Dated 1 Nov 1785, proved

DAVID CRAIG          wife: name not stated

Sons: William Johnston, John, David

daughter mentioned, but not named.   Unborn child mentioned.

Executors: Friends William McCauley, John Craig, Samuel Craig.
Witnesses: Samuel Hunter, Aaron (x) Hunter, Wm.(x) Lagan
- - -

A-362  Will in Archives. Dated 3 May 1785, proved - no date.

ROBERT FOSSETT          wife: name not stated

sons: George, Robert, Thomas

daus: Fanny, Elizabeth

grandsons: Robert, son of George; Edward, son of Thomas.
                  -continued-

A362, Will of Robert Fossett, continued -

Witnesses: John Walker, Hugh Crawford. No executor named.

— — —

A- 363.          Not in Archives. Dated 1 March 1786, proved
GEORGE ALLEN          DEED OF GIFT to his          May 1786.

grandson George Mebane (a minor),"son of daughter Margaret,
wife of James Mebane," and his

granddaughter Elizabeth Mebane,"sister of George Mebane ".

Witnesses: Absolom Tatom,Wm. McCauley, A. Lytle.

— — —

A-364 BILL OF SALE, from BENJAMIN CHAPMAN to William Newman.

Dated 26 June 1784, proved Nov 1785.

Witnesses: Bern M. Gurkin (?), Benjamin Newman.

— — —

A-365 BOND . ASA BLAKE of Wake County for James Blake's
standing security for Asa Blake to the Administrators of
Benjamin and Jones Blake.
Witness: Jno. G. Rencher.          Dated 25 Nov 1785

— — —

A-366 BILL OF SALE from SAMUEL GUTHRIE of Gloucester Co., Va.
to Edward Trice of "Orange County and State of Virginia."

Dated 8 October, no year given.  Witnesses: John Butler
                                              A. Tatom.

— — —

A-366 BILL OF SALE from WILLIAM RHOADS to Joseph Moore.

Dated 21 July 1786, proved Aug 1786.
Witnesses: Josiah Watts, John Moore.

— — —

A-367 DEED for a negro from JOHN EDWARDS to "friend Margaret
Edwards, and at her death to her son Henry Edwards."
Dated 14 June 1785          Witnesses: John Durrum,
                                       Sarah Durrum.

— — —

A-368 BILL OF SALE from JOHN MURRAY to John Elliott
Dated 6 July 1785, proved May 1786 Witness: David Pasmore.

64

A-369  Bond between Alexander Mebane, for County Court and
John McVinch. Binding "JOHN RILEY, now of the age of 2 yrs"
to John McVinch as a servant, until he becomes 21 yrs old.

Dated 24 Nov 1784.          Witness: A. Tatom.

- - -

A-370 Agreement (Easement) , between Jesse Benton and
William Shepperd of Hartford, both of Orange County, N.C.

Dated 4 June 1783.          Witnesses: James Boswell,
- - -                                   James Gooch.

A-371  Bill of Sale. John Stacy sells negroes to
William Galbreath.

Dated 17 March 1786, proved Nov 1786.
Witnesses: Geo. Hodge, Lewis Jones.

- - -

A-372  Will in Archives. Dated 10 March 1786,proved Nov '86.

JOBE FARMER               wife: name not stated

sons: Athniel Farmer, James Farmer

daus: Ann Farmer, Drucilla Farmer.

Executors: wife, and Daniel Green.
Witnesses: Daniel Green, Grisham Forrest, John (x) Edwards.

- - -

A-373 Bill of Sale from PHILIP PENDLETON to James G. Hunt,
for a negro, "now in possession of Henry Thompson".

Dated 21 July 1786, proved Nov 1786.
Witness: Henry Thompson.

- - -

A-374  Bill of Sale from GRISCAL McCALLISTER to Mary Clark.
Dated 25 March 1786, proved Nov 1786. Witness: John Ray.

- - -

A-375 Power of Attorney from JOSEPH BRAWNER to
James Hester of Mecklinburgh County, Va.    Dated 30 May 1787
Witness: J. Benton, C.C.                     proved May 1787.

- - -

A-376  Deed from WILL HOOPER to his daughter Elizabeth.
Dated 24 Oct 1787, proved - -
Witnesses: Walter Alves, Wm. Watters (or Walters).

---

A-377  Bill of Sale from JOHN MURRY to James Neal, for a negro.

Dated 30 May 1787, proved May 1787.
Witnesses: Andrew Gibson, Tho. Johns.

— — —

A-377 Bill of Sale from WILLIAM SHEPPERD to John Williams, Esq. of Chatham County, for a negro.

Dated 1 March 1788.                    Witness: S. Pinto.

— — —

A-378 Deed of Gift from CARNES TINNEN to son Robert Tinnen.

Dated 4 Oct 1787, proved Feb 1788.
Witnesses: Jacob Lake, Wm. Tate.

A-379 Bond from ROBERT ABERCROMBIE to Charles Abercrombie.

Dated 5 Feb 1784, proved Nov 1788.
Witnesses: John Michaux, Harris Grisham.

— — —

A-380 Power of Attorney from JAMES WILLIAMS "late of Hills-bourough  in North Carolina but now in Washington in the County of Wilkes and State of Georgia Esquire" to John Estes of Hillsborough, Esquire, and John Williams, Esq. of Chatham Co., N.C.
                              Witness: Thomas Watts.
Dated 6 Oct 1787, proved Aug 1788.

———

                    End of BOOK A.

BOOK B, page 1. Will in Archives. Dated 20 May 1785,

JOHN BUTLER                    wife: Anne

Executors: wife Anne, William Rainey, Esq.
Witnesses: Moses Crawford, Wm. Shannon.

— — —

B-2  Will in Archives. Dated 10 Jan 1787

DANIEL HOGAN                    wife: name not stated

sons: Thomas Lloyd Hogan; another son, name not stated.

daughters, names and number not stated.

Executors: "well-beloved-friends" John Hogan and
                William McCauley.
Witnesses: Henry Morras, Sam Craig, Alec Piper.

— — —

B-3 Will in Archives. Dated 17 Oct 1785, proved --

SARAH MORGAN            Sons: John Morgan, Hardy Morgan

daus: Anne Hart,     and   Sarah Yeargan, wife of Benjamin.

granddaughter: Charlotte Yeargin

"the surviving children she (Sarah Yeargin) has by Ben Yeargin".

Executors: Benjamin Yeargin, Daniel Hogan.
Witnesses: Robt. Campbell, Nicholas Quesenbury, Dan Boothe.

— — —

B-5 Deed of Gift from JOHN SHEELS to his wife Mary Sheels,
for 1 negro girl.          Witness: John Nichols.
Dated 2 March 1787, proved ...

— — —

B-6 Will in Archives. Dated 4 August 1786, proved ..

WILLIAM STROUD           wife: Elizabeth

sons: John Stroud, Anderson Stroud, Wm. Stroud,
       Marshal Stroud, Thomas Stroud, Dickson Stroud.
dau: Margaret Douglass
daus: Mary Thrift, Salley King, Fanney Howell, Eliz. Stroud.

Executors: wife Elizabeth, and "trusty friend John Hogan".
Witnesses: William Willis, William Buckner, Mary Buckner.

— — —

B-11 Power of Attorney from ABSOLOM TATOM of Hillsboro, N.C.
to Charles Taylor.         Dated 2 April 1785.

— — —

B-13 Will in Archives. Dated 10 March 1786, proved ..

JOB FARMER            wife: name not stated

sons: Nathaniel Farmer, James Farmer.

Anne Farmer, Drucilla Farmer

Executors: wife, and Daniel Green.
Witnesses: Daniel Green, Gresham Forrest, John Edwards.

— — —

B-14 JAMES (or FAMUS) S...?..(impossible to read) , assigns
his right in a tract of land to "Eliza Simons relict of
Henry Simons deceased."    Dated 24 Sept 1782, proved ..
Witnesses: Ralph Jackson, Eliza Williams.

— — —

B-15  Will of RICHARD HOPSON. Dated 12 Dec 1786, proved ..

Wife: Elizabeth Hopson

sons: Younger Hopson, Mar/<sup>tin</sup> Hopson, Daniel Hopson.

daus: Sarah Hopson, Mary Hopson

sons-in-law: Ephriam Barcor, Isaac Kirk, William Baucom.

Executors: wife Elixabeth, John Jenkins.
Witnesses: Nathan Almond, George Taylor.

－ － －

B-17 Will in Archives. Dated 5 July 1787, proved ..

NICHOLAS HOLT              wife: Eve

sons: Francis Holt, John Holt, Nicholas Holt, James Holt.

dau: Rachel Holt

grandson: Michael Holt

Executors: Francis Holt, Nicholas Holt.
Witnesses: Michael Holt, Joshua Holt.

－ － －

B-19 Power of Attorney from MICHAEL SAMPSON of Wilmimgton,
Merchant, to Joseph Dickson.
Dated 1 Feb 1787, proved ··        Witness: T. Benton, C.C.

－ － －

B-20 Will in Archives. Dated 18 July 1877, proved ..

ANDROSS RANDALL      Wife: Catherine

daughter, Mary Randall.            No executor named.

Witnesses: Robert Cate, Joseph Cate, Thomas Cate.

－ － －

B-22  Will in Archives. Dated 18 June 1787, proved ..

WILLIAM WILLIAMS          wife: Elizabeth

son: William gets land given to testator by the State of
    N.C. for his services "as Captain in the Continental
    line of this State."

brother: Sam Williams
nephew: William Williams, son of Sam.

His wife gets house and lot in town of Hillsborough, and
land which he purchased from Jacob Richards in Orange Co.
Executors: wife Elizabeth, George Doherty.
Witnesses: J.Watts, Will Lytle.

－ － －

B-25 Deed from PATRICK McCOLLOCH to John Woods, son of
Hugh Woods, for 100 acres of land after the death of
Patrick McColloch and his wife. Dated 20 August 1785.
Witnesses: Andrew Patterson, John Elliott.

— — —

B-26 Will in Archives. Dated 31 Oct 1787, proved --

JOHN SHEELS                  wife: Mary Cumming

Executrix: wife Mary Cumming.
Witnesses: Wm. McCauley, Will Lytle, A. Tatom.

— — —

B-28 Will in Archives. Dated Dec 1787, proved --

THOMAS PRATT     Nephews and nieces are the chief legatees.

nephew: James Pratt L 100 "hard money", etc
"       George Pratt L 100 "hard money",Gilt Stock Buckle,
                     1pr Shoe Buckles
nieces: Peggy Pratt, Lucy Pratt, money, etc.

relationship, if any, not stated to: James Grant, David
Ray, John McWhitney, Walter Alves, Samuel Benton.
"James Taylor son of Frederick Taylor" L 25."paper money".

Executor: David Ray. Witnesses: John McWhitney,
                                 Mary (x) Pratt.
— — —

B-32 Will in Archives. No date.

CHRISTIAN GRADY   Heirs are Isaac Gaddes and his wife.

Executor: James Hogg. Witnesses: Wm. Parks, Elizabeth Parks.

— — —

B-32 Will in Archives. Dated 25 March 1779, proved --

JAMES FEW                  wife: Frances

son: James

"My three daughters Elizabeth, Ann and Bethiah".

Executrix: wife Frances.
Witnesses: John Wood, Ann Wood, John Flinthem.

— — —

B-34 Will in Archives. Dated 8 Nov 1787, proved --

ARCHIBALD HAMILTON          nephew: Joseph Hamilton

"First son, Joseph Hamilton ....

The will is unfinished, and unsigned - no witnesses.

— — —

B-35 Will in Archives. Dated 21 April 1786, proved --

JOHN (x) REED                    wife: Lydia Reed

His property is on Stagg's Creek and Hico Creek.

daughters: Rebecca Reed, Jemimah Reed.

Executor: Henry Cole.
Witnesses: Thomas Cole, Wm. McMennamy, John McMennamy.
— — —

B-36 Will in Archives. Dated 26 Oct 1788, proved --

JAMES (x) VAUGHAN            second wife: Mary Vaughan

Son, Grief Evand Vaughan and daughter Susannah Selton,
given "one shilling apiece".

Children of second wife: John Vaughan, Sarah, Peggy,
Betsey, Polly, to receive all property.

Executors: Mary Vaughan, James Walker.
Witnesses: Wm. Smallwood, Julius King.
— — —

B-37 Will in Archives. Dated --, proved --

SAMUEL PARKS               wife: Mary Vaughan Parks

sons: Thomas, Samuel, Alexander, John, James

daus: Tine, she has a son William , name not stated.
      Nancy," "  " "  Alexander, name not stated.

The Executors are ordered to sell 100 acres of land
adjoining James Bracken on Stony Creek.

Executors: wife Mary, John Robinson, William Rainey.
Witness: William Rainey.
— — —

B-38 Agreement between THOMAS KING and JEREMIAH EDGE,
both of Orange County, N.C. Dated 14 October 1788.

THOMAS KING proposes to leave wife Sophia and children,
to travel. Under this agreement he binds himself to Jeremiah Edge. Agrees to divide personal and real property
(land bought of John Duke and taken up in parternership
with Jeremiah Edge.) Edge is to look after King's wife
and children.   Witnesses: Archibald Harris, John Duke.
— — — — — — —

B-39 Will in Archives. Dated 6 July 1788, proved --

JOSIAH WATTS    wife: Susannah       daughter: Susannah

Partners in business: Courtney Watts, Wm. Lytle, Esq.
                              - continued -

70

B-39  Will of JOSIAH WATTS continued -

Executors: brother Thomas Watts, John Grant Rencher.
Witnesses: Vincent P. Williamson, William Courtney.

- - -

B-40 Will in Archives. Dated 1 July 1788, proved

THOMAS SEARES                wife: Elizabeth Seares

sons; William, Joseph, Thomas, John, Henry

daus: Elizabeth, Mary Surls (?)

Executors: Elizabeth Seares, Thomas Seares, John Seares.
Witnesses: Wortham Glenn, Henry Seares, Elizabeth (x) Seares.

- - -

B-41  Will in Archives. Dated 13 July 1786, proved ..

PETER (x) HENDRICKS        wife: Amy

sons: Isaac, Abraham, William

daus: Ann Hendricks, Mary Hendricks Balander, Eliz. Hendricks

Executrix: Amy Hendricks.
Witnesses: John Cabe, Thomas Reding.

- - -

B-42  Will in Archives.  Dated 22 August 1787, proved ..

WILLIAM (x) LOGAN        Wife: Agnes

son: John Logan        daughter Elizabeth
  grandson: William Logan.

Executors: John Hart, Senior; James Hart.
Witnesses: William Hart, John Hart Jr.

- - -

B-50  Will of NATHANIEL (x) LEWIS. Dated 11 Nov 1788,
                              proved ..
Wife: Elizabeth

sons: John Lewis, William Lewis

daus: Lydia, Sarah, Rebeccah, Mary

Executors: wife Elizabeth, son John.
Witnesses: John Wood, Anne Wood.

- - -

B-54  Will in Archives. Dated 25 Oct 1785, proved ..

JAMES PAULL                wife: Elizabeth

sons: James, William, John.

dau: Rachel.              grandau: Elizabeth Carregan.

Executors: Elizabeth Paull, John Paull.
Witnesses: Margaret Collins, Joseph Collins, Jesse Benton.
- - -

B-57  Will in Archives. Dated 19 Jan 1789, proved ..

JEAN (x) BOWLING

Sons: Archibald, Abraham, Alexander, and Andrew Bowling.

daus: Isabel Butler wife of John Butler,
      Susannah Boswell, Elizabeth Bowling.

relationship not stated: Nancy Flintom.

Witnesses: Sam'l Wray, William Nunn, Joseph Hart.
- - -

B-63  Will in Archives. Dated 20 April 1789, proved ..

ELI McDANNELL (signed McDANIEL).   wife: Margaret

son John, land on Quaker Road adjoining Peter Woolf and
      Samuel Campbell- bought of C. Lytle.

son James, land formerly occupied by Daniel McVey, and also
      land bought from James Williams.

son Eli, land adjoining above tracts.

daus: Elizabeth, Susannah, and two younger ones not named.

Executors: wife Margaret, son John.
Witnesses:Ruth Christmas, Robert Scoby.
- - -

B-65  Will in Archives. Dated 15 March 1789, proved ..

ADAM MARLEY                wife: Rosannah

sons: Robert, Adam, and Samuel Marley.
                                        Robert.
grandsons: Robert Marley son of Adam, Adam Marley son of /

" I give to my beloved son Adam Marley Mary Douglas Hannah
White Nancy Hall Robert Marley's son Adam, and my son Adam
Marley's son Robert .." (No punctuation given.)
                              - continued -

B-65 Will of ADAM MARLEY continued -

Executor: Samuel Marley.
Witnesses: Arthur Lovins, John Stark, Alexander Robbs.
－ ——

B-70   Will of JOSEPH ALLISON.   Dated 7 April 1789, proved ..

Wife: Elizabeth

Sons: David Allison(land on Duck River),Joseph Allison.

daus: Margaret, Mary, Sarah, Nancy Allison.

sons-in-law: John Thompson, Asiriah Thompson, Samuel Woods.

Executors: Elizabeth Allison, David and John Thompson.
Witnesses: John Wilson, Sarah (x) Gomage.
－ － －

B-72   Will of WILLIAM CLARKE.   Dated 25 July 1789, proved ..

Heir: "George Daniel, for his trouble and care of me".

Executor: Samuel Daniel.
Witnesses: William Findley, John Daniel, Mary Castlebury.
－ － －

B- 73  Will in Archives. Dated 3 Sept 1788, proved ;;

STEPHEN TATOM             wife: Mornin

sons: Stephen and John lands on Camp Creek.
      William, 1 shilling.

daus: Sarah, Anna, Elizabeth, Francis, Tizia, Mary, Jemima.

Executors: "trusty friends Towland Gooch and John Wilburn".
Witnesses: Fowler Jones, William (x) Tatom.
－ － －

B 74-77. Will in Archives. Dated 9 June 1789, proved ..

CHARLES JOHNSTON             wife: Martha Johnston

son: George

sons-in-law: John Freeland, Chaldous (?) Bailey,
             Samuel Craig, John Strayhorn, Matthew McCauley.

grandsons: William Craig, John McCauley.

Charles McCauley and Charles Strayhorn mentioned, but no
relationship stated.
                              - continued -

B-74-77 Will of CHARLES JOHNSTON continued -

He says "all my children" , but does not give names.

Executors: "trusty and well-beloved friends, Samuel Craig
and William McCauley."
Witnesses: Wm. Blackwood, Joseph Blackwood, James Blackwood.
— — —

B-78  Will in Archives. Dated 1 May 1789, proved ..

JAMES DIXON            wife: Nancy

sons: James, Stewart, Robert, William, Thomas, "my five sons"

daus: Polly, Margaret.

Executors: wife Nancy, and Stewart.
Witnesses: James Freeland, Joseph Hodge.
— — —

B-79  Will in Archives. Dated 12 Dec 1786, proved Feb 1790 ?

JOHN FOUST            wife: Barbara Foust

sons: Philip, John, Jacob, Christian, and George each get
5 shillings.
" 3 youngest sons George, Peter and Daniel Foust" get
all his real estate.

daus: Barbara Clap, and Judith Clap, get 5 shillings each.

Executors: " two sons George and Peter Foust".
Witnesses: Joseph Stout, Samuel Stout, Jacob Marshall.
— — —

B-81  Bill of Sale from JOHN McDANIEL of Cane Creek Settlement of Orange Co,,and Mary his wife, to Daniel Foust.

Dated 20 Jan 1790     Witnesses: John Murray (?), James Neal.
-- — —

B-82  Will in Archives. Dated 19 March 1789, proved 1790.

THOMAS (x) ASPEN         wife: Sarah

Relationship, if any, to Souths and Paschalls not stated

"Benjamin South is to pay her (Sarah) 3 pounds a year and
William Paschall 2 pounds a year, then I will my plantation
to William Paschall during his life and his wife's life,
and at their demise to William Paschall's son Thomas".

                     - continued -

B-82 Will of Thomas Aspen continued -

"Benjamin South and his wife"...
"Dilly South and Gemima South"...

Executors: "Trusty friends John Armstrong and John Woods."
Witnesses: Jno. Armstrong, Jno. Allison.

— — —

B-84  Bill of Sale from VINCENT PETER WILLIAMSON of town of
Hillsborough, N.C. to Charles Holeman of Caswell Co., N.C.

For Lots #70, 71, 89, 90, dwelling house, one negro woman,
gray horse, etc.                    Dated 25 Feb 1790

Witnesses: William Cumming, Will Rountree.

— — —

B-85 Bill of Sale from ROBERT ASHLEY to Jeremiah Edge, both
of Orange Co., N.C.   Witnesses: Wm. Smallwood, Wm. Dyar.

— — —

B-85 Will in Archives. Dated 11 June 1789, proved Feb 1790.

ANTHONY STANFORD            wife: Elizabeth

sons: Charles, Robert, James and William Stanford.

daus: Agnes, Jean, Martha, Elizabeth, Mary, Margaret.

granddau: Fanny King.

Executors: "my wife Elizabeth and my son James".
Witnesses: Daniel (x) Hanley, J. Galbreath.

— — —

B-87  Bill of Sale from GEORGE DOHERTY to James Hogg, Esq.,
both of Orange Co., N.C.  Dated 2 Jan 1790, recorded Feb '90.
(James Hogg is guardian for Polly Burke.)

Witnesses: Theopilus Thompson, Wm. Comb, Walter Alves.

— — —

B-89  Deed of Gift from ELIZABETH PAUL of Orange Co., N.C.
"for love" .., "to my son James Paul of Washington Co., Ga."
and for 1 shilling paid, a negro boy named Peter.

Dated 30 Nov 1789, proved May 1790.
Witnesses: Robert Faucet, Jacob Walters.

-- — —

B-90  Will in Archives. Dated 17 March 1789, proved May 1790.

ROBERT NELSON             wife: Mary

"to my two sons James and Robert the plantation whereon I
now live " .. " but my wife to have the benefit until they
arrive to the age of 17 and 16 years".        - continued -

B-90 Will of ROBERT NELSON continued -

"daughter Jean Scott one lot in the town of Randolph Courthouse in the County of Randolph."

Witnesses: John Umstead, Peter Wrightman.

— — —

B-92  Will in Archives. Dated 27 Sept 1789, proved May 1790.

ZACHARIAH ALLEN            wife: name not stated

sons: George; William;
      James gets land in "Lincorn County on S. Side of Ca-
      tawba (River)."
      John, under age.

"rest of my children, Mary Jean, Sarah, Robert
Ruth Lovda(?) Joseph & Zachariah." (punctuation very poor.)

Executors: "my worthy friends John Thomson son of Thomas
           and James Allen."

Witnesses: James Allen, Daniel McDaniel.

— — —

B- 93  Will in Archives. Dated 29 March 1790, proved May
                                                    1790.
CHRISTIAN (x) HUFFMAN

brother: Peter Huffman

"friend and brother Jesse Acock"

Elizabeth Huffman, no relationship stated.

"I give and bequeath to Suffice (?) Ingle, if her mother
swears her to me one shilling, if not nothing."

"my brothers and sisters" mentioned, but not named.

Executors: friends George Clap and Barney Troxler.
Witnesses: Michael Charles, Jacob Clap.

— — —

B-94  Deed of Gift for 1 negro girl from SAMUEL DANIEL to
his son John Daniel, for love.

Dated 17 Feb 1790, proved May 1790.
Witnesses: Edward Trice, Robert T. Daniel.

— —

B-95    Will in Archives. Dated 11 Sept 1789, proved May 1790

JOHN (x) HOLSTEIN

brother: Jacob Holstein "land on Adcock Creek in Granville
         County, N.C."

**B-95 Will of JOHN HOLSTEIN continued -**

brother-in-law : Henry Streider "land in Granville on
                Adcock Creek".
"three sisters Mary, Susannah and Barbaryman".

Executors: Henry Streider, Jacob Holstein.
Witnesses: William Jacob, George (x) Streider.

- - -

B-97  Will in Archives. Dated 28 Jan 1790, proved Aug 1790.

ANDREW PATTEN (or PATTON)

wife: Margaret " to receive an equal part with the children
      who are boys and girls."

"to sons Robert and Thomas all my Cumberland lands- one
survey."
"to sons John and Andrew land in Orange County."

daughter; Sarah Hughes.

He speaks of "wife and younger children."

Executors: "friends Joseph Thompson and James Hughes."
Witnesses: Henry Campbell, Robert Tinnen, John Thompson.

- - -

B-98  Deed of Gift from THOMAS (x) BIBINGS "to the two
children Robert Carter and Thomas Bebins junior" , horse,
cow, etc. No relationship stated.    Witness: Joseph Sharp.

Dated 15 August 1790, proved August 1790.

- - -

B-99 Will in Archives. Dated 25 Aug 1790, proved -- 1790.

SAMUEL McCADDAMS or McADAMS.    wife: Catherine.

mother: Sarah McCaddams.    brothers: Joseph and William.

dau: Mary

"my children, Sarah, Catherine, Ellender, John, Joseph,
and William."

Executors: "my trusty friends John Sloss and Andrew Murdock."
Witnesses: Thos. Mulhollan, Jno. Unstead, Alex. Kirkpatrick.

- - -

B-100 Will in Archives. Dated 24 Nov 1789, proved .

ARTHUR MANGUM              wife: Lucy

sons: William Mangum, Arthur Mangum                - continued -

B-100   Will of Arthur Mangum continued -

daus: Sally Bobitt, Clarey, Chaney.
        Holley "land adjoining John Mize's and James Bobbitt's
              and William Mangum's."

Executors: "trusty friends John Carrington and
              William Mangum, junior."
- - -

B-102   Will in Archives.   Dated 6 July 1782, proved Oct 1790.

JACOB CANTRELL                          wife: Mary

daus: eldest Margaret Cantril, Jane, Hannah, Sarah, Susannah.

sons: Zebedee Cantril, Thomas Cantril, Joseph Cantril.

Sole Executor: wife Mary.
Witnesses: John Hinslee, Rachel (x) Robinson.
- - -

B-105   Will in Archives.   Dated 20 Feb 1790, proved Nov 1790.

JOHN JENKINS                            wife: Mary

Children listed in the order they are named in the will.
daughters, Nancy Fennel, Patty Allen,
sons, Sanford Jenkins, John, Thomas, Mansfield Jenkins,
daughters Betsey, Polly, Patience, Catherine Jenkins.

"granddaughter Higgerson" (under 18 years of age). See below.

Executors: wife Mary Jenkins, and friends William Merritt
              and Joseph Fennel.
Witnesses: William Halliburton, Massey Chrismus Medearis,
              William Merritt.
- - -

B-124 The will of JOHN JENKINS exactly as above, except that
the granddaughter is called Polly Higgerson.
- - -

B-107   Will in Archives.   Dated 3 Nov 1790, proved Nov 1790.

JOHN (x) ALBRIGHT               wife: Hester (is pregnant ?)

sons: John Christian plantation on Beaver Creek joining
                                        John Clap.
"If I should have more sons than the one mentioned ...."

daughters: Elizabeth, "rest of her sisters..."

Executors: brother William Albright, neighbor Adam Smith.
Witnesses: William Harp, Jacob Clap.
- - -

B-109 Receipt. ROBERT RAY, Junior and JOHN RAY, sons of Robert Ray, Senior, do acknowledge that we have received our full part of the real estate of Robert Ray, our father.

Dated 31 Dec 1789. Witnesses: Joseph Clendenning, Thomas Holgan.

— — —

B-110 Bill of Sale from NORMAN BIGELOW to John Umstead, both of Orange Co., N.C. for "one negro fellow".

Dated 9 Feb 1791, proved Feb 1791. Witness: James Grant.

— — —

B-111 Bill of Sale from JAMES WIRES of Chatham Co., N.C. to George Foust of Orange Co., N.C., for "one negro man".

Dated 8 Nov 1790, proved Nov 1790. Witness: Jno. Ray.

— — —

B-112  Will in Archives. Dated 18 Sept 1790, proved Feb 1791.

SAMUEL CRAIG                    wife: Mary

sons: William Craig, David Craig, Samuel Craig, all under 20.

dau: Martha , for others, see below.

"My children together with my wife to wit Martha, Margaret, Elizabeth, Jenney, Issabel, and my wife."

Executors: wife Mary, "trusty friend George Johnston." Witnesses: Wm. McCauley, John Craig, Matthew McCauley.

— — —

B-114 Bill of Sale from HENRY STEPHENS to John Ross, both of Orange Co., N.C.          Witness: Thomas Mulhollan. Dated 30 Jan 1791, proved Feb 1791.

— — —

B-116 Bill of Sale from HARDY SANDERS of Wake Co., N.C. to John Grant Rencher of Orange Co., N.C., for a negro girl.

Dated 3 March 1790, proved Feb 1791. Witness: Joseph Taylor.

— — —

B-117  Power of Attorney from JOHN MORGAN to "trusty friend John Grant Rencher" to manage his plantation. He speaks of "my children" but they are not named.

Dated 3 March 1791 ?, proved Feb 1791. Witnesses: Henry (x) Sears, Jacob Flowers, Jr., Mark Morgan.

— — —

B-119-120 Power of Attorney.       JOHN LATTA of Orange Co.,
N.C. Attorney for John Evans of Philadelphia to prosecute
a suit against Orange County merchants, deputizes his
"worthy friend Johnathan Lindley" to act for him under
this Power of Attorney.       Feb 1791.

— — —

B-120  Will in Archives. Dated 6 Jan 1791, proved Feb 1791.

WILLIAM RHODES                wife: Mary

"My three children Hannah Rhodes, Elizabeth Rhodes,
Alexander Rhodes."

Executors: wife Mary, brother Aquilla Rhodes.
Witnesses: Richard Rhodes, Thomas Rhodes, Henry Burch? or
                                                  — Bunch.
— — —

B-121  Will in Archives. Dated 25 Nov 1790, proved Feb 1791.

JOHN ARMSTRONG                wife: Margaret

son: William, land on Haw River joining John Holmes, Moses
     Crawford and Richard Christmas.

daus: Elizabeth (under 18 years),
      Mary, Margaret, Rachel.

Executors: wife, and Richard Christmas.
Witnesses: Richard Goff, William Trousdale.

— — —

B124  Will of JOHN JENKINS, already given on page B-105.

— — —

B-126  Will of JACOB DEBLEY. In Archives. Dated 17 May 1790,
                                        proved Feb 1791.
Wife: Margery Debley

"boys Jacob, James and John Debley, my three sons."

daus: Mary Debley, Fanny Debly.

The children are all minors. Sons are to be apprenticed to
trades when they reach 14 years of age.

Executors: John Steele, John Thompson.

Witnesses: William Clendennin, William Morrow.

— — —

B-128 Will in Archives. Dated 10 July 1790, proved May 1791.
JOHN PATTERSON, Senior      wife: Margaret

sons: David, Isaac, William, James, John.

daus: Jean, Margaret Abbott, Mary Patterson, Agnes.

Executors: wife Margaret, son David.
Witnesses: Jacob ...?.., Nathaniel Matthews.
— — —

B-130  Bill of Sale from JOHN MITCHELL to James Comb of
Orange Co., N.C., for 4 negroes.
Dated 30 Nov 1791, proved May 1791 (dates that way in book).
Witnesses: John McKerrall, Mary Comb.
— — —

B-130  Bond. Dated 1 Sept 1789, proved May 1791.

JOHN RICE of Davidson Co., N.C. and JESSE BENTON of Orange
Co., N.C. bound unto ROBINSON MUMFORD of Orange Co., N.C.
Eleven hundred pounds.  John Rice purchased "15,000 acres
of land situate on the Western waters"from Robinson Mumford.

Witnesses: James Mumford, John Umstead.
— — —

B-132  Will in Archives. Dated 25 Dec 1789, proved May 1791.

NATHANIEL PATTERSON          wife: Issabel

daus: Jenny Ward, Margaret Swift, Susannah Ray,
        Elizabeth Baker, Mary

"John Ward son of my daughter Margaret Swift deceased".

Executors: wife Issabel, son William, "John Ray my son-in-
        law", Issabel Ray (relationship not stated).

Witnesses: William Hodges, Jr., Andrew Murdock.
— — —

B-136  Will in Archives. No date, proved Aug 1791.

SAMUEL (x) TOLBY (this will is indexed in the Archives
                as TALLEY.)
wife: Elizabeth

no relationship stated: Elizabeth Faddis.

son: William Hitchcock Tolby
daus: Milly Whitaker, Mary Kennady, Elizabeth Rhodes.

Executors: James Kennady, Richard Rhodes.
Witnesses: A. Tatom, Wm. Strayhorn.
— — —

B-136  Will in Archives. Dated 8 April 1789, proved Aug 1791.

ALEXANDER (x) CARSON        wife: name not stated.

sons: Robert Carson, Samuel Carson.

grandson: Alexander Carson. grandson: David Clenny.

daus: Elizabeth, Mary Carson, Alice Clenny wife to Wm. Clenny

Executors: wife, and John Grant Rencher.
Witnesses: Wm. McCauley, Wm. Ansley, Henry McCollum.

- - -

B-141  Will in Archives. Dated 2 August 1791, proved
                                          August 1791.
WILLIAM COMB              wife: Ann

sons: James (under 21), John

daus: Mary Comb, Nancy Comb, Betty Mitchell, Ellender Trice.

granddau: Sarah Miller.

Executors: wife Ann, sons James & John,
           daughters Mary & Nancy Comb.

Witnesses: John Turrentine, Caleb Harvey.

- - -

B-143  Bill of Sale from WILLIAM HALL of Orange Co., N.C.
to William Watters, for 7 negroes.

Dated 26 May 1786, proved August 1791.
Witnesses: John Hall, James Grange (?).

- - -

B-144  Will in Archives. Dated 21 Oct 1790, proved Aug 1791.

JESSE BENTON              wife: Nancy

This will is four pages long.

Testator has several children, all minors, but their names
are not given.

Executors: wife Nancy, Colonel Alfred Moore, William Walters,
           Absolom Tatom.

Witnesses: S. Benton, A. Benton.

- - -

B-149  Bill of Sale from ABNER NASH of Craven Co., N.C. to

William Nash of Orange Co., N.C. for 2 negroes.
Dated 25 March 1791, proved Aug 1791. Witness: And. Murdock.

- - -

B-149  Deed of Gift from ABNER NASH of Craven Co., N.C. to William Nash of Orange Co., N.C., for a negro boy "for love".

Dated 25 March 1791, proved Aug 1791.
Witness: Andrew Murdock.

— — —

B-149  Will in Archives. Dated 2 June 1791, proved
Feb. 1792.
WILLIAM HAMILTON

son: Joseph Hamilton

daus: Elizabeth, Jean, Margaret, Nancy.

Executors and "trustees for my daughters": son Joseph, and
Thomas Bradford.
Witnesses: William Bradford, Thomas Bradford.

— — —Receipt
B-151/entered on book 18 Feb 1792 from "John Craven, late Treasurer of the Board of Trustees of The University of North Carolina." (Long document.)

— — —

B-152  Will in Archives. Dated 28 July 1791, proved 179-

JOHN RILEY (or RIELEY)    wife: Mary

sons: William, Robert, Samuel

daus: Jane Riley, Mary Donaldson, Nancy, Elizabeth.

Executors: "trusty friends John Armstrong and Mary Ruby (?)"
Witnesses: John Armstrong, James Riggs.

— — —

B-154  Will in Archives. Dated 10 April 1791, proved 179-

THOMAS LOVE    only heir: Peggy Love, relationship not
given.
Executors: Thomas Love, James Love.
Witnesses: Joseph Armstrong, William Love.

— — —

B-156  Will in Archives. Dated 28 July 1791, proved 179-

JACOB ALBRIGHT, SENIOR    wife: Catherine

sons: George, John, Jacob, Joseph, Henry, Daniel.

daus: Sophia, Catherine.

Executors: son John Albright, Strudwick Clap.
Witnesses: William Ray, Boston Sharp.

— — —

B-160   Will in Archives. Dated --, proved Feb 1792.

ELIZABETH PAUL          daus: Margaret Reddin, Elizabeth Gray.

grandchildren: Elizabeth Carrigan, William Reddin,
               James Gray, James Paul, Elizabeth Gray,
               Elizabeth Paul.

Executor: Enoe Robert Fassetts.
Witnesses: Francis Wilkinson, Samuel McCracken.

— — —

B-162   Will in Archives. Dated 9 Feb 1792, proved Feb 1792.

DANIEL (x) SULLIVAN          wife: Margaret

sons: "oldest son Joseph Sullivan", Ben Sullivan,
      Isaac,Daniel, John, "youngest son Edmund Sullivan".

daus: "oldest daughter Mary", Sarah, Margaret.

Witnesses: George Spous, John Melvin, Edmund (x) Melvin.

— — —

B-166  Will in Archives. Dated 17 Jan 1792, proved May 1792.

CHRISTOPHER BARBEE          wife: Dicy Barbee (she is pregnant)

Daughters mentioned, but names not given.

Executors: "loving friends Goin Barbee and Joseph Barbee".
Witnesses: Goin Barbee, Ephriam Beasley, Ransom (x) David.

— — —

B-168   Will in Archives. Dated 9 Jan 1792, proved Feb 1792.

ENOCH DAVIS          sons: Abraham Davis, John Davis.

"loving son William Eavins"

dau: Ellenor Darker          he mentions "four daughters"...

Sole Executor: son Abraham Davis.
Witnesses: Stephen Merritt, Mary (x) Houge.

— — —

B-170   Will in Archives. Dated 7 Feb 1792, proved May 1792.

THOMAS LLOYD          sons: Thomas Lloyd, Frederick Lloyd.

daus: Sarah Hogan, Mary Hogan

sons-in-law: John Hogan,John Maxeden,Adlai Osborne,

grandchildren: Thomas Hogan, John Hogan,William Hogan,
               James Hogan, Alexander Hogan,
               Margaret Lloyd Hogan,
               Thomas Lloyd son of Stephen Lloyd. -continued-

B-170 Will of THOMAS LLOYD continued -

Executors: "trusty friends John Hogan and Baxton King".
Witnesses: Benjamin Howell (?), Wm. Forester, Wm. Brasher.
─ ─ ─

B-174  Will in Archives. Dated 10 Sept 1791, proved May 1792.

JEAN (x) HALL

sons: William Hall, John Hall, Robert Hall, Thomas Hall.

daus: Rebecca Kell, Mary Nichols, Sarah Hall, Rachel Hall.

Executors: Thos. Rountree, Robert Hall.
Witnesses: Charles Rountree, Lydia Rountree.
─ ─ ─

B-177 Will in Archives. Dated 11 Feb 1792, proved May 1792.

JAMES ROACH                wife: Ann Roach

son: Absolom

He has sons under age, names and number not stated.

He has 3 daughters under 18. His mother is living.

Executors: wife Ann, Absolom Roach, John Thompson (miller).
Witnesses: James Thompson, Wm. Thompson, Wm. (x) Roach.
─ ─ ─

B-180  Will in Archives. Dated 7 June 1788, proved May 1792.

JOHN CONNER                wife: Elizabeth

"James Watson and Margaret his wife"
"Said Watson's children".. James Watson, Jr.

No executor named. Witnesses: William Railey, James Railey.
─ ─ ─

B-182  Will in Archives. Dated 6 April 1792, proved May 1792.

THOMAS HORN, SENIOR        sons: Thomas Horn, James Horn.

"Joshua Horn Senior, "young Henry Horn son of Joshua Horn",
"Nelly Horn daughter of James Horn .. and her mother Margery"
William Horn Senior and John Horn 1 shilling each.

No executor named. Witnesses: John Adams, Thomas Holloway.
─ ─ ─

B-185  Deed of Gift from MARK MORGAN of Orange Co., N.C. to
"three sons Mark Morgan, John Morgan and Solomon Morgan of
the same county"... for love ... certain tracts of land.

Dated 31 May 1792, proved May 1792.
Witnesses: John Scott, Phillip Allan, Albert Sears,
           William Goodwin.

— — —

B-188  JOHN SHAW and SEANY SHAW renounce title to land on
Bolings Creek in Orange County, conveyed to Seany Jones in
"her infancy" by John Boothe. Seany is now John Shaw's wife.

Dated 18 March 1792, proved May 1792;
Witnesses: James Trice, Mark Barbee, Zachariah Boothe.

— — —

B-199 Will in Archives. Dated 10 Aug 1792, proved Aug 1792.

JUDITH (x) STAGG

All her property to grandchildren Charles and Celia Stagg.

Witnesses: James Hogg, Gavin Alves.

— — —

B-191 Will in Archives. Dated 24 Feb 1792, proved Nov 1792.

JAMES WOODY              wife: Rebecca Woody.

"two youngest brothers Joseph and Lewis Woody", both
under 21.

Executors: Johnathan Lindley, James Woody.
Witnesses: Ezekiel Hornaday, Peter Duks, Zachariah Duks.

— — —

B-193 Will in Archives. Dated 5 June 1792, proved 1792.

ISAAC SEBASTION or SURBASTEN.          wife: Sarah

"Estate to support wife and her family".

Executor: "Friend Stephen Conger".
Witnesses: John Eubanks, Samuel Williams.

— — —

B- 194  Will in Archives. Dated 24 Aug 1786, proved 1792.

CATHERINE LOCKHART of the town of Hillsborough, N.C.

son: William Lockhart

daus: Catherine Roads, Jean Holt, Sarah Parker,
      Elizabeth Mucklejohn, Mary (?) Smith.
Executors: son William, son-in-law James Parker.
Witnesses: John Allison, William Kennedy, Martin Palmer.

— — —

B-197  Will in Archives. Dated 17 May 1792, proved Nov 179-

JOHN WOODS                    wife: Margaret Woods

sons: Matthew; John and Richard, both under 21.

daus: Margaret Woods, Nancy Woods, Sarah Woods,
      Hannah Kirkpatrick.
He speaks of "my two young daughters".."youngest daughters".

son-in-law: Samuel Kirkpatrick.

Executors: wife Margaret, son Matthew.
Witnesses: Abe Allen, Reuben Smith, Thomas Bradford.

— — —

B-204 to 208. Will in Archives. Dated 1 May 1792,
                                        proved Aug 1792.
FRANCIS CHILD          wife: Frances

"My 3 sons Samuel (eldest), Wilson and Francis." All are
under 21 years of age.

daughter-in-law: Fanny McKerall

"My natural son James Floyd".

Executors: wife Frances, Robert Freeman, Jno. Casey.
Witnesses: Jno. Casey, David Sloan, Will McKerall.

Codicil appoints " friends John Haywood and William Watters
Esquires" .. " guardians to my three sons Samuel, Wilson
and Thomas". Same witnesses as the will.

— — —

B-209  Will in Archives. Dated 19 June 1792, proved
                                              Aug 1792.
MARY (x) WALTON

daus: Mary Collins, Jemima Ward, Keziah Bane.

She mentions "my late husband Nathaniel Walton". (He died in
1786 ?).

Sole Executor: son-in-law Thomas Bane.
Witnesses: Thomas Armstrong, William Clarke.

— — —

B-211 Bill of Sale from HENRY (x) WHITE to William Nash,
both of Orange Co., N.C., for 1 negro girl.

No date, proved Feb 1793.

Witnesses: Michael Holt, Jr., Robert Mitchell.

— — —

B-211 Bill of Sale from HENRY (x) WHITE to William Nash, for a slave, Kesiah and her daughter Lucy.

Dated 21 Aug 1793 ?, proved Feb 1793.

— — —

B-212  Bill of Sale from WILLIAM NEWMAN to William Nash, both of Orange Co., N.C., for 4 negroes.

Dated 10 Nov 1792, proved Feb 1793. Witness: S. Benton.

— — —

B-213  Power of Attorney from CHARLES MILLIKEN to Alexander Hatch.  Dated 18 Jan 1793, proved Feb. 1793. Witness: John Thompson.

— — —

B-215 Deed of Gift from THOMAS TRICE to his daughter Ann House and son-in-law House, for love.. 200 acres of land during their lives, then to his granddaughter Betsey House.

Dated 26 Feb 1793, proved Feb 1793. Witnesses: Daniel Carlton, Sam'l Daniel.

— — —

B-216  Will in Archives. Dated 30 April 1789, proved Feb '93.

ALEXANDER MEBANE            wife: Name not stated

sons: William, Alexander, James, John

daus: Jennett Anderson, Ann Morrow, Margaret Murdaugh.

granddaughter: Margaret Anderson.
grandson: Alexander Anderson.

Executors: Alexander Mebane; James Mebane.
Witnesses: Thos. Mulholland, Edward Wilson, William Wilson.

— — —

B-220  Will in Archives. Dated 2 March 1792, proved Feb 1793.

ROBERT RAY                  wife: Hannah Ray

"Eldest daughters Isabella, Fanny, Margaret, Silly, Mary, Martha and Nancy".

sons: Robert, John, Matthew (under 21).

dau: Kassey under 21.        step-daughter: Ann Massey.

"granddaughter Rebecca daughter of Robert".

Executors: wife Hannah, William Clendennin.
Witnesses: Jas. Freeland, Joseph Pindar, Matthew Hunter.

— — —

B-222 Will in Archives. Dated 13 March 1792, proved Feb 1793.

WILLIAM (x) JAMISON, SENIOR          wife: Rachel

daus: Rachel Jamison, Mary Parks, Margaret Lindsey.

sons: John, Ellis, Thomas, William.

Executor: friend Sterling Harris.
Witnesses: Theopilus Thompson, Sterling Harris.

— — —

B-224 Bill of Sale from PETER BURTON of Mecklenburg Co., Va.
to Abraham Thompson of Orange Co., N.C. for 1 negro girl.

Dated 24 Aug 1791, proved May 1792. Witness: John Thompson.

— — —

B-228 Bill of Sale from JOSEPH BRADFORD of St. Asaph's
Parish, Orange Co., N.C. to Benjamin Piggott of Orange Co.

Dated 21 May 1792, proved May 1792.
Witnesses: Jas. Stoneman, Jos. Stoneman, Lewis Hornaday.

— — —

B-229 Will in Archives. Dated 29 Dec 1791, proved Feb 1792.

JAMES WALKER          Wife: Elizabeth

"My five children that I had by my first wife (viz) Ann
Cimbol, Sanders Walker, Lydia Wright, Jeremiah Walker and
William Walker." .

"My three children that I had by my second wife
Sarah Colbert, Elizabeth Horton, James Walker."

Sole Executor: James Walker.
Witnesses: Thomas Latta, Samuel Garrard.

— — —

B-231 Inquest on the body of PETER NOE. 7 November 1787.
Jurymen were : Joel Burrow, farmer, Nicholas Coonee,
Frederick Kimbrough, Jacob Jones, Philip Burrow, Philip
Eulice (?), Abraham Jones, Conrad Kimbrough, Joshua Holt,
Martin Shofner, Henry Kimbrough. They found that Peter Noe
died from natural causes.

— — —

B-233 Bill of Sale from GRAHAM BELL to William Nash for
a slave.  Dated 20 April 1793, proved May 1793.
Witness: J. Estes.

— — —

B-234  Will in Archives. Dated 4 Jan 1793, proved May 1793

PETER (x) EFLAND          wife: Catherine

son: Daniel Efland 5 shillings.

"To my son John Efland, Catherine Noe, Mary Gibbs,
Elizabeth Nance, Sarah Graves and Philis Sharp an equal
share."

Executors: "friends John Albright and Obed Green."
Witnesses: John Bullock, James Holmes.
- - -

B-236  Will in Archives. Dated 10 Oct 1791, proved Aug 1793.

GEORGE DOHERTY

"to my wife Mary, and her three daughters Polly W. Burke,
Frances Daugherty and Nelly Daugherty, share and share alike"

Executors: wife Mary, James Gillespie Esq. of Duplin County.
Witnesses: James Grant, John Casey.
- - -

B-237  Will in Archives  Dated 6 May 1793, proved Aug 1793

WILLIAM LEWIS

All estate "to my brothers James, Howell, Robert, Charles,
Nicholas and my sister Jane Mereweather Lewis."

Executors: brothers James, Howell and Robert Lewis.
Witnesses: Eliza Ridley, Charles Lewis, Thos. Hines.
- - -

B-238 Quit-claim-deed from JOSHUA (x) HORN to Jesse James
and his wife, formerly Betsey Horne.

Dated 27 Aug 1793, proved Aug 1793. Witness: James H. Keys
- - -

B-239 Power of Attorney from JAMES WILLIAMS of Wilkes Co.,
Georgia to John Willis Esq. of Orange Co., N.C. to sell
land on the Allamance in Orange Co., N.C.

Dated --, proved August 1793.
Witnesses: S. Benton, A. Tatom, John Taylor.
- - -

B-240  Will in Archives. Dated 11 Dec 1792, proved Aug 1793.

JAMES ROSS          wife: Margaret

daus: Jane Smith, Levinia Minnis.          - continued -

B-240 Will of JAMES ROSS continued -

Executors: wife Margaret, Levinia Minnis, John Minnis.
Witnesses: A. Tatom, John Casey, John Allison.

- - -

B-241  Will in Archives. Dated 12 Jan 1791, proved Aug 1793.

ROBERT ANDREW                wife: Sarah

sons: Robert, David, Thomas and William Andrew.

"grandson Robert Andrew, son of John Andrew Deceased."

"My four daughters, namely Jane, Katherine, Ann and Sarah."

Executors: sons William and Thomas Andrew.
Witnesses: John Carter, James Woody.

- - -

B-243 Indenture. HERMAN (x) HUSK  binds himself to
John Sloss Esq. as a servant for 1 year

Dated 31 Aug 1793, proved Aug 1793. Witness: Andrew Burke.

- - -

B-245 Power of Attorney from SAMUEL STRUDWICK of the State
of N.C., Planter, to Henry Shepperd of the State of N.C.
" to receive such sums as may be due me from Michael Wooley,
Robert Christmass, or any other persons, of, in, or belonging to the State of Georgia in America."

Dated 24 Nov 1793, proved Nov 1793.
Witnesses: Wm. Shepperd, W.F.Strudwick

- - -

B-246  Power of Attorney from D. WITHERSPOON to William
Nash Esq. to sell land on Flat River in Orange County, N.C

Dated 22 Oct 1792, proved Nov 1793. Witness: Wm. Courtney.

- - -

B-247 Bill of Sale from JOHN BILLUPS and RICHARD K. CARROLL
to John Scott, for 1 negro and her child.

Dated 30 July 1791, proved Nov 1793.
Witnesses: John Ray, George Ray.

- - -

B-248 Bill of Sale from ENOCH LEWIS to John Scott, both of
Orange Co., N.C. for 1 negro boy.

Dated 25 Feb 1793, proved Nov 1793.
Witnesses: John Dannel, Ezekiel Trice.

- - -

B-249 Bill of Sale from JAMES G  BOHUN of Warren Co., N.C
to Michael Shofner, for a negro boy.  Dated 17 Feb 1794.
Witness: Augustine Willis.

— — —

B-249  Will in Archives  Dated 18 Feb 1794, proved 179-

JAMES HUNTER                    wife: Christian

relationship not stated: James Hunter Andrew,
                         Richard Hunter.

brother: Andrew Hunter.

Sole Executrix: wife.
Witnesses: Reuben Harris, James Walker,
           Priscilla (x) Montgomery.

— — —

B-251 to 254  Will in Archives. Dated 20 Aug 1793,
                                        proved Nov 1793
JOHN STEEL              wife: Mary

daus: Agnes (youngest), Elizabeth Steel, Mary Steel (2nd),
      Sarah. All the daughters are under 16 years of age

son: Joseph Steel under 20 years of age.

"right of Margery Carrigan's third"...

Executors:"wife Mary and trusty friend Joseph Hodge."
Witnesses: Wm  Steel, John Pickard, Charles Clendennin.

— — —

B-255    Will  in Archives  Dated 27 Feb 1793, proved
                                             Nov 1793
PHILIP (x) SNOTERLY        wife: Elizabeth

sons: Henry, Jacob

"3 youngest daughters Susannah, Rachel Catherine" all under
age. No other daughters are named.

Executors: "Trusty friends Peter Foust and Jacob Antony".
Witnesses: William Ray, Henry (x) Lay.

— — —

B-257  Will in Archives. Dated 15 Jan 1774, proved Nov  1793

GEORGE GOBEL (COBLE ?)    sons: Henry, David.

Witnesses: George Cortner, Solomon Ly..?.., Simeon Anderson.

Codicil dated 25 Feb 1786 names same heirs.
Witnesses: David Thornburg (?), ...?..

The above will is indexed in OLDS as COBLE.

B-259  Will in Archives. Dated16 July 1793, proved Feb 1794

RICHARD CATE            wife: Emelia

"My eight children .. James, Jesse, Richard, Thomas,John,
Martha, Susannah, Emilia"

son: Benjamin            dau: Martha Hastin (Hastings ?)

Several tracts of land are devised. One tract joins Charles
Kelly, Another, "100 acres which I purchased from James
Crawford". "50 acres on Cain Creek". "Land purchased from
Thomas Moore", "tract bought of Richard Tinnen on E. side
of Cain Creek", "my mill on west side of Cain Creek".

Executors: Sackfield (?) Brewer, brother John Cate,
           son James Cate.

Witnesses: Bernard Cate, Lewis Kirk.

— — —

B-262  Will in Archives. Dated 3 March 1790, proved Feb 1794

DANIEL (x) HANLEY            wife: name not stated

daus: Ester and Susannah, both under age.
      Ann Linnin, Elizabeth, Grace, Ruth,

"My only son William"...

grandson: "Grace's son Daniel".

Testator devises "lands on the Cumberland".

Executors: Alexander Mebane, James Mebane.
Witnesses: William Allen, Daniel Mason.

Codicil dated March 3 1790. "If son dies without heir,
daughters are to share equally in estate".

Witnesses to codicil: Henry Beason, Daniel Mason.

— — —

B-264  Bill of Sale from JOHN WILLS of Orange Co., N.C, to
William Falkner of Warren Co., N.C. for slaves, etc.

Dated 16 Sept 1793, proved Feb 1794.

— — —

B-265  Bill of Sale from  WILLIAM O'NEAL to Thomas Cole,
both of Orange Co., N.C., for slaves.

Dated 26 Nov 1793, proved Feb 1794.
Witness: William Nash.

— — —

B266 Deed of Gift from THOMAS DABNEY of Caswell County to his niece Barshaba Crumbie of Orange County, for love , "Fifty pounds in property on or before she comes to age of 21 years". Dated 15 Nov 1793, proved Feb 1794.

Witnesses: Frances Moreland, John Wood.

— — —

B-267 Will in Archives. Dated 30 Aug 1793, proved Feb 1794.

ISRAEL (x) STANTEFER        wife: Cassander

sons: Ephriam eldest, Joshua.
      Isarel "100 acres of land called by name of William
             Baker's place."
      Benjamin Stantefer.

daus: Sarah Rhoades, Rossaner Rhodes, Casander Hendon.
      "to daughters Mary Stantefer and Elizabeth Stantefer
      land adjoining Thomas Guyns, John Cabe's, William
      Tesmon (?)."

granddaughter: "Sarah Rhoades daughter Cassandra."

grandson: Israel Turner "son of Ruth Turner, wife of Wm. Turner, 88 acres on the north side of William Pickett's cart road joining on Benjamin Peeler's land."

Executors: wife Casander, son Joshua.
Witnesses: Joshua Standeford, Mary (x) Stantefer,
           Henry Bunch.

— — —

B-270 Bill of Sale from EDWARD WILSON to William Wilson, both of Orange Co., N.C. for ..."three entries of land ... in the Hawfields in Orange County... adjoining lands of Samuel Strudwick." Dated 23 Sept 1793, proved Feb 1794.

Witnesses: James Tate, George Tate.

— — —

B-271 Deed of Gift from LEWIS KIRK to granddaughter Martha Williamson Kirk, both of Orange Co., N.C., for love, a "Negro girl Agnes, one year old."
Dated 2 Dec 1793, proved Feb 1794.

Witnesses: Nathaniel Christmas, Reubin Smith.

— — —

B-272  Deed of Gift from EDWARD WILSON to "my loving daughter Mary Wilson", both of Orange Co., N.C. "All goods and chattels now being in my dwelling house". A signed inventory is given.        Dated 23 Sept 1793, proved Nov 1794.

Witnesses: James Tate, George Tate.

— — —

B-274 Will in Archives. Dated 24 Oct 1793, proved Feb 1794.

JOHN MOORE, JUNIOR.            wife: Name not stated.

"Only son Asahel, plantation whereon I now live with an obligation for 900 acres of land in Cumberland".

dau: Elizabeth.

Executors: "trusty friends James Moore and David Turrentine". Witnesses: Jno. Umstead, Samuel Turrentine, James Turrentine.

— — —

B-275 Will not in Archives. Dated 20 Oct 1793, proved
                                                    Feb 1794.
JOHN LINDSEY            wife: Mary Lindsey

"Three sons Athanatious Lindsey, John Lindsey, Caleb Lindsey".

dau: Dille Lindsey.

"All my children that are not married"...

Executors: son Athanatious Lindsey,
           son-in-law Henry Edwards.
Witnesses: David Durham, Benjamin Davis, ..(torn) Lindsey.

— — —

B-277 Quit-claim-deed from DAVID BRADFORD to George Bradford "parcel of land bequeathed by George Bradford's father Davis Brandford to George Bradford (name is spelled 3 ways in deed). Speaks of land forming Andrew Pattin's line.

Dated 25 Feb 1794, proved Feb 1794.
Witnesses: John Armstrong, John Allison.

— — —

B-279 Will in Archives. Dated 15 June 1790, proved
                                                    Nov 1795 ?
ANDREW MITCHELL            son: James Mitchell

"All my children", names and number not stated.

Executors: Sam'l Woods, James Carr.
Witnesses: Wm. McCauley, George Long.

— — —

B-281 Bill of Sale from WILLIAM BAYLEY or BEEZELY ? of Chatham Co., N.C. to James Motley (Moseley ?) of Oring (Orange) Co., for a negro. Dated 22 Nov 1794, proved Nov 1794.

Witnesses: Ephriam (x) Beasley, Thomas Hopson.

— — —

B-282  Bill of Sale from JOHN FAIRMAN of town of Hillsbor -
ough, Orange Co., N.C. to Joseph Dixon, for 2 negroes.
Dated 25 Nov 1794. Witnesses: A. Tatom, Walter Alves.

- - -

B-280  Will not in Archives. Dated 2 November 3 o'clock A.M.
                                          no year.
ARCHIBALD LYTLE

"All to my brother William Lytle to dispose of".

"Step-mother Sarah Lytle to have use of plantation she lives
on during her life for the use of her children."

Witnesses: George Doherty, Jno. Hawkins.

- - -

B-284  Deed of Gift from PATERSON (x) DANIEL to brother
Roger Daniel a tract of land, 100 acres, for love, adjoining lands of Roger Daniel, Christopher Daniel, John Daniel,
Thomas Trice, and Joseph Bough".. about 13 miles from the
town of Hillsborough.  No date, proved 1794 ?

Witnesses: Francis Nash, J or I. Walker.

- - -

B-285  Power of Attorney from FRANCIS STRUDWICK to Henry
Shepperd, both of Orange Co., N.C. "to demand and receive
money or negroes " due from (blank)  Patterson of the State
of South Carolina.  Dated 27 Oct 1794, proved 179-

- - -

B-286  Power of Attorney from MARTHA STRUDWICK of N.C. (sole
Executrix of Samuel deceased) to Henry Shepperd of N.C. to
sue for "money due to me from Michael Watley or Robert
Christmas, or any other person or persons in the state of
Georgia in America".  Dated 27 Oct 1794, proved 179-

Witnesses: Wm. Shepperd, Morgan Hart (?).

- - -

B-287 Bill of Sale from WILLIAM FALKENER of Warren Co., N.C.
to James F. Brehan of Warren Co.  Falkener sells stock of
hogs which he bought from John Wills of Orange Co., N.C. in
a bill, dated 16 Sept 1793.

Dated 28 Jan.1795, proved Feb 1795.

- - -

B-288 Bill of Sale from JOHN FAIRMAN to Thomas O'Harro, both
of Orange Co., N.C., for slaves.
Dated 3 Dec 1794, proved Feb 1795.

Witnesses: Joseph Dixon, James Coghlin.

- - -

B-289  Will in Archives. Dated 10 Sept 1794, proved Feb 1795.

WILLIAM SHANNON

Estate to "Loving cousins Thomas and Robert Shannon".

Sole Executor: "My trusty friend Richard Christmas."
Witnesses: Moses Crawford, Rachel Crawford.

− − −

B-290 Will in Archives. Dated 5 March 1793, proved Feb 1795.

GEORGE MILLER          sons: Jesse Miller, James Miller.

daus: Sarah Ray, wife of John Ray
      Lydia, widow of Joseph Ray, deceased
      Mary, wife of Zachariah Dickey

grandsons: Joseph Miller, son of Wm. and Ann Miller.
           George Ray, son of John and Sarah Ray.
           George Ray, son of Lydia and Joseph Ray deceased.
           George Miller, son of Martha and Jesse Miller.
           George Dickey, son of Mary and Zachariah Dickey.

Sole Executor: son James Miller.
Witnesses: James Jackson, James Ray, Jean (x) Turentine.

− − −

B-292  Will in Archives. Dated 26 Nov 1794, proved Feb 1795.

HENRY (x) DUNWEDDEE       wife: Elizabeth      son: John

daus: Nancy Long, Sarah Gresham.

grandsons: Absolom and James, sons of John Dunweddee,
           John Jackson.

Executors: Josiah Warren, John Redman.
Witnesses: Jonathan (x) Dollar, Tho. Gresham,
           Maryan (x) Gresham.

− − −

B-294  Bill of Sale from WILLIAM G. SMITH of State of New
York, to DANIEL MAY, Senior, for negroes.
Dated 12 Aug 1794, proved Feb 1795.

Witnesses: Francis Nash, ...?... Patterson.

− − −

B-294  Bill of Sale from HENRY WHITE to Adam Smith, for
a negro. Dated 9 July 1794, proved Feb 1795.

WITNESSES: ...?.. Patterson, Joshua Holt.

− − −

B-296 Bill of Sale from JOHN STROUD to Obed Green, for a negro.  Dated 15 Aug 1794, proved Feb 1795.

Witnesses: James Patterson, Thos. Whitehead.

— — —

B-297  Bill of Sale from JOHN ELLIFF (ELLIS ?) to Thomas Cole, for a negro. Dated 20 Nov 1794, proved Feb 1795.

Witnesses: Absolom Holt, Jeremiah Holt.

— — —

B-298  Bond. JAMES MEBANE agrees to sell to Thomas Lloyd, Sr a tract of "land on which Col. Hogan now lives"

Dated 5 Jan 1795, proved Feb 1795.
Witnesses: B. Stanford, R. Morris, Isaac Blackwood

— — —

B-299 Power of Attorney from ZACHARIAH BOOTHE of Hancock Co., Ga. to friend William Trice of Orange Co., N.C. to make lawful deed to James Trice of lands in Chatham Co., N.C. on the waters of White Oak. Dated 7 Nov 1794, proved Feb 1795.

Witnesses: Jas. Trice, Edward Trice.

— — —

B-300 Bill of Sale from JOSEPH HODGE, Sheriff of Orange Co., N.C. John Allison of town of Hillsborough. "Allison was in debt to the estate of William Armistead.)

Dated 17 Oct 1795, proved Nov 1795. Witness: John Kelly.

— — —

B-301 Receipt to JOHN RAY, Administrator of William Jameson deceased, for the just and full sum of Thirteen hundred and twenty-nine pounds, Eleven shillings and ten pence in full of his administration upon the Estate of William Jameson deceased, by me Jean Jameson, Guardian of Margaret Jameson, John Jameson, Mary Jameson, Jean Jameson, William Jameson and Robert Jameson. I say rec'd the above sum by me.
Jean (x) Jameson
Witness: Andrew McBroom.

This is the last entry in WILL BOOK B.

— — — — — —

Book C, page 1. Will in Archives. Dated 3 Feb 1794
proved May 1794.
THOMAS (x) MORTISE    wife: Mary Mortise

daughter, name not stated.

Witnesses: John Adams, Joseph Hastings.

— — —

98

C-2 Will in Archives. Dated 20 Jan 1794, proved May 1794.

GRIZZEL McCALLISTER

Heirs named as follows, relationship not stated to some of
them. David Allison, John Allison son, Margaret Allison,
Grizzle Thompson, Mary Clark daughter, Jane Allison,
James Donaldson, Elizabeth Allison, Sarah Allison.

Sole Executor: David Allison.
Witnesses: James Mordah, Elizabeth Allison.

– – –

C-3 Power of Attorney dated 24 May 1794 from Ezekiel Mace,
    John Darris & Angel his wife ... The said John Darris
in right of his wife heretofore Angel Mace ... the said
Ezekiel Mace and Angel Darris being the only surviving children of Josias Mace heretofore of Dorchester County, Md,
deceased ... do constitute Edmond Brannock of Dorchester Co.
Md. their lawful att'y to sell their share of the property
of John Brannock of Maryland known as Grace Ridings ...
which Josias Mace purchased of Lewis Woolford and Mary his
wife ...
Witnesses: Hardy Hurdle, Stephen Mareign, Jacob Etterton,
– – –      Alex. Robbs.

May Court 1794 the heirs deputize "Our uncle Alex. Robbs to
act for us and to sell property in Dorchester Co., Maryland
known as Buttons Intent" ... this 24 May 1794.

Witnesses: Hardy Hurdle, Stephen Maragn, Jacob Mortise.

– – –

C-8 Bill of Sale dated 12 October 1792

JOHN GREGORY & PETER BURTON deliver to MRS. FRANCIS CHILD
one negro boy, 14 years old, for 160 Spanish dollars.
Witness: John Casey.

– – –

C-9 Bill of Sale dated 16 Feb 1793 from
MITCHELL RUSSOM to MRS. FRANCES CHILD, Exec'x of Francis
Child, dec'd, for slaves.        Witness: John McKerral.

– – –

C-9 Bill of Sale dated 16 Feb 1793 from HENRY WHITE to
MRS. FRANCES CHILD, Exec'x of the will of Frances Cdild,
dec'd, for five slaves.        Witness: John Casey.

– – –

C-10, C-11, and C-12 have other transactions concerning
MRS. FRANCES CHILD. JOSEPH NICHOLS sells .... etc.

C-13 Deed of Gift from RICHARD RHODES "for love and good
     will to the Church and the Gospel..." He gives two
acres for a meeting house on Kennady's ..   Date 18 Jan./
                                                      1794

C-14 Deed. Dated 25 Dec 1794? from GEORGE RIDENS to
      John Tilley, for land, etc.     Witness: Wm. Hopkins.

- - -

C-16 Bond. Dated 20 Feb 1794, proved Aug 1794.

THOMAS HORNE, SR to Stephen Carroll & Henry Bunch a bond
that said Carroll & Bunch joined with Thos. Horne to give
to John Latta for 125 pounds for which I make over my tract
of 250 acres.               Signed: Thomas Horne, Sr.
Witnesses: Wm. Horn, John Riley.

- - -

C-17 Bill of sale dated 26 August 1794.   AMBROSE GREGORY
      of Mecklenburg Co., Va. sells to William Nash of Orange
Co., N.C. two negro boys.     Witness: Jas. Philips.

- - -

C-18  HARDY MORGAN "for the good will that I have for my
      friend & neighbor JAS. PATTERSON of Chatham Co.,N.C.
give him the privilege of cutting all large pine trees for
sawing to Sam'l Allen's line .. to land adjoining Christopher Barbee's.                Dated 18 Nov 1793,
Witness: John McCauley,Jr.    proved August 1794.

- - -

C-20 Bill of sale. Dated 4 April 1794, proved Aug 1794.

JOHN WILLIS sells to JAMES G. BRECKON of Warren Co., N.C.
household furniture, etc.
Witnesses: Thos. Glasier, Will Kirkland.

- - -

C-19 Will in Archives. Dated 24 July 1794, proved Aug 1794.

THOMAS (x) HULGAN                 wife: Fanny

sons: Robert, Stephen

daughters: Margaret Neely, Rosannah, Mary.

Executors: wife Fanny, William Ray, John Ray.
Witnesses: Samuel Mebane, Steward Dickson.

- - -

C-21 Will in Archives. Dated July 1794, proved Aug 1794.

JAMES THOMPSON     He speaks of "my seven children" ...

son: James gets one fourth "of tract I purchased of Stephen
          Hart" and "land purchased from Robert Burnside"
son: Joshua (he is under 21) gets land purchased of Thomas
          Norris, and land purchased of James Riley.
son: John (he is under 21)

daughters: Ellinor, Martha , both under 18 years of age.
          Sarah Lindley, Elizabeth Hadley.
                                        - continued -

C-21 Will of JAMES THOMPSON continued -

son-in-law: Owen Lindley

brother: Joseph

no relationship stated to William Rily.

Executors: Samuel Chambers brother-in-law, and brother
            Joseph Thompson.
Witnesses: Will Raily, Jno. Bowle, Sarah Chambers.

- - -

C-25 Deed dated 7 Nov 1793, proved Aug 1794.

GOIN BARBEE of Wake County, N.C. "for 100 pounds paid to me
by JOHN BARBEE, sell him land in aforesaid county, being part
of land surveyed for John Barbee, Sr containing 263 acres on
N. East (Creek)". Witnesses: Phebe Barbee, Benj. Barbee.

- - -

C-26 Deed dated 27 Nov 1793, proved Aug 1794.

GOIN BARBEE of Wake County, N.C. sells to BENJAMIN BARBEE
land "surveyed for John Barbee, Sr" ..."lying on prong of the
N. East of New Hope (Creek)". Witnesses: Jos. Burnett,
                                          John Barbee.

- - -

C-28 Will in Archives. Dated 24 Dec 1793, proved Aug 1794.

JOSEPH CATE                          wife: Ann

sons: Solomon, Charles, Steven

daughters: Esther, Sall

Testator's property is on Cane Creek. Neighbors mentioned are
John Cate, Thomas Baskett, Thomas Durham, W. or Mr. Brewer.

Executors: wife Ann, brother Thomas.
Witnesses: John Cate, Elizabeth Cate, John Workman.

- - -

C-30 Indenture between MARY STONE and KENNETH ANDERSON ....
Dated 13 Feb 1794.    Witnesses: Thos. Smith, Ruben Smith.

- - -

C-33 through C-48 are blank.pages.

- - -

C-49 Bill of Sale dated 12 Feb 1793, proved Nov 1794.

FRANCES CHILD, widow of Francis Child, sells to Miss Frances
McKerrall, a negro woman ..... Witness: John McKerrall.

- - -

C-50 Bill of Sale dated 12 July 1794.

JOHN BILLUPS & WM. G. GOOCH sell to MRS FRANCES CHILD
three sleves, etc.                Witness: John McKerrall.

C-50 Bill of Sale dated 10 May 1793. JOHN McKERRALL sells
to MRS. FRANCES CHILD, one negro woman. Witness: Jos. Dixon.

- - -

C-52 is blank.

C-53 Will in Archives. Dated 10 Feb 1794, proved Aug 1795.

JAMES BURCH                        wife: Mary

sons: John, George, William, James Johnston.

daughters: Sareh, Agnas.

Executors: wife Mary and son John.
Witnesses: John Kennedy, Caleb Burch, John Sloss.

- - -

C-56 Will in Archives. Dated --, proved August 1795.

ANNE HOOPER

sons: William, Thomas

daughter: Elizabeth Watters or Walters.

grandson: Henry Walters.

Executors:sons William and Thomas, and daughter Elizabeth.
Witnesses: Gavin Alves, Sam'l Benton.

- - -

C-53 to 56 Will in Archives. Dated 3 July 1795, proved Aug /
                                                        1795
ALEXANDER MEBANE

wife: Ann, has property in Philadelphia.

sons: John Alexander, William, Robert, James.

daus: Jannet Stanford, Mary Hodge,
        Sarah, Fanny, Susannah, Elizabeth, Nancy.

grandchildren: Arriana and Mary Stanford.

Executors: son James, brother James, and Robert Hodge.
Witnesses: Wm. Hodge, John Matthews.

- - -

C-57 Will in Archives. Dated 20 Aug 1778, proved Aug 1795.

THOMAS SMOTHERS                    wife: Susannah

sons: William, John, James, Thomas          - continued -

C-57 Will of THOMAS SMOTHERS continued -

daus: Sarah Smothers, Rebecca Sumner or Summer,
    Elizabeth Pickard, Mary Smothers.

Executors: wife Susanna and Alex. Summers ?.
Witnesses: John Daniely, Jonathan Clampit.

- - -

C-58 Will in Archives. Dated 27 Feb 1793, proved Aug 1795.

JOHN SHY            wife: Martha

"Brother Ike and his heirs ..."

Executors: wife Martha and Robert Harrison.
Witnesses: Samuel Hill, Caleb Harvey.

- - -

C-59 Will in Archives. Dated 7 March 1794, proved Aug 1794.

JOHN MOORE          wife: Elizabeth

sons: James, Henry

daughters: Elizabeth, Martha

grandson: Ashahel Moore

cousin: Martha Moore.

Executors: James Moore, Charles Robinson.
Witnesses: James Watson, Henry Moore, Margaret Watson.

- - -

C-61 Will in Archives. Dated 21 Feb 1793, proved Nov 1795.

JOSEPH BUCKINGHAM               wife: Margery

brothers: James, William

"To my brother James Buckingham's son Joshua Buckingham"
half of estate.

"To my brother William Buckingham's son William" 40 sh.

"brother-in-law's son Jeremiah Piggott's son Jeremiah ..."
"brother-in-law Jeremiah Piggott's daughter Rachel"...

no relationship stated to: Barbara Carter.

Executors: wife Margery, Joshua Buckingham.
Witnesses: Benj. Piggott, Mary Piggott, John Piggott.

- - -

BOOK C, page 62  Will in Archives. Dated Nov. 1795,
Proved Nov. 1795
PHILLIP WALKER

names wife and children, but names are not given.

Executors: John Trusdale, John Walker.

Witnesses: John Walker, Wm. Walker.

- - -

C-62  Will in Archives. Dated 22 June 1795. Proved Nov. 1795
BENJAMIN THOMPSON            wife: Sarah

sons: Robert, Richard, Stephen, Samuel.

dau: Frances Thompson

Executors: wife Sarah, and Caleb Harvey.

Witnesses: Caleb Harvey, Joseph Anderson.

- - -

C-64  Will in Archives. Dated April 1795, Proved Nov. 1795
ATHENATIUS ROBERTSON         wife: Dilley

Son: Nathaniel              dau: Mary Lindsay

grandson: Athenatious Lindsay.

Executors: John Snipes and grandson Athenatious Lindsay.

Witnesses: Thos. Snipes, Wm. Snipes, Alex. Hatch.

- - -

BOOK C, page 65  Will in Archives. Dated 27 August 1795
Proved November 1795
ALEXANDER McCRACKEN

wife: Abigail

sons: Samuel (eldest), Thomas, John, William,
Robert, Alexander.

daus: Mary Andrew, Hannah Tinnen,
Abigail Davis, Ruth Chamness.

-continued on next page-

Will of Alexander McCracken continued

Executors: son Samuel McCracken, Francis Wilkinson.

Witnesses: David Gilston, Samuel Chambers, Thomas Bradford.

- - -

C-67  Will in Archives. Dated Oct. 7, 1795, proved Nov. 1795.

TENTS MASSEY               wife: Ruth

son: James                dau: Mary

Executors: wife Ruth, and "my mother Hannah Ray".

Witnesses: Eli Harvey, Nathan Hicks.

- - -

C-68  Will in Archives. Dated 2 July 1795, proved Nov 1795.

SAMUEL CLENEAY (spelled Clenny in Probate.)

sons: William, Samuel, Johnathan.

3 daughters to get "claim of land on the western waters",
their names not stated.

Sole Executor: son-in-law William Belvin.

Witnesses: John Wood, Ann Wood, Rebecca Wood.

- - -

C-69 Will in Archives. Dated 9 Dec. 1795, proved Feb. 1796.

MATHEW DURHAM              wife: Susanna Durham

son: Mark Durham           no Executor named.

Witnesses: Wm. Stroud, Lysias Durham.

- - -

C-70  Will in Archives. Dated 17 March 1794, proved Feb 1796

THOMAS THOMPSON of Eno, Orange Co., N.C.      wife: Ann

son: Samuel "150 acres of land on which he now lives joining
     Maddon's and Chamberlan's lands."

-continued - next page

Will of Thomas Thompson continued

son: Abraham "home tract oh which I now live"

grandson: John Debow.

Sole Executor: son Abraham.

Witnesses: Jacob Lake, Wm. McMun.

— — —

C-71  Will in Archives. Dated 30 July 1795, proved Feb 1796.

JAMES CLARK                wife: Elizabeth

"son William Clark deceased's sons James Clark, Thomas Clark, William Clark, Jesse Clark, Joseph Clark".

"dau. Elinor wife of John Clark"

Dau: Catrenah

son: James Clark gets "plantation where I now live".

"granddaughter Sarah that now lives with me"...

Executors: "my son James Clark", and"my friend John Ray".

Witnesses: Jesse Clark, Thomas Clark.

— — —

C- 73 POWER OF ATTORNEY Dated 1 Dec 1795, proved Feb. 1796.

From DAVID LYNCH of Orange Co. to his brother Jesse Lynch.

Witnesses: Empson Bird, J.P., William Bird.

— — —

C-73 POWER OF ATTORNEY  dated 19 Sept 1795, proved Feb 1796.

From JOHN HOGAN to "trusty friend" John Grant Rencher, both of Orange Co., N.C. To empower said attorney to convey 100 acres of land to Baxter King.

Witnesses: Thomas Lloyd, John Kimbel.

— — —

BOOK C, page 75  Will in Archives. Dated 8 December 1795
                                    Proved  February 1796

JOHN ALLISON                  wife: Martha

son: Joseph Allison , 20 shillings
     James Allison " 240 acres of the entry joining David
     Allison's tract "

     John Allison, Charles Allison, Hamilton Allison.

daus: "Jennet wife of James Ray"
      "Mary wife of Thomas Curtis"
      "Martha wife of Samuel Garat"
      Grisel Allison, Agnes Allison, Elizabeth Allison.

Executors: wife Martha, and son Joseph Allison

Witnesses: John Ray, Andrew McBroom.

- - -


C-76 Will in Archives. Dated 2 Sept. 1795, proved Feb  1796

JAMES (x) HUTCHINSON          wife: Margaret

sons: Samuel, James, Ross

daus: Margaret Kelly,  Jane Lynch.

Executors: wife Margaret, and son James.

Witnesses: William Mebane, John (x) McCrory
           Judah (x) Griffith.
- - -


C-78  Will in Archives  Dated 17 Dec. 1795, proved Feb 1796

ALEXANDER (x) CHISENHALL          wife: Celah

sons: Samuel Chizenall, Reuben Chizenall, John Chizenall.

daus: Elizabeth Ridgeway,  Sarah Manning
      Markey Wood.

Executors: wife Celah and son Samuel.

Witnesses: William Ansley, John (x) Reaves.


- - -

BOOK C, page 79   Will in Archives.  Dated --- , proved
Feb. 1796.
MARY (x) PATTERSON

All her estate " to be equally divided among the surviving
children of John Couch and Betsey his wife deceased "..
"The names of the several children now living being Mary
Couch, Letitia Couch, July Couch, Elenor Couch, Elizabeth
Couch". (They are all under 18 years of age.)

Executors: "Worthy friends Robert Campbell, Roger Daniel,
      and John Couch."

Witnesses: Robert Campbell, Roger (x) Daniel.

- - -


C- 80  Will in Archives. Dated 29 Feb. 1796, proved May 1796.

THOMAS MULHOLLAND           wife: Martha

daus: Mary
      Elizabeth "lands in Cumberland and this county".

"As to my four sons Hugh, John, Thomas and Henry, I leave
my whole Mumford lands". Hugh gets surveying instruments.

Executors: wife, and son Hugh.

Witnesses: John Umstead, Samuel Nelson, John Nelson.

- - -


C-81  Will in Archives. Dated18 July 1796, proved Aug. 1796.

JOHN LACKEY

wife: Elizabeth gets all his estate "to raise and school my

      children." The number of children is not stated, no

      names given. He mentions " my sons". All the children

      are under 21 years of age.

Executors: wife Elizabeth and son Robert Lackey.

Witnesses: John Moody (Woody ?), Hugh Lackey.

- - -

C-82 Will in Archives. Dated 22 March 1796, proved Aug/
1796

JAMES HALL                    wife: Mary Hall

son: Levi, blacksmith tools, etc
son: Jehu, plantation, etc.

daughters: Mary Garrison, Lydia Faucette, Tamar Server,
           Deborah Davis, Margaret Garrison, Elizabeth
           Hall, Phebe Anderson.

Executor: son Jehu Hall.
Witnesses: Hardy Hurdle, Isaac Hall, Garrit Garrison.

— — —

C-83 Bill of Sale from ROBERT SCOBY to ROBERT TINNEN,
     both of Orange Co.,N.C., for one negro boy.
Dated 13 Nov 1795, proved Aug 1796.
Witnesses: Jo. Moore, William Fitch.

— — —

C-84 Will in Archives. Dated 15 Oct 1795, proved Aug 1796

JOHN MURDOCK                  wife: Ann

son: William          daughter: Prudence "one loom"

grandsons: John Murdock, John Ray

William Pain and his wife Rebecca 5 shillings.

"My son-in-law Robert Ray and his wife Elinor ..."

Executors: wife Ann and son William.
Witnesses: John (x) Thompson, Levi Thompson.

— — —

C-85 Will in Archives. Dated 8 May 1796, proved Aug 1796

GEORGE HERNDON                wife: Sarah

sons: James, George, Zachariah, Reuben, Edmund, Lewis.

daus: Mary Roberts, Ruth Roberts, Salley McCoy,
      Betty Cole,  Ester Barbee, Delilah Rhodes,
      Maryanne Trice.

grandson: George Roberts.

Executors: wife Sarah, Zachariah Herndon, James Herndon
Witnesses: Joseph Booth, Jos. Bilbo, David (x) George.

— — —

C-88 Will in Archives. Dated 6 April 1794, proved Nov /
1796

JAMES (x) ARMSTRONG           Slave Cicero is set free.

son: William Armstrong                    — continued —

C-88 continued -
daughters: Sarah Allen, Susannah Lloyed.
"To the heirs of my daughter Mary Mebane..."
"To the heirs of my daughter Elizabeth Lapsley...

grandsons: Thomas, James & Wm. Armstrong, all under age.
granddaughter: Mary Tinnen.

Executors: "well beloved friends John Taylor and Robert
Faucette".        Witnesses: William Elliott, Robert Taylor.
- - -

C-90 Will in Archives. Dated 12 Sept 1796, proved Nov 1796.

JOHN (x) BOYLE                    wife: Martha Boyle

sons: John Boyle and William Boyle each 500 acres of
     land "lying in Cumberland in company with Jesse
     Benton and Charles Parate."

grandson: "John Boyle son to my son James" 500 acres.
"To each of my grandsons and daughters a Bible."

Executors: sons James and John Boyle.
Witnesses: Samuel Thompson, Wm. Boyle, James Boyle.
- - -

C-91 Will in Archives. Dated 30 -- 1793, proved Nov 1796.

THOMAS SEARLES     wife a legatee, name not stated.

sons: Coventon Searles "100 acres lying in Wake Co., N.C.
     where he now lives".
     Henry, 100 acres in Orange joining George Herndon.
     Ephriam, land in Orange.
     Francis "100 acres in Orange joining Joseph Clark".
     Edward Searles.

daughters: Winney Searles,Betty Searles,Peggy Cook.

Executors: sons Henry and Francis Searles,
          "son-in-law Joseph Searles".
Witnesses: Dan Green,Bartholomew (x) Stovall,
- - -       Othniel (x) Farmer.

C-92 Bill of Sale from JOHN TAYLOR, Esq. of Orange to
     WILLIAM LYTLE, Esq. and ANDREW GIBSON, one bay
mare and seven negroes. Dated 28 Feb 1797, proved Feb '97.
- - -

C-93 Will in Archives. Dated 9 Nov 1796, proved Feb 1797.

WILLIAM BELVIN

Wife Magdalene "lot I now live on in Hillsboro (#29)" etc.

Executors: wife Magdalene and William Whitted, Jr.
Witnesses: Wm. Courtney, John Faddis, Wm. Whitted, Jr.
- - -

Book C, page 94. Will in Archives. Dated 17 Feb 1797, proved
May 1797.

JOHN KING

sons: Thomas King (oldest), Edward King, Armour King,William
King, get $1 each.

John King gets estate.

Sole Executor: son John King.

Witnesses: Thomas Bradford, D. Bradford.

‒ ‒ ‒

C-94. Will in Archives. Dated 6 March 1797, proved May 1796.

JOHN FOSSETT (signed John Faucette)    wife: Pherebe

son: Thomas Fossett "plantation joining Jpseph Hastings"

dau: Polly Fossett.

Executors: Thomas Cate, Ezra Cate, "my brother Sam Fossett".

Witnesses: Richard (x) Fossett, Thomas (x) Faucette.

‒ ‒ ‒

C-96 POWER OF ATTORNEY from JEMIMA (x) BARBEE to Benjamin

Barbee, both of Orange. Dated 23 April 1794, proved May 1797.

Witnesses: George Herndon, George (x) Holder.

‒ ‒ ‒

C- 97  Will in Archives. Dated 1 April 1797, proved May 1797.

JAMES K.D.BYRN              wife: Mary

sons: Thomas Byrn, James Byrn, Absolom Byrn, Resin Byrn.

daus: Elizabeth, Mary.

Some of the children are under age.

EXECUTORS: wife Mary and son James.

Witnesses: William Ray, James H. Ray.

‒ ‒ ‒

BOOK C, page 98   Will in Archives.      Dated 22 April 1797
                                          Proved May 1797
HARDY MORGAN

wife: Sarah " and if she should have an heir or heirs"

sons: Samuel and Allen

Executors: wife Sarah, John Daniel.

Witnesses: John Daniel, C.P.Patterson.

— — —

C-100   Will in Archives. Dated 1 August 1797, proved
                                          August 1797.
ROBERT BARNHILL              wife: Margaret

sons: "eldest son James"
       John - "plantation whereon he lives"

Sole Executor: wife Margaret

Witnesses: Thomas Johnston, George Fausett.

— — —

C-101 Will in Archives. Dated 6 June 1794, proved Aug. 1797.

WILLIAM O'NEAL

wife: Elizabeth "all my estate during her life".

relationship not stated:

" William O'Neal Perkins and his brothers and sisters.".
" Thomas H. Perkins and Mary his wife and children"...

Executors: "Trusty Friends Thomas H. Perkins and
             Elizabeth O'Neal."

Witnesses: Andrew Gibson, Joseph Culbertson, Robert Dickson.

— — —.

C-102 MORTGAGE from THOMAS CONNALLY,SR. to John McCawley

on "negro man Jack"    Dated 3 Feb. 1796, proved August 1797.

Witnesses: George Johnston, Alexander Borland.

— — —

112

Book C, page 103  Will in Archives. Dated 11 March 1795
proved August 1797

CONRAD LONG        wife: Catey

"2 sons Jacob and Conrad"

sons Henry and Casper

daus: Mary, Elizabeth

Executors: wife Catey, son Henry.

Witnesses: William Rainey, Mary (x) Rainey.

— — —

C-104  Will in Archives.  Dated 27 May 1797, proved Nov. 1797

WILLIAM (x) RODGERS of the Hawfields

wife: Elizabeth

sons: Abraham Rodgers, Theopelous Rodgers, Nathan Rodgers

daus: Rachel Garner        Jemima Green
      Morning Perkins      Leasey Rodgers
      Wilthy Bryant        Laney Rodgers, youngest

Executors: wife Elizabeth, son Theopelous.

Witnesses: Thomas Bradford, Moses Cate.

— — —

C-105  BILL OF SALE from SAMUEL DANIEL of Orange Co., N.C.
to John Daniel for a "negro woman and her sucking child".
Dated 12 Sept. 1797, proved Feb. 1798.

Witnesses. Thomas Trice, Robert T. Daniel.

— — —

C-106  BILL OF SALE from SARAH (x) MURRELL "of the county of
Orange, N.C., late of the State of Virginia, Granville Co.,
to Robert Tinnen of Orange Co., N.C." .. one negro girl.
Dated 16 August 1797, proved Feb. 1789.

Witnesses: Thomas Armstrong, John Paul.

— — —

C-107 Will in Archives. Dated 18 Jan 1797, proved Feb 1798.

JOHN (x) FANN          wife: Elizabeth

"Five youngest daughters, Rebecca, Patsey, Tabby, Anne and Betsy Fanns..."

"Three youngest sons, Elijah, Willie and Rawley Fanns..." all three are under age.

"My elder children"...(not named except for son Macky) have received their parts."

Executors: wife Elizabeth, and friend John Wilson.
Witnesses: John Walker, Mack Fann, William Dodd.
– – –

C-109 Will in Archives. Dated 19 Nov 1794, proved Feb 1800.

WILLIAM BROWN          wife: Hannah

sons: Joel Brown, William Brown

daughter: Deborah Brown

..."sons who are living at wife's decease ..."
..."daughters who are living at wife's decease ..."
"I give five shillings to each of my married children."

Executors: son Joel Brown, friend Jacob Marshall.
Witnesses: William Brown, Jacob Brown, William Stout.
– – –

C-110 Will in Archives. Dated 23 May 1786, proved Feb 1800.

THOMAS (x) WOOD of Eno River.          wife: Mary

| | |
|---|---|
| dau: Lydia Good | son: Henry Wood |
| son: Edward Wood | dau: Meley Gwin |
| "    william Wood | "    Theaney Wallace |
| "    Blayton Wood | "    Mary Woods |
| dau: Sarah Forrest | "    Elizabeth Acory |

All the above children are to receive one shilling each.

..."sons James Wood and Joseph Wood all the remainder."

Executors: sons James and Joseph.
Witnesses: James Alston, Elias Turner, Frederick Geer.
– – –

C-111 Will in Archives. Dated 19 Nov 1799, proved Feb 1800

ELIZABETH SHARP "of the Town of Hillsboro, N.C."

Daughter Elizabeth to receive entire estate.

Sole Executrix: daughter Elizabeth.
Witnesses: I or J Casey, Catlett Campbell,
– – –          James Yarborough.

114

C-112   Will in Archives.  Dated 11 Feb 1797, proved Feb 1798.

GEORGE HOLT

wife Cise receives half his estate.  She appears to be his second
     wife, as he provides for "paling of my grave where my wife
     now lieth."

₺ 5 for repairing the meeting house at Joshua Holt's.

relationship not stated: Elizabeth O'Neal receives half estate.

No executor named.

Witnesses: Wm. Rainey, Harmon (x) Lowe.

— — —

C-113   Will in Archives.  Dated 7 July 1797, proved Feb 1798.

ISAAC FORREST            wife a legatee, her name not stated.

sons: Silous and William, both under age.

"my 3 daughters, Mary, Sarah and Milly"...

Executors: brother Shadrack Forrest, and James Curry.

Witnesses: Thornberry Anderson, Silas Forrest, Philon Forrest.

— — —

C-114   Will in Archives.  Dated 6 April 1773, proved May 1798.

JAMES (x) TINNEN                    wife: Elizabeth

other legatees, relationship not stated:
"Alexander, son of John Tinnen", "Cearns Tinnen's son Robert",
"Robert Tinnen's son Robert" and "to his brother Cearns",
"James Tinnen the son of Robert Tinnen".   Sarah Johnston.

Executors: wife Elizabeth and John Thompson Miller.

Witnesses: John Reading, Arch'd Campbell, William Campbell.

— —

C-115 Power of Attorney from JAMES SHEPPARD of Washington
Co., Ga. to William Francis Strudwick of Orange Co., N.C.
to receive a negro from Andrew Murdock of Orange Co., N.C.

Dated 31 Oct 1797, proved May 1798.
Witnesses: Jarret Groce, H. Shepard.
The above P of A had been recorded in "Lyncoln County, Ga."

— — —

C-117  Will in Archives.   Dated 31 March 1798, proved
                                          May 1798.
RAINEY PHILLIPS

wife Mary gets "estate to raise my children"

stepson: Henry               stepdaughter: Leander

dau: Polly "100 acres on N. Side of Haw River bought of /
                                          Widow Parks"
dau: Rachel              son:.Ben Rainey
 "   Hannah Johnston     dau: Lucretia.

Executors: wife, and brother William Phillips.

Witnesses: Sarah Phillips, William Madray.
— — —

C-118  Will in Archives.   Dated 8 Feb 1798, proved May 1798.

ZACCHEUS TATE               (no wife mentioned)

Heirs given in the order in which they occur in the will.
Most of the children are under age.

son: John Tate          granddaughter: Jean Mechum Tracy

daus: Jean Tate, Lydia Tate, and Udose Tate

sons; Zaccheus Tate, Velentine Tate, Uriah Tate,
      Zephaniah Tate, Uzziah Tate, Zenas Tate,
      Simpson Tate (he is married).

dau: Sally Spruce wife of Quinton Spruce.

Executor: son John Tate.

Witnesses: Wm. Brackin, James McClary.
— — —

C-120  Will in Archives.   Dated 20 Aug 1798, proved Aug 1798.

ABIJAH (x) MASSEY           wife: Jemima

"my children" number and names not stated.
He mentions a tract of land bought from John Conally.

Executors: brother Abner Massey,
        "William Pendergrass my Honorable Father-in-Law".
Witnesses: Matthew McCauley, Jobe (x) Pendergrass,
— — —       John Pendergrass.

Book C, page 122          "Petersburg  12th June 1798

Mr. John McKerall, Sir-    In consequence of Mr. Kirkland's agreement with you to collect the debts of William McQuiston assigned to me as attorney for Miss Watson sister to the late Andrew Watson, I hereby confirm Mr. Kirkland's appointment of of you as collector." ...

Witness: Wil. Kirkland          CHARLES DUNCAN

Recorded November 1798.

— — —

C-122  Will in Archives.  Dated 27 May 1798, proved Nov 1798.

JOHN PIPER          daughter: Mary Brown

relationship not stated: Sarah Findley, Ruth Brown,
                            Jemima Cabe
son: John Piper

"my daughters"mentioned, no names.

Sole executor: John Piper

Witnesses: Samuel Piper, Wm. Cabe, Stephen Scarlet.

— — —

C-124  Will in Archives.  Dated 28 Oct 1798, proved Nov 1798.

THOMAS (x) SMITH          wife: Sarah

son: Abraham

"3 daughters, Elizabeth, Mary and Hannah"

Executor: Alexander Boling.

Witnesses: Thos. Reding, John Whitaker.

— — —

C-126  Will in Archives.  Dated 6 April 1798, proved Nov 1798.

GEORGE RIGGS          wife: Sarah

sons: William Riggs, James Riggs

"my six daughters, namely Mary Newton, Jane Eakins, Sarah Montgomery, Ann Cell (?), Susannah Watson & Elizabeth Watson."

"my three daughters namely Margaret Riggs, Agnes Riggs, and Rachel Riggs."

grandson: James Woods

"my daughter Elizabeth's two eldest children", names not stated.

Executors: wife Sarah and John Latta, Senior.

Witnesses: John Latta, Elizabeth (x) Latta, Eliz. Latta, Jr.

— — —

Book C, page 127   Will in Archives.   Dated 30 Nov 1798,
                                        proved Feb 1798.
DAVID CARSON

father: James Carson receives all estate.

"to my beloved son known by the name of Ecklon Woods" $100
if he lives to become 21 years old.

Sole executor: father James Carson.

Witnesses: Robert A. Carson, Moses Carson.

— — —

C-128   Will in Archives.   Dated 7 Jan 1799, proved Feb 1799.

JOHN PATTON        wife a legatee, name not stated.

sons: William, John

daus: Jean, Mary

Executor: Matthew Patton.

Witnesses: Joseph Clendennin, John McDaniel.

— — —

C-129   Will in Archives.   Dated 4 Sept 1791, proved Feb 1799.

JONATHAN HILL              wife: Rezzy

"my three younger children "

son: Elzy Hill.

Sole executrix: wife Rezzy.

Witnesses: John Hervey, John Starr.

— — —

C-131   Will in Archives.   Dated 18 March 1793, proved
                                                Feb 1799.
HENRY (x) PARISH               wife: Mary

sons: Henry Parish, William Parish

dau: Tenah Sanders.

Executors: wife Mary, and Moses Cox.

Witnesses: Jno. Thompson, Joseph Woody,
           Thomas McMullin, Robert Thompson.

— — —

Book C, page 132  Will in Archives. Dated 3 Sept 1798,
                                    proved Feb 1799.
ABRAHAM MASSEY

wife: Gwen Massey

sons: Daniel, Enoch, Thomas, Abner.

daus: Anne, Mary, Lydia Herndon.

Executors: Abner Massey, Daniel Massey.

Witnesses: Bethier Bragg, John Bragg, James Trice.

— — —

C-134  Will in Archives.  Dated 29 Dec 1795, proved May 1798.

JOHN (x) LOWRY

"to Thaipiah Henderson daughter of Margaret Henderson"...

Witnesses: John Daniely, James Ross, Thomas Phillips.

"N.B. I the said JOHN LOWRY further appoint the above said
Margaret Cleft Executrix."

Mary Cleft qualified as Executrix.

— — —

C-135  Will in Archives.  Dated --- proved May 1799.

WILLIAM DUNNAGAN, SENIOR            wife: Sarah

This is a very poorly worded will, relationships not clear.

son: William

sons ? Ashby Dunnagan, Sherod.

dau: Peggy.

He has married children, and unmarried daughters.

He mentions "the three boys" ... "all the girls".

Executors: Ashby Dunnagan, William Dunnagan.

Witnesses: Alex. McMullan
           Winnifred (x) McMullan.

— — —

Book C, page 136  Will in Archives.   Dated 2 Dec 1798,
                                      proved May 1799.
BENJAMIN (x) CATE

wife: Mary to receive 1/6th part of estate.

He is to "be buried at the Reading House".

"5 sons viz: John Cate, Timothy Cate, Jesse Cate,
William Cate and James Cate."

dau: Mary Cate, under age

"to Henry Hunt's oldest boy Elijah Hunt"...
"to David Nutt's oldest son John Nutt"...

Executors: brother Richard Cate, William Cain, merchant.

Witnesses: Alex'r McMullan, Edward Wortham,
            William (x) Cate.
— — —

C-137  Will in Archives.   Dated 30 April 1799, proved
                                              May 1799.
SUSANNAH (x) DURHAM

sons: Matthew Durham, Lysias Durham, Mark Durham.

dau: Mary Mechum

"daughter Jane's children Susannah Piper and Sarah Piper".

Executor: Lysias Durham.

Witnesses: Alexander Hatch, Frances (x) Durham, Oney Hutson.

— — —

C- 139  Will in Archives. Dated 8 Dec 1793, proved May 1799.

JAMES (x) MORDAK              wife: Elizabeth

son: James Mordak

daus: Ketren, Mary Behanon, Ann Mordak.

son: William Mordak

grandson: William Riggs.

Executors: wife Elizabeth and son William.

Witnesses: Wm. Bowls, Fanney (x) Bowls.
— — —

120

Book C, page 140  Will in Archives.  Dated --  proved May /
1799.

JAMES NELSON

brothers: John, Abraham  and Archer Nelson

sisters: Elizabeth Waldrop and Milly Meredith.

"to John Nelson Rencher and Sarah Rencher son and daughter
of Jno. G. Rencher and Nancy Rencher."
"to James son of above"...

"to Sarah Nelson daughter of Archer"...
"Nelly Nelson daughter of Archer"...

sister: Nancy Rencher

"Lydia and Elizabeth Harold daughters of Edy Harold"...

"my honored father"...

Executors: George Johnston, Alexander Bowland.

Witnesses: James Strayhorn, Adam (x) Stowers.

-- -- --

C-142  Will in Archives.  Dated 1 Aug 1799, proved Aug 1799.

EDWARD GAINS                    wife: Susannah

sons: Thomas Gains, Joseph Gains, Francis Gains,
      Solomon Gains, Broadus Gains, Wilson Gains.

daus: Susannah Gains, Elizabeth Gains, Mary Gains,
      Nancy Gains.

Executors: wife, and son Thomas.

Witnesses: Isaac Rainey, Asa (x) Kent, Rob't (x) Pinkerton.

-- -- --

C-144  Will in Archives.  Dated 17 Oct 1796, proved Aug 1799.

JOSHUA WYATT                    wife: Elizabeth

sons: Joshua Wyatt, Frederick Wyatt get land bought of /
                                        Isaac Dorris

daus: Elizabeth Wyatt, Mary Simpson.

Executors: wife Elizabeth, sons Joshua and Frederick.

Witnesses: Will Wilkins, Mary (x) Wilkins.

-- -- --

Book C, page 145  BILL OF SALE from JOHN TROUSDALE to
Joseph Allison, for one negro.  Dated 12 Aug 1797, proved
Aug. 1799.                Witness: John Campbell.

– – –

C-146  Will in Archives.  Dated 17 April 1799, proved Aug 1799.

FRANCES THOMPSON

daughter Margaret "half of estate left me by my father Benjamin Thompson at the decease of my mother Sarah Thompson."

son: Anderson (under age) other half of estate.

Executors: brothers Robert and Richard Thompson.

Witnesses: Samuel Thompson, Caleb Harvey.

– – –

C-147  Will in Archives.  Dated 9 Feb 1799, proved Aug 1799.

JOHN MOORE                      wife: Mary

4 oldest sons: James, John, Nathan, Alfred (a minor), get
               land on waters of Laughlens Creek.

daus: Mary, Martha, Sarah

Executors: wife Mary, son James.

Witnesses: James Boyle, Lem'l C. Jepson, Robert Moore.

– – –

C-149  Will in Archives.  Dated 23 Jan 1798, proved Aug 1799.

MICHAEL HOLT                    wife: Jean

children by first wife...

son: Joseph Holt
daus: Margaret Powell, Elizabeth Smith

dau: Sarah Hardin
sons: Joshua Holt, Isaac Holt
daus: Mary Thompson, Catherine Holt
sons: Michael Holt, William Holt.

Executors: wife Jean, sons Isaac and Joshua.

Witnesses: J. Scott, Wm. Rainey, John Holt.

– – –

C-153 Deed in Archives, dated 19 Aug 1799, proved Nov 1799.

From HENRY COOK, SR to ."my three children Ann Cook, Augustin Cook and Hamlin Cook" five negroes.
Witness: Hardress Hawkins.

— — —

C-153 Will in Archives. Dated 29 May 1781, proved Nov 1799.

JOHN ESTES of the Town of Hillsborough.

To wife Eliza "all my estate".

Executors: wife Eliza, Col. Robert Rowan of Cumberland Co.
Witnesses: Francis McKerall, A. Tatom.

— — —

C-154 Bond from THOMAS MULHOLLAND to DAVID ENGLISH on land joining lands of John Parks, James McCanlis and Thomas Person.      Witnesses: Jno. Armstrong, J. Baldridge.

— — —

C-155 Will in Archives. Dated 17 Oct 1799, proved Nov 1799.

CONRAD MESSER SMITH

sons: Leonard, Stephen, Conrad, Phette.

daus: Elizabeth Cates, Mary "10 sh. to disinherit her".

Witnesses: Jno. McMullan, Alexander Turrentine.
Executor named by the Court, Samuel Turrentine.

— — —

C-156 Will in Archives. Dated 28 Jan 1799, proved Nov 1799.

ENOCH LEWIS

Bequests to: John Moore, Joseph Trice,
Abner Massey "land lying on Crooked Creek waters of New Hope",
Gwen Massey-see note below, Thomas Massey, Enoch Massey,
Ann Massey dau of Gwen Massey, Mary Gray wife of Thomas Gray,
Daniel Massey, Lydia Herndon -see note below.

Executors: "trusty friends John Moore and Abner Massey".
Witnesses: Thomas Trice, Mann Patterson, James Trice.

Note by Ruth Herndon Shields.  Notice that these are the same Massey heirs named in the will of Abraham Massey, C-132.
Gwen Massey was the sister of ENOCH LEWIS. Lydia Massey married Benjamin Herndon, and thus became my great-great-great-grandmother. Her descendants are given in PART FOUR of THE HERNDON FAMILY OF VIRGINIA by Dr. John Goodwin Herndon.

Also in the same book are the descendants of George and his wife Sarah Herndon  (see C-85) my great-great-great-grandparents in my father's maternal line.

— — —

C-157 Will in Archives. Dated 18 Oct 1799, proved Nov 1799.

GEORGE LOY           wife: name not stated.

sons: John, Jacob, George, Henry, William

daughter: Sally
daus: Elizabeth Moser, Caty Albright,
      Margaret Clapp,  Rachel Albright.

Executors: wife, and son John.
Witnesses: Michael Holt, John Loy.

— — —

C-159 Will in Archives. Dated 5 May 1799, proved Nov 1799.

JOHN BARBEE      wife: Sarah (she was Sarah Patterson)

Three sons Mark, Young, William, get 440 acres in Chatham
County near Torrinton's (Farrington's ?) Mill.

Relationship not stated, but we know from deeds that they
are children: Joseph, Patt/ , John, Sylve, Edie, have had
their parts.        (Martha)
"rest of my children Sally, Elizabeth, Rosanna and Theina"..

granddaughter: Frances (under age) sirname not stated.

Executors: wife Sarah Barbee, brother Christopher Barbee.
Witnesses: Mark Patterson, James Rainey, Syntha Rhodes.

— — —

C-161 Will in Archives. Dated 16 July 1799, proved Feb 1800.

JOSEPH COURTNEY

wife: Hannah, receives land "lately belonging to my brother
      Wm. Courtney which he purchased from Wm.
      Courtney, Sr". And other lands bounded by
      lands of Gilbert Strayhorn. Bond on Robert
      Glenn of Person County.

father: William Courtney

Executors: Major Absolom Tatom, William Whitehead, Jr.
Witnesses: Robert Bell, Abner Tapp.

— — —

C-162 Bill of Release, dated 2 Nov 1799, proved Feb 1800.

From JOHN McRAE to Capt. JOHN CARRINGTON. He relinquishes

all property involved except land sold to Col. William
Hunt of Granville County.

Witnesses: Wm. Hunt, Duncan McRae, George Jimmason.

A STUDY OF THE BARBEE FAMILIES OF CHATHAM, ORANGE & WAKE
COUNTIES, NORTH CAROLINA   Compiled by Ruth Herndon Shields
Belle Lewter West, Kathryn Crossley Stone. Published 1971

124

C-163 Will in Archives. Dated 7 March 1799, proved Feb 1800

**DAVID COPELAND, SENIOR**          wife: Elizabeth

sons: David, Douglass, Hugh, John.

daughter: Elizabeth Nunn.

Executors: sons David and Douglass Copeland.
Witnesses: John Wood, Isaac Holden, John Holden.

- - -

C-164 Will in Archives. Dated 19 March 1799, proved Feb /
                                                          1800
WILLIAM WARD          wife: Susannah

sons: Stephen, Anthony, William, Thomas, James

daughters: Susanna Pike, Sarah Clark,
           Priscilla Ferree, Esther Wells.

son-in-law: Daniel Ferree land joining Adam Coble.

Executors: wife Susanna, son Stephen.
Witnesses: Jacob Marshill, Jesse Hinshaw, Jr.

- - -

C-166 Will in Archives. Dated 29 Nov 1799, proved Feb 1800.

BENJAMIN PEELOR

wife: Christiana "land known by the name of my Anthony
              place, as also Boney tract."

son: Samuel receives "lands bounded by lands of Jno. Holt,
         Thos. Browning and William Pickett."

sons: Pleasant, Allen, Abner.

daughters: Franky, Polly, Esther.

son: Benjamin receives "place where Thomas McFarland lives
         and Mark Browning's place."

Executors: wife Christiana, friend Jno. G. Rencher.
Witnesses: J.G.Rencher, Christian Peelor.

- - -

                    END OF BOOK C

D-1 Will in Archives. Dated 18 Jan 1794, proved May 1800.

HUGH WOODS                    wife: Mary Woods

sons: Joseph Elihugh, John

daus: Susanna wife of James Faucette,
      Sarah, Elizabeth, Mary Ann

granddau: Milly, dau. of George Riggs & wife Rebecca.
grandson: Hugh,   son  "   "      "      " "      "

Executors: wife Mary, and son-in-law James Faucett.
Witnesses: David Turrentine, James Grimes, Hugh Montgomery.
- - -

D-3 Will in Archives. Dated 22 July 1799, proved May 1800.

FREDERICK MOSIER, SR.

sons: John, Frederick, Jacob, Michael,
      Abraham, Phillip, Nicholas.

daus: Caty Kimbro, Barbara Huffman, Lizy Sharp,
      Eve Sharp, Magdalene Bulcher.

Executors: son Phillip and son-in-law Peter Sharpe.
Witness: Richard Cochran.
- - -

Note by Ruth H. Shields. Here are a few genealogies I
happen to know about, that have information about families
of Caswell, Chatham, Orange and Wake Counties of N.C.
Some of them are out of print, I give information on those
I know about.

BROOKS and Kindred Families by Ida Brooks Kellam (1950)
Much information on Chatham and neighboring counties.

WILLIAMS and MURPHY Records by R. Murphy Williams (1949)

The ALSTONS and ALLSTONS of North and South Carolina
by Joseph A. Groves, M.D. First published in 1902.
Re-issued in 1957. Price $10.00 order from
The Seeman Printery, Inc., Durham, N.C.

HAPPY VALLEY, by Thomas Felix Hickerson of Chapel Hill,N.C.

The NEVILLE family of Orange County is given in
Historical Southern Families, Vol 2, by John B. Boddie.

HERNDONS of The American Revolution, Part Four
by John Goodwin Herndon has Caswell and Orange families.

Descendants of William and Sarah (Poe) Herndon
of Caroline County, Va. and Chatham County, N.C.
Price $10.00, order from Mrs. C. W. Shields, Chapel Hill.

126

D-4 Will in Archives. Dated 22 July 1799, proved May 1800.

DEBORAH TURRENTINE
sons: Samuel, Daniel, James, Alexander.

daus: Elizabeth Baldridge, Martha Baldridge, Jean Watson.

Executors: sons Samuel and Alexander Turrentine.
Witnesses: James Roark, William Roark, Thomas Wilson.

- - -

D-5 Will in Archives. Dated 9 April 1800, proved May 1800.

URIAH SPRINGER            wife: Margaret Springer.

sons: George, Adam, David.

daus: Mary, Eve Porter.

Executors: Stephen Ward, John Whiter.
Witnesses: Ebenezer Doan, John Bullack.

- - -

D-6  Will in Archives. Dated 6 March, proved May 1800.

ROBERT TURNER            wife: Mary Turner

son: James Turner.    daus: Eliza Agnew, Jane, Sarah.

Executors: wife Mary Turner, and John Agnew.
Witnesses: Hardy Hurdle, Thomas Rippy, Joseph Rippy.

- - -

D-7  Will in Archives. Dated 20 June 1800, proved Nov 1800.

EDWARD TRICE            daus: Ruth Higgins, Betsy.

sons: John, Harrison, William, George,
      Andrew, Charles, Zecel (Ezekiel).

Executors: wife Tabitha, and William Trice and John Moore.
Witnesses: John Moore, Enah Massey, Martha Casselberry.

- - -

D-9  Will in Archives. Dated 25 Sept 1800, proved Nov 1800.

ELIZABETH STROUD

Leaves property to children to wit - " Margaret Douglass,
John Stroud, the children of Fanny Howell, Mary Thrift,
Sally King, Anderson Stroud, William Stroud, Elizabeth Rane,
Marshall Stroud, Dixon Stroud."

Executors: John Stroud, Anderson Stroud.
Witnesses: John King, Nancy Hogan, Elizabeth King.

- - -

D-10 Will in Archives. Dated 25 Jan 1794, proved Nov 1800.

JAMES FRUIT or FRUTH      wife: Grizel (spelled Girzel)

son: John

daus: Elinor, Jennett, Hannah, Nancy, Mary.

Executor: John Fruth
Witnesses: Moses Crawford, Ann Crawford.

— — —

D-11 Will in Archives. Dated 9 Nov 1800, proved Nov 1800.

ENOCH BRADLEY, Blacksmith.     wife: Rachel Bradley.

sisters: Mary Jackson, Ann Hill.

To "brother Charles Bradley and his 3 sons, George, Enoch,
and Josiah".
To " sister Mary's 6 children: Jain Morgan, Baldwin, Ruth,
John, Sarah and Deborah."
To " sister Ann Hill's 3 children - Elizabeth, Hannah,
and Samuel."
"To sister Elizabeth Collin's children, namely, John,
Catherine, Enoch, Mary Brice, Elizabeth, Jain, Joseph,
and Margaret."
"To Nathaniel Carter's son Enoch."
"To Robert Green's son Enoch."

Sole Executor: James Newlin.
Witnesses: George Maden, John Newlin.

— — —

D-12 Will in Archives. Dated 9 Sept 1799, proved Nov 1800.

JOHN MURRAY             wife: Jean Murray

sons: Thomas, John, Joseph.
daus: Rebekah, Mary, Elizabeth, Jean, Lydia.

Executors: wife Jean, and friend Jesse Towel.
Witnesses: Nathan Dicks, Isaac Harvey, Jacob Marshall.

— — —

D-14 Will in Archives. Dated 13 Feb 1800, proved Aug 1800.

JAMES ANDERSON             wife: Jennet

sons: John, William.

daus: Margaret, Elizabeth Clendenning, Jennet Achles.
(Eccles)

Executors: Benjamin Roney, Samuel Mebane.
Witnesses: Benjamin Roney, Samuel Mebane.

— — —

128

D-15  Will in Archives. Dated 4 March 1800, proved Aug 1800.

JACOB BEASON          sons: John, Frederick, Joseph.

daus: Margaret, Hannah, and Catherine.

Executors: brother Henry Beason, brother-in-law Aron Sharpe.
Witnesses: W. Mebane, Richard Bull, Thomas Dixon.

- - -

D-16  Will in Archives. Dated 20 June 1800, proved Aug 1800.

JOHN HARVEY              wife: Mary

sons: David, Absolom, Jonathan.    daus: Mary, Alice.

"To John Harvey son of Jonathan Harvey"

Executors: son David, "true friend Wm. Fausett".
Witnesses: Levi Hall, James Hall.

- - -

D-18  Will in Archives. Dated 4 Jan 1799, proved Aug 1800.

WILLIAM GALBREATH         wife

sons: Walter, William (2nd son), John ("3rd and youngest").

daus: "Cathron (oldest) now MacKieney",
      "Elizabeth, now Cunningham".
      "Mary, now Dickson".
      Ann.

sons-in-law: Francis McKieney, Matthew Cunningham.

grandsons: Wm. McKieney, Wm. Dickson, Wm. Galbreath.

No Executor named.  Witnesses: Mac Cunningham, Wm. Kirk.

- - -

D-20 Will in Archives. Dated 12 Jan 1789, proved Aug 1800.

GEORGE LAWS, SENIOR.

sons: William, George.     daus: Elizabeth, Sarah Harris.

grandson: George Laws, son of William Laws.
granddaus: Nancy Laws daughter of Wm. Laws.
           Mary Laws daughter of George Laws.
           Betty Edge
son-in-law: Jeremiah Edge.

Executors: sons George Laws and William Laws.
Witnesses: Joseph Guess, Wm. Madison, Richard Bohannon.

- - -

For 19 other wills recorded in Book D see A-212-

MARRIAGES FOUND IN ORANGE COUNTY , N.C. WILLS RECORDED IN
WILL BOOKS A, B, AND C, WHICH DO NOT APPEAR IN THE ORANGE
COUNTY MARRIAGE RECORDS.

       Not all of these marriages took place in Orange County.
All we can be certain of is that some time before the will
was written in which they are mentioned, such marriages
took place.

       The date of the will in which they are given, and the
date of the will, follows the name of the bride and groom.
The last name in the line is the name of the person making
the will. Anyone wishing to obtain a copy of one of these
wills can write to the CLERK OF COURT, Hillsboro, N.C.

       These marriages are presented first with the name of
the bride indexed. They are then given with the name of the
groom alphebetized.

| BRIDE | GROOM | DATE OF WILL | TESTATOR |
|---|---|---|---|
| Abercromby, Jenny | ...... Mebane | May 1779 | Rob. Abercromby |
| Allen, Margaret | James Mebane | Mar 1786 | George Allen |
| Anderson, Jennett | ..... Achles | Feb 1800 | James Anderson |

Bond found -Jean Anderson 5 March 1792 John Eccles

| BRIDE | GROOM | DATE OF WILL | TESTATOR |
|---|---|---|---|
| Asten, .... | Peter Downey | Nov 1766 | Wm. Asten |
| " , .... | Archibald McLeroy | " " | " " |
| Berry, Margaret | James Morrow | Apr 1761 | Thomas Berry |
| Blake, Martha | Elisha Cain | Apr 1783 | Benj. Blake |
| " , Rebecca | ...... Mason | " " | " " |
| " , Sarah | ...... Braswell | " " | " " |
| Bohannon, Frankey | ...... Boyd | .. 1760 | Duncan Bohannon |
| Bowling, Isabel | John Butler | Jan 1789 | Jean Bowling |
| " , Susannah | .... Boswell | " " | " " |
| Bowls, Elizabeth | .... Murdak | 1798 | Thomas Bowls |
| Breazier, Eliz. | .... Jameson | May 1770 | Thos. Breazier |
| " , Hannah | .... Teague | " " | " " |
| " , Sarah | .... Pyle | " " | " " |
| Breese,(or Bruce) Jannet | ..... Robeson | Feb 1784 | Thos. Breese |
| Carson, Alice | Wm. Clenny | Apr 1789 | Alex. Carson |

Bond found - Alce Cearson 26 August 1787 William Clenny

| BRIDE | GROOM | DATE OF WILL | TESTATOR |
|---|---|---|---|
| Christmas, Ann | ..... Pickat(?) | Aug 1783 | John Christmas |
| Coharon, Minny | Joseph Guy | Oct 1775 | Alex Coharon |
| Comb, Betty | .... Mitchell | Aug 1791 | Wm. Comb |
| " , Ellender | .... Trice | " " | " " |
| Cox, Catherine | Elizor Hunt | Jan 1767 | William Cox |
| " , Marjory | Isaac Nichols | " " | " " |
| " , Martha | Wm. Terrell | " " | " " |
| " , Mary | James Lindley | " " | " " |
| " , Rebecca | ..... Dixon | " " | " " |
| Craige, Abigail | ..... Pasmore | Jan 1785 | William Craige |
| " , Bathsheba | ..... Crayton | " " | " " |
| " , Joanna | ..... McMullin | " " | " " |
| " , Mary | ..... Sheart | " " | " " |
| " , Ruth | ..... Simmons | " " | " " |
| Davis, Ellenor | ..... Darker | Jan 1792 | Enoch Davis |
| Deal, Jean ? | John Hall | Feb 1775 | John Hall |
| Dixson, Anne | Caleb Bailey | Dec 1769 | Joseph Dixson |
| Donaldson, Margaret | Wm. Ray | Mar 1770 | Rob. Donaldson |
| Dunweddee, Nancy | ... Long | Nov 1794 | Henry Dunweddee |
| " , Sarah | .... Gresham | " " | " " |
| Durham, Jane | .... Piper | Apr 1799 | Susannah Durham |
| Foust, Barbara | .... Clap | Dec 1786 | John Foust |
| " , Judith | .... Clap | " " | " " |
| Galbreath, Cathron | Francis McKieney | Jan 1799 | Wm. Galbreath |
| Geer, Mary | .... Burnett | Aug 1769 | John Geer |
| George, Mary | .... Hinsford | Feb 1770 | Joseph George |
| " , Catherine | .... Riddle | " " | " " |
| Greason, Marg't | .... Lowe | Sep 1768 | Isaac Greason |
| " , Unitie | .. Lionburger | " " | " " |
| Hadley, Mary | .... Piggott | Sep 1760 | Joshua Hadley |
| " , Ruth | .... Marshal | " " | " " |
| " , Sarah | .... Ford | " " | " " |

| BRIDE | GROOM | DATE OF WILL | TESTATOR |
|---|---|---|---|
| Hall, Rebecca | ..... Kell ? | Sep 1791 | Jean Hall |
| Hanley, Ann | ..... Linin ,or Tinin ? | Mar 1790 | Daniel Hanley |
| Harrison, Anne | (John ?) Ware | May 1773 | Andrew Harrison |
| " , Milley | (Wm ?) Moore | " " | " " |
| " , Lenora ? | ..... Burks | Jun 1773 | Nath. Harrison |
| " , Unity | ..... Callahan | " " | " " |
| Hendricks, Mary | ... Balander | Jul 1786 | Peter Hendricks |
| Herndon, Eliz. | (Wm.) Cole | May 1796 | George Herndon |
| " , Mary | .... Roberts | " " | " " |
| " , Maryanne | (Ezekiel) Trice | " " | " " |
| " , Ruth | .... Roberts | " " | " " |
| " , Sally | (Henry) McCoy | " " | " " |
| Holloway, Eliz. | .... Horner | Nov 1776 | Rob. Holloway |
| " , Mary | .... Readen | " " | " " |
| Holt, Eliz. | .... Smith | Jan 1798 | Michael Holt |
| " , Margaret | .... Powell | " " | " " |

(Two of Michael Holt's daughters were married in Orange Co. Mary in 1787, Sarah in 1785.)

| | | | |
|---|---|---|---|
| Hooper, Eliz. | ..... Walters or Watters | Apr 1793 | Anne Hooper |
| Hulgan,Marg't | ..... Neely | Jul 1794 | Thomas Hulgan |
| Jamison, Mary | .... Parks | Feb 1793 | Wm. Jamison |
| " , Margaret | .... Lindsey | " " | " " |
| Jenkins, Nancy | .. Fennell (Ferrell ?) | 1790 | John Jenkins |
| " , Patty | .. Allen | Feb 1790 | " " |
| Johnston, ... | Chaldous ? Bailey | Jun 1789 | Chas. Johnston |
| " , ... | Samuel Craig | Jun 1789 | " " |
| " , ... | John Strayhorn | " " | " " |
| Jones, Seaney | John Shaw | March 1792, Deed, B188 | |
| Larkin, Eliz. | .... Boring | Aug 1792 | Alex. Larkin |
| " , Mary | Mordecai Moor | " " | " " |
| Laws, ... | Jeremiah Edge | Jan 1798 | Geo. Laws, Sr. |
| " , Sarah | .... Harris | " " | " " |
| Leak, Eliz. | James Terry | Feb 1784 | Richard Leak |
| " , Mary | ..... Moor | " " | " " |
| " , Jean | ..... Harley | " " | " " |
| " , Susannah | ..... Campbell | " " | " " |
| " , .... | ..... Slatter | " " | " " |

| BRIDE | GROOM | DATE OF WILL, TESTATOR |
|---|---|---|

Lindley, Deborah  .... Newlin      Mar 1780 Wm. Lindley
"  , Elinor     .... Mauriss (Morris?) "    "    "
"  , Katherine   .... White       Mar "    "    "    "
"  , Ruth       .... Hadley       "    "    "    "

Lloyd, Mary       (John?) Hogan      Feb 1792 Thomas Lloyd

Lockhart, Cath.     ..... Roads       Aug 1786 Cath. Lockhart
"  , Elizabeth   .. Mucklejohn      "    "    "    "
"  , Jean       ..... Holt        "    "    "    "
"  , Mary       ..... Smith       "    "    "    "
"  , Sarah       James Parker      "    "    "    "

Mace, Angel       John Dorris       May 1794 Power of Att'y

Mangum, Sally     .... Bobitt       Nov 1789 Arthur Mangum

Massey, Lydia      (Benj.) Herndon       1798 Abr. Massey
"     ,     "           "        Feb 1799 Enoch Lewis

                                                   ter
McCallister, Marg't/Andrew Patent      Jul 1768 John McCallis-
                (or Poteat?)

McCracken, Abigail .... Davis       Aug 1795 Alex. McCracken
"  , Hannah     .... Tinnen       "    "    "    "
"  , Mary       .... Andrew       "    "    "    "
"  , Ruth       .... Chamness      "    "    "    "

Mebane, Ann       .... Morrow       Apr 1789 Alex. Mebane
"  , Jennett    .... Anderson      "    "    "    "
"  , Margaret   .... Murdaugh      "    "    "    "
"  , Jennett    .... Stanford      Jul 1795 "       "

Miles, or Meler, or Mills,
    Hannah         .... Slade        Mar 1766 Thomas Miles
"  ,......         .... Pottiett ? "    "    "    "

Miller, Lydia      Joseph Ray       Mar 1793 George Miller
"     , Mary     Zach. Dickey      "    "    "    "
"     , Sarah    John Ray        "    "    "    "

Mordak, Mary      .... Behanon      Dec 1793 James Mordak
(Probably Mary Murdock who m 17 June 1786 Thos. Buchanon.)

Morgan, Anne      ..... Hart        Jan 1787 Sarah Morgan
"  , Sarah       ..... Yeargan      "    "    "    "

Mosier, Barbara    ..... Huffman      Apr 1796 Frederick Mosier
"  , Caty        ..... Kimbro       "    "    "    "
"  , Lizy        ..... Sharp        "    "    "    "
"  , Magdalene   ..... Bulcher      "    "    "    "
(Their sister Eve m in Orange 31 Aug 1795 Peter Sharp.)

| BRIDE | GROOM | DATE OF WILL, TESTATOR |
|---|---|---|
| Nelson, Jean | .... Scott | Mar 1790 Robert Nelson |
| Parish, Tenah | .... Sanders | Mar 1793 Henry Parish |
| Patterson, Jenny | .... Ward | Dec 1789 Nath. Patterson |
| " , Margaret | .... Swift | "    "     "     " |
| " , " | .... Abbott | Jul 1790 John Patterson |
| Phillips, Hannah | .... Johnston | May 1798 Rainey Phillips |
| Pike, Ann | .... Hughes | Mar 1771 John Pike |
| " , Elizabeth | .... Stuart | "    "     "     " |
| " , Rachel | .... Williams | "    "     "     " |
| " , Ruth | .... Winner | "    "     "     " |
| " , Sarah | .... Piggott | "    "     "     " |
| " , Susannah | .... Lee | "    "     "     " |
| Pryor, Elizabeth | .... Flournoy | Sep 1771 John Pryor |
| " , Leah | .... Perkins | "    "     "     " |
| " , Lucy | .... Tapley | "    "     "     " |
| " , Mildred | David Womack | "    "     "     " |
| " , Rachel | .... Pope | "    "     "     " |
| " , Rhode | William Stone | "    "     "     " |
| Rea, ... | James Mordah (k?) | Oct 1769 William Rea |
| " , ... | John Mordah (k?) | "    "     "     " |
| " , ... | Michael Robbins | "    "     "     " |
| " , ... | Patrick Rutherford | "    "     "     " |
| Rice, Hannah | Jesse Towell | Jan 1783 John Rice |
| Riggs, Ann | .... Cell (?) | Apr 1798 George Riggs |
| " , Eliz. | .... Watson | "    "     "     " |
| " , Jane | .... Eakins | "    "     "     " |
| " , Mary | .... Newton | "    "     "     " |
| " , Mary | Barnaba Grymes | Mar 1776 William Riggs |
| Riley, Mary | .... Donaldson | July 1791 John Riley |
| Robbinson, Esthy | .... Thompson | Apr 1774 Alex. Robbinson |
| " , Ellenor | John Ceasey | "    "     "     " |
| Robertson, Mary | .... Lindsay | Apr 1795 Ath. Robertson |
| Robison, Mary | .... Lindsay , deed, | May 1785 Athanasius Robison |
| Ross, Jane | .... Smith | Dec 1792 James Ross |
| " ; Levinia | (John?) Minnis | "    "     "     " |
| Sanders, Fanny | Wm. Sanders,Sr | Feb 1776 James Sanders Sr |
| " , Sarah | William Trigg | "    "     "     " |
| " , Susannah | Robert Terry | "    "     "     " |

| BRIDE | GROOM | DATE OF WILL | TESTATOR |
|---|---|---|---|
| Scoby, Margaret | .... Tait | Oct 1782 | Matthew Scoby |
| Seares, Mary | .... Surls | Jul 1788 | Thomas Seares |
| Smith, Elizabeth | .... Cates | Oct 1799 | Conrod M. Smith |
| Smothers, Eliz. | .... Pickard | Aug 1778 | Thomas Smothers |
| " , Rebecca | .... Sumner | " " | " " |
| Springer, Eve | .... Porter | Apr 1800 | Uriah Springer |
| Stantefer,Casander | ... Hendon | Aug 1793 | Israel Stantefer |
| " , Rossaner | ..... Rhodes | " " | " " |
| " , Sarah | ..... Rhoades | " " | " " |

(Ruth Stantefer m in Orange 14 Aug 1781 William Turner.)

| BRIDE | GROOM | DATE OF WILL | TESTATOR |
|---|---|---|---|
| Stanford, ... ? | ..... King ? | Jun 1789 | Anthony Stanford |
| Stroud, Margaret | ..... Douglass | Aug 1786 | Wm. Stroud |
| " , Mary | ..... Thrift | " " | " " |
| " , Salley | ..... King | " " | " " |

These 2 Stroud marriages also found in will of Elizabeth
Stroud, Jan 1794.

| BRIDE | GROOM | DATE OF WILL | TESTATOR |
|---|---|---|---|
| Thomas, Ann | ..... Wilks | Mar 1769 | Owen Thomas |
| " , Mary | .... Hart, or Hard | " | " " |
| Thompson, Eliz | .... Hadley | Jul 1794 | James Thompson |
| " , Sarah | Owen Lindley | " " | " " |
| Tolby or Talley, | | | |
| Elizabeth | (Richard?) Rhodes | Aug 1791 | Samuel Tolby ? |
| " , Mary | (James?) Kennady | " " | " " |
| " , Milly | ..... Whitaker | " " | " " |
| Turner, Eliza | (John ?) Agnew | Mar 1800 | Robert Turner |
| Turrentine, Eliz | .. Baldridge | Jul 1799 | Deb. Turrentine |
| " , Martha | .... Baldridge | " " | " " |
| " , Jean | .... Watson | " " | " " |
| Wade, Eliz. | .... Talley | Jan 1757 | Joseph Wade |
| " , Lucy | Joseph Powel | " " | " " |
| " , Mary | .... Strawther | " " | " " |
| " , Sarah | .... Fountain | " " | " " |
| " , Susannah | .... Hart | " " | " " |
| Waggoner, Eliz. | .... Johns | Jul 1784 | Geo Waggoner |
| " , Susannah | .... Smith | " " | " " |
| Walker, Ann | .... Cimball | Dec 1791 | James Walker |
| " , Elizabeth | .... Horton | " " | " " |
| " , Lydia | .... Wright | " " | " " |
| " , Sarah | .... Colbert | " " | " " |

| BRIDE | GROOM | DATE OF WILL, TESTATOR |
|---|---|---|
| Watson, Helen | William Reed | Dec 1776 James Watson |
| Wood, Elizabeth | .... Acory | May 1786 Thomas Wood |
| " , Lydia | .... Good | "    "    "    " |
| " , Meley | .... Gwin | "    "    "    " |
| " , Sarah | .... Forrest | "    "    "    " |
| " , Theaney | .... Wallace | "    "    "    " |
| Woods, Rebecca | George Riggs | Jan 1794 Hugh Woods |
| " , Susanna | James Faucette | "    "    "    " |
| Wyatt, Mary | ..... Simpson | Oct 1796 Joshua Wyatt |

| GROOM, | BRIDE | DATE OF WILL, TESTATOR |
|---|---|---|
| Abbott, ... | Margaret Patterson | Jul 1790 John Patterson |
| Achles, ... | Jennett Anderson | Feb 1800 James Anderson |
| Acory, ... | Elizabeth Wood | May 1786 Thomas Wood |
| Agnew, John (?) | Eliza Turner | Mar 1800 Robert Turner |
| Allen, ... | Patty Jenkins | Feb 1790 John Jenkins |
| Anderson, ... | Jennett Mebane | Apr 1789 Alex. Mebane |
| Andrew, ... | Mary McCracken | Aug 1795 Alex. McCracken |
| Bailey, Caleb | Anne Dixson | Dec 1769 Joseph Dixson |
| " , Chaldous ? | ..... Johnston | Jun 1789 Chas. Johnston |
| Balander, ... | Mary Hendricks | Jul 1786 Peter Hendricks |
| Baldridge, ... | Eliz. Turrentine | Jul 1799 Deb. Turrentine |
| " , ... | Martha Turrentine | "    "    "    " |
| Behanon, ... | Mary Mordak | Dec 1793 James Mordak |
| (Probably Thomas | Buchanan who m 17 | June 1786 Mary Murdock.) |
| Bobitt, ... | Sally Mangum | Nov 1789 Arthur Mangum |
| Boring, ... | Elizabeth Larkin | Aug 1772 Alex. Larkin |
| Boswell, ... | Susannah Bowling | Jan 1789 Jean Bowling |
| Boyd, ... | Frankey Bohannon | 1760 Duncan Bohannon |
| Braswell, ... | Sarah Blake | Apr 1783 Benj. Blake |
| Bulcher, ... | Magdalene Mosier | Apr 1796 Fred. Mosier |

| GROOM | BRIDE | DATE OF WILL, TESTATOR |
|---|---|---|
| Burks, ... | Lenora? Harris | Jun 1773 Nath. Harris |
| Burnett, ... | Mary Geer | Aug 1769 John Geer |
| Butler, John | Isabel Bowling | Jan 1789 Jean Bowling |
| Cain, Elisha | Martha Blake | Apr 1783 Benj Blake |
| Callahan, ... | Unitie Harris | Jun 1773 Nath. Harris |
| Campbell, ... | Susannah Leak | Feb 1784 Richard Leak |
| Cates, ... | Elizabeth Smith | Oct 1799 Conrod M. Smith |
| Ceasey, John | Ellenor Robbinson | Apr 1774 Alex. Robbinson |
| Cell ?, ... | Ann Riggs | Apr 1798 George Riggs |
| Chamness, ... | Ruth McCracken | Aug 1795 Alex. McCracken |
| Cimboll, ... (Kimball ?) | Ann Walker | Dec 1791 James Walker |
| Clap, ... | Barbara Foust | Dec 1786 John Foust |
| " , ... | Judith Foust | " " " " |
| Clenny, William | Alice Carson | Apr 1789 Alex. Carson |
| Colbert, ... | Sarah Walker | Dec 1791 James Walker |
| Cole, (Wm.) | Eliz. Herndon | May 1796 George Herndon |
| Craig, Samuel | .... Johnston | Jun 1789 Chas. Johnston |
| Crayton, ... | Bathsheba Craige | Jan 1785 William Craige |
| Darker, ... | Ellenor Davis | Jan 1792 Enoch Davis |
| Darris, John | Angel Mace | May 1794 deed, Will Bk. C |
| Davis, ... | Abigail McCracken | Aug 1795 Alex. McCracken |
| Dickey, Zach. | Mary Miller | Mar 1793 George Miller |
| Dixon, ... | Rebecca Cox | Jan 1767 William Cox |
| Donaldson, ... | Mary Riley | Jul 1791 John Riley |
| Douglass, ... | Margaret Stroud | Aug 1786 Wm. Stroud<br>Jan 1794 Eliz. Stroud |
| Downey, Peter | ..... Asten | Nov 1766 William Asten |
| Eakins, ... | Jane Riggs | Apr 1798 George Riggs |

| GROOM | BRIDE | DATE OF WILL, TESTATOR |
|---|---|---|
| Edge, Jeremiah | .... Laws | Jan 1798 George Laws,Sr. |
| Faucette, James | Susanna Woods | Jan 1794 Hugh Woods |
| Fennell, .... (or Ferrell) | Nancy Jenkins | Feb 1790 John Jenkins |
| Flournoy, .. | Elizabeth Piper | Sep 1771 John Piper |
| Ford, ... | Sarah Hadley | Sep 1760 Joshua Hadley |
| Forrest, ... | Sarah Wood | May 1786 Thomas Wood |
| Fountain, ... | Sarah Wade | Jan 1757 Joseph Wade |
| Good, ... | Lydia Wood | May 1786 Thomas Wood |
| Gresham, .... | Sarah Dunweddee | Nov 1794 Henry Dunweddee |
| Grymes, Bannaba | Mary Riggs | Mar 1776 William Riggs |
| Guy, Joseph | Minny Coharon | Oct 1775 Alex. Coharon |
| Gwin, ... | Meley Wood | May 1786 Thomas Wood |
| Hadley, ... | Ruth Lindley | Mar 1780 Wm. Lindley |
| " , ... | Eliz. Thompson | Jul 1794 Jas. Thompson |
| Hall, John | Jean ? Deal | Feb 1775 John Hall |
| Harley, ... | Jean Leak | Feb 1784 Richard Leak |
| Harris, ... | Sarah Laws | Jan 1798 Geo. Laws Sr. |
| Hart or Hard,. | Mary Thomas | Mar 1769 Owen Thomas |
| Hart, ... | Susannah Wade | Jan 1757 Joseph Wade |
| Hendon, ... | Casander Stantefer | Aug 1793 Israel Stantefer/ |
| Herndon, Benj. | Lydia Massey | L..1798 Abr. Massey |
| " " | " " | Feb 1799 Enoch Lewis |
| Hinsford, ... | Mary George | Feb 1770 Joseph George |
| Holt, ... | Jean Lockhart | Aug 1786 Cath. Lockhart |
| Horn, James | Margery ... | Apr 1792 Thos. Horn,Sr. |
| Horner, ... | Eliz. Holloway | Nov 1776 Rob. Holloway |
| Horton, ... | Eliz. Walker | Dec 1791 James Walker |

138

| GROOM | BRIDE | DATE OF WILL, TESTATOR |
|---|---|---|
| Hart, ..... . | Ann Morgan | Jan 1787 Sarah Morgan |
| Huffman, ... | Barbara Mosier | Apr 1796 Fred. Mosier |
| Hughes, ... | Ann Pike | Mar 1771 John Pike |
| Hunt, Elizor | Catherine Cox | Jan 1767 William Cox |
| Jameson, ... | Eliz. Breazier | May 1770 Thos. Breazier |
| Johns, ... | Eliz. Waggoner | Jul 1784 Geo. Waggoner |
| Johnston, ... | Hannah Phillips | May 1798 Rainey Phillips |
| Kell, ... | Rebecca Hall | Sep 1791 Jean Hall |
| Kennady, (James?) | Mary Tolby or Talley | Aug 1791 Samuel Tolby ? |
| Kimbro, ... | Caty Mosier | Apr 1796 Fred. Mosier |
| King, ... | .... Stanford | Jun 1789 Anthony Stanford |
| " , ... | Salley Stroud | Aug 1786 Wm. Stroud |
| '' | '' '' | Jan 1794 Eliz. Stroud |
| Lee, ... | Susannah Pike | Mar 1771 John Pike |
| Lindley, James | Mary Cox | Jan 1767 William Cox |
| " , Owen | Sarah Thompson | Jul 1794 Jas Thompson |
| Lindsay, ... | Mary Robertson | Apr 1795 Ath. Robertson |
| " , .... | Mary Robison, deed, May 1785, Athanasuis / Robison. | |
| Lindsay, ... | Margaret Jamison | Feb 1793 Wm. Jamison |
| Linin, .. (or Tinin ?) | Ann Hanley | Mar 1790 Daniel Hanley |
| Lionburger, .. | Unitie Greason | Sep 1768 Isaac Greason |
| Long, .. | Nancy Dunweddee | Nov 1794 Henry Dunweddee |
| Lowe, ... | Margaret Greason | Sep 1768 Isaac Greason |
| Marshel, ... | Ruth Hadley | Sep 1760 Joshua Hadley |
| Mason, ... | Rebecca Blake | Apr 1783 Benj. Blake |
| Mauriss, ... (Morris ?) | Elinor Lindley | Mar 1780 Wm. Lindley |
| McCoy, (Henry) | Sally Herndon | May 1796 George Herndon |

| GROOM | BRIDE | DATE OF WILL, TESTATOR |
|-------|-------|------------------------|
| McKieney, Francis/Catherine Galbreath | | Jan 1799 Wm. Galbreath |
| McLeroy, Archibald | ...... Asten | Nov 1766 Wm. Asten |
| McMullin, ... | Joanna Craige | Jan 1785 Wm. Craige |
| Mebane, ... | Jenny Abercromby | May 1779 Ra⁺ Abercromby |
| "  , James | Margaret Allen | Mar 1786 George Allen. |
| Minnis, John ? | Levinia Ross | Dec 1792 James Ross |
| Mitchell, ... | Betty Comb | Aug 1791 Wm. Comb |
| Moor, Mordecai | Mary Larkin | Aug 1772 Alex. Larkin |
| "  , ... | Mary Leak | Feb 1784 Richard Leak |
| Moore, (Wm.?) | Milley Harrison | May 1773 And. Harrison |
| Mordah (Murdock ?) | | |
| James | ...... Rea | Oct 1769 Wm. Rea |
| John | ...... Rea | "    "    "    " |
| Morrow, James | Margaret Berry | Apr 1761 Thomas Berry |
| "   , ... | Ann Mebane | Apr 1789 Alex. Mebane |
| Mucklejohn, .. | Eliz. Lockhart | Aug 1786 Cath. Lock-/hart. |
| Murdak, .... | Eliz. Bowls | 1798 Thomas Bowls |
| Murdaugh, ... | Margaret Mebane | Apr 1789 Alex. Mebane |
| Neely, ... | Margaret Hulgan | Jul 1794 Thomas Hulgan |
| Newlin, ... | Deborah Lindley | Mar 1780 Wm. Lindley |
| Newton, ... | Mary Riggs | Apr 1798 George Riggs |
| Nicholas, Isaac | Marjory Cox | Jan 1767 Wm. Cox |
| Parker, James | Sarah Lockhart | Aug 1786 C. Lockhart |
| Parks, ... | Mary Jamison | Feb 1793 Wm. Jamison |
| Pasmore, ... | Abigail Craige | Jan 1785 Wm. Craige |
| Patent (Poteat?), Andrew | Marg't McCallister | Jul 1768 John McC. |
| Perkins, ... | Leah Pryor | Sep 1771 John Pryor |
| Pickard, ... | Eliz. Smothers | Aug 1778 Th. Smothers |
| Pickat, ..... (Pickett ?) | Ann Christmas | Aug 1783 J. Christmas |

| GROOM | BRIDE | DATE OF WILL, TESTATOR |
|---|---|---|
| Piggott, ... | Mary Hadley | Sep 1760 Joshua Hadley |
| "      , ... | Sarah Pike | Mar 1771 John Pike |
| Piper, ... | Jane Durham | Apr 1799 Susannah Durham |
| Pope, ... | Rachel Pryor | Sep 1771 John Pryor |
| Porter, ... | Eve Springer | Apr 1800 Uriah Springer |
| Pottiett, ... | ... Miles, Meler, or Mills | Mar 1766 Thos. Miles ? |
| Powel, Joseph | Lucy Wade | Jan 1757 Joseph Wade |
| Powell, ... | Margaret Holt | Jan 1798 Michael Holt |
| Pyle, ... | Sarah Breazier | May 1770 Thos. Breazier |
| Ray, John | Sarah Miller | Mar 1793 George Miller |
| "    , Joseph | Lydia Miller | "    "    "    " |
| "    , William | Marg't Donaldson | Mar 1770 Rob. Donaldson |
| Readen, ... | Mary Holloway | Nov 1776 Rob. Holloway |
| Reed, William | Helen Watson | Dec 1776 James Watson |
| Rhoades, ... | Sarah Stantefer | Aug 1793 Israel Stantefer |
| Rhodes, (Richard?) | Elizabeth Tolby (or Talley) | Aug 1791 Samuel Tolby ? |
| Rhodes, ... / | Rossaner Stantefer | Aug 1793 I. Stantefer |
| Riddle, ... | Catherine George | Feb 1770 Joseph George |
| Riggs, George | Rebecca Woods | Jan 1794 Hugh Woods |
| Roads, ... | Cath. Lockhart | Aug 1786 Cath. Lockhart |
| Robbins, Michael | .... Rea | Oct 1769 William Rea |
| Roberts, ... | Mary Herndon | May 1786 George Herndon |
| "      , ... | Ruth Herndon | "    "    "    " |
| Robeson, ... | Janet Breese (or Bruce) | Feb 1784 Thos. Breese |
| Rutherford, Pat. | ..... Rea | Oct 1769 William Rea |
| Sanders, Wm. Sr. | Fanny Sanders | Feb 1776 James Sanders |
| "      , ... | Tenah Parish | Mar 1793 Henry Parish |
| Scott, ... | Jean Nelson | Mar 1790 Robert Nelson |
| Sharp, ... | Lizy Mosier | Apr 1796 Fred. Mosier |

| GROOM | BRIDE | DATE OF WILL, TESTATOR |
|---|---|---|
| Shaw, John | Seaney Jones | Mar 1792 deed |
| Sheart, ... | Mary Craige | Jan 1785 Wm. Craige |
| Simmons, .. | Ruth Craige | "      "      "      " |
| Simpson, ... | Mary Wyatt | Oct 1796 Joshua Wyatt |
| Slade, ... | Hannah Miles, (or Meler, Mills) | Mar 1766 Thos. Miles ? |
| Slatter, ... | ...... Leak | Feb 1784 Richard Leak |
| Smith, ... | Eliz. Holt | Jan 1798 Michael Holt |
| "      , ... | Mary Lockhart | Aug 1786 Cath. Lockhart |
| "      , ... | Jane Ross | Dec 1792 James Ross |
| "      , ... | Sus. Waggoner | Jul 1784 Geo. Waggoner |
| Stone, William | Rhode Pryor | Sep 1771 John Pryor |
| Strawther, ... | Mary Wade | Jan 1757 Joseph Wade |
| Strayhorn, John | .... Johnston | Jun 1789 Chas. Johnston |
| Stuart, ... | Elizabeth Pike | Mar 1771 John Pike |
| Sumner, ... | Rebecca Smothers | Aug 1778 Thos. Smothers |
| Surls, ... | Mary Seares | Jul 1788 Thomas Seares |
| Swift, ... | Marg't Patterson | Dec 1789 Nath. Patterson |
| Tait, ... | Margaret Scoby | Oct 1782 Matthew Scoby |
| Talley, ... | Elizabeth Wade | Jan 1757 Joseph Wade |
| Tapley, ... | Lucy Pryor | Sep 1771 John Pryor |
| Teague, ... | Hannah Breazier | May 1770 Thomas Breazier |
| Terrell, Wm. | Martha Cox | Jan 1767 William Cox |
| Terry, James | Elizabeth Leak | Feb 1784 Richard Leak |
| "      , Robert | Sus. Sanders | Feb 1776 James Sanders |
| Thompson, ... | Esthy Robbinson | Apr 1774 Alex. Robbinson |
| Thrift, ... | Mary Stroud | Aug 1786 Wm. Stroud |
| "      | "      " | Jan 1794 Eliz. Stroud |
| Tinnen, ... | Hannah McCracken | Aug 1795 Alex. McCracken |
| Trice, ... | Ellender Comb | Aug 1791 William Comb |
| "      , (Ezekiel) | Maryanne Herndon | May 1796 George Herndon |

142

| GROOM | BRIDE | DATE OF WILL | TESTATOR |
|---|---|---|---|
| Trigg, William | Sarah Sanders | Feb 1776 | James Sanders |
| Towel, Jesse | Hannah Rice | Jan 1783 | John Rice |
| Wallace, ... | Theaney Wood | May 1786 | Thomas Wood |
| Walters, ... | Elizabeth Hooper | 1795 Power of Attorney | |
| Watters, ... | "          " | Apr 1793 | Anne Hooper |
| Walton, Nath. | Mary ... | Jun 1786 | Mary Walton |
| Ward, ... | Jenny Patterson | Dec 1789 | Nath. Patterson |
| Ware, (John ?) | Anne Harrison | May 1773 | Andrew Harrison |
| Watson, ... | Elizabeth Riggs | Apr 1798 | George Riggs |
| "       , ... | Jean Turrentine | Jul 1799 | Deb. Turrentine |
| Whitaker, ... | Milly Tolby (or Talley) | Aug 1791 | Samuel Tolby ? |
| White, (Wm.) | Katherine Lindley | Mar 1780 | Wm. Lindley |
| Wilks, ... | Ann Thomas | Mar 1769 | Owen Thomas |
| Williams, ... | Rachel Pike | Mar 1771 | John Pike |
| Winner, ... | Ruth Pike | Mar 1771 | "       " |
| Womack, David | Mildred Pryor | Sep 1771 | John Pryor |
| Wright, ... | Lydia Walker | Dec 1791 | James Walker |
| Yeargan, ... | Sarah Morgan | Jan 1787 | Sarah Morgan |

— — — — — — — — — — — — — —

SUGGESTION : One way to prove where a marriage took place is to learn where the person who made the will lived at the probable time of the marriage.

Land Grants and deeds are the best source of information. Orange County was formed in 1752 almost entirely from Granville. Granville was formed from Bertie in 1746. Bertie was formed from Chowan in 1722. Thus a person who settled in Orange at the time of its earliest formation, may have a grant or deed in either or all of those counties.

The Secretary of State has a wonderful record of all the North Carolina Land Grants in his office at Raleigh, N.C.

— — — — —

See page 28

144

INDEX

BAILEY, Ann (Dixson), Caleb A114; Chaldous ? B74
   Claud, Thomas A310; Thomas A77
BAKER, Eliz (Patterson) B132; John A70,350 ;
   John, Joseph, Mary A205; Joseph A259; William B267
BALANDER, Mary (Hendricks) B41
BALDRIDGE, Eliz (Turrentine, Martha (Turrentine) D4; I,C154
BANE, Keziah (Walton), Thomas B209
BARBEE, Benjamin C06; Benj, Goin, John, J.Sr, Phebe C25,26
   Christopher, Edie, Eliz C159; Esther (Herndon) C85
   Chris.,daughters, Dicy (...), Goin, Joseph B166
   Jemima C96; John, John Jr, Mark, Patt, Rosanna, Sally;
   Sarah (...), Sylve, Theina, William, Young C159
   Mark B188; Thomas A330; William A150 ; genealogy C159
BARCOR ?,Ephriam B15                       BARBET, William A150
BARKER, Lewis; William A63
BARNETT, John, Joseph, Mary, Rachel,(...), Samuel, Sarah,
   Thomas, unborn child A166; Robert A81
BARNHILL, James, John, Margaret (...), Robert C100; Rob. A80
BARTLETT, Francis (Inventory of Sale has 26 names) A306
BARTON, Sam A59; Thomas A177       BARTOW, Lewis A48
BASKETT, Ann (..), James, John, Thomas, William A135
   Eliz, John, Mary, Ruth (..), Ruth, Thos, Wm, Wm Jr, A72
   John, A95,124
BASON, see BISHIND
BAUCOM, William B15                 BAYLEE ?, Wm B281
BEACH ?, Thomas A68                 BEALE, Thos. A37
BEASLEY, Ephriam B166, 281          BEEZELY ?, Wm B281
BEASON, Catherine, Fred., Hannah, Henry, Jacob, John,
   Joseph, Margaret D15; Henry B262
BEHANON, Mary (Mordak) C139 see BOHANNON
BELL, Graham B233; Robert C161; Samuel A189
BELVIN, Madgelane (...), William C93; William C68
BENNEHAN, R.C. A217; Richard A333,337
BENTON, A. B144; J. A340,341;        Samuel B28, C56
   Jesse A213,214,370, B54,130;      S., B144,212,239. ,
   Jesse, children, Nancy (..), B144
BERKS, John A296
BERRY, Benj, Eliz (...), Eliz, James, Jane, Margaret, Nancy,
   Thomas, Thos Jr., William, Wm. Jr., A19; Robert A231
BIBINGS (BIVINS ?), Thomas, Thos. Jr. B98
BIGELOW, Norman B110               BILBO, Joseph C85
BILLUPS, John B247, C50
BIRD, Empson, William C73; James (note about his will) A212
BISHIND (BASON), Cath. (..), Hannah, Jacob,J.Jr, John A172
   (BEASON in Index in State Archives.)
BLACK, Elinor A329; H., A286; Josiah A158,181
BLACKWOOD, Ann, Eliz, Eliz (...), James, Jennet, John,
   Martha, Mary, William, Wm. Jr., A129; Isaac B298
   James, Joseph, William B74; William A290
BLAKE, Ann, Benj., Benj. Jr., Bethana, Jones, Martha,
   Penelope, Rebecca, Sarah, wife, A275
   Asa, Benjamin, James, Jones A365
BLOUNT, Col. William A245
BOBITT, James, Sally (Mangum) B100
BOGGAS, Richard A179                 BOGS, Joseph A86

INDEX

BOHANNON, Benj, Betty, Duncan, Frankey, John, Mary, Richard,
   Susannah (..), A5; Richard D20 (See Behanon)
BOLING, Alexander C124 (See Boring, Bollin, Bowling)
BONNEY, Daniel, John, John Jr, Richard, Simon, wife, Wm A27
BOOKER, James, John, Patience (...), Patience A23
BOOTH, Joseph C85
BOOTHE, Dan B3; John, John Jr A277; John, Zachariah B188
   Zachariah B299
BORING, Eliz (Larkin) A117; Eliz (..) A187
   Charles, Joseph, William A93
   James, John, Mary, Nicy, Ribecca A187
BORLAND, Alexander C102                    BORNAL, Peter A37
BORRIN, Becky, David, Isaac,James, John, Joseph, Jos Jr,
   Phebe, Sara, Susan, Susannah (...), William A188
BOSWELL, James A370; Susannah (Bowling) B57
BOUGH, Joseph B284
BOWER, George, daughters, Margaret (...), sons A128
BOWIE, Jno., Mary A309
BOWLAND, Alexander C140                    BOWLE, Jno. C21
BOWLING, Abraham, Alex, Andrew, Arch., Eliz, Isabel, Jean,
   Susannah B57
BOWLS, Fanney, Wm. C139
BOYD, Frankey (Bohannon) A5; James A13
BOYLE, James C90;147; John (3), Martha, William C90
BRACEWELL, see BRASWELL and BRANWELL
BRACKEN, Abigal A70; James B37          BRACKIN, Wm. C118
BRADFORD, David, George B277; D, Thomas, C94, Joseph B228
   Thomas B197, C65,104; Thomas, William B149; Wm.,  A67
BRADLEY, Ann, Charles, Enoch, Enoch Jr, George, Josiah,
   Mary, Rachel (..) D11
BRAGG, Bethier, John C132
BRANNOCK, Edmund, George, John C36
BRANTLEY, Hannah, John, Jos A5; James, William A97
BRANWELL, or BRACEWELL, Henry, Joyce (..), Mary, Richard,
   Tabitha, Valentine, A16
BRASHER, Wm. B170
BRASWELL, Sarah (Blake) A275
BRAWNER, Joseph A375                    BRAYNS, Wm. A355
BREAZIER, Aquliia, Cassa, Eliz, Hanah, James, Jean, John,
   Mary, Rachel, Samuel, Sarah, Thomas, Thos Jr A286
BRECKON, James G. C20        BREHAN, James F. B287
BREESE or BRUCE, James, Janney, John, Martha, Martha (...),
   Robert, Richard, Thomas, Thos Jr, William A296
BREEZE, Lidy A185                      BREVARD, Wm. A23
BREWER, Katy (note about her will) A212; Sackfield B259
BRIDGES, John A200                 BRISON? Wm    A 34
BROOKS, Eliz, James, Joel, John, Mary (...), Mary A34
   Joab Jr A114
BROWN, Anson A278; Deborah, Hannah (...), Jacob, Joel,
   William, Wm Jr C109; Howil A114; Jesse A301
   Mary (Piper), Ruth C122; Susannah A23; William A31,A34
BROWNING, Jas A128; Mark, Thomas C166
BRUER (BREWER), Sackfield A298

CARROLL, Richard K.  B247; Stephen  C16;
CARSON, Alex, Alex Jr, Alice, Eliz, Mary, Robert,
    Samuel, wife  B136;  David, James, Moses, Robert A., C127
    James  A226;
CARTER, Barbara  C61; Enoch, Nathaniel  D11
    John  A252; Robert  B98
CASEY, I or J, C111; John  B204,236, C8,9,50
CASSELBURY, CASSLBURY, CASTLEBURY, Martha  D7; Mary  B72
    Eliz, David, Dise, Gilley, Joseph, Mary, Paul, Patsy,
    Rosy, Ruth, Solomon, Sukey (Susannah),  A278
CATE, Ann, Eliz (...), Joseph, Richard, Robert, Sarah, Th.  A64
    Ann, Charles, Eliz, Esther, John, Joseph, Solomon,
    Steven, Thomas  C28; Benjamin  A3, C136; Ezra  C94
    Barnard, Benj, Emilia (.:.), Emilia, James, Jesse, John,
    Martha  B259; Eliz, John, Thomas  A135; Moses  C104
    Benj, James, Jesse, Jojn, Mary (...), Mary, Tim., Wm. C136
    Joseph, Robert, Thomas  B20; Richard  A211,257, C136
    Richard, R'd Jr, Susannah, Thomas  B259
    Thomas  A124, C94; Thomas son of Robert  A95
CATES, Eliz (Smith)  C155
CEASEY, David, Ellenor (..), James, John  A147
CELL? (KELL?), Ann (Riggs)  C126
CHAMNESS, Anthony  A12
CHAMNESS, Ruth (McCracken)  C65
CHAMBERLAIN, Jeremiah  D18
CHAMBERS, Sarah, C21;  Samuel  C65
CHAPMAN, Benj  A364
CHARLES, Michael  B93                      CHASSEN, Robert  A121
CHILD, Mrs. Frances  C9,10,11,12
    Feances, Francis, Fr. Jr, Samuel, Thos, Wilson B204, C87
CHRISTMAS, Ann, Charles, Henrietta, Henry, James, John, J.Jr,
    Mary (...), Mary Eliz, Richard, Robert, Thos, Wm., A264
    Nathaniel  B271; Richard  B121,289; Robert B245,286
    Ruth  B63
CHIZENALL, Alex  C78; Celah (...), Eliz, John, Markey  C78
    Reuben, Samuel, Sarah  C78
CIMBOL.(KIMBALL?),Ann (Walker)  B229
CLAMPIT, John  C57
CLAP, George, Jacob  B93; Jacob B107; Strudwick  B156
CLAPP, daughters, John, Lodowick, sons, wife  A203
    Margaret (Loy)  C157
CLARK, Abner, Catherine, Mary, Sarah, Susanna (..), Thomas,
    Thomas Jr, William  A226; Catrenah  C71; Elinor (...) C71
    Eliz (...), C71; Hannah, James, John, Mary (...), Susan-
    nah, William, Wm Jr,  A243; James, Jas Jr, Jesse, John,
    Joseph, Thomas, William (2), C71; Mary  A374, C2
    Sarah (Ward)  C164; William  A27,122,239
CLARKE, Patty  A188; William  B72,209
CLAYTON, Richard  A249
CLEFT, Mary, Margaret  C134          CLENDENIN, Wm. A212
CLENDENNIN(G), Eliz (Anderson)  D14; Charles  A288, B251
    Joseph  B109, C128; William  B126,220
CLEANEAY (CLENNY?), daughters, Johnathan, Samuel, Sam Jr,
    William  C68
CLENNY, Alice (Carson), David, William  B136

CURRIE, James A187,188;John A93
     James, John, Margaret, Mary Ann, Mary  All
CURRY, James Sr (note about will), A212;  James  C113
CURTIS, Mary (Allison) C75; Thomas  C75

DABNEY, Thomas B266          DAEL ?, Jane  A72
DALEY, John A272
DANIEL, Christopher, John, Patterson, Roger  B284
     George, John, Samuel  B72; John C98,105; Robert T.  C105
     John, Robert T, Samuel  B94; Roger C79;  Samuel  C105
     Melchi, Margaret (see McDANIEL)  A35
DANIELY, John C134                      DANNEL, John  B248
DARK, Andrew A52             DARKER, Ellenor (Davis)  B168
DARRIS, Angel (Mace),John  C86
DAUGHERTY, Frances, Nelly  B236 (see Doherty)
DAVEY, Gabriel  A201        DAVID, Ransom B166
DAVIS, Abigail (McCracken)  C65; Benjamin  A300, B275
     Abraham, daughters, Enoch, Ellenor,John, William  B168
     Charles  A12; Deborah (Hall)  C82; Hadawick  A304
     James  A201, John  A215,304;  Robert  A304
DEAL, William  A319                              B126
DEBLEY, Fanny, Jacob (2), James, John, Margery (..), Mary  ∧
DEBOW, Ann, Benj, Eliz, Fred., Hannah (..), Hannah, Jane,
     John, Mary, Sarah, Solomon  A74; John  C70
     John, Liney (...), Solomon, Stephen  A259
DELEY, William (note about his will)  A212
DENNIS, Isaac, John, Mary, Rachel  A13
DENT, Michael  A105
DESERN, James  A209,350
DICKEY, George, Mary (Miller), Zachariah  B290
DICKINGS, James  A184
DICKS, Nathan  D12; Zacharaih  A252
DICKSON, Joseph B19;  Mary (Galbreath), William  D18
     Robert  C101; Steward  C19
DIXON, James, Jas Jr, Margaret, Nancy (...), Polly, Robert,
     Stewart, Thomas, William  B78; John A333, Penelope  A352
     Joseph B282,288, C50;  Rebecca (Cox)  A53; Thomas  D15
DIXSON, Anne, Eli, George, Jesse, Joseph, Jos Jr, Mary (..),
     Nathan, Samuel, Solomon, Stephen  A114
DOAN, Ebenezer  D5
DOBBINS, Eliz, Hugh, John, Margaret, Nancy, Rachel (...),
     Rachel, Thomas, Thos Jr  A169;  Thomas  A189
DODD, William  C107
DOHERTY, George, B22,87,280; George, Mary (...)  B236
DOLLAR, Jonathan  B292
DONALDSON, Eliz, Hannah, Hannah (...), Jean, Margaret, Mary,
     Robert, Rob Jr, Thomas  A106;  James  C2;
     Mary (Riley)  B152
DORRIS, Isaac  C144  (see DARRIS)
DORSET, Francis  A7
DOSSETT, Philip, Selah (...), Seney, Susannah, Wm  A298
DOUGLAS(S), John, Margaret  A57; Margaret (Stroud)  D9
     Mary B65; Thos  A106
DOWD, Owen  A49          DOWNEY, Peter, Wm. Asten  A52
DOWNS, Ann  A13

DRISHALL, David  A330
DUDLEY, Thomas  A143
DUKE, John  A38,309        DUKS, Peter, Zachariah  B191
DUNCAN, Charles  C122
DUNNAGON, Asby, Peggy  C135; Sarah, Sherod  C135
   Sherwood (note about his will)  A212; Wm, Wm Jr,  C135
DUNNEVIN, John  A272
DUNWEDDEE, Absolom, Eliz (...), Henry, James, John  B292
   Nancy, Sarah  B292
DURBIN, Wm.  A131
DURHAM, David  B275; Frances  C137; John  A300
   Jane, Lysias, Mark, Mary, Matthew , Susannah  C137
   Lysias, Matthew, Mark, Susannah (...)  C69
DURRUM, John, Sarah  A367
DYAR, Wm.  B85

EAKINS, Jane (Riggs)  C126        EASON, Joshua  A255
ECTOR, Samuel  A272               ECCLES, Jennett (Anderson)
EDGE, Betty, Jeremiah  D20;  Jeremiah  A38, B85        D14
EDWARDS, Henry  B275; Henry, John, Margaret  A367
   John  A372, B13; John Sr,John, sons, William  A300
EFLAND, Catherine (...), daughters, Daniel, John, Peter  B234
ELLETT, Michael  A1
ELLIFF, John  B297                ELLIMAN, Enos  A137
ELLIOTT, James  A306; John  A368,B25; William  C88
ELLMORE, Enos  A27
ENGLISH, David  C154
ESTES, Eliza (...), John  C153;  J.  B233; John Esq.  A380
ETTERTON, Jacob  C3
EVANS, Amoss  A45; Jas.  A107; John  A345

FADDIS, Elizabeth  B136; John  C93
FAIRMAN, John  B282,288
FALKNER, William  B264,287
FANN, Ann, Betsy, Eliz (...), Elijah, John, Macky  C107
   Patsey, Rawley, Rebecca, Tabby, Willie  C107
FARLEY, Eliz, John James, Josiah, Moses, Sarah (...)  A196
FARMER, Ann, Athniel, Drucilla, James, Job, wife  A372
   Anne, Drucilla, James, Job, Nathaniel, wife  B13
   Job  A330, Othneil  C91, Susanna  A229
FARRAR, Thomas  A240
FASSETTS, Enoe Robert  B160
FAUCET, Robert  B89
FAUCETTE, James, Susanna (Woods)  D1; John  C94, see FOSSETT
   Lydia (Hall)  C82; Pherebe (...), Polly, Sam, Thomas  C94
   Robert  C88
FAUSETT, George  C100; William  D16  (see Fossett)
FEN, James  A208
FENNEL, Nancy (Jenkins), Joseph  B105
FENTON, Mildred (...), Thos  A333
FERGUSON, Andrew, John  A189
FERREE, Daniel, Priscilla (Ward)  C164
FEW, Ann, Bethiah, Eliz, Frances (...), James, Jas.Jr.  B32
FIELDS, John, his wife,John Jr, Rachel Roger  A56

FINCHER, Benj, Hannah, Jonathan, Jon. Jr, Joseph, Mary  A3
    Richard, wife  A3; Benjamin, Richard  A57, Joshua A3
FINDLEY, Sarah  C122;  William  B72
FINLEY, Andrew  A32; George  A52;  Hugh  A128
FITCH, William  C84
FLINTHUM. John  B32              FLINTOM, Nancy  B57

FLOURNOY, Elizabeth (Flowers)  A160
FLOWERS, Jacob Jr  B117
FLOYD, Buckner  A257;  James  B204
FOGLEMAN, Catherine (...), Eve, George, Geo Jr; Henry  A323
    John, Malachi, Peter  A323;  George  A86,89, 194
FORBIS, Arthur, children, George, Hugh, John,Margaret (..),
    Rachel, William, Wm Jr  A32
FORD, Sarah (Hadley)  A7
FORESTER, Wm  B170
FORREST, Benj, Stephen  A298; Gresham  B13, Benjamin A212
    Gresham, Isaac, Jesse, Joel, Lovina (Louisa?) (...),
    Shadrack, William, Wm Jr  A207: Grisham  A372
    Isaac, Mary, Milly, Philon, Sary, Silous, Shadrack C113
    Sarah (Wood)  C110;  William  C113
FOUNTAIN, Sarah  (Wade)  A67
FOSHEE, Charles, Chas Jr, Susannah (...), William  A2
    Charles, Chas Jr, Joseph, Susannah (...), William  A62
FOSSETT, David, Elane, Margrete, Rich'd, William, W.Jr A339
    Edward, Eliz, Fanny, George, Robert, Rob.Jr (2),  A362
    Thomas, wife  A362;  John, Richard  C94  see FAUCETTE
FOUST, Barbara (...), Barbara, Christian, Daniel. Geo. B79
    Daniel B81; George  B111; Peter  B255; Jacob B79
    John, John Jr, Judith, Peter, Philip  B79
FOWLER, Grace, William  A191
FRAZER, James  A213
FREELAND, James  A44, B78,220; John  B74
FREEMAN, Rebecca, Samuel  A329; Robert  B204; William  A212
FRUIT or FRUTH, Elinor, Grizel, Hannah, James, Jennett  D10
    John, Mary, Nancy  D10
FULLER, Joseph  A5
FULTON, David  A52

GADDES, Isaac and wife  B32
GAINS, Broadus, Edward, Eliz, Francis, Joseph, Mary  C142
    Mary, Nancy, Solomon, Susannah , Susannah (..)  C142
    Thomas, Wilson  C142
GALBREATH, Ann, Cathron, Eliz, John, Mary, Walter, D18
    William, Wm Jr  D18; J., B85; R.,Wm  A225; Wm.  A371
GANT, Cary, Edward, Eliz (...), John, Sary, Thomas  A279
    John (note about his will)  A212
GARAT, Martha (Allison), Samuel  C75
GARDNER, Catherine (...), Edward  A333
GARHURT, Henry  A207
GARNER, Rachel (Rodgers)  C104
GARRARD, Jacob Jr  A105; Samuel  B229
GARRISON, Garrit  C82; George C90; Margaret (Hall)  C82
    Mary (Hall)  C82
GEE, Philip  A83

INDEX

HALLIBURTON, Charles, David, D.Jr, John, Thos, wife, Wm  A68
   Wm.  B105
HAMILTON, Ann (...)  A333; Archibald, Joseph (20,  B34
   Eliz, Jean, Joseph, Margaret, Nancy  B149
   George  A280;  William  B149
HAMLETT, Ann, John  A41               HANCE, Eliz.  B234
HANCOCK, Henry  A257
HANLEY, Ann, Daniel, Eliz, Ester, Grace, Ruth, B262
   Daniel  B85;  Susanna, William, wife  B262
HANNAH, William  A158,330
HARD or HART, Mary  A95
HARDIN, Edmund, children,Mary (...), Jonathan  A124
   Sarah (Holt)  C149
HARGROVE, Henry, Martha (Harris)  A337
HARLEY, Jean (Leak)  A288
HARMON, Paul  A19; Zach.  A277      HARP, Wm.  B107
HARPER, Margaret  A268
HARRILSON, Burgis  A160; Burges, Drusilla, Elishiba  A152
   Eliz (...), Ezekiel, Jimima, John  A152 Elkanah  A152
HARRIS, Archibald A38; Archer, Charles, Edward, Ellender (..),
   Lenora ?, Nathaniel, Nat.Jt, Unity  A146, Ed., Mary A146
   Edward, Eliz, Hannah (...), James, Jas.Jr, John  A337
   Martha, Mary, Richmond, Sarah, Susannah  A337
   REUBEN  B249; Sarah (Laws)  D20; Sterling  B222
HARRISON, Andrew, And. Jr, Anne, Eliz, Jane (...), John A140
   Milley, Molly, Ninian, Thomas ,Wm  A140; Mary, James A333
HARROLD, Edy (...), Eliz, Lydia  C140
HART, Benjamin  A150; Maj.David, Nathaniel, Col.Thomas  A182
   Eliz  A37; James, John, John Jr, Wm  B42; John  A127
   Joseph  B57; Morgan  B286; Susannah (Wade)  A67
   Thomas  A213,214,333; Anne (Morgan)  B3
HARVEY, Absolom, Alice, David, Jonathan, John, John Jr, D16
   Caleb  B141; C58,62,146; Eli  C67; Isaac A212, D11
   James  A45; Mary (...); Mary  D16
HARWOOD, Joseph  A215,315
HASTIN, Martha (Cate)  B259
HASTINGS, Henry  A182; Joseph  C1,94
HATCH, Alexander  B213, C64,137
HATLY, John W., Wm. A233
HAWKINS, Hardress  C153; Jno.  B280
HAYGOOD, Benj, George, James, Jas Jr, Rebecca, wife, Wm  A83
HAYNIE, Bridger  A174
HAYWOOD, John  B204
HENDERSON, Margaret, Thaipiah ? C134; Nath'l  A240
HENDON, Casander (Stantefer)  B267
HENDRICKS, Abraham, Amy (...), Ann, Eliz, Isaac, Mary B41
   Peter, William  B41
HERNDON, Delilah, Edmund, Eliz, Ester,James, Lewis C85
   George  C85,91,96, A99; Lydia (Massey) C132,156
   Mary, Maryanne, Reuben, Ruth, Sarah, Sarah (...),Zach C85
HESTER, James  A375
HERVEY, John  C129
HICKS, Joseph  A160; Nathan  C67
HIGGERSON, Polly  B105
HIGGINS, Ruth (Trice)  D7

HILL, Ann (Bradley), Eliz, Hannah, Samuel D11; Samuel C58
 children, Elzy, Jonathan, Rezzy C129; Thomas A176
 children, George, Henry, wife A210
HINES, Thos. A13; B237
HINSFORD, Mary (George) A125
HINSHAW, Jesse,Jr C164       HINSLEE, John B102
HODGE, Geoege A371; John A259,
 Joseph B78,251,300; Robert C53; William C56
HODGES, Wm Jr B132
HOGAN, Alex, James,John,John Jr, Margaret Lloyd, Mary (Lloyd)
 Sarah, Thomas, William B170; Colonel B298; Daniel B3
 Daniel, daughters, John, son, Thomas Loyd, wife B2
 John A255,290,B6,C73
HOGG, James A214,283,333, B32,87,189; John A316
HOLEMAN, Charles B84
HOLDEN, Isaac, John C163      HOLDER, David C96
HOLDERNESS, Ann, John, Thos Sr A57
HOLDING, Isaac, Isaac Jr, Sarah (...), Thomas, Thos Jr A57
HOLLINGSWORTH, Reubin A311
HOLLODAY, Henry, Mary A311
HOLLOWAY, Ann, Brigett, Eliz, Jane, Litici, Martha (..),
 Mary, Priscilla, Rachell, Robert, Ruth, Samuel, Stephan,
 Susannah A205; Thomas B182
HOLMAN, Richard A229
HOLMES, James B234; William A7
HOLSTEIN, Barbaryman, Jacob, John, Mary, Susannah B95
HOLT, Absolom B297; Cise (...) C112; George C112
 Catherine, Eliz, Isaac, Jean (...), John; Joshua, Joseph,
 Marg't, Mary, Michael, Micheal Jr, Sarah, Wm. C149
 Eliz, Michael, Michael Jr; Nicholas Jr, Peter A76
 Eve (...), Francis, James, John, Joshua, Michael, Nicholas
 Nicholas Jr, Rachel B17; Jean (Lockhart) B194
 Jeremiah B297; John C166; Joshua B294,C112
 Michael B211, C157
HOLYGAM (HOGAN?), Thos A31     HOOD ?, John A80
HOOPER, Anne, Eliz, Thomas, William C56; Eliz, Will, A375
 Eliz, Thomas Hogg, William, Wm Jr A316
HOPKINS, James, Wm A1; Wm C14
HOPSON, Daniel, Eliz (...), Martin, Mary, Rich'd, Sarah B15
 Thomas B281; Younger B15
HORN, Betsy Rebe A321; Henry, James, John, Joshua B182
 Joshua B238; Margery (..),Nelly B182,
 Thomas, Thos Sr, Wm B182; Wm C16
HORNADAY, Ezekiel B191; Lewis B228
HORNE, Thos Sr C16
HORNER, Eliz (Holloway) A205; George, Geo Jr, James A354
HORTON, Eliz (Walker) B229
HOUGE, Mary B168
HOUSE, Ann (Trice), Betsey B215;
HOWARD, Thomas A343
HOWELL, Benjamin B170;. Fanny B6,D9
HUFFMAN, Barbara (Mosier) D3;
 Christian, brothers & sisters, Eliz, Peter B93
HUGHES, Anne (Pike) A176; Daniel, Gabriel A184; Sarah B97
HULGAN, Fanny (...), Margaret, Mary,Robert, Rosannah C19
 Stephen, Thomas C19

INDEX

McCADDAMS, Catherine, Cath (...), Ellender, John, Joseph,(2),
    Mary, Samuel, Sarah (...), Sarah, William  B99
McCAFFRITY, Joseph  A121
McCALEB, John  A294
McCALISTER Grizzel (...)  C2
McCALLISTER, Eliz, I (?), James (2), John, Joseph, Margaret,
    Martha, Mary, Rosannah (...), Sarah  A84; Griscal  A374
McCANE, John  A200
McCANLIS, David, Eliz, James, Jas Jr, Jane (...), John A295
    James  C154; William  A295
McCANN, A127
McCAUL, Robert  A231
McCAULEY, Charles, John, Matthew, Wm  B74; James  A42;
    John  C102; John Jr  C18; Matthew  A340,B26,112,136,279
    Matthew  C120; William  A340,342,361,363, B2
McCAVAY, Daniel  A49
McCLARY, James  C118
McCLINTOCK, Wm. Brown  A31
McCOLLOCH, James, John, John Jr, Mary, Robert  A355
    Patrick, wife  B25
McCOLLUM, Henry  B136
McCOMB, Darcas, Eliz, Harrow, Jane, Jesse, John, Margaret,
    Mary, Rachel (...), Sarah  A94
McCONKEY, Elizabeth  A185
McCOOL, Benjamin  A211
McCOY, Eliz, children, Francis, John, wife, William  A92
    Sally (Herndon)  85
McCRACKEN, Alex, Alex jr, Abigail (...), Abigail, Hannah C65
    Jeremiah  A212; John,Mary, Robert, Ruth, Samuel, C63
    Samuel  B160; Thomas, William  C63
McCRORY, C76
McDANIEL, Daniel  B92; Eli A158,353; John, Mary B81;Jo. C128
    Eli, Eli Jr, Eliz, James, John, Margaret (...), Sus.  B63
    Melchi, Marget (...), children  A211
McFARLAND, Thomas  C166
McGEE, Michael  A217
McGOWN, Ettar, James, Jas Jr, Mary, Sus., wife of J, Wm A116
McKERRALL, Frances  C49; Fanny  B197; Francis  C153
    John  B130, C9,50,122; Will B204
McKIE, Wm  A319
McKIENEY, Cathron (Galbreath), Francis, William  D18
McKINLEY, Eliz  A235
McLEROY, Archibald, Thomas S.  A52
McLESTER, Jos A29,45
McMATH, Wm  A19
McMENNAMY, John, Wm  B35
McMULLAN, Alex C135,136; Jno.  C155;Joanna (Craige)  A329
    Thomas  C131; Winnifred  C135
McNAIR, Ralph  A25
McNEIL, Anne Sr, Thomas A168; Thos  A112 (see MACKNEEL)
McMUN, Wm  C70
McRAE, Duncan, John  C162
McVEY, Daniel  B63
McVINCH, John  A369          McVINCHEY, John  A57
McWHITNEY, John  B28

MEBANE, Alex  A44,129,369; Alex, James  B262
  Alex, A Jr, Ann, James, John, Jennet, Margaret, wife,
  William  B216; Alex, Ann (...), Eliz, Fanny, James (2),
  Jannet, John, Mary, Nancy, Robert, Sarah, Sus., Wm  C56
  Eliz, George, James, Margaret (Allen)  A363
  James  A359,B298; Jenny (Abercromby)  A209; Robert  A116
  Mary (Armstrong)  C85;  Samuel  C19,D14; Wm  C78, D15
MECHUM, Mary (Durham)  C137
MEDEARIS, Massey Crismus  B105
MELER, see MILES
MELVIN, Edmund, John  B162
MEREDITH, Milly (Nelson)  C140
MERRETT, William  B105            MERRITT, Stephen  B168
MICHAUX, John  A379
MIDDLEBROOKS, John  A179
MIER, Christopher, George, wife  A194
MILES, Abraham  A112,174,48; Aquilla, Hannah, Han. (...).A48
  Charles, John, J jr, Mary (...), Thomas, William  A119
  Jacob, John, Moses, Thomas, Thos Jr  A48; William  A166
MILLER, Amn (...),Geoerge  A164; John Thompson  C114
  George, G Jr, James, Jesse, Joseph, Lydia, Mary  B290
  Martha (...), Sarah, Wm  B290; Sarah  B141; Susannah A214
MILLIKEN, Charles  B213
MINNIS, John, Levinia  B240
MITCHELL, Andrew, children, James  B279; Betty (Comb)  B141
  Andrew, Jinnet, John  A359; Mary  A36; Robert  B211
MIZE, John  B100
MOFFITT, Wm.  A53,114
MOGAR, Josias  A86
MOLBOROUGH, Simeon  A111
MONTGOMERY, Alex A59,81; Ann, Eliz, John, Mary,wife, Wm  A81
  Hugh  D1; John A277; Sarah (Montgomery)  C126
MOODY (WOODY ?), John  C81
MOOR, John  A199;Mary (Larkin), Mordecai  A117
MOORE, Alfred  A283,b144,C147;  Ephriam  C147
  Asahel, Eliz, James, John, wife  B274, James  C59
  Asahel, Eliz (...), Eliz, Henry, James, John, Martha C59
  James, John, John Jr, Martha, Mary, Mary (...), C147
  Nathan, Robert, Sarah  C147; John  A212, C84,156, D7
  John, Jos  A366; John, Mary (Leak), Richard Leak  A288
  Milley (Harrison)  A140; Thomas  A320, B259
MORDAGH, Agness, Catrin, David, Eliz (...), Eliz, James,
  Janet, John, John Jr  A139  (see MURDOCK)
MORDAH, Eliz, James  A250; James A154, C2; John  A154
MORDAK, Ann, Eliz (...),James, Jas Jr, Katren, Mary, Wm  C139
  John, Mary (...), Robert, unborn child  A248
MORELAND, Frances  B266
MORGAN, Allen  C98; Anne,Hardy,John,Sarah,Sarah (...)  B3
  Hardy C98,187; Hardy, Sarah  A310,315; John A315,James A56
  John, children  B117; Mark A150,B117,185; Mark Jr  B185
  John, Solomon  B185; Sarah (...), Sam  C98; Thos  A9,32
MORRAS, Henry  B2
MORRIS, James  A202; R., B298; Richard  A290
MORRISON, Robert  C58

INDEX

MORROW, Ann (Mebane) B216; Hugh, James, Mary, Sarah  A268
    James, Margaret (Berry)  A19;  William A206,B126
MORTISE, Jacob C3; Mary (...), daughter, Thomas  C1
MOSELEY (MOTLEY ?), James  B281
MOSER, Elizabeth (Loy)  C157
MOSIER, Abraham, Barbara, Caty, Eve, Fred., Fred Sr, Jaocb,
    John, Lizy, Magdalene, Michael, Nicholas, Philip  D3
MOTHEREL, John, Joseph, Robert &wife, Rob Jr, Samuel  A109
MUCKLEJOHN, Eliz (Lockhart)  B194
MULHOLLAND, Eliz, Henry; Hugh, John, Martha (...), Mary  C80
    Thomas A359, B99,114,216, C80,154;  Thomas Jr  C80
MULLINS, James  A249
MUMFORD, James, Robinson  B130
MURDAUGH, Margaret (Mebane)  B216
MURDOCK, Andrew B99;132,149, C115;
    Ann (...), Elinor, John (2), Prudence, William  C84
MURPHEY, Archibald A169,Roger,Sr, Roger Jr, A56
MURRAY, Eliz, Jean (...), Jean, John, John Jr, Joseph  D12
    John A368, B81; Lydia, Mary, Rebekah, Thomas  D12
MURRELL, Sarah  C105
MURROW, Adam, Charles  A80
MURRY, John  A262,353,377


NALL, Frederick, Martelenor  A79                         B284
NASH, Abner (2)  B149; Edward All, Francis A25,341, B294/
    William  (2) B211, (2) B149, B233,246,265,  C17
NEAL, James  A377, B81
NEELY, Margaret (Hulgan)  C19
NELSON, Abraham, Archeer, Eliz, James, John, Milly, Nancy,
    Sally C140;  Ann (...), Elinor, Hannah, Rachel, A358
    James, Jean, Mary (...), Robert, Rob Jr  B90; Robert A247
    David, Samuel  A359; John, Samuel  C80;
    Rebecca, Ruth, Samuel, William  A358
NEVILLE, James  A158
NEWLIN, Deborah (Lindley)  A252, James D11; John A252, D11
    John Sr (note about his will)  A212
NEWMAN, Benjamin  A363; William  A364, B212
NEWTON, Mary (Riggs)  C126
NICHOLS, Isaac, Marjory (Cox)  A53;  John  B5
NICHOLSON, Benjamin  A306
NICKS, Honor  A106
NOE, Catherine B234; Hannah (...), John, Joseph, Peter  A237
    Peter, Inquest on, (names of the 12 jurymen listed) B231
NORRIS, Daniel, Matthews (...), A37
NORTON, Anne, Eliz, Jane (...), John, Margaret  A179
    Stephen, Richard, William  A179
NUNN, Eliz (Copeland) C163; William  B57
NUTT, David, John  C136


OFFILL, Wm  A1                    O'HARRO, Thomas  B288
OLIVER, John  A86,89
O'NEAL, Eliz C112; Eliz, William C101;  Wm  B265
OSBORNE, Adlai  B170
OSTIN, Joseph  A59
OWEN, John  A315

PICKAT, Ann (Christmas), James I or J, A264
PICKETT, William B267, C166
PIGGOTT, Benjamin A352, B228, C61; John, Mary, Rachel C61
    Jeremiah, Je. Jr C61; Jeremiah, William A60
    Mary (Hadley) A7; Sarah (Pike) A176
PIKE, Abigail (...), Anne, Eliz, John, John Jr, Nathan A176
    Priscilla, Rachel, Ruth, Samuel, Sarah, Susannah A176
    John A12; John Jr, Samuel A60; Susannah (Ward) C164
PILLS ?, John A29
PINKERTON, David, Dav. Jr, John, Margaret (...), Martha A164
    Mary, William A164; Robert C142
PINDAR, Joseph B220
PINTO, S. A377
PIPER, Alec B2; Jane (Durham), Sarah, Susannah C137
    John, daughters, Mary, Samuel C122
POCOCK, Abel, James, Nancy, Temperence (...) A321
POE, John A119
POOR, Ann, Phillipinia, Eliz (...), Eliz, Eva Catarina ,
    Mary Ann, Peter, Peter Jr A86
PORTER, Eve (Springer) D5
POPE, Rachel (Pryor) A160
POTTIET, POTEAT ?, .... A48 See PATENT
POWEL, Joseph, Lucy (Wade) A67
POWELL, Margaret (Holt) C149; William A147
PRATT, George, James, Lucy, Mary, Peggy, Thomas B28
PRICE, William A196
PRYOR, Abner, Betty Green, Dorothy, Eliz, Green, John, J Jr,
    John Henry, Leah, Lucy, Margaret (...), Martha, Mildred,
    Rachel, Rhoda, Robert A160; John A125
PUGH, John A288
PYLE, Sarah (Breazier) A286

QUESENBURY, Nicholas B3

RAILEY, James, Wm B180 see RILEY
RAINEY, David A212,172; Isaac C142; James C159
    John, Wm A156; Mary A279, C103, William A279, B1,
    William A279, B1,37, C103,112,149
RAMSEY, John A277
RANDALL, Andross, Catherine (...), Mary B20
RANKIN, Victory A125
RAY, David B28, Elinor (...) C84; George, John B247
    Fanny, Isabella, Kassey, Marg't, Mary, Mary, Reb. B220
    George (2), James, John, Lydia (Miller), Joseph B290
    Hannah (...) C67; Issabel B132; James C75; Jas H. C97
    Jennet (Allison) C75, John, Wm C19; Margaret A31
    John A226,341,374, B109,132,111,301, C71,75,84
    Robert B109,220, c85; Robert Jr B109,220; Silly B220
    Sarah (Miller) B290; Sus. (Patterson) B132
    William B156,B255,C97
REA, Catherine (...), David, James Jr, William, Wm Jr A154
    Robert A64,92
READ, Robert A333
READING, John C114 READEN, Mary (Holloway) A205
(see Reddin and Redding)

REAVES, John C78                    REEVES, John A131
RECORD, Comfort (...), David, John, Mary, Sion A97; John A17
REDDIN, Margaret (Paul), William B160
REDING, Thomas B41, C124
REDMAN, John B292
REED, Helen (Watson, James, Robert, Watson, William A202
    Jemimah, John, Lydia (...), Rebeccah B35
    Mary (...), Samuel A102
REGEN, Eliz A237
RENCHER, John Grant A365, B116,117,136,39, C73,140,166
    John Nelson, Nancy (Nelson), Sarah C140
RHOADES, Sarah (Stantefer), Cassandra B267; William A366
RHODES, Alex, Aquilla, Eliz, Hannah, Mary (...), Richard,
    Thomas, William B120; Eliz (Talley) B136
    Delilah (Herndon) C85; Richard B136, C13, Syntha C159
    Rossaner (Stantefer) B267
RICE, Cairin (...), Hannah, John A262, Jesse A212
    Joel A259; John B130; Moses A124
RICHARDS, Jacob B22; Mary A23; William A264; Jacob A351
RIDDLE, Catherine (George) A125
RIDENS, George C14
RIDGE, Susannah A237
RIDGEWAY, Eliz (Chizenall) C78
RIGGINS?, Ruthey (Trice) D7
RIGGS, Ann, George, Henry, James, Jane, John, Mary (...) A270
    Mary, Samuel, Thomas, William A270;
    Agnes, Ann, Eliz, George, James, Jane, Margaret, Mary C126
    Rachel, Sarah (...), Sarah, Susannah, William C126
    George, Hugh, Milly, Rebekah (Woods) D1; James B152
    William C139
RIGHTENHOUS, Kathereana A237
RIDLEY, Eliza B237
RILEY, Eliz, Jane B152; John A182,C16; Mary B152
    John, Mary (...), Mary, Nancy, Robert, Samuel, Wm B152
RILEY or RAILY, Will C21
RIPPY, Joseph, Thomas D6
ROACH, Absolom, Ann (...), daughters, James, mother, sons,
    William B177
ROADS, Catherine (Lockhart) B194  see RHODES, etc
ROARK, James, Wm D4
ROBBINS, Michael A154
ROBBINSON, see ROBINSON, ROBISON, ROBERTSON, ROBSON
ROBBS, Alex B65, C3
ROBERTS, Edward A185;  George C85; James A168; Thos A278
    Mary (Herndon), Ruth(Herndon) C85; William A314
ROBERTSON, Athanatious, Dilley (...), Mary, Nathaniel C64
    John A101,280 (note about his will) A212
ROBINSON, or ROBERTSON ?, Alex A147
"          " ROBESON ?, Jannet (Bruce), Martha, Rachel A296
    Charles C59; Eliz A333; John A333, B37; Rachel B102
    William A81
ROBISON, Athanisius, Nathaniel A353
ROBSON, Henry, Mary (...) A333
ROBUCK, Isaac A48
ROCHESTER, Nathaniel A202,243

RODGERS, Abraham, Eliz (...), Jemima, Laney, Leasey, Morning,
    Nathan, Rachel, Theopelous, William, Wilthy  C104
ROGER, Adam, Elmore, Hugh, Isabel, John, John Jr, Mary, wife,
    unborn child, William  A64
ROGERS, Peter  A160; William  A158
ROONEY or RONEY, Ann, Benj, Eliz, James, Thos  A42; Benj  D14
ROPER, James  A105; Jesse  A257
ROSS, James  A249,B240, C134; Jane, Levinia, Margaret  B240
    John  B114
ROUNDTREE, Thomas  A229
ROUNTREE, Chas, Lydia, Thos  B174; Thos, Wm  A319; Will  B84
ROWAN, Col. Robert  C153
RUBY?,        Nelly  A127
RUSSELL, Alex, Alex Jr, Elenor, Eliz, James, Jane (...),
    Jane, Margaret  A158
RUSSOM, Mitchell  C9
RUTHERFORD, Patrick  A154; William  A137
RUTLEDGE, John, John Jr  A245


SAMPH, Samuel  A154
SAMPLE, John  A44; Mary  A42,129
SAMPSON, Michael  B19
SANFORD, A.  A44
SANDERS, Hardy B116; James, Jas Jr, Richard, Sarah, wife of J,
    Susannah, William  A197; Tenah (Parish)  C131
SAXON, William  A209
SCARLETT, James  A200; Stephen  C122
SCOBY, David, Jenet (...), Margaret, Matthew, Robert  A273
    Robert  B63, C84
SCOTT, J.  C149; Henry, Jesse, John, Mary (...), Molly A314
    Jean (Nelson)  B90; John  B185,247,248;
    Richard, Robert, Vaughan, William  A314
SEARES, Eliz, Eliz (...), Henry, John, Joseph, Mary, Thomas,
    Thomas Jr, William  B40    see SEARS
SEARLES, Betty, Coventon, Edward, Ephriam, Francis, Henry,
    Joseph, Peggy, Thomas, Winney  C91    see SURLS
SEARS, Albert B185; Barby, Edward, Harry, Henry, John A150
    Henry B117; John  A277; Nancy, Rose (...), Sally  A150
SEBASTION, Isaac, Sarah (...)  B193
SEE, George  A112
~~LEIGLE~~, Richard A223 (this should be LEIGH)
SERJANT, Eliz, James, Jos, Sarah (...), Stephen, Thomas A77
    William Sr  A77
SERVER, James (Hall)  C82
SHANNON, Robert, Thomas, William  B289; Wm  B1
SHARP, Aron  D15; Boston B156, Eliz, Eliz Jr  C111
    Bostian, Christian, Eliz, Isaac, John, Peter, Phillipina,
    Phil. (...), unborn child  A241; Isaac A207, Jno. T. A293
    Eve (Mosier), Lizy (Mosier, Peter  D3; Joseph  B98
    Philis  B234
SHAW, John, Seany (Jones)  B188
SHEART, Mary (Craige)
SHEELS, John, Mary (Cumming)  B26
SHEETS ?, John, Mary (...)  B5
SHEPHEARD, Mary (...), Mary  A17
SHEPPARD, James  C115
SHEPPERD, H.  C115; Henry  B245,285
    William  A370,377, B245,286

SHOFNER, Michael  B249
SHY, Ike, John, Martha (...)  C58
SIMMONS, Lius  A279; Ruth (Craige)  A329
SIMONS, Eliza (...), Henry  B14
SIMPSON, Mary (Wyatt)  C144
SINKLER, Ann (...), Charles, Chas Jr, Catherine  A45
SINOW, Hugh  A49
SLADE, Hannah (Miles ?)  A48
SLATOR, Jacob, John  A17
SLATTER (SLAUGHTER ?), Richard, Walter  A288
SLOAN, David  B204
SLOSS, John  B99,243, C53
SMALLWOOD, William  B36,85
SMITH, Adam  A212,323, B294; Andrew, Eliz, Isabel  A121
  Abraham, Eliz, Hannah, Mary  C124; Charles, Chris.  A119
  Ann, Cunningham, Jonathan, Marg't, Mary (...), A280
  Conrad Messer, Conrad Jr, Eliz, Leonard, Mary, Phette,
   Stephen C155; Cunnungham A325; Eliz, John  A94;
  Eliz (Holt)  C149; Jas.  A144; Jane (Ross)  B240
  John, Mary A121; John Pryor A160; Mary (...) B194
  Reuben B197,271, C30; Robert, Rob Jr, Wm  A121
  Robert, Samuel, William, Wm jr A280; Samuel A325
  Sarah (...)  C124; Susannah (Waggoner, Stephen  A330
  Thomas  C30,124, Wm  A64; Wm Bailey  A179; Wm. G.  B294
SMOTHERS, James, John, Rebecca, Sarah, Susanna (...),
  Thomas, Thos Jr, William  C57
SMYTH, Step.  A231
SNIPES, John, Thos, Wm.  C64
SNOTERLY, Catherine, Eliz, Henry, Jacob, Philip, Rachel,
  Susannah  B255
SOUTH, Benjamin, Dilly, Gemima  B82
SPOUS, George  B162
SPRINGER, Adam, David, Eve, George, Marg't (...) Mary, D5
  Uriah  D5
SPRUCE, Quinton, Sally (Tate)  C118
STABLER, Edward  A333
STACY, John  A371
STAGG, Judith, Celia, Charles  B189
STALCOP, John (note about his will)  A212
STANFORD, Agnes, Anthony, Charles, Eliz (...), Eliz, B85
  B. B298; Jannet (Mebane)  C56
  James, Jean, Marg't, Martha, Mary, Robert, William  B85
STANTEFER, Benjamin, Casander (...), Casander, Eliz B267
  Israel, Is. Jr, Joshua, Mary, Rosanner, Sarah  B267
STARK, John  B65
STARR, Adam  A323; John  C129
STEEL, Agnes, Eliz, Mary (...), Mary, John, Joseph  B251
  John A206,342, B126; John & J. Jr  A343; Samuel  A343
  Sarah, William  B251
STEPHENS, Abraham, Arthur, Eliz, Leviner, Sarah, sons A200
  Henry B114, Mary (...), Thomas A351
STEWART, James  A99,189; Samuel  A102    see STUART
STONE, Mary  C30; Rhode (Pryor), A160; Susannah  A185
  William  A152,160
STONEMAN, James. Joseph  B228

STARNES, Abeneasor, Ann (...)  A56

STOUT, Chas. A34; Joseph & Samuel A358,B79; William C109
STOVALL, Bartholemew C91
STOWERS, Adam C140
STRAIN, Wm. A226
STRAWTHER, Joseph, Mary (Wade) A67
STRAYHORN, Charles, John B74; Gilbert C161; James C140
    William B136
STREIDER, George, Henry B95
STROUD, Anderson, Dickson, Eliz (...), Eliz, Fanney, John,
    Marg't, Marshal, Mary, Salley, Thomas, William, W.Jr B6
    Anderson, Dixon, Eliz (...), Eliz, Fanny, John, D9
    Margaret, Marshall, Mary, Sally, William D9, John B296
    William C69
STRUDWICK, Francis B285; , Martha B286;
    Samuel B245,270,286; William Francis B245, C115
STUART (see STEWART), Abigal, Alex, Eliz (...),John, Rob A60
    Elix (Pike) A176; Samuel A49
SULLIVAN, Ben, Daniel, Dan Jr, Edmund, Isaac, John, B162
    Joseph, Margaret (...), Marg't, Mary, Sarah B162
SUMNER, Alex, Rebecca (Smothers) C57; Josiah A13
SURLS (see SEARLES), Mary (Seares) B40
SUTTON, Joseph A184
SWIFT, Margaret (Patterson) B132
SWING, Lodowick A203
SYNNOTT, Michael, Richard A217


TAIT, Margaret (Scoby) A273    see TATE
TALLEY, Eliz (Wade) A67
  "   (or TOLBY), Eliz (...), Mary, Milly, Saml.,Wm H. B13&
TAPP,Abner C161
TALBERT, Benj, daughter, father, mother, James, John A112
    Joseph, Loran, Mary (...) A112
TAPLEY, Hosea, Hos. Jr, wife, John Pryor A125,
    Lucy (Pryor) A160
TARVER, Benjamin A257
TATE, Agnes, Keturo , Eliz, George, James, Jinnet, Jinnet Jr,
    Lettice, Margaret A359; Eliz A127; George A116, B272
    Akness, George, Geo Jr, Kitturah, Litia, Janet, Margaret,
    Eliz; Mary, wife of Geo, William A144; James A272
    Jean, John, Lydia C118; William A129,259,378
    Sally, Simpson, Udose, Valentine, Uriah, Uzziah C118
    Zaccheus, Z. jr, Zenas, Zephaniah C118
TATOM, A. A366,369, B26,136,239,282, C153
    Absolom A363, B11,144, C161; Anna, Eliz, Francis B73
    Jeremiah, John, Mary, Mornin (...), Sarah, Stephen B73
    Stephen Jr, Tizia, William (2) B73
TAYLOR, Charles B11; Fred., James B28; George B15
    John B239, C88,92; Joseph B116; Robert C88
TEAGUE, Abraham, Moses A29, Hannah (Breazier) A286
TELFORD, Eliz, Eliz (...), Hugh, Robert, Rosannah A325
    Samuel, Thomas, Thos Jr, William A325
TERRY, Eliz (Leak), James, John, Richard Leak A288
TILFORD, Thomas A280
TENNING, Eliz. (note about her will) A212 See TINNEN etc

INDEX

INDEX

WILKS, Ann (Thomas)  A95
WILLIAMS, Benj. A185; Eliza  B14; Frederick  A95
    Eliz (...), Sam; William, Wm Jr  B22; James  A380,B63,239
    John Esq.  A377,380; Rachel (Pike)  A176; Ralph  A277
    William  A70,226,239
WILLIAMSON, Vincent Peter  B39,84
WILLIS, Augustine  B249; Hugh, John, Martha, Thomas, Wm  A32
    John  B239, C20
wills, list of 19 dated 1800 or earlier, recorded in 1801
    or later  A212
WILLS, John  B264,287
WILLSON, Edward  A359; Hugh  A144; Robert  A154
WILSON, Edward  B216,270,272; John  B70, C107; Margaret  A249
    Gregory, James, John, Mary (...), Mary, Samuel, Wm  A229
    Mary  B272; Thomas  D4; William  B216,270
WINNER, Ruth (Pike)  A176
WIRES, James  B111
WITHERSPOON, D.  B246
WITT, Ezecaia  A199
WOMACK, Abraham Jr  A107; David, Mildred (Pryor)  A160
WOOD, Ann & John  B32,50, C68; Blaton  A298; Fanny  A57
    Blayton, Eliz, Edward, Henry, James, Joseph, Lydia  C110
    James, Joseph  A210; John  A57, B266, C163; Rebecca  C68
    Markey (Chizenall)  C78; Mary (...), Mary, Meley  C110
    Sarah, Theaney, Thomas, William  C110
    Elihugh, Eliz, Hugh, John, Joseph, Mary (...), D1
    Ecklon  C127; Hannah, John, John Jr, Margaret (...)  B197
    Hugh, John  B25; James  C126; John  A13, B82; Sam.  B279
    Margaret; Matthew, Nancy, Richard, Sarah  B197
    Mary Ann, Rebekah, Susanna  D1
WOODWARD, Christopher  A63
WOODY, James (2), Joseph, Lewis, Rebecca (...)  B191
    Joseph (26 names of purchasers at sale of estate)  A306
    Joseph  C131, John  C81
WOOLEY, Michael  B245
WOLF, Peter  A79, B63
WOOLFORD, Lewis  C3
WORKMAN, John  C28
WORTHAM, Edward  C136
WRAY, Sam'l  B57    see RAY
WRIGHT, Lydia (Walker)  B229
WRIGHTSMAN, Peter  B90
WRITE, Isaac, I. Jr, Mary(..), Mary, Providence, Zach. A174
WUFNER, Michael  A49
WYATT, Eliz (...), Eliz, Fred.,Joshua, Josh. Jr, Mary  C144
WYLIE, Wm.  A283

YARBOROUGH, Eliz, John, Lewcey, Samuel, Sam Jr, Sarah  A107
    James  C111; Sarah, William  A107; Wm.  A201
YEARGIN, Benj. A315,B3; Sarah (Morgan), Sharlotte  B3
YOUNG, Catrin (...), George, son, William  A36. A36 is LONG
    John, John Jr, Joseph, unborn child, wife  A225
YOUNGER, James  A125

ZACHARY, William  A169

- - - - - - -

ABSTRACTS OF WILLS

RECORDED IN

ORANGE COUNTY NORTH CAROLINA

1800 - 1850

Compiled by

Ruth Herndon Shields

TABLE OF CONTENTS                                    pages

— — — — — — — —

ORANGE COUNTY was formed in 1752, largely from Granville,
partly from Bladen and Johnston Counties.
From ORANGE COUNTY were taken:
all of Chatham, Guilford and Wake in 1771
all of Caswell in 1777 (Person was formed from Caswell 1792)
all of Alamance in 1849, part of Durham in 1881.
The eastern halves of Randolph and Rockingham Counties were
formed from that part of Guilford which was taken from ORANGE.

— — — — — — — — —

FOREWORD

   Abstracting the wills of Orange County to 1850 has been a
project of the Genealogical Records Committee of Davie Poplar
Chapter NSDAR for the last four years. Work was begun in 1955
with Mrs. Robert Lester as chairman, and Mrs. B.B.Lane as our
Regent. Knowing how valuable these abstracts would be to the
thousands of descendants of Orange County pioneers, I undertook publication of them. The volume for 1752-1800 was com-
pleted in 1957.
   For the sake of historical accuracy, whenever a will was
signed with a "mark", I have noted the fact. Some of the committee did not do this. I personally abstracted all of Book D,
Book E from page 251 to the end; and parts of Book F. Writing
of some of the clerks  was poor, and their capital letters impossible to decipher. Dozens of the abstracts have been checked with the original wills in the Archives.
   I  was amazed to find that with the exception of nine wills
(see page 221) every will listed in this book is preserved in
the Archives in Raleigh. Photostats can be ordered through the
Archives at about $1 per page.
   My grateful thanks to each and every member of·the committee
who labored so long and patiently on this project, but most of
all to Mrs. Lester and Mrs. Lane who were untiringly faithful.
   Since  marriage bonds were not required to be returned until
about 1782, I listed all marriages mentioned in the wills up to
1820. This list was ckecked against the collected marriage
bonds of Orange County, and seventy were found that are not
listed in the collected bonds. They will be found on page 268.
Many of those marriages may have taken place in other counties.

Ruth Herndon Shields (Mrs. C.W.) Chairman
Genealogical Records Committee, Davie Poplar Chapter, NSDAR
Chapel Hill, N.C.
November 17, 1958

ABSTRACTS OF WILLS, ORANGE COUNTY, N. C. 1800 - 1850

Book D, page 22   Will in Archives. Dated 7 Jan 1800,
proved Aug 1800
SHERID DUNNAGAN

Wife: Dice gets whole estate "to support the children until
the youngest child is 21 years of age"

Sons: William, Sherid

"Two daughters Amelia and Mary"

Executors: wife, and her brother George Carington.
Witnesses: George Newton, Edward Worsham
- - -

D-23   Will in Archives.  Dated 4 Nov 1800, proved Feb 1801.

BENJAMIN (x) FORRESTER                Wife: Sarah

Sons: Ila  gets land after mother's death
Edmund,(10 shillings),  Josiah, Benjamin

Daus: Jemimah Woods wife of Harris Woods
Drucilla Dosset wife of William Dorset
Nancy, Betsy, Milly

Executors are to sell 50 acres of land joining George Carington and John Gains.

Executors: "friends James Woods and Joseph Woods".
Witnesses: Walter Alves, William Bennehan.
- - -

D-24   Paper dated 26 Feb 1801.  THOMAS BROOKS of the Town of

Hillsborough revokes a Power of Attorney made in the year

1784 to his son And'w Brooks, which was never used.
- - -

D-25   Will in Archives.  Dated 17 June 1790, proved Feb 1801.

WILLIAM CLENDENNIN                Wife: Mary

Sons: Younger, William, John, Joseph

Daus: Polly, Rebecca, Ann, Fanny, Jenny

"My niece Ann, daughter of John Clendenning deceased"

Sons: James and Fisher get 200 acres of land.

"Two youngest sons William and John the home plantation after
they arrive at lawful age" They are to be bound out to trades.

Executors: John Thompson, Esquire, and Andrew Murdock.
Witnesses: James Johnston, John Johnston.
- - -

D-25  Will in Archives.  Dated 6 May 1800, proved Feb 1801

JOHN MOORE                          Wife: Mary Moore

Legacies " to each of my children as they shall arrive
at lawful age." (Their names and number not stated.)

Executors: "brother James Moore and my trusty friend
          James Martin and my beloved wife Mary Moore."

Witnesses: James Lindsey, John Martin.

— — —

D-28  Will in Archives. Dated 10 Sept 1800, proved Feb 1801.

JOHN KELL                           Wife: Rebeckah

"My children" mentioned, but number not stated.

"My boys Thomas and John" are to be bound to a trade .

Executors: Robert Hall and William Kell.
Witnesses: Jno. Riggs, Rachel (x) Millan.

— — —

D-29  Power of Attorney dated 16 Feb 1801, proved Feb 1801.

from JOSEPH HART of Caswell County, N.C. "to my trusty

friend JAMES MOORE, Cap't" of Orange County, N.C., to col-

lect debts and accounts in Orange and Rockingham Counties,

N.C.   Witnesses: H. Brown, John Murray.

— — —

D-30  Will in Archives.  Dated 10 July 1800, proved Feb /
                                                      1801.
KATY (x) BREWER

"My four children, to wit: Candice, Charlotte, William
and Polly."

Exec's: "Trusty friends Samuel Carothers and Wm. Forsythe."
Witnesses: Wm. Strowd, James (x) Lloyd, Eliza. (x) Lloyd.

— — —

D-30  Will in Archives. Dated 25 Dec 1800, proved May 1801.

JOHN GANT              Wife: Ann ,"all the land on the S.
                                 Side of Haw River", etc.
Sons: William Gant, John Gant,
      James Gant, Isam Gant, Zacharia

Daus: Keziah Rippey, Sarah Gant, Mary Riggins,
      Hannah Boish ?

Executors: wife Ann, and son Isom Gant.
Witnesses: W. Mebane, W.B.? Mebane.

— — —

D 33  Will dated 20 Feb 1801, proved May Court 1801.

WILLIAM EVANS                    wife: Margaret Evans

"my two sons Samuel and William Evans all my land"

daus: Catey, Betsey, Susanna Evans.
"All my furniture to be equally divided among my three girls"

Samuel Davis (no relationship stated)

Executors: "My son Samuel Evans and Margaret Evans."
Witnesses: Almon Mullan,Nathaniel Carrington.
- - -

D 34  Will dated 23 Feb 1801, proved May Court 1801.

BAXTER KING                    wife: Elenner King

daus: Mary, Hannah King, Nancy King, Dolley King,
      Elizabeth King.  "until my young daughter comes of age"

sons: John, Nathaniel (he is to have "proper schooling")

"Mosby tract of land to be rented out"

Executors: wife Elinor and son John King.
Witnesses: John Adams, William Hogan, Charles King.
- - -

D 36  Will dated 1 March 1801, proved May Court 1801.

EDWARD HARRIS              wife: Mary to have "plantation on
                                 Mountain Creek", etc.
sons: Sterling & Edward

daus: Mary & Elizabeth Harris, Delila

sons: Nathaniel and Willie all "my land and plantation
      lying upon Eno River" .. when they arrive at age 21.
      Willie (also spelled Wylley) is the youngest.

Executors: wife Mary Harris and friend James Walker.
Witnesses: Jesse Trice, James Moore, James Carrington, Jr.
- - -

D 38  Will dated 14 Jan 1800, proved May Court 1801.

SAMUEL (x) TURRENTINE        wife: Mary

"Two youngest sons Absolom and Daniel" (they are under 21)

son: John "100 acres joining the lands of George Wilson"

son: Samuel "land lying on the east side of Buffalo Creek
            joining the lands of James Watson Senior."

                                        - continued -

son: James "100 acres ... turning from Roark's corner west to
        Jane Jamison's line .... to James Roark's."

daus: Lydia & Susanna (they are unmarried)
        Sarah ...."and her son is to have 1 year's schooling"

"my Jane $10 " (no word omitted)

daus: Mary, Deborah and Martha $4 each

Executors: Wife, and son Samuel
Witnesses: John McMullen, Jno. Alston.

Codicil about burying ground dated 6 May 1801. Same witnesses.

— — —

D 40  Will dated 1 Nov 1800, proved May Court 1801.

JAMES GUTHRIE                    wife: Elizabeth

sons: James Guthrie, Robert Guthrie

"My four oldest daughters Ann, Mary, Margaret & Martha"

daus: Jean Guthrie, youngest Elizabeth Guthrie

grandsons: James & Robert Guthrie, sons of James Guthrie

grandsons: James Shanon, James Barnett, James Forrest,
        James Mimenemy ? (McManamy ?)

Executors: "trusty friend David Mitchell and Isaac Raney".
Witnesses: Wm. McManamy, Jno. Sanders.

— — —

D 42  Will dated 25 March 1801, proved May Court 1801.

JOHN JOHNS                    wife: Elizabeth Johns

sons: Henry Johns, Thomas Johns

son-in-law: Thomas William Grice

"To my Kitty ? Johns" (no word omitted)

daus: Susannah, Elizabeth Johns, Patsey Johns

Executors: "Trusty friend John McCollock Sr and
        James Allison."
Witnesses: Wm. Keeling, Wm. (x) Whitfield, George (x) Welsh.

— — —

D 43  Will dated 4 Dec 1800, proved May Court 1801.

WILLIAM FREEMAN

wife: Sarah Freeman "to raise and maintain my children"

son: George Freemen  100 acres "joining the land of David
...... and Thomas Dixon"
dau: Polly Trotman

sons: John Freeman and William Freeman

After wife's death her share of the estate to be divided
equally among "my chilren Christian Freeman, Nancy Freeman,
John Freeman, Betsey Freeman, Sally Freeman & Wm. Freeman."

Executors: wife Sarah Freeman, and George Freeman.
Witnesses: Hardy Hurdle, Joseph Terrill.
- - -

D 34  Will dated 19 Feb 1801, proved May Court 1801.

GEORGE NEWTON                wife: Mary

"My two youngest children Sarah and John, and my daughter
Lette's child Elizabeth to be schooled".

He speaks of "my children under age".

After wife's death property to be divided "between all my
children and grandchild Elizabeth viz: Lette Newton, William
Newton, James  Newton, Henry Newton, Isaac Newton, George New-
ton, Robert Newton, Sarah Newton, John Newton, Elizabeth New-
ton daughter of Lette."

Executors: wife Mary and two sons Henry and George Newton.
Witnesses: James Latta,Jr., Henry Newton.
- - -

D 46  Will dated 6 June 1800, proved May Court 1801.

JOHN ROBERTSON          wife a legatee, name not stated

sons: Hugh Robertson, Andrew Robertson

grandsons: John, Zachrias & Andrew Robertson

daus: Margaret Wilson, Elenor Johnson, Rebekka Guin

granddaus: Molly Robertson, Marget Robertson, Elenor Robert-
          son, daughters of Andrew

Executors: wife, and Hugh Robertson
Witnesses: John Douglass, Robert Hatrick.
- - -

D 47A  Will dated 20 April 1801, proved August Court 1801.

LEWIS (x) BREWER "weak in body"    wife: Patience (one third)

daughter Nancy other 2/3 at her arrival at lawful age.

Executors: Nathan Dicks and Eli Harvey
Witnesses: John Stout, Adam Rinehart.
- - -

D 48   Power of Attorney from MARY (x) WILSON to "trusty
       friend William Cocke (Cooke ?) ". Dated 17 June 1801,
       proved August Court 1801.
       Witnesses: John McCanless, Abraham Moore.

— — —

D 49        Will dated  2 July 1801, proved August Court 1801.

JAMES WATSON, SR.                    wife: Rosanna

sons: John, James, David, Jonathan

grandson: James, son of James

dau: Peggy "plantation I purchased of Henry Moore at the death
              of my wife ..."
dau: Elizabeth

Sole executor: son James Watson
Witnesses: James Moore, John Moore.

— — —

D 50  Will dated 3 July 1801, proved August Court 1801.

HENRY MORRAS        "dear and loving wife"

At wife's death property to be divided "amongst my children
and my son Henry's children."

sons: Thomas Morrass, Richard

grandson: John Morris  ( notice three spellings of name)

Executors: "trusty friends William Hogan and Thomas Brewer".
Witnesses: Wm. McCauley, David Hogan, Robert (x) Blackwood.

— — —

D 52  Will dated 14 July 1801, proved August Court 1801.

PHEBE (x) GRIMES        eldest daughter Elizabeth Grimes

daus: Phebe Grimes, Lydia Grimes, Ann Grimes

sons: eldest James Grimes, Charles Grimes

"to Rebekah 5 shillings" (no relationship stated)

"My four children that is at home with me, viz: Elizabeth,
Phebe, Lydia and Ann Grimes".

Executors: daughter Elizabeth Grimes and Thomas Wilson.
Witnesses: John Latta, Caleb Wilson

— — —

D 53  Will dated 12 Feb 1800, proved November Court 1801.

ELIZABETH (x) TINNING "being weak of body"

"To Elizabeth Grahams, daughter of John Grahams ..."

D 53 continued          "to Mary Gresham"

"to my sister's daughter Sarah Thompson"
                    daughter
"to Fanny Walker/to John Walker" L 10 when she comes of age.

"to Fanny Hall daughter to John Hall ten pounds when she is
of such age to receive it."

"unto my cousin Richard Ball L hard money."
"unto my cousin Wilson Ball L hard money."

The remainder of her estate "unto John Grahams Sr. and his
two sons James Grahams and George Grahams."

Executor: John Grahams
Witnesses: Caleb Simmons, James Tate.

– – –

D 55  Will dated 17 March 1801, proved November Court 1801.

JOHN HOLDER                    wife: Mary Holder

youngest son: Aron Holder

10 shillings each to Abram Holder, Rhoda Vallentine, John
Holder, Jr., Anny Morgan, Elijah Holder, Dannel Holder, David
Holder. (No relationship stated to these 7 persons.)Children ?

Executors: "my loving Mary Holder and my two sons William
                and John Holder."
Witnesses: John Scoggins, Wm. Holder, Aron Holder.

– – –

D 56  Will dated 2 April 1796, proved November Court 1801.

JOHN EDWARDS "very aged and infirm"

wife: Mary Edwards all estate during her life.

son: John Edwards 10 shillings

daus: Susannah Odean & Mary Campbell, 10 shillings each

sons: David Edwards, William Edwards, Sell Edwards and their
          children, 1 negro each.

He sets free a  negro woman.

"To my son Henry Edwards" 5 negroes, etc.

Executors: son Henry Edwards and Zackfield Brewer.
Witnesses: Thomas Brewer, Elizabeth (x) Brewer).

– – –

D 57  Will dated 27 July 1901, proved February Court 1802.

RICHARD WILLIAMS "in decline of life"    Wife: Rachel

son: James 302 acres of land "and the money that is coming to
me in Pennsylvania." ( £113 money due him mentioned"in a letter from my brother dated November
27, 1799."

daus: Hester, Martha, Rachel, Ann.
Rebeckah wife of John Wilkerson.

son: John Williams

Executors: wife Rachel, and son James Williams
Witnesses: Isaac Jackson, Owbert ? Faucett.

- - -

D 59  Will dated 2 April 1798, proved February Court 1802.

ADAM SMITH                    wife: Elizabeth

"My two sons and three daughters by my first wife".

Two plantations .. "one on which I now live containing about
197 acres, and another in Rowan County containing about 200
acres shall be divided into equal shares among all the children of my second wife Elizabeth ... 4 parts "

Executors: David Thornbury and George Brown, both living in
Guilford County.
Witnesses: Adam Smith, Martin Strother, David Coble.

- - -

D 61 Will dated 11 October 1796, proved February Court 1802.

MARGARET CARSON "widow and relict of Alex'r Carson"

sons: Robert Carson, Samuel

"My three daughters Alice Mary and Elizabeth"

granddau: Margaret Clenny

Executor: son-in-law William Clenny
Witnesses: J. G. Rencher, Anne Rencher.

- - -

D 62  Will dated 5 February  1801, proved  Feb Court 1802.

JOHN (x) GANDLEY        to wife Mary 2/3 of estate

"to her (wife's)  daughter Jean, other 1/3"

Witnesses: John Wilkinson, Francis Wilkinson, Robert Fossett.

- - -

D 62  Will dated 4th day 7th month 1800, proved May 1802.

ISAAC HARVEY (malster)               wife: Martha Harvey

"Isaac  Hannah  Rachel  Martha and Ruth  one English shilling each".

"Five shillings to be divided among my deceased son William Harvey's children."

"Five shillings to be divided among my deceased daughter Edith Madden's children."

Son Nathan Harvey gets plantation.

Sole exceutor: son Nathan
Witnesses: James Newlin, ..... .......

— — —

D 64  Will dated 24 February 1802, proved February Court 1802.

SAMUEL (x) McMULLEN "weak of body"        wife a legatee

son: John $20

daughters Sarah, Margaret, Mary, Jane, and Rachel $1 each

sons: Samuel and Thomas $1 each

daughters Ann and Rebecca $1 each

son: James gets remainder of estate after mother's death

Executors: wife, and son James
Witnesses: Jesse Towel, John Towel.

— — —

D 66  Will dated 24 December 1794, proved August Court 1802.

JEREMIAH McCRACKEN               wife: Sarah

brother: John

Executors: "Brother John McCracken and Sary McCracken."
Witnesses: William Clendennin, James Clendennin.

— — —

D 67  Will dated 20 April 1802, proved August Court 1802.

CHARLES (x) WILSON "in decline of life"

daughter Sally Wilson half of lands and plantation
"        Rachel Dunn   "    "   "       "    "

granddaughter: Elinor Dunn

Executors: "trusty friend Isaac Rainey and Robert McKee"
Witnesses: Sale Hatch, John Raney, Polle (x) McKee.

— — —

D 68   Will dated 7 June 1800, proved August Court 1802.

DAVID RANEY                        wife: Siney or Liney

"daughters Susannah Rainey, Jenny R., Margaret R., and Mary
Rainey" each get a cow, etc, "when they see cause to leave
their present home"

sons John Rainey and David Rainey and daughter Cathrin get
five shillings each

son James Rainey gets all lands, etc

daughter Jinny

Executors: son James, and William Horne
Witnesses: Zaccheus Boroughs, Mark Barbee, Wm. Horn.
― ― ―

D 70  Will dated 24 May 1802, proved August Court 1802.

SARAH HERNDON, Widow  (see note below)

daughter: Delilah Rhodes          granddau: Sarah Jordan

sons: Lewis, James, George and Zachariah Herndon

daus: Mary Roberts, Sarah McCoy            son: Reuben

Zachariah Herndon, Edmond Herndon, Ruth Roberts senior,
Maryan Trice, Elizabeth Cole, Esther Barbee and Delilah Rhodes

Executors: Zachariah Herndon and Edmond Herndon
Witnesses: Thomas Steele, Joseph Bilbo.

Note by Ruth Herndon Shields:  SARAH was the widow of George
Herndon, whose will dated 8 May 1796 was proved at August
Court 1796 and is recorded on page 85 in Will Book C.  All the
heirs named are identical except that George names his grandson
George Roberts and does not name a granddaughter.

     The descendants of George and Sarah Herndon are given in
PART FOUR, HERNDONS OF THE AMERICAN REVOLUTION. See ad on last
page of this book. I am a descendant through Delilah Rhodes.
― ― ―

D 71  Will dated 12 April 1802, proved August Court 1802.

THOMAS SHELTON          wife: Catherine gets all estate

son  James Shelton & daughter Mary Collar 5 shillings each

sons: Buckner, Frederick, Jeremiah and Thomas Shelton 5 sh.
                    - continued -

D 71 continued
dau: Rhoda Shelton feather bed, etc
son: John Shelton horse worth $40
dau: Elizabeth Shelton feather bed, etc
son: Edmund Shelton  $40

Sole executrix: wife Catherine
Witness: Isaac Gattis.

— — —

D 73  Will dated 30 August 1801, proved August Court 1802.

SAMUEL PYLE            son: Joseph Pyle

brother-in-law John Hall, his son Samuel Hall

brother Joseph Pyle and his son Samuel Pyle

Deborah Newlin, Daniel ...?....

Executor: John Newlin
Witnesses: ...?... ...?..., Dan'l Foust.

— — —

D 75  Will dated 27 March 1802, proved August Court 1802.

FRANCIS MORELAND            wife: Nancy, all during her life

nephew: Joseph Moreland

Thomas Cooke, Francis Asbury and Richard Walcot.

"To John Major son of William Major deceased,
to Francis Moreland son of William Moreland,
to Francis Ashly son of William Ashly deceased " land, etc,
after the death of wife, Nancy Moreland.

Executors: Wm. Rhodes Jun'r, Page Patterson, John Major.
Witnesses: Thos. Steele, J. Dixon, John Hampton.
This will is signed by both Francis and Nancy Moreland.

— — —

D 76  Will dated 12 July 1802, proved November Court 1802.

ROBERT HUNTER            wife: Nancy Hunter

daughter Frances Hunter to be made "equal with other daughters
        in household furniture"

sons: Samuel Hunter, James Hunter, Robert Hunter

daughters Marget and Jean and son Robert have had their full
shares.

Executors: wife Nancy Hunter, and John Thompson, Esquire.
Witnesses: Robert Whitaker, Robert Hodge.

— — —

D 79  Will dated 2 March 1801, proved November Court 1802.

DANIEL BOOTH                          wife: Prissley

son: Gray Booth 20 shillings
"    John Booth "plantation where he now lives known by the
                name of Hutson's plantation"
"    Mark Booth 150 acres on "west of my mountain tract"
"    Tapley Booth 125 acres joining Mark's
"    Joseph Booth 175 acres joining Tapley
"    Daniel Booth 245 acres known by name of Caselweary place
"    Solomon Booth "one half of home plantation including
                dwelling house"
"    Alphred Booth "other half of my Home Tract"

"My lot at the University to be sold".

daughter: Sarah Dixon  20 shillings

"To my six daughters namely Ruthey, Polly, Betty, Silvey,
Ritty and Patty" ....

Executors: wife Prissley, son John Booth, and John Moore.
Witnesses: John Moore, Samson Moore, James (x) Daews ?.
- - -

D 80  Will dated 7 August 1802, proved November Court 1802.

JOHN (x) POWEL "weak in body"              son: Oliver

wife? "loving Margaret Powel"

"Daughter Mary shall have just as much as the rest of her sisters"

"To all my sons"

Executors: "loving son Josiah Powel and Thomas Powel"
Witnesses: Arthur Lovin ?, Lewis (x) Rhodes.
- - -

D 82  Will dated 18 July 1802, proved November Court 1802.

SAMUEL FREELAND          wife Seely gets all estate for life

After wife's death "all my children to have an equal part".

No executor named.
Witnesses: Benjamin Shoarman, Joseph Rumbley,
           John (x) Whitten ?
- - -

D 83  Will dated 20 June 1802, proved November Court 1802.

JOSEPH BARBER                     wife: Marjary Barber

"My two children David and Elizabeth Barber " who are under
age "to be schooled".
                                    - continued -

D 83 continued

"My stepdaughter Sarah Moore who is in the Western Territory".

Executors: "wife Marjary Barber and my brother Matthew Barber".
Witnesses: Jas. Boyle, Jean Barber, W.F.Thompson.

- - -

D 84  "State of North Carolina, Newberry District" Deed of Gift

from THOMAS CATES to his son Thomas Cates of Orange County, N.C.
for a negro boy.  Dated 29 November 1802, proved Feb Court 1803.
Witnesses: James S. Gilliam, Thos. Wadlington, Archibell Durham
Proved by the oath of Archibell Durham.

- - -

D 84  "State of North Carolina, Newberry District" Deed of Gift

from THOMAS CATES to his "loving daughter Ann Durham the wife
of William Durham" of Orange County, N.C., for a negro girl.
Dated 29 November 1802, proved February Court 1803.
Witnesses: Thos. Wadlington, James S. Gilliam,
          William Bedire ?, Archibell Durham.
Proved by the oaths of James S. Gilliam and Wm. Beaire ?.

- - -

D 85  Will dated 4 October 1800, proved February Court 1803.

HUGH CRAWFORD "old and infirm"

He leaves his wife Jenny "to the care of my only son Samuel".

daughter: Elizabeth Walker

Witnesses: William Freshwater, John Galbraith.

- - -

D 86  Power of Attorney from THOMAS H. PERKINS to "trusty

friend Francis Bullock" to collect debts due to the firm of
Vestal and Perkins. (Vestal is deceased.) Witness: ..?.. Holt.
Dated 10 October 1801, proved February Court 1803.

- - -

D 87  Will dated 15 January 1783, proved February Court 1803.

GILBERT STRAYHORN

sons: David, John, William, James

"Grandsons Gilbert and John, sons of David" .... "house where-
in I now dwell with 170 acres". They are both under 21 years.

son-in-law James Hart
grandchildren: Sarah and John Hart sons of James Hart

14
D 87 continued

William Ansley (?) Ł 20,no relationship stated.

son-in-law John Strain

Executors: "My two sons-in-law John Strain and James Hart."
Witnesses: John Allison, John Ward ?, Thomas Scarlett.
— — —

D 89  Will dated 4 September 1802, proved February Court 1803.

LAZARUS (x) CATE "very weak of body"      wife: Margaret

sons: William, John, Isaiah, Thomas and Benjamin Cate
      "my five sons"

Executors: Culbird ? Burton, Henry Bunch.
Witnesses: Culbird (x) Burton, Henry Bunch,
           Christian (his mark x) Burton.
— — —

D 90  Power of Attorney from JACOB SHORB of Frederick Co., Md.

to Archibald D. Murphey of Orange County, N.C.
Dated 16 Dec 1802, proved Feb Court 1803.  Witness:
                                          George Wilkins.

— — —

D 91  Will dated 22 December 1802, proved February Court 1803.

BARTHOLEMEW (x) STOVALL

wife Ann to have all his estate to use at her discretion "in
raising my younger children."

This will is so confusing that I quote the following as
written:
    "My will and desire is that my executors shall pay unto my
five children  the wife of David Chandler five shillings spe-
cie - Thos. Stovall  Bathew Stovall  Mathew Griffin, George
Stovall the same have already give them & they to have no other part of my estate unless my wife shall think to give it to
them."

"My remaining children to witt / Susanna  William  Jane Frederick  Henery & Anna  Phebe & Nancy Wily & their ares (heirs)
forever " ..

Executors:"wife Ann and real (?) friend & William Stovall
           and Frederick Stovall."
Witnesses: Daniel Green, Elisha Manum (?)
           Benjamin (x) Barber.
— — —

D 93  Will dated 12 December 1802, proved Feb Court 1803.

PETER (x) HELTON "very sick"        wife: Susannah

son: Abraham Helton 100 acres "he now lives on"
 "     Peter Helton   100 "      " he formerly lived on"
 "     James Helton   170 "      "including the old plantation"

"My eight daughters", names not stated.

Executors: Samuel Fogleman, and "John Cobble son of Adam".
Witnesses: Abraham (x) Helton, John Cobble,
           Samuel Macq....?, Adam Starr.

— — —

D 94-99  Will dated 17 December 1802, proved Feb Court 1803.

ABSOLOM TATOM "of the Town of Hillsborough but now in the
              city of Raleigh."

"To my friends John Hogg, Catlett Campbell, David Ray, William
Kirkland and Duncan Cameron "

"To Mary Willott wife of William Willott in the County of
- (blank)- in the State of Tennessee" ... land on Harpeth
River in the County and State aforesaid."

"To nephew Samuel Goodwin of the town of Fayetteville" ... "my
house and lot in the town of Hillsborough".

"To my eldest brother Barnet Tatom" ...
"To my sister Elizabeth Hicks of Granville County" ...
"My brothers Abner Tatom, John Tatom, and William Tatom"
"To the children and heirs of my deceased brother Abel  Tatom"
"To the children of my deceased sister Haritta Tulbylove"
"To the children of deceased sister Meriah Goodwin alias Newby,
 Samuel Goodwin excepted who is otherwise provided for".

Testator and William Moore have "interests in certain lands
lying in Randolph County".

Executors: Samuel Goodwin, John Hogg, Catlett Campbell,
           Duncan Cameron.
Witnesses: William Norwood, Ed. Jones, Gavin Alves,
           W. L. Strudwick.

Codicil dated 17 December 1802 leaves to "Thomas Hogg the son
of James Hogg" $200 to be placed at interest until he reaches
21 years of age. Same witnesses as above.

Friends to handle Tennessee lands: Major Abraham Maury (?),
Gen'l Daniel Smith.

— — —

16

D 100  Will dated 24 January 1803, proved May Court 1803.

JAMES SHAW          wife a legatee, name not stated

"To Betsy Shaw daughter of William Shaw (son of Sam'l)" ...

"My eight children"

sons: Joseph and William Shaw          daughter: Fanny

"To my grandson James Shaw son of Levi"

Executors: "trusty friend James Dixon and my nephew Wm. Shaw."
Witnesses: Daniel Turrentine, Samuel White.

- - -

D 101  Will dated 24 March 1803, proved August Court 1803.

WILLIAM MEBANE          wife: Rebecca 1/3 of estate

Robert Murdock large Bible, etc, and plantation after wife's
death.

brother James 1/3 of estate
  "       David 1/3 of estate

"To my supposed son William Brown Mebane" he gives a slave.

Executors: "My brother James Mebane and my father-in-law
              Benjamin Rainey"
Witnesses: James Hutcheson, Ross Hutcheson.

- - -

D 103  Will dated 22 May 1803, proved August Court 1803.

THOMAS DURHAM          wife: Lucey ? Durham

daus: Elizabeth Durham, Rebecca Durham, Susey ? Durham

sons: Aron, John, Thomas, Iley I., and Ezra Durham.

Executors: "friends William Durham and Thomas Cate".
Witnesses: Lysias Durham, William Hopson.

- - -

D 104  Will dated 26 February 1803, proved August Court 1803.

STWPHWN WILLSON          wife: Sarah 1/3 of estate

to son John and daughter Sarah "land joining Mr. Tilley's "

"To William Dollar one English Crown besides what I have given
him".
"To William Guess  "     "       "      "       "  I "     "
him"

Executors: William Cain and "my loving wife Sarah".
Witnesses: Thomas Latta, John Latta, Jr.

- - -

D 105   Will dated 25 August 1794, proved August Court 1803.

WILLIAM (x) DELEY "weak in body"

wife: Isble Deley, gets plantation during her lifetime,"then
                  it falls to William Deley son of John Deley"

"Sister's children", names not given.

son-in-law James Gibens - his wife Catherine Gibens.
"   "   "    George Reed  - "   "     Mary Reed.

Wm. Deley Reed son of George Reed

Resey and Isbel Deley daughters of John Deley

William son of Samuel Ector

Executors: wife Isbel, and James Ector.
Witnesses: Samuel Ector, Joseph (x) Ector, Jr.
- - -

D 107   Will dated 4 November 1802, proved August Court 1803.

JAMES BALDRIDGE                wife: Martha

"Female children", names and number not stated.See below.
"Youngest daughter Martha White Baldridge"

sons: Malcolm and Josiah Walker Baldridge

"All my children to live with my wife until they marry".
                                                     ough.
Executors are to sell McDade plantation and lots in Hillsbor/

son: Stephen White Baldridge

"To Ann Baldridge"

daus: Elizabeth, Mary, Susanna, Charity, Jean, Margaret (all
      named Baldridge)

step-daughter: Elizabeth Moore

"940 acres of land upon Gasper River in the Western Country
to be divided among my three sons Malcolm, Stephen W., and
Josiah Walker."

Executors: trusty friends Samuel Turrentine, David White,
           James H. Bowman and Malcolm Baldridge.
Witnesses: David Allison, Joseph Hughes.
- - -

D 109   Agreement between the heirs of the Estate of JAMES

ROBINSON, dec'd.   William Robinson gets land on Little Creek. Others mentioned are Elisha Robinson, James Robinson. The paper is signed by Jesse (x) Beckum, James Robertson, Jane (x) Robertson, Elisha (x) Robertson.

Witnesses: J. Cook, Augustine Willis, Jacob Mosier ?. Dated 15 July 1803, proved August Court 1803.

– – –

D 110   Will dated 15 February 1803, proved Nov Court 1803.

JOHN (x) CARRINGTON   "weak in body"

wife: Mary gets all estate during her life

son: Thomas Carington (1 bed and furniture)

Executors: "my two sons Nath'l Carington and Ephriam." Witnesses: Jesse Rice ?, Benjamin (x) Carington.

– – –

D 111   Will dated 1 January 1798, proved Nov Court 1803.

JESSE RICE of Wake County, N.C.         wife: Elizabeth

Executors: "my wife Elizabeth and my friend James Walker" No witnesses.

– – –

D 112   Power of Attorney from JAMES MEBANE SENIOR to his son Alexander Mebane, both of Orange County, N.C., to sell land in Tennesse (county left blank) on Bartow's (Barton'n ?) Creek, "1000 acres granted by State of North Carolina to me for my military services." Dated 30 November 1803. Witness: Archibald Murphey.

– – –

D 113   Power of Attorney from PATSEY ATKINSON of Caswell Co. N.C. to Archibald Murphey of Caswell Co., N.C., to collect the estate of her late brother RANSOM ATKINSON, late of Wayne Co. An advertisemant about his estate was published in the Raleigh Register.... money is in the hands of Simpson Smith. Dated 17 November 1803.       Witness: Solomon Parks.

– – –

D 113   Power of Attorney from SAMUEL THOMPSON, weaver, of Orange County N.C. to John Boyle Junior of Orange County to sell land in Beautetort Co., Va.  A tract containing 400 acres "entered in my name and at the instance of a certain Samuel Findley of the County of Beautetort". Dated 26 November 1803; proved November Court 1803. Witnesses: James Davis, James Palson ?.

– – –

D 114-118  Will dated 24 August 1801, proved Nov Court 1803.

THOMAS TRICE

"To my wife Sarey Trice one half of my property in Brunswick County, Virginia", etc.

Thomas Trice Carlton 400 acres "bounded by my home plantation Christopher Daniels and Robert Cambel's".

Polly Barby "200 acres bounded by my brother Edward Trice, Wm Cain and Page Patterson, running up Second (Creek) to the Cow Lick".

Ritty Barby   200 acres
Polly House   300 "
Nancy Carlton gets a negro girl

dau: Sally Barby wife of Joseph Barby gets two negroes
"    Nancy House gets two negroes

Betsey Carlton wife of Leonard Carlton gets two negroes

"These six grandchildren Thomas Trice Carlton, William Carlton, Polly Barby, Ritty Barbee, Polly House, Betsey House" get 11 negroes.

Executors: brother Edward Trice, Lennard Carlton, John Moore.
Witnesses: Wm. Trice, Edward Trice, John Moore.
- - -

D 119  Will dated 27 November 1803, proved Feb Court 1804.

AQILIIA JONES           wife: Hephsebeth

"My three sons John, Aquilla and James"

"Her (wife's) son William Hargis".

daughter Mary Jones

Testator's wish is that all the family stay together.

Executors: wife, and Reubin Smith.
Witnesses: David Ray, John Butner.
- - -

D 120-122  Will dated 13 April 1800, proved Feb Court 1804.

WILLIAM (x) PARTIN "weak in body"      wife: Jane or Jean

To heirs of "my son John Partin deceased" 1 shilling.
To son-in-law Jesse Rigsby  1 shilling.

Sons: William Partin, Lennard  1 shilling each.
                                        - continued -

20          D 120-122 continued
sons-in-law: Henson Colther and Thomas Connaly 1 shilling
son: Charles Partin  1 shilling
son-in-law: Waller Herndon  1 shilling
son: Bennet Partin land joining Wm. Brewer, Alex. Strain,
              and John McCauley.
son: Lewis Partin  land after wife's death

Executors: "trusty friend William Brewer and my son Charles
              Partin".                              her
Witnesses: Isham Brewer, Waller Herndon, Holley  x  Rigsby,
              Bennett Partin.                    mark

- - -

D 122  Will dated 8 January 1804, proved Feb Court 1804.

SAMUEL DICKIE              wife: Cathren

(The name is signed DICKIE, but spelled two other ways.)

son: James Dicky
"    Samuel Dickey, land in Caswell County

daus: Rachel Burd, Hannah Linch, Hester ? Cantrill

son: William Dickey, land in Caswell County.

dau: Susannah Linch

Executors: sons Samuel and William Dicky.
Witnesses: Sam'l Ector, Savana (x) Garison, her mark.
- - -

D 124  Power of Attorney from BENJAMIN PEELER  to John Grant
Rencher of the City of Wake.    Dated 2 April 1804.
Witnesses: Thos. (x) Browning, John (x) May.
- - -

D 125  Will dated 10 July 1800, proved May Court 1804.

JOHN (x) STALCOP "sick and weak"        wife: Elizabeth

sons: Solomon Stalcop, Thomas Stalcop (he is under 20 years)

daus: Elizabeth Stalcop Jr, Nancy Stalcop, Rachel Stalcop,
      Lydda Stalcop, Susannah Stalcop.

Executors: wife Elizabeth and son Solomon.
Witnesses: James Pyle, William Pyle.
- - -

D 127  This will is so confusingly worded that I copied it
verbatim from the original in the Archives in Raleigh, N.C.

"July the 21st 1800

I, Samuel Thompson of the County of Orange and State
- continued -

of North Carolina     Just Account & legs (legacies ?)

    Henry O'Daniel to Thirty Pounds Dr (debtor ?)
    Joshua Thompson to Eighteen Pounds Dr
    Samuel Thompson to Six Pounds Dr

I leave to my son Joshua Thompson
son Joshua son of Mary Paynes
Twenty Pounds

Samuel Bartly to have a child's part

Witness: Thomas Bradshaw ? "      Signed: his
Proved May Court 1804         Samuel x Thompson
                            mark

— — —

D 127  Will dated 3 January 1804, proved May Court 1804.

JOSEPH (x) CANTERIEL

sons: Isaac Canteriel, Benjamin Canteriel

daus: Rachel Hensley, Sally Davis

Sole executor: son Isaac Canteriel.
Witnesses: Andrew McClary, Conoley Walker.

— — —

D 129  Will dated 2 April 1804, proved May Court 1804.

SIMPSON (x) TAIT        wife: Catherine Tait

son: Zacheus Tait

Executors: "well beloved friend Anthony Tait, and wife Cath-
        erine."
Witnesses: Edmond Gilam, Wm. Street, Joseph Street, Senior.

— — —

D 130  Will dated 17 November 1803, proved May Court 1804.

JAMES (x) LINCH "very sick"      wife: Jean Linch

William Hughes and his wife.

"My three children (to wit) Elizabeth Linch, James Linch,
and Aron Linch". All three are under age.

Executors: "my wife and her brother James Hutcheson."
Witnesses: Anth. Lovins, John (x) McCrory ?.

— — —

D 136  Will dated 13 March 1804, proved May Court 1804.

JEHU WHITTED          daughter: Anna

wife: Susanna "tract of land adjoining William Pickett, Eli
                                - continued -

22        D 136 continued
Hill and others on Hill's Creek being part of the land that
Wm. Courtney died possessed of."
"One house and part of lot #6 in the town of Hillsbouough now
occupied by James Child."

daughter Anna         brother Levi
"Should my wife have a child before my death ..."

He leaves L 100 in trust with his father Wm. Whitted and brother Wm. Whitted Jr. for the benefit of a mulatto child Fanny. She
is to have 6 months schooling, and be emancipated.

Samuel Bigeloe a legatee.
Testator has lands "in the Western Country."

sisters: Mary Bird (testator is guardian for her children)
        Hannah Harris, Elizabeth Thompson, Susannah Thompson

Executors: father Wm. Whitted, brothers Levi and Wm. Whitted Jr,
        and William Harwood.
Witnesses: Will I ? Cain, Gavin Alves.

─ ─ ─

D 137  Will dated 20 December 1800, proved August Court 1804.

JAMES (x) CURREY "weak in body"        wife a legatee,
                                       name not stated

sons: James
        John "land joining Chisenhall's line"
"The three girls that is single", names not stated.

Executors: wife, and son James.
Witnesses: Silus Forest, Isaac Jones, James Currey.

─ ─ ─

D 138  Will dated 14 September 1804, proved Nov Court 1804.

SARAH McCRACKEN widow

"To Mary Paton wife of Robert Paton at whose House I now reside, and Polly Patton daughter of said Robert Patton"... (a
long list of articles is given, and a list of notes due her.)

Executors: "trusty friends Robert Patton Senior and David
        Turrentine."
Witnesses: Robert Hodge, Robert Patton, Senior.

─ ─ ─

D 140  Will dated 20 February 1804, proved Nov Court 1804.

JOSEPH WELLS, Senior

son: William Wells "land on both sides of Cane Creek"
sons: John, Joseph, Nathan, Isaac Wells, $7 each

daughters: Margrate Gifford, Charity McDaniel $7 each
        Mary A. Jamison ?, Rachel Underwood $7 each
                - continued -

D 140 continued                                                23
granddaughter: "daughter of Jesse Wells deceased"

Elizabeth Wells (no relationship stated)

Executors: sons Isaac and William Wells.
Witnesses: Wm. Pike, John Pike Jr., John Marshill.

— — —

D 141  Division of the negroes in the Estate of RICHARD
COCHRAN to Mrs. Turner, the widow of Richard Cochran, and
his daughter Polly Dilhu Cockran.
Signed by: Joshua Holt, J. Scott, J'se ? Hall.

— — —

D 142  Will dated 19 March 1804, proved November 1804.

FREDERICK LOYD                          wife: Mary Loyd

sons: Lacey Loyd, Frederick and John Loyd.

Executors: "well beloved friend Thomas Brewer and Lacey Loyd"
Witnesses: Sackfield Brewer, Elizabeth (x) Brewer.

— — —

D 143  Will dated 2 January 1805, proved February Court 1805.

WILLIAM MURRAY

wife: Margaret to have all estate "for her and her children's
               support as it is this day for twelve years."
               James Barnhill & Isaac Hall are to help settle
               any disputes that arise during the twelve years.

sons: William, Robert Murray
          "3 youngest" Andrew, Eli and John Murray

daughter: Margaret Bird

Testator has a saw mill and a grist mill.
He has land claims in Cumberland.

Executors: sons Robert and William.
Witnesses: Christ'r Swindell, Walter Murray, Rob't Tate.

— — —

D 146-148  Will dated 19 March 1804, proved Feb Court 1805.

JAMES HOGG                 sisters: Mary Elizabeth and Jean

neice: Jean Burgess
brother: Robert Hogg, deceased

"To my son Gavin Alves"
daughter: Robina Norwood

"My children Walter Alves, Gavin Alves, Helen Hooper and
Robina Norwood, and to my grandchildren John Huske and Ann
                     - continued -

24
Alves Huske."

D 146-148 continued

Executors: son Walter Alves and Gavin Alves.
Witness: James Wells.

— — —

D 148  Will dated 13 September 1803, proved May Court 1805.

THOMAS ROUNTREE              wife a legatee, name not given

son: Joseph Rountree gets land on condition that he care for
     his mother.
sons: John and Thomas Rountree 5 shillings each

Lydia Cate and Rachel Jacobs 5 shillings each (daughters ?)

Money left in estate after wife's death to be divided into
8 shares and divided as follows: (no relationships stated)
Andrew & Thomas 2 shares each, John, Charles, Lydia and Joseph, 1 share each.

Rachel, one cow
granddaughter: Elizabeth Hannah

No executor named.
Witnesses: Thompson McKissick, Wm. McKissick.

— — —

D 150  Will dated 4 May 1805, proved May Court 1805.

JONATHAN (x) JENKINS "sick and very weak"        wife: Ann

Executors: wife, and "trusty friend John Wilbourn."
Witnesses: Ownley ?(x) Owen, Samuel (x) Owen.

— — —

D 151  Will dated 25 February 1805, proved May Court 1805.

THOMAS LEWIS                      wife: Jane
                                               lives"
son: William "land on east side of Henry Lewis where he now/
"    Fielding  "land where I now live"

daughters: Frances, Elizabeth, Mary

sons: Robert, Henry, John

son-in-law: Nicholas Durning

Executors: "My two sons Fielding and Henry Lewis, and John
           Rhodes of Benjamin, and my loving wife Jane."
Witnesses: John Rhodes, Ben. Rhodes.

— — —

D 152  Will dated 25 June 1805, proved August 1805.

JOHN (x) KING  "weak of body"

"Wife and two children Calvin and John five shillings each".

"My two sons Thomas King and Jeremiah King " under age.

Sole executor: father, Thomas King.
Witnesses: Julius King, John King.

- - -

D 154  Will dated 6 August 1803, proved August Court 1805.

MARTHA STRUDWICK

"to grandson Samuel Strudwick when he arrives at twenty..."
"in case of Samuel's death I give property to Edmund ..."

Sole executor: son Wm. F. Strudwick.
Elizabeth Kirby to have $50 "if she is with me at my death"
Witness: Elizabeth Sheppard.

- - -

D 155  Will dated 24 October 1793, proved August Court 1805.

JAMES BIRD                    (no wife mentioned)

"Youngest son Thomas Bird all my land I now possess."

"... the whole of my children saying Richard Empson Thomas
Sarah Mary Susanna and Catherine each to have share and share
alike" in moveable estate. (No punctuation.)

Executors: sons Richard and Empson Bird.
Witnesses: Alex. Mebane, Jas. Mebane, Jun'r.

- - -

D 156  Will dated 28 October 1804, proved August Court 1805.

HENRY McCLUER                  wife: Mary

son: James 150 acres and ½ of grist mill and all of saw mill
"    John  180 "
"    Henry (he is under age) 150 acres and "plantation I now
           live on" and ½ of grist mill

daughters: Elizabeth and Susannah 50 acres each
           Sarah 5 shillings
           Mary, Ann, and E.D. 50 acres each

granddaughter: Elizabeth (dau. of Sarah) 50 acres

Executors: sons James and John.
Witnesses: Wm. Hatchett, John McCullock, Eliz. McCullock.
"N.B.  I will to my beloved son William 5 shillings."

- - -

D 158  Will dated 10 November 1800, proved August Court 1805.

GEORGE (x) FRIDDLE                    wife: Mary

sons: Casper, John and Henry Friddle, 1 shilling each
dau: Caty Garrot wife of Averot Gattot 1 shilling
"    Peggy Lue wife of Michael Lue 1 shilling

"I say that it may be fully understood all my children by my
first wife shall have one shilling each."

"My three youngest children (to wit) Caty Friddle Purley
Friddle and Martin J. Friddle."

Executors: friends Ludwick Allbright Junr. and Jacob Graves.
Witnesses: Michael Holt, John ...land ?

— — —

D 160  Power of Attorney from JAMES TRICE to his brother
William Trice, both of Orange County.
Dated 30 October 1805, proved November Court 1805.
Witnesses: Francis Barbee, Isaiah Marcum.

— — —

D 160  Will dated 20 August 1805, proved November Court 1805.

JOHN McKEE                    wife: Catherine "and family"

son: John McKee  500 acres
daus: Alizabeth McKee 250 acres, Mary McKee 250 acres
He speaks of "my three children"

Executors: Wife Catherine, James Clark and Robert McKee.
Witnesses: Thomas Clark, Agness Anderson.

— — —

D 162  Will dated 8 June 1805, proved August Court 1805.

JOHN NEWLIN

son: Nathaniel Newlin "the plantation I now live on"

"My other children namely Jas Newlin John Newlin Hannah
Holladay and Mary Hadley."

"Five grandchildren of my son Eli Newlin deceased five pounds
(to wit) Joshua and John Newlin  Ruth Vestal  Edith & Mary
Newlin ..." (no punctuation)

No executor named.
Witnesses: John Carter, Anne Carter, Hannah Carter.

— — —

D 163A  Will dated 17 December 1805, proved Feb Court 1806.

JAMES (x) COZART                    wife: Sarah

son: Hiram Brinkley Cozart "all my lands lying in Person Co.
     viz 1303 acres with the grist mill." He is under age.

sons: Hiram, David and William, all under age.

daus: Lively Brinklry Cozart, Edy Brinkley Cozart, Jemimah
      Cozart, Sarah Cozart, all under age. The three last are
      the youngest.

"I have left in the possession of James Tomison who married
Charlotte four negroes ..."

Executors: wife Sarah,"and Court of Orange to appoint an
           Executor to act with my widow."
Witnesses: Alex. (x) McMullan, Rachel (x) Hopkins.

— — —

D 166  Will dated 2 February 1806, proved Feb Court 1806.

MARTHA WILLIAMS

sisters: Hester Williams and Nancy Williams
brother: James Williams

No executor named.
Witnesses: Isaac Jackson, John McMullin.

— — —

D 167  Will dated 9 September 1805, proved Feb Court 1806.

JAMES (x) MILIKEN                    wife: Rachel

sons: James (eldest), Elias, and George (youngest)

Executors: wife Rachel, and Jesse Miliken.
Witnesses: William Moore, William Robertson.

— — —

D 169  Will dated 15 February 1806, proved May Court 1806.

JOHN (x) ANDERSON                    wife: Lettice

daughters: Mary, Pheby and Ann

sons: Robert, John

Executors: sons Robert and John.
Witnesses: Thos. Armstrong, Robert Anderson, Wm. Anderson.

— — —

D 170   Will dated 9 May 1804, proved May Court 1806.

ROBERT (x) BURNSIDE     He says "my seven children"

sons: Benjamin Burnside (eldest), John and James Burnside

daughters: Ruth, Hannah, Ann

Executors: Joseph Thompson, Owin Lindley.
Witnesses: Wm. Morris, James Lindley, Gracy ? Lindley.
- - -

D 172   Indenture bewteen ROBERT (x) BURNSIDE and Thomas
Faucett, both of Orange Co., N.C.  BURNSIDE sells land on
Eno and Haw Rivers to Faucett. Dated 9 Nov 1798, proved 1806.
Witnesses: Owin Lindley, Chas ? Stubbins.
- - -

D 174   Will dated 26 September 1803, proved August Court 1806.

FRANCIS WILKINSON        sons: John and William

He speaks of "my six children" but names only the two above,
and David below.
Executors: sons John and David.
Witnesses: Joseph Thompson, ..?.. Hart, Thos. McCracken.
- - -

D 175   Will dated 29 August 1805, proved August Court 1806.

JAMES MURRAY                 wife: Sarah

son Jonathan, daughter Ann, and son James, 1 shilling each.

daughter Elizabeth everything after wife's death
   "        Ruth

Executrix: daughter Elizabeth.
Witnesses: Wm. Rainey, Jonathan (x) Murray.
- - -

D 176   Will dated 2 March 1803, proved August Court 1806.

GEORGE ALLEN

sons-in-law: James Mebane, David Mebane, David White,
             James Armstrong

son: Samuel Allen plantation joining lands of Robert Hodge
              and Robert Patton.

sons: William Allen George Allen, Alexander  Allen

Executors: son-in-law David White, and Robert Hodge.
Witnesses: James Patton, Alexander Patton.
- - -

D 178   Will dated 13 January 1806, proved Nov Court 1806.

JACOB SENIOR ALLEN

son: Jacob Allen   land on South side of Eno River
 "      William Allen land on North side of Eno

daus: Sally Allen; Betsey Allen, Hannah Allen
      Nancy Latta, Syntha Scarlett

Executors: son-in-law James Latta, son Jacob Allen.
Witnesses: Wm. Cain Sr., John Kelly Sr., Cuthburt (x) Burton.

- - -

D 179   Will dated 13 October 1806, proved Nov Court 1806.

JOHN FAUCETT                     wife: Mary

"I leave my land to be divided equally to my children that
shall live to come of age." Number and names not stated.

Executors: "friends John Ray and William Bradford."
Witnesses: Samuel Faucett, Thos. Bradford.

- - -

D 180   Will dated 23 September 1806, proved Nov Court 1806.
        her
LESEY    x    ROGERS
        mark

son: Laban Rogers (under age) all estate, including "my pro-
portionate part of my deceased father's estate after my mother's death."

Executors: Richard Goat, Nathan Rogers.
Witnesses: James Sykes, Wm. A. Freshwater.

- - -

D 181   Will dated 19 November 1806, proved Nov Court L806.

EPHRIAM MITCHELL            wife a legatee, name not stated

"Six of my sons Henry, David, Randall ?, James, Efram, and
William."
                              (This will has been
daughter Patsey               checked with the
                              original in the Ar-
children: Noah and Happey ? $15 each.   chives. The writing
                              is very bad.)
No executor named.
Witnesses: Stephen Robart, Nancy (x) Robart.

- - -

D 183  Will dated 15 Nov 1806, proved Nov 1806 or Feb 1807.

ISHAM GANT                              wife: Sally

"My children", all under age, names and number not stated.

Executors: brothers William Gant and James Gant.
Witnesses: J. Webb, A. Murray.

– – –

D 184  Will dated 8 July 1806 ?, proved February 1807.

MICHAEL ROBINSON

son: William 20 shillings
"    David Robinson 20 shillings, a negro, 500 acres of land
                   on Duck River
"James Robinson son of Alexander Robinson deceased" 20 sh.

daughter: Catherine Moore 5 shillings
son: Michael Robinson                                      Ray"
grandson: John Robinson son of Michael "by his first wife Jane/
son: James Robinson "my large Bible"
daughter: Mary Moore 5 shillings
daus: Jinnett Ray wife of James Ray
      Martha Ray, Nancy Rountree
son: Joseph Robinson  300 acres of land "lying on the waters
                   of Duck River in the State of Tennessee,
                   it being the third part of a tract of
                   1500 acres."
son: John Robinson  500 acres on Duck River
"    Charles Robinson

"To heirs of my daughter Margaret McCallister" 5 shillings.
"To Jane Anderson daughter of Samuel Anderson" one negro child.
grandson: Michael Robinson Moore $20 "to help with his educa-
                                               tion."
Executors: friends Wm. Cooke, Thomas Roundtree, David Ray.
Witnesses: James Whitfield, Nancy (x) Wilson.

– – –

D 186  Will dated 18 November 1807, proved Nov Court 1807.

JOHN KING

"To friend George Wagoner 10 gallons of the whiskey  James
Walker promised to pay me."
To friend Charles Roberts, all his estate.

Executors: George Wagoner, Ephriam Roberts, James Walker.
Witnesses: Abner (x) Roberts, William Harris,
           Milly (x) Arnold, Winnifred (x) Roberts.

– – –

D 187   Will dated 30 April 1806, proved February Court 1807.

JAMES McCADDAMS                    wife: Rebeckah

sons: James McCaddams, James Hopkins

grandson: Absalom McCaddams

Executors; sons Jos'h McCaddams, James.
Witnesses: James McCaddams Jr., William Crutchfield.

— — —

D 189   Will dated 3 February 1807, proved Feb Court 1807 ?

WILLIAM MORROW of the Hawfields, "old and infirm"

son: William Morrow "plantation whereon I now live"
 "      James Morrow    ""         "         he now lives"

daughters: Elizabeth Andrews ?, Margat Bryen ?, Jane Pickhard

"My son John Morrow doter Janey Banks (Parker ?) Morrow"
Janey is under age, her mother is Sarah Morrow.

Executors: son William Morrow and James Morrow and Jno.
            Thompson.
Witnesses: Robert Grahams, William (x) Grahams, Jno. Thompson.

I have examined the original will in the Archives in Raleigh.
The writing is poor, name is spelled MURROW in the body of
the will but the signature is MORROW.

— — —

D 190   Will dated 11 August 1807, proved November Court 1807.

JONATHAN NICHOLS

grandchildren: Hannah and Nancy Riggs, Irven and John Riggs
                John Nichols
"Heirs of my beloved daughter Hannah Riggs".

"To sons Jonathan Baldwin John and Amos Nichols"

Executors: sons Jonathan and Amos.
Witnesses: Jno. McMullen, James Daugherty.

— — —

D 192-4   Will dated 9 May 1807, proved May Court 1807.

WILLIAM (x) PICKET              wife: Elizabeth

"To India  Pickett daughter of my son Jesse Picket.

granddaus: "Tempy and Edy Rigsby daughters of Jesse Rigsby"

daughter Elizabeth Rigsby                - continued -

D 192-4 continued
sons: Mark Picket, Thomas Picket

"Thomas Picket and Jesse Picket .. the land and plantation
where they live during their lives."

daughter Peggy Perry
grandson: Arche ? Rigsby "land where he now lives, formerly
                        the property of David Grisham"

Executors: "worthy friends Mann Patterson, Wm. Rhodes Trice."
Witnesses: C. P. Patterson, William Rhodes.

— — —

D 194  Will dated 18 December 1806, proved May Court 1807.

JAMES RODGERS              wife and "children as they grow up"

son: John "140 acres joining the line of Ceason ? Capps"
sons: James and William each get half of lands "joining George
                Fost and others", 150 acres

"My daughters, viz, Jean Ann Nelson and Polly"
Polly is the youngest.

Executors: "brother William Rodgers and my loving wife."
Witnesses: J. Scott, James Partin.

— — —

D 197   Will dated 5 February 1806, proved August Court 1807.

JEAN (or JANE) (x) McCANLESS     No relationship stated to
                                any of the legatees.
John McCanless
John Commins Senior, James McCanless, Elizabeth Hammetton
David McCanless "the mansion house", William  McCanless

Executors: James H. Bowman, James Murdock.
Witnesses: John Trimble, Marget (x) Trimble, Sarah (x) Trimble.

— — —

D 199   Will dated 27 July 1805, proved August Court 1807.

JAMES FREELAND

grandchildren: Thomas Freeland "son of my son Thomas deceased"
               Susan Freeland, daughter of Thomas deceased.

sons: James $1, John $50, have already received plantations

daus: Mary, "Jean Gibson wife of Andrew Gibson"

son: Joseph "all land I now possess"

Executors: Andrew Murdock; "and my son John Freeland."
Witnesses: Thomas Dickson, Stewart Dickson, Wm. Rainey.

— — —

D 201-203  Will dated 18 May 1807, proved August Court 1807.

JAMES MEBANE                    wife gets plantation, etc

daus: Elizabeth, Jenny, Nancy, Polley, Peggy

son: Alexander "200 acres in the State of Tennessee on the
                 waters of Harpeth where he now lives."
"    George "200 acres in Tennessee on waters of Harper"
"    Robert "2000 acres in Tennessee in Jackson County"
"    William "200 "    "  "        on waters of Harper"
"    Allen    200 "    "  "            "  "      "  "
"    Nathaniel 200 acres in Tenn.    "  "        "  "
"    James  home plantation after wife's death
Other lands in Orange Co., N.C. and Tennessee are to be sold.

Executors: brother David Mebane, James Mebane, John Thompson.
Witnesses: Samuel  Nelson, John Nelson, Edward Willson.

- - -

D 203  Will dated 14 September 1806, proved Nov Court 1807.
JOHN LINER

"My six children Mary  James  Sarah  John  Nancy  Margaret".
Mary, Sarah and Margaret are living with their father.

Executors: "loving friends John Scott and Isaac Holt."
Witnesses: A. (x) Thompson, John Cook.

- - -

D 205  Will dated 27 March 1806, proved May Court 1806.

JOSEPH LOFTIN of Chapel Hill, N.C.    Wife: Elizabeth

"My three children who are unmarried"
"To two sons Leonard and William ... lands I bought of John
 Morgan".
dau: Catherine "lands I bought of Bonds where Underhill lives".
daus: Vineter ?, Betsey
"Lands I bought of Thos Heath to be sold ".. in Craven County.

Executors: son Leanord Loftin and friend Daniel West.
Witnesses: Wm. Croom, Geo. Lane (Love ?), Thomas Collier ?.

- - -

D 206  Will dated 19 November 1806, proved Nov Court 1807.

JAMES CRUTCHFIELD

wife: Mary  all estate, household furniture, etc, including
            "wheat at John Crawford's mill." This property to
            be divided among her children after her death.
            "All the property willed to her by John Steel."

James Crutchfield (under 21 years) "my road tract" 128 acres.

brother: Benjamin Crutchfield gets a slave, provided he com-
            pletes a wagon on hand at Mathew Wilson's and Benja-
            min Crutchfield's shop.          - continued -

34          D 206 continued
brothers: John, William, Stephen ?, Anderson
"Property coming to me at the death of my mother I leave to
 Thomas and Stapleton."

John Pitts

Executors: wife Mary, and friend Jacob Geer (Greer ?).
Witnesses: Thomas Bradshaw, Wm. Shaw.

‒ ‒ ‒

D 208  Will dated 16 September 1807, proved Nov Court 1807.

ELIHU WOOD "a farmer"                    wife: Elinor

"My four daughters Margaret Mary Rebecka and Lucy".

sons: William (under age), Hugh, Elihu (youngest)

Executors: "faithful friends David Ray and Robert Fausett, Sr."
Witnesses: Jno. Kelly Sen'r, John Trimble, Joseph Wood.

‒ ‒ ‒

D 211  Will dated 16 June 1806, proved November Court 1807.

GEORGE McRAY                    wife: Sarah

son: James "land bought of Monhollen adjoining James Duke's"
daus: Susanna, Margret, Ann (she is under 18 years of age)
son: George (under 20) land joining John Hall & John Graham
dau: Sarah
son: John

Executors: wife Sarah, son James
Witnesses: Jonathan Harvey, James King.

‒ ‒ ‒

D 213  Will dated 5 March 1805, proved Nov Court 1807.

HENRY (x) HORTON               grandson: Henry McFarlan gets
                                          all lands
granddau: Mary Copley
son: Hugh Horton
dau: Elizabeth McFarlaine        Thomas McFarlaine
"To my grandchildren of Sarah each and each to share alike
(viz) Winnfred McMullen  Susana Adams  Mary Copley
James McFarlain and William McFarlain." (No punctuation.)

Sole executor: grandson John McFarlain.        his
Witnesses: Jas. Walker, Moses Jones, Larcan  (x) McFarlain.
                                             mark
‒ ‒ ‒

D 215  Will dated 18 October 1808,     proved Feb Court 1807 ?

ALEXANDER (x) ROBBS "sick and weak"

All his estate goes to Benjamin Cantril, who is to set free
his negro slave Peter, after ten years.

Witnesses: Hardy Hurdle, John Layne.

- - -

D 216  Power of Attorney from JAMES ALLAN MORGAN "being about
to leave the State of North Carolina" to Chesley P. Patterson,
"to lease, rent or sell ... lands bounded by Lemuel Morgan,
Solomon Morgan, Christopher Barbee and Jarratt Yeargin."
Dated 19 November 1807, proved February Court 1808.
Witnesses: C. Barbee, John Morgan.

- - -

D 218  Power of Attorney from CASAN SWINDLE to Christopher
Swindle, both of Orange County, N.C.    Witness: James Mebane,/
Dated 28 October 1805, proved Feb Court 1808.               Jr.

- - -

D 219  Will dated 5 September 1807, proved Feb Court 1808 ?

JAMES CARSON                    son: Robert Carson

wife: Mary all estate during her life, including plantation
      and land that "now belongs to John McDade."

Executors: wife Mary, and William Clark.
Witness: Jesse Clark.

- - -

D 220  Will dated 11 November 1807, proved Feb Court 1808.

SABUT WOOD

grandchildren: Sabet Wood, Mary Wood, Hardy Wood, children of
               "my son Levin Wood."
dau-in-law: Elizabeth Wood, wife of Levin Wood
dau: Kezzia Wood
son: Isaac

Sole executor: son Levin Wood.
Witnesses: Joseph Clendennin, Jos. Harlow, George Coble.

- - -

D 221  Deed of Gift from MARGARET RIGGS to Sarah Hall' Shelton
Hall and Jenny Hall (under age), all of Otange County, N.C.
Dated 19 September 1807, proved February Court 1808.
Witnesses: Jno. Riggs, James Woods, John Jimmason ?.

- - -

D 222  Will dated 23 November 1802, proved Feb Court 1808.

DAVID DENNING or DINNING

Dau: Margery Barber all estate, land on Laughlen's Creek, etc.

grandchildren: David Barber, Betty Barber
son: David Denning
dau: Isabella Moore

Executrix: Margery Barber.
Witnesses: John & James Boyles (Boylen ?), James Davis.
- - -

D 224  Will dated 20 November 1807, proved Feb Court 1808.

JOHN DUGLASS                          wife: Mary

"My five children John Duglass, George Duglass, Adam Duglass,
Rosanna Duglass and Hannah Duglass."

"Peggy Walls and her son William Walls."

Executors: wife Mary, and son John.
Witnesses: James Cain, Thomas Holden, Henry Bunch.
- - -

D 226  No date on will, proved May Court 1808.

JONATHAN NICHOLS

mother: Sarah Dickson               father: Jonathan Nichols

Witnesses: Jas. H. Bowman, Thomas Ray.
- - -

D 228  Will dated 10 June 1807, proved May Court 1808.

WILLIAM (x) BUSICK, SR  "old and weak in body"

son: Caleb Busick
dau: Elizabeth Wood 5 shillings
son-in-law: Samuel Green 5 shillings
daus: Mary Willcox, Polly Conner ?  5 shillings each

"Son William Busick and Elizabeth Busick and Nancy Busick
and Phebe Busick to be equally divided among them."

Executors: son William Busick and Henry Brannon.
Witnesses: William Brannock, Leah Branock.
- - -

D 229-231  Will dated 12 February 1808, proved May Court 1808.

ROBERT SR MORRISON

son: James all lands in Randolph County
 "    William "land where I now live and a piece of land I pur-
                chased from Wm. Carter adjoining the said place."

D 229-231 continued
son: Robert "land whereon my son William now lives"
daus: Hannah and Deborah  $80 each    207 acres bought from
                                Isaac Reynolds to be sold to pay them
"My daughters (viz) Jean, Catherine, Mary, Ruth, Hannah and
Deborah."

Executors: son Robert, and James Newlin.
Witnesses: Wm. Carter, Danell Towell, Duncan Darroch.

- - -

D 231  Will dated 14 November 1807, proved May Court 1808.

DAVID (x) RAY "very sick"        wife a legatee

sons: William (eldest),John, David, Hugh, James, Henry get
      5 shillings each

daus: Rachel Gibson, Mary Becom  5 shillings each
      Jenny Jones, Nelly Ricketts, 5 shillings each.

"son and youngest child Alexander", horse, etc.

Executors: wife, and John Pickard, elder.
Witnesses: John H. Pickard, John Grimes.

- - -

D 233  Will dated 18 Jan 1808, proved May or August Court 1808.

DAVID HALL              wife: Elizabeth  all lands

son: Hardy Almond  lands after wife's death
"    Thomas   5 shillings
dau: Delila   5 "
"daughters Sally Rebecca Betsey and Estey (Elsey ?)" get
personal estate.

Executors: Abner Massey, wife Elizabeth.
Witnesses: Leonard Carlton, Wm. Shepard, J. Dixon.

- - -

D 235  Will dated 24 October 1807, recorded August Court 1808.

JOHN HARDIN              wife: Sarah

son: John
"Four youngest daughters Polley, Sally, Betsy and Peggy."

No executor named.  Witnesses: Jean Holt, Wm. Holt.

- - -

D 236  Mortgage from JAMES RIGGS to Andrew McBroom on a mare
and a colt, etc, dated October 5, 1805, proved Nov Court 1808.
Witness: Ashahel Moore.

- - -

D 237  Will dated 19 June 1808, proved Nov Court 1808.

WILLIAM WOLF

Ann (relationship not stated, wife ?) gets plantation

sons: Peter, John, William (he is youngest)
daus: Barbara and Mary

His negro man to be hired out until he earns enough to repay
his purchase price, when he is to be freed.

Witnesses: Benjamin Jackson, Joseph Clendennin.

— — —

D 239  Will dated 28 September 1808, proved Nov Court 1808.

PETER (x) FOUST "weak in body"    wife: Mary, is pregnant

son: John Foust "plantation I bought of Joseph Stout", etc.
daus: Elizabeth Clap, Sarah Amick
son: Peter Foust under age
brother: Daniel

Exceutors: wife, and son John
Witnesses: Thomas Lindley, Jacob Marshall.

— — —

D 241  Will dated 8 October 1808, proved Feb Court 1809.

ELI McDANIEL          wife: Elizabeth

sons: John and James, both married
daus: Peggy, Salley, Susy  all under age

Executors: John McDaniel, James McDaniel.
Witnesses: Joshua O'Daniel, Jesse Miliken.

— — —

D 243  Will dated 10 October 1804, proved Feb Court 1809 ?

THOMAS ROBERTSON          wife: Susannah

son: Abijah Ray

Executor: wife Susannah
Witnesses: John Clendennin, James (x) Daniels.

— — —

D 244  Will dated 25 November 1808, proved Feb Court 1809.

PETER (x) JEFFREYS          wife: Lucy

Two slaves are to be emancipated.

Executor: John Young of the town of Hillsborough.
Witnesses: Robert Tinnen, James Lapslie.

— — —

D 244  Bill of Sale from WILLIAM BUSSICK, SR. to William
Bussuck Jr. for $60, a sorrel mare and cow and calf.
Dated 24 February 1808, proved May Court 1809.
Witnesses: Elizabeth Bussick, Catherine (x) Bussick.

— — —

D 246  Power of Attorney from WILLIAM FORSYTHE to "trusty
friend and son James Forsythe", both of Orange County.
Dated 17 July 1809, proved August Court 1809.
Witness: Barnett Forsythe.

— — —

D 247  Power of Attorney from WILLIAM BOND of Hillsborough,
N.C., to friend James Webb of Hillsborough.
Dated 10 March 1809, proved August Court 1809.
Witnesses: William Whitted, James Whitted.

— — —

D 248  Will dated 13 April 1809, proved August Court 1809.

HUGH (x) McCADDAMS                wife: Caty

sons: James, John, William and Isaac McCaddams $1 each
daus: Nancy McCaddams, Elizabeth Bason, Mary McCaddams $1 each
son: Hugh McCaddams  land
"    David McCaddams $1
"    Tinnen McCaddams land
dau: Franky McCaddams  one negro
son: Joseph, land, slaves

Executors: friends Joseph Moore and Robert Fossett.
Witnesses: Edward Fossett, Robert Tinnin, George Fausett.

— — —

D 250  Will dated 3 October 1808, proved August Court 1809.

REBECCA (x) McAdams

son: James and his daughter Rebecca
daus: Egness, Elizabeth Blair.

Witness: Samuel Crawford.

— — —

D 251  Will dated 9 May 1809, proved August Court 1809.

SAMUEL CHAMBERS                wife: Sarah

son: James Chambers $1
sons: Samuel and William "land I purchased of John Railey"

daus: Mary Chambers, Elizabeth Railey, Hannah Lindley,
      Grace Lindley

Executors: wife Sarah, and Owen Lindley.
Witnesses: John Thompson, Bennett Watson ?.

— — —

D 253  Bill of Sale from ANTHONY (x) COZART to Josiah Davis,
both of Orange Co., N.C., for a slave girl Tamar for Ł 500.
Dated 20 May 1809, proved November Court 1809.
Witnesses: John Carrington, William Brinkley, Jr.

– – –

D 254  Will dated 25 May 1809, proved November Court 1809.

HENRY (x) PICKET "sick of body"     wife: Indy or Judy

son-in-law: Ellick Grayham
granddau: Elizabeth Grayham

Executors: Ryly Vickers, ..?.. Guess.
Witnesses: Jesse (x) Picket, Lucy (x) Dolar, Mo. Guess.

– – –

D 256  Will dated 31 August 1809, proved Nov Court 1809.

DAVID (x) DUNN

sister: Nancy Love one half of property
brother: Drury Dunn  other half of property

Witnesses: Isaac Hudson, Nathaniel Dunn.

– – –

D 257-258  Will dated 21 November 1809, proved Feb Court 1810.

ONLY (x) OWENS "sick and weak"          wife: Sarah

daus: Nancy Jenkins and Elizabeth Lingo 5 shillings each
son: Belitha  Owens 5 shillings
daus: Lear Pettigrew and Lavinia Pettigrew, 5 shillings each
sons: Samuel and John Owens 5 shillings each
son: Thomas Owens balance of estate

Executors: "trusty friends John Wilbon and John Jenkins."
Witnesses: Wm. Meadows , Charles Jenkins.

– – –

D 259  Will dated 10 October 1809, proved Feb Court 1810.

JOHN GRAHAM          wife: Mary gets plantation etc, "to
                              raise the children"
"Three sons James, George and Thomas Graham" all under age,
to "be schooled".

daus: Jenny Walker $5; Ann Hall $5 and 1 negro man
sons: John Graham $25, etc, Robert Graham $25
dau: Fanny Walker $5
daus: Elizabeth Graham, Mary Graham, Charity Graham get a
        horse, cows, saddle, etc, each

Executors: wife Mary, and son John Graham.
Witnesses: David Bradford, James (x) Tate.

– – –

D 261   Will dated 12 March 1808, proved February Court 1810.

DARKIS (x) HAYS

Friends: Milly Beasley, Nancy Martin, Rachel Blanchard,
          Ruthy Stark, the widow Stark, Phebe Stark,
          Elizabeth Stark, Christin Hurdle

Executrix: Ruthy Stark
Witnesses: Hardy Hurdle, James Hurdle.

- - -

D 262   Will dated 14 August 1809, proved February Court 1810.

WORHAM GLEN                    wife: Nanny Glen

"My children (viz) Firy ? Glen, James Glen, David Glen,
Nancy Wood, John Glen, Robert Glen and Sally Garrard."

Executors: Fery ? Glen and David Glen.
Witnesses: Thos. Reavis, Sally (x) Scoggins.

- - -

D 263   Will dated 11 September 1809, proved May Court 1810.

JESSE NEVILL                   wife: Elizabeth

"First children that have married off and gone from me, that
is to say, Goodwick Kirk, Elizabeth Barby, Solomon Nevill,
Benjamin Nevill, Jesse Nevill Jr", these have had their shares.

son: Samuel Parke Nevill
dau: Selah Nevill
son: Goodman Nevill (spelled Goodwin below)
"    Wiley Whitwell Nevill
dau: Cynthia Aris ? Robertson

Executors: sons Goodwin Nevill and Samuel Parke Nevill.
Witnesses: Wm. Brewer, James Miles, Joshua Brewer.

- - -

D 265   Will dated 18 March ----, proved May Court 1810.

CHARLES COLLIER                wife: Patty all estate

"My dear children", names and number not stated.

Executors: wife Patty, and friend Samuel Hopkins.
Witnesses: Edward Rigins, Rob't Campbell.

- - -

D 267   Bill of Sale from JOSHUA WEEDON of Orange County, N.C.
to Quinton Anderson, horses and cow. Witness: James Anderson.
Dated 9 February 1810, proved August Court 1810.

- - -

D 267  Will dated 8 September 1806, proved August Court 1810.

JNO. ARMSTRONG                    wife: Anne Armstrong

sons: Joseph, Thomas and James Armstrong 20 shillings each
dau: Margaret wife of James Willson       20 "
 "    Jinnet wife of John Hanks           20 "
 "    Mary wife of John Jesse             20 "
 "    Elizabeth wife of Isaac Jackson     20 "
 "    Catrenah wife of Absolom Cooper     20 "

Executors: wife Anne, "and my son John Hanks."
Witnesses: And'w McBroom, John Ray.

- - -

D 269  Will dated 6 July 1809, proved August Court 1810.

JOHN GATTIS

sons: Thomas & Alexander Gattis, land joining Joseph Kirkland
"To my daughter Martha or John Caldwell" 5 shillings
son: Samuel Gattis 5 shillings
"To my daughter Jinnet Morrow or William Morrow" 5 shillings
""  "  "       Sarah King or Nathaniel King"    5 "
sons: William Gattis and Isaac Gattis 5 shillings each

Executors: sons Thomas and Alexander Gattis.
Witnesses: Geo. Johnston, Mary Johnston, Joseph Kirkland.

- - -

D 271  Will dated 17 May 1810, proved November Court 1810.

WILLIAM (x) SCOTT                 wife: Mary Scott

sons:"John and William Mitchell Scott", Alexander and Thomas
daus: Jennet, Faney, Elizabeth, Mary

Executors: James Hutcheson, James Mc adam.
Witness: Samuel Crawford.

- - -

D 272  Will dated 20 August 1810, proved November Court 1810.

ABNER TAPP                        wife: Frances

He says "my fore children ... to raise my children.."

son: Richard Tapp
four daughters: Elizabeth, Susannah, Elethe

No  executor named, no witnesses.

- - -

D 276  Will dated 28 August 1810, proved November Court 1810.

SAMUEL BENTON    All estate goes to "John Taylor the younger
                 my son-in-law of Hillsboro."
Executors: son-in-law John Taylor, friend Duncan Cameron.
Witnesses: Richard Henderson, Ed. Jones.

- - -

D 277  Will dated 4 December 1810, proved Feb Court 1811.

WILSON CHILD                    mother: Frances Child
of the town of Hillsborough

brother: Francis Child

"John Bruce, Charles Bruce & William Bruce sons of my brother-in-law Abner Bruce."

Executors: friends Archibald D. Murphey and John Taylor, Jr.
Witnesses: Henry Shutt, And. Brooks.
— — —

D 278  Will dated 9 March 1798, proved February Court 1811.

JOHN (x) COOK                   wife: Sarah Cook

son: Archibald Cook  "plantation whereon he now lives"
"      David Cook      ""          "         "  "  "  "
"      Robert Cook
"All my children", number not stated.

Executors: son David Cook, and friend Hardy Hurdle.
Witnesses: Hardy Hurdle, H'm (?) Corgin.
— — —

D 280  Will dated 3 March 1810, proved February Court 1811.

LUDWICK ALBRIGHT

dau: Caty Holt wife of Jeremiah Holt
"     Barbara Powel wife of Elias Powel

sons: John, Philip, Jacob, Ludwick, George & Daniel $10 each

"All my children tp wit: John, Barbara, Philip, Jacob, Ludwick, Caty, George and Daniel."

Executors: sons Ludwick and Daniel Albright.
Witnesses: Michael Holt, Rachel Holt.
— — —

D 282  Will dated 7 November 1810, proved Feb Court 1811.

CHARLES KING                   wife: Elizabeth

oldest son: Shurley gets land which was surveyed by Nathaniel
                        and William King.
youngest son: Charles under age.

dau: Biddy
"son-in-law Charles Shaw and his wife Betsey" 10 shillings
grandchildren: William Franklin Shaw and Louisa Shaw

"To my bound servant John Cole ..."          — continued —

Executors: Richard Blackwood, son Shurley King and wife Eliz.
Witnesses: Edwd. Robson, Wm. King.

— — —

D 286   Will dated 17 April 1811, proved May Court 1811. This will
        is not in the State Archives.

BENJAMIN RAINEY                        wife: Nancy

Michael Holt and Neil Bhon ? have bought land from testator.

daus: Nancy, Sally, Milly
son: John   land in Tennessee on Turnbull Creek, 500 acres

"Sons and sons-in-law (to wit) John King, Isaac Rainey, Benjamin Abel Rainey and William Holt" land in Orange County, N.C.
joining Guilford County line, Anthony Coble, etc.

grandson: Austin
He leaves his surveying instruments to his son Isaac.

Executors: son Benjamin Able Rainey and son-in-law Wm. Holt.
Witnesses: John Gant, Mason Tapley.
This will is also recorded on pages 295-299 in Book D.

— — —

D 289   Will dated 24 February 1807, proved Nov Court 1808.

LEWIS KIRK               wife: Sarah

son: John Kirk

"My four eldest children viz William  James  Rebecca and
Josiah."

Executors: friends Richard Stanford and Thomas Snipes.
Witnesses: Jon. Umstead, H. Forest, David Roach.

— — —

D 291   Deed from JAMES A. MORGAN to William Kirkland.
        Witnesses: William Barbee, Edward ...?...
        Dated 22 May 1809, proved November 1809.

— — —

D 292   Will dated 4 October 1799, proved May Court 1803.

JAMES ELLIOTT   (no relationships stated except to wife)

wife: her name  not stated, William Elliott is to care for her.

"To William Elliott all my lands on franchbord(French Broad ?)
on James River on Haw River on Canocogiy ? Creek in Pennsylvania". (Seem to be four tracts in N.C. and another in Pa.)

- continued -

D 292 continued

Two shillings each to: John Murray, William Carter, James ..ad,
Thomas Blak, William Pasmore.

Executor: William Elliott
Witnesses: John Murray, David Pasmore.

— — —

D 293   Will dated 16 September 1802, proved Feb Court 1804.

WILLIAM RHODES                wife: Mary Rhodes

son: Benjamin Baker Rhodes
"     John Rhodes (he has already received his part)
"     William Rhodes

These eight daughters have already received their parts:
Hannah Wotle (Whatley ?), Nanny Grism, Elizabeth Grisum,
Molly Pattishall, Michel Horn, Amelia Herndon, Rebecca Herndon,
Franky Barbee.

Executors: Chesley Page Patterson, John Rhodes,
           Benjamin Rhodes' son John, Benj. Baker Rhodes.
Witnesses: James Wilson, William Herndon, Henry (x) Trice,
           James Hutchins.

— — —

D 295-299 BENJAMIN RAINEY will. See D 286.

— — —

D 300   Power of Attorney from THOMAS HOUSE or HORNE "formerly
        of Orange County, N.C. but now of Chester District in the
        State of South Carolina" to William Holt. He revokes let-
        ters of Administration granted to John Strowd on the es-
        tate of his deceased son LILLTLEBURY HORNE ? who died in
        North Carolina.  Dated 21 June 1811. Witness: B.A.Rainey.

— — —

D 301   Will dated 31 May 1808, proved November Court 1808.

W. A. FRESHWATER            wife: Sally "to raise my children"

"My children to wit: Thadeus Freshwater, Chloe, Polley, Betsey,
Luraney David Sally and Susanna Freshwater."

Executors: wife, and Hardy Hurdle.
Witnesses: Hardy Hurdle, Benj. Simpson.

— — —

D 303   Agreement between WILLIAM MINOR (now of age) and his for-
mer guardian JOHN STROWD (who was his guardian by the Chatham
County, N.C. Court ..;  Witnesses: Bryant Strowd, Henry Strowd.
Dated 14 January 1807, proved November Court 1807.

— — —

D 304   Will dated 26 March 1806, proved May Court 1806.

RICHARD CATE                    wife: Elizabeth

son: Abner Cate "land where he is settled"
sons: John Cate; Ephriam Cate
daus: Mary Hunt, Nancy Dossett

"My five children - Mary Hunt, Nancy Dossett, John, Ephriam
and Abner Cate."

Executors: sons Ephriam and Abner.
Witnesses: James Latta, Shardick (x) Channeller.

— — —

D 306   Will dated 19 July 1810, proved August Court 1810.

JOHN (x) CRESWELL            son: John Creswell

daus: Margaret Morrow, Easter Creswell
sons: William Creswell, Alexander Creswell

Executors: "trusty friends John Ray and Robert Faucett."
Witnesses: Thomas Vincent, Thomas Barnwell.

Codicil dated 30 July 1830 gives daughter Easter loom, etc.
Witnesses: John (x) Noble, John Creswell.

— — —

D 308   Power of Attorney from GEORGE RAY of Tennessee to
JAMES MILLER of Orange County, N.C. Dated 11 May 1808, proved
May 1808.   Witnesses: Sampson Moore, John Hart.

— — —

D 309-311   Will dated 18 July 1801, proved May Court 1811.

JAMES FAUCETTE              wife: Susannah

dau: Rachel Faucett
  "     Margaret Woods wife of Nathan Woods
  "     Mary Watham wife of Charles Wortham (spelled both ways)
  "     Lucy Smith wife of William Smith

He has unmarried daughters, names and number not stated.

Executors and friends to care for property: "well beloved
            friends Robert Faucett, Mathew Woods, Charles
            Watham and James Latta."
Witnesses: A. Tatom, George Anderson, Dun. Cameron.

— — —

D 312   Will dated 22 April 1811, proved May Court 1811.

HENRY SHUTT of the town of Hillsborough   wife: Elizabeth

"My children" all under age, names and number not stated.

Executors: wife Elizabeth, and Thomas Ruffin.
Witnesses: J. Webb, J. Taylor.

— — —

D 314  Will dated --- 1811, proved May Court 1811.

SAMUEL ECTOR                    wife: name not stated

sons: Joseph, James, William
son: Hugh "land where John Dunnivan now lives"
daus: Margaret, Keziah                son: Thomas

Executors: wife, and son Joseph
Witnesses: David Bradford,Sr., John Hughes.

- - -

D 316  Will dated 18 December 1810, proved May Court 1811.

SOLOMON BOOTH                    mother: Priscilla Booth

brother: Alfred Booth        "my brothers"

Executor: brother Tapley Booth
Witnesses: John Moore, Sampson Moore, Betsey (x) Booth.

- - -

D 317  Power of Attornet from JONATHAN LINDLEY to "trusty friend
JOHN NEWLIN.  Witnesses: Thos. Whitted, Jon. Thomson.
Dated 1 May 1811, proved May Court 1811.

- - -

D 317A   Power of Attorney from JAMES RAY to friend JAMES WILLI-
AMS, both of Orange County, to sell land on a branch of Little
River in Orange County conveyed from Rebecca McClennin to James
Ray, and a tract conveyed by William Lindley to James Ray on the
waters of Eno.  Money is due James Ray from the estate of
Michael Robinson, dec'd, who "removed before his decease to the
State of Tennessee."  Dated 17 November 1810, proved Aug 1811.
Witnesses: John Street, Justice Peace
              David Ray, W. Cain.
                            signed:"James Ray of John."

- - -

D 318  Power of Attorney from WILLIAM KIRKLAND to GEORGE
McNEILL and THOMAS RUFFIN, all of Orange County, N.C., to sell
any of his property not devised by will to his wife Margaret
Kirkland and his sons John Umstead and Alexander McKinzie.
Dated 1 August 1811, proved August Court 1811.
Witness: Wm. Norwood.

- - -

D 320  Will dated 3 November 1792, proved August Court 1811.

JOHN (x) HODGE                wife: Agness Hodge
"in low state of health"

son: Robert

"Two grandsons William & Joseph's sons John" each £ 10, when
they come of age.
                        - continued -

sons: George, Samuel

Executors: wife Agness, and son Robert
Witnesses: Wm. Hodge, Jno. Herman.

− − −

D 322  Will dated 1 September 1811, proved Feb Court 1812.

CHARLES CHRISTMAS

All his estate is left in trust for the children named below,
no relationship stated.   He mentions a note he holds from his
brother Nath. Christmas of the Mississippi Territory.

Estate left for the "raising of six children of Sarah Smith's
(viz) John, Charles, Nancy, Patheny, William & Susannah & the
raising and schooling of a child of Nancy Willocks (viz) Rebeckah."

Executors: Richard Christmas, Thomas Brewer, William Moore.
Witnesses: Wm. Moore, Joel Parish.

− − −

D 324  Will dated 20 December 1811, proved Feb Court 1812.

MATHAIS WILSON        sister: Rachel Wilson plantation, etc.

friend: George Brown

"To William Wilson son of my brother Edward Wilson $20 to
help with his schooling".

Executors: sister Rachel and brother William Wilson.
Witnesses: Thomas Gill, David Mebane.

− − −

D 326  Will dated 31 December 1811, proved Feb Court 1812.

JAMES CRAWFORD            wife: Margaret

sons: William, Samuel      he says "all my sons"
"Girls that is at home" names and number not stated.
dau: Hannah

Executors: son John Crawford and James Crawford.
Witnesses: Thos. Whitted, Jno. Thompson, James Morrow.

− − −

D 327  Will dated −−−, proved February Court 1812.

DANIEL CLOUD            wife: Nancy

sons: Joel, "to Daniel and David the tract of land on New
      Hope and mill I bought of John Mitchel"

daus: Martha, Margaret                    − continued −

son: John                          No executor named.

**Witnesses:** Wm. Palmer, John Comb, Jesse ..?..

— — —

D 328   Will dated 16 December 1811, proved Feb Court 1812.

ANDREW BROOKS                  mother a legatee, name not stated

sisters: Hannah, Sally Terrill

To Nelly Bryant all household furniture and bedding.
"Children of my brother William Brook and Joseph Terrill".
"Nephew James Brooks son of my sister Hannah."

No executor named. Will is not signed or witnessed.

— — —

D 331   Will dated 24 February 1809, proved Feb Court 1812.

JOHN (x) SHADDY            wife: Elizabeth
He owns a mill.

"All my children"
Molly wife of John Coble
Caty   "     "   George A. Fogleman
John Shaddy
Rachel wife of George Fogleman
Jacob Shaddy
"youngest daughter and wife of Henry Steel"

Executors: "friend Michael Holt and my son Jacob Shaddy".
Witness:   Frederic Kinney

— — —

D 333   Will dated 11 March 1812, proved May Court 1812.

JAMES TAYLOR                sister: Ann Taylor

father: John Taylor        Executor: Thomas Taylor.
Witnesses: John Anderson, Daniel Wilkerson, John Wilkerson.

— — —

D 334   Will dated 25 May 1801, proved May Court 1812.

WILLIAM (x) CRABTREE        granddaughter: Amelia

sons: Samuel, Abraham, James

Executor: son Samuel.
Witnesses: Samuel Thompson, Thos. Barton Jun'r,
           Chas. Hughes.

— — —

D 335    Will dated 30 March 1812, proved May Court 1812.
JAMES THOMPSON                    wife: Elizabeth

"All my children", number not stated.
sons: Levi (gets family Bible), John Thompson
dau: Sarah Woody

Executors: "beloved friends John Woody and Samuel Woody sons
           of James Woody."
Witnesses: John Whitted, Joshua Woody.

- - -

D 336  Will dated 17 March 1810, proved May Court 1812.

JOHN WALKER                       (no wife mentioned)

son: Peter Walker  100 acres on Duck River in Tennessee
dau: Mary Picket
Walter Picket
grandsons: John and James Walker, sons of William.
son: Andrew "remainder of my land on Duck River in Tennessee"
            and "plantation on which he lives".
grandsons: Peter and John, sons of Andrew Walker.
dau: Matty McCauley

Executors: sons Peter and William Walker.
Witnesses: James Mebane, John Wilson, James Murray.

- - -

D 338  Will dated 18 May 1811, proved May Court 1812.

BENJAMIN YEARGIN

wife: Sarah Yeargin "500 acres in Wilkes County on Cub Creek,
                    on S.Side of Yadkin River, and near the Court
                    House, Wilkesborough."
"Three of my children, Mark M. Yeargin, Harriett Forsythe,
Bartlett Yeargin."
dau: Charlotte H. Young
son: Mark M. Yeargin 700 acres in Wilkes on Mulberry Creek.

Executors: wife Sarah, James Forsythe and Bartlett Yeargin.
Witness: David Strain.

- - -

D 339  Will dated 10 May 1812, proved May Court 1812.

HENRY (x) HASTINGS       (heirs given in the order they are given
                         in the will.)
dau: Mary Hastings
grandson: John Young
dau: Margaret Adams
grandson: Thomas Crabtree
daus: Isbell Collins, Elizabeth Watson, Ester Thompson
sons: James, Joseph, John, William and Henry Hastings.

Executor: son James Hastings
Witnesses: Andrew Watson, Arch. Crabtree.

- - -

D 342  Will dated 27 September 1810, proved --

MICHAEL SHOFNER

youngest son: Peter Shofner, "his four brothers"
son: Michael Shofner
dau: Magdalane

Executors: "sons-in-law Jacob Antony, Mathea (?) Fogleman."
Witness:  Henry Cook, Jr.

- - -

D 344  Will dated 23 June 1812, proved --

ISHAM (x) THRIFT

wife: Mary gets land in Orange County "deeded from Wm. Strowd,
      deceased", and land in Chatham Co., N.C. "deeded
      from Jesse Buckner on the N.Side of Haw River on
      Wilkerson Creek."

"All my children, namely, Elizabeth Snipes, Susannah Booker,
Perry Thrift, Sally Thrift, Delila Petty, Peggy Thrift, Wil-
liam Thrift, David Thrift, Drury Thrift, Isham Thrift, Polly
Thrift, Frances Thrift, Nancy Thrift and Levicy Thrift." (14)

Executors: wife Mary Thrift and son David Thrift.
Witnesses: Bryant Strowd, P. Willis, Henry (x) Andrus.

- - -

D 346  Will dated 9 July 1812, proved --

PHILIP (x) EULICE          wife: Elizabeth

sons: Henry Eulice, John Eulice, Actum (?) Eulice.

daus: Margaret Kimbro, Mary Linn, Molly Huffman, Eve Ross ?,
      Susanna Kimbro, Elizabeth Jones, Barbara Tracy.

"Children of my daughter Catherine Lineberry ... her daughter Eleanor Jones, ... Sophia Coble, George Lineberry and
William Lineberry."

Executors: sons Henry and John Eulice.
Witnesses: Jonathan Hadley, John Arwick, Andrew (x) Shatterly.

- - -

D 347  Will dated 13 May 1812, proved --

EDWARD WILSON          wife: Rachel

daus: Polly (unmarried), Nancy, Rachel
sons: William, Edward, Hugh
grandson: "my son Edward's son William"

Executors: daughter Polly and son William.
Witnesses: David Mebane, B. Burnsides.

- - -

D 351  Will dated 15 February 1812, proved --

JOHN PICKARD                    wife: Peggy

dau: Sally (unmarried), her brother Alex is named as guardian.

"My three youngest sons, viz, Daniel, Jesse and Thomas."

.."rest of my sons and daughters, to wit, my sons Henry
James John Alex'r Isaac Richard Elisha Michael and my
daughters Rebecca Steel  Fanny Crutchfield and Catherine
Efland." (No punctuation.)

Executors: son Alex'r Pickard and grandson John H. Pickard.
Witnesses: Thomas Lasley, John Grimes.

- - -

D 352-358  Will dated 3 January 1812, proved --

GAVIN ALVES                    cousin: Jane Burgess

aunts: Elizabeth Hogg, Jean Hogg

He sets free his slaves John and Esther. A negro boy, son of
Esther, is to be bound out to learn a trade until he reaches
21 years of age, when he is to be emancipated. Legacies to
each of these slaves.

brother: Walter Alves
sisters: Mrs. Hellen Caldwell, Mrs. Robina Norwood
sister-in-law: Mrs. Amelia Alves
neices: Ann Alves Webb, Mrs. Anne Henderson, Elizabeth Alves,
        Elizabeth Norwood.
nephews: John Huske, William, James and Thomas Hooper,
        James Alves, William Alves.
friends: the Rev. Joseph Caldwell,  Dr. James Webb,
        Richard Henderson, Esq., Wm. Norwood, Esq.
        Catlett Campbell, Esq.

Executors: brother Walter Alves and friend Dr. James Webb.
Witnesses: James Child, A.B.Bruce.

- - - -

D 359-362  Will dated 29 January 1812, proved --

JOHN ALLEN                     wife: Jennett

daus: Peggy, Sally, Jane ("Jenny"), all unmarried
sons: Abraham, George, Samuel
daus: Elizabeth, Nancy
grandson: John Allen

Executors: son Samuel, and Alexander Russell.
Witnesses: Ezekiel B. Currie, Alexander Russell,
        John C. Russell.

- - -

D 362  Will dated 4 November 1812, proved --

JOHN WILSON                 wife: Nancy

"My children",names and number not stated

Executors: "trusty friends James Walker and Herbert Sims."
Witnesses: James Webb, Thos. Latta.

- - -

D 364  Will dated 23 October 1812, proved --

PETER (x) SMITH

mother: Hannah Smith to have all his estate during her life

"my four sisters namely Nancy, Susanna, Barbary and Polly
Smith" to divide estate after mother's death.

Executors: "trusty friends John Hilton and John Cook."
Witness: Henry Cook,Jr.

- - -

D 365  Will dated 13 August 1812, proved --

JACOB RILEY, SR.

son: Jacob Riley        plantation, money, furniture, etc,
dau: Susanna Riley      divided between these two children.

sons: Peter Riley, John Riley, 1 shilling each
dau: Caty Findly wife of Jacob Findly   1 shilling
"    Mary Gray    "    "  James Gray    1 "

Executors: sons Peter and Jacob Riley.
Witness: James Webb.

- - -

D 366  Will dated 10 February 1813, proved --

WILLIAM RAY             wife: Nancy Ray

son: James Ray
dau: Elizabeth Ray.          No executor named

Witnesses: Elizabeth (x) Allison, Moses Gwinn.

- - -

D 367  Will dated 9 January 1813, proved --

JOHN (x) McCRARY or McCRORY

sons: Robert and John  land on Boyd's Creek
"     Andrew McCrory; David McCrory
daus: Agness Fossett, Jane Scarborough

Witnesses: Samuel Crawford, James Murray. No executor named.

- - -

54

D 368  Will dated ?              proved --

WILLIAM HORN        Wife: Agnes, all estate during her life.

"Unmarried children viz- John Tapley William Wesley Thomas
Anderson & Nancy Ann Horn." (No punctuation, see below.)

Married children: Abel Horn, Sarah Griffin, Edith Younger.

three sons John Tapley  William Wesley & Thomas Anderson
Horn to receive plantation after wife's death.

Executors: wife, and John Tapley Horn.
Witnesses: G. Campbell, Peter Walker.

- - -

D 369  Will dated 17 December 1811, proved --

THOMAS CATE                 wife: Martha Cate

sons: Thomas Cate and John S. Cate, both under age
dau: Doratha Cate, under age
daus: Polly Cate, Martha Cate
sons: Isaih Cate, Thomas Cate

Executors: wife Martha, and "well beloved friend John Sykes."
Witness: Susannah (x) Durham.

- - -

D 371  Power of Attorney from JOHN C. McLEMORE of town of
Nashville, County of Davidson, State of Tennessee, to HUGH
MULHOLLAN of Orange Co., N.C., to make a deed to John Crutchfield for land on waters of Cane Creek joining Thomas Kirk and
others, being the same land conveyed by William Kirkland ..."
Dated 28 December 1812, recorded in Davidson Co., Tenn.,
4 January 1813, in Orange County, N.C. --

- - -

D 373  Will dated 9 March 1812, proved --

DAVID HERNDON

dau: Frances
son: Larkin
daus: Clary, Martha
sons: Edmond, George
daus: Nancy, Rachel, Elizabeth, Rebecca
son: Martin Pearce

Executors: sons Edmond and George Herndon.
Witnesses: Jno. Landers, Elisha Rowark.
Note by Ruth Herndon Shields: Descendants of David Herndon
are given in PART FOUR, HERNDONS OF THE AMERICAN REVOLUTION,
by John Goodwin Herndon. See last pages of this book.)

- - -

55

D 374  Power of Attorney from JOHN (x) GEE planter of Rollins
Fork of Salt River in Casey County, Kentucky, to HANSON COUL-
TER of Orange Co., N.C., to collect a legacy from the estate
of Thomas Odian (?) of Chatham Co., N.C.
Dated 9 April 1812, proved August Court 1812.
Witness: John Pendergrass.

- - -

D 375  Power of Attorney from JACOB ALBRIGHT of Madison County
Georgia, to THOMAS POWELL of Orange Co., N.C., to collect from
the executors of "my father LUDOWICK ALBRIGHT'S estate" ....
Dated 27 April 1812, proved August Court 1812.
Witnesses: Jas. Patterson, Thomas Kirk.

- - -

D 375  Power of Attorney from MARK M. YEARGIN of Orange County,
N.C. to his brother BARTLETT YEARGIN, to sell land in Wilkes
County, N.C.  Dated 13 September 1812, proved Nov Court 1812.
Witness: James Forsythe.

- - -

D 376  SARAH YOUNGER administratrix of HENRY YOUNGER dec'd,
"died on 2nd day of December 1812", gives her account of the
slaves belonging to the estate, among Robert A. Younger the
oldest son, John Younger the second child, and Richard Younger
"the third and last child". Sarah is guardian to John and
Richard.  Dated 27 May 1813, proved May Court 1813.

- - -

D 377  Will dated 16 May 1813, proved May Court 1813.

HENRY O'DANIEL

Three brothers, Samuel, John and Joshua O'Daniel.
Four sisters, Susannah Pickard, Jane McDaniel,
                Sally Hastings and Peggy Pickard.

Executors: James O'Daniel and Thomas Hastings.
Witnesses: Arch'd Holmes, John Grimes.

- - -

D 379  Will dated 24 July 1797, proved August Court 1813.

WILLIAM (x) RANY                  wife: Mary

son: David Rany
grandsons: William Baker (under age),
                Wm. Rany Gwin (under age), William Rany

John Baker (no relationship stated)
brother: David Rany

Executors: wife Mary, and son David Rany.
Witnesses: Wm. Thrailkill, John Gil, Robert Duncan.

- - -

D 380   Deed of Gift from THOMAS HOLLOWAY of Orange County, N.C.
to his son WILLIAM HOLLOWAY for a mare.
Dated 26 August 1813, proved August Court 1813.
Witnesses: Reuben Farthing, Thomas Holloway, Sr.

— — —

D 380   Will dated 15 June 1812, proved August Court 1813.

JOHN TAYLOR

son: Joseph Taylor            daughter: Ann Taylor
"All my sons and daughters", names and number not stated.

Sole executor: Thomas Taylor.
Witnesses: Thomas Clarke, James McCord.

— — —

D 381   Will dated 14 July 1813, proved August Court 1813.

JAMES (x) WATSON, SR.                wife: Margaret

sister-in-law: Elleanor Witted (?)

"My eight children-to wit- Helen Riley, James Watson,
Rebecca Watson, Elizabeth Comb, Andrew Watson, Nancy Watson,
John Watson and Robert Watson."

grandchildren: "Three children of Helen Riley -viz- Washing-
               ton Riley, Elizabeth Riley and Rachel Riley."

Executors: wife Margaret, and son-in-law John Combs.
Witnesses: Abner Bailiff, John Dockery.

— — —

D 383   Will dated 16 January 1813, proved August Court 1813.

JOSEPH MOORE              brother: John Moore

sister: Mary Ferguson plantation, slaves, etc, and after
        her death it goes to his brother John Moore.

Executors: John Moore, Sampson Moore, and sister Mary Ferguson.
Witnesses: John Allison, James Allison.

— — —

D 384   Will dated 2 June 1810, proved August Court 1813.

SACKFIELD or ZACKFIELD BREWER        son: Thomas Brewer

granddaughter: Patsey Lindsey

great-grandchildren: "Two oldest children of my granddaughter
                     Sarah Edwards" names not stated.
son: Ezekiel Brewer
- continued -

D 384 continued
grandsons: Sackfield and Henry Brewer, sons of Ezekiel
granddaus: Patsey and Polly Brewer, daughters of Ezekiel

dau: Elizabeth  land on West side of Cane Creek joining Wm./
                                                        Hopson
granddaus: Mary Meachum, Sarah Edwards, Patsey Lindsey

"Great-grandson Peter Brewer son of my grandson Peter Brewer".

"My four surviving children Ezekiel and Thomas Brewer,
Elizabeth Brewer and Rebecca Thompson."

Executors: sons Ezekiel and Sackfield Brewer.
Witnesses: A. Stanford, William Moore.
- - -

D 387  Will dated 14 September 1818, proved August Court 1813.

STERLING HARRIS

wife: Hannah "tract whereon I now live", slaves, lot in
               Hillsborough, etc.

dau: Charlotte Street wife of John Street of Hillsborough

Executors: wife Hannah, and "trusty friends Levi Whitted,
           James Phillips and William Kirkland."
Witnesses: John Young, J. Taylor, Theopilus Thompson.
- - -

D 389  Power of Attorney from PATSEY (x) RHODES to her
father ACQUILLA RHODES to collect money due her from William
Barbee.  Dated 15 May 1813, proved November Court 1813.
Witnesses: Mann Patterson, David (x) Hinchey.
- - -

D 390  Will dated 29 September 1813, proved Nov Court 1813.

ROBERT (x) MILLIKEN              wife: Jane  gets land and mill

sons: John, Charles, Jesse; Robert and William get planta-
      tation after wife's death ; Haberson.

Executors: wife Jane, and sons Robert and William.
Witnesses: Joel Strong, Wm. Moore.
- - -

D 392  Will dated 19 July 1809, proved November Court 1813.

JOHN LINCH, SR.

sons: Jackson Linch and Cleaton Linch get plantation

daus: Rachel Linch, Gillee Linch
                                    - continued -

58          D 392 continued
sons: Darling Linch, John Linch
daus: Sarah Jenkins, Olive Horner

Executors: James Latta and son Jackson Linch.
Witnesses: Henry Bunch, Rachel (x) Linch, Gillee (x) Linch.
— — —

D 393  Will dated 29 June 1808, proved November Court 1813.

JOHN WOODS                 wife: Ann Woods

son: David Woods

"All my children- viz- William woods, John Woods, Samuel
Woods and Thomas Woods except Joseph Woods alias Joseph Baldridge."

Executors: sons Samuel and David Woods.
Witnesses: Jas. H. Bowman, John Hanks.
— — —

D 395  Will dated 7 October 1809, proved Nov Court 1813.

JACOB HUGGINS          wife: Mary one-half of estate

son: Jacob Huggins other half of estate

Executors: "worthy friends John Campbell and Aaron Walker."
Witnesses: Jno. Campbell, Jas. Campbell, Joseph Hodge.
— — —

D 396  Will dated 4 August 1813, proved November Court 1813.

GEORGE CLANCY, SR. of the Town of Hillsborough, N.C.

wife: Rebecca
daus: Jenny Clancy, Polly Clancy & Sally Clancy, all under age.
son-in-law: William Palmer
sons: Jack Clancy and William Clancy to be sent to school, and
          then to be bound to trades.

Executors: wife Rebecca, and son Thomas Clancy.
Witness: A. B. Bruce.
— — —

D 398  Will dated 10 December 1813, proved Feb Court 1814.

JOHN WILKERSON              wife: Rebecca

daughter Rebecca, under age, to be educated

Executors: "trusty friends James Lapslie and Daniel Wilkerson."
Witnesses: Moses Guin, Thomas Wilson, Jas. D. Hughes.
— — —

D 399  Will dated 8 February 1814, proved Feb Court 1814.

ELIZABETH (x) MURDOCK widow of James Murdock.

dau: Ann Murdock      grandson: David Murdock, son of Ann

oldest daughter: Caty Murdock  5 shillings
dau: Mary Buchannon 5 shillings
sons: James and William Murdock  5 shillings each
grandchildren: John Murdock and Mary Murdock, ch. of James.
grandson: Robert, son of John Murdock deceased
granddau: Elizabeth Riggs, dau. of John Murdock deceased
"        Elizabeth Murdock, dau. of James Murdock

Executrix: daughter Ann Murdock.
Witnesses: Thos. B. Patterson, Wm. Bowls.

- - -

D 401-404  Will dated 9th day 9th month 1813, proved Feb. 1814

JAMES NEWLIN "farmer"              wife: Deborah

son: John
"     Thomas "land on which I now live on the N. Side of
            Cane Creek" .. approximately 350 acres
"     Nathaniel "my place over the creek ... 200 acres ...
            known by the name of Wait's place."
"     William  "plantation known by name of Waugh's place.."
"     Jonathan "tract of land I lately purchased of Robert
            Green .. also my lot in Haywood."
daus: Deborah, Sarah, Mary, Ruth, Hannah

Executors: sons John and Thomas, and brother Nathaniel.
Witnesses: Jeremiah Hubbard, Margaret Hubbard.

- - -

D 4-4 Power of Attorney  from SAMUEL TURRENTINE of the town
of Hillsborough to JOHN TAYLOR and THOMAS CLANCY,ESQ.
Dated 27 Jan 1814, proved Feb 1814.  Witness: Wm. Norwood.

- - -

D 406  Deed from JOSEPH COLLINS to ENOCH COLLINS for a mare.
Dated 1 April 1814, proved May Court 1814.
Witnesses: Edward McDade, Thomas Ray, Ashby Dunnagan.

- - -

D 407  Will dated 21 March 1814, proved May Court 1814.

DAVID H. NUNN          mother: Elizabeth Nunn

brothers: Ilai Nunn; Hugh Nunn
sisters: Sally Nunn, Edith (Nunn) Thompson

Executors: brother-in-law Richard Thompson, and Thomas
            Clancy of Hillsborough.
Witnesses: I or J Witherspoon, F. Burnett.

- - -

60

D 408  Will dated 16 April 1812, proved August Court 1814.

ROBERT BERRY                    wife: Elizabeth

dau: Elizabeth Berry and her daughter Mary

sons: Robert Berry, Joshua Berry, Thomas Berry
      Isaac Berry (not of sound mind, Henry   care for him)
      Henry Berry, David Berry, William Berry
"daughter Mary Kemp deceased's heirs one pound"
"son John Berry deceased's heirs one negro girl."

Executors: wife, and son Henry Berry.
Witnesses: J. Rountree, Wm. R. Robinson.

— — —

D 410  Will dated 23 March 1807, proved August Court 1814.

JAMES WILKINSON                 wife: Caty Wilkinson

son: William Wilkinson plantation, etc
dau: Mary Wilkinson "bed & furniture, mare & colt, etc"
daus: An Wilkinson and Susannah Ray  5 shillings each
sons: John Wilkinson, James Wilkinson  5 shillings each

Executors: "my wife Caty Wilkinson and my son Joseph Ray."
Witnesses: John Ray, James Clarke.

— — —

D 411  Will dated 14 July 1814, proved November Court 1814.

PAUL (x) MORGAN    "very sick"

All estate to Isaac Jackson Senior. He is named executor.

Witnesses: Benoni Jackson, Hezekia s (x) Revel.

— — —

D 412  Will dated 21 October 1814, proved Nov Court 1814.

JOHN SAUNDERS          All estate to mother, Lydia Saunders.

If anything is left after his mother's death it is to be divided between Patsy Proctor and Nancy Saunders.

Trustee and executor: William Henry Merritt.
Witnesses: Wm. Merritt, Thomas Merritt,

— — —

D 412  Will dated 17 September 1814, proved Nov Court 1814.

ISAAC JACKSON, JUNIOR  farmer

No relationship stated to any of the legatees.
"To James Jackson, to Benoni Jackson " ...    - continued-

61          D 412 continued
"to Elizabeth Randles and Mary Thompson" ...
"to Elizabeth McCain" ..
"to Isaac Jackson, .. to James Jackson"
"and Hetty Williams owes 3 dollard in which I allow to be
  buried."

Executor: J. Jackson.
Witnesses: Benoni Jackson, Mary (x) Jackson.

- - -

D 413  Deed from WILLIAM FAUCETTE to RALPH FAUCETTE for a
negro girl and child.          Witness: Philip Walker.
Dated 28 November 1814, proved November Court 1814.

- - -

D 414  Will dated 6 September 1814, proved Nov Court 1814.

GEORGE RAY          wife, name not stated , is pregnant ?

son: Michael Ray
daus: Jenny, Polly, Sally, Delilah, Matheran (Martha Ann ?)
"If my wife should have a male child ..."

Executors: "friend John Ray and Rankin McKee."
Witnesses: James Miller, R.R.Reade, Martin Murphey.

- - -

D 416  Will dated 26 August 1808, proved November 1814.

WILLIAM ARMSTRONG                    wife: Nancy

"My five children"
eldest son: Joseph Armstrong
daus: Isabella Armstrong, Marget Armstrong
sons: William Armstrong, James Armstrong

grandsons: Jesse Armstrong, James Watson Armstrong

Executors: sons Joseph and William Armstrong.
Witnesses: J. Rountree, Charles Rountree Jun'r.

- - -

D 418-420  Will dated 20 September 1814, proved Nov 1814.

SARAH HARDEN

son: John Harden "he having been provided for in the will
                of his father"
dau: Mary Prather tract of 150 acres called Powell's Place
"my three youngest daughters Sarah, Betsey and Peggy"
Peggy gets "tract whereon I now live, .. also the Rainey
      tract", etc.

Executors: "my good worthy friends Archibald D. Murphey,
            John L. Prather, and John Harden."
Witnesses: Thos. Scott, Rebekah Harden.

- - -

D 421-423  Will dated 24 November 1814, proved Feb Court 1815.

WILLIAM HOBBS, SENIOR                    wife: Easther

son: James Hobbs $1, he has had his share
daus: Mary Cheek, Elizabeth Chambers $1 each
sons: Thomas Hobbs, William Hobbs  $1 each
son-in-law: Thomas Durham $1
sons: Jonathan, David, John, Harbard Hobbs
dau: Susannah Hobbs

Executors: wife Easther Hobbs, and trusty friend Thomas Latta.
Witnesses: Andrew Watson, Joseph (x) Weeks.

— — —

D 423  Deed of Gift from JOHN L. KIRK to his son JOHN L.F.
KIRK for a negro girl.  Dated 20 Nov 1812, proved Feb 1815.
Witness: Sarah Kirk.

— — —

D 423  Receipt from SARAH KIRK. "Received of THOMAS GRIFFIN
Ⴑ 200 for a negro woman.  Dated 4 Jan 1810, proved Feb 1815.
Witnesses: John L. Kirk, James Minnis. "

— — —

D 424  Power of Attorney from GEORGE CHARLES of Russell Co.,
Va. to JOSEPH GIBSON of Guilford Co., N.C.  to collect his
part of the estate of "my father Michael Charles lately deceased of Orange County." Dated 22 July 1813, proved Feb 1815.
Witnesses: Andrew Gibson, Zachariah Phillips.

— — —

D 424  Bill of Sale from JAMES MINNIS to JAMES CHAMBERS both
of Orange County, N.C.  Dated 2 March 1815, proved Feb Ct 1815.
Witnesses: Andrew Watson, Joseph Stubbins.
Secutity: Thomas (x) Griffin.

— — —

D 425  Will dated 14 July 1814, proved February Court 1815.

JOSEPH WOODY                    wife: Sarah Woody

sons: Joshua Woody, Joseph Woody, Robert Woody
"All my children", number not stated.
"Patsy Jones which was bound to me"..

Executors: sons Joshua and Joseph Woody.
Witnesses: John Whitted, Thomas Whitted, Jun'r.

— — —

D 427  Will dated 20 September 1814, proved Feb Court 1815.

HENRY EVANS                    wife: Elizabeth (she is pregnant)

son: Asa  land in Wake County, N.C.(he is under 9 years old)

D 427 continued
"Archelus M. Thompson be sent to school 18 months" .. he is
"to continue with my wife if they can agree".

Executors: "trusty friends Chesley P. Patterson, William
          Rhodes and Benjamin Rhodes."
Witnesses:John Rhodes, Thomas (x) Hutchings.

- - -

D 429  Will dated 18 April 1815, proved May Court 1815.

MARY (x) BIRD "in a low state of health"

son: John                  daughters, names not stated

Sole executor: son John
Witnesses: I or J Mebane, Alfred Compton, Jno. Umstead.

- - -

D 430  Will dated 27 February 1806, proved May Court 1815.

JAMES FULTON, "planter"

son: James gets estate
dau: Mary Rhodes wife of Thomas Rhodes  10 shillings
 "   Esther Warren  wife of James Warren 10 shillings
 "   Jane   "       "     "  William Warren  10 shillings
 "   Margaret Garrard  wife of James Garrard  10 shillings
 "   Sarah Edwards     "     "  Thomas Edwards 10"

Executor: son James.
Witnesses: Thomas Latta, Jun'r, J. Watson.

- - -

D 431  Will dated 24 July 1814, proved May Court 1815.

HENRY (x) MARTIN            wife: Sarah

sons: Robert Martin, George Martin
dau: Jane Browning wife of Edmund Browning
children: Elizabeth, Sally Wamick (Warnick ?) Rebecca  Polly
          Nancy & Peggy Martin (only one comma)

Executrix: wife, "in whom I much confide."
Witnesses: Caleb Wilson, J. Watson.

- - -

D 432-434  Will dated 30 March 1815, proved May Court 1815.

GEORGE COBLE            wife: Catherine

sons: John, David, Peter, William
daus: Elizabeth, Mary

Executors: Wife Catherine, and friend Isaac Patterson.
Witnesses: Levin Wood, M.G.Clay.

- - -

64

D 434  Will dated 8 March 1815, proved May Court 1815.

WILLIAM (x) MONTGOMERY                    wife: Eady
"weak in body"

sons: Hugh, John, Jonathan, James, David, Alexander
dau: Nancy
grandsons: "son Hugh's two sons James and Alexander"

Executors: John Latta Jun'r, and William Baldwin.
Witnesses: Hugh Montgomery, William (x) Woods.

- - -

D 436-438  Will dated 23 September 1814, proved May Court 1815.

WILLIS (x) ROBERTS                    wife: Sarah Roberts

stepchildren: Rebecca Harris, Ephriam Harris, Elzy Harris

"My own six children" to "be schooled".
daus: Menday Roberts, Loviney Roberts
sons: James Roberts,  Jesse Roberts
daus: Sarah Roberts,  Polly Roberts

Executors: Thomas Latta Sr., and Samuel Turrentine.
Witnesses: Joseph Armstrong, Peggy Armstrong, Eliz. (x) Trimble.

- - -

D 438  Will dated 18 April 1815, proved August Court 1815.

THOMAS LYNCH    (This will is not in the Archives.)

brother: Jesse Lynch 300 acres joining William Paisley, James
                     Forrest and others.
brother: Moses Lynch balance of 640 acre grant, etc.

Executor: brother Moses Lynch. Witness: Thomas Reeves.

- - -

D 439  Will dated 24 September 1814, proved August Court 1814.
        his
ASEY    x  BROWN            Leonard Sears a legatee
        mark

"My mother Susannah Castlebury"
"My brothers and sisters", not named.

Executors: friends David George and Sampson Moore.
Witnesses: John Riggins, Gilly (x) Henderson.

- - -

D 440  Will dated 12 September 1814, proved August Court 1815.

JOHN ALSTON SR.

son: John 5 shillings "and all property I gave him when he
        left me"                          - continued -

sons: George, James, Phillip, Lemuel, Alfred
daus: Polly, Patsy, Sally Pickett
son: Absolom 5 shillings & property "I gave him when he left/
                                                          me"
"grandson (son of Absolom) Calvin Alston"

Executors: son Absolom Alston and William Cain Jun'r.
Witnesses: William Cain Sen'r, William Smith.

- - -

D 441  Will dated 20 July 1813, proved August Court 1815.

WILLIAM (x) BOYLE "weak in body"        wife: Ann

youngest son: John Boyle
son: James Boyle is to look after his brother John
daus: Mary Boyle, Jean Denning
grandson: Henry Boyle

Executors: son James Boyle, wife Ann.
Witnesses: John Boyle, James Boyle, Jas. Boyle.

- - -

D 443  Will dated 3 April 1815, proved August Court 1815.

JOHN BOYLE              wife: Elizabeth

son: Hugh Boyle
"My three married daughters Rachel, Lavinia and Elizabeth."
"Two married daughters Ann and Martha."

Testator has land on Obine River in West Tennessee.

Sole executrix: wife Elizabeth.
Witnesses: George Garrison, Jas. Boyle, Mary (x) Moor.

- - -

D 445  Will dated 4 July 1815, proved August Court 1815.

NATHAN (x) ROGERS "sick of body"

wife: Nancy  land on Boyd's Creek        dau: Celia Ann
son:  Idelet

Executors: wife Nancy, and "respected friend Lodwick Fear."
Witnesses: Thos. Scott, Alex Allen.

- - -

D 446  Will dated 17 February 1815, proved May Court 1815.

MARY (x) PRATT "very sick and weak"    son: George Pratt

daus: Margaret Paul, Alsa Flintum, Caty Taylor

No executor named. Witnesses: Jas. Kerr, Jno. Piper.

- - -

66

D 447 Will dated 28 June 1815, proved August Court 1815.

JOHN COBLE                          wife: Catherine

sons: Peter, Samuel
"My four children that has had some property ", George,
Catherine, Peggy, Mary.
"My three youngest children Henry & David & Milly" (Milly
is youngest of all.)
sons: David (deceased ?),
       Henry and Daniel get land on Stinking Creek

Executors: Jonathan Hadley and Adam Ingold.
Witnesses: Richard Proctor, Daniel Shofner, Eli (x) Rose.

- - -

D 449 Will dated 24 June 1811, proved August Court 1815.

HANNAH SHUGART

sons: William, Isaac and Nathan 1 shilling each
daughter: Rachel Shugart

Sole executrix: daughter Rachel.
Witnesses: Thomas Newlin, Nathaniel Newlin.

- - -

D 450 Agreement between the heirs of JOHN ALSTON. George
Alston gives up claim. Signed by: A. Alston, Patsey (x) Al-
ston, Solomon Jones, Christian Jones, Phillip Alston, L. Al-
ston, Alfred Alston, Mary K. Alston, Mathew Pickett.
Witnesses: Susannah (x) Beaver, Henry Avrett.
(This original paper is in the State Archives.)

- - -

D 451 Will dated --, proved May Court 1813.

LEVI PENNINGTON                     wife: Margaret

Executors: wife Margaret, and worthy friend Archibald
           Murphey.   No witnesses.
Proved by the oaths of John Umstead, John Stockard, and
James W. Russell.

- - -

D 451 Will dated 1 October 1815, proved Nov Court 1815.

WILLIAM WILKINSON                   wife: Ann , whole estate

Executors: wife Ann, and David Wilkinson.
Witnesses: Samuel McCracken, John Plummet.

- - -

D 452  Will dated 19 April 1811, proved Nov Court 1815.

FISHER CLENDENNIN            wife: Ann, is pregnant

oldest son: Thomas (under 21 years)
"My five sons, Thomas, Joseph, William, James & Fisher".
dau: Sarah (under 18 years)

"My apprentice William Izzel"

Executors: wife, and William Bradshaw Jun'r.

‒ ‒ ‒

D 454  Will dated 24 June 1815, proved Nov Court 1815.

GEORGE LAWS          wife: Sarah Laws

"To heirs of my deceased son William Laws, deceased son George
Laws, deceased son Thomas Laws" 10 shillings each.

"My sons now living" names and number not stated.

Executors: sons Ezekiel and Leonard Laws, Thomas Latta,
           James Walker and Sterling Harris.
Witnesses: William Dollar, Thomas Latta.

‒ ‒ ‒

D 455-457  Will dated 13 October, proved Nov Court 1815.

JOHN (x) NEALY or NEELEY             wife: Mary

dau: Sally Cates 5 shillings , her son Nealy Cates
son: Isaac Nealy 5 shillings and Ŀ 50 to be divided among
        his lawful children
dau: Nelly Turrentine 5 shillings and Ŀ100 to her lawful ch.
 "     Elizabeth Bryant 5 "          "  Ŀ100 "  "    "      "
 "     Rachel Pickle    5 "          "  Ŀ100 "  "    "      "
 "     Polly Green      5 "          "  Ŀ100 "  "    "      "
sons: John Nealy, Thomas Nealy
dau: Nancy Harris  5 shillings and Ŀ50 to her children
 "    Hannah Nealy Ŀ30 and to her son Green Nealy, etc.

Executors: friends Samuel Turrentine Sr and Benjamin Bullock
           "and my son John Nealy Jr."
Witnesses: Chas. Holman, Thos. Wilson, Joseph Woods.

‒ ‒ ‒

D 457  Will dated 30 July 1815, proved November Court 1815.

DUNCAN D. BRIGGS

half-sisters: Mary I or J Alston, Kitty Alston
brothers: Samuel Briggs, John J or I Briggs.
half-brother: Calvin J. Alston
Duncan Briggs son of Samuel Briggs
Absolom Alston "all my books"

Executor: Absolom Alston  Witnesses: James Webb, A.M.Dickson.

‒ ‒ ‒

68

D 458  Will dated 9 February 1816, proved Feb Court 1816.

HIRAM (x) LOVE          Hugh Finley "all my hogs"

sister: Margaret Harvey
brother: William Love
Mary Megomery ?
"brother Robert Love's child Dilly Ann Love"
brother-in-law: James Finley
brothers: John Love, James Love    sister-in-law: Mary Love

No executor named. Witnesses: D.H.Harvey, William (x) Redum.

— — —

D 458  Will dated 21 February 1816, proved Feb Court 1816.

ROBERT (x) ANDERSON

"to Augusta Anderson and William Anderson the plantation
where William Anderson did live, and 48 acres bequeathed
to me Robert Anderson by my father John Anderson."

sisters: Mary, Phebe and Ann Anderson, and Letty Clark
brothers: John Anderson, Stewart Anderson
John Clark, John N. Clark

Executors: "trusty friend Wiley Shaw, Esq., and Major James
            Lapslie."
Witnesses: James McCluskey, Joseph Anderson, Alex. Anderson.

— — —

D 459  Will dated 9 February 1816, proved Feb Court 1816.

JAMES (x) TATE "very sick & weak"       wife: Margaret

sons: Abner, Jesse, Joel, Robert
"Margaret Tate widow of James Tate deceased"
daus: Susannah, Elizabeth, Alse, Margaret

Executors: sons Abner and Jesse.
Witnesses: D. Bradford, Sr., James McCrory.

— — —

D 461  Will dated 19 February 1816, proved Feb Court 1816.

ZEPHANIAH TATE                  wife: Hannah

daughter: Polly Tate (under age)

Executor: "worthy friend Anthony Tate."
Witnesses: Jno. McMullan, John Hevy ?.

— — —

D 462  Will dated 10 January 1816, proved Feb Court 1816

VINSON (x) ROBERTS     wife: Beersheba is pregnant ?
              - continued -

D 462 continued                                           69

sons: James, Morgan, George, Zephaniah.
      Calvin Henderson Roberts
daus: Lidda, Clary, Jemima, Peggy, Mary, Rebeckah
"My wife's daughter Nancy" 5 shillings

Executors: Thomas Compton and James Boling.
Witnesses: John Creswell, Jno. Landers, Erasmus (x) Compton.
- - -

D 464  Will dated 21 April 1815, proved Feb Court 1816.

ELIZABETH (x) WYATT "old and weak"

"My three children Joshua Wyatt, Frederick Wyatt, and
Elizabeth Benson" get all her slaves.
"My son-in-law Benjamin Simpson" $1.

Executors: sons Joshua and Frederick Wyatt.
Witnesses: Anderson King, David King.
- - -

D 465  Will dated 4 January 1815, proved Feb Court 1816.

WILLIAM FAUSSETT, SEN'R

wife: Lydia  land on Cane Creek
son: Ralph Faucett ₤5 "in addition to what I have given him"
 "    George  "      ₤5  "   "      "   "   I  "    "      "
son-in-law: Abner Walker-₤5 "in addition to what I have
                already given him with my daughter Polly"
son-in-law James Watkins and daughter Margaret
 "    "    "    Robert McCauley
daus: Eleanor Faussett, Lucia Faussett
sons: Robert, Eli, James Faussett

Executors: sons Ralph Faussett and George Faussett.
Witnesses: Rob't L. Mitchell, Caleb Wilson, James McCrory.
- - -

D 467  Will dated 29 December 1815, proved Feb Court 1816.

CHARLES ROUNTREE              wife: Nancy

"My children, as they come of age", names and number not
stated.

Executors: brothers Thomas Rountree and Joseph Rountree.
Witness: Jno. Rountree.
- - -

D 468  Will dated 24 March 1814, proved February Court 1816.

WILLIAM WHITTED, SR.

daus: Mary Bird, Hannah Harris ("she has but one child"),
      Elizabeth Holden, Susannah Thompson
- continued -

grandsons: Samuel Bigelow, William Whitted son of Levi
son: William Whitted
"     Levi Whitted "land joining Isaac Holden's Mill Tract"

Testator emancipates his mulatto slave Dick.

Executors: sons William and Levi.
Witnesses: Thomas Flint, Henry Neal.

Codicil dated 4 August 1815. Daughter Mary Bird has died.
Her legacy goes to "William Bird, James Bird, Sarah Walker,
Nancy Thompson, Susannah Anderson, John Bird and Fanny Ham-
ilton (children of the deceased Mary Bird) ..."

Witnesses: David Yarborough, J or I McKerall.

— — —

D 471-474  Will dated 10 March 1809, proved Feb Court 1816.

JOHN MOORE                    wife: Nancy

children under age: Mary, Nancy, Susannah, Lewis, Betsey,
                    Sarah.
dau: Frances wife of John Hart
son: Thomas Moore ½ of tract of land in Tennessee on Bloom-
                    ing Grove Creek in Montgomery County. Thomas
                    is living there.
son: Sampson  Moore ½ of land in Tennessee, and tract in Orange
                    joining Colonel Greene
son: Lewis  other half of land in Orange County

Executors: wife Nancy, son Sampson, friend Mann Patterson.
Witnesses: P. Henderson, James (x) Davis, Richard (x) Davis,
            Christopher (x) Daniel.

— — —

D 475  Will dated 28 January 1814, proved August Court 1814.

JEREMIAH (x) GLENN              wife: Patsey Glenn

sons: James, Thomas Anderson Glenn, George Washington Glenn
"To my daughter Nancy Woods's heirs"-Ƚ3
"To my daughter Feriby Watson's heirs"-Ƚ5
dau: Permelia Glenn
"To my daughter Polly Etheridge's heirs"-Ƚ5
daus ?: Kitty Horton Glenn, Lucy Glenn

Executors: brother William Glenn and James Latta,  ～q.
Witnesses: Jno. Marshall, Demsey Wood.

— —.—

D 476  Agreement about a road between LUDWICK ALBRIGHT and
MICHAEL HOLT. Dated April 1816, proved May Court 1816.

— — —

D 477 Will dated 10 February 1816, proved May Court 1816.

MILDRED (x) GARRARD   "very weak"

William Carrington and William Garrard 5 shillings each
"My son-in-law Joshua Childres" 5 shillings
"Heirs of my son-in-law George Bryant" 5 shillings
son: Daniel Garrard  5 shillings
dau-in-law: Elizabeth Garrard 5 shillings
sons: John Garrard, Jacob Garrard  5 shillings each
son: Carter N. Garrard  bed, chairs
"    Samuel Garrard     "   , "      , and land
dau: Susy Garrard  furniture, stock, etc.

Executors: friend James Walker, and Carter Garrard.
Witnesses: Lot G. Watson, Chuza Hopkins.
– – –

D 478  Will dated 1816, proved May Court 1816.

JAMES HANCOCK                    wife: Clarissa

sons: William and James Hancock  $1 each
To deceased son Stephen Hancock's children $1 each.
dau: Betsey Franklin
sons: Robert Hancock, Nathan Hancock, Roger Hancock
dau: Polly
"two youngest children": sons Stanley and John Hancock.

Executors: wife Clarissa, and son Nathan
Witnesses: Tyree Glenn, Martin (x) Crutcher.
– – –

D 480  Will dated 11 April 1816, proved May Court 1816.

NATHAN HANCOCK

"brothers Robert Hancock & Roger Hancock & my sister
Polly Hancock"
"My sister Polly's little daughter Henrietta" $100.

Executor: James Kimbrough.
Witnesses: Thomas Cottrell, Ira E. Arnold.
– – –

D 481  Will dated 19 February 1816, proved May Court 1816.

JOHN DOUGLASS

wife: Margaret all estate. Land bounded by William Cannon,
          James Graham, David Bradford and Jacob Gar-
          rison.

brothers: William, David and Henderson Douglass $2 each
                         - continued -

72          D 481 continued

"Heirs of my brother James Douglass" $2

Executors: friends James Graham and George Garrison son of
          Jacob Garrison.
Witnesses: David Bradford Jr, Thomas (x) Bradford,
          George Graham.

— — —

D 482  Will dated 1st day 4th month 1816, proved May 1816.

ANNA ELIZABETH (x) CULBERSON

dau: Anna Elizabeth Culberson
 "    Rhoda McCracken

Executors:"Isaac Shugarts and my brother John"
Witnesses: Thomas Newlin, Henry Quakenbush.

— — —

D 483  Will dated 21 April 1816, proved May Court 1816.

ELI LINDSEY                     wife: Jane

sons: Josiah Bowman Lindsey, Martin Luther Lindsey.
daus: Ann Hodge, Polly Clark, and Sally Hodge "money now
      in hands of Willie Shaw, Esq."
dau: Eunice Lindsey  bed & furniture, etc.
sons: John, Robert and James Lindsey, $3 each

Executors: wife Jane, and William McCluskey.
Witnesses: William Woods, J. Allison, John McDade.

— — —

D 484  Will dated 24 February 1816, proved May Court 1816.

ANN (x) BOYLE "weak in body"

dau: Jane Denning $5; etc
granddaus: Ann Boyle, Martha Boyle
son: John Boyle
dau: Mary Boyle gets most of estate

Executrix: daughter Mary Boyle.
Witnesses: Caleb Wilson, James Boyle.

— — —

D 485  Will dated 13 May 1816, proved May Court 1816.

JAMES (x) CARRINGTON "weak in body"     wife: Ankey

sons: John & William $1 each with what they have already had
dau: Elizabeth $1 with what she has already received.
"The above the children of my first wife Jemima."
                              - continued -

D 485 continued                                              73

son: James $1 besides what I have already given him
dau: Mary $1
"The children of my second wife Ankey"

Sole executor: James Latta.    Witness: Thomas Latta, Sen'r.
- - -

D 486  Will dated 25 December 1812, proved May Court 1816.

RICHARD STANFORD            wife a legatee

"Two oldest daughters Ariana and Mary Mebane"
"Two youngest children Lawrence and Adeline"

Executors: friends Thomas Snipes Esq. and John Newlin.
Witness: Mark Durham.
Codicil dated 22 January 1814. No witness. Same heirs.
- - -

D 489  Will dated 11 August 1810, proved August Court 1816.

EDMUND (x) GILLIAM                wife: Sarah

sons: Edmund Gilliam
      Charles and Burwell land on South-west side of Haw Riv.
      David  land on North-east side of Haw River
daus: Sarah Hurbin (?), Susannah Smothers,
      Mary Bracken,    Elizabeth Stalcop

Executor: son Edmund Gilliam.
Witnesses: Thomas Bradford Jun'r, David Bradford Sr.
- - -

D 490  Will dated 2 April 1812, proved August Court 1816.

THOMAS CATE            wife: Sarah Cate

son: Moses "150 acres where he now lives"
"    John  "150 acres "   "  "   "   "
"    Ephriam "100 acres whereon he did dwell"
"    Thomas  100 "    "whereon I now dwell"

"My eleven children - Moses Cate, John Cate, Fanny Sykes,
Martha Moore, Winney Sykes, Milly Roach, Huldah Cate,
Tabitha Smith, Elizabeth Cate, Thomas Cate, Ephriam Cate."
                        her
Witnesses: Barnard Cate, Jean  x  Cate .
                        mark
- - -

D 491-493  Will dated 19 April 1816, proved August 1816.

LUDWICK ALBRIGHT            wife: Elizabeth

son: John Albright "tract of land he now lives on" etc.
"    George       "  "   "   "   "   "   "   "  " "  "
                                  -continued-
married daughters: "Mary Fogleman, deceased wife of John"
"Elizabeth Albright, wife of John"

son: Daniel "land whereon he now lives"
"Daughters not married-namely-Barbara, Martha and Sarah".
son: Isaac (unmarried, under 25) "land on S.Side of the Alle-
                                mance"
son: Ludwick (unmarried, under 25) land on the S. Side of the
                                Allemance.

Executors: "my brother Daniel Albright and my son John"
Witnesses: Mich'l Holt, Elias Albright, S. Harris.

— — —

D 494  Will dated 8 June 1816, proved Nov Court 1816.

HEZEKIAH (x) RHODES            wife: Alementor Rhodes
"weak of body"

sons: Wesley and William
granddau: Mary Linnington Rhodes daughter of Wesley Rhodes
granddaus: Lucy Hall and Alsy C. Hall get cow and heifer
            "now in the possession of Henry Hall"

Executors: Wesley Rhodes and Absolom Alston.
Witnesses: L. Alston, Elizabeth (x) Cabe ?.

— — —

D 494  Will dated 22 March 1816, proved Nov Court 1816.

AARON BOLES

Henderson Haney "now about two years old", Nancy Haney
brother: John Boles $1
"$1 to each of my sisters"

Executor: friend Walter Murray.
Witnesses: Walter Murray, William (x) Criswell, Robert Fulton.

— — —

D 495  Will dated 2 March 1816, proved Nov Court 1816.

JACOB UMSTEAD            mother, and "her daughter Jane"

"my brothers and sisters"
"my brother David's sons"
"" "        John's "    "

Executor: Elisha Umstead.    Witness: Thornton McFarling.

— — —

D 496  Will dated 5 August 1816, proved Feb Court 1817.

JOHN CRAIG

He is to be buried near his wife Mary "who is gone before me"

son: Samuel (unmarried),      son: Abraham
dau: Peggy  ("       )        "   James      -continued-

D 496 continued
"Elizabeth Russell and her children"
dau: Polly
grandson: John Long
granddau: "Elizabeth Craig of David"
"To each of my grandsons named for me $6."
son: Alexander
"My three granddaughters by David viz- Nancy Murdock, Polly
and Sally Craig 5 shillings each"

Executors: nephew Isaac Craig and son-in-law Alex'r Russell.
Witnesses: Alex'r Russell, Isaac Craig.

- - -

D 498  Will dated 26 December 1815, proved Feb Court 1817.

ANDREW MURDOCK                  wife: Margaret

sons: Robert Nurdock, James Murdock
grandchildren: Andrew (under 21) and Betsey Murdock ,
               children of James
"              Andrew and Peggy Ann Craig, children of
               Abraham Craig
"              Andrew Steel son of Joseph Steel, Peggy Steel
"To Andrew Murdock son of Thomas Murdock.."

Executors: son-in-law Abraham Craig and nephew James Mebane.
Proved by the oaths of James Mebane, William Sheppard,
                    Reuben Smith and Thomas Whitted.

- - -

D 500  Will dated 24 November 1816, proved Feb Court 1817.

NANCY (x) MOORE

daughters Nelly, Margaret and Betsey get all estate,
"cutting out all other heirs with five cents apiece."

Executors: Edward Couch, Alexander Gattis.
Witnesses: Thomas Gattis, Elizabeth Mason.

- - -

D 501  Will dated 31 July 1815, proved February Court 1817.

THOMAS (x) HATWOOD "low in body"      wife: Nancy all estate

sons: Thomas Hatwood, John Hatwood   50¢ each
son-in-law: Robert Gee 50¢
dau: Jean Hatwood $1

Executors: friends Laban Andrews and George Smith.
Witnesses: James Reeves, Lacey Loyd.

- - -

D 502  Power of Attorney from SOLOMON NEVILL to his brother
GOODMAN NEVILL.  Dated 28 February 1816, proved Feb 1817.
Witness: John Craig.

- - -

76

D503   Will dated 21 April 1814, proved February Court 1817.

JOSEPH (x) McCULLOCH      Testator owns a mill-stone quarry.
"weak in body"
son: John McCulloch "tract whereon he now lives on the S.
                     Side of Toms Creek."
sons: George, William
son: Joseph "tract whereon he now lives which I purchased of
            John Tate, lying on both sides of Watson's Creek"

daus: Mary Johnston, Deborah Walker, Elizabeth

Executors: son George McCulloch and son-in-law Wm Walker.
Witnesses: Robt L. Mitchell, Thos. McCullock,
           Sam'l Edmiston, Andrew McCullock.

— — —

D 505   Will dated 22 February 1817, proved May Court 1817.

JAMES WHITTED          wife: Attelia  is pregnant

son: Nash Whitted

Executor:  friend James Webb.
Witnesses: James Phillips, William I. Nash.

— — —

D 506   Will dated 8 June 1816, proved May Court 1817.

SUSANNAH (x) FULTON "low in health"

sons: Jesse Fulton, David Fulton, Samuel Fulton  $2 each
granddaughter: Elsy Tate "my walnut chest"
son: Robert Fulton
great-granddau: Celia, daughter of Susannah Tate

Executor: "trusty friend William Bradford.
Witnesses: James Mebane, John Hughes.

— — —

D 507   Will dated 26 March 1814, proved May Court 1817.

BARNEY (x) TROXLER           wife: Elizabeth $50, etc.

"Unto the heirs of Philipena Coble wife of David Coble" 5 sh.
"Daughter Mary's son John Albright"  5 shillings
son: Jacob  Troxler  5 shillings
"Daughter Elizabeth Huffman wife of Peter Huffman" $20
"  "        Catherine McCamey "    " James McCamey" $1
son: David Troxler "my chest and clothes and $50"
"     Powell  $30
"     Barney  5 shillings
"     George  balance of estate

Executors: George Troxler and Isaac Holt.
Witnesses: Is'c Holt, Christopher Coble, Daniel Albright.

— — —

D 508  Will dated 7 January 1817, proved May Court 1817.

MATTHEW (x) RIPPY "old and weak in body"

He devises several slaves, land, etc. Mentions land he has already given away. Balance of estate to be sold and the money divided among "all my sons & daughters and the children of my daughter Jinney Garrett that is now dead." Daughters names are not stated.

Sons: John, Edward, Joseph, Thomas, James and Jesse Rippy.

Executors: friend Samuel Scott and son John Rippy.
Witnesses: Samuel Scott, John McCrackin.

– – –

D 509  Will dated 8 April 1817, proved August Court 1817.

HANNAH (x) RAY          This will is so puzzling I give most of
                        it as written. Checked with original.

.."to my eldest son James Massey James Lindley, to my youngest son Matthew Ray & my two grandsons the youngest sons of my daughter Lydia  West, & Ann Wolf, at the decease of my two daughters a certain note of hand now in my possession on my son Matthew Ray for the sum of $95.  Also all the money which I may die seized and possed of".

eldest daughter: Lydia West
youngest daughter: Ann Wolf

Executors: son Matthew Ray and John Stockard.
Witness: John Stockard.

– – –

D 510  Will dated 6 July 1817, proved August Court 1817.

STEPHEN SCARLETT                wife: Sally

daus: Rachel and Cynthia Scarlett are unmarried
sons: James Scarlett (youngest),John Scarlett (eldest)

"7 daughters - Elizabeth Cain, Mary Latta , Sally Latta, Jane Latta, Susannah Cole, Rachel Scarlett and Cynthia Scarlett."

Executors: wife Sally and son James.
Witnesses: William Lewis, Henry Bunch, Abraham (x) Crabtree.

─────

D 512  Will dated 16 August 1816, proved August Court 1817.

WILLIAM LAWS            wife: Frances plantation on Flat River

son: Jonathan Laws land lying in Orange and Granville
"     James Laws
sister: Elizabeth Laws                    - continued -

daughters: Jinney Waller, Polly Ferguson, Nancy Laws,
           Rebecca Laws,  Sally Laws,    Margaret Laws,
           Alsey Laws,    Frances Laws

"My grandson David Laws son of my deceased son George Laws
the tract of land on which my daughter-in-law Margaret Laws
now lives." In case of his death it goes "to my grandson
Charles Laws."

son-in-law: Elisha Umstead  $5
granddaughter: Jemima Umstead

Executors:"Worthy friends Thomas D. Bennehan, William Roberts,
           Sr., and my son Jonathan Laws."
Witnesses: Mark Veazey, William Veazey.

– – –

D 514  Will dated 25 February 1817, proved Nov Court 1817.

MARY WOODS

niece: Emeline Dortch (under age) one-half of estate
nieces: Sally Dortch, Polly Dortch and Lucy Dortch, other half

Executor: Duncan Cameron.
Witnesses: James ? Kelly, Senior, Hugh Cain, Junior.

– – –

D 515  Will dated 13 November 1817, proved Nov Court 1817.

POMPHRETT HERNDON         brother: James Herndon Jr half of
                                                   estate
father: James Herndon  $5
sisters: Polly Gorman, Nancy Barbee, Elizabeth Dickson $5 ea.
brother-in-law (half-brother) Macharine C. Herndon $5
Teresa N. Herndon (his half-sister) $5

sister: Sally Herndon other half of estate

Executor: brother James Herndon, Jr.
Witnesses: Ja mes Lynn, Charles H. Collier.

– – –

D 517  Will dated 29 March 1813, proved February Court 1818.

WILLIAM McPHERSON     Checked with original will, writing bad.

wife: Phebe

"I give to my children as follows:
to Thomas and Mary Braxton,
to Othail (Othneil ?) & C ristain McPherson,
to Ruth Jonson (Tomson ?),
to Wm. & Betty McPherson,
to Daniel and Mary McPherson,
to Margaret & Jesse Pierce,"                  - continued -

79       D 517 continued
"to John and Hannah McPherson,
 to Aaron and Phebe Lindley,
 to Mary and Edward Stuart (Stewart ?),
 to Ann and John Crutchfield,
 to Edith and Mark Morgan, each two of them a Crown besides
 what they have already had".

"to my grandson Wm. McPherson(ye son of Enoch)" ..
"son Enoch and his wife Paray (Panay ?) .."

Executors: Daniel McPherson and John McPherson.
Witnesses: Jacob Nugent, Daniel McPherson, James Neal,
           Enoch McPherson.

– – –

D 518  Will dated 18 July 1817, proved February Court 1818.

LEWIS HERNDON   (See back of this book for HERNDON genealogy)

wife: Polly "to keep our children together" and educate them
His lands in Wake County, N.C. to be divided among his 4 sons.

sons: Joseph (oldest), George, Lewis, Willis
dau: Polly

Executors: friends Joseph Boothe Jr. and Sampson Moore,
           and wife Polly.
Witnesses: Mark Beasley, Polly (x) Beasley,
           David (x) Castleberry.

– – –

D 520  Will dated 1 December 1817, proved Feb Court 1818.

JOHN EDWARDS,SR.              wife: Lucy

son: Young Edwards 60 acres in Ash County -mill-on Dead Creek
"    Allen Edwards
"To Stokes Edwards' children by his first wife to wit:
Richard, Isaac & Allen, John, Nancy, Lucy & Cathery."

"great-grandchildren Rhoda, William & Mary, children of
Richard Ricketts & Rebecca his wife."

sons: Stokes Edwards, John Edwards
daus: Elizabeth, Roda Ball

Executors: wife Lucy, son Allen, Brother Barry Cate, and
           Reuben Smith.
Witnesses: Elijah Graves, Ariana Graves.

– – –

D 521  Will dated 5 April 1817, proved Feb Court 1818.

ANNE WOOD widow of John Wood

daus: Nancy Robinson, Jane Wilson, Rebecca Thompson
nieces: Sally Wood, Ann Wilson
sons-in-law: Thomas Wilson, Samuel Thompson
                                        - continued -

Executors: Thomas Wilson and Samuel Thompson "both of Orange".
Witnesses: Richard Holeman, Charles Holeman.

- - -

D 522  Will dated 14 August 1817, proved May Court 1818.
EVE (x) SMITH
cousin-in-law: Peter Smith all estate

Witnesses: Frederick (x) Kimbro, Richard Proctor,
           Isaac (x) Sharp.

- - -

D 523  Will dated 17 February 1818, proved May Court 1818.

JOHN (x) WALKER           wife: Judy

daus: Nelly Walker, Polly Ryals, Rebeckah Walker,
      Betsy Walker, Letty Walker.
son: Benjamin Walker (under age)
daus: Emily Walker, Lucy Walker (both under age)

Executors: "Friends Herbert Collier & William Oldham & Judy
           Walker".
Witnesses: George Oldham, John (x) Oldham.

- - -

D 525  Will dated 8 February 1817, proved May Court 1818.

JOHN LATTA          wife a legatee, name not stated

children "to be schooled"
son: John "Little River plantation"
dau: Moriah

Executors: John Latta, Sr., and John Cabe, Esq.
Witness: Hugh Montgomery.

- - -

D 526  Will dated 24 July 1817, proved May Court 1818.

JAMES WILKINSON           wife: Susannah "to raise and
                                 school all our children"
sons: James and William, both under age
daus: Cata, Patsa and Sysannah Wilkinson

Executors: wife Susannah, and William Wilkinson.
Witnesses: Samuel Madden, Joseph Ray.

- - -

D 527  Will dated 11 January 1813, proved May Court 1818.

JAMES TURNER, SR.           wife: Mary

daus: Hannah, Sarah and Jane, all unmarried
sons: David Turner plantation, etc, James Turner 10 shillings
daus: Nelly Craig, Mary Holland, Ann, Christian Milligan 10 sh.

son: John Turner   10 shillings

Executors: wife Mary, and son David.
Witnesses: J. S. Smith, William (x) Smith.

- - -

D 529  Will dated 8th day 8th month 1813, proved May 1818.

BENJAMIN PIGGOTT

sons: Joshua (eldest), John Piggott
daus: Patience Cox(oldest), Elizabeth Wheeler $1 each
son-in-law: Jeremiah Cox  $1
dau: Mary Keggs  $1
son-in-law: Charles Davis  $1
dau: Ruth Horniday  $1
youngest son: Benjamin Piggott
grandchildren: Benjamin Piggott son of Joshua
               "         "       "   "  John
               Hannah Piggott dau of Benjamin
               Mary Piggott    "    "    "

Witnesses: Jeremiah Piggott, Thomas Marshall, Benj. Wheeler.
- - -

D 530  Will dated 25 March 1818, proved May Court 1818.

MORDECAI SOUTHERLAND

sons: Samuel (plantation); Ransom, William  10 shillings
daus: Frances Turner, Susannah Glen  10 shillings each
      Polly Glen, Elizabeth Burton  10 shillings each

Executor: son Samuel.
Witnesses: Kennedy Haughton, Jas. Kimbrough.

- - -

D 531  Will dated 10 Febriary 1817, proved May Court 1818.

ROGER HANCOCK              wife: Nancy

daus: Susannah Hancock, Polly W. Hancock, Betsy Hancock.
sons: Wesley Hancock "my big Bible"
      Fletcher Hancock  "my small Bible"

Sole executrix: wife Nancy Hancock.
Witnesses: Reubin Cardin, Jesse Branch.

- - -

D 533  Will dated 6th month 26th day 1816, proved May 1818.

JACOB MARSHILL              wife: Margaret

son: Francis Marshill
dau: Ruth Hadley
dau-in-law: Ruth Marshill          - continued -

sons: William and John Marshill land on E side of Mary's Creek.
"heir of my son Jacob Marshill 5 shillings if demanded"
"  "   "   " daughter Mary Hinshaw 5 shillings if demanded"
dau: Anna Thompson "2/6 if she comes to demand it"
"heir of my daughter Margaret Jones 2/6"
"  "   "   "   " Elizabeth Freeman 2/6"
"Ann Dunn feather bed ana furniture"

Executrix: wife.
Witnesses: Richard Thompson, Samuel Freeman, James Murray,
           Joseph Murray, J or I Hinshaw.

— — —

D 535  Deed of Gift from MORDECAI SOUTHERLAND to friend
FEBE DOSSETT, bed and furniture, cow and yaerling, pine chest,
etc.  Dated 17 March 1818, proved August Court 1818.
Witnesses: Jas. Kimbrough, Tyree Glenn.

— — —

D 535  Will dated 10 July 1818, proved August Court 1818.

JOHN BARBEE                    wife: Esther

son: King Barbee              dau: Sally
 "   Reuben Barbee $1 "with what he has already received"
 "   Zachariah
dau: Elizabeth (under age)
son: John "160 acres where I now live, etc."
 "   Gray "100 acres .. joining Bilbo and others.."

Executors: "worthy friend (actually his wife's brother) Zach-
            ariah Herndon" and King Barbee.
Witnesses: Zach.  Herndon, William Hall, John Herndon.

— — —

D 537  Will dated 24 January 1813, proved August Court 1818.

JAMES WILSON

sisters: Maryann and Elizabeth get plantation, etc., they
           are to support his father and mother.

Executors: James Lapslie and Thomas Armstrong.
Witnesses: William Shepperd, Egbert Shepperd.

— — —

D 538  Will dated 28 January 1813, proved August Court 1818.

EDWARD WILSON                  wife: Mary

dau: Elizabeth $1, she has had her share.
son: Charles Wortham "all that I gave him when he left me"
dau: Sarah Hall  gets a mare
son: William Wortham  "all that he had when he left me", etc.
dau: Nancy Wilson $10 and what she had "when she left me"
son: John Wortham "all that I gave him when he left me", etc.
 "   James  "   "  "   "   " he got from me when he left me,"
                                     - continued -

D 538 continued

son: Alfred Wortham "plantation I now live on .. known as
                Walker Tract .. he to have full possession after
                the death of Mrs. Sarah Dunnagan."
"        Samuel Wortham "tract where Mrs. Sarah Dunnagan lives"

Executors: wife, and son Samuel.
Witnesses: Joseph Armstrong, Peggy Armstrong.
- - -

D 539  Will dated 18 March 1818, proved August Court 1818.

WILLIAM LEWIS                        wife: Agnes

sons: Charles Lewis and Parsons Lewis
"only daughter Franky Lewis"

Executrix: wife Agnes Lewis.
Witnesses: James Nutt, Pomphrett Gooch.
- - -

D 540  Will dated 30 May 1818, proved August Court 1818.

JOSEPH HAMILTON                      wife: Martha
sons: James, John and William Hamilton

Executors: friends William Pickett and Archibald Hamilton.
Witnesses: Robert Gragson,  Samuel McCaddams.
- - -

D 542  Will dated 18 June 1818, proved August Court 1818.

LEMUEL ALSTON

sisters: Christian Jones wife of Solomon Jones;  Patsy
brothers: Absalom Alston, Philip Alston & Alfred Alston
sister: Mary Scott wife of Robert Scott
brother: George L. Alston
sister: Sally Pickett wife of Matthew Pickett
nephew: Lemuel Alston son of James Alston

Executors: "worthy friends and brothers Solomon Jones and
                George L. Alston."
Witnesses: W. E. Roberts, Freeman Broadwell.
- - -

D 543  Will dated 14 July 1818, proved August Court 1818.

JACOB JEFFRIES

wife: Jane all estate, including "the Bounty Ticket of $3000
                due by Major Thomas Donahoo".
"To each of my first wife's children, viz: Reuben Jeffries,
Mourning Jeffries, John Jeffries, Katie Ammons, Betsy Gray,
to each a  dollar."

Sole executrix: wife Jane.
Witnesses: Rob't L. Mitchell, David (x) Hathcock.
- - -

D 544  Will dated 6 January 1812, proved August Court 1818.

STEPHEN WHITE

wife: Ann  land on waters of Back Creek and Haw River
"To heirs of James Baldridge deceased " $2
sons-in-law: Samuel Mebane, William Hodge  $2 each
sons: Stephen White, John White  $2 each
sons: David  land;  James a mare
sons: Samuel  $2;  Joseph "land I now live on"

Executors: sons David and Joseph White.
Witnesses: James Palmer, Wm. Shaw, David Bryan.

— — —

D 454  Power of Attorney from JOHN ATKINSON to WESTWARD A.
JONES, to collect from the "Sec'y of State of N.C. all the
pay, bounty lands that is due ... from the state aforesaid
for my services as a soldier of the Continental Line and on
that Establishment ..." Witnesses: Wm. Leathers, John Darby.
Dated 28 July 1808, proved February 1816.

— — —

D 546  Mortgage from GEORGE (x) PICKET to SAMUEL WILSON on
a horse.  Dated 23 February 1819, proved Feb. L819.
Witness: Joseph A. Woods.

— — —

D 547  Bond - ROBERT HARRIS and WM. MONTGOMERY to RICHARD
UMSTEAD. Robert Harris has purchased from Richard Umstead
his interest in the estate of his brother Jacob deceased.
Dated 20 January 1818, proved February Court 1818.
Witnesses: Ezekiel Umstead, Jonathan Montgomery.

— — —

D 547  Deed from RICHARD CATE to SALLY CATE for a mare.
Dated 9 June 1818, proved February 1819. Witness: Huldah Cate.

— — —

D 548  Deed from ALFRED or ALFORD CATE to NANCY CATE for
two cows and calves. Dated 28 May 1822, proved August 1822.
Witness: Huldah (x) Cate.

— — —

D 549  Will dated 21 March 1813, proved November Court 1818.

JOHN JOHNSTON                    wife: Isabel

sons: eldest David, second John, both under age
"each of my daughters as they arrive at age", not named

Executors: wife Isabel, and John Craig.
Witnesses: John Blackwoof, Margaret Johnston.

— — —

D 550   Will dated 10 April 1818, proved November Court 1818.

JOHN THOMAS                    wife: Elizabeth

Executor: worthy friend
Witnesses: Alexander Morphis, Micajah Thomas.

— — —

D 550   Will dated 5 September 1818, proved Nov Court 1818.

ALEXANDER RUSSELL              wife: Elizabeth

sons: John Craig Russell, David, Robert Paistly Russell (under
son: Wright "land he now lives on"                    age)
dau: Jane Rodgers
son: Alexander "land I hold in Guilford bought of Jessup"
nephew: Joseph, surname not stated
unmarried sister, name not stated

Executors: sons John and Wright Russell, and Mathew Ray.
Witnesses: James Webb, James Turner.

— — —

D 552   Will dated 26 December 1818, proved Feb Court 1819.

ABRAM CRAIG                    wife: Jane

"Two oldest children are to receive a considerable legacy
from the estate of Andrew Murdock dec'd. ..."
"My other children" , names not stated

Executors: friends James Mebane, George Johnston and John
            Freeland.
Witnesses: James Webb, James Craig.

— — —

D 553   Will dated 19 January 1819, proved February Court 1819.

JOHN WELBORN or WILBOURNE          wife: Mary

"unto Duran  Hampton wife of Nolan Hampton"
Alves and Nolan Hampton sons of Nolan Hampton
brother: Richard Wilborn
Robert Wilborn son of Richard
Lewis Wilborn
brothers: Edward and Zachariah Welborne  50¢ each
brother Thomas Welborne's children 50¢ each
sisters: Temperance Marshall, Susannah Ludlo Jones,
         Lida Slaughter
friends: Roland Cook, and John Hampton son of my wife,
He leaves 100 acres to his slave Jeremiah, who is to be freed.

Executors: friends Thomas Bennehan, Benjamin Bullock, and
            Nathaniel Carrington.
Witnesses: Samuel (x) Rush, John Suit, Jr., Robert Ashley.

— — —

D 555   Will dated 7 October 1815, proved February Court 1819.

ISAAC DALE                wife: Margaret Dale   whole estate

daughter Margaret Haddock   $10

Executors: friends Thomas Holaday Sr."and my step-son Robert
             Andrew".
Witnesses: Lewis Hornaday, Dinah (x) Bittick.

— — —

D 556   Will dated 5 June 1818, proved February Court 1819.

WILLIAM (x) WOODS "sick and weak"      mother: Elinor Woods

sister: Margaret Hopkins   $1
brothers: Hugh Woods, Eli Woods
"brother-in-law Eli Woods husband of my late sister Lucy Woods
deceased "my part of her part of the money coming from our
grandfather Hugh Woods' estate."

Witnesses: Wm. Baldwin, Hugh Montgomery, Joseph Woods.
Executors: (named in Codicil) "My uncle Robert Faucett and my
             trusty friend James Jackson son of James Jackson Sr."

— — —

D 558   Will dated 14 March 1819, proved May Court 1819.

BENJAMIN WHIDBEE            wife: Sally

son: Joseph (under age)
"All my children" (they all seem to be minors).

Executors: wife Sally, and brother-in-law William Holt.
Witnesses: John Harden, Lewis Holt.

— — —

D 559   Will dated 15 February 1816, proved May Court 1819.

THOMAS CARMICHAEL            wife: Mary

sons: John Henry Carmichael, Archibald Carmichael
daus: Margaret Street, Nancy Smith, Jane Isley

Executor: son John Henry Carmichael.
Witnesses: John McMullan, Vance Laffatee.

— — —

D 560   Will dated 14 January 1819, proved May Court 1819.

WILLIAM FORSYTHE            wife: Ma

"My children James Barnet John Margaret & Gilla & one sixth
part to Anna Bailey's children" (no punctuation)
sons: John and Barnet get   "landed estate"        — continued —

daughter: Anna $10
"Friends Thomas Snipes and Elijah Graves trustees and guardian for my son John and his property for life".

Executors: son Barnet Forsythe and friend William McCauley.
Witnesses: Jno. Caruthers, Archibald Durham.

— — —

D 560  Will dated 30 March 1819, proved May Court 1819.

EDWARD PICKETT

son: John Pickett               dau: Mary Murry
 "    William Pickett            "    Margaret Roney
 "    James Pickett
daus: Sarah McDaniel, Martha Murray
son: Walter Pickett

Executors: sons John and James.
Witnesses: James Mebane, J. A. Mebane.

— — —

D 562  Will dated 13 March 1819, proved May Court 1819.

JAMES (x) PYLE "sick in body"          wife: Elizabeth

daughter Sally, "all my children" names not stated

Executors: wife Elizabeth, son William.
Witnesses: Wm. Hatchett, James Hicks, John Hicks.

— — —

D 563  Will dated 15 March 1819, proved August Court 1819.

THOMAS MOORE              wife: Diana

"Four daughters- Elinor Moore (eldest), Diana Moore, Mary
Moore, Sarah Moore."
"Daughters Jeney Moore, Marthy Moore and Elizabeth Moore"
sons: James Moore 10 shillings besides what he has received
      Andrew Moore 10 "       "      "     "    "    "
      Thomas, Mathew, Robert

Executors: sons Andrew and Thomas Moore.
Witnesses: James Moore, Daniel Atkins.

— — —

D 564  Will dated 25 August 1819, proved November Court 1819.

JAMES WOOD

dau: Betsy Latta wife of John J. Latta
son: Willie Wood
dau: Nancy Lewis wife of Fielding Lewis
 "   Sally Wallace wife of Owen Wallace      - continued -

88        D 564 continued

dau: Polly Chisenhall wife of Delancy Chisenhall

Executors: son Willie Wood, and John J. Latta.
Witnesses: Frederick Moize, Marstain (x) Crotckett ?

— — —

D 565   Will dated 22 November 1819, proved Nov Court 1819.

SAMUEL CARUTHERS                        wife: Sary

sons: John Caruthers, William Caruthers
"All my daughters", none named, some are married.

Executors: sons John and William.
Witnesses: William Brown, Levi Andrews.

— — —

D566   Will dated 10 January 1820, proved Feb Court 1820.

WILLIAM SMITH

"To William Smith son of John Smith (the grandson of my
brother John) $50."
"To Ferze daughter of Robert Smith (son of John Smith) $50
"To Allen Compton the son of Erasmus Compton " $50
"To William O'Kelly the son of William O'Kelly" $50
"To Elender Smith the daughter of Polly Smith  a note of $16
     on John Ward."
"Unto Polly's children Jane, Ellender, Entricans (?) and
Nancy" .. a tract of land. They are under age.

"My sister Mary McMund, Robert Smith (son of John Smith my
brother), Joseph Smith and John Smith sons of Robert my
brother" .. another tract of land.

Executors: Robert Smith (son of John Smith), and Robert
             Campbell.
Witnesses: John Landers, John Ward, Jacob (x) Huggins.

— — —

D 567   Will dated 11 June 1818, proved February Court 1820.

JOHN ECCLES                      wife: Jennet

daus: Elizabeth Eccles, Mary Eccles, Sarah Eccles,
     Martha Eccles (the last three under age ?)
son-in-law: Thomas Murray $1 besides what he has received
son: William Eccles

Sole executrix: wife Jennet.
Witnesses: Robert G. Mitchell, Junia Hall, James Barnard.

— — —

D 568   Will dated 30 September 1817, proved Feb Court 1820.

JOHN THOMPSON                    wife: Jennet

son: Thomas
dau: Rachel wife of John Russell
sons: James, William and John Thompson
dau: Jennet wife of George Johnston
daus: Ann Thompson, Elizabeth Grahams, Elender Thomas

Executors: brother Robert Thompson, son William Thompson.
Witnesses: W. Thompson, William (x) Gorly ?.

- - -

D 571   Will dated 20 November 1819, proved Feb Court 1820.

WILLIAM KING                     wife: Sarah

dau: Senea gets 1 filly
son: John $1
daus: Fanny, Elizabeth, Peggy  $1 each
sons: William D. King, Marshal King, Pleasant King
dau: Sarrah  gets bed and furniture

Executors: wife, and sons John and Wm. D. King.
Witness: Jonathan Tapp.

- - -

D 572   Will dated 8 December 1818, proved Feb Court 1820.

ROBERT (x) ANDERSON              wife: Nancy

daus: Charity (she is married), Mary
sons: Robert, William (he is married), Alexander

Executors: friend William Maris, and son Alexander.
Witnesses: John Anderson, Wiatt Hickman.

- - -

D 573   Will dated 15 July 1811, proved February Court 1820.

MARY (x) McMUNN                  granddaughter: Ann

Executrix: daughter Sarah.
Witnesses: Alexander Findley, James Smith.

- - -

D 574   Will dated 25 November 1814, proved May Court 1820.

ROBERT McCULLEY        He says "my seven children" ..

sons: Moore ? McCulley, William McCulley
dau: Sally McCulley

Executors: son Moore, and daughter Sally McCulley.
Witnesses: Daniel Johnston, John Boon.

- - -

D 575   Will dated 9 April 1820, proved May Court 1820.

JACOB GRAVES                        wife: Furby

dau: Betsy , unmarried
No relationship to : Mary Glass, Catherine Glass,
    is stated. Daus ? Nelly (or Milly) Nease,
                      Barbara Graves, Betsy & Sarah Graves
son: Daniel Graves "tract whereon he lives"
sons: Elias, David, Bostian and John Graves

Testator owns a mill. His land joins that of Malachi Isley,
Doctor Brehon, Frederic Shofner.

Executors: George Isley, Boston Graves, David Graves.
Witnesses: Is. Holt, Martin Nease, Jacob Anthony.

— — —

D 577   Will dated 25 July 1815, proved May Court 1820.

THOMAS HOWARD, SR.              wife: Elizabeth

son: James Howard          dau: Henrietta (unmarried)
"    John Howard            "    Betsy Watson
sons: Thomas Howard, Richard Howard

Executors: wife Elizabeth, and son Richard.
Witnesses: Thomas Scott, Stephen Glass.

— — —

D 579   Will dated 10 December 1819, proved August Court 1820.

HENRY KECK              wife: Elizabeth

son: Daniel
unmarried daughters: Sally and Caty
married daughters: Mary, Elizabeth and Barbara
"All my children, namely, Mary John Henry Elizabeth George
Daniel , Barbara, David, William, Sally and Caty."

Executors: sons George Keck and David Keck.
Witness: Mich'l Holt.

— — —

D 580   Will dated 28 July 1820, proved August Court 1820.

THOMAS ROUNTREE              wife: Victory

He gives a  rifle to Neil (?) Cate

Executrix: wife Victory.        Witness: Wm. Armstrong.

— — —

D 581   Will dated 30 June 1820, proved August Court 1820.

JOHN (x) COPLEY, SR.                wife: Sarah
    "sick and weak"
son: Iley Copley              dau: Jiney Copley

Executors: wife Sarah, and Moses McCown.
Witnesses: John Redman, Jr, Aquilla Roades.

— — —

D 581   Will dated 6 March 1820, proved August Court 1820.

ISAAC (x) JACKSON            father: James Jackson
    "very sick"

sisters: Elizabeth and Ruth Jackson
sister:  Sarah Cloud   $1

Executor: trusty friend Levi Jackson.
Witnesses: A. G. Jackson, Jacob Jackson, Benoni Jackson.

— — —

D 583   Will dated 30 January 1819, proved August Court 1820.

JOHN BREEZE                  wife: Jenney Breeze

daughters: Patsy Breeze, Rachel Breeze, Polly Breeze,
           Jinney Breeze, Susa Breeze

Executors: friends Richard Breeze and Abner Bruce.
Witnesses: John McDade, A. B. Bruce, Patsy Breeze.

— — —

D 584   Will dated 24th day 2nd month 1820, proved Nov 1820.

NATHAN ALAN

wife: Martha  her own land , which joins Robert Rains
              and Jacob Cox , inherited from her father.

Children: Ruth, Job, Miles, all under age.

Sole executor: trusty friend Ephriam Doan.
Witnesses: Soloman Alan, William Alan.

— — —

D 585   Will dated 12 October 1820, proved Nov Court 1820.

ISAAC HOLDEN                 wife: Elizabeth

son: Thomas Holden "my mills on Eno River", etc.
sons: Isaac (under 21 years)
"My children Thomas W. Holden, Sally Holden, Elizabeth Holden, William Holden, Mary Holden, Harriett Holden and Isaac
Holden ".                                    - continued -

92          D 585 continued

Executors: wife Elizabeth, son Thomas W. Holden, and friend
            John Taylor, Jr.
Witnesses: Tho. J. Faddis, Thomas Holden.

— — —

D 586   Will dated 27 August 1820, proved Nov Court 1820.

ANN (x) WILSON "low in health"        son: John Wilson

granddaughter Polly "that lives with me"
"             Betsy ""    "      "   " "
grandson: Robert Wilkinson
son: Thomas Wilson   $1
son-in-law: John Wilkinson   5 shillings
son: James Wilson   $10
dau: Elizabeth Wilson   balance of estate

Executors: Thomas Wilson and Elizabeth Wilson.
Witnesses: Joseph Latta, Caleb Wilson.

— — —

D 588-589  Will dated 11 January 1818, proved Jan Court 1821.

JAMES LAPSLIE

sister: Elizabeth Lapslie half of estate during her life
"I loan to Sally Bryant mother of my two supposed daughters ..
Lavinia Isabelle Bryant and Jane Bryant".. both under age,
half (of estate) now, rest after death of sister Elizabeth.

"Anderson Armstrong and Thomas Lapslie Armstrong sons of my
nephew Thomas Armstrong"
"Seney Armstrong and Mitchell Armstrong children of the said
Thomas Armstrong"

Executors: trusty friends Thomas Armstrong and Willie Shaw,Esq.
Witnesses: A. B. Bruce, Chs. Bruce.

— — —

D 590   Will dated 20 January 1821, proved Feb Court 1821.

MARY (x) RAINEY "in low state of health"

grandson: William W. Rainey
"grandchildren Mary A. Rainey & Pemelia E. Rainey"
dau-in-law: Ann P. Rainey

Executrix: daughter-in-law Ann P. Rainey.
Witnesses: Sam'l Craford, George Allison.

— — —

D 591   Will dated 8 July 1820, proved February Court 1821.

THOMAS READING                    wife: Mary
                                       - continued -

"Children, namely: John Reading, Stephen Reading, Martha Beever, Mary Whitaker, Elizabeth Horm, Thomas Reading."

Sole executor: son John Reading.
Witnesses: John Redmon, Jones Cardin.

— — —

D 592  Will dated 15 July 1820, proved February Court 1821.

JAMES (x) ROBERTS            wife gets all estate

"Two youngest sons James & Ellis" land after wife's death.
"All my other children" 10¢

Executors: William Roberts and Lewis Roberts.
Witnesses: Nathaniel Harris, Matthew (x) Ellis.

— — —

D 592  Will dated 23 September 1820, proved Feb Court 1821.

ELIZABETH F. (x) SAWYER "very weak and feeble"

All estate to sister Mary C. Sawyer.

Sole executor: friend and Uncle John Campbell.
Witnesses: E. Turner, John Landers.

— — —

D  593  Will dated 19 October 1819, proved Feb Court 1821.
JOHN LEIGH         dau: Jane  5 shillings

son: Richerson  5 shillings
daus: Aleus (?), Caty, Lear, 5 shillings each
      Susannah  $20; Patsy & Dianna bed & furniture each

"Rest of estate to be sold and money divided between my under named children to wit: Jack B. Leigh, Sullivan Leigh, Washington Leigh, Richard Leigh, Samuel Leigh, Thomas Leigh, Ewel Leigh, Patsy Ellice, Nancy Garrard, Betsy Leigh and Dianna Leigh, eleven in all."

Executors: sons Jack B. Leigh and Sullivan Leigh.
Witnesses: Anderson Clements, Philip Alston, Isaiah Marcom.

— — —

D 594  Will dated 8 December 1820, proved Feb Court 1821.

JAMES (x) MILLER "low in health"

wife:"plantation I now live on"
daus: Susan, Jane, Lydia, Polly, Rebeckah
son: William "the plantation I bought of the Widow Trice"
 "   Jesse  "200 acres joining Robert Walker and others"
                          - continued -

94             D 594 continued

sons: John and George land after mother's death

Executors: son William Miller and Rachel Miller.
Witnesses: James Williams, John Riley, Joseph Latta.
— — —

D 595  Will dated 28th day 7th month 1816, proved May 1821.

JOSEPH ALBRIGHT              wife: Barbara

dau: Sarah Nicholson
son: John Albright "the plantation on the Alamance"
"     Andrew Albright "the plantation where I now live"

Executors: son Andrew Albright and son-in-law James Nicholson.
Witnesses: John Marshill, John Marshill Jr., Jacob Marshill.
— — —

D 596  Will dated 14 January 1820, proved May Court 1821.

JOHN BROWNING               wife: Elizabeth

dau: Mary Browning         son: Soloman Browning

grandchildren: "My four granddaughters children of Rachel
               Browning Elizabeth Sarah Frances & Milly"
               "The two sons of Edward Browning Isaac &
               Edward Elim."
son: Richard Browning 10 shillings (he owes his father $200)

Executors: worthy friend Robert Browning, and Soloman Browning.
Witnesses: James Hurdle, James Douglass.
— — —

D 597-598  Will dated 1 March 1820, proved May Court 1821.

JAMES MURRAY "old - infirm"      wife: Jennit plantation, etc.

sons: John Murray, William Murray
daus: Rachel Walker, Elizabeth Craig, Margaret MCadams, Mary
son: James Murray
"my four sons" mentioned twice, only 3 are named.
He mentions "unmarried children"
nephew: James Madison Murray son of Walter Murray

Executors: William Murray, Elder, and son John Murray.
Witnesses: John McCawley, William Murray.
— — —

D 599  Will dated 12 March 1821, proved May Court 1821.

SAMUEL THOMPSON              wife: Rebeckah plantation

"sons John B., Robert & Richard T. & my daughter Sally" get
land in Tennessee.
sons: Ralph and Samuel get plantation after wife's death
"Three youngest daughters Betsy, Rebeckah & Patsy" all minors
                                          - continued -

Executors: wife Rebeckah, Thomas Thompson and Joel Cloud.
Witnesses: Joseph Anderson, David W. Anderson.

- - -

D 600   Will dated 19 July 1821, proved August Court 1821.

SAMUEL STRAYHORN              (no wife mentioned)

Son James and daughter Sally are both under age. They are
to be educated.

Executors: friend Sampson Moore and Gilbert Hart.
Witnesses: J. Webb, James Hart.

- - -

D 601   Will dated 30 May 1821, proved August Court 1821.

RICHARD (x) GOTT in "low state of health"

wife: Catherine Gott 2/3 of estate
"Sarah Squires daughter of Thomas Squires" 1/3 of estate.

No executor named.
Witnesses: Jno. Umstead, Thomas Gill, Thomas Squires.

- - -

D 601   Will dated 28 May 1821, proved August Court 1821.

CULBIRTH BURTON              wife: Christian Burton

sons: John, Samuel (youngest), Williamson, William

Executors: wife Christian, and sons Williamson and John.
Witnesses: John Link, Elizabeth Horner, John Burton,
          Henry Bunch.

- - -

D 602   Will dated 21 January 1818, proved August Court 1821.

ALEXANDER BORLAND            wife: Susannah

sons: Andrew, Archibald, Abraham
"To William and John Borland living in the State of Ga." Ŀ25 ea
"Three daughters Susannah Jenney and Nancy" unmarried
"My daughters Elizabeth Moulder, Mary Stout, Sally Strayhorn"

Executors: wife Susannah, John Cabe, Andrew Borland, and
            Archibald Borland.
Witnesses: John Scarlett, Aron (x) Hunter, Robert Taylor.

- - -

D 603   Will dated 8 January 1817, proved August Court 1821.

JAMES CRAIG, SR.            wife: Rebecca

son: William  10 shillings                - continued -

daus: Nancy Mellett, Margaret Nichols 10 shillings each
son: Isaac   10 shillings
dau: Rebecca (unmarried)
son: David   plantation

Executors: wife Rebecca, and friend John Blackwood.
Witnesses: John Blackwood, Samuel Strayhorn, Thomas Faucett.

- - -

D 605   Will dated 30 May 1821, proved August Court 1821.

GEORGE REEVES                    (no wife mentioned)

sons: John, George, James and Frederick Reeves
daus: Sarah Durham, Nancy Baldwin.

Executors: John Reeves and George Reeves.
Witnesses: William Brown, James Bishop, John Brown.

- - -

D 606   Will dated 20 September 1820, proved Nov Court 1821.

STEPHEN BECKHAM or BERKHAM          wife: Catherine

daus: Nancy and Tabitha
sons: Joshua Joseph Thomas Leonard Caswell (no punctuation)
"John my grandson that lives with me" (surname not stated)
dau: Elizabeth  has had her share

Executor: son Joshua.
Witnesses: D. Patterson, Isaac Patterson.

- - -

D 606   Will dated 20 October 1821, proved Nov Court 1821.

FREDERICK REED               wife: Penny Reed

William Anderson a legatee, no relationship stated.

Executor: William Anderson.

Witnesses: Redding George, Sampson Moore.

- - -

D 607-609  Will dated 31 July 1821, proved November Court 1821.

DAVID RAY                wife: Jane

brother: Robert Ray
son: Peter has already had land deeded to him
sons: Griffin, George and Tyree
Remaining estate to be divided into eight parts "to each of
my children Peter, Ellen, Griffin, George, Petronilla, Peggy
Jane and Tyree"
                              - continued -

D 607-609 continued                                                97
"William B. Jamison the husband of my daughter Ellen"
"To my friends Duncan Cameron and James Webb .. 1/8 part in
trust for my son William."

"Duncan Cameron, James Webb, and Thomas Ruffin the guardians
of all my infant children". These three also named executors.

Witnesses: Wil. Kirkland, Favid Woods.
— — —

D 610   Will dated 19 June 1821, proved November Court 1821.

DAVID GREESON                          wife: Mary

"My children William Elias Peter and Polly Greeson", no punctuation.

Executor: friend Ludwick Lowe.
Witnesses: W. R. Holt, Jas. Gibson.
— — —

D 611   Will dated 7 February 1811, proved Nov Court 1821.

MATHEW McCAULEY                        wife: Martha

sons: John, Charles, William, George and Mathew McCauley
daus: Jenny (Jane), Martha, Elizabeth and Elender
"Three youngest children George and Elender and Mathew" are
under age.

Executors: friends George Johnston and John McCauley.
Witnesses: Wm. Brewer, Isham Brewer,
           Cressy (Cassy ?) (x) Pickett (her mark).
— — —

D 612   Will dated 8 August 1821, proved Nov Court 1821.

ARCHIBALD NICHOLSON        (Checked with original will, very
                            bad writing.)
dau: Diley or Dilcey ? Davis Nicholson
daus: Caty Davis Nicholson, Nancy Nicholson
dau: Sukey Maras  10 shillings
grandson: Young Antony  10 shillings

Executors: George Fogleman and David Fogleman. No witnesses.
Proved by the oaths of Delilah Nicholson, George Fogleman,
William Clendennin, Joseph Murray and John Marshall.
— — —

D 614   Receipt from AMELIA (x) MORGAN to SARAH MORGAN, Exec-
utrix of Hardy Morgan deceased.
Dated 11 January 1803, proved May Court 1810.
Witnesses: John Daniel, J.G.Rencher, Ch. Barbee.
— — —

D 614  Bill of Sale from THOMAS R. CATE to JOHN S. CATE.
Dated 7 November 1818, proved Feb Court 1819.
Witness: Solomon Cate.

— — —

D 615  Bill of Sale from JAMES BARTON (or BOSTON) HORNE to
ARCHIBALD HORNE for a gray mare colt, $150.
Dated 4 May 1817, proved February Court 1819.
Witnesses: Reuben Carden, Jacob Lemmons.
This original paper is preserved in the State Archives.
_____                    Last entry in Book D                    _____

ORANGE COUNTY WILL BOOK E

E 1  Will dated 18 November 1821, proved Feb Court 1822.

ADAM (x) WHITSEL                    wife a legatee, name not stated

daus: Elizabeth, Polly, Nancy

Executors: John Boon, Esq., John Troxler.
Witnesses: John Boon, David Troxler.

— — —

E 2  Will dated 7 January 1821, proved Feb Court 1822.

WILLIAM WHITTED, Sr. of Hillsboro, N.C.        Wife: Mary

brother: Levi                deceased brother: John
neice: Anne, daughter of Jehu
son: William Henry Whitted
dau: Eliza I.
grandchildren: "William Nash Whitted and Mary T. Whitted,
                 children of my son James Whitted, deceased."
Attelia Whitted, widow of James.
"Anne Whitted deceased, daughter of Jehu".

Executors: James Webb, James Phillips.
Witnesses: Wm. Horton, John Scott.

— — —

E 7  Will dated 19 July 1821, proved Fenruary Court 1822.

JAMES LINN                    wife: Mary

"Wife Mary to make children with her equal with those that
have left her." All children to have equal shares in estate.

Executors: Henry Barnhart and Eli Euliss.
Witnesses: John (x) Euliss, WM. Causey, Peter Linn.

— — —

E 7  Will dated 3 January 1818, proved Feb Court 1822.

ADAM (x) WHITSEL                    - continued -

sons: Ludowick (deceased), Jacob, Daniel, John, Henry,
      and Christian Whitsel have all had land deeded to them
dau: Barbara is to have an amount equal to "my other daugh-
      ters who are now married and left me."
daus: Caty, Mary. and Elizabeth Turley

Witnesses: Wm. Montgomery, John Boon.

— — —

E 9   Will dated 10 January 1822, proved Feb Court 1822.

TINNIN (x) McADAMS "in low state of health"

wife: Ann            "My four children" to be "schooled"

son: Joseph Armstrong
daus: Mary, Peggy, Catey

Executor: John A. Mebane.
Witnesses: James Mebane, J. A. Mebane.

— — —

E 10   Will dated 10 August 1813 ?, proved Feb Court 1822.

DAVID ANDERSON               son: Joseph

daus: Hannah Hill, Martha  Anderson, Elizabeth Anderson

Executors: daughters Martha and Elizabeth, James Lapslie.
Witnesses: Thomas Armstrong, Robert Mitchell.

— — —

E 10   Will dated 30 January 1822, proved Feb Court 1822.

JOHN BRACKEN               wife: Nancy

daughter: Julia Ann
brother: Joseph

Executors: brother Joseph, and Caleb Wilson.
Witnesses: James Blackwell, Wm. Ector.

— — —

E 11   Will dated 14 January 1819, proved Feb Court 1822.

GEORGE GARRISON               wife: Margaret

daus: Lidia Brown, Susanna Phillips
son: Wm. H. Garrison
dau: Margaret Simpson
son: Zimree

Executor: Hall Garrison.
Witnesses: James Nicholson, Wm. Boswell.

— — —

100

E 13   Will dated 8 March 1813, proved February Court 1822.

MOSES HUTCHINS                    son: Thomas Hutchins

daus: Nelly Herndon, Hannah Herndon,
      Elizabeth Evans, Peggy Turner

Executors: son Thomas, and C. P. Patterson.
Witnesses: C. P. Patterson, Sarah Patterson.

— — —

E 13   Will dated 7 February 1822, proved Ma y Court 1822.

NATHANIEL CARTER

sons: Enoch, William, Henry, Brice
dau: Rebecca
sons: Nathaniel, Joshua

Executors: son Enoch, and John Newlin.
Witness: Elizabeth Rinstaff.

— — —

E 14   Will dated 28 December 1821, proved May Court 1822.

WILLIAM BRADFORD           sons: Thomas and Joseph

dau: Sarah McCauley
grandsons: Hamilton and Grandison, sons of daughter Sarah
daus: Elizabeth Douglas, Margaret Ray, Jane Ray wife of Wm.

Executors: son David, and Robert Ray.
Witnesses: James Bradford, Thomas Reeves.

— — —

E 15   Will dated 15 May 1822, proved May Court 1822.

DANIEL (x) HUFFHINES "low in body"       wife: Lucretia

daus: "heirs of Mary Farmer", Betsy Tickle, Caty Lowe,
      Mary May, Susa (Lucy ?) Cornodle, Sally Lowe,
      Christiner Cotner

sons: John, Jacob, George
He mentions George Cornable (Cornodle ?) as having a note.
George's father is also named George.

Executors: sons-in-law David Lowe and George Cornodle.
Witnesses: Joseph Gibson, Jeremiah Holt.

— — —

E 17   Will dated 8 December 1818, proved May Court 1822.

EPHRIAM CARRINGTON       wife: Priscilla

sons: Morgan, John, Linton (?)
daus: Charlotte, Dicey, Polly        - continued -

Executors: Herbert Lines, John I. Carrington "friends".
Witnesses: James S. Harris, Thomas Cottrell.

– – –

E 18  Will dated 7 March 1817, proved May Court 1822.

SUSANNA WARD                    son: William

son: James 20 shillings,
sons: Stephen, Thomas
daus: Sarah Clark, Asther Wells
son: Antony Ward
dau: Priscilla Free (?)
"To my daughter Susanna Pike heirs 20 shillings"

Execytors: son Stephen Ward, and David Patterson.
Witnesses: Isaac Patterson, John Coble.

– – –

E 19  Will dated 4 April 1822, proved August Court 1822.

JOHN (x) TICKLE                 wife: Mary

dau: Margaret Millar "tract on which she now lives"
daus: Catheriner Trollinger, Mary Huffhines, Barbary Tate.

"Grandson David Tickle's daughter Sally"
son: John

Executor: son John.
Witnesses: John H. Carmichael, Daniel Ockelreas.

– – –

E 20  Will dated 20 June 1822, proved August Court 1822.

JACOB (x) JOHNSON     (Checked with original in Archives)

wife: Amy (?) "land I now live on which I purchased of
            Clement Massey."

Executrix: wife.
Witnesses: Sanders Riley, Warden Riley, Austin (x) Wesson.

– – –

E 20  Will dated 6 August 1822, proved August Court 1822.

GEORGE GRESHAM (or GRISHAM), SR.          wife: Sarah

grandsons: George Washington Clinton, John Linnington Clin-
            ton; Samuel Harrison Clinton (youngest is under
            age, but can't tell which is youngest)
granddaughters: Sarah Clinton, Elizabeth Clinton,
            Nancy  Clinton, Mary Ann Clinton.

Executors: "worthy friends Aquilla Rhodes and James Dollar
            son of Jonathan."
Witnesses: Moses McCown, James Dollar.

– – –

102

E 21   Will dated 9 June 1822, proved August Court 1822.

JOHN NELSON                          wife: Janet.
sons: William, David, John, Samuel, Alfred, Paisley
dau: Isabella
son: James
daus: Marey (or Nancy), Margaret

no executor named
Witnesses: Samuel Nelson, James Tate.
- - -

E 22   Will dated 6 August 1821, proved November Court 1822.

JAMES JACKSON, SR.

sons: William, Jacob and James Jackson  $5 each
daus: Susannah Latta, Mary Cloud, Sarah Cloud  $10 each
daus: Elizabeth Jackson and Tuth Jackson "plantation where
          Abner Jackson now lives"

Executrix: daughter Elizabeth Jackson.
Witnesses: Wm. Nichols, Sr., Abner Jackson, Bradley Collins.
- - -

E 23   Will dated 23 October 1822, proved Nov Court 1822.

JOHN YOUNG of the Town of Hillsboro

wife: Nancy "my plantation bought of James Hastings", etc.

"Tiny children" mentioned, names and number not stated.

Executors: friends Levi Whitted and Thomas D. Watts.
Witnesses: James Webb, James L. Smith.
- - -

E 24   Will dated 6 April 1821, proved November Court 1822.

WILLIAM SHEPPARD

children: Wm. Sheppard, Betsy Ashe, Mary Ashe, & Susan Jane Hay
dau: Sally Grove
sons: Egbert Sheppard, Henry James Sheppard
dau: Margaret L. Sheppard "640 acres in Tennessee in the Chick-
          asaw Purchase", etc.

Executors: Dr. James Webb, David Yarborough.
Witness: John Haywood.
- - -

E 25   Will dated 29 July 1818, proved November Court 1822.

JOSEPH (x) COURTNEY "weak and indisposed"

Friend, relation, Thomas D. Watts  all estate.      - continued

Elizabeth Christmas is to be allowed to live where she is
   now for her lifetime.

"Loving friend and sister Frances Courtney"

Executor: friend Thomas Clancy.
Witnesses: Robert Glenn, Jane Glenn.
— — —

E 26  Will dated 2 October 1820, proved Nov Court 1822.

MARY WOODS, widow  (See will of Hugh Woods Jan 1794, D 1)

dau: Susanna Faucett
granddau: Rebecca P, Ray, daughter of Thomas Ray and his Mary.
dau: Sarah Ray
granddaus: "son John Woods two daughters Susanna and Peggy"
great-grand-dau:"Mary Mecia (?) Wood, daughter of my grand-
               son Timothy Wood."
daus: Elizabeth Woods,Mary Ann Ray

Executors: son Joseph Woods, friend Robert Walker,
Witnesses: William Dunagan, Eli Woods, Wm. Baldwin.
— — —

E 27  Will dated 22 May 1822, proved November Court 1822.

MARTHA (PATSEY) BREWER

sisters: Polly Miner, Fanny King, Elizabeth O'Daniel
         Biddy Brewer (under age), Aris Brewer
brothers: William Brewer, Ransom Brewer, Morris Brewer,
          John Brewer

Her mother is living.

Executors: "beloved friends Thomas Brewer Sr, and Sackfield
           Brewer."
Witnesses: Thomas Brewer, Ezekiel Brewer.
— — —

E 28  Will dated 27 February 1821, proved Nov Court 1822.

JAMES WOODY              wife: Mary

sons: Hugh, Samuel, John
daus: Sarah, Mary, Rebecca, Charity, Hannah,
      Susannah, Jane, Ruth, Ellenor

Executors: sons Hugh and Samuel.
Witnesses: Enoch Morrison, Robert Graham.
— — —

E 29  Will dated 25 October 1822, proved Nov Court 1822.

JAMES HASTINGS                    daughter: Easter Cate

sons: Thomas, Henry
daus: Nance Smith, Sarah Hastings, Hannah Smith,
    Margaret Lashley
youngest sons: James, John, Joseph

Executors: sons Thomas and Henry.
Witnesses: A. Watson, Joseph H. Latta.

- - -

E 30  Will dated 14 November 1822, proved Feb Court 1823.

JOSEPH PICKETT                    wife: Nancy

"Supposed son, John Copley, son of Dolly Copley.".. "Lives
with me, raised by me, and bound by me - 17 February 1816."

Witnesses: Jacob Whitaker, Isley Copley.

- - -

E 31  Will dated 12 February 1819, proved Feb Court 1823.

ANNA ARMSTRONG          son-in-law: Isaac Jackson

"To all my sons and daughters 10 shillings each", none named.

Executor: son-in-law Isaac Jackson.
Witnesses: Robert Whitted, Levi Whitted.

- - -

E 32  Will dated 5 October 1822, proved Feb Court 1823.

WILLIAM McKEE                    wife: Dolly or Polly

daus: Polly or Dolly McKee, Anne Wood
son: Rankin
dau: Victory Boring
sons: James, William
dau: Betsy Hargis
son: David

Executors: wife, and son Rankin.
Witnesses: William B. Roberson, James Murdock.

- - -

E 33  Will dated 25 July 1822, proved May Court 1823.

PETER (x) TICKLE "low and weak"

children: Mary Whait, John Tickle, Peter Tickle,
        Elizabeth Huffhines, Conrad Tickle, Henry Tickle.
son-in-law: Daniel Whait

Executor: Joseph Gibson.        Witness: Anthony Coble.

- - -

E 34  Will dated 25 February 1823, proved May Court 1823.

MARY WHITTED

daughter: Eliza J. Whitted
son: Henry Whitted
grandchildren: Nash Whitted and Mary Jemima (or Terminia ?)
            Whitted get 1/3 of estate

Executor: James Webb
Witnesses: William Whitted, James Webb.

— — —

E 35  Will dated 25 July 1822, proved May Court 1823.

SAMUEL PEELOR          wife: Elizabeth

son: Benjamin "when he comes of age".."old place whereon
            Iley Browning now lives"
grown sons: Cader Peelor, Michael Sherman Peelor,
            Pleasant Peelor, Anthony Redwine Peelor,
            Thornberry Peelor
daus: Sarah Peelor, Catherine Peelor

Executors: Moses Guess and Moses McCown.
Witnesses: Anthony Cole, Thomas James.

— — —

E 36  Will dated 5 February 1823, proved May Court 1823.

WILLIAM ANDERSON          wife a legatee, name not stated

"Money put to interest till my youngest child comes of age
then equally divided between my children."

Executors: worthy friends Joseph Allison and William Maris.
Witnesses: J.D.Hughes, Thomas Armstrong, Joseph Allison.

— — —

E 36  Will dated --  , proved August Court 1823.

DANIEL MAY          wife: Barbary May

sons: David, William, Daniel, Jacob
daus: Mary Allbright, Barbary May, Catherine May

Executors: sons Jacob and William.
Witnesses: James Nelson, Samuel Curtis.

— — —

E 37  Will dated 7 February 1816, proved August Court 1823.

WILLIAM KEELING          wife: Polley

"son William's three sons: John youngest, oldest son Benjamin, William"                    - continued -

"son James Keeling and his two sons James and William"
son: Gregory Perry Keeling
"My other five children: Thomas, Rachel, Betsey, Polly
and Ceney."

Executors: William and James Keeling and John Dunn.
Witnesses: Richard Breeze, Ast. Moore.

- - -

E 39  Will dated 6 February 1822, proved August Court 1823.

LUCY HILLYARD

She leaves all her estate to her daughters, because it is
so small, though she loves her sons dearly.
Eldest daughter Nancy is to be guardian of the three other
daughters, Lucy, Martha and Mary.

sons: William and John
Unimproved lot in Chapel Hill, N.C. is to be sold.

Executor: "Elisha Mitchell of Orange County."
Witnesses: William Pannill, Samuel Pannill.

- - -

E 40  Will dated 15 April 1820, proved August Court 1823.

JAMES PYLE            wife: Sarah

sons: Isaac and Caleb  $5 each
grandson: Henry Pyle son of Caleb
sons: William gets property, John $5, Joseph $50 "if living"
daus: Mary Whittenton, Rachel Cooke  $5 each
grandson: Moses Pyle son of Isaac
"           Garrett Pyle son of John
great-granddaughter: Rebecca Pyle (under 21)

Executors: William Matkins, William Brinkley.
Witnesses: Thomas Brown, James Danieley.
(Note: Mary Pyle married 15 Sept 1802 John Whittington.)

- - -

E 41  Bill of Sale  from WILLIAM HINCHEY of Orange County
to THOMAS M. JOHNSTON for bay horse, saddle and bridle, all
household furniture, etc.  Dated 13 July 1823, proved August
Court 1823.  Witnesses: C.W.Johnston, Matthew McCauley.

- - -

E 42  Will dated 15 December 1820, proved Nov Court 1823.

ISAAC HOLT            wife: Mary

youngest sons: Archibald M. Holt and Isaac , not of age
son: Thomas S. Holt                    - continued -

E 42    Will of Isaac Holt continued                    07

Maria D. Foust wife of George Foust
Emily Ray wife of William Ray
Thomas Rowan and wife Emily and to her children
"I leave on the Guliford Plantation of my wife .." etc.

Executors: Thomas Scott and George Foust, Jr.
Witnesses: Daniel Coble, Austin Coble, Frederick Kemruce ?,
          Thomas Scott, Wm. D. Murphey, A. D. Murphey.
Codicil dated 23 June 1821 names no new legatees.

- - -

E 47  Will dated 18 August 1823, proved Nov Court 1823.

JONATHAN DAVIS              wife a legatee, name not stated

  All children to have equal shares in estate. They are all
under age now.

Executors: wife, and Colonel Joseph Allison.
Witnesses: E. Graves, Abram Parish.

- - -

E 48  Will dated 9 September 1823, proved Nov Court 1823.

PERRY MITCHELL

wife: Polly  "land left me by will of my father at the
             death of my mother."

Executors: wife Polly, and Eli Murray.
Witnesses: Benjamin Burnside, John Compton.

E 48  Will dated 4 December 1807, proved Nov Court 1823.

LUDWICK WAYNICK

wife: Margaret "all to my wife unless she marry again , then
              to be returned to my children"

sole executrix: wife Margaret.
Witnesses: Thomas C. Scott, John Southard.

- - -

E 49  Will dated 15 February 1820, proved Feb Court 1824.

WILLIAM ANDREW, SR. (Indexed in Archives as ANDRUS)
"very aged"
sons: Starling land lying west of the Haw Branch
      Archibel, Laborn  5 shillings
grandchildren: "lawful heirs of Elizabeth Edwards" 5 sh.
sons: Mark, John  5 shillings each
dau: Patsy Cheek 5 shillings
son: Henry 5 shillings      dau: Ginney Cheek 5 shillings
                - continued -

108   E 49   Will of WILLIAM ANDREW, SR continued

sons: William 5 shillings, Archibald

Executors: sons Laborn and Mark.
Witnesses: Thomas Brewer, John ...?..

- - -

E 50   Will dated 19 April 1823, proved February Court 1824.

THOMAS LASHLEY (LESLEY in Archives)   wife: Hannah

daus: Fanny, Hannah, Nicy, Henry Ray's wife, Jean, Rachel
sons: Thomas, Elijah, Alexander
Betsy, David Ray's wife

Executor: friend James Thompson.
Witnesses: Thomas Bradshaw, James Bradshaw.

- - -

E 51   Will dated 1821, proved February Court 1824.

WILLIS (x) MONK                    wife: Mary

sons: Andrew, John
"I have given all my children their portion I alloted for them."

Executors: wife Mary Monk, and Ezekiel Hailey.

- - -

E 52   Will dated 5 February 1824, proved Feb Court 1824.

RACHEL (x) MILLER   "in low state of health"

sons: William, Jessey
daus: Lydia Miller, Polly Miller, Rebecca Miller
sons: Jarge (under age), John
sister: Sally Hall "my loom"
sons-in-law: Samuel Bird, James S. Cate  5 shillings each

No executor named.
Witnesses: John I. Freeland, Daniel Cloud.

- - -

E 53   Will dated 1 January 1823, proved Feb Court 1824.

JOHN McCAULEY

wife: Mary R. "land I may inherit from my father by Will at
              his death ...: to be divided between my chil-
              dren, if any, if none then in that case whole
              shall be divided equally between Maria and Mar-
              tha Lea, daughters of Gabriel B. Lea, Esq."
sister: Mary Ann Lea
brother: Robert W. McCauley
brother-in-law: William M. Lea

Executor: Joel B. Lea.                    Witness: Robert Morrow.

- - -

E 54   Will dated 26 November 1823, proved May Court 1824

WILLIAM PICKETT                    wife: Elizabeth

sons: Edward, Joseph and William (youngest)

"The whole of my children, Edward, Patsy, Polly, Eliza, Emily, Joseph, Lucretia, William."

Executor: Gabriel B. Lea.
Witnesses: I. S. Smith, Elizah Pickard.

— — —

E 55   Will dated 11 May 1824, proved May Court 1824.

JOHN HOLT              wife: Melly

"My three children: Elizabeth, Hezekiah, Milly."

Executor: cousin William Holt.
Witnesses: Peter L. Ray, Mason Tarpley.

— — —

E 56   Will dated 9 January 1823, proved May Court 1824.

JOHN HUTCHINS         dau: Polly wife of William Lewis

Executors: daughter Polly lewis, and son-in-law Wm. Lewis.
Witnesses: Philip Alston, William Lynn, J. Dickson.

— — —

E 57   Will dated 8 January 1824, proved May Court 1824.

DAVID HARDEE                wife: Winney

sons: John, William, Thomas
daus: Polly Wells, Elizabeth Crisp, Sally Hardee,
      Martha  Carlton Thompson
granddaughter: Martha Winnefred Thompson
                                                    Wells.
Executors: wife, and Sally Hardee , Mr. Willie Shaw, Miles /
Witnesses: Alston Moore, John Moore.

— — —

E 58   Will dated 31 October 1816, proved May Court 1824.

THOMAS KELL               son: William

"Three children Robert, Thomas, Elizabeth

Executors: William Kell and Thomas Riggs.
Witness: John Latta.

— — —

110

E 59  Will dated 18 February 1824, proved May Court 1824.

SAMUEL PYLE                    wife: Susannah

sons: Joel, Alfred, William
 He speaks of property to be kept in hands of executors for
"all my children", but only the three above are named.

Executors: Isaac Patterson, Alexander Albright
Witnesses: Stephen Ward, Leven Woods, John Pike,Jr.

— — —

E 60  Will dated 20 May 1824, proved August Court 1824.

WILLIAM MARSHILL               wife: Mary

daus: Elizabeth (unmarried), Rachel, Ann
son: William "plantation he now lives on"
sons-in-law: Benjamin Dixon, Winlock (?) Reynolds, Solomon Stout
dau-in-law: Elizabeth Marshill

Executors: son William, and son-in-law Benjamin Dixon.
Witnesses: Solomon Allen, John (x) Sheirdan (?).

— — —

E 61  Will dated 2 March 1824, proved August Court 1824.

NATHANIEL KING, SR.            wife: Sally

son: Thomas
daus: Polly, Sally, Fanny

..."property equally divided between all my children now
living."

Executors: wife Sally; and sons Nathaniel and William.
Witnesses: John Adams, John McCauley, N. I. King.

— — —

E 62  Will dated 16 November 1823, proved August Court 1824.

JOHN McDANIEL                  wife: Margaret

sons: Eli, John, Alexander
daus: Elenor, Elizabeth, Margaret, Jean, Susannah
son: James

Executors: sons Eli and James.
Witnesses: John Stockard, Richard Thompson.

— — —

E 64  Will dated 3 July 1824, proved November Court 1824.

PETER WALKER                   wife: Elizabeth

nephew: William Walker son of William Walker deceased

- continued -

nephew: Peter Walker, son of "my brother Andrew"
"Lemuel Pickett son of John"
neice: Sarah Walker "daughter of my brother Andrew"

Executors: brother Andrew Walker, and nephew John Pickett.
Witnesses: Wm. I. Bingham, Vicy King, Nancy Hamilton.
- - -

E 65  Will dated 18 August 1824, proved Nov Court 1824.

JOHN LONG                    aunt: Polly Freeland

uncle and aunt: Samuel Craig and Peggy Craig
cousin: Elizabeth Craig
half-brothers: George Long, Thomas Long, James Long,
              Charles Long; Anderson Long, 5 shillings each
half-sisters:   Nancy Long, Catherine Long,5 "          "
"To my brother William Long's children he had of his wife
Peggy"  5 shillings each.
"To the man who succeeds me as Captain of my Company, my
Military equipage .."etc.

Executors: friends Isaac Craig, John Freeland.
Witnesses: Isaac Craig, James Freeland.

- - -

E 66  Will dated 1 April 1824, proved November Court 1824.

JOSEPH LATTA            wife: Sarah

"All my children: Mary P. Latta, John Cabe Latta, Nancy A.
Latta, Elizabeth L. Latta, Caroline L. Latta."(John a minor.)

Executors: trusty friends Thomas Latta and James Latta.
Witnesses: John Riley, John Ray, Sr.
- - -

E 68  Will dated 28 July 1824, proved November Court 1824.

JOHN RHODES                wife: Patsy

sons: Pleasant, John, Benjamin
daus: Polly, Sally, Betsy, Patsy

Executors: Christopher Barbee Jr, Pleasant Rhodes, and
            Benjamin Rhodes.
Witnesses: Sampson Moore, F ? H. Ta ylor.
- - -

E  67  Will dated 5 June 1823, proved November Court 1824,

JOHN LATTA                son: Thomas

"son John's two children John and Maria"        - continued -

sons: James, Joseph
sons-in-law: Robert Walker, Robert Davis
           William Faucett, Thomas Holloway Jr.
grandsons: William and John Holloway

Executors: sons Thomas and John Latta.
Witnesses: James Allison, Robert Davis.

- - -

E 70  Will dated 10 January 1823, proved August Court 1824.

State of Tennessee, Roane County 4th Monday in April 1823
Court.  "An instrument in writing was produced in Open Court
and proved by oath of Samuel Eskridge and Abigail Johnston
who made oath that the said FRANCIS CHILDS signed, sealed
and published the said instrument as his last will and testament in their presence.

   I, FRANCES CHILDS of Orange County, N.C. now in Roane County Tennessee, and I give and deliver to my son, Samuel, one-
halfof my estate.  To my wife, Martha, rest of estate. Hereby
appoint executors: Simon Turner of Murray County. "

- - -

E 71  Will dated 12 August 1822, proved February Court 1825.

HENRY THOMPSON                    wife: Priscilla

dau: Mrs. Nelly Baldridge
dau: Sally - her estate is to be held in trust for her during
           her life by Catlett Campbell, James Child, William
           Huntington.
granddaughter: Susan Thompson "daughter of said Sally"

Executors: Thomas Clancy, John Scott.
Witnesses: James Phillips, J. H. Hand.

- - -

E 73  Will dated 4 July 1822, proved February Court 1825.

JACOB ALBRIGHT           "beloved wife"

sons: John, Solomon, William
"After just debts paid money to be equally divided between my
daughters" names and number not stated.

Executors: son Solomon and son-in-law John Albright.
Witnesses: Andrew Albright, Henry Garrott.

- - -

E 74  Will dated 5 May 1817, proved February Court 1825.

WILLIAM (x) HOLDER            wife: Mourning

Children: Chesley, William, Daniel, Polly, John, Hosea,
      Lydia, Nancy, Elijah, Elisha.
Executor: son Chesley.  Witnesses: Thos. Flint, Harrison
                                  Christian.
- - -

Will dated 6 December 1824, proved Feb Court 1825.

LESLIE O'KELLY                    wife: Nancy

"My children", names and number not stated.

Executor: brother Franklin O'Kelly and brother-in-law John
          McCuiston.
Witnesses: Henry Moring, William Hudson.

- - -

E 76  Will dated 24 August 1823, proved Feb Court 1825.

SARAH YEARGAN      daus: Charlotte Nunn, Harriet Forsythe

son: Mann Patterson
Milly , daughter of Mann Patterson
"Four oldest daughters of Mann Patterson", not named.
son: Bartlett Yeargan

Executor: Mann Patterson
Witnesses: B. Cheek, W. I. Dillard.

- - -

E 76  Will dated 29 July 1824, proved Feb Court 1825.

WILLIAM HENRY WHITTED              wife: Frances

sister: Eliza Jane Murphey
brother James
brother's children: William Nash Whitted
                    Tarmesia Mary Whitted

Executor: Dr. James Webb.
Witnesses: Thomas Ruffin, James Child, James Webb, John Street

- - -

E 78  Will dated 20 April 1821, proved February Court 1825.

JOHN O'DANIEL

sons: John, Henry, James, Jesse, Green
daus: Jane Cates, Peggy Thompson
"Peggy Thompson's three daughters Nance, Jane and Anne
    Thompson are to have her part" (is Peggy deceased ?)
"Nancy Basket, John Basket, and William Basket sons and
    daughter of Susannah Basket"

Executors: son James, and Thomas Thompson.
Witnesses: Ezra Durham, John Durham, Henry O'Daniel Sr.

- - -

E 80  Will dated 29 November 1824, proved May Court 1825.

ELIZABETH HOWARD           daughter: Henrietta

granddau: Elizabeth Christmas Howard, daughter of Richard

Executor: Stephen Glass
Witnesses: W. Thompson, Reuben Smith.
- - -

E 81  Will dated 12 July 1812, proved May Court 1825.

JAMES WILSON                        wife: Henrietta

son: Samuel gets a colt          son: William  "small colt"
daus: Dicey, Sally, Henrietta, Jean
"Granddaughter Mariah daughter of my deceased daughter
  Dradeyann (?)."
sons: John D. Wilson and George Wilson, both under age.
   "     Hiram "my plantation"; James to "live where he is for 3 yrs"
son-in-law: James Turrentine $1   After wife's death her share t
"All my children, namely: James, Archelaus, William, Samuel,
  John D, George Wilson, also Nancy, Polly, Dicey, Sally,
  Henrietta and Jeane,"except Hiram, who has land left to him."
       wife
Executors:/Henrietta and Samuel Turrentine.
Witnesses: S. Turrentine, Alex. Turrentine, Arch. Turrentine.

Proved by oaths of Thomas Clancy and William Hall who swore
that they were acquainted with the handwriting both of Samuel
and Alex Turrentine and that they believe their names sub-
scribed as witnesses to the foregoing will are in the proper
handwriting of the said Samuel and Alex Turrentine."

— — —

E 82  Will dated 12 March 1825, proved May Court 1825.

JAMES BARNWELL              wife: Susan

"Three youngest daughters Susan, Nancy and Elenor".

Children: Robert, Catherine, John, William, Susan, Nancy,
          Elenor, James

Executors: wife Susan, and son John.
Witnesses: Ellis Malone, William Murray, Andrew Murray.

— — —

E 84  Will dated 28 January 1825, proved May Court 1825.

THOMAS VINCENT

sons: John, William, James, Thomas
daus: Sarah Morrow, Polly Byrd, Elizabeth Vincent

Executors: sons John and William.
Witnesses: Thomas Reeves, Wm. Creswell, Gab. B. Lea.

— — —

E 86  Noncupative will of WILLIAM W. HALL dated 4 June 1825,

proved by the oaths of William Hall Sr., Joseph Allison and
Joel Reynolds at August Court 1825.
All estate left to Alex G. Hall, no relationship stated.

— — —

E 86   Will dated 7 September 1824, proved August Court 1825.

JOSEPH BOOTHE, SENIOR                wife: Sarah

son: Joseph

"Grandchildren Joseph B. Herndon, George Herndon, Lewis,
    Willis and Mary Herndon are to receive the share of their
    deceased mother, Mary Herndon."

daughter: Rosy Reach (Beach ?)
granddaughter: Mary Yates daughter of Rosy Reach
daus: Elizabeth Stone, Tabitha Hudson, Delilah Yates,
      Sally George

Executors: Wm. Yates, Sampson Moore, and wife Sarah Boothe.
Witnesses: David George, David Castleberry.

Note by Ruth Herndon Shields: This BOOTHE family and their
descendants are given in HERNDON-HUNT and ALLIED FAMILIES
by Lillie Boothe Nesbitt and Edna Hilliard White Wood, published 1930.  The HERNDON grandchildren's ancestry will be
found in HERNDONS OF THE AMERICAN REVOLUTION, PART FOUR, by
John Goodwin Herndon. (See last page in this book.)
- - -

E 87   Will dated 10 March 1825, proved August Court 1825.

WILLIAM LEATHERS

" ... property to be divided equally between my wife and
children .... to be kept together until one of them marries
or comes of age ..." Number and names of children not given.

Executors: brother Fielding Leathers, and Tignal Jones.
Witnesses: James Webb, Westward A. Jones.
- - -

E 88   Will dated 20 August 1822, proved August Court 1825.

JOHN FLINTHOM (FLENTHOM ?)        wife: Alsey

son: Clement
daus: Elizabeth Campbell, Sally Flinthum
Legacy to Nancy Carr (relationship not stated) .."if she
    will come into this county and visit her relations, nothing
    if she will not come."
son: James                    No executor named.

Witnesses: Archibald Borland, Thomas W. Holden.
- - -

E 89   Will dated 28 August 1818, proved Nov Court 1825.

PETER INGOLD            wife a legatee, name not stated

son: Adam                              - continued -

He says he leaves "nothing to other heirs".
William Ingold is mentioned in description of land boundaries,
  no relationship mentioned.

Executor: son Adam.
Witnesses: Jacob Sherer, John Garrett, Peter Ingold.

— — —

E 90  Will dated 6 April 1825, proved Nov Court 1825.

CHARLES HOBSON          wife: Zernah

daus: Peninah and Lydia, both under age.

Executor: William Thompson.
Witnesses: John Thompson (two of them), Libri ? Moffitt.

— — —

E 90  ADAM SPRINGER          sisters: Mary Springer, Eve Partin

brothers: David Springer, George Springer

Executor: "Trusty and beloved friend Sebastian Graves."
Witnesses: Benj. Burnside, John Coble.

— — —

E 91  Will dated --, proved November Court 1825.

DAVID NELSON          brother-in-law: David Craig

brothers: William, John, Samuel and Alfred Nelson.
sisters: Mary Nelson, Margaret Nelson
brother: Paisley Nelson
mother: Jennett Nelson

Executors: James Tate and David Mebane.
Witnesses: David Mebane, James Tate.

— — —

E 92  Will dated 16 April 1824, proved November Court 1825.

JOHN DAVIS          wife: Elizabeth

sons: Anderson, James, John, William
daus: Sally Beville, Nancy Raney, Frances Beville
son: Robert
daus: Mary Davis, Elizabeth Gattis
son: Wyatt

Executors: son  James, and Sampson Moore.
Witnesses: Jack B. Leigh, Anne Leigh.

— — —

E 94  Will dated 20 November 1822, proved Nov Court 1825.

JONATHAN JORDAN          wife: Mary

son: George              daughter: Nancy

grandson: Jacob          granddaughter: Polly Jordan

"To each and all my other children the property they have
   already received of me." Names and number not stated.

Executors: James Hutcheson, George Hurdle.
Witnesses: David Perkins, James Paul.
– – –

E 95  Will dated 13 September 1825, proved Nov Court 1825 ?

JOHN B. VINCENT

brothers William and James, and sister Betsey

niece: "Elizabeth Bird, daughter of my sister Polly Bird."

Executors: Brothers William and James.
Witnesses: Gabriel  B. Leigh, Ashford Walker,
– – –        Wm. C. Patrick, James Weldon.

E 96  Will dated 24 April 1820, proved February Court 1826.

RICHARD BENNEHAN          daughter: Rebecca Cameron

son: Thomas D. Bennehan

"1,000 for the propagation of the gospel of Jesus Christ."

Witnesses: Samuel Yarborough, Wm. M. Shaw
Executors: son Thomas D. Bennehan, and Duncan Cameron.

– – –

E 97  Will dated 3 April 1818, proved February Court 1926.

WILLIAM McCAULEY       James Allison's lot in Hillsboro is
                                         mentioned.
son: John
dau: Jane McCollum
sons: Matthew, Charles
grandson: William, son of John
grandsons: Benjamin and James, sons of Matthew
"          James Reeves;  William, son of Charles
dau-in-law: Catred ? McCauley, widow of son James
son-in-law: William Trousdale and Catred his wife

Executors: George Johnston, Alex. Gattis, Wm. Kirkland.
Witnesses: Matthew McCauley, James McCauley.

– – –

E 99  Will dated 22 March 1823, proved February Court 1826.

JUDY CLAPP

"Children of my daughter Barbara formerly wife of John Powell."
son: John
daughter: Caty, wife of John Hobbs
"         Sophia, wife of Jacob Foust

Executor: son John Clapp.
Witnesses: Joel C. Yancey , Wm. Smith.

— — —

E 99  Will dated 28 January 1826, proved Feb Court 1826.

JOHN STRAIN                  wife: Marian ? Miriam ?

sons: David, Alexander, James, Samuel
dau: Mary Strayhorn
daus: Elizabeth Strain, Sarah Strain
grandchildren:  Jane Strayhorn and Samuel Strayhorn

Executors: son David Strain, and son-in-law Bryant Strayhorn.
Witnesses: Charles W. Johnston, Wm. Kirkland, Chas. R. Yancey.

— — —

E 101  Will dated 29 October 1825, proved Feb Court 1826.

GEORGE TROXLER             son: John, under age

eldest daughter: Adeline Warren, wife of Briscoe Warren
daughter: Franky Rich, wife of Henry Rich
unmarried daughters, names not stated: "my two other daugh-
     ters that may remain after one other is married."

Executors: son-in-law Briscoe Warren, and Wm. Montgomery.
Witnesses: D. Albright, B. Troxler.

— — —

E 103  Will dated 29 October 1825, proved Feb Court 1826.

MARY CRAIG

She is to be buried at New Hope (Presbyterian) Meeting House
where "my husband and many of my relatives are buried."

grandchildren: "William, Peggy and Polly, children of my
     deceased son Samuel."

Executors: Wm. Kirkland and Charles D. Johnson.
Witnesses: George J. Johnston, Joseph Kirkland.

— — —

E 105  Will dated 11 November 1825, proved Feb Court 1826.

JOSEPH TATE        wife: Mary              - continued -

E 105 Will of JOSEPH TATE continued
daughters: Polly and Alice
son: Griffith Tate. Legacy to him "if said Griffith Tate
ever return to the county."
sons: James, Joseph, William, Robert
dau: Elizabeth Taylor
"All property divided between five sons and three daughters,
Polly and Alice."

Executors: sons William and Robert
Witnesses: John Hughes, William Gattis.

— — —

E 106 Will dated 6 September 1824, proved Feb Court 1826.

ROBERT DOCKERY                 wife: Caty

nephew: "Sister's son John Withey (?)

Executors: Richard Breese and Caty Dockery.
Witnesses: S.M.McCracken, John (x) Dockery, R. Breese,
Paton ? Dockery.

— — —

E 107 Will dated 22 December 1825, proved Feb Court 1826.

ROSANNAH COTNER              grandson: Aaron Cotner

relationship not stated to : Barbary Hunt, Eve Stonor,
Mary Alexander, Peter Cotner, Susannah Kinney

"To Louis Cotner, Grace Cotner and Rosannah Gifford all
rest of my property."

Executors: Isaih Hornaday and Samuel Hymer.
Witnesses: Micajah Thompson, Job Evans.

— — —

E 107 Will dated 6 February 1826, proved May Court 1826.

ROBERT WALKER               wife: Elenor

daughter: Elizabeth Patterson "to be excluded"
sons: John, William, Robert, Philip, and George W. Walker
(George is under age)
daus: Sally, Polley, Peggy, Jane
granddaughter: Elizabeth Walker

"To Rev. WM. M. Green in trust for Protestant Episcopal
Church in this state, $25."

Executors: sons John and William.
Witnesses: Wm. B. Jamison, Ezekiel Laws.

— — —

E 109  Will dated 5 March 1826, proved May Court 1826.

PHILIP WALKER, SR.        sons: James, Alexander

dau: Jinney
sons: Conley, John, Philip
dau-in-law: Peggy Walker
dau: Mary Crawford

Executor: son Connerly Walker.
Witnesses: Thomas Reeves, Ralph Faucett.

- - -

E 111  Will dated 1 December 1825, proved May Court 1826.

WILLIAM SHEPPERD          son: James

"Heirs of Henry Shepperd"
daus: Mary, Caty, and heirs of Elizabeth
"Rest of property divided between my six daughters" names
  not stated.

Executors: "Sampson Moore as an executor for Susanna Thrower",
        Christopher Barbee and Sullivan Leigh.
Witnesses: Richard Leigh, Berry Holden.

- - -

E 112  Deed from HENRY EDWARDS, SR. to JOHN EDWARDS of Chatham
Co., N.C., for a  negro boy. Dated 10 April 1826, proved May
Court 1826.  Witnesses: Henry Edwards, Jr., Isaac Durham.

- - -

E 113  Will dated 20 April 1824, proved ....... 1826.

HENRY NEAL               wife: Lydia

Part of property to be "divided between my children and my
Wife's sister Nancy Furguson."
dau: Martha Turner wife of James Turner
grandson: Henry Turner son of James

Executor: James Webb.
Witnesses: F.B.Phillips, W. Whitted.

- - -

E 115  Will dated 19 May 1817, proved August Court 1826.

JOHN KELLY, SR.          wife: Mary

granddaughters: Peggy and Sally Lockhart, $50 each
grandsons: Isaac, John K., Billy and David Lockhart, $1 each
Remainder of estate to "wife Mary Kelly and her six children,
to wit: Kesiah Bane, Nancy Kelly, Dolly, Betsy, my son John,
and Charity Kelly."

Executors: James Cain, Archibald Cain, Thomas Bain.

- - -

E 117  Will dated 1 July 1824, proved August Court 1826.

ISAAC JACKSON, SR.                 wife: Mary

daus: Elizabeth Reynolds, Ruth Pickett
"daughter Mary Thompson's children" their mother's portion
To Benoni Jackson (relationship not stated) 50 acres
son: James Jackson "my plantation"
To "rest of lawful children 50¢ ... which have all been
portioned off before."

Executors: James Jackson, Benoni Jackson.
Witnesses: Brice Jackson, Jno. Jackson.

─  ─  ─

E 118  Will dated 3 April 1826, proved August Court 1826.
       This will is not indexed in the State Archives.

MASON TARPLEY

wife: Elizabeth, plantation and ten slaves, etc.
sons: James, Abraim, William, Henry

unmarried daughters Sarah, Elizabeth, Dolly, Milly, Nancy,
"if they should marry they be furnished by my executors such
things as can be spared & value it that the other married
daughters may be equal."

Witnesses: Peter L. Ray, John Isley.

─  ─  ─

E 120  Will dated 26 May 1826, proved August Court 1826.

WILLIAM ANDREW          wife: Hannah, west end of land joining
                               Joseph Thompson's.
son: Isaac
granddaughter: Olive Newlin
grandson: William Andrew son of John Andrew
"Sons and daughters, namely, Henry, Sarah, John, Robert,
Samuel, William, James, Aaron and Hannah."

Executors: son Isaac, and son-in-law Nathaniel Newlin.
Witnesses: Joseph Marshill, Thomas Thompson.

─  ─  ─

E 121  Will dated 17 June 1826, proved Nov Court 1826.

LEONARD (x) SMITH          wife: Mary

son: Daniel Smith "all lands" after wife's death

Executors: Andrew Shearen, Daniel Smith, John Furguson.
Witnesses: Peter Spoone, Robert  Marshill.

─  ─  ─

122

E 122  Will dated 13 September 1825, proved Nov Court 1826.

BENJAMIN (x) JACKSON                    wife: Letty

sons: John, Alfred, Malehu
daus: Nancy, Charity, Bien ?, Polly, Ruth, Love, Edy

Executor: John Long, Jr.
Witnesses: D. Patterson, Jones Rivers.

— — —

E 122  Will dated 23 December 1825, proved Nov Court 1826.

BENJAMIN (x) BARBEE                     wife: Phoebe

son: Gabriel
daus: Jemima Rainey, Polly, Betsey
grandson: Francis, son of Gabriel
son: Gray

Executors: Gabriel Barbee, William Cooke.
Witnesses: Isaiah Marcum, William Cooke.

— — —

E 124  Will dated 16 August 1826, proved November Court 1826.

DANIEL (x) FOUST                        wife: Sarah

Friend Robert Graham plantation known as Lindley place,
  226 acres.
Nephew, Daniel Foust, son of Peter "plantation known as
  Marshill place".  Also "new entry".

Executor: Robert Grahams.
Witnesses: John Newlin, Solomon Allen, William Allen.

— — —

E 125  Will dated 18 September 1826, proved Nov Court 1826.

HENRY (x) COBLE

wife (name not stated) "to live on and be suppotred by sons
    on plantation."

sons: George, Henry (plantation), David, Peter
daus: Elizabeth, Eve, Peggy, Mary, Barbara, Sally, Catherine

Executor: son Peter.
Witnesses: John Long, Sr., William Patterson.

— — —

E 125  Will dated 8 August 1826, proved November Court 1826.

WILLIAM FLINTOFF            wife: Mary Flintoff

daughter: Jane Flintoff "clock of Library"        - continued -

son: William R. Flintoff "at lawful age my watch", etc.
"     John T. Flintoff "at lawful age my desk and six vol-
                umes of books"

Executors: wife Mary, and William Robson.
Witnesses: John Blackwood, William Hinchey.

- - -

E 127-129  Will dated 26 October 1826, proved Nov Court 1826.

THOMAS BAIN            wife: Keziah

daus: Rachel, Keziah, Sarah
"three youngest children, Ellenor, Mary and Charity"
son-in-law Thomas Heartt and his four children Harrul Walton Heartt, Henry Jackson Heartt, Harrison Bain Heartt, and
Julian Heartt.

sons: Nathaniel (oldest), John

Executors: sons Nathaniel and John.
Witnesses: E. Graves, Thos. Armstrong, Wm. Clark.

- - -

E 130-133  Will dated 17 November 1826, proved Nov 1826.

JOHN ALAN  name is spelled Allen in will, but signed Alan.

sons: John Allen (Chatham Co.), Peter (Chatham Co.),
     Joseph, Herman (land in Randolph Co. on Mill Creek),
     Nathan Allen (Orange Co.) deceased
grandchildren: Ruth Allen, Job Allen, Miles Allen, children
     of Nathan
sons: Solomon Allen (Orange Co.), William Allen

wife: Rachel
dau-in-law: Martha Allen, widow of Nathan $1
son: Joel
daus: Phoebe, Hannah

Executors: sons Joseph, Herman, Solomon and William.
Witnesses: Peter Stout, Jesse Dixon, Joseph Dixon.

- - -

E 134-136  Will dated 3 March 1824, proved November 1826.

BARNARD CATE              wife: Jane

grandsons: Joel, Joshua, sons of Joseph
son Bernard's heir David
son David's two sons: James and Sanders
son Thomas' "    "   : Joseph and Vinson
                                    - continued -

daus: Rebecca Cate, Ann Cate, Mary Cate, Sarah Cate,
      Jean Cate, Rosannah Cate

Executors: John Sykes, Robert Hastings, Wm. Thompson.
Witnesses: John Workman, Wm. Workman, W. Thompson.

- - -

E 137-138  Will dated 3 August 1822, proved February Court 1827

ROBERT FAUCETT

"To Mrs. Martha Strudwick- my faithful old slave Luce- if
Mrs. Strudwick dies before I do, I leave Luce to Mrs. Grove,
widow of late Wm. B. Grove of Fayetteville."

Legay to son Robert Faucett if he returns to North Carolina
to claim it. He does not know where he is.
sons: James Faucett, William Faucett
"To Wm. Tudor, whom I have raised ..."

Executors: Rev. John Hanks, cousin James Faucett, John Fau-
           cett, son of Henry.
Witnesses: Thomas Ruffin, Patrick H. Winston.

- - -

E 139  Will dated 17 August 1826, proved  May Court 1827.

JESSE THOMAS              son: Nehemiah Thomas

To Elenor Ripper "case of drawers"
daus: Jane Donnerly,  Caty Thomas, Mary Hubbert
grandson: Thomas Thomas
grandchildren: Nancy, Caty (surnames not stated)

Executor: Nehemiah Thomas
Witnesses: Robert Lackey, John (x) Underwood.

- - -

E 140  Will dated 7 December 1826, proved May Court 1827.

JAMES (x) DAVIS              wife: Elizabeth

sons: Sampson Moore, James Roberson

Executors: Dr. Hudson N. Cave, nephew James Davis.
Witnesses: R. Henderson, Isaac Molett, Abner (x) Parry.

- - -

E 141  Will dated 21 January 1827, proved May Court 1827.

GEORGE FAUCETT              wife: Martha

son: Ray      daughters: Nancy, and another not named

Executors: brother Edward, Samuel Tate Sr, Wm. Murray.
Witnesses: Willis Sellars, Sam'l Crawford.

- - -

E 143  Will dated 13 February 1823, proved August Court 1827.

RACHEL ARMSTRONG

niece Anne Glass, daughter of Stephen and Betsy Glass

Executors: Thomas Ruffin, Archibald D. Murphy.
Witnesses: A. D. Murphy, Victor M. Murphy.

— — —

E 143-145  Will dated 25 March 1825, proved August Court 1827.

BENJAMIN (x) RONEY          wife: Catherine

daus: Margaret Eason, Nancy Bryan, Catherine Pickett
        Mary Clendennin, Sally McCadams, Elizabeth Trowlinger
Catherine and Benjamin Clendennin children of Mary
sons: James Roney, Andrew Roney, John Roney
grandchildren: Benjamin and Catherine (under 21) McAdams,
               children of daughter Sally McAdams

Executors: son Andrew Roney, son-in-law John Trolinger.
Witnesses: Robert A. Younger, Joseph Barker.

— — —

E 145  Will dated 2 June 1827, proved August Court 1827.

SAMUEL (x) STEWART          wife: Elizabeth

daughter: Anna (unmarried)
sons: Samuel, James, Charles, John
grandson: Samuel Stewart

Executors: friend Joseph Thompson, and son James Stewart.
Witnesses: Wm. J. Clendennin, Robert Thompson, Wm. Bradshaw.

— — —

E 146  Will dated 10 June 1827, proved August Court 1827.

JAMES CRAIG, SR.          wife: Ellen

daughter: Ann Craig
son: John M. Craig gets plantation after mother's death
"     James A. Craig "plantation where he now lives"
"     William I. Craig

Executor: John McCauley.
Witnesses: John Lewis, John M. Craig, John McCauley.

— — —

E 147  Will dated 7 March 1827, proved November Court 1827.

SALLY LEWIS REEVES          sister: Martha E. Reeves

brother George Washington Reeves gets three negroes "provided
                    - continued -

my brother John Claiborn Reeves shall succeed in obtaining
property left him by his brother William B. Hill, deceased,
to amount of the three last named negroes."

Executor: father Willis Reeves.     Witness: W. Reeves.

– – –

E 148-149  Will dated 19 February 1820, proved Nov Court 1827.

JESSE (x) RIGSBY "weak in body"   wife: Elizabeth all estate

Executors: wife Elizabeth, and friend and relation Mark
            Pickett.
Witnesses: C. P. Patterson, John Anderson.

– – –

E 149  Will dated --, proved November Court 1827.

WILLIAM HALL, SR.          son: Alexander G. Hall

daughters: Polly, Jinney

Witnesses: Sam Woods, Thomas Bowls.

– – –

E 150  Will dated 30 October 1827, proved Nov Court 1827.

LETTY (x) SANDERS

grandson: Henry Neal, son of John Neal
"         James Monroe Neal, son of John Neal
granddau: Eliza Neal, daughter   "   "   "
"To John Rhodes, son of Benjamin Rhodes, deceased."
sons: Jordan and Henry, 5 shillings each "if demanded"
dau: Franky "5 shilling if demanded"

Executor: friend James Rainey.
Witnesses: Alfred Horne, Riley Neal.

– – –

E 151  Will dated 23 December 1826, proved Nov Court 1827.

DAVID COBLE

son: George "plantation whereon his widow now lives"
"    John "part of plantation known as Horniday Place"
"    Eli "plantation whereon I now live"
"    David  other part of Horniday place

Daughters Barbary, Mary, Margaret, Catty, Elizabeth,
          Sally, and Nancy have already received their parts.

Executors: son John Coble, and Michael Writsel.
Witnesses: D. Patterson, ....?   .....? (illegible).

– – –

E 152  Will dated 9 July 1827, proved November Court 1827.

SARAH MORGAN

All estate after debts are paid to grandchildren Thomas Morgan, Hardy Morgan, Sally Morgan, Lemuel Morgan, James Ruffin Morgan and Mary Emeline Morgan.

Son James A. Morgan is to be testamentary guardian and executor until youngest grandchild reaches 21 years of age.

— — —

E 153  Will dated 16 February 1828, proved Feb Court 1828.

THOMAS (x) NICHOLS

His wife Hannah is to have all his property and slaves. At her death property is to be divided between his brothers and sisters , names not stated.

Witnesses: John Bane, Tho. Jeff. Faddis.

— — —

E 153  Will dated 31 January 1828, proved Feb Court 1828.

WILLIAM (x) TATE                wife: Rachel all property

children: Joseph, Alfred, Margaret, Mary

Executors: wife Rachel Tate, and friend Joseph Eaton.
Witnesses: Robert Tate, James Tate.

— — —

E 155  Will dated 7 July 1827, proved February Court 1828.

JOSIAH CLIFTON            wife: Catron is pregnant

"My three daughters- Emily, Amy and Mahala Cliftons"
sons: James K. Clifton, John J. Clifton, James Clifton

Executors: son John J. Clifton, and friend Isaac Kirby.
Witnesses: John Moring, William H. Lewter.

— — —

E 156  Will dated 8 May 1827, proved February Court 1828.

JAMES (x) ADAMS            wife: Nancy

dau: Isabella Allen  5 shillings
sons: James Adams, John Adams  5 shillings each
dau: Dianna Adams, property after wife's death

Executrix: daughter Diannah Adams.
Witnesses: Thomas Brown, Robert Lackey.

— — —

E 157  Will dated 10 April 1827, proved May Court 1828.

MARY (x) HALL            mother a legatee

brothers: Anderson Hall, Junah Hall
friend: Sarah Pyle side saddle and one fly wheel

Witnesses: Jehu Hall, William Hall.

- - -

E 159  Will dated 27 March 1828, proved May Court 1828.

SAMUEL (x) GARRARD            sister: Susan Garrard to have
                             "rent of my old place with
James Garrard                exception of store house"
Ann Leathers daughter of Fielding Leathers
Mary  Webb Warren
Henry Warren "all other lands- watch- kitchen furniture
Willie Shaw Jr "books bonds property real and personal be-
     longing to concern of Garrard and Shaw, and should he go
     into mercantile business I give him the storehouse - all
     with the understanding that he marry with the consent of
his father and Uncle- otherwise to Anny Warren.

Executors: Henry Warren,  Samuel  Yarborough

- - -

E 160  Will dated 19 February 1816, proved -- 1828

STEPHEN MESSER (x) SMITH            wife: Susannah

daus: Catherine Gates - 5 shillings, Mary Smith,
     Johannah Parker,  Elizabeth Horner - 5 shillings
sons: Leonard Smith and William Smith under age, to receive
          plantation and grist-mill, etc, when of age
daus: Sarah  Smith, Dice, Agnes
granddaughter of daughter Mary named Jinnet
"My grandson of my daughter Sarah named John" 2 years school

Executors: Jacob Waggoner, John .
Witness: Thomas Hall.

- - -

E 161  Will dated 13 January 1827, proved August Court 1828.

WILLIAM ANDERSON            wife: Lucinda

dau: Margaret Anderson
sons: Henry Anderson and William Anderson, both under age
dau: Minerva Anderson

Executor: William Merritt.
Witnesses: Franklin O'Kelly, Pleasant Barbee.

- - -

E 162   Will dated 17 March 1828, proved August Court 1828.

ISAAC McCADAMS              wife: Peggy

son: Wiley
daus: Jane (youngest, under age), Rebeckah,
      Fanny Long (oldest) wife of William Long

Executor: son-in-law Moses Whitsett.
Witness: John Trolinger.

- - -

E 163   Will dated 10 April 1828, proved August Court 1828.

RICHARD FAUCETT            wife: Rebecca

"My two single daughters Nancy and Elizabeth"
daughter Susannah Durham
son: Thomas Samuel Faucett, under age

Executors: wife Susannah, and Samuel Strayhorn.
Witnesses: Samuel Faucett, Thos. Latta, Jinney Faucett.

- - -

E 164   Will dated 19 July 1827, proved August Court 1828.

HARDY HURDLE

sons: James  Hurdle, Henry Hurdle, George Hurdle
dau: Nancy Garrison and her children
"    Sarah McCulley  $5, Rachel Hurdle
sons: Thomas Hurdle, Benjamin Hurdle, Josiah Hurdle
son:  Jacob Hurdle (under 21)
grandson: Hardy Beasley "land I purchased from Jonathan Jordan"
"my son-in-law Samuel Beasley and his wife Milly Beasley"
"to the children of my daughter Sarah McCulley wife of John
McCulley viz: William McCulley, Hardy McCulley, Miles McCulley
Milley McCulley and Sarah McCulley."
daughter Milly Beasley's children  $25 each

Executors: "My seven sons"
Witnesses: Robert A. Younger, James M. Scott.

- - -

E 167-171  Will dated 22 September 1824, proved 1828.

"JONATHAN LINDLEY of Orange and State of Indiana"

Wife: Martha              daughter: Gubelma (under age)
son: Jonathan                "my big Bible"
dau: Catherine McVey
sons: Thomas Lindley, William Lindley
daus: Sarah Hadley, Deborah James, Hannah Braxton, Mary Dixon,
      Quine Esther Clark, Ruth Farlow, Ellenor Chambers
to Rebecca Henley 8 acres of land
                                    - continued -
"To sister Deborah Newlin, $100"

"To William and Jonathan Dicks ....
son: Zaccheus $5, "I deeded him his plantation some time ago"

He devises many tracts of land in Orange County, N.C. and in Orange County, Indiana.

Executors: sons Thomas and William "my sole and whole executors in the State of Indiana and all the Western Country", and John Newlin "my sole executor in the State of North Carolina."
Witnesses: Owen Lindley, Thomas Maris, Aaron Maris.
Probated in Paoli, Orange County, Indiana, 25 July 1828.

— — —

E 173   Will dated 3 July 1827, proved November Court 1828.

STEPHEN (x) CARROLL indexed in State Archives as CARRELL
"weak in body"

wife: Elenor                    son: Benjamin

Executors: wife Elenor, and William Lewis.
Witnesses: James Berry, James Dollar.

— — —

E 174   Will dated 19 September 1827, proved Nov Court 1828.

MARY WORTHAM          All estate to daughter Elizabeth Wilson.

Sole executor: son-in-law Samuel Wilson.
Witnesses: Joseph Armstrong Jr, John Wilson, Peggy Armstrong.

— — —

E 174   Will dated 10 March 1823, proved February Court 1829.

BENJAMIN (x) WHEELEY                    wife: Dorothy
  "weak in body"

son: Benjamin Wheeley
daus: Susannah Wheeley, Dorothy Wheeley and Betsey Wheeley
son: Philip Wheeley
He says "my seven children" only five named.

Executors: sons Benjamin and Philip.
Witnesses: Edward Eubanks, James (x) Blackwell.

— — —

E 175   Will dated 10 August 1827, proved February Court 1829.

JOHN RAY, SR.          wife: Sally

dau: Margaret Robinson wife of James
daus: Sally Robinson, and Lydia McKee wife of Rankin McKee
"Susy Ray, widow of my son Joseph Ray, deceased."
- continued -

sons: John Ray and David Ray
dau: Susan Ray

Executors: son David Ray; and Richard Nichols.
Witnesses: Samuel Madden, Alex. Smith.

— — —

E 178  Will dated 9 September 1828, proved Feb Court 1829.

SAMUEL BYRD            Father and mother are living.

"My desire is that my daughter Susannah Byrd be taken by my
sister Caty Kimbrough to raise"

"My two sisters-in-law and two brothers-in-law namely:
Rebeckah, Polly, George and John Miller."

"To my brother Thomas Bird's daughter Mary $50"

"Brothers and sister: James Bird, Empson Bird, Caty Kimbrough,
and Elizabeth Flowrence"

Executors: Thomas Lynch and Gabriel B. Lea.
Witnesses: Gabriel B. Lea, Thomas Bird, Sr.

— — —

E 180  Will dated 1 February 1827, proved Feb Court 1829.

JOHN WILSON                     wife: Eunice

daus: Rhoda Wilson, Martha Wilson, Ann Atwater
"To my daughter Nancy Tripp's children, to wit, Martha Tripp,
Elizabeth Tripp, Eunice Tripp, Polly Tripp, Millicent Tripp,
John Wilson Tripp and William Blumer Tripp, $50 each."
grandson: Wilson Atwater
daus: Millicent Pritchett, Lois Cole, Elizabeth McCauley

Executors: friends Wilson Atwater and Charles McCauley.
Witnesses: Wm. McCauley , Goodman Neville, Richard Thompson.

— — —

E 182  Will dated 25 June 1829, proved May Court 1829.

JOHN UMSTEAD

"To Morgan Hart .. home plantation where I now reside."

His slave Dicey and her two children are to be freed.

To friend John Umstead Kirkland "land on Obion River in State
of Tennessee."

Executors: Catlett Campbell and Thomas D. Bennehan.
Witnesses: James Webb, Wil Kirkland, Hugh Waddell.

— — —

132

E 183   Will dated 21 April 1829, proved May Court 1829.

CHARLES McCAWLEY                        wife: Mary

daus: Eliza McCawley, Sarah McCawley, Mary Jane McCawley
sons: William McCawley, James McCawley
"       Johnston, Archibald and Henry Crawford McCawley,
         the last three are all under 21 yaers of age

Testator's father, now desceased, was William McCawley.

Executor: John McCawley, son of Matthew.
Witnesses: Joseph Kirkland, James Long.

— — —

E 185   Will dated 8 November 1826, proved May Court 1829.

JOHN LINK                  wife a legatee, name not stated

sons: Silas M. Link, William
"When all my children come of age", only two (above) named.

Executor: son Silas M. Link.       Witness: Ed. Strudwick.

— — —

E 186   Will dated 5 May 1819, proved May Court 1829.

GARRETT GARRISON           daughter: Mary  $5

sons: Levi Garrison, John Garrison
daus: Rebecca 5 shillings, Eleanor Garrison
sons: George, Jehu

Executors: sons Levi and George
Witnesses: William Bribkley, Henry Hurdle.

— — —

E 188-190   Will dated 22 November 1828, proved August 1829.

THOMAS WILSON                   wife: Jane

daus: Nancy, Fanny
sons: Anderson, Caleb
dau: Elizabeth wife of Solomon Latta
grandsons: Jackson Latta, Asahel M. Latta, Caleb H. Latta
"My sons that have married and left me" not called by name.
"Children of sons Charles and Robert"

Executors: sons Anderson and Caleb.
Witnesses: James Holeman, Richard Holeman.

— — —

E 191   Will dated 7 January 1829, proved August Court 1829.

WILLIS (x) TREWIT or TRUET or TRUETT, spelled three ways
 "weak of body"
Wife: Nancy                           - continued -

E 191   Will of WILLIS TREWIT continued                133

two oldest sons: John and Levi  $1 each
two youngest sons: Spencer and Willis
daus: Gatsey Hall and Mary Danley  $1 each
three youngest daughters: Eleanor, Elizabeth and Nancy

Executors: son Levi Truett, and Robert A. Younger and
           William Brinkley.
Witnesses: Josiah Hurdle, William Benson.

- - -

E 192   Will dated 23 June 1829, proved August Court 1829.

WILLIAM (x) CLARK (ROCK) signed with a mark CLARK.
(This will is not in the State Archives.)

Daughter: Nancy Clark

Executor: friend James Clancy.
Witnesses: James Webb, Henry Yarborough.

- - -

E 193-195   Will dated 5 June 1829, proved August Court 1829.

JAMES JACKSON, SR.                 wife: Nancy

He devises many tracts of land, among them land "willed by
George Riggs Sr. to his daughter Nancy my wife and Rachel
wife of Amos Nichols and Nancy Riggs". He has bought land
from Levi Whitted, Jacob Jackson, Margaret Jackson, James
Glenn, James & Ruth Jackson, John & Polly Collins, .....
Carter & wife Catherine, Betsy & Ruth Jackson.

sons: James, George and Anderson Jackson.

Executors: wife Nancy, and son James.
Witnesses: Michael Ray, Thos. W. Holden.

- - -

E 195-200   Will dated 6 January 1813, proved August 1829.

SAMUEL THOMPSON               wife: Isabell

son: Richard Thompson and his son Samuel
dau: Nelly Barton wife of John Barton "Kennedy's place
          adjoining lands of Wm. Strayhorn" 200 acres
grandson Stephen Barton son of Nelly Barton
unmarried daughters: Frances, Hannah, Phoebe

Executors: wife Isabell, and William Norwood.
Witnesses: David Yarborough, James Child.
Codicil dated 11 Nov 1815 says grandson Samuel Thompson has
died. Witnesses: Wesley Debruler, Levi McCollum.
Another codicil dated 20 August 1823, same witnesses.
A third codicil dated 28 Sept 1824 says that daughter Phoebe
is now married to James Clancy, names son James Thompson.

- - -

E 201  Will dated 12 May 1824, proved November Court 1829.

JOHN FADDIS, SR. of the Town of Hillsborough

wife: Nancy all estate during her life

"My two children, Nancy Womack and Thomas J. Faddis."
granddaughters: Eliza Womack, Mary Jane Womack
Jacob P. Womack, husband of daughter Nancy, also called Ann.

Executors: wife and son Thomas J. Faddis, and Jonathan P. Sneed.
Witnesses: James Webb, F. B. Phillips.

– – –

E 202  Will dated 3 August 1824, proved November Court 1829.

RICHARD BIRD                          wife: Rachel

daughters Catherine Kimbrough and Elizabeth Florence

"My granddaughter Nancy Bird, daughter of my son Thomas Bird
deceased" under age.

sons: Samuel, James and Empson Bird

Executors: sons James and Samuel.
Witnesses: Thomas Reeves, John Reeves.

– – –

E 203  Will dated 16 October 1829, proved Noc Court 1829.

WILLIAM PIKE                  son: John Pike

daus: Abigail Pike, Mary Pike, Nancy

"Heirs of daughters Hannah and Priscilla deceased"

Executor: friend William Thompson.
Witnesses: Wm. Albright, John Thompson, John Thompson.

– – –

E 204  Will dated 19 October 1829, proved Nov Court 1829.

THOMAS or JOSEPH (x) LAYCOCK, SR.  This will is in the Archives.
                                   It is endorsed on the back
wife: Rosea $1                     "Will of Thomas Laycock".

sons: William and Joseph get land on both sides of Eno River

daus: Nelly Cates, Elizabeth Scarlett, Sally Scarlett, Delilah Scarlett, Disey Laycock, Easter Laycock

Executors: son Joseph, and Frederick Moize.
Witness: John (x) Warren.

– – –

E 205  Will dated 20 August 1829, proved Nov Court 1829.

RICHARD (x) MARCUM                 wife: Anna

son: Wilie "tract he now lives on"
"    William "tract he now lives on"
sons: John and Spencer "land where my father lived and died"
son: Aaron "plantation I now live on"
daus: Cynthia (unmarried), Polly Sorrell
son: Willis  $40 (mentioned in codicil, made same day)

Executors: worthy friends Thomas Bilbo and John Bilbo.
Witnesses: William B. Williams, John D. Carlton.

- - -

E 207  Will dated 28 May 1829, proved  November Court 1829.

JOSHUA (x) HORNE, SR.          wife: Mikey
   "very weak"                (She was Michel Rhodes)

sons: John and Joshua  "all my land"

daus: Milly Redding, Alsey Cates, Viney Hinchey ?, Betsy
    Brockwell, and Polly Neel 5 shillings each

Executor: friend James Rainey.
Witnesses: Pleasant Rhodes, Young E. Rainey.

- - -

E 208  Will dated 22 November 1820, proved Nov Court 1829.

HENRY O'DANIEL            wife: Margery

sons: Samuel, John, Joshua
daus: Susana Pickhard, Jeane McDaniel, Sally Hastings,
    Margaret Pickhard
grandson: William O'Daniel son of John
grandsons: Henry and William sons of William

Executors: Thomas Hastings and Thomas Brewer.
Witnesses: John O'Daniel Jr., Jesse O'Daniel.

- - -

E 209  Will dated 27 August 1829, proved February Court 1830.

MELCHI McDANIEL
                                            place"
son: William McDaniel "plantation known as the Henry Hasten /
dau: Martha Smith wife of William Smith "my plantation"
Elizabeth Britt daughter of Celia Britt "my plantation known
    as James Minnis plantation on E Side of Cane Creek"
Eli Britt son of Celia Britt "plantation where I now live" on
    E Side of Cane Creek.

Executors: David Roach and William Thompson.
Witnesses: Thomas G. Willis, Alfred Pickard, Henry O'Daniel.

- - -

136

E 211  Will dated 5 December 1829, proved Feb Court 1830.

ELIZABETH (x) WALKER

sisters: Margaret McCullay, Nancy Byrd
Andrew Walker
"To John Picket's children: Juliann and John Quincy"
"To William Picket's (deceased) Children: Joseph, Lucrecey,
   William, and Vicey Byrd."

Executor: worthy friend James Forest.
Witnesses: Thomas Lynch, James Forest, John Forest.

— — —

E 212  Will dated 2 December 1829, proved Feb Court 1830.

ANN (x) LONG                    daughter: Nancy Long
"weak in body"                 "         Mary Long

sons:  James Long, Thomas Long, Anderson Long, George Long,
       and Charles Long, 50¢ each
"My granddaughter Eliza Long daughter of Mary Long"

Executor: son George.
Witnesses: Wm. H. Woods, John Brown, William McCauley.

— — —

E 213  Will dated 23 January 1830, proved Feb Court 1830.

LETTICE (x) McCULLEY

Albert Hamilton, son of William Hamilton
Thomas McCulley  "all my pewterware"
William Hamilton "all balance of estate"

Executor: "friend Henry Hurdle".
Witnesses: Chesley F. Faucette, Edward Fausett.

— — —

E 213  Will dated 6 August 1828, proved February Court 1830.

MARY KELLEY              sister: Keziah Bane

sisters: Nancy and Betsy to have her share of the undi-
              vided estate of their father
"To Sally  Lockhart $15 for her services to me in my sickness"

Executor: Thomas W. Holden.
Witnesses: Hugh Cain, John Lockhart.

— — —

E 215  Will dated 10 May 1826, proved May Court 1830.

JOHN (x) IVEY           wife: Mornning

daus: Nancy Holder $1, Sally        - continued -

sons: Joseph Ivey, Andrew Patterson, John $2, William $2

Executor: friend John Carethers.
Witnesses: Archibald Durham, Thomas Lloyd.

- - -

E 216-218  Will dated 3 May 1830, proved May Court 1830.

NICHOLAS JONES

wife: Nancy "land which joins Samuel Evans and Ephriam Car-
          rington deceased"
wife's father David Parker of Granville County, N.C.
son: William land in Granville County on "Nap of Reed Creek"
          joining land of George Roberts deceased, James
          Roberts, Edward Jones Sr, and others
son: Washington Jones (under age)
dau: Polly Jones (under age)
daus: Ma rtha Ann Jones and Rebecca Jones (both under age)
son: Willis Simpson Jones  land on Flat River

Executors: brother Henry W. Jones of Granville County, and
          son Washington Jones.
Witnesses: Willis Bowling, John J. Carrington.

- - -

E 219  Will dated 30 April 1830, proved May Court 1830.

MIRIAM (x) STRAIN  "low in health"

sons: James, Samuel, and David get ,land, Alexander 50¢
granddaughters: Mary Strayhorn, Jane Strayhorn
dau: Mary Strayhorn wife of Bryant Strayhorn
dau: Elizabeth Elkins

Executor: John McCauley.
Witnesses: Wm. D. Strain, John Strayhorn.

- - -

E 220  Will dated 25 September 1827, proved May Court 1830.

ELIZABETH (x) BREWER "old and infirm"

nieces: Betsy Oldham, Mary Ann Bracher ?
brothers: Ezekiel Brewer, Thomas Brewer
sister: Rebeckah Hopson

Executor: friend Thomas Snipes of Chatham County.
Witnesses: W. S. Snipes, George W. Morrow.

- - -

E 221  Will dated 25 February 1830, proved May Court 1830.

SARAH (x) STRAIN    brothers: James and Samuel Strain

She holds a note on her mother Maryann Strain (actually
Miriam, see E 219)                    - continued -

sister: Mary Strayhorn wife of Bryant Strayhorn
"       Elizabeth Elkins

"My six nieces: Mary Strayhorn, Jane Strayhorn, Elizabeth Strayhorn, Mary Strain, Elizabeth Strain and Sarah Strain."

Executor: Bryant Strayhorn.
Witnesses: Samuel Strain, Alex, Gattis, Mary Strayhorn.

— — —

E 222   Will dated 7 May 1827, proved May Court 1830.

THOMAS (x) HART, SR.  "weak of body"

daughters: Rebecca and Susannah get all his land
son: Fin Hart

Executor: son Fin Hart, and Thomas McCracken.
Witnesses: Jo. Hart, John W. McCracken.

— — —

E 223   Will dated 3 January 1826, proved August Court 1830.

EDWARD (x) BOSWELL    "weak in body"

two eldest sons: Craven and John
"Mary Boswell widow of my son Thomas Boswell deceased"
"three other sons: Edward, Mathew and James Boswell"
grandson: Brown Boswell
"My three married daughters, namely, Susannah Leachman (?), Nancy Wilkerson, Catherine Graham."
daughter: Charlotte Boswell
son-in-law: Thomas Sulivan  $1
"      "     "      James Wilkerson  $1
granddaughters: Julia Ann Bracken (under 18), Catherine Graham
grandchildren:  William Sulivan, Craven Sulivan,
                "Nancy, Catherine and Elizabeth Sulivan"

Executors: son James Boswell, and George Graham.
Witnesses: Andrew Hughs, Thomas Fitch.

— — —

E 224   Will dated July 1827, proved August Court 1830.

ROBERT MOORE                     wife: Isabel

granddaus: Keziah Moore, Sally Tate, Isabel Tate
"To Anthony Tate, James Faucett Moore, David Moore, Robert Moore, William Moore, 10 shillings each"
His plantation to grandsons, sons of Thomas Moore: Robert Moore, William Moore, David Moore, Absalem Moore.

Executors: Absolem Harvey and Juneah Hall.
Witnesses: James Moore, Thomas Moore.

— — —

E 226  Will dated 8 December 1825, proved August 1830.

HUGH MONTGOMERY          wife: Rebecca

sons: James and Alexander (legacy), William  $1
dau: Lydia Woods wife of Alfred Woods  $1
"To Hambleton James Alexander and Hugh one dollar as they
    arrive to age 21" (no punctuation)

Executors: wife Rebecca, and friend Thomas Holden.
Witnesses: Eli Woods, John Woods.

- - -

E 227  Will dated 11 August 1828, proved August Court 1830.

WILLIAM MILLER          wife: Rebecca

"My children", names and number not stated.

Executors: friends Dr. Edmund Strudwick and William Bowls.
Witnesses: James Webb, Jesse Miller.
Codicil dated 2 Feb 1830 says that wife is to have life es-
tate.  Witness: James Webb.

- - -

E 228  Will dated 4 February 1823, proved August Court 1830.

MARY (x) THOMPSON   "weak in body"

"To my sister Hannah Thompson all my money in the hands of
my brother John Thompson." (Her father was Thomas Thompson.)

Executors: friends Thomas Thompson and Robert Thompson.
Witnesses: Jo Clendennin, John Thompson.
Codicil mentions Thomas, Nelly and Mary Thompson.

- - -

E 229  Will dated 31 July 1830, proved August Court 1830.

EDWARD McDADE

daughter: Peggy McDade
niece: Peggy McDade daughter of brother John McDade
"Mrs Elizabeth Wilfong saddles, etc. in my shop"

Executors: friends John McDade and Thomas Clancy.
Witnesses: J.W ? Smith, Wm. Nelson.

- - -

E 229  Will dated 23 November 1829, proved August 1830.

WILLIAM BLACKWOOD

daus: Hannah Selph, Elizabeth Allen, Mary Craig  50¢ each
son:  John Blackwood  50¢
daus: Martha Craig, Jane McCauley, Ann Potts  50¢ each
daus: Margaret Long, Sarah Gattis  50¢ each    - continued -

sons: William Blackwood, James Blackwood  50¢ each
daus: Nancy, Catherine and Fanny "all my land, furniture", etc.
grandson: Anderson, son of daughter Ann Potts

Executors: sons John and William Blackwood.
Witnesses: Wm. C. Blackwood, Franklin L. Blackwood.

- - -

E 231  Will dated 4 August 1830, proved August Court 1830.

SOLOMON WOOD              wife: Elizabeth all during her life

Henry Wood
brother James Wood          brother-in-law Ezekiel Haley

Executor: wife Elizabeth, and brother-in-law Ezekiel Haley.
Witnesses: Arch'd Cain, J. B. Leathers.

- - -

E 231  Dated 15 October 1830, proved Nov Court 1830.

JOHN (x) ALBRIGHT SR.   "weak of body"

daughter: Barbara Garrat "all the land I own with all appur-
                         tainances."
daus: Betsey Clap and Philipenia Swing
Sally Holt wife of Thomas Holt
Abraham Clap

Executors: Andrew Albright, John Garrat Sr.
Witnesses: Henry (x) Thomas, William (x) Holt.

- - -

E 232  Will dated 13 August 1830, proved November Court 1830.

PETER L. RAY              wife: Elizabeth B. Ray

children: David L. Ray (under age), Mary E. Ray, Griffen L. Ray

Executors: William Holt, Sr, and Jeremiah Holt, Sr.
Witnesses: James Bleat, William Tarpley.

- - -

E 233 Will dated 28 August 1830, proved Nov Court 1830.

WILLIAM CRESWELL         wife: Jane is pregnant ?

nephew: William Brown Creswell
  "      Wesley Morrow

Executor: George A. Mebane.
Witnesses: B. Breeze, William Mebane.

- - -

E 235  Will dated 21 March 1825, proved Feb Court 1831.

ELIZABETH (x) FAUCETT

son: Joseph Faucett , estate of late husband David Faucett
"    James Faucett  $50
granddaughter Elizabeth Ann Bain (under age)

Executors: James Faucett and Joseph Faucett.
Witnesses: A. Armstrong, WM. B. Ringstaff.

- - -

E 236  Will dated 25 September 1830, proved Nov Court 1830 ?

WILLIAM WOODS          wife: Elenor all during her life

daus: Anne and Asenath
He mantions "all my children", seems to have married daughters.
David Dickey is to have board and lodging for 1 year.

Executors: son John S. Woods and son-in-law Robert Redden.
Witnesses: Samuel Paisley, James Clark.

- - -

E 237  Will dated 15 January 1831, proved Feb Court 1831.

EMPSON BIRD            wife: Polly

"Two oldest daughters Eliza Bird and Citty Bird"
"Three youngest Martha Bird, John Bird, Richard Bird"
"Land I bought from Catherine Redding to be sold".
"Sister Betsy Florence should take and raise Eliza"
"Sister-in-law Nancy Kirkpatrick should take and raise Citty"
"Cousin Sarah Walker take and raise my daughter Martha"
"Uncle James Dickey should take and raise my son John"
"Friend George Jordan find a place for Richard if necessary"

Executor: George Jordan.
Witnesses: Jehu Bird, James Bird, Charles Jordan.

- - -

E 239  Will dated 17 February 1831, proved Feb Court 1831.

RICHARD DAVIS    sons: Archibald and Miles Davis 50¢ each

daus: Dellila King, Sarah Montgomery, Mary Jenkins 50¢ each
son: John Richard Davis 50¢
"    Thomas Capper Davis  half of estate
daus: Winnifred Beville and Fanny Trice other half

Executors: friends John L. Moore and James N. Patterson.
Witnesses: J. L. Moore, Nancy Moore, James N. Patterson.

- - -

E 240  Will dated 8 March 1831, proved February Court 1831.

JOHN (x) CARRIGAN "sick and weak"      "present wife "

"wife and daughter Tempe" (unmarried)    - continued -

"son Hugh (he is under age) by my present wife to share equally
 with other children"

Executor: trusty friend Samuel Child.
Witnesses: Alves Cheek, James Cheek.
Codicil, dated same day, says son-in-law James Roach has "my
permission to build himself a house near where Thomas Dodson
now lives, and at end of Dodson's rent take over possession
of 10 acres around house as long as wife and daughter Tempe
live"._ _

E 241  Will dated 14 January 1831, proved Feb Term 1831.

NATHANIEL CARRINGTON

son: Nathaniel M. Carrington all real estate
daus: Ruth Carrington, Dolly Cozart, Polly Cozart wife of Dovy
daus: Fanny wife of J.J.Carrington and Dessy Harris wife of
      Edward Harris, 10¢ each, they have had their portions
sons: William Carrington (10¢), Eaphriam and Alfred

Witnesses: James Webb, P.H.Ma ngum.

_ _ _

E 243  Will dated 28 March 1831, proved February Court 1831.

STEPHEN GARROTT          wife: Betsey all property for life

Children to receive property after wife's death.

Executrix: wife Betsey.
Witnesses: F. Moize, Lewis Hutchins.

_ _ _

E 243  Will dated 16 May 1829, proved February Term 1831.

PRISCILLA DUNCAN          dau: Elizabeth White  $1

estate to daughter Lucy Duncan and son Charles N. Duncan

Executor: friend James Forest.
Witnesses: Wm. P. Forest, A. Forest.

_ _ _

E 245  Will dated 28 January 1831, proved Feb Court 1831.

BARNABAS O'FAIRHILL          wife: Nancy one third

"No bequests to any of her (his wife's) children".
sister: Jane Woods
niece: Anne Kelly

Executor: Thomas Clincy of Hillsborough.
Witnesses: Thomas D. Watts, John Scott.

E 247  Will dated 22 May 18--, proved August Court 1831.

JOSEPH MOORE

sons: William Stanford Moore 100 acres, Carter Moore (married)
daus: Patsey Bird, Celia Reynolds, Susan (unmarried)
sons: Peyton P. Moore and Joseph Moore balance of land

Executors: Peyton P. Moore and Jehu Bird.
Witnesses: James Mebane, James Picket.

- - -

E 248  Will dated 4 June 1831, proved August Court 1831.

SUSANNAH (x) RAY  "weak of body"

She leaves slaves and household furniture to her step-mother
Sally Ray, and after her death to brother David Ray.

sister: Sally Robertson wife of Joseph Robertson
Lydia McKee wife of Rankin McKee
"To the heirs of George Ray dec'd, the heirs of Joseph Ray,
John Robertson and Michael Robertson sons of James Robertson
deceased, James Ray and John Ray, that is to say, six equal
parts."    Peggy Jane Ray, daughter of David Ray.
Witnesses: Robert Reding, J.H.Mangum.
Executor: Richardson Nichols.

E 250  Will dated 30 May 1830, proved August Court 1831.

LYDIA (x) DILLARD "weak of body"

"Four youngest daughters viz: Eliza, Caroline, Martha and
Mary Jane"
She has thirteen children, but only four are named.

Executor: son Willis.
Witnesses: Wm. R. Herndon, Polly (x) Blake, David Roberts.

- - -

E 251  Will dated 20 July 1831, proved August Court 1831.

WILLIAM WHYTE "of the Village of Chapel Hill"

wife: Lucy
"My three children namely Thomas Whyte Rebecca Ann Whyte
and Joseph Whyte."

Executor: friend John McCauley.
Witnesses: D. B. Alsobrook, Thomas E. Taylor.
Codicil dated 8 August 1831, signed with a mark, same wit-
nesses, mentions "my plantation which I lately purchased of
William Barbee Sr known as Creage (?) Mill Tract".

- - -

144

E 253  Will dated 16 February 1831, proved August Court 1831.

ANDREW HUNTER               wife: Susannah

son: Alexander Hunter
daus: Elizabeth Hunter, Jane Loyd, Frances Hunter,
     Frances Hunter, Eliza Hunter, Christa Hunter,
     Harriet Hunter
son: Thomas Hunter
"... that my first wife's children have nothing more than
they have received .."
daus: Nancy Loyd and Sary Cate

Executors: Thos Hogan and John Careathers.
Witnesses: Hasten Poe, Reuben C. Poe.

— — —

E 255  Will dated 10 May 1825, proved August Court 1831.

ELIZABETH (x) HALL

daus: Phebe Dickey, Joannah McAdams  $1 each
sons: Jeremiah Hall, Samuel C. Hall  $1 "
dau:  Mary Hall
daus: Nancy Plummer, Elizabeth Harvey, Sarah McAdams  $1 each
son: Anderson Hall

Executor: son Anderson Hall.
Witnesses: John Hall, William Hall.

— — —

E 256  Will dated 24 October 1830, proved August Court 1831.

JOSEPH BAKER SR.

daus: Margaret Murray, Susey Clarke
"My granddaughter Eliza H. Baker daughter of my son Nathaniel
 Baker (now deceased). She is under 21.
son: Joseph Baker

Executors: friend John Trolinger, and son Joseph Baker.
Witnesses: Wm. H. White, James A. Craig.

— — —

E 257  Will dated October 1819, "republished" 13 September
       1827, proved August Court 1831.

LUCY (x) JEFRES        granddaughters: Milly and Lucy

grandsons: Ja mes Samuel and Cato (surnames not stated)

Executor; Fielding Leathers.
Witnesses: Robert Faucet, James Webb.

— — —

E 258  Will dated 1 May 1831, proved August Court 1831.

HENRY (x) MOIZE                    wife: Lucy

Daughter Frances Moize gets his land.
"My children Allen Moize Nancy Roberts Elizabeth Tilly Keziah
  Tilly and Frances Moize."

Executor: brother John Moize.
Witnesses: Frederic Moize, Willia P. Mangum.

- - -

E 259  Will dated 26 February 1831, proved 1831.

ROBERT HARRIS                    wife: Casserna

"sons Marcus ? Harris William Harris & Harrison Harris"
daus: Bulia;  Tempy and Edny (last two under age)
sons: Nathaniel, Archer

Executors: Silas M. Link, and son Marcus Harris.
Witnesses: Duncan Cameron, Thomas D. Bennehan.

- - -

E 261  Will dated 17 October 1831, proved Nov Court 1831.

ISAAC (x) JONES                    wife: Catherine

sons: Samuel Stockard Jones, John Orange Jones
daus: Elizabeth Jones and Frances Jones, both under age

Executor: brother Samuel Jones.
Witnesses: Jeremiah Holt, V. M. Murphey.

- - -

E 262  Will dated 24 August 1831, proved November Court 1831.

SARAH (x) THOMPSON

oldest daughter: Ann Thompson
"next eldest daughter Jilsey ? Roundtree
daughter Rebecca Bird and her children
sons: John Thompson (eldest), James, Thomas Thompson
"      Lawrence, Joseph and Nicholas Thompson

Executors: son Nicholas, and friend James Forest, Esq.
Witnesses: Peter Walker, Mathew Brown.

- - -

E 263  Will dated 14 January 1829, proved Nov Court 1831.

MARGARET WATSON            dau: Helen Riley

son: James Watson
daus: Rebecca Watson, Elizabeth Comb
son: Andrew Watson                    - continued -

146   E 263  Will of MARGARET WATSON continued
dau: Nancy McCamal ?
son: John Watson and his daughter Margaret Watson
"     Robert Watson

Executor: son Robert Watson.
Witnesses: Js. R. Watson, Farmer Smith.

- - -

E 265  Will dated 8 June 1831, proved November Court 1831.

SAMUEL WARE                    wife: Gilly

"My daughter and son", names not stated.

Executrix: wife.
Witnesses: Chesley M ? Patterson, Isreal (x) Turner.

- - -

E 265  Will dated 22 October 1831, proved Feb Court 1832.

DANIEL LYNCH          wife: Polly "may be pregnant"

He purchased tracts of land from John Horner, Thomas W. Holden
and Alves Nichols.

children: Sarah Ann Lynch, Logan Lynch

Executrix: wife Polly.  Witnesses: John Allen, John Horner.

- - -

E 267  Will dated 11 September 1829, proved Feb Court 1832.

ELIZABETH (x) ROGERS "weak and infirm"    son: Theopilus

Elizabeth Webb, daughter of John Webb

  All her grandchildren to have equal shares "except Idlett
Rogers who I consider has gotten a good share from his grandfather William Rogers's Estate".

Executor: James A. Craig.
Witnesses: John Cheek, Sarah (x) Freshwater.

- - -

E 268  Will dated 15 February 1832, proved Feb Court 1832.

THOMAS (x) JAMES                    wife: Elizabeth

He speaks of his children .."until my youngest child comes of
age ... my three sons ..."

Executor: "worthy friend James Rhodes".
Witnesses: Silas M. Link, Wm'son Burton.

- - -

JOSEPH THOMPSON

".. children taht arc herein named  Elizabeth, Abel, Enoch,
Thomas, Edith, Lydia and Sarah .."

Executors: "my two sons Abel and William Turner".
Witnesses: Samuel McCracken Sr., Samuel McCracken Jr.

- - -

E 270  Will dated 5 February 1832, proved May Court 1832.

WILLIAM WHITAKER                wife: Nancy

daus: Polly Cardin, Nancy Whitaker, Ann Whitaker
son: John (schooling 1 year), Burton
"     Thomas, Isaac, William and David Whitaker

Executor: son William Whitaker.
Witnesses: Robert Gresham, James Horn.

- - -

E 271  Will dated 7 January 1823, proved August Court 1832.

FRANCES CHILD "of the Town of Hillsborough"

son: Samuel Child "lot where I now live, lot # 117"
grandsons: Samuel Child and William McKerall

Executors: "worthy friends James Webb and F. Nash"
Witnesses: Thomas Clancy, James Child.

- - -

E 272  Will dated 13 January 1832, proved August Court 1832.

WILLIAM (x) BRANNOCK

sons-in-law: David Gilliam and William Taylor 10 shillings ea.
sons: William Brannock 10 shillings, Alexander N. Brannock
"My two daughters Delilah Brannock and Angel M. Brannock my
   lands".

Executor: "my son-in-law Henry Brannock in whom I much confide"
Witnesses: Wright Brannock, George Thomas, Henry Brannock, Sr.

- - -

E 273  Will dated 14 June 1832, proved August Court 1932.

PARRIS PEARSON               wife: Mary

"My children- to wit- Stephen Thomas John M Joel Jane Marcom
Sarah Trice Rachel Massey and Eliza Colliear" (no commas).
"To my son Green  50¢"
"To my grandson Silas Green Clark"
"daughter Ann Collier and Mary Moore $2 each"

Executors: "sons William and Edward Collier".
Witnesses: R. S. Leigh, W. D. Carlton.

- - -

148

E 275  Will dated 5 May 1829, proved August Court 1832.

JACOB GARRISON

"grandson Henry Garrison plantation on which I now live,
joining the lands of Henry Hurdle and his mother Nancy Garrison"

son-in-law: Henry Hurdle
grandsons Jacob and John Jorden plantation on Tom's Creek
son-in-law Job Walker "plantation on Stoney Creek known by
   the name Bracken's old place" 200 acres
son-in-law Thomas Bradfprd  $500
daughter Rachel Walker 100 acres on Stoney Creek known as
   "Burch's old place, and "each of her children $50"
"My grandchildren, children of my daughter Mary Dickey $100
   each except George"
granddaughters: Mary Jordon and Levina Jordon
grandchildren: Elizabeth and George King
daughter: Margaret Hurdle
grandson: Granderson Garrison
"That John Walker pay to Rachel Walker" note due.

Executors: son-in-law Henry Hurdle, and friend William Brinkley.
Witnesses: Thomas Trewett Sr, Thos Trewett, Jonathan Harvey.

- - -

E 277-279  Will dated 27 February 1826, proved August 1832.

JOSEPH SHAW          grandson: Benjamin J. Kinnion

daughter Maria Kinnion, and to her children
son: Joseph B. Shaw
"daughters of my son Joseph"
grandson: Joseph John Shaw
daughter Drusilla Ann Hargis .. "her daughters"
daughter Catherine H. Horton "and to the children of her daughter Maria B. Hargis"
daus: Elinor Ann Ray, Rebecca E. Shaw, Fantitina Joys Shaw
son: Neal H. Shaw
grandsons: Neal H. Horton, Anthony W. Horton
sons-in-law: John Warren, James M. Wheat (?) 10 shillings each
"   "   "   Paul Kennion, Dennis Hargis 10 shillings each

Executrix: daughter Fantitina J. Shaw.
Witnesses: Murrell Breesse , Thos. V. Hargis, J. P. Sneed.

- - -

E 280  Will dated 7 June 1831, proved August Court 1832.

HENSON (x) COULTER, SR.        wife: Lizzy

sons: Anderson Coulter, Charles Coulter , 50¢ each
"deceased son Thomas Coulter or his heirs" 50 ¢
daughter Jane Fan
sons: Allen Coulter, Asa Coulter, Ashley Coulter
                        - continued -

daus: Miloy  Pendergrass and Fanny Pendergrass  50¢ each
dau: Milly Coulter  $200
"My illegitimate daughter now bearing and known by the name
   of Eliza Coulter , $200."
"My three last sons viz  Sherly ? Coulter, Bartlett Coulter
   and Fanning Coulter," lands, etc.

Executors: friends William Barbee Sr., and Thomas H. Taylor.
Witnesses: Henry Thomson, John Sparrow, Chas. R. Yancey,
           Ashley Coulter.

- - -

E 282  Will dated Jul7 1832, proved November Court 1832.

JAMES (x) CRABTREE

sons: Richard, John and Abram Crabtree, $1 each
dau: Charlotte wife of James Jackson  $1
dau: Fanny      "    "  James Crabtree, land
daus: Sally, Elizabeth and Polly Crabtree, land
son: Clement Crabtree

Executor: Son Clement Crabtree.
Witnesses: Allen Cain, James Myrick.

- - -

E 283-285  Will dated 16 September 1832, proved November 1832.

JOHN McCAULEY          wife: Nancy F. McCauley is pregnant

sons: William, James, Mathew McCauley
son: Charles John Franklin McCauley
dau: Marthy E. Morrow and her husband John Morrow
daus: Nancy Flutcher McCauley, Mary McCauley,
      Ellen Jane McCauley, Orella Dow McCauley,
      Verlina Ann McCauley, Lucinda

Executor: brother Mathew McCauley.  Witness: Thos. D. Watts.
- - -

E 285  Will dated 6 May 1831, proved November Court 1832.

JOHN HICKS                 son: John Hicks

daus: Frances Hicks, Jane Hicks
sons: John Hicks, Thomas M. Hicks

Executors: sons James and John.
Witnesses: James Trewett, Wm. Brannock.
- - -

E 287-288  Will dated 30 June 1830, proved February 1833.

JAMES (x) STRAYHORN, SR. "weak in body"    wife: Rachel

daus: Elizabeth Strayhorn, Polly Strayhorn   - continued -

sons: James, John, William

He devises "tract which I purchased of James Hart", "
"tract which I purchased of my nephew Gilbert Strayhorn and
   John Strayhorn sons of my brother David deceased, and which
   was willed to them by their grandfather Gilbert Strayhorn, Sr."

Executor: son John Strayhorn.
Witnesses: J. M. Kerall, Thomas Crabtree, Wilsom McKerall.

— — —

E 289   Will dated 1 February 1833, proved Feb Court 1833.

AARON WALKER                    wife: Sarah

sons: Levi Walker, Empson Walker
"daughter Nancy Shaw wife of John W. Shaw"
"daughter Harriett Crawford wife of Philip Crawford"
son: Freeman Walker

Executor: son Dr. Levi Walker.
Witnesses: J. S. Smith, John Walker, James Walker.

— — —

E 290   Will dated 11 November 1832, proved Feb Court 1833.

JOHN FARRAR            Wife a legatee, name not stated.

Children, names not stated, to "be schooled".

No executor named.  Witnesses: Hunter McCauley, Joseph Barbee.

— — —

E 291   Will dated 10 September 1827, proved May Court 1833.

JOSEPH (x) WOOD                 wife: Polly

dau: Elizabeth Chisenhall       son: James Wood

Children: Solomon Wood, Henry, Joseph, Sukey Glenn, Nancy King,
          Mary Chisenhall, $1 each.

Executor: son James Wood.
Witnesses: Frederick Moize, Dempsey Wood.

— — —

E 292   Will dated 3 March 1832, proved May Court 1833.

BETSY (x) LEIGH  "sick in body"

sisters: Nancy Garrett; Anna Leigh
brothers: Thomas Leigh, Sullivan Leigh

Executor: brother Sullivan Leigh.
Witnesses: Joseph Dickson, William Leigh.

— — —

E 294   Will dated 21 April 1833, proved May Court 1833.

WILLIAM GUESS

"My seven children Margaret, Sarah, James, Nancy, Frances,
   Joseph and Wilson"  $400.
son: Moses
"Balance to be equally divided among all my children, Mary
   intermarried with David Warren, Rebecca intermarried with
   James Dollar; John, Elizabeth, George, Thomas, Margaret,
   Moses, Sarah, James, Nancy, Frances, Joseph and Wilson."

Executor: son Moses.

- - -

E 294   Will dated 31 January 1833, proved May Court 1833.

WILLIAM BARBEE            wife: Sarah

"infant daughter June (or Jane ?) Barbee"
son: James Barbee "tract where he now lives"

Executor: "worthy friend" John W. Wilson.
Witnesses: Caleb Wilson, An. Watson.

- - -

E 296   Will dated 18 January 1832, proved May Court 1833.

JOSEPH WARD              wife: Charity

Son Robertson, daughters Sally Parham, Patsy Blailoc, Bethany,
sons Ransom, William and Josiah, daughter Elizabeth Moor,
sons Isham (or Isaac ?) and John, 50¢ each.  These all seem
to be children of his first wife.

Daughters Rebecca Moor, Mary Ward, Jennet, son Edwin, daughter
Louisa, sons James and Marvil, daughter Nancy Ann (unmarried),
"my last wife's children aforementioned".

Executors: wife Charity, and brother-in-law James Law.
Witness: Thomas Howard.

- - -

E 297   Will dated 20 March 1833, proved May Court 1833.

DAVID RAY           Wife a legatee, name not stated.

step-mother: Sally Ray
sister: Susannah Ray deceased
daughter Peggy Jane Ray

He says "until my youngest child that may be living arrives
at age of twenty-one."

Executor: Richerson Nichols.
Witnesses: John Hanks, John Smith, Charles Ray.

- - -

E 298 Will dated 10 May 1831, proved May Court 1833.

WINNEY   her<br>
       x  HARDEE                daughter:  Sally Shields<br>
      mark<br>
daughter: Polly Wells $1 "besides what I have given her
son: William Hardee
daus: Martha Carlton Thompson, Eliza Wells
grandchildren: Luiza Hardee, Caroline Gordan,
                    Whitmell H. Hardee
"Three of my son John's children, namely Henrietta, Luvina
  Daniel and Frances W. Hardee."
"All my son William's children" (not named)
"All my daughter Martha C. Thompson's children"
"All my daughter Eliza Wells' children"

Executors: son William Hardee, son-in-law Benjamin Wells.
Witnesses: J. A. McDade, H. C. McDade.

- - -

E 300  Will dated 25 June 1830, proved May Court 1833.

RICHARD CHRISTMAS   (He devises many slaves and other property.)

To Miss Betsy Cooper for her care of him in his infirmities,
$100, slave, furniture, etc.

Legacies to Richard Glass, son of Stephen and Betsy Glass,
and to his parents.
Dr. James A. Craig
Niece Mary G. Christmas
   "    Nancy Christmas daughter of my deceased brother James
   "    Henrietta Christmas dau. "  "  "      "      "
nephews: John and William sons "  "  "     "     "
"My niece Mary Edward Green daughter of my nephew John Green
of Warrenton."
Niece, Mary Young widow.
Ann Christmas Lytle ? niece of my deceased wife.
Mary Smart          "     "    "    "     "
Peggy Lankston       "    "  "  "     "
"My niece Mary Powers wife of Richard Powers"

Executor: Dr. James A. Craig.
Witnesses: A. D. Murphey, Arch'd Murphey, V. M. Murphy.

- - -

E 302  Will dated 16 October 1828, proved August Court 1833.

ELIZABETH (x) LAWS         friend: Thos. D. Bennehan

Mary Furgerson wife of John Furgerson
"To William Laws son of my nephew Leonard Laws"

Executor: Thos. D. Bennehan.
Witnesses: Wm. Horner, Sam'l Yarborough.
Young Dorch, A. Williams.

- - -

E 303-305  Will dated 2 April 1826, proved August 1833.

WILLIAM (x) BREWER          wife: Dorothy

"Four sons of my son Isham Brewer (viz): Joseph, Benjamin,
   Washington and Isham."

grandchildren: William Hatch, George B. Hatch,& Sally Hatch.
"My three grandchildren (viz) William B. Bredges, Elizabeth
   C. Bredges, and Mary I. Bredges."
"Jane Brewer and her six children Joseph and Benjamin &
   Washington & Isham & July & Polly."

Executors: trusty friends Thomas Weaver and Joseph Brewer.
Witnesses: Jessey Nevills, John Crabtree, William Thompson.
- - -

E 306  Will dated 9 July 1833, proved August Court 1833.

MOSES HARVEY or HERVEY ?          wife: Hannah

"All my children", not named except daughter Grace.

Executors: Worthy friends Samuel Woods and John Newlin.
Witnesses: Robert Cheek, Isaac Andrews.
- - -

E 307  Will dated 21 June 1833, proved November Court 1833.

JOHN HOLMES               wife: Catherine

son: Nicholas              unmarried son: William
unmarried daughters: Ann and Jane
"their three married sisters who have left me"

"All my children namely, Mary, Hannah, Sarah, William,
   Henry, Ann, Joseph, Nicholas and Jane."

Executor: son William  Holmes.
Witnesses: William Paine, John Stockard, John (x) Paine.
- - -

E 308  Will dated 2 November 1833, proved Nov. Court 1833.

CASON CAPPS               wife: Mary

sons: Robert and James, "William now in the Western Country"
"Nelly McDaniel, Milly Carter & Mary Stout & their children"
None of the property shall fall into the hands of their hus-
bands Joseph McDaniel, Joseph Carter and Samuel Stout.

Executors: sons Richard and James.
Witnesses: James Moore, Thomas Scott.
- - -

E 309  Will dated 10 May 1832, Proved November Court 1833.

BETSY (x) GRAVES                    son: Elijah

"My two granddaughters Selina F. Graves and Betsy C. Graves
   my four wheel carriage and harness."
"Grandson Ralph Lewis Graves son of Elijah"
"Grandsons Jessey Dixon Graves and Elijah Calvin Graves, sons
   of my dear Henry."

Executor: son Elijah.
Witnesses: Archibald Andrews, Isaac Durham.

- - -

E 311  Will dated 13 August 1822, proved February Court 1834.

JOHN (x) DANNELLEY "frail and old"          wife: Nancy

dau: Rosanna Smothers  $1       son: James Dannelley  $1
 "    Priscilla Rumbley $1        "    John Dannelley  $1
daus: Sarah and Margaret Dannelley

Executors: daughters Sarah and Margaret Dannelley.
Witnesses: Robert Lackey, Thomas Woody.

- - -

E 311  Will dated 3 December 1833, proved Feb Court 1844.

ARCHIBALD (x) FINDLY "weak in body"          Wife: Ann,
                                              all estate.
"My children Brice Andrew and Morau" (no punctuation)
children are under 21 years of age.

Executors: trusty friends John A. Faucett & Levi McCollum.
Witnesses: Geo. W. Bruce, John Newman.

- - -

E 313  Will dated 23 October 1833, proved Feb Court 1844.

WILLIAM (x) PRICHARD          wife: Milly

dau: Rodah Prichard
son: Nelson "land on south side of Price's Creek"
son: Wilson
dau: Nancy Prichard (under age)
son: Edmond Prichard

Executors: "trusty friends Wilson Prichard and Nelson Prichard."
Witness: Goodman Nevill.

- - -

E 315  Will dated 2 February 1832, proved May Court 1834.

JOHN (x) ROBERTS          "son's daughter Mary Roberts"

"son William's son John Wesley Roberts"
Executor: son William. Witnesses: Nath. Newlin, Sarah Andrews.

- - -

E 315  Will dated 18 January 1832, proved May Court 1834.

THOMAS (x) KING "far advanced in years"

wife: Elizabeth land adjoining James Walker and others
youngest son: Thomas King
daus: Dicey King and Marsha ? Ann King

executors: friend James Leathers, and wife Elizabeth.
Witnesses: W. J. Duke, James Leathers.

— — —

E 316  Will dated 13 February 1833, proved May Court 1834.

WILLIAM RAY, SR.

son: James Ray            dau: Jane Hopkins
 "    William Ray          "    Sally Rhew
 "    John Ray

"Grandsons James and John Ray sons of Thomas Ray deceased"
(other children of Thomas) William, Rebecca, Charles & Bogan.

Executor: Richison Nichols.
Witnesses: Adam Dikson, Wm. Dickson.

— — —

E 317  Will dated 5 September 1829, proved May Court 1834.

JOHN REDMOND, SR.   (Names is spelled Redmon in will but is
                     signed Redmond.)
Daughter Margaret Redmon gets all estate during her life.
Grandson John Riley,Jr gets land after Margaret's death if
  he stays to care for her.
John Redmon, Jr.
Sally Riley wife of John Riley
Nancy Redden wife of John Redden
Elizabeth Browning wife of James Browning

Executor: worthy friend Willoughby Hudgins.
Witnesses: William Chamblee, John Riley.

— — —

E 318  Will dated 18 March 1833, proved May Court 1834.

WILLIAM (x) M'CADDAMS "on the decline"     wife: Fanny

daus: Nancy M'Caddams and Margaret M'Caddams
son: Hugh,"and his son William M'Caddams"
 "    Samuel
 "    James M'Caddams "my plantation in the North East corner
                      of the county called the Robson place"
dau: Catherine Thomas
son: William M'Caddams

Residue of estate "equally divided between ....... M'Caddams,
Samuel M'Caddamd James M'Caddams Catherine Thomas  Martha
                                        - continued -

156    E 318  Will of WILLIAM M'CADDAMS continued

Redden  William M'Caddams  Nancy M'Caddams  Margaret M'Caddams."

Executor: Edward Benson.
Witnesses: Stephen Benson, William Benson.

- - -

E 319  Will dated 12 March 1832, proved May Court 1834.

JOHN REEVES              All estate to son Thomas Reeves.

Executor: Thomas Reeves.        Witness: Thomas Lynch.

- - -

E 319  Will dated 12 May 1834, proved May Court 1834.

JOSEPH DICKSON "far advanced in years"

Daughter Mary M. Herndon, and her two sons Maturine C. Herndon
and Coslett M. Herndon.
"My granddaughter Mary Ann now the wife of Anderson Ferrell."
son: Alexander C. Dickson
granddaughters: Mary Ann Dickson and Caroline Dickson
"Respected friends Hugh Waddell and Robert William Dickson
and Presley H. Mangum Esquires attorneys-at-law" trustees to
hold estate for "my daughter Julia Newell Dickson and my
grandson Robert William Dickson" until he arrives at mature age.

Caroline Dickson now the wife of Joseph Marcom.

Executors: Hugh Waddell, Robert WM. Dickson, Presley H. Mangum.
Witnesses: Joseph Marcom, F. Bilbo, Elizabeth (x) Rigsby,
           Mary (x) Marcom.

- - -

E 321-323  Will dated 5 February 1823, proved May Court 1834.

CHRISTOPHER BARBEE       He devises numerous slaves, etc.

son: Francis
son: William lands on Morgan Creek, and "lands on Bolind's
            Creek which I bought of Tapley Booth"
dau: Elizabeth who married Samuel Allen
"    Nancy    "    "      Edward Jones
"    Susanna  "    "      Wm. Henry Merritt
"Some years ago being visited by my granddaughter Polly Allen
daughter of my daughter Elizabeth who then lived in the State
of Tennessee, I loaned to her a certain negro ..."
grandsons: Christopher Allen, Willis Jones

Executors: son William, and friend Mann Patterson.
Witnesses: J. Henderson, N. I. King, Maurice Henderson.

Codicil dated 31 January 1826 annuls legacy to grandson
Willis Jones.  Witnesses: Wm. Chalmers, John Hutchins,
                          Wm. McCauley.
- - -

E 324-328  Will dated 14 December 1827, proved November 1834.

WILLIAM CAIN the older.

daughter: Polly Southerland "tract called Fannings ... which
            formerly belonged to my brother Timothy Cain"
son-in-law (married to Charity Cain) Willie P. Mangum, lot
            in Hillsborough
son: William Cain
daughter Ann Davis and her husband Edward Davis and children
"grandsons William Cain, William R. Southerland and William
  Cain Davis"
"To Eliza Moore (daughter of Philip Moore) a bureau, one of
  those used by my deseased daughter Martha."
dau: Peggy Cain

Executors: friend Duncan Cameron, and son William Cain.
Witnesses: Thos. D. Bennehan, Sam'l Yarborough.

- - -

E 329  Will dated 28 October 1834, proved Nov Court 1834.

WILLIAM RHODES  (He was a son of William and Delilah (Herndon)
                  Rhodes. See Delilah's will, F 6.)
WIFE (name not stated, but she was Penelope Trice) gets
estate to "raise" and "school" children.
"All my children" mentioned, names and number not stated.

Executor: "worthy friend Zachariah Trice".
Witnesses: Henry Trice, Sr., Chesley P. Trice, Henry D. Trice.

- - -

E 330  Will dated 6 December 1834, proved Feb Court 1835.

JONATHAN (x) DOLLAR "far advanced in years"

daus: Milly, Sally, Cynthia
Mary Rhodes (relationship not stated)
son: Jonathan Dollar

Executor: son Jonathan Dollar.
Witnesses: W. S ? Pratt, T(homas) Bilbo, William Lynn.

- - -

E 331  Will dated 13 February 1834, proved Feb Court 1835.

ALEXANDER WALKER

brothers: Conoley Walker, James Walker, Philip Walker
"Margaret Walker widow of William Walker"
Samuel Crawford $1        John Walker

Executor: brother Conoly Walker.
Witnesses: C. F. Faacette , Robert Fausett.

- - -

E 332  Will dated 8 December 1834, proved Feb Court 1835.

ROBERT H. FAUCETT                    "my mother Phebe Dickey"

"My two sisters and brother (viz) Aby Dickey Elizabeth Dickey
and Isaac Newton Dickey all my land ..."

Executors: "Uncle Absolem Harvey and Junia Hall."
Witnesses: James Pickett, James Hart.

- - -

E 334  Will dated 22 November 1834, codicil dated 5 Dec 1834,
                                     proved February Court 1835.
MARY (x) THRIFT "weak of body"

daus: Nancy Rosser, Elizabeth Snipes, Polly Lloyd
"son Isham Thrift's children"
She says "all my children", but does not give number.

Executor: James Rosser.
Witnesses: B. Strowd, Wilson Atwater.

- - -

E 335-338  Will dated 18 August 1834, proved Feb Court 1835.

STEWART DIXON

wife: Sally home plantation and part of Hulgan Tract
eldest son: James Dixon "Turrentine Tract" of land
son: Joseph Dixon "Kirk Tract of land which runs to Haw River"
                   joins Hufman.
son: Thomas Dixon "Patton Tract"
"    John Dixon "McCracking Tract"
"    William Dixon  "balance of Hulgan Tract" & "Freeman Tract"
daughter Mary Wilkins wife of William Wilkins
daus: Martha Morrow, Hannah Dixon, Margaret Dixon,
      Nancy Dixon, Sally Dixon

Executor: son Thomas Dixon.
Witnesses: John Trolinger, Alex Mebane, Elijah Pickard.

- - -

E 338  Will dated 31 July 1828, proved May Court 1835.

JACOB (x) ANTHONY, SR          daughter: Mary Moser

"My other twelve children" names not stated.
eldest son: Jacob

"I was born the first day of May 1745".

Executors: son Henry Anthony, Adam Wrightsel.
Witnesses: A. W. Albright, ...?.. ...?.... (a foreign name).

- - -

E 339  Will dated 16 June 1833, proved May Court 1835.

THOMAS (x) McCRACKEN, SR. "weak of body"      wife: Priscilla

"All my children- viz- Joseph, Robert, Stephen, Alexander,
Abigail, Martha, Thomas."

Executor: son Thomas McCracken.
Witnesses: John Hart, Samuel McCracken.

— — —

E 341  Will dated 21 April 1835, proved May Court 1835.

THOMAS FREELAND               "all my brothers"

father: John Freeland "my land which he now lives on adjoin-
            ing Charles Johnston, John Blackwood and others"
sister: Martha Cloud

Wxwcutor: worthy friend John Blackwood.
Witnesses: James J. Blackwood, David K. Blackwood.

— — —

E 342  Will dated 25 April 1835, proved May Court 1835.

WILLIAM (x) LOYD,SR.            wife: Hannah

sons: Thomas, William, Pleasant, Green and John Loyd
daus: Sarah Loyd, Mary Poe, Nancy Jones, Elizabeth Loyd
daughter Rebecca William's children

Executor: John Careathers..
Witnesses: Levi Andrews, William Careathers.

— — —

E 343  Will dated 11 February 1835, proved May Court 1835.

MARY (x) DICKIE in "feeble state of health"

"son Zachariah Dickie - and his children"
grandsons: E. M. Dickie, Franklin Dickie
granddaus: Margaret Dickie and Mary Dickie
dau: Margaret Dickie

Executor: J. D. Hughes.
Witnesses: James Clark, John Reding, Jr.

— — —

E 344  Will dated 1 November 1830, proved May Court 1835.

DIANNA (x) MOORE

All to daughters Elennor Moore and Mary Bowls.

Executors: worthy friends Thomas Moore and Anderson Moore.
Witnesses: Isaac Jeffreys, James Moore.

— — —

160

E 345  Will dated 19 February 1831, proved May Court 1835.

ANDREW (x) McCULLOCK, SR. "weak of body"

friend: James Kerr of Caswell County
niece: Polly Smith land joining William Barbee
Land and slaves to "my nephew Andrew Forgason, now of Ireland",
provided he comes to America.

Executors: worthy friends James Kerr and James Hurdle.
Witnesses: Solomon Browning, Wm. Cantrell, Connoly Walker.
- - -

E 247-249  Will dated 3 March 1835, proved May Court 1835.

THOMAS ARMSTRONG                  wife: Elizabeth

son: Anderson Armstrong
"My children Anderson, Asenath, Thomas Lapslie and Frances
E. Armstrong (Frances is under 21) "

"Daughter Asenath Curree and son-in-law John Currie" ... "her
children Thomas Anderson, Ann Elizabeth and such other children as she may have..."
son: Thomas Lapslie Armstrong  slaves, and "all my interest
        in a tract of land lying in Montgomery County, Ga."
son: James Armstrong has had his part

Executors: Anderson Armstrong and Thomas L. Armstrong.
Witnesses: William Clark, Jno Bane, Thos. P. Paul.
- - -

E 350  Will dated 27 October 183-, proved May Court 1835.

FREDERICK FONVILLE         Wife a legatee, name not stated.

sons: Asa and Brice, both under age
married daughter Hannah and her son Brice
"         "      Edna   "   "   dau Palina
"         "      Sarah
daus: Mary, Fanna
sons: William ($1) and his son Washington, James ($3), John $1

Executor: son-in-law Thomas Grahams.
Witnesses: Jacob Somers, Chesley F. Faucette.
- - -

E 351-352  Will dated 21 September 1834, proved May Court 1835.

THOMAS RHODES, SR.          son: Noah Rhodes

"My granchildren Jane Medley (Medlin), Wesley Rhodes, Wiley
Rhodes and Artemesia Rhodes children of my son Noah Rhodes."

son: Thomas Rhodes , his children, "his present wife Sally"
        get "tract where he now lives that I purchased from
        William Riley."                        - continued -

E 351   Will of THOMAS RHODES, SR continued              161
son:   James Rhodes "tract whereon he now lives"
dau:   Hannah Rhodes                                      Bunch.
"      Belinda wife of Abel Cain "tract I purchased of Henry/
"      Elizabeth Guess wife of Thomas Guess now of the State
          of Kentucky
"To the children of David Warren which he had by my daughter
   Polly Rhodes"

Sole executor: Silas M. Link.
Witnesses: Archibald Cain, Wmson Burton.
(Names of other grandchildren will be found in equity suit
papers about the settlement of this estate. In State Archives)
- - -

E 353   Will dated 10 September 1834, proved May Court 1835.

MANN PATTERSON

Wife Mary Patterson and her seven children namely Jane,
Martha, Caroline, Mann, William, David and Robert, 2200
acres on the waters of New Hope adjoining the lands of
William Cain, Wm. Jenkins, Wm. Robertson and others...

son: John T(apley) Patterson
"Caroline and Ferdenon M. Patterson daughter and son of
John T. Patterson."
son: James N. Patterson
daus: Sarah M. Rhodes,  Nancy M. Strayhorn
"      Amelia H. Boroughs, Mary A. Patterson

Executors: friends James Webb, James N. Patterson and
              John C. Rhodes.
Witnesses: Robert Davis, Elias Batchelor, Thomas (x) Henderson.
- - -

E 355-357   Will dated 18 November 1834, proved May 1835.

THOMAS HOLLOWAY, SR.                    wife: Lydia

"My children John, Williamson, Sarah, Lydia Caroline, and
Milly Holloway".   "Said three daughters" all under age ?
son: Bennehan Holloway
"children of my son Samuel Holloway"
Susannah Whitaker
"the heirs of my daughter Polly Woods"
daughter Lucy Whitaker
David Holloway, William Holloway
"heirs of Elizabeth Trice"
Hannah Latta, Ann Farthing, Agatha Harward (married)
Thomas Holloway; Sarah Holloway, Fanny Leathers,
James  Holloway, John Holloway, Williamson Holloway,
Lydia Caroline and Milly Holloway.

Executors: friends James Latta, John Leathers, and
              Williamson Burton.
Witnesses: Archibald Cain, William Piper.

162   Codicil to will of THOMAS HOLLOWAY, SR.

Daughter Ann Farthing, her son Hargis Farthing, his deceased
father Reuben Farthing.   Witness: Silas M. Link.

— — —

E 358-361   Will dated 26 July 1831, proved August Court 1835.

MARTIN PALMER

William Huntingdon and Thomas Clancy trustees for property
left to son William Palmer, and then to his children.

son James Palmer and his children
daughter Mary and her husband Roswell Huntingdon
    "      Sarah and her husband John Rasberry
son-in-law Thomas Clancy and his wife Nancy
daughter Elizabeth Peacock wife of Richard Peacock
    "      Temperance Faucett wife of John Faucett
    "      Agnes wife of Henry G. Parish

Executors and trustees: Thomas Clancy and Wm. Huntingdon.
Witnesses: J. W. Norwood, James Faucett.

— — —

E 362   Will dated 23 July 1834, proved May Court 1835.

THOMAS BIRD, SR.

wife: Nancy ... "I lay no claim to the property that my wife
        Nancy possessed when I married her".
son: Thomas
"All my children", names and number not stated.

Executors: son William, and friend Thomas Reeves.
Witnesses: Thomas Reeves, William Bird.

— — —

E 363   Will dated 17 March 1835, proved August Court 1835.

WILLIAM G. CLENDENNIN              wife: Isabel

"All my children", names and number not stated.

Sole executor: James Johnston.
Witnesses: Alfred Thompson, Patterson Thompson,
        James Clendennin.

— — —

E 363   Will dated 26 September 1817, proved August Court 1835.

JOSEPH CALDWELL                   wife: Helen

step-son: William Hooper, Esq.   niece: Margaret Caldwell

Executors: William Hooper, Esq., James Webb.
Witnesses: John L. Bailey, Pleasant H. May.

— — —

E-365  Will dated 15 December 1832, proved Nov Court 1835.

THOMAS FITCH

"Grandson Thomas Fitch son of my son James Fitch" tract on
west side of Stony Creek joining Jacob Greeson, to Tom's
Creek .... James Graham's line... "
son: Empson Fitch
dau: Mary Fitch
"     Barbara Barker wife of George Barker
"     Susanna Younger wife of Joseph
son: James Fitch  $1
"     William Fitch  $2

Executors: friend George Martin, and son Empson Fitch.
Witnesses: Caleb Wilson, John Fitch.

- - -

E 366  Will dated 5 October 1833, proved Nov Court 1835.

BENJAMIN (x) TUTTERTON in "feeble state of health"

dau: Elizabeth Blalock $1 "besides what I have given her"
son: Barenton Tutterton $1 "         "    I  "    "     him
daus: Lainey Tutterton and Polly Tutterton get all estate

Executor: William Paul.
Witnesses: J. D. Hughes, R. Thompson.

- - -

E 367  Will dated 25 January 1834, proved Nov Court 1835.

PETTER WAGGONER                    wife: Margaret

son: Daniel
Daughters Barbary Elizabeth Catherine Margaret Mary
Rosanna Hannah (no punctuation).
"Granddaughter Nancy Waggoner daughter of Peter , deceased."

Executors: son Daniel Waggoner, and George Smith.
Witnesses: John Boon, Jonathan Harvey.

- - -

E 368  Will dated 19 )ctober 1835, proved Feb Court 1836.

TEMPERANCE PRIMROSE

"Six of my children (viz) William Primrose, Rachel Wheeler,
Frances Culberhouse, Ann Chisenhall, Thomas Primrose, and
George Primrose."
"To heirs of James Primrose deceased"
"To Aga Primrose daughter of Pegga Primrose Dec'd."
Nine shares to "John Primrose  Elizabeth Garrard Mary Stem
William Primrose  Rachel Wheeler  Frances Culberhouse
Ann Chisenhall  Thomas Primrose and George Primrose."
                    - continued -

Executors: son and daughter John Primrose and Elizabeth Garrard.
Witnesses: Thomas Flint, Lewis Hutchins.
This will is recorded again in Book F page 114.

— — —

E 369  Will dated 5 June 1825, proved February Court 1836.

JOHN O'DANIEL

All his estate to his brothers Henry and Jesse O'Daniel.
If brothers die without issue property goes to Anne Waddleton
and John Baskett of South Carolina.
No witnesses. Ececutors: brothers Henry and Jesse O'Daniel.

— — —

E Will dated 10 November 1832, proved Feb Court 1836.

PHEBE (x) GRIMES

sisters: Elizabeth Grimes $5, Anna Grimes  $5,
          Rebecca Montgomery widow of Hugh Montgomery  $5
sister: Lydia Grimes  land and all other property

Executors: "Loving friend Anderson Wilson", and sister Lydia.
Witnesses: Caleb Wilson, Samuel Turrentine,
          Martha Wilson, Absolem Turrentine.

— — —

E 371  Will dated 5 February 1834, proved Feb Court 1836.

SARAH YOUNGER widow, "aged and infirm"

son: Robert Younger  all money on hand
"Heirs of my son John E. Younger" $1
to son Richard Younger , plantantion, etc; and to his son
John, "my plantation on Boyd's Creek where I lately resided"

Executor: son Richard Younger.
Witnesses: Jas. Grahams, Robert Fausett.

— — —

E 371  Will dated January 1835, proved Feb Court 1836.

ROBERT MOORE                    father: James Moore

"sister Margaret, James and sister Sally Crutchfield and
John Moore"
"sister Margaret Jones"
He devises lands on waters of Cain Creek -to wit- Lashley
Tract .. joining James Moore & Wm Morrow', the Griffin Tract
joining Wm. Smith & John Crofford (Crawford) ...

Executors: John Jones and John Moore.
Witnesses: Henry O'Daniel, Elizabeth (x) Moore,
Jesse O'Daniel.

— — —

E 372  Will dated 22 December 1835, proved Feb 1836.

PETER S. CLARK                  sister: Elizabeth Weaver.

wife: Susannah, land near Woody's Ferry, etc.

Executors: wife, & " friend Jediah Smith of Guilford County."
Witness: John Moore.

— — —

E 373-375  Will dated 10 September 1835, proved Feb 1836.

ALEXANDER ALLEN             Wife a legatee, name not stated.

Infant son Alexander, son John, daughters Fanny, Mary, Jane
and Nancy. (All the children seem to be minors.)

Executors: "friend and kinsman George Mebane and my brother-
                in-law John Scott."
Witnesses: James Patton, James White.

— — —

E 375  Will dated 22 April 1830, proved Feb 1836.

ROBERT TINNEN          sons: Thomas and David

sons: Catlett C. Tinnen & Robert Tinnen "plantation which
        joins Joseph Allison".
"My four daughters Margaret, Jennet, Elenor and Mary" ...
Grandsons: "Robert Clark (of Jos) and Robert Tinnen (of Thos)"
"My bound girl Polly Deneal ..."

Executors: sons David Tinnen and Robert Tinnen.
Witnesses: J. Taylor, James Lindsey.

— — —

E 377  Will dated 12 January 1836, proved Feb 1836.

MARTHA (x) PRICE.  All estate to grandson Thomas Johnson
                        Crabtree.
Executor: "trusty friend John Crabtree".
Witnesses: Goodman Nevill, John Couch.

— — —

E 378  Will dated 18 November 1834, proved May 1836.

MARTHA (x) MULHOLLAN, widow of Thomas.

To friend Samuel N. Tate all her property in trust for
sons John Mulhollan and Samuel Mulhollan. At their deaths
to "the children of my son Hugh Mulhollan deceased."

Executor: Samuel N. Tate.  Witnesses: C. C. Smith, James Tate.

— — —

E 379  Will dated 14 April 1827, proved May 1836.

JOHN HUGHS, SR.            Wife a legatee, name not stated.

son: Thomas Hughs.        daughter: Elizabeth

166       E 379  Will of JOHN HUGHS, SR continued

son: Samuel Hughs  land on Reedy Fork
sons: John and Andrew Hughs have already received land

Sole executor: son Andrew Hughs.
Witnesses: Robert Bevell, Michael Strader.

— — —

E 380  Will dated 11 May 1836, proved May Court 1836.

WILLIAM H. PARKER "weak in body"

wife: Jane  plantation in Person County "known by the name of
              the Aldrige Tract ... lying on waters of Flat River"
dau: Anzalette M. Parker
His plantation in Orange County known as Vincent Tapp tract to
be sold.

Executor: George C. Ray.
Witnesses: Hugh Woods, H. Terry, Edward Riley.

— — —

E 381  Will dated  11 May 1836, proved May Court 1836.

PHILEMON HOLT              wife: Sarah

"My children namely Mary S. Holt, Jane Holt and Wilkins Holt"
all minors.
"My bound boy Granville Simpson now living with me to be
schooled."

Exceutors: wife Sarah, and brother Jacob Holt.
Witnesses: Sarah Holt, Jonah Dobyna, Elizabeth W. Waggoner.

— — —

E 382  Will dated 18 April 1835, proved May Court 1836.

WILLIAM KELL              wife: Anna

dau: Sally                granddaughter: Charlotte Kell
grandson: William Gates
great-grandson: Allen Kell son of Charlotte Kell

No executor named.  Witnesses: James Webb, James Webb, Jr.

— — —

E 382-384  Will dated 17 May 1828, proved May Court 1836.

GEORGE FOUST              wife: Barbara

son: Daniel Foust 250 acres in Guilford County "which I
          bought from my brother John Foust and John Cook"
son: George Foust plantation where he now lives, with a piece
          joining it "which I bought from William Ray"
                                        - continued -

son: Peter Foust "land which I bought from Old Woman Ray and
       her son Robert".."likewise a part of the tract I bought
       from James Ray from the Fayetteville Road to the Ala-
       mance".."land I bought from Old Aaron Sharp"
son: William Foust  "plantation I bought from John Ray"
       "100 acres I bought from the heirs of the Widow Ray"
son: Henry Foust "plantation whereon I now live" and 50 acres
       bought from James Tinnen, & "plantation I bought from
       David Efland"

daughter: Catherine  wife of John Clap
    "        Barbara    "    "  Joseph Bason
    "        Sally      "    "  Jeremiah Holt
granddau: Sally daughter "of my son John Foust Deceased",
       half of plantation John Foust lived on.
great-granddaughter: Barbara Catherine Albright
He owns other tracts of land which are to be sold.

Executors: sons George, Peter, William and Henry Foust.
Witnesses: Joseph Clendennin; John Holmes, A.D.Murphey.
All the above witnesses died, and the will was witnessed
again 18 September 1833 by: Thomas Ruffin, Will K. Ruffin.

- - -

E 385   Will dated 18 January 1836, proved May Court 1836.

VINES GUYE         wife: Elizabeth "to raise my children"

Children (names and number not stated) all seem to be minors.

Executors: wife Elizabeth, and James Womble.
Witnesses: Tho. Prendergast, William Miles.

- - -

E 385   Will dated 6 April 1836, proved August Court 1836.

ELIZABETH (x) KING widow of John   "weak in body"

James Wyate $1 - "his son John Wyate my well-beloved grand-
                 son" (under age)
Empson Byrd $1-"his oldest sons Thomas & John Byrd $2"
Daughter Levina King and sons John and Hezekiah King "tract
whereon I now live".

Executors: son John, and daughter Levina King.
Witnesses: Thomas A. Horn, Levi Truet.              . .

- - -

E 386   Will dated 8 July 1836, proved August Court 1836.

DICY (x) HARRIS "weak in body"   brother: William Harris

"Brother William Harris' four oldest children -- Narcissa
Ann, Rufust, Mary, Lucy."                    - continued -

Amelia Ball, Temperance Harris, Eliz. Mangum, Nathaniel Harris

"Elenor Piper, Drady Parker, Temperance Harris, Edna Harris,
Elizabeth Harris, Ducey Harris my neices."

Sole executor: nephew Williams Harris.
Witnesses: James C. Roberts.

- - -

E 387   Will dated 24 September 1824, proved August Court 1836.

EDWARD THOMAS                    wife: Elizabeth

sons: Neamia Thomas, Richard Thomas
"Six daughters Nelly Hollen, Hannah Cook, Nancy Hubbert *,
Elizabeth Thomas, Jenney Thomas & Caty Thomas."
* (Nancy Thomas married in Orange Co. 24 March 1809 James Hub/
                                                            bard.)
Executrix: wife Elizabeth.
Witnesses: D. Albright, Israel Holt.

- - -

E 388   Will dated --, proved August Court 1836.

JAMES MOORE

"The property that will fall to" daughter Patsey Smith not
to be subject to any debts of Hosea Smith.

Sons Robert and John Moore to be guardians of property.
Witnesses: Jesse O'Daniel, Henry O'Daniel.

- - -

E 388-390   Will dated 16 October 1829, proved -- ?

WILLIAM KIRKLAND                 wife: Margaret

His estate is very involved. He is indebted to David Yarborough. He appoints his son John Kirkland and his-son-in-
law Thomas Ruffin Trustees and Executors.

"My four children Alexander, Mary, Susan and Phebe"
Married daughter Martha.
He speaks of "my four younger children", it is not clear
whether they are the four named above.

No witnesses.

Page 391 is blank.

E 392   Will dated 4 July 1836, proved November Court 1836.

MOSES ATWATER                   wife: Anney or Amey ?

sons: Gehiel, Jahaza, Wilson get lands which join James Nor-
       wood, Maderson Cook, Isham Smith.        - continued -

E 392  Will of MOSES ATWATER continued              169
He speaks of his mill purchased from Fearington.

daughters: Lois Strowd and Celia Strowd.
"All my children (viz) Wilson, Edmund, Jahaza, Gehiel,
Lois Strowd and Celia Strowd."

Executors: sons Wilson and Jehaza.
Witnesses: J. H. Norwood, Martha Bilbow.
- - -

E 393  Will dated 4 August 1836, proved November Court 1836.

ISABEL JOHNSTON              youngest daughter: Fanny

daughter: Jane Thompson
"All my children", number not stated.

Sole executor: James Johnston.
Witnesses: Ja mes Patton, Samuel Patton.
- - -

E 394  Will dated 15 November 1836, proved Nov Court 1836.

JOHN (x) MINNIS "weak of body"

son: James (he has had his part) $1
dau: Jane Taylor  $1
son: William Minnis    half his land joining Jos Thompson
dau: Lavinia Minnis    "    "    "    "        "    "
grandson: Ashburn Minnis
son: Allen Minnis  $1
dau: Margaret Gant $1
"My pension if any be due" to be collected.

Executor: friend William F. Jones, and son William Minnis.
Witnesses: Samuel Jones, Alf. Nelson.
- - -

E 395  Will dated 19 October 1836, proved Nov Court 1836.

JAMES MELVIN              wife: Catherine

sons: Louis, John (to be educated), James, Elias
"Four daughters Mary, Elizabeth, Nancy and Matilda."

Executors: son Elias, and Boston Iseley.
Witnesses: Julius S. Bracken, Christian Iseley,
           James Melvin, Jr.
- - -

E 396-400  Will dated 5 August 1824, proved August 1836.

ANTHONY (x) THOMPSON              wife: name not stated

son: Anderson Thompson
"    William    "        land "whereon he now lives"
                                    - continued -

E 396  Will of ANTHONY THOMPSON continued
son: Marmaduke Michael Thompson "land on Beaver Creek join-
      ing Barney Clap & others"
son: Anthony
Daughter Polly has had one of her hands injured. She is to
have $150 more than other children.

"My children- to wit- Nancy Jane Anderson Letty William
Dilly Marmaduke and Anthony and my daughter Polly."

Executrix: wife.
Witnesses: Michael Holt, Alfred A. Holt, Joel C. Yancey.

Codicil dated 7 June 1826 revokes bequest to daughter Jane,
wife of John James.
Daughter Nancy has been advanced $50 "for the moving of her
and her family from the State of Tennessee."
$50 to Archibald D. Murphey, who advanced this $50 to Nancy
"without my consent."
Witnesses: Michael Holt, Alfred A. Holt.

— — —

E 400-401  Will dated 12 January 1836, proved Nov Court 1836.

JOHN LONG, SR.              wife: Mary W. Long

son: Alphonso to continue at school until he is 18½ years old
"My store to be kept in operation", store goes to Alphonso.
"His sister Flora (Alphonso's) "
"Each of my first wife's children Nancy, John, Rebecca, Sally,
Polly, Rachel"  $200, with what they have already received.

Executors: "John Newlin and his son James Newlin."
Witnesses: D. Patterson, A. Shearer, Fred'k Brown.

— — —

E 402  Will dated --, proved November Court 1836.

JAMES MOORE     "The property that will fall to my daughter
                Nancy Sykes and to the heirs of her body" not
                to be subject to the debts of William Sykes.
Guardians of property: sons Robert Morre and John Moore.
Witnesses: Jesse O'Daniel, Henry O'Daniel.

— — —

E 402-403  Will dated 9 February 1837, proved Feb Court 1837.

DAVID (x) STRAIN              wife: Jane

son: John Strain
unmarried daughters: Sarah and Elizabeth Strain
son: William Strain

Executors: sons William and John.
Witnesses: N. I. King, J. Mullchey, David McLean.

— — —

E 404  Will dated 16 December 1836, proved Feb Court 1837.

CHARLES McCAULEY                wife: Elizabeth ½ estate

son: Matthew other ½ of estate- he is to be educated
brother: Matthew McCauley  150 acres on Cub Creek and
          land on E side of Morgan Creek known as Brewer
          or Tilly land "including my saw mill"
brother: George McCauley "who now resides in the State of
                                         Tennessee"
He speaks of "wife and my family".

Executors: brother Matthew McCauley and friend Bryant Strowd.
Witnesses: Charles King, Henry McColum, John Cheek.

- - -

E 406-407  Will dated 18 December 1836, proved Feb Court 1827.

RACHEL (x) STRAYHORN widow of James

son: William Strayhorn
grandsons: Thompson and James Strayhorn
granddaughter: Rachel Strayhorn
son: John Strayhorn
dau: Polly Bowland
grandchildren: Willie Strayhorn Malcacy A. Strayhorn
sons: John Thompson, John Strayhorn

Executors: friends Andrew Bowland and Samuel Strayhorn.
Witnesses: Aaron Strayhorn, William (x) Strayhorn.

- - -

E 408  Will dated 11 January 1837, proved Feb Court 1837.

JAMES RAY, SR.         legatee: Sally Daugherty

grandson: James Ray            granddaughter: Elizabeth Ray
granddaughters: Polly Cole and Rosanna Jones

Executors: grandson James Ray and worthy friend Hezekiah
            Terry.
Witnesses: Charles Wilson, Jon R. McKee.

- - -

E 409  Will dated 12 March 1830, proved February Court 1837.

JOSEPH FREELAND        wife a legatee, name not stated

sons: William and Thomas, both under age
daus: Sally and Mary, both under age

Witnesses: W.F.Hogan, James Gattis.
Executor: brother John Freeland, appointed in codicil
            dated December 1836.
Witnesses to codicil: W.F.Hogan, Thomas Hogan.

John J. Freeland qualified as executor.

- - -

E 410  Will dated 7 December 1836, proved Feb Court 1837.

ELIZABETH (x) Strayhorn                niece: Rachel Strayhorn

nephews: Thompson and James Strayhorn
Emmely Malone
sister: Polly Bowland
"Three brothers William,  John and James Strayhorn"
mother: Rachel Strayhorn

Executors: worthy friends Andrew Bowland and Bryant Strayhorn.
Witnesses: S. Strayhorn, J. S. Smith.

— — —

E 410  Will dated 12 December 1836, proved Feb Court 1837.

PHEBE (x) BARBEE

daus: Gemima Hopkins, Mary King
grandson: Francis Barbee
granddaughters- "all the daughters of Gabriel Barbee" ...
              "Durcilla Nancy Noe Phebe Ann Barbee" (no
                 punctuation)
"To Luvinia Matley 50¢ she is to have no more of my estate"
dau: Elizabeth Rencher

Executor: Gabriel Barbee.
Witnesses: Isaah Marcum, David Malone.

— — —

E 411  Will dated 13 July 1832, proved May Court 1837.

NANCY (x) CLOUD  "weak of body"

daughter Martha Bailiff wife of Abner Bailiff
"My children Samuel Cloud; Martha Bailiff, Joel Cloud,
Daniel Cloud, David Cloud, John Cloud, Mary Beavers and
Sarah Nichols & my grandchildren Nancy Cloud daughter of
Samuel, Nancy Cloud daughter of Joel, Daniel Cloud son of
Joel, Daniel Bailiff son of Abner Bailiff, and Daniel Cloud
son of David Cloud."
Nathaniel J. Palmer, Esq.

Executor: friend Catlett Campbell.
Witnesses: David Murdock, Matthew Futral.

— — —

E 412  Will dated 24 April 1837, proved May Court 1837.

JOHN SCARLETT                wife: Scyntha

sons: Allen, Page and Henderson Scarlett
daus: Nancy, Mariah and Delilah Scarlett.
grandson: John Gaston Carrell
dau: Nancy Elizabeth Carrell

Executor: son Page Scarlett.
Witnesses: Silas M. Link, Susan McQuiston.

— — —

E 414  Will dated 6 May 1834, proved May Court 1837.

WILLIAM ROBERTS

"Five of my children- Winnefred, John, Jacob, David and
Mahala" (Winnefred and Mahala are unmarried)
sons: Willis, William, Charles and Elisha
"My son Richard's two children Wesley and Eliza"

Executors: sons Jacob and John.  Witness: Elisha Umstead.
- - -

E 415  Will dated 9 February 1837, proved May Court 1837.

DAVID (x) McCROREY  "sick in body"

son:  David "my plantation adjoining Wm. Faucett, ... Sellers,
           James Mebane .."
son: William
"brother John McCrorey's son Thomas McCrorey"

Executor: "Anderson Thompson, true and faithful friend."
Witnesses: Samuel Tate, Thomas McCrorey.
- - -

E 416  Will dated 30 July 1834, proved May Court 1837.

NATHAN (x) HARVEY  "my advanced age"          wife: Agness

son: Anthony
daus: Mary and Elizabeth
son: Isaac

Executor: "worthy friend Samuel Woody".
Witnesses: John Newlin, Z. Bingham, Elenor Guthrie.
- - -

E 417  Will dated 3 January 1833, proved May Court 1837.

STEPHEN WARD         wife: all estate during her life

Stephen Ward    son of William Ward    ⎫
   "     Pike    "    "  William Pike   ⎬
   "     Elliott son of Abraham Elliott ⎬  $50 each
   "     Wells   "    "  Nathan Wells   ⎭
   "     Moon    "    "  James Moon $25
Leah Siler wife of Jeremiah Siler  $100

Remainder of estate in 7 equal parts to: 1 part to Susannah
Ward's children, 1 part to William Ward's children, 1 part to
..?.ster Wells' children, 1 part to Priscilla Free, 1 part to
James Ward's children, 1 part to Thomas Ward's children, 1
part to Antony Ward.

Executors: John Long, Jr., and Benjamin Way.
Witnesses: A. Shearer, Geo. C. Mendenhall.
- - -

174

E 418  Will dated 29 July 1836, proved May Court 1837.

SALLY MITCHELL

"My graddaughter Frances E. Potter daughter of Thomas Potter
late of the County of Granville deceased" (Frances is a minor).
"My granddaughter Caroline Mildred Pratt daughter of Moses S.
Pratt late of Orange County deceased" (Caroline is a minor).
"My daughter-in-law Caroline Mitchell widow of my son James"
"Granddaughters Lucy and Martha Mitchell daughters of Robert
B. Mitchell deceased."

Executors: "James Mallory late of the County of Granville in
           this State but more recently of the State of Ala-
           bama", and friend John Hutchins of Orange County.
Witnesses: J. W. McGee, John Hutchins.

- - -

E 420  Will dated 30 April 1835, proved  August Court 1837.

ROBERT KING "aged and infirm"

son: Benjamin King
"To heirs of my daughter Foster $1"
dau: Rebecca Walker wife of Philip Walker  $1
 "   Nancy Wallis   "    "  Peter Wallis   $1
 "   Sally Barber
 "   Clarecy Faucett wife of Robert Faucett

Executors: son-in-law Robert Faucett and friend James Grahams.
Witnesses: William Barber, Nathan Findley.

- - -

E 421  Will dated 10 July 1837, proved May Court 1837.

ELIZABETH (x) SNIPES                Willis Snipes  $1

Mary Shelby wife of John Shelby  $1
Sarah Masey "    " Lonnie ? Masey  $1
Dempsey Snipes $1, Oren Snipes  $1

Thomas Snipes and Robert Snipes, Martha Snipes and Elizabeth
Snipes get proceeds of sale of "my land in Chatham County".

Executors: friends Thomas M. Durham and James Rosser.
Witnesses: James Lloyd, Mary Lloyd.

- - -

E 422  Will dated 27 April 1837, proved August Court 1837.

JOHN (x) DANIEL "advanced in age"          wife: Susannah

After wife's death property to: "David Carlton & Nancy his
wife & their sons William & Henry & daughters Margaret Marcum and Nancy Leigh " ..
"Henry Trice Sr ... during his life and at his death to Henry
Pearson".  Henry's daughter Amelia Trice, his son Page Trice ,
his daughter Sarah Lynn, his daughter Frances, son Henry Trice,

daughter Susannah."                                                175
"To my grandson John Carlton" the Patterson tract of land.
"To John Couch's three children he had by Susannah Carlton"
    $100 each.
"To Wesley Carlton's three children , $100 a piece"
"grandson Page Trice" 150 acres .. "where he now lives"
    "        Henry Trice  "balance of my land"
    "        William Carlton
granddaughter Elizabeth Marcum

"Daniel Carlton guardian for John Couch's and Wesley Carlton's
children as to the money I left them."

Executors: Henry Trice Sr. and Daniel Carlton.
Witnesses: R. Henslee, Mark (x) Pickett, Joseph White.

- - -

E 424  Will dated 7 July 1837, proved August Court 1837.

WILLIAM (x) STRAYHORN

Mother-in-law is to take his "children to raise them."
Children are to be "schooled." Names and number not stated.

Executor: William Duskin or "Heart or my brother Aaron".
Witnesses: E. Strudwick, Walter A. Norwood.

- - -

E 425  Will dated 30 June 1837, proved August Court 1837.

JOSHUA (x) THOMPSON                    daughter: Polly Thompson

son: James Thompson
dau: Patsy Curry wife of William Curry
 "   Ruth Thompson wife of James Thompson

Executors: son James Thompson, and Richard Tapp.
Witnesses: Geo. W. Bruce, W. H. Thompson, Abel Thompson.

- - -

E 426  Will dated 9 October 1834, proved August Court 1837.

SAMUEL NELSON, planter.        daughter: Ibby Allen

son: David Nelson (of Tennessee)
dau: Betsey Stephens (of Tenn.) "three slaves she received
        from me when she removed to Tennessee"
daus: Peggy Dunn, Ginney
sons: George, Samuel
"Samuel Allen son of my daughter Ibby"

Executor: son George. Witnesses: Alf Nelson, James A. Craig.

- - -

E 428-429 and here the number skips to 500.
Will dated 14 May 1837, proved August Court 1837.

ENOCH McPHERSON                    wife: Sarah           - continued -

dau: Sarah
"    Mary Dask ?  "land I purchased of John Pyle"
son: Eli  "the Nall place"
"Grandchildren the children of my son James, by name Enoch
John Aren William & Wright".
dau: Phebe  "the Dowdy place"
He frees his two slaves.

Sole executor: son William McPherson.
Witnesses: James McPherson, Isaac Andrew, John Davis.

— — —

E 501  Will dated 24 February 1837, proved August Court 1837.

LEWIS (x) HORNADAY                 wife: Dinah

son: William "plantation on which he is now living" and Cot-
                ner place.
son: John  land "known as the Dale plantation"
Brother: Simon shall have the benefit of the Pike plantation
                for three years.
daus: Susannah Foust, Polly Stafford, Ruth Wells, Rebecca Hill,
      Hester Alexander
sons: Simon, Ezekiel
son: Lewis "the Dixon place"
Dinah Marshall

Executors: son William Hornaday and friend William Thompson.
Witnesses: John McPherson, R. Freeman.
Codicil made orally during his last illness 25 August 1837.
Witnesses: Henry Stout, Dinah (x) Hornaday.

— — —

E 508-509  Will dated 11 July 1833, proved November Court 1837.

DAVID WHITE                        wife: Betsy

grandchildren: David White Kerr, Margaret Graham Kerr
son-in-law: Samuel Kerr
Fanny White daughter of Samuel White
John Allen son of Alexander Allen

Executors: son-in-law Samuel Kerr, and brother-in-law
                Alexander Allen.        Witness: James A. Craig.

— — —

E 509  Will dated 18 August 1837, proved Nov Court 1837.

REBECCA (x) BIRD    Son, James J. Bird, to be educated.

Executor: James Bird.        Witness: Thomas Reeves.

— — —

Book E has been re-bound, and the last few pages are
badly scrambled, hence the confusion in page numbers here.

E 503-505  Will dated 6 January 1837, proved August 1837

ALFRED MOORE "of Moorefields"

"My son-in-law Francis Nash Waddell of the State of Louisi-
ana" whole estate. Waddell has looked after the affairs of
testator during his long illness.
Sister, Sarah Moore to have use of Moorefields plantation
in Orange County, she is unmarried. His daughters, Augusta,
Emma and Caroline (all unmarried) to live with their Aunt
Sarah at Moorefields.

Sole executor: son-in-law Francis Nash Waddell.
No witnesses. The will was found among his valuable papers
1 August 1837, after his death.

- - -

E 505  Will dated 31 January 1837, proved Nov Court 1837.

SAMUEL THOMPSON              wife: Elizabeth

daughter: Rebecca Cloud
sons: William, Solomon and David Thompson
Daughter Nancy Sytayhorn is not of sound mind.
granddaughter: Rachel Strayhorn
dau: Rachel Lindley

Executors: wife Elizabeth, and son Solomon.
Witnesses: J. Allison, John McDade.

- - -

E 507  Will dated 25 October 1837, proved Nov Court 1837.

ANDREW WILLIAMS, Blacksmith              wife: Phebe

He speaks of his blacksmith shop at Staggsville.

"My children", number not stated.                      made.
Daughters, Sally, Matildy and Annis to have beds they have /

Executor: James Leathers.
Witnesses: P. C. Cameron, Fendal Southerland.

- - -

E 510  Will dated 17 July 1837, proved November Court 1837.

RALPH (x) FAUCETT, SR.              wife: Martha

daus: Sarah Weedon, Emelia Wilson
son: William Faucett
daus: Martha Wilson, Charity Dickey, Rachel
sons: Ralph Faucett, Bracken Faucett
dau: Clarissa (unmarried)

Executor: friend Robert Gillam.
Witnesses: Robert Faucett, Snelson Love.

- - -

E 511  Will dated 1823, proved Nov Court 1837.

GEORGE (x) THOMAS

sons: William Thomas $1, Josiah Thomas  $3
daughter  Mary Thomas     to have all his lands
"         Elizabeth to live with Mary

Executors: Sam'l Crawford and John McCauley.
Witnesses: A. McCauly , Joseph Tate.

— — —

E 512  Will dated 15 May 1834, proved November Court 1837.

ANDREW BURNS "weak and infirm"          wife: Martha

eldest son: William Burns  gets "Blackwood tract" of land
son: Samuel Burns  "land joining Alex. Craig ... David Stray-
                    horn's line"
son: Andrew Johnson Burns land joining Wm Robson and Mary /
                                                    Flintoff
dau: Margaret Mitchell Burns (unmarried)
"    Mary Strain wife Alex Strain

Executors: sons William and Samuel Burns.
Witnesses: C. W. Johnston, William Duskin, John Boroughs.

— — — — — — — — — END OF BOOK E — — — — — — — — — — — — —

BOOK F, page 1   Will dated 9 Sept 1837, proved Feb Court 1938.

JOHN SHAW

Daughters Jane Walker, Elinor Street, Kitty Armstrong,
            Clarissa Crawford, Verlinda D. Vincent.
sons: John W. Shaw, William V. Shaw, Joseph W. Shaw
John W gets land he lives on, on Jordan Creek ... corner of
 William Cantrell's line and the land he bought from Anderson
 Watson .. another tract on West side of big branch running
 with James Walkers' line
Joseph W gets land on S side of Jordan Creek near Connaly
 Walker's .. to Gibson's corner ..., etc
William W ... land joining Samuel Couch.. and Rachel Walker

Executors: son John W. Shaw, and son-in-law James Walker of
            Caswell County.
Witnesses: Obediah Hurdle, John Squires, Edmisten ? Love.

— — —

F 3  Will dated 5 September 1837, proved Feb Court 1838.

LYSIAS DURHAM

daughters: Tabitha Gear, Mary Jane ( a minor), Susannah L.
sons: David, Dudley, Tarleton

Executors: friends Wilson Atwater, Manly Snipes.
Witnesses: R. C. Poe, Antho. Durham.

— — —

F 4  Will dated 9 September 1837, proved Feb Court 1838.

ANN PHILLIPS                    son: Benjamin

daus: Polly, Hannah, Rachel
daughter Lucretia is non compos mentis- she is to live with
    brother-in-law Boston Iseley and his wife. Her share to go
    to Boston Iseley and Rachel.

Executor: Boston Iseley.
Witnesses: Jesse Thompson, John Lewis, Abner (x) James.

- - -

F 6  Will dated 18 December 1837, proved Feb Court 1838.

DELILAH RHODES

"Son Zachariah Rhodes' three children (viz) Lowry Jane,
Cozby Ann, Claudeus Jasper"

children: Sarah Hutchins, George W. Rhodes, Dicey Rhodes,
Caroline Jane Rhodes, Penney Patteshall, Mary Hurley,
Delilah Patteshall, Milley Smith.

Son William Rhodes' children"

Witnesses: Samuel Couch, Wm. Trice, Jr.
The above will does not state that these are her children,
but papers in the equity suit for distribution of the estate
give all the relationships. Delilah is the widow of William
Rhodes, and the daughter of George Herndon and Sarah. See D70.

- - -

F 7  Will dated 3 July 1838, proved August Court 1838.

ANN WILKERSON           sons: James, Francis & John Wilkerson

daus: Frances Wilkerson, Polly Wilkerson, Nancy Pickett,
    Margaret McDaniel, Elizabeth Wilkerson

Executors: son Francis Wilkerson, and John Wilkerson.
Witnesses: William Wilkerson, Robert G. Tinnen.

- - -

F 8  Will dated 23 December 1836, proved August Court 1828.

SAMUEL McCRACKEN           sons: John and Thomas

Executors: son Thomas McCracken, and James Tate.
Witnesses: Sam'l N. Tate, Thomas Squires.

- - -

F 8  Will dated 15 December 1837, proved August Court 1838.

JAMES TATE

son: David "home plantation at present occupied by Chas Cox"
sons: George and Samuel N. Tate                - continued -

180      F 8  Will of JAMES TATE continued
George Marlet (no relationship stated)
son-in-law: John Squires
Thomas Gill "$70 to be paid by my son Sam'l N. Tate"

Executor: son Samuel N. Tate.
Witnesses: C. C. Smith, Thomas McCracken.
- - -

F 9  Will dated 22 June 1838, proved August Court 1838.

WILLIAM SUTHERLAND          Mother: Mary A. Sutherland

Executor: William Cain of Hillsboro.
Witnesses: George W. Jones, Menerva R. Cain.
- - -

F 10  Will dated 7 November 1837, proved May Court 1838.

JOSEPH (x) FENNELL  (or FERRELL ?)

"To my five daughters namely Betsy Williams, Patsy Lester,
Nancy Kelley, Catherine W. Castleberry, Sally S. Lewter, what
they have received" and $1 each.
Daughter Patience F. Fennell, all estate.

Executrix: Patience F. Fennell.
Witnesses: Henry Moring, John S. Moring.
- - -

F 11  Will dated 11 March 1837, proved May Court 1838.

MARTHA RAY "wife of George Ray, deceased"

dau: Martha Ann wife of Anderson Jackson
daus: Delila Nickols, Polly Jackson, Jenny Collins
To friend James Jackson (of James) in trust "for my daughter
Sally Hopkins, wife of Cuza Hopkins" ...
sons-in-law: Bradley Collins and Cuza Hopkins  $1 each
sons: Michael Ray, James Collins
granddaughters: Martha A. Collins and Martha D. Hopkins

Executor: James Jackson (of James).
Witnesses: Levi Whitted, Thos. W. Holden.
- - -

F 13  Will dated 10 December 1837, proved May Court 1838.

ISAAC CANTRELL          wife: Rutha

"Children", number and names not stated.

Executrix: wife Tutha Cantrell.
Witnesses: John Tapscott, Joseph Simpson, George W. Taylor.
- - -

F 14  Will dated 10 May 1834, proved May Court 1838.

EZEKIEL VEAZEY of Granville County          wife: Frances

daughters: Mealey Jarrot and Thersday (?)
son: Leonard
Other children he does not name.

Executors: son Edward Veazey, and friend Elijah Hester.
Witnesses: William Veazey, John C. Veazey.

- - -

F 16  Will dated 12 July 1838, proved November Court 1838.

JOHN PATTON

Sisters Margaret and Elizabeth to live on home plantation.
"Andrew Patton to have a support as long as he continues
with them."

Executor: friend John Thompson.
Witnesses: Stephen Scarlett, John Hamilton.

- - -

F 17  Will dated 12 July 1838, proved February Court 1839.

THOMAS MARCOM

sons: Nathan, Isaiah, Thomas.
"Son Edmond's children, William and Henderson M. Marcom."
granddaughters: Mary Moring and Nancy Marcom.
dau: Elizabeth Carlton
daus: Amelia Dodd, Celia Cates, Polly Shepherd,
      Patsey Williams
Lewis Caudle (no relationship stated)

Executors: sons Isaiah and Nathan Marcum.
Witnesses: Cornelius (x) Cook, Benj. Marcom.
This family and descendants are given in HERNDONS OF THE
AMERICAN REVOLUTION, PART FOUR, See last page in this book.

- - -

F 19  Will dated 7 December 1838, proved Feb Court 1839.

WILLIAM TRICE, SR.          wife: Frances

sons: Zachariah, William, James
dau: Penny
granddaughter: Penny Dillard
Willis Dillard "land adjoining Widow Daniel... to repay him
               cost of Philpot and Barbee debts which he paid
               as security for my son James Trice."

Executors: sons Zachariah and William Trice.
Witnesses: Richard Henslee, F. Bilbo.

- - -

F 21  Will dated 12 December 1832, proved Feb Court 1839.

LETTY (x) NEECE

"My oldest daughter Milly" ... "balance of my girls"
son: Elias
Powel Anthony, Eli Sharp, Polly, Prisee (relationship not
                                                      stated)
Executors: Powel Anthony, Eli Sharp.
Witnesses: Hiram Steel, Isaac Sharp.

— — —

F 22  Will dated 18 December 1838, proved May Court 1839.

REBECCA MONTGOMERY                    daughter: Lydia Woods

sons: Hamilton, Hugh, James, Alexander

Executor: son Hamilton Montgomery.
Witnesses: John Woods, James T. Roberts.

— — —

F 23  Will dated 9 June 1839, proved August Court 1839.

ANDREW McCAULY                    wife: Mary

daughter: Jane Long
niece: Martha Nobel tract including the place where John Fitch ?
                    now lives "
John Nobel (note on George & James Graham); Robert Nobel
niece: Mary Nobel (note on Gabriel B. Lea)
son: Johnson McCauly  tract adjoining Margaret Watson

ExecutorsL Johnson McCauly and John Nobel Jr.
Witnesses: Robert Fausett, C. F. Faucette.

— — —

F 25  Will dated 30 May 1839, proved August Court 1839.

JOANNA FARTHING "widow of Reuben Farthing"

sons: Hargis Farthing, Thomas Farthing, John Farthing
dau: Nancy Watkins Farthing
sons: William Farthing, Abner Farthing.

Executors: William Farthing and Abner Farthing.
Witnesses: Harris Wilkerson, I. Gooch.

— — —

F 26  Will dated 16 March 1832, proved August Court 1839.

WILLIAM BROWN                    wife: Ruth

dau: Ann Brown          granddaughter: Polly Ann Cabe
sons: Mathew, John, William, Jehu, and Allen Brown

Executors: sons Mathew Brown and Allen Brown.
Witnesses: Daniel Wilkerson, John Wilkerson.

— — —

Will dated 27 May 1839, proved August Court 1839.

WILLIAM HORNADAY                    wife: Mary

son: Alfred   plantation that formerly belonged to Christopher
              Hornaday
son: Balam home plantation, "including land devised to me by
              my brother Lewis Hornaday deceased."
minor daughters: Anna, Hester, Jemima, Mary Ann, Ruth Elinor
daus: Sally, Rebecca

Executors: son Alfred Hornaday, and friend Wm. Thompson.
Witnesses: Jer. Piggott, B. Adams.

— — —

F 29  Will dated 25 May 1835, proved November Court 1839.

JAMES HART

son: Samuel  land "where he now lives on E side of Raleigh Rd.
sons: David, William, James
daus: Betsy, Miriam, Jane
grandchildren: Sarah Strayhorn James Strayhorn
sons: John, Gilbert, Samuel

Executors: son David Hart, and friend Catlett Campbell.
Witnesses: A. Mivkle, John U. Kirkland.

— — —

F 31  Will dated 19 February 1838, proved Nov Court 1839.

JAMES HERNDON                       wife: Mary M. Herndon

son: Maturine C. Herndon "part of tract bought ftom Robert
              Campbell and a lso the Hall tract"
son: Coslett M(axwell) Herndon
daus: Elizabeth Carlton, Terminia Herndon, Nancy Barbee
grandson: Lorenzo J. Vann
"Children of my son James" $1

Executors: Thomas Bilbo, Anderson Ferrell.
Witnesses: Aquilla Herndon, Sullivan Leigh.
James Herndon was a son of George and Sarah Herndon. See D70.

— — —

F 33  Will dated 17 August 1839, proved November Court 1839.

WILLIAM TAYLOR

eldest son: Harrison Taylor "plantation called Faucett place"
"      dau: Nancy Taylor
second son: Henderson Taylor
"      dau: Juda Betsy Taylor

Executor: Harrison Taylor
Witnesses: William Bowls, Hugh Woods.

— — —

184
F 34   Will dated 8 March 1837, proved November Court 1839.

WILLIAM L. DURHAM

son: Archibald Durham        "children of my son Thomas"
"granddaughter Nancy Durham wife of Mark Durham"
"children of son Isaac Durham deceased"
"  "        "   daughter Susannah Jolley deceased"
"  "        "   daughter Frances Lacy deceased"
"My five sons: Archibald, Isaiah, William, John and Thomas"

Executors: "three sons Archibald Durham, William Durham,
            John Durham".     Witnesses: R. C. Poe, B. Strowd.

- - -

F 35   Will dated 27 July 1835, proved November Court 1839.

HARDEMAN DUKE

Daughter Betsy and her husband John Duke - after Betsy's
death her children to have her part.

Executors: trusty friends Willie P. Mangum, John Moize.
Witnesses: Benjamin Hester, Charity A. Mangum, William P. Mangum.

- - -

F 38   Will dated 17 January 1834, proved Nov Court 1839.

THOMAS LLOYD            wife: Delilah

sons: Sidney S. Lloyd, Thomas M. Lloyd
"two youngest sons Lorren O. Lloyd, Atlas J. Lloyd"
daughters: "Sintha Hunter and her children"
            Elizabeth Lloyd, "Frances Barbee and her children",
            Cornelia A. Lloyd, Sephonia C. Lloyd
Testator's land is on Phill's Creek.

Executors: wife Delilah, and sons Sidney S. and Thomas M. Lloyd.
Witnesses: B. Strowd, Henry McCollum, Hasten Poe.

- - -

F 41   Will dated --, proved --   JAMES MILES or MILER ?

Wife: Nancy Miles          No witnesses or executor.

- - -

F 42   Will dated 7 January 1840, proved Feb Court 1840.

ELI WOODS            wife: Margaret R. Woods

son: John Washington Woods
daus: Lucy Ann Woods, Ellen Woods, Margaret Ray Woods,
      Adaline Woods, Elizabeth Brown Woods

Executors: wife Margaret R. Woods, and Samuel Turrentine.
Witnesses: Hezekiah Terry, Charles Wilson.

- - -

F 43 Will dated 4 January 1840, proved Feb Court 1840. 

JAMES BARBER wife: Ellen

daughters: Sarah Jane, Mary Ann
friend: Samuel Ellett

Executor: John W. Wilson.
Witnesses: Nathan Findley, A. N. Watson.

- - -

F 45 Will dated 28 November 1839, proved Feb Court 1840.

JAMES PATTEN wife: Elenor

"All my children, namely, Samuel, Margaret, James, Jane, Isabel, Johnston, Mary, George, Nancy, Elenor, William and Alexander." "Younger children shall get as much schooling as the older ones have had."

Executors: Wife Elenor, and James Johnston.
Witnesses: Alexander Patton, Sam'l King.

- - -

F 46 Will dated 11 July 18 , proved February Court 1840.

JESSE MILLER wife: Margaret

"Jesse Miller and other five children".... not named.

Executor: Henry Whitted.
Witnesses: A. C. Murdock, Alvis Nichols.

- - -

F 47 Will dated 7 October 1839, proved Feb Court 1840.

MARY A . PALMER

sons: James N. Palmer, Nathaniel Palmer, John C. Palmer.

No executor. Witnesses: Thomas Fawcett, R. W. Lassiter.

- - -

F 48 Will dated 11 April 1840, proved May Court 1840.

HENRY (x) TRICE sons: Chesley P. Trice, Henry D. Trice

daughters: Nanny Pearson, Frances Trice, Amelia Trice, Elizabeth Marcum, Sarah Lynn

Executors: Chesley P. Trice and son-in-law William Pearson.
Witnesses: James N. Patterson, David Vickers.

- - -

F 50   Will dated 21 March 1839, proved May Court 1840.

EUPHENCE B. KERR                son: Samuel Kerr

daughters: Eliza Jane Kerr, Susan Kerr (both under 18 ?)
She speaks of "the boys" but names only one son, Samuel.

Executors: "trusty friends Samuel Kerr and James Whitsett."
Witnesses: Austin Whitsett, John McJean ?.

— — —

F 51   Will dated 26 February 1840, proved May Court 1840.

ELEANOR HOPKINS            son: Gilbert

daughters: Bashaba, Mary.

Executors: two daughters Bashaba and Mary.
Witnesses: Nathaniel Harris, Oxford Moize.

— — —

F 52   Will dated 19 January 1835, proved May Court 1840.

STEPHEN JUSTICE   (The name is spelled Justus in the will, but
                   is signed Justice. I have checked the orig-
wife: Anna         inal will in the Archives, writing very bad.)

"Beloved friend Stephen Pleasants" gets a slave.
"Stephen Farthing son of William Farthing deceased" $100.
"To the children of Elder William Worel (?) deceased" $200.
Heirs of my two brothers Davy and Allen Justus $300.
 "      "    "  sister Kyer (?) or Lizy (?) Robertson $300.
 "      "    "  sister-in-law Mary Lloyd (?) Floyd (?) deceased
Matildy Perry $100
William Roberts, son of Paschal Roberts $100
Stephen Brown  $300,  Phelemon Lacy  $300
$1000 to foreign missions

Executors: Anna Justus, and Stephen Pleasants, Sr.
Witnesses: Thomas Weaver, William Roberts.

— — —

F 53   Will dated 17 October 1839, proved May Court 1840.

HENRY FOUST            wife: Caroline R. Foust

sons: Robert M. Foust, William M. Foust

Executor:  brother-in-law William M. Mebane.
Witnesses: William Holt, Mich'l Wm. Holt.

— — —

F 54   Will dated 18 April 1840, proved August Court 1840.

JANE ALLEN    sons: John Allen, Alexandrico

daughter: Mary Jane                Executor: John Scott.
Witnesses: James White, Thomas Lashley.

— — —

F 56   Will dated 21 June 1840, proved August Couty 1840.   187

JOHN (x) CHRISTOPHER                wife: Pollay

sons: James Christopher "my Finley tract"; John Christopher
grandsons: "Pollay Stuerts two sons John C. Stewart, Calvin
                 B. Stewart"
other children: Elizabeth Compton; Jane Scott,
                Nancy Christopher, Sideny Smith,
                Frances Ward, Eliza Ward, Matty Christopher.

Executor: Thomas Lynch. Witnesses: James Ward, Empson Walker.
- - -

F 57   Will dated 18 October 1838, proved August Court 1840.

MARY (x) WILBOURN  sons: Nolen Hampton, John Hampton

grandson: Noah, son of Nolen

Executors: John Hampton and Allen Waller.
Witnesses: Wm. J. Roberts, G. Hopkins.
- - -

F 58   Will dated 22 May 1838, proved August Court 1840.

JOHN (x) POOL,SR.          daughter: Sarah

sons: Isaac Pool, John Samuel

Executor: Lewis Hutchins.
Witnesses: Harris Wilkerson, Thos. W. Gooch.
- - -

F 59   Will dated 28 August 1837, proved August Court 1840.

HENRY ALBRIGHT              son: Joseph Albright

daughters: Catheron, Elizabeth, Polly

Executors: "my sons, Nickolas and Joseph."
Witnesses: Levin Wood, Daniel Coble.
- - -

F 60   Will dated 6 March 1838, proved August Court 1840.

GEORGE NEASE              wife: Molly

sons: Jacob, Sampson, Anson, George
daughters: Sally and Polly

Exceutor: Jacob Nease.
Witnesses: Mich. Holt, Edwin N. Holt, W. A. Carrigan.
- - -

F 62  DAVID McCRORY          No date, proved August Court 1840.

son: James                  daughter: Mary Jane
brother-in-law John Albert

Executor: James Johnston. Witnesses: Giles Mebane, Robt. S. White.

- - -

F 63  Will dated 5 April 1840, proved August Court 1840.

SAMUEL WILSON                wife: Elizabeth

sons: Charles and John, plantation after wife's death
son: Felix "plantation where he now lives"
His two other plantations known as the Turner place and the
Ray place to be rented.
daughters: Sally Roundtree, Elizabeth Dickson,
           Nancy Nichols, Harriet Walker.
"My three daughters now in the west: Lotty Cates, Jane Taylor
and Polly Roland (or Robards ?)".

Executors: sons Charles and John Wilson.
Witnesses: Jas. Holeman, Alex. Robinson.

- - -

F 65  Will dated 14 December 1827, proved August Court 1840.

JOHN SOUTHWARD      daughters: Sally, Polly, Tempey

sons: Macklen Southward, Gilliam, Charles, James, Carter,
       John
"My sons Macklen and James guardians for my son John".

Executors: sons Macklen and James.
Witnesses: James Moore, Daniel Barnet.

- - -

F 68  Will dated 23 June 1840, proved August Court 1840.

JOSHUA JOHNSON               wife: Sarah

sons: Hiram, and Calvin (youngest, under 21)
dau: Anna Johnson
"     Mary, wife of Joseph Haskins "land on Deep River in
        Guilford County whereon my sister now resides".
daus: Susanna, Lydia

Testator owns a tannery in Chatham County with Wm. Albright.
He owns mills in Guilford County, and stock in Cain Creek Cotton Factory.

Executors: Joseph Huskins, Calvin  Johnson, Anna  Johnson.
Witnesses: Jno Long, Jesse Hargrave.

- - -

E 72  Will dated 26 May 1840, proved November Court 1840.

WILLIAM MORTON                      wife: Sarah

sons: Benjamin F. Morton, Jacob Morton, Henry H. (under 21)
daughter: Martha Morton
Joseph Gillam , husband of daughter Mary deceased $5.

Executor: son Benjamin F. Morton.
Witnesses: James Hicks, Lemuel W. Simpson.

– – –

F 72  Will dated 5 October 1840, proved Nov Court 1840.

GEORGE KEEK or KECK ?               wife: Polly

son: George Alexander
"All my children", number not stated, they all seem to be
minors.

Executors: wife Polly, and William A Carrigan.
Witnesses: Jonathan Job, John C. Troxler.

– – –

F 76  Will dated 23 May 1839, proved November Court 1840.

JOSEPH ARMSTRONG

wife: Peggy, is to receive numerous items, including "settee
          now in the possession of James B. Leathers" also
          "all my right in the sale of the Jonathan Watson
          lands". He speaks of "her own four children or
          her grandchildren."
daughters: Mary Ann Parker, Parthenia Leathers, Nancy Coggin
This is a long will, many pieces of land are devised, and
many slaves. His father was William Armstrong.

Executors: Jesse P. Parker, George T. Coggin, John B. Leathers.
Witnesses: Andrew Gray, S.C.M. Gray, Wm. J. Gray, Enos Ross.

– – –

F 80  Will dated 23 August 1838, proved  Nov Court 1840 ?

JOHN HENDERSON              wife: Frances
sons: Pleasant, Thomas, James, and John Henderson
daughters: Elizabeth Pearson, Sarah Perry, Dicey Perry,
          Martha Henderson, Eliza C. Henderson.
"Heirs of daughter Polly Stowers"

Witnesses: A. W. Clemebts, John D. Carlton.
Executrix: wife Frances Henderson.

– – –

F 82  Will dated 20 May 1835, proved November Court 1840.

SARAH FREEMAN  (This will is not in the State Archives.)

husband: Richard Freeman, land in Chatham County on Rocky River.

Executor: John Newlin. Witnesses: John Pope, M. H. Britt.

- - -

F 83  Will dated 26 May 1840, proved Feb Court 1841.

ABNER (x) MASSEY (this will is very confusingly worded.)

sons: William Massey $1, Armon
married daughters: Christilly Prosper ?, Corrinda Chancery $1
other children John Massey, Hardy Massey, Joel (under 21),
Kellister Massey, Valinia or Lavinia Massey, Louisey Massey,
Miriam Massey" $118 debt due me by John Massey to be paid to
the seven children named above.

"I will that my seven children single stay together until Joel
Massey becomes 21."

Executors: sons John Massey and Armon Massey.
Witnesses: S. W. Fowler, Thos. R. Shepherd.

- - -

F 84  Will dated 11 January 1839, proved Feb Coyrt 1841.

ZERNAH HOBSON widow

daughters: Lydia Hadley, Peninah Hobson, Emily Hobson.
"Peninah to have the motherly care of my young daughter
Emily Hobson."

Executor: friend Frederick Stafford.
Witnesses: Wm. Thompson, Peninah Hobson, John Thompson.

- - -

F 86  Will dated 12 February 1834, codicil dated 14 Feb 1837,
                                   proved February Court 1841.
ISBELL (x) THOMPSON

daus: Fanny, Hannah, Ellen Barlow
son: Richard
"to Phebe Clancy"

Executor: friend James Webb.
Witnesses: Wm. Norwood, John Bylers ?.

- - -

F 87  Will dated 14 March 1841, proved May Court 1841.

DRURY (x) JEFFRAS                wife: Sylvia

sons: Andrew, Eaton, Stephen, Henry, Addison    - continued -

F 87  Will of DRURY JEFFRAS continued                    191

daughters: Betsy, Sylvia, Partha, Tempy Corn, Polly Burnett.

Willy Corn (grandson ?)        granddaughter: Peggy Jeffrass

Executors: Andrew Jeffrass, Eaton Jeffrass.
Witnesses: Hugh Jeffrass, Charles Jeffrass.

– – –

F 89  Will dated 1 November 1833, proved May Court 1841.

JOSEPH KIRKLAND, SR.              son: Joseph King

daughters: Ann King, Elizabeth, Jinney Strayhorn
"Children of deceased son William: Samuel Kirkland, Joseph
Kirkland; Johnston Kirkland, William and John Kirkland, Peggy
Kirkland, Betsy Kirkland, Isabel Kirkland."
granddaughters: Margaret King and Jinney King
grandchildren: Mary, Peggy and Patsy Craig

Executors: Charles W. Johnston and Joseph Kirkland.
Witnesses: Alex. Gattis, C. W. Johnston, Thomas Gattis.

– – –

F 92  Will dated 29 March 1826, proved May Court 1841.

LAZARUS TILLEY              wife: Elizabeth

sons: John and Thomas  $1 each

Executrix: wife Elizabeth.
Witnesses: Wm. Horner, Robert Edwards, Willie P. Mangum.

– – –

F 93  Will dated 25 January 1841, proved August Court 1841.

WILLIAM LEIGH              brother: Richard Leigh

sister: Susan Trice
The will mentions that testator's wife was a daughter of
David George.

Executor: father, name not stated.    Witness: S. W. Fowler.

– – –

F 94  Will dated 15 January 1837, proved August Court 1841.

MARY (x) GRAHAM              daughter: Mary Garretson

grandson: John Graham, son of James
"Mary Graham, daughter of my son George"

Executor: son James.  Witnesses: Thomas Reeves, Wm. Hamilton.
At date of probate, the witnesses having removed from the
State, the will was proved by Chesley F. Faucett, Esq., and
Lemuel Lynch.

– – –

F 96  Will dated 12 June 1841, proved August Court 1841.

MARGARET J. McDADE        Father: John McDade, Sr.

Mother: Lavinia        relationship not stated: Lucinda McDade

Executor: John McDade.        Witnesses: Ast. Moore.

– – –

F 97  Will dated 1 September 1828, proved August Court 1841.

HENRY BRANNOCK, SR.        wife: Elizabeth

sons: William, Henry, Edmund, James, Wright, Thomas
daughter: Sarah

Executors: Henry Brannock and Edmund Brannock.
Witnesses: John Foster, Alex. N. Brannock, William Makins.
Codicil dated 6 May 1833, after the death of Henry.

– – –

F 100  Will dated 12 September 1834, proved August Court 1841.

THOMAS TATE        daughters: Ann and Ginny

son: Samuel Tate        granddaughter: Luiza

Executor: son Samuel.        Witnesses: Joseph Tate, Samuel Tate.

– – –

F 101  Will dated 4 January 1841, proved August Court 1841.

ABNER TATE        sister: Alsa Tate        brother: Jesse Tate

Executor: brother Jesse.        Witnesses: Andrew Ross, David Barber.

– – –

F 102  Will dated 18 November 1836, proved August Court 1841.

THOMAS THOMPSON        wife: Elizabeth

son: John        son-in-law: William Thompson
"All my children", number and names not stated.

Executor: son John Thompson.
Witnesses: W. Bradshaw, Jno. Thompson.

– – –

F 104  Will dated 9 January 1840, proved August Court 1841.

CHRISTOPHER (x) HORNADAY        John Tague ? (Teague ?)

"The four daughters of John Tague (?): Polly, Patty, Kisiah, and Jemiah"
"The four sons of John Tague: Isiah, William, Christopher, Edward," $25 each.
sons: John, Solomon, Samuel, Isaiah Hornaday. - continued -

grandson: Christopher, son of John Hornaday  $100
"        Daniel, son of Isaiah Hornaday  $25
granddaughter: Priscilah, daughter of Isaiah  $25

Executor: friend David Patterson, Sr.
Witnesses: John Foust, Benj. Way, Weston (x) Low (or Law).
- - -

F 106  Will dated 22 October 1840, proved Nov Court 1841.

EDWIN G. (or T) THOMPSON          wife: Eliza

son: George Sidney Thompson

Executrix: wife Eliza.
Witnesses: James N. Thompson, Wm. Pickard.
- - -

F 107  Will dated 4 April 1837, proved Nov Court 1841.

SAMUEL SCOTT                      wife: Nancy

sons: John Scott, Henderson Scott
daughters: Jane Allen, Fanny Scott and Hannah Murphy
granddaughter: Nancy Scott "daughter of my son John Scott"
"Fanny Allen, daughter of Alexander Allen deceased"
Executors: John Scott, Henderson Scott.
Witnesses: John Trolinger, Benjamin Trolinger.

- - -

F 110  Will dated 13 April 1841, proved November Court 1841.

JESSE (x) JAMES, SR.          son: Thomas James

wife: Elizabeth "tract whereon I now live"

Other heirs: William James, Milly Redmon, Sarah Rhodes,
George James, Elizabeth Dollar, Jesse James, Rebecca Rhodes,
Russell James, Riley James, Polly Baldwin.
"To the children of my son Thomas James $1."

Executor: "trusty friend James Latta, Sr."
Witnesses: Silas M. Link, John Holloway, Jr.
- - -

F 112  Will dated 17 August 1841, proved Nov Court 1841.

HANNAH KIRKPATRICK          sons: Joseph, Paisley

daughter-in-law: Nancy Kirkpatrick
granddaughters: Hannah Kirkpatrick, Elizabeth Kirkpatrick,
                Caroline Kirkpatrick, Sarah Jane Kirkpatrick,
                Frances Kirkpatrick
grandson: Samuel

Executor: Paisley Kirkpatrick.
Witnesses: Thomas Jones, Alex N. Wood.
- - -

194

F 114   Will dated 19 October 1835, recorded May Court 1836.
TEMPERANCE (x) PROMROSE. This will is recorded in Book E on
page 368. With the will is a statement of the property she has
already given the legatees.

— — —

F 115   Will dated 23 March 1840, proved February Court 1841.

THOMAS S. COX                    Father: Charles Cox

sisters: Margaret, Nancy, Caroline, Elizabeth, Isabella
Trustee to hold property for his mother Elizabeth Cox, then
it goes to his father, then to his sisters.

Trustee and executor: Osmond F. Long.
Witnesses: Steve Moore, Jas. Sneed.

— — —

F 116   Will dated 30 March, 18--, proved February Court 1841.

WILLIAM NORWOOD                  wife: Robina

sons: John W. Norwood, Joseph Norwood, James H. Norwood,
      William, Walter
daughters: Eliza, Jane, Helen
"Son James H. Norwood's wife and children", names not stated.

Executors: sons Joseph and John.
Witnesses: O. F. Long, H. Webb.

— — —

F 119   Will dated 18 December 1840, proved Feb Court 1842.

ABNER (x) ROBERTS "weak and low"

daughters: Elizabeth Casey, Sarah Roberts, Vinney Roberts
sons: Thomas Roberts, Moses Roberts, Abner Roberts
son: Ivey Roberts $1
"granddaughter Susan Rew, daughter of my son Jesse Roberts,
      deceased"
"granddaughters Elizey Ann, Caroline & Winny Roberts, daugh-
      ters of my son Moses Roberts"

Executor: friend Elijah Hester.
Witnesses: Mark Roberts, Presly Roberts.

— — —

F 121   Will dated 6 March 1841, proved February Court 1842.

THOMAS LATTA                     wife: Elizabeth

sons: Joseph H. Latta, John W. Latta
daughters: Ann Durham, Mary Long
"My seven daughters Elizabeth, Elenor, Jane, Arena, Amelia,
Rachel and Fanny" (unmarried).

Executors: sons Joseph H. Latta and John W. Latta.
Witness: James C. Latta.

— — —

F 124  Will dated 20 December 1842, proved Feb Court 1842.

DANIEL WILKINSON              wife: Elizabeth

sons: Thomas (oldest), John, William and Samuel Wilkinson
Daughters mentioned, names and number not stated.

Executors: sons Thomas and John.
Witnesses: Samuel McCracken, Allen Brown.

— — —

F 126-129  Will dated 20 January 1842, proved May Court 1842.

MICHAEL HOLT  "I was born 11 July 1778"

sons: William and Edwin M. Holt.
"My two grandchildren, children of my deceased daughter Jane-
to Edwin M. Holt,Jr., to Eliza Ann ..."
"My grandchildren, children of my daughter Nancy M Carigan,
namely Alfred William Robert John and James   Carigan certain
slaves now in the possession of their father Wm. A. Carigan."

Many tracts of land and many slaves are devised.
$200 to enclose with brick or stone burying plot "graves in
the garden."

Executors: sons William R. and Edwin M. Holt, and Wm. A.
            Carigan.
Witnesses: Wm. Smith, A. T. Finley.

— — —

F 130  Will dated 5 October 1837, proved May Court 1842.

LABAN (x) ANDREWS "weak in body"        wife: Rebecca

son-in-law: Aron Trip
son: Green                daughter: Hannah
"    John
"My children- David, William  Henry  Nancy Cates Berry
Willie Elizabeth Trip Green & Delia Robards" (no commas).
He says "my four daughters".

Executors: sons David and Berry.
Witnesses: E. Graves, A. Graves, J. Caruthers,
            Ruffin Andrews.

— — —

F 132  Will dated 27 October 1817, proved May Court 1842.

GEORGE (x) SMITH        wife a legatee, name not stated

"All my children, viz, David Smith Joseph Smith William
Smith, George Smith & Wesley & Suckey Smith Nancy Smith &
Sally Smith". "Two youngest sons George & Wesley".

Executors: friends Thomas Whitted and Thomas Brewer.
Witness: Thos. Brewer.(He was blind when the will was proved.)

196

F 134   Will dated 24 March 1842, proved May Court 1842.

JOSEPH THOMPSON                    wife: Elizabeth

sons: Samuel and Thomas to have his mill together

"Daughter-in-law Lavina Thompson tract whereon she now lives",
after her death "to my son Robert Thompson's children, to wit:
Jinnett Elizabeth Joseph Samuel Elender Lavina Thompson"
son: John Thompson
daughters: Elinor Foust and Rachel Morrow, land which is to be
                  "divided by Daniel Foust and John Morrow"
son: Joseph Thompson

Executors: son Thomas Thompson, and son-in-law Daniel Foust.
Witnesses: John Thompson, James Paris, Jno. Thompson.
- - -

F 136   Will dated 8 March 1842, proved May Coyrt 1842.

JAMES (x) CARRELL               wife: Polly

youngest daughter: Ellin (under age)
sons: Lemuel, John, Dixon get land; William gets $2
grandson: James McColum  $2
"My nine children Lemuel & John & William & Dixon Candis &
Cinthy & Martha & Elizabeth & Ellin."

Executor: son William Brewer.
Witnesses: James Reaves, Calvin Carrell.

- - -

F 137   Will dated 29 June 1842, proved August Court 1842.

ANDREW WATSON                    wife: Nancy

dau: Tempy T. Watson
 "      "Margaret Watson wife of Wilson Watson and her two
        children Alexander Watson and Juliana Watson"
sons: Julius Watson, James M. Watson
"Daughter Elizabeth Durkey dec'd wife of ..... Dorkey"
son-in-law: Samuel Riley $5

Executors: son Julius Watson and son-in-law Wilson Watson.
Witnesses: Levi McCollum, S? L. Turner.
- - -

F 139   Will dated 23 January 1839, proved August Court 1842.

WILLIAM DUKE, SR.        sons: John Duke, William Duke

daughter: Polly Leathers wife of Moses Leathers
son: Green
"Heirs of daughter Dicey Bobbitt".
daughter: Reny Mangum wife of W.G.Mangum
 "        Bedy Oakley wife of Vincent Oakley
                                                    Moize.
Executor: Ellison G. Mangum. Witnesses: Jeff Horner, Orford /

F 142  Will dated 7 June 1842, proved Nov Court 1842.

NANCY MOOR (She was the widow of John Moore. See D 471)

To William F. Strayhorn
son-in-law: Samuel Strayhorn
granddaughters: Mary E. M. Strayhorn, Nancy Craig
grandsons: Samuel Strayhorn, Thomas Strayhorn
daughters: Frances Hart, Nancy Hart, Susannah Yergan,
          Sally Pratt, Elizabeth Allen

Executor: grandson William F. Strayhorn.
Witnesses: D. W. Craig, James N. Craig.

— — —

F 143  Will dated 17 October 1842, proved Nov Court 1842.

WILLIAM (x) McCULLOCK                wife: Patience Jane

"All my children", names and number not stated.

Executor: uncle John McCullock.
Witnesses: Alex. Dickson, Joseph McCullock.

— — —

F 144-152  Will dated 7 April 1842, proved Feb Court 1843.

DAVID MEBANE                wife: Elizabeth

sons: Alexander, George A., Wiley, Anderson and Sidney.
daus: Betsy Mitchell, Jane (Jenny) Thompson, Fanny Walker,
     Martha Ann Holt
grandau: Julia Ann Curry
"Elizabeth Elbridge daughter of my deceased son Elbridge"
grandson: David son of George A. Mebane
son-in-law John Thompson

Executors: sons Alexander and George A. Mebane.
Witnesses: James A. Craig, Samuel Tate.
Codicil dated 26 April 1842.

— — —

F 152 Will dated 22 December 1834, proved Feb Court 1843.

JAMES (x) STANFORD              son: Robert Stanford

daus: Peggy Stanford, Jinny Stanford, Elizabeth Dixon.
grandson: James Stanford son of Alexander

Executor: son Robert. Witnesses: Peyton P. Moor, Wm. McCrory.

— — —

F 153  Will dated 24 May 1836, proved February Court 1843.

ALEXANDER GATTIS              wife: Rosanna

"My four sons John, William, Alexander & Thomas " all lands.
Son James has already received land.

198    Will of ALEXANDER GATTIS concluded
daughters: Elizabeth, Jane and Margaret

Executors: wife Rosanna, son John M., and friend Charles W.
          Johnston.
Codicil: same date, "to son Samuel $1".
Witnesses: Thomas Gattis, C. W. Johnston.

— — —

F 155  Will dated 25 April 1842, proved May Court 1843.

PETER F. PERRY                    wife: Patty

"My three sons Samuel, William, Persullas (?)" $100 each.
"My five sons Manly Murphy Peter Henry John A. Mangum Edward
Norris"(no punctuation) "all my land".

Executors: son William Perry and George Johnston.
Witnesses: Nathaniel Newlin, Samuel Perry.

— — —

F 157  Will dated 10 August 1842, proved May Court 1843.

ELENOR (x) WOODS

grandchildren: James Hopkins, Rebecca Hopkins, Harriet Hopkins.

Executor: "Trusty friend Henry Whitted."
Witnesses: James Montgomery, Lydia (x) Grimes.

— — —

F 158  Will dated 17 February 1843, proved May Court 1843.

NANCY (x) ROBINSON        All to Alexander Robinson.

Executor: Alexander Robinson.        Witness: Jas Holeman.

— — —

F 159  Will dated 3 September 1838, proved May Court 1843.

JAMES ALLISON                     wife: Elizabeth

son: John gets land adjoining Edward Riley
 "     Joseph

Executor: friend Caleb Wilson. No witnesses.
Proved by the testimony of Joseph Allison.

— — —

F 160  Will dated 7 January 1843, proved May Court 1843.

JAMES (x) HUTCHERSON              wife: Sarah

"Daughter Patian and her husband George McCrary" land joining
said McCrary, Thomas Tyrell and others ... adjoining Sally Allen
                                    - continued -

Will of JAMES HUTCHERSON concluded
and A. Mebane and others"

Balance of estate to be divided between "all my children."

Executors: George McCray, and friend George Hurdle.
Witnesses: Henry Bason, Stephen White.

— — —

F 162  Will dated 8 August 1841, proved August Court 1843.

PETER (x) MOSER                    wife: Barbara

Executors: Ephriam Mitchell, Levy Moser.
Witnesses: Martin Moser, Bostian Moser.

— — —

F 163  Will dated 13 1842, proved August Court 1843.

MIRIAM (x) STRAIN

sons: David Strain, Samuel D. Strain, John Strain
dau: Miriam Strain          son: William D. Strain
D. Strain "interest in estate of son Alexander Strain,dec'd"
granddaughters: Miriam Crutchfield, Miriam Tate, Miriam Nelson.
          Miriam Freeland, Miriam Davis

Executor: son Samuel D. Strain.    Witness: Samuel S. Clayter.

— — —

F 164  Will dated 7 June 1843, proved August Court 1843.

POLLY (x) RONEY

"My two daughters Catherine Prater & Mary Ann McCray".
"My only and beloved grandson William R. Prater."

Executor: friend John Roney.
Witnesses: Henry Bason, John White.

— — —

F 165  Will dated 30 November 1842, proved August Court 1843.

JOHN STRAYHORN          daus: Jane, Patsy Trice

sons: David Strayhorn, Bryant Strayhorn
dau: Polly Davis
"grandchildren whose father and mother is dead."

Executors: son Bryant Strayhorn and son-in-law Alex. Craig.
Witnesses: David Hart, David Craig.

— — —

200

F 167  Will dated 16 January 1843, proved August Court 1843.

HENRY (x) DOLLAR                    wife: Elizabeth

son: William Dollar
daus: Mildred and Cinthia Ann Dollar

Executrix: wife Elizabeth.
Witnesses: Silas M. Link, John C. Burton.

－ － －

F 168  Will dated 20 September 1842, proved Nov Court 1843.

THOMAS WEAVER                    wife: Sarah

eldest daughter: Winnie C  Lloyd
"       son: William G. Weaver  $10
second son: Isham S. Weaver
grandsons: Samuel and George Weaver, sons of Isham
son: John H. Weaver
daus: Mary C. Weaver, Elizabeth C. Weaver
youngest son: Thos S. Weaver

Executors: William G. Weaver and John H. Weaver.
Witnesses: W. H. Merrett, George W. Purify.

－ － －

F 170  Will dated 13 March 1843, proved November Court 1843.

SARAH WALKER (See the will of Aaron Walker, E 289)

sons: Levi Walker, Empson Walker
daus: Harriet Crofford(Crawford), Nancy Shaw
son: Freeman Walker

Executor:son Levi Walker.
Witnesses: Thos Lynch, John Compton.

－ － －

F 171  Will dated 17 September 1835, proved Nov Court 1843.

OSBOURNE SNIPES            All estate to wife Martha Snipes.

He leaves "to any other legal representatives or heirs" 50¢.

Executor: Bennett T. Blake.
Witnesses: Ellis G. Blake, Jno P. Cook.

－ － －

F 172  Will dated 8 March 1843, proved November Court 1843.

JOHN WALKER                    wife: Hannah

Two daughters Mary (Polly or Dolly) Walker and Hannah M. Walker.
son: Adam D. Walker pnantation called "the Tate place".

Executors: friends Sam M. Douglas, Absalom Hervey.
Witnesses: John C. Douglas, James Gilliam.

－ － －

F 174   Will dated 9 November 1843, proved Nov 1843.

JOHN BLACKWOOD                    wife: Mary

He devises property "in Town of Hillsboro adjoining lot of
Thomas Faucett ... now occupied by Charles Cooley."  And a
tract of land on Eno River joining John McCauley. A tract
called "the Mountain Tract."

daus: Mary Strayhorn, Margaret McCauley
sons: David K. Blackwood, John J., and Johnston Blackwood

Executor: David K. Blackwood.
Witnesses: C. W. Johnston, James Gattis.

- - -

F 175   Will dated 26 November 1842, proved Nov Court 1843.

JESSE O'DANIEL     All estate to his brother Henry O'Daniel.

Witnesses: Wm.(x) O'Daniel, William Perry.

- - -

F 176   Will dated 5 August 1826, proved May Court 1843.

DANIEL ALBRIGHT              wife, name not stated

"Son-in-law William Montgomery and daughter Sarah."
"My grandchildren", number and names not stated.
His wife is to choose an executor.
Witnesses: Elias Albright, John Clapp.

- - -

F 178   Will dated 27 March 1841, proved February Court 1844.

THOMAS (x) GRIFFIN "weak in body"

"I lend to Peggy Griffin the use of my plantation which
Alfred Pickard now lives on".
"Peggy Pickard wife of Alfred Pickard"
"Peggy Pickard's two sons James Pickard and Thomas Pickard"
"brother James Griffin and his wife"
"Lilla Wicks & Rebecca Wicks daughters of Jenny Wicks" both
under age, $1000 each.
friend Hugh Waddell $500
friends Jesse O'Daniel and Henry O'Daniel balance
stepson Thomas Griffin  $200

Executors: friends Hugh Waddell and Jesse O'Daniel.
Witnesses: B. Strowd, Thos. M. Durham, R. Stanford.

- - -

F 179   Will dated 21 November 1843, proved Feb Court 1844.

WILLIAM CLENDENNIN             wife: Jean

"..daughters Hanor S ?, Nancy Ann, Sarah M., and Letitia ? or
Lavinia ? Cornelia ? Bradshary ? so long as they live single "
In another place Sarah Margaret is mentioned. - continued -

202 F 179 Will of WILLIAM CLENDENNIN continued

son: William Clendennin (unmarried)
"daughter Caroline who is married"

Executor: "friend and neighbor John Stockard."
Witnesses: George Clendennin, Fisher Clendennin.

— — —

F 181-184  Will dated 20 July 1843, proved Feb Court 1844.

HENRY (x) TROLINGER, SR.            wife: Polly

eldest son: John Trolinger
"      dau: Betsy Gant        son-in-law: Jonathan Gant
sons: Henry Trolinger Jr, Joseph
dau: Catherine Freshwater                                age".
"children of my deceased son Jacob Trolinger as they arrive at /
dau: Mary Raney
"daughter Peggy Tarpley and her husband Henry Tarpley"
grandson: Moses Trolinger
granddaughter: Adaline Freshwater

Executors: sons John and Joseph Trolinger.
Witnesses: Daniel A. Montgomery, Thos. Dixon.

— — —

F 184  Will dated 23 July 1836, proved February Court 1844.

JOHN COOK, SR.          daughter: Sarah Thomas

granddaughter: Elizabeth R. Wagner

Sole executor: William Brannock.
Witnesses: Daniel White, John Hicks.

— — —

F 186  Will dated 30 September 1841, proved Feb Court 1844.

ANDREW (x) McCAULEY        grandson: John W. McCauley

"Sarah McCauley, widow of my son Robert dec'd"   $2.
son-in-law: Gabreal B. Lea
grandsons: John and Andrew Lea (under 21)
granddaus: Hannah Moore, Martha Lea
Andrew J. McCauley

Executor: Gab. B. Lea. Witnesses: Wm.Ward Sr, John Barnwell.

— — —

F 187  Will dated 23 August 1840, proved February Court 1844.

MARY (x) JONES            brother: Johnson Jones

sister Margaret Jones, and sister Levina Woods and her daughter Matilda Woods

Executor: Johnson Woods. Witnesses: Wm. Shaw, Alex'r M. Woods.

— — —

F 188-190  Will dated 18 March 1843, proved Feb 1844.

JOHN PICKETT                    wife: Catherine

dau: Julia Ann Pickett (unmarried)
sons: Samuel & John Quincy Pickett
dau: Elizabeth W. Wilkinson

Sole executor: friend Thomas Lynch, Esq.
Witnesses: J. Allison, C. E. Tinnen.

- - -

F 190  Will dated 23 April 1843, proved May Court 1844.

PRISCILLA (x) CARRINGTON "advanced in years"

son: Morgan
dau: Polly Parrish wife of James Parrish
"    Dicey Cozart wife of Wm. Cozart of Person County

Executor: George W. Jones.
Witnesses: Willis Bowling ?, David Parrish, George W. Jones.

- - -

F 191  Will dated 12 December 1842, proved May Court 1844.

JAMES CLARK                     wife: Ann

dau: Grace (unmarried)          son: James W. Clark
"    Sarah Hughs
Hannah H. Dickey                His land on Eno River
granddau: I.B.Bethiah Lindsey   joins John Compton,
grandson: James C. Lindsey      Wm. Allison, & others.
son: Stephen Clark  $1

Executors: sons James W. and Stephen Clark.
Witnesses: Lemuel Wilkinson, Alexander Findley.

- - -

F 193  Will dated 8 April 1844, proved May Court 1844.

JOSEPH D. HUGHES      daughters: Jane, Eliza

"My wife Sarah and her four children Rice (?) Ann John and
Sidney are to have my lands lying near Person County" 500
acres. Children all seem to be minors.

"My eight children Anderson Thomas Samuel Jane Joseph
Franklin Paisley and Eliza" (no punctuation).

"Whatever may be coming to me from the estate of James Clark
deceased" ...

Executors: sons Anderson and Samuel.
Witnesses: Monroe Allen, I or J. C. McDaniel.

- - -

204

F 195   Will dated 27 March 1844, proved May Court 1844.

JOSEPH (x) WHITE                    wife: Nancy

mother: Mary Couch
daus: Susanna Craig, Nancy Cole
sons: Thomas White, Joseph White
Land he purchased of Moses H. Turner to be rented.

Sole executor: Thomas White.
Witnesses: Jas. N. Patterson, Sam Couch, Anderson (x) Rhodes.
- - -

F 197   Will dated 18 March 1839, proved May Court 1844.

JOHN (x) RUMBLEY              wife: Elizabeth

"Two infant children John Severn (?) Rumbley and Rachel L. (?)
Rumbley".
son: Thomas Rumbley 150 acres "Adam's Old Tract" which he now
                        lives on
sons: James, Edward and William, $1 each with what they have had
"son Aron Rumbley's heirs $1"

Executrix: wife Elizabeth. Witnesses: Benj. Hurdle, John Pyle.
- - -

F 198   Will dated 8 February 1841, proved May Court 1844.

FRANCIS JONES "late of the county of Chatham, but now of the
              town of Hillsboro" .."in advanced age and feeble"
son-in-law James S. Smith of Hillsboro plantation on Pokeberry
   Creek joining John Hackney, Joseph Bynum, James Kirby & others
   2000 to 2700 acres (in Chatham) in trust for "only child and
   daughter Delia Smith wife of the said Dr. James S. Smith"

grandson: Dr. Francis J. Smith  another plantation in Chatham
              joining Isaiah Cole, Wm. Merritt, 1800 acres.
grandson: James Sidney Smith
granddau: Mary R. Smith plantation in Orange on Price's Creek

Sole executor: James S. Smith.
Witnesses: A. Parks, Thomas Faucett.
- - -

F 200   Will dated 24 February 1839, proved May Court 1844.

JOHN FREELAND, SR.              wife: Nancy

"All my children", number and names not stated.
Deceased son Thomas Freeland.
                                                        cett.
Executors: son John J. Freeland, grand-son-in-law Ralph Fau-/
Witnesses: C. W. Johntson, John Blackwood, James J. Blackwood.
- - -

F 203-205  Will dated 15 June 1841, proved May Court 1844.

THOMAS HORNER, SR.                  wife: Sarah

daus: Mary Parker, Elizabeth Cabe, Lucretia Holeman $1 each
"Three sons William Horner, John Horner & Jefferson Horner
land on Flat River joining Nathaniel Harris & Elizabeth King."

Executors: sons William and Jefferson Horner.
Witnesses: Francis Epperson, L.C.Ellis ? (Ellus ?)

- - -

F 204-206  Will dated 8 May 1844, proved May Court 1844.

NICHOLAS ALBRIGHT                   wife: Ann

eldest son James P. Albright "tract on which he now lives"
son: John G. "tract on which he now lives" on Haw River
sons: Henry Albright, William P. Albright (under 21)

Executors: wife Ann, and William M. Rogers.
Witnesses: Calvin C. Graves, Mich'l M. Holt.

- - -

F 206  Will dated 2 June 1844, proved August Court 1844.

JOSEPH W. ALLISON                   wife: Susan

oldest daughter: Margaret Jane Allison
daus: Mary N. Allison, Susan G. Allison
son: Joseph Washington Allison (undera age)
He speaks of his wife's "raising the children".

Sole executrix: wife Susan.
Witnesses: Hezekiah Long, James Allison.

- - -

F 208  Will dated 25 July 1844, proved August Court 1844.

JOHN McDADE                         wife: Levina
                                                      death
sons: James B. & Patterson H. McDade plantation after wife's /
son: Henderson C. McDade "100 acres where he now lives"
"    John A. McDade    "100 "      "       "  "    "    "

Executor: friend Joseph  Allison.
Witnesses: John Kelly, Joseph Smith.

- - -

F 210  Will dated 26 July 1844, proved August Court 1844.

ELIZABETH GASKELL        "younger daughter Drusilla Gaskell"

"My three daughters Mary Gaskell Susan Gaskell & Drusilla."

Executor: friend James A. Craig.
Witnesses: Randolph C. Mabrey, George Crawford.

- - -

F 212  Will dated 18 April 1844, proved August Court 1844.

WILLIAM GATTIS                          wife: Rebecca

"All my children", names and number not stated.

Executrix: wife Rebecca.  Witnesses: D.D.Pane, Nath'l ? Bain.

— — —

F 213  Will dated 29 December 1842, proved August Court 1844.

ELIZABETH (x) CLINTON                son: Jesse Clinton

"Milly Watson's daughter Elizabeth Ann Watson"
No relationship stated to: Milly Anderson, Susan Clark,
    John Clinton, Samuel Clinton, Mary Dollar  $1 each.

Executor: son Jesse Clinton.
Witnesses: James Stag, Washington Duke.

— — —

F 214  Will dated 27 March 1843, proved August Court 1844.

REEVES MANGUM                           wife: Martha

"All my children", names and number not stated.

Executor: son William.
Witnesses: Thos. W. Gooch, Harris Wilkerson.

— — —

F 215  Will dated 13 June 1840, proved August Court 1844.

NATHAN MANN    Nancy Lasley "pension money due me".

Sole executrix: friend Nancy Lasley.
Witnesses: Thos. Pendergrast, Andrew J..?...

— — —

F 216  Will dated 8 April 1839, proved August Court 1844.

SOLOMON CATE                            wife: Mary

"son Thomas and Anna"
"little William must be bound to  some trade"

Executor: son Thomas.  Witnesses: Thomas Sykes, Anna (x) Cate.

— — —

F 217  Will dated 30 March 1841, proved August Court 1844.

ELENOR (x) ROGERS       youngest son: Will Rogers (unmarried)

son: James Rogers
"Four daughters Jane Holt (?), Ann Albright, Elenor Johnson,
and Mary Foust."                              - continued -

"only sister Jane Rogers wife of Wm. Robess (?) the elder"
grandsons: sons of daughter Elenor Johnston, John and James,
            both under 21 years of age
son: John Rogers

Executor: son William Rogers.
Witnesses: Thomas Ruffin, Milton S. Holt.
Codicil, no date . Daughter Elenor has died. Granddaughter
Sally Rogers (unmarried" has waited on "me most kindly and
faithfully". Witnesses: John Rogers, Milton S. Holt.

— — —

F 220  Will dated 17 September 1843, proved August Court 1844.

MARY (x) HERNDON, widow  (She was the widow of Elias Herndon
                         who died intestate in 1828.)
"My children, that is, Elizabeth Mason wife of John Mason,
Reaney Jenkins wife of Joseph Jenkins, Matilda George wife
of Ezekiel George, William Herndon and Martha Herndon my (two)
grandsons the heirs of Gustin Herndon, and Madison Herndon
my grandson son of Stanford Herndon, heirs of my daughter
Mary wife of Berry Mason; Joseph Mason, Adison Mason, Leroy
Mason, Elizabeth Mason, Nancy Mason."

Berry (Littleberry) Mason $1

Executor: friend John Mason.
Witnesses: John Marcom, Willis Marcom.

— — —

F 222  Will dated 8 July 1844, proved August Court 1844.

DANIEL HUFFMAN              wife: Elizabeth

married daughters: Rachel, Polly or Patty, Catherine Lydia
                   and Sally
youngest daughter: Susan
son: John "200 acres on which he now lives"

Executor: son John.
Witnesses: Joseph J. Trolinger, Daniel A. Montgomery.

— — —

F 224-226  Will dated 5 May 1838, proved November Court 1844.

THOMAS BREWER          wife a legatee, name not stated

son: Thomas
daus: Elizabeth Oldham, Maryann Bradshaw, Margaret Snipes
      Martha Lindsey

granddaus: Polly Strowd, Rosanna Turner, Nancy Cate
grandsons: Wesley Edwards, William Edwards, Thomas Edwards

Executors: son Thomas Brewer, Thos. Oldham & Wm. Bradshaw.
Witnesses: David Roach, David Williams.

— — —

F 227  Will dated 25 September 1844, proved Nov Court 1844.

WILLIAM (x) O'DANIEL                brother: John O'Daniel

sisters: Lavina and Margaret

Executor: brother John.  Witnesses: John Jones, Henry Ray.

— — —

F 227  Will dated 21 September 1838, proved Nov Court 1843.

CATHERINE (x) HORN              son: John Horn   $1

"Daughter-in-law Elizabeth Horner (?) and her three children
namely Nancy Catherine Horn, William Page Horn and Norflet
Anderson Horn". (It is Horner in the book in Hillsboro. I have
not checked the original will which is in Raleigh. R.H.S.)

Sole executor: James N. Patterson.
Witnesses: Jane Cole, Susannah (x) Rainey.

— — —

F 229-233  Will dated 10 October 1838, proved Nov Court 1844.

BARNEY (x) CLAP          wife a  legatee, name not stated

son: Emanuel land on Bever Creek
daughter Polly "of unsound mind"
"Daughter Penny John Lacy's (?) Lue's (?) wife".(The clerk's
writing is very poor. There were Lacy and Lue families near.)

Daughters: "George Clap and wife Barbara, Frederick Sherer ?
and wife Peggy, John Lue ? and wife Penny, Ceatty ? Clap wife
of Isaac Clap, Sally Kime ?, John Lowe and wife Nelly".

Executors: sons David Clap and Emanuel Clap, and son-in-law
            John Low.
Witnesses: Wm. Smith, Wm. Artz, Mich'l Holt.
Codicil dated 5 February 1842, names no new heirs.

— — —

F 233  Will dated 20 August 1844, proved November Court 1844.

SARAH MONTGOMERY            mother: Elizabeth Albright

"My four youngest children Harriett Cornelia Barbary & William .... until the youngest child shall reach the age of 15"
"All my children", names and number not stated.

Executor: son Daniel A. Montgomery.
Witnesses: James B. Montgomery, Hiram Whitsell.

— — —

ARMOUR KING, SR.            wife: Rach

sons: Jennison or Jeremiah  $2, Armer
daus: Elender, Margret, Sarah
sons: Samuel, Henry $2, Garrison $2
daus: Rachel, Nancy and Mary  $2 each
"granddaughter Mary the daughter of Elender"

No executor named. Witnesses: Jas Lover ?, Jas MCray.

- - -

F 236  Will dated 3 February 1843, proved --

ELENOR (x) GARRISON         legatee: Brise F. Garrison

brother: George Garrison          brother: John 1 shilling
brother Levi Garrison's heirs 1 shilling
sister Mary Pyle's heirs 1 shilling each
sister Rebecca Pyle's heirs 1 shilling each

Executor: brother George Garrison.
Witnesses: Benj. Hurdle, Edward (x) Thompson.

- - -

F 238  Will dated 5 Debruary 1842, proved August 1844.

WILLIAM RILEY

sons: Samuel, Copeland and William Riley
sons: Warden and Judson Riley land on McGowan's Creek bought
                              from Enoch Thompson.
dau: Polly

Sole executor: son William Riley.
Witnesses: Hugh Waddell, F. N. Waddell.

- - -

F 238  Will dated -- , proved November 1841.

JOHN HUFFIND            wife: Rachel

Jackson Mury (or Munn)  no relationship stated.

No executor named. No witnesses.

- - -

F 240  Will dated 20 July 1844, proved February Court 1845.

JOHN (x) COBLE (listed as CABLE in index in Archives)

wife: Catherine        youngest son: Benjamin Coble
oldest son: John       second son:  Phillip
daus: Barbary Wirick ?, Elizabeth Tickle, Sarah Wirick ?
"..unto Warner Cardin if he stays and works with family until
he is twenty-one..."

Executors: son Benjamin Coble, and George Tickle.
Witnesses: Adam (x) Strader, Lewis Lowe ?, Archibald Murphy.

- - -

F 242  Will dated 9 December 1844, proved Feb Court 1845.

HENRY (x) EULIS                    sons: George and John

daughter Peggy wife of Tobias Clapp
    "        Catherine wife of Daniel Spoon
son: Allen
daughter Reney $1, her daughter Lucritta (?)   $200
    "        Nancy wife of N. Holt
"George son of Elizabeth Kimbrow " $50

Executors: Powel Kimbro, George Eulis, Peter Eulis.
Witnesses: William Moser, John Kimbro.

- - -

F 244  Will dated 3 January 1845, proved Feb Court 1845.

GEORGE (x) BAKER "low state of health"    wife: Barbary
(Indexed in State Archives as BARKER)

"sons Thomas Isreal & John Baker having left me and married"..
C.B. Baker  George Baker  Mary Baker  & Susan Baker (no punctuation, and no relationship stated)

Executor: son John Baker.
Witnesses: Snelson Love, Samuel P. Foster.

- - -

F 245-247  Will dated 11 January 1845, proved Feb Court 1845.

CATLETT CAMPBELL    He speaks of "my kindred in Virginia."

"Children of my deceased sister Mary Ann Burke"
sister Nancy Marbury ?          sister Sally Turner
nephew James Burke of Alleghany County, Va.
sisters: Permelia Waugh, Judy McGinnis

Executors: Nephew James Burke, friends John U. Kirkland,
          Osmond F. Long and John W. Norwood.
Witnesses: Jas C. Norwood, Thos N. Burke, Wm. Ward.

- - -

F 248  Will dated 5 March 1845, proved May Court 1845.

JEMIMA (x) CABE "weak and feeble"

"To my daughter Mary Burton the plantation I purchased of
my son-in-law John Brown"        grandson: John Burton
granddau: Mary A. Burton
son: William Cabe
dau: Rachel Claytor
"All my children"

Executors: son-in-law John Brown and Samuel S. Claytor.
Witnesses: Allen Brown, Thomas Piper.

- - -

F 249  Will dated 26 October 1841, proved May Court 1845.

ELIZABETH ESTES

"My neices Mary Jane & Caroline Evans" lands on Eno River,
and "my residence in the Town of Hillsborough"
neice: Catherine Evans "house on Churton Street"
neices: Isabelle Bridges, Mariah Dodd
sister: Mrs. Peggy Nash
Mrs. Sarah Grove widow of Wm. B. Grove
"Mary Whitted daughter of my late neice Eliza Whitted" (the
3rd Codicil says "of Alabama")
"friends Mrs. Josiah Turner, Mrs. Attelia Whitted and Mrs.
Eliza Bingham"
"To Mrs. Elizabeth Thompson my neice a daughter of Mrs. Mary
Seawell & wife of Mr. Thomas"
Harriet Barton
"To Eliza Turner & Mary Turner daughters of Josiah Turner"
"Mrs. Susan Mebane wife of James Mebene Jr."

Executors: friends John W. Norwood and James Dodd of Fayette/
Witnesses: O.F.Long, A. Mickle.                          ville.

Codicil #1 dated 18 Nov 1843, Witnesses: J.Webb Jr., H.Y.Webb.
Catherine Evans is now the wife of John Turner,
Isabella Bridges wife of Young Bridges.

Codicil #2 dated 24 Feb 1844 revokes bequest to Harriet Barton
"      #3 dated 10 March 1844, and #4 dated 2 August 1844
name no new heirs.

- - -

F 253-255  Will dated 24 February 1844, proved Feb Court 1845.

JAMES LEATHERS                    wife: Elizabeth

son: John Leathers
"    William Leathers "tract where he now lives joining
        Wm Lipscomb & others" (200 acres)
"    Moses Leathers   500 acres
"    Kintchin Leathers land joining Durham Hall (200 acres)
daughter: Elizabeth
Zachariah Rhodes "who married my daughter Sally", & children
"My children, viz, John Leathers William Leathers Moses
Leathers Kintchin Leathers Patsey Holloway wife of James Hol-
loway  Edney Green wife of William Green & Elizabeth single"..

Executors: sons John and Moses Leathers.
Witnesses: Harris Wilkerson, Benton Ray.

- - -

F 256  Will dated 22 April 1845, proved May Court 1845.

SAMUEL McDANIEL            "my dear father"

"My three single sisters Sally Peggy & Jane"    - continued -

"My two single brothers William and Jesse"
brother Henry and sister Elizabeth

Executor: brother William McDaniel.

- - -

F 256   Will dated 24 March 1843, proved May Court 1845.

POLLY (x) HARRIS

son Arlos Harris land joining John Brewer & Josiah Turner.

Exceutor: son Arlos.  Witnesses: J. Turner, Jas. R. Brewer.

- - -

F 257   Will dated25 September 1844, proved May Court 1845.

ALVIS NICHOLS              wife: Polly

"My children" names and number not stated.
He mentions "plantation whereon William & Elenor Faucett now
live" and "plantation whereon Jacob Jackson Sr now lives"

- - -

F 258-260   Will dated 7 April 1845, proved May Court 1845.

JAMES GARRARD

sons: William, James and Sherwood Garrard
son Wilson Garrard to make deeds (Clerk's writing very bad)

Executors: sons James and Sherwood Garrard.
Witnesses: Silas M. Link, James Latta.

- - -

F 260   Will dated 30 April 1845, proved May Court 1845.

ELZY HOPKINS            all estate to wife Sarah

"My children ... as they grow up"  no names given.

Executors: "my father-in-law John Ray and his son Benton Ray".
Witnesses: E. Strudwick, J. B. Leathers.

- - -

F 261   Will dated 22 June 1844, proved May Court 1845.

WILLIAM (x) HOPSON              wife: Harriett

deceased son Wiley
son: Wm. Henry Harrison Hopson plantation on N.E.Creek of New/
dau: Rebecca Tapp wife of Richard Tapp $10                    Hope
 "   Rosannah Tapp wife of Vincent Tapp $10
 "   Sally Barbee  $10

Executor: friend William Thompson.
Witnesses: W. Bradshaw, Elijah Pickard, R. Stanford.

- - -

F 262   Will dated 16 July 1830, proved May Court 1845.

GEORGE (x) PAISLEY                    wife (see note below)
"low and weak"

sons: Joseph and John         (All the children seem to
daus: Luisa and Mary Ann        be minors.)

Guardians and executors: Johnston Freeland and Moses Gibson.
Witnesses: Joseph Gibson, Josn Freeland, John Paisley.
George Paisley married in Orange Co,1 Feb 1810 Elizabeth
Freeland, bondsman was Johnston Freeland.

- - -

F 264   Will dated 28 May 1845, proved August Court 1845.

THOMAS McCRACKEN        wife: Susan all estate, except

$100 to "my nephew Thomas McCracken son of my brother John"

Executor: Thomas P. Paul.        witness: Sam'l N. Tate.

- - -

F 265   Will dated 13 February 1845, proved Nov Court 1845.

THOMAS COUCH

All estate goes to his brother William Couch except one
slave girl to Thomas White.

Witnesses: Abner Copeland, James N. Patterson.

- - -

F 266   Will dated 2 July 1844, proved November Court 1845.

SAMUEL TURRENTINE            wife: Ann

"brother Absalom Turrentine's two oldest children Samuel W.
Turrentine (under age) and Mary I. (or J) Turrentine"
neice: Seliny Ann Turrentine
Martha A. Wilson
brothers: Absalom and Daniel 100 acres called "Kell Tract"

Executors: Charles Wilson and Daniel Turrentine.
Witnesses: Joseph Brown, John L. Brown, C. Wilson.

- - -

F 267   Will dated 21 September 1840, proved November 1845.

CONNALLY WALKER "far advanced in age"     wife: Elizabeth

All estate to daughters Jane Walker and Mary Walker.
His three sons William, Samuel and Phillip Walker have all
received their portions.

Executors: son Samuel and daughter Jane Walker.
Witnesses: John W. Shaw, Obediah Hurdle.

- - -

F 268  Will dated 4 April 1845, proved November Court 1845.

REBECCA (x) DOLLAR

daughter Susan Dollar all money on hand, all notes due her,
and "pension due me from the United States"
"My grandson William Glenn son of James Glenn"

Executrix: daughter Susan. Witnesses: J. Turner, James Turner.

- - -

F 269  Will dated 19 December 1839, proved Nov Court 1845.

ROBERT MORROW                wife a legatee, name not stated

sons: Vincent, Josiah, Robert J, and George W. Morrow.
daus: Eliza A., Mary Jane, Elizabeth M., Julee Nancy
sons: Sidney Mebane, George Washington Morrow
"son Elbridge's heirs"

Executors: sons Vincent and Josiah.
Witnesses: Thomas Reeves, Robert Whitted.

- - -

F 271  Will dated 14 June 1839, proved February Court 1846.

JOSEPH ARMSTRONG              wife: Frances

sons: John Armstrong, Thomas D. Armstrong
daus: Frances Clendennin, Jinney Walker, Elizabeth Tate,
      Henrietta Tate, Parthena Faucett
grandchildren: Joseph McAdams, Mary Rippy, Peggy McAdams,
               Catherine McAdams
"Little grandson Joseph Tate, Betsy Tate's son" .. "my shotgun"

Executors: sons-in-law John Tate and John Faucett.

- - -

F 273  Will dated 22 August 1845, proved February Court 1846.

NANCY (x) CRUTCHFIELD         grandson: John Workman

daughter: Nancy Stubbins
sons: John, Enoch and James Crutchfield

Executor: son Enoch.
Witnesses: Richard Tapp, James H. Thompson.

- - -

F 274  Will dated 3 November 1845, proved Feb Court 1846.

BENJAMIN (x) CARROLL          wife: Nancy

son: Alsey Carroll
"Ilai Copley and his wife Claricey"
Dicey James, Luvico ? Glenn                    - continued -

F 274  Will of BENJAMIN CARROLL continued                215

sons: Eli Carroll, Archibald Carroll, Charles Carroll, Benja-
    min Carroll, Clement Carroll and Stephen Carroll 50¢ ea.

Executor: son Alsey Carroll. Witnesses: W.N.Pratt, Thos. White.

- - -

F 276  Will dated 25 June 1845, proved February Court 1846.

TIRZA (x) SWEANEY

neices Nancy and Martha Oakley, daughters of Barton and
Amelia Oakley (both neices are under age)

Executor: George W. Jones. Witnesses: John Duke, John Hill.

- - -

F 277  Will dated 23 May 1840, proved May Court 1846.

JOHN (x) NOE "under bodily affliction"

sons: George Noe, Daniel Noe
daughters Sally, Nelly Noe land on Stinking Quarter Creek
son: Solomon balance of land
married daughter Mary 5 shillings

Executor: Edwin Holt, Esq.
Witnesses: Mich. Holt, Jno.A.M.Fadyen, Christian --

- - -

From this point I give only the name of the testator, date
of the will and date of probate, except for the two or three
I had already abstracted earlier. All are in Book F.

| Book F page # | testator | date of will | proved |
|---|---|---|---|
| 279-281 | FREDERICK (x) SHOFFNER | 23 October 1845, | May 1846 |
| 283 | SAMUEL PATTON, SR . | 25 July 1846 | Aug 1846 |
| 285 | HANDY WOOD | 8 August 1846 | "   " |
| 286 | EDWARD J. WARD | 31 July 1846 | "   " |
| 288 | JOHN WALKER | 15 November 1844 | "   " |
| 290 | ANDERSON HALL | 7 March 1846 | "   " |
| 293 | ROBERT McCADAMS | 13 June 1846 | "   " |
| 294 | JAMES THOMPSON, SR. "old and feeble" | 22 July 1833 | "   " |
| 296 | MARY (x) FINN or FENN | 14 February 1846 | "   " |
| 297-300 | LOFTIN K. PRATT | 4 August 1846 | "   " |

| Book F | name of testator | date of will | proved |
|---|---|---|---|
| 301 | MARGARET (x) WALL | 16 August 1838 | Aug 1846 |
| 304 | ELI EULISS | 8 September 1846 | Nov 1846 |
| 303 | JOHN MORROW | 23 July 1846 | " " |
| 305 | MARTHA (x) BENSON | 10 August 1842 | " " |
| 306 | WILLIAM HOLT | 20 April 1842 | " " |
| 308 | WILLIAM FOUST | 18 August 1846 | " " |
| 309 | AQUILLA (x) JONES, SR. "old and weak" | 26 November 1843 | " " |
| 310 | JOSIAH ATKINS, SR. | 23 November 1839 | " " |
| 312 | JOSEPH A. WHITE | 3 October 1846 | " " |
| 314 | JOSHUA SUMMERS | 25 August 1846 | " " |
| 315 | YOUNG (x) DORCH | 1 October 1846 | " " |
| 317 | DANIEL ALBRIGHT | 30 October 1846 | " " |
| 319 | MARTHA (x) McCAULEY | 24 October 1846 | " " |
| 322-6 | JOHN (x) EULISS | 10 December 1845 | " " |
| 327-9 | EMANUEL CLAPP | 2 August 1846 | " " |
| 330 | SUSANNAH ESTHER BAKER | 23 October 1843 | " " |
| 331 | MARTIN COBLE | 8 August 1846 | Feb 1847 |
| 331-3 | MASTING CHEEK | 26 March 1841 | " " |
| 334 | JOHN WOODS | 30 July 1845 | " " |
| 336 | HENRY O'DANIEL | 2 February 1846 | " " |
| 337-9 | MOSES GUESS | 19 March 1842 | " " |
| 240-2 | JOHN JONES | 17 October 1846 | " " |
| 343 | MARGARET (x) McCULLOCK | 24 January 1845 | " " |
| 344-5 | THOMAS BOWLS | 13 February 1839 | " " |
| 346 | EDWIN ISELEY | 16 September 1846 | " " |
| 348 | JAMES (x) ECTOR | 1 September 1846 | May 1847 |
| 349 | WILLIAM WILKINSON | 29 May 1845 | " " |

| Book F | name of testator | date of will | proved |
|---|---|---|---|
| 350 | CHARLES (x) PETTIGREW | 31 October 1844 | May 1847 |
| 351 | ELIZABETH BURTON | 16 July 1845 | " " |
| 354 | JAMES LINDSEY | 7 April 1847 | Aug 1847 |
| 355 | JAMES (x) CARTER | 8 March 1831 | " " |
| 357-8 | JOHN THOMPSON | 17 February 1847 | " " |
| 359-61 | JOSEPH ANDERSON | 3 July 1847 | " " |
| 362-4 | STEPHEN GLASS | 31 July 1847 | " " |
| 365 | MARGARET (x) PATTON | 6 August 1846 | " " |
| 366 | THOMAS (x) BARTON "weak in body" | 14 June 1847 | " " |
| 368-9 | DAVID (x) CASTLEBERRY | 19 May 1847 | " " |
| 371 | JAMES PHILLIPS | 27 October 1847 | Nov 1847 |
| 373 | REBECCA (x) DAVIS | 11 July 1844 | " " |
| 375-7 | THOMAS D. BENNEHAN | 28 April 1845 | " " |
| 378 | JAMES (x) HAILEY | 22 October 1847 | " " |
| 379 | MARGARET (x) HERNDON | 16 August 1847 | " " |

379 MARGARET (x) HERNDON. All her estate to her sister Elizabeth. It consists partly of her share of the undivided estate of her father William Herndon. Wits: Wm. Trice, Noah Trice.

| 380-3 | GEORGE FOGLEMAN | 28 February 1843 | Nov 1847 |
| | " " codicil | 3 September 1846 | " " |
| 383 | JAMES W. McCAULEY | 21 July 1847 | " " |

383 "late of the State of Tennessee, but now at the home of Wm. McCauley (his relative) of Orange County."

| 386 | DAVID PATTERSON | 4 December 1839 | Nov 1847 |
| 388 | JOHN TAYLOR | 13 November 1847 | " " |
| 389 | JAMES RIGGS | 24 July 1847 | " " |
| 390 | ARLAS (x) HARRIS "weak in body" | September 1847 | " " |
| 392 | JAMES ROSS | 11 January 1836 | Feb 1848 |
| 394 | ISABELL (x) CLENDENNIN | 22 October 1847 | " " |
| 395 | SIMPSON RHEW | 20 June 1847 | " " |

218

| Book F | name of testator | date of will | proved |
|---|---|---|---|
| 396 | FRANCES (x) COOK "weak in body" | 10 August 1846 | Feb 1848 |
| 398 | NATHAN HOOKER | 24 December 1847 | " " |
| 400 | ELIZABETH (x) BLACKNALL | 5 January 1848 | " " |
| 401 | FIELDING (x) LEWIS | 27 February 1847 | " " |

wife: Nancy          daughters: Mary and Nancy
"sons and daughters" ... "rest of my children that has married and left me"
Executor: son John C. Lewis.
Witnesses: Joseph Proctor, John Pool.

| | | | |
|---|---|---|---|
| 402 | HARVEY I. ROUNDTREE | 29 October 1847 | Feb 1848 |
| 404 | GEORGE (x) FOSTER | 29 January 1846 | May 1848 |
| 406-9 | JOSEPH FREELAND | 2 July 1846 | " " |
| 409-11 | MARGARET (x) KERR "old" | 4 July 1843 | " " |
| 412 | ELIZABETH THOMPSON | 13 August 1842 | " " |
| 413 | RACHEL (x) JACKSON | 13 April 1848 | " " |
| 414 | WILLIAM ROGERS | 27 January 1845 | " " |
| 416-8 | WILLIAM ECTOR | 26 June 1848 | " " |
| 419-21 | GEORGE ISELEY | 24 February 1845 | Nov 1848 |
| 422-4 | SARAH F. DURHAM | 8 April 1847 | " " |
| 425 | JANE (x) STEVENS | 2 March 1845 | " " |
| 427 | HETTY (x) WILLIAMS | 24 September 1847 | " " |
| 428 | WILLIAM (x) FOGLEMAN | 8 December 1848 | Feb 1849 |
| 430 | NATHANIEL HARRIS | 30 June 1846 | " " |
| 432 | MARTIN MURPHY | 26 September 1848 | May 1849 |
| 433-7 | RICHARD CRABTREE " " codicil | 21 May 1841 13 October 1843 | " " " " |
| 439-43 | LEVI WHITTED " " codicil | 10 June 1845 17 April 1849 | Aug 1849 " " |
| 443 | DANIEL HOGAN | 7 May 1844 | " " |
| 445 | MARGARET (x) RIGGS | 18 May 1828 | " " |
| 447 | ANN (x) GRIMES | 27 March 1846 | " " |

| Book F | name of testator | date of will | proved |
|--------|------------------|--------------|--------|
| 449 | WILLIAM BOWLES | 1 September 1827 | Nov 1849 |
| 451 | ROBERT (x) BLACKWOOD<br>"low state of health" | 28 September 1849 | Feb 1850 |
| 452 | JOHN (x) GATES<br>"in affliction" | 30 January 1849 | " " |
| 453 | JANE (x) WILSON | 5 September 1841 | " " |
| 455 | DANIEL GREEN | 22 April 1850 | May 1850 |
| 456 | ALEXANDER HATCH | 21 November 1845 | " " |
| 458-62 | WILLIAM H. MERRITT | 18 July 1850 | Aug 1850 |
| 462-5 | DANIEL PARKER<br>"in advanced age" | 24 August 1844 | " " |
| 466 | HENRY EDWARDS, SR. | 20 July 1844 | " " |
| 467 | DAVID ROBERSON | 24 December 1849 | " " |
| 469 | DAVID (x) WILLIAMS<br>"in feeble health" | 27 April 1849 | " " |
| 470 | DICEY (x) SPARROW | 14 June 1850 | " " |
| 472 | DANIEL BOOTHE | 18 August 1850 | Nov 1850 |
| 474 | ANNA DEBRULER | 29 August 1850 | " " |

This concludes the wills probated during the year 1850.

———————  ———————  ———————  ———————  ———————

I found six original wills among the second series of Orange County wills preserved in the State Archives in Raleigh, N.C. which are not now on record in the will books in Hillsboro. The date of probate on these wills is not known. I give them in order of their dates.

GENET (x) McCOWN, widow    "very weak"    dated 9 July 1785

grandsons: James Johnston and James Odonel  $20 each
granddaus: Jean Johnston and Jean Odonel (O'Donnel)
daus: Jean Johnston and Agness Odonel
"My grandchildren Thomas John Jean & Charles Johnston  and likewise Jean Susiana William John and Henry Odonal ... above named nine children...."

Executors: John Thompson Miller and Thomas Brad .... (torn).
Witnesses: Chas Clindennin, Wm. Clindennin, Thomas Bradshaw.

220    Codicil to the will of GENET McCOWN    dated 10 Oct. 1792.

"my son-in-law John Johnston married to my eldest daughter
Jean " 5 shillings
"my son-in-law John ODonal married to my youngest daughter
Agness"  5 shillings

Witnesses: James Thompson, Thomas Thompson, Chas. Clindennin.

- - -

JAMES McMUNN        Will dated 31 December 1802, proved --

wife a legatee, name not stated        son: William 5 sh.
daughter: Ginny Brease 5 shillings
Ann Hargis 20 shillings        James Lindcey  5 shillings
daughter: Elizabeth  5 shillings

Witnesses: Alexander Finley, Wm. Smith.

- - -

ABRAHAM I. (x) WHITAKER        Will dated 10 December 1803,
                                               proved --
wife: Martha
sons: William and Abram Whitaker land bounded by John Redmond's
                              Cardin's & Jacob Allen's lands
son: Jacob land "where John Poteet formerly lived now belonging
             to Thomas Holloway"
youngest son: James Whitaker
sons and daughters Isaac Whitaker
daus: Joana Holliway, Hannah Barbee, Elizabeth Riley, Mary Riley

Executors: John Cabe and Henry Bunch.
Witnesses: Henry Bunch, John (x) Morris.

- - -

THOMAS (x) GUINN        Will dated 18 June 1822, proved --

wife: Mildred all estate during her life
son: Joseph Guinn  $1
dau: Elizabeth Vickers wife of David Vickers  $1
"    Mary Jane Quinn estate after wife's death

Executors: friends Reuben Cardin & Frederick Moize Esq.
Witnesses: Thomas (x) Christian, Benton Clark.

- - -

THOMAS (x) CRABTREE        Will dated 10 March 1826, note on back
                              says "recorded February 1833"
wife: Caty

"Children Harriet Tempe Martha Anne Abram, George, Jacob Samuel" (punctuation as given)
"To my children John Thomas William, Peggy, Nancy Hunter (?)
Hetty, Susanna Elizabeth one shilling each having heretofore
advanced them".                                        - continued -

Executors: "brother William Crabtree and James Crabtree son
           to my brother Abram."
Witnesses: J. Taylor, Thos. Hargis.

- - -

THOMAS COUCH There are two drafts of this will, the first is
dated 14 January 1828, the second is dated 27 January 1829.

son: Thomas Couch "one-half the land I bought of Wm White and
                  part of the tract I bought of Joseph White
                  ... lying on the W side of Piney Mountain Cr.
son: Hardin Couch "Peelor tracts adjoining Aquilla Rhodes and
                  the heirs of Benjamin Rhodes."
sons: Isaac Couch, Jacob Couch, William Couch, Samuel Couch
daughter Rachel White  $10, Thomas White  $10, Joseph White Jr
$10, Nancy White  $10, Susannah White  $10.

No executor named, no witnesses, but signed by Thomas Couch.

- - - - - -

Every will abstracted in this book is preserved in the State
Archives with the exception of the nine listed below.

| name of testator | date of will | recorded in Book |
|---|---|---|
| LYNCH, THOMAS | April 1815 | D 438 |
| MOORE, JAMES | proved 1836 | E 402 |
| MURDOCK, ANDREW | December 1815 | D 498 |
| RAINEY, BENJAMIN | April 1811 | D 286 |
| STRAYHORN, GILBERT | 1783 | D 87 |
| TARPLEY, MASON | April 1826 | E 118 |
| TATE, JOSEPH | November 1825 | E 105 |
| WOOD, SABUT | November 1807 | D 220 |
| WORTHAM, MARY | September 1827 | E 174 |

- - - - - -

CORRECTIONS

D203  The name is JOHN LINN instead of Liner. He is "advanced
      in age and infirm."
D263  Nancy McDaniel instead of Nancy McCamal. A check of
      Orange County marriages shows that Nancy Watson married
      18 September 1817 John McDaniel.
E207  Vicey instead of Viney Horne.
E417  After "Susannah Ward's children, Wm Ward's children" it
      should read Esther,  instead of Stephen, Well's children

During the period covered by this book Orange County Inferior
Court met quarterly, in February, May, August and November.
For part of this time it began on the fourth Monday of the
month and lasted several days, sometimes going over until the
first of the following month.

- - - - -

BARBEE, BENJAMIN, Betsy, Francis, Gabriel, Gray, Jemima,
  Phoebe (..), Polly E122; Christopher D614,E68; C. D216,614;
  Chris Jr E68; CHRISTOPHER, Eliz, Francis, Nancy, Susanna,
  William E321; Drucilla, Eliz, Francis, Gabriel, Gemima,
  Mary; Nancy, PHEBE (...), Phebe Ann E410; Francis D160;
  Eliz, Esther (H),Gray, JOHN, John Jr, King, Reuben, Sally,
  Zachariah D535; Esther (Herndon) D70; Franky (Rhodes) D293;
  Hannah (Whitekar) 220; James, Jane, Sarah (..), WILLIAM E294;
  Joseph E290; Mark D68; Nancy (Herndon) D515,F31; Wm Sr E251
  Pleasant E161; Sally (Hopson) F261; Wm D291,389,E345,280
BARBY, Polly, Ritty, Joseph, Sally D114; Eliz (Nevill) D263.
BARBER, Benjamin D91; Betty, David, Margery D222; David F101;
  Ellen (..), JAMES, Mary Ann, Sarah Jane F43;
  Frances (Lloyd), her children F38; Sally (King), Wm E420;
  David, Eliz, Jean, JOSEPH, Marjary (..), Matthew D83;
BARKER, Barbara (Fitch), George E365; Joseph E143
BARLOW, Ellen (Thompson) F86
BARNARD, James D567
BARNET, Daniel F65          BARNETT, James D40
BARNHEART, Henry E7
BARNHILL, James D143
BARNWELL, Catherine, Elenor, JAMES, Jas Jr, John, Nancy,
  Robert, Susan (..), Susan, William E82; James D306; John F186
BARTON, Harriet F247; THOMAS F366; Thomas Jr D334;
  Nelly (Thompson), John, Stephen E195
BASKET, John E369;
  John, Nancy, Susannah (O'Daniel), William E78
BASON, Barbara (Foust) E382; Elizabeth (McCaddams) D248;
  Henry F160,164; Joseph E382
BATCHELOR, Elias E353
BEAIRE ? or BEDIRE ?, William D84
BEASLEY, Hardy, Milly (Hurdle) & her children, Samuel E164;
  Mark, Polly D518; Milly D261
BEAVER, Susannah D450;     BEAVERS, Mary (Cloud) E411
BECKHAM, Caswell, Catherine (..), Eliz, Isabella, Joseph, D606
  Joshua, Leonard, Mahaly, Nancy, STEPHEN, Tabitha, Thos D606
BECKUM, Jesse D109          BECOM, Mary (Ray) D231
BENNEHAN, Rebecca, RICHARD, Thomas D E96;
  Thomas D. D512,553, E182,259,302,324, his will F375; Wm D23
BENSON, Eliz (Wyatt) D464; Edward, Stephen E318;
  MARTHA F304; William E191,318
BENTON, SAMUEL D276
BERRY, David, Eliz (..), Eliz, Henry, Isaac, John, Joshua D407
  James E173; Mary, ROBERT, Rob Jr, Thomas, William D407
BEVELL, BEVILLE, Francis (Favis), Sally (Davis) E92;
  Robert F379; Winnifred (Davis) E239
BHON ?, Neil D286
BIGELOE, Samuel D136;      BIGELOW, Samuel D468
BILBO, F. E319,F19; John E205; Joseph D70; Martha E392;
  Thomas E205,330, F31
BINGHAM, Mrs. Eliza F249; Wm.I. E64; Z. E416
BIRD, Catherine, Empson, JAMES, Mary, Richard, Sarah, (see BYRD)
  Susannah, Thomas D155; Citty ?, Eliza, EMPSON, John, Martha,
  Polly (..), Richard E237; Eliz, Polly (Vincent) E95;
  James, John, Nancy, Susannah, Wm D468; Jehu, Patsy (M) E247;
  James, Jas J, Rebecca E509; John, MARY, her daughters D249;
  Jehu E247; Margaret (Murray) D143; Mary (Whitted) D136,468;

BIRD, Nancy (..), THOMAS SR, Thos, other children, Wm  E362;
  Patsy (Moore) E247; Rebecca (Thompson) E262; Sam. E52 see BURD
BISHOP, James  D605                      and BYRD
BLACKNALL, ELIZABETH  F400
BLACKWELL,  James  E10,E174
BLACKWOOD, Ann, Catherine, Fanny, Franklin L, Hannah, James,
  Jane, John, Marg't, Martha, Mary, Nancy, Sarah, WILLIAM,
  Wm Jr  E229; David K. E341,F174; James J. E341,F200;
  JOHN, John J, Johnston, Margaret, Mary (..), Mary  F174;
  John  D549,600, E125,341, F200;  Richard  D282; Robert  D50;
  ROBERT  F451
BLACLOE ?, Patsy (Ward) E296
BLAIR, Elizabeth (McAdams)  D250
BLAKE, Bennett T, Ellis G. F171; Polly E250;  Thomas  D292
BLALOCK, Elizabeth (Tutterton)  E366
BLANCHARD , Rachel  D261
BLAND, J.H.  E71               BLEAT, James  E231
BOBBITT, Dicey (Duke) F139     BOISH ?, Hannah (Gant)  D30
BOLES, AARON, John, sisters  D494
BOLING, James  D462   see BORLAND and BOWLING
BOND, William  D247
BOOKER, Susannah (Thrift)  D344
BOON, John  D574, E1,7,367
BOOTH, Alphred, Betty, DANIEL, Dan Jr, Gray, John, Joseph D79
  Mark, Patty, Polly, Prissley (..), Ritty, Ruthy, Sarah  D79
  Sarah, Silvey, Solomon, Tapley  D79;
  Alfred, Betsey, Priscilla (..), SOLOMON, Tapley  D316;
BOOTHE, DANIEL  F472; Delilah, Eliz, Joseph, JOSEPH SR E86
  Joseph Jr  D518; Mary, Rosy, Sarah (..) Sally, Tabitha E86
BORING, Victory (McKee)  E32
BORLAND, Abraham, ALEXANDER, Andrew, Archibald, Eliz, Jenny,
  John, Mary, Nancy, Sally, Susannah (..), Sus., Wm. D602;
  Archibald  E88;  see BOLING and BOWLAND
BOROUGHS, Amelia H. (Patterson) E353; John E512; Zaccheus D68
BOSWELL, Brown, Catherine, Charlotte, Craven, EDWARD, E223
  Ed Jr, James, John, Mathew, Mary (..), Nancy, Susannah  E223
  Thomas  E223; Wm.  E11
BOWLAND, Andrew, Polly (Strayhorn), E406,E410
BOWLING, Willis F190
BOWLES, WILLIAM  F449
BOWLS, Mary (Moore) E344; Thomas E149, THOMAS F344; Wm D399,E227
BOWMAN, James H. D107,197,226;393
BOYLE, Ann (..), Henry, James, John, Jean, Mary, WILLIAM  D441;
  Ann, Eliz (..), Eliz, Hugh, James, JOHN, Lavinia, Martha,
  Rachel  D443; Jas  D83; John Jr  D114;
  ANN (..), Ann, James, Jane, John, Martha, Mary  D484;
BOYLES or BOYLEN ?, Jas, John  D222
BRACHER (BRASHEAR ?), Mary Ann  E220
BRACKEN, JOHN, Joseph, Julia Ann, Nancy (..) E10;
  Julia Ann E223; Julius S. E395; Mary (Gilliam)  D489
BRADFORD, David D259,481; David Sr D460,489,314; D.Jr  D481;
  David, Eliz, Jas, Jos, Marg't, Sarah, Thos, WILLIAM  E14;
  Thomas D179,481,E275; Thos Jr D489; William  D179,506.
BRADSHAW, James E50; Maryann F224; Thomas D127,206,E50, p219
  W. F102,261;  William E145,F224; Wm Jr D452

BRANCH, Jesse  D530
BRANNOCK, Alex N, Angel M, Delilah, Henry, Henry Sr, WILLIAM,
   Wm. Jr, Wright  E272; Alex N, Edmund; Eliz (..), HENRY SR,
   Henry, James, Sarah, Thomas, William, Wright  F97;
   Henry, Leah, Wm  D228; Wm. E285,F184
BRAXTON, Hannah (Lindley) E167; Mary (McPherson), Thomas D517
BREDGES, Eliz C, Mary, Wm B. E303  see BRIDGES
BREASE, Ginny (McMunn) page 220
BREESE (BREEZE), B. E233; Murrell E277; Richard E37,E106;
   Jenney (..), Jinney, JOHN, Patsy, Polly, Rachel, D583
   Richard, Susa  D583
BREWER, Aris, Biddy, Dolly, Eliz, Ezekiel, Fanny, John, Martha,
   Norris, PATSY, Ransom, Sackfield, Thomas, William  E27;
   Benjamin (2), Dorothy (..), Isham (2), Jane, Joseph (2),
   July, Polly, Sally, Washington (2), WILLIAM E303;
   Candice, Charlotte, KATY, Polly, William  D30;
   Eliz; Sackfield D56,142; ELIZ.,Ezek., Rebeckah, Thos E220;
   Eliz, Ezek, Henry, Patsy, Polly, Peter (2), Rebecca,
   SACKFIELD, Sackfield Jr (2), Thomas  D384; Isham D120,161;
   Eliz, Marg't, Martha, Maryann, THOMAS, his wife, Thos  F222;
   John F256; Joshua D263; LEWIS, Nancy, Patience (..)  D47;
   Thomas D50,56,142,322, E49,208, F132;
   William D120,263,565,611, F136
BRIDGES, Isabella, Young  F249    see BREDGES
BRIGGS, DUNCAN D., Duncan, John, Samuel  D457
BRINKLEY, William  E40,186,191, 275;  William Jr  D253
BRITT, Celia, Eli, Elizabeth  E209; M.H.  F82
BROADWELL, Freeman  D452
BROCKWELL, Betsey (Horne)  E307
BROOKS, Andrew  D24,277;   Thomas  D24;
   ANDREW, Hannah, James, mother, William  D328
BROWN, Allen F124,248; ASEY, his brothers & sisters  D439;
   Allen, Ann, Jehu, John, Mathew, Ruth (..), WILLIAM, Wm F26;
   Fred'k E400; George D59; H. D29; Jas R. F256; Joseph F265;
   John  D605,F212,248; John L. F265; Lydia (Garrison) E11;
   Mathew E262; Stephen  F52; Thomas E40,E156; William D605
BROWNING; Edmund, Jane (Martin) D431; Iley  E35;
   Edward, Ed Elim, Eliz (..), Eliz, Frances, Isaac, JOHN,
   Mary, Milly, Rachel, Richard, Robert, Solomon, Sarah D596;
   Eliz (Redmond), James E317; Solomon E345; Thos. D124
BRUCE, A.B.  D352,396,583,588;  Charles D588; Geo. W. E245;
   Abner, Charles, John, Willson D277
BRYAN, David D544; Nancy (Roney) E143; Marg't (Morrow) D189
BRYANT, Eliz (Nealy) D455; George  D477; Nelly  D328;
   Jane, Lavina Isabella, Sally  D588
BUCHANNON, Mary (Murdock) . D399
BUCKNER, Jesse  D344
BULLOCK, Benj.  D456,553;  Francis  D86
BUNCH, Henry  D89,392,510,601, page 220
BURCH, Henry  D224
BURD, Rachel (Dickie)  D122  see BIRD and BYRD
BURGESS, Jean D146
BURKE, James, Mary Ann F245
BURNETT, F.  D407; Polly (Jeffrass) F87
BURNS, Anderson J, ANDREW, Margaret M, Martha (..), Mary E512
   Samuel, William  E512

Name of the testator is in capitals.

BURNSIDE, Ann, Benj, Hannahm James, John, ROBERT, Ruth  D170
   B. D347;  Benjamin  E48,90; Robert  D172
BURTON, Christian, Culbird  D89; Cuthburt  D178;
   Christian (..), CULBIRTH, John, Samuel, Wm, Williamson  D601;
   Eliz (Southerland) D530; ELIZABETH  F351; Wm'son  E268,351,355;
   John C, John, Mary (Cabe), Mary A.  F248
BUSICK, Caleb, Eliz, Mary, Nancy, Phebe, WILLIAM SR, Wm Jr  D228;
BUSSICK, Catherine, Eliz, William, Wm Jr  D244
BUTNER, John  D119
BYLERS ?, John  F86               BYNUM, Joseph  F198
BYRD, Dicey; Nancy  E211;
   Catherine, Eliz, Empson, James, Mary, Rachel (..), RICHARD,
   Samuel, Thomas  E202; Empson, John, Thomas  E385;
   Caty, Eliz, Empson, James, Mary, SAMUEL, Susannah, Thomas,
   father & Mother  E178; Polly (Vincent)  E84.  see BIRD, BURD


CABE, Eliz  D494; Eliz (Horner)  F202; John  D525,602, page 220;
   JEMIMA, Mary, Rachel, William  F248; Polly Ann  F26
CABLE see COBLE
CAIN, Abel, Belinda (Rhodes)  E351; Allen  E282; Hugh  D514,E213;
   Archibald  E115,231,351,355; Eliz (Scarlett)  D510;
   Ann, Charity, Martha, Peggy, Polly, Timothy, WILLIAM, Wm  E324;
   James  D224,E115; Manerva R.  F9; W.  D317a;
   William  D104,114,136,E353,F9; Wm. Sr  D178,440; Wm. Jr  D440
CALDWELL, Helen, Rev. Joseph  D352,E363: Margaret  E363;
   John, Martha (Gattis)  D269
CAMERON, Duncan, D94,276,309,514,608, E96,259,324,137;
   P. C.  E507; Rebecca (Bennehan)  E96
CAMPBELL, Catlett D94,352,E29,182,411, his will F245; G.  D386;
   James  D395; John  D395,592; Mary (Edwards)  D56; Rob't  D265,F31
CANNON, William  D481
CANTERIAL, Benj, Isaac, JOSEPH, Rachel, Sally  D127;
CANTRELL, Isaac  Fl; ISAAC, Rutha (..), children  E13; Wm  E345,Fl
CANTRIL, Benjamin D215;   Hester ? (Dickie)  D122
CAPPS, Ceason  D194; CASON, James, Mary (..), Mary, Milly,
   Nelly, Richard, Robert, William  E308
CARDIN, Jones  D591; Polly (Whitaker)  E270;
   Reubin  D530,615, page 220; Warner  F240
CAREATHERS, John, William  E342   see CARRUTHERS
CARLTON, Betsey (Trice), Leonard,Nancy, Thos Trice, Wm  D114;
   Daniel, David, Henry, John, Marg't, Nancy (..), Nancy  E422;
   Wesley, William  E422; Eliz (Herndon)  F31; Eliz (Marcom)  F17;
   John D.  E205,F80; Leonard D233; W. D.  E273
CARMICHAEL, Archibald, Jane, John Henry, Margaret, Mary (..),
   Nancy, THOMAS  D559; John H.  E19
CAROTHERS, Samuel D30  see CAREATHERS, CARUTHERS
CARREL, Calvin, Candis; Cinthy, Dixon, Eliz, Ellin, JAMES  F136
   John, Lemuel, Martha, Polly (..), William  F136
CARRELL, Nancy Eliz (Scarlett), John Gaston  E412  see CARROLL
CARRIGAN, Alfred, James, John, Nancy (Holt), Rob, Wm, Wm A.  F126
   Hugh, JOHN, children, wife,Tempe  E240; Wm A.  F60,72
CARRINGTON, Alfred, Dessy, Eaphriam, Fanny, Holly, J.J., E241;
   NATHANIEL, Nath Jr, Polly, Ruth, William E241; George D22,23;
   Ankey (..), Eliz, JAMES, Jas Jr, Jemima (..), John, D485,
   Mary, Wm D485; Dicey, Morgan, Polly, PRISCILLA (..)  F190;

CARRINGTON, Charlotte, Dicey, EPHRIAM, John, Linton, Morgan,
 Polly, Priscilla (..) E17; James Jr D36; John D253;
 Benj, Ephriam, JOHN, Mary (..), Nathaniel, Thomas  D110;
 John J. E216; Nathaniel D33,553; William D477
CARROLL, Alsey, Archibald, Charles, Clement, Eli, Stephen,
 BENJAMIN, Ben Jr, Nancy (...) F274;
 Benjamin, Elenor (..), STEPHEN E183      see CARREL
CARSON, JAMES, Mary (...), Robert D219;
 Alice, Eliz, MARGARET, Mary, Robert, Samuel D61
CARTER, Ann, Hannah, John D162; Catherine E193;
 Brice, Enoch, Henry, Joshua, NATHANIEL, Nat Jr, Rebecca E13;
 JAMES F355; Joseph, Milley (Capps) E308; Wm. D229,292,E13
CARUTHERS, Jno D560; John E215,253; J. F130;
 John, Sary (..), SAMUEL, daughters, William D565
CASEY, Eliz (Roberts)  F119
CASTLEBERRY, Cath W (Fennell) F10; David D518,E86,
 DAVID F368; Susannah D437
CATE, Alfred or Alford D548;
 Abner, Eliz (..), Ephriam, John, Mary, Nancy, RICH'D D304;
 Ann, BARNARD, Bar Jr, David, James, Jane (..), Jean E134;
 Joel, Joseph (2), Joshua, Mary, Rebecca, Rosannah  E134;
 Sanders, Sarah, Thomas, Vinson E134; Barnard D490,520;
 Anna, Mary (..), SOLOMON, Thomas, William F216;
 Benj, Isaiah, John, LAZARUS, Marg't (..), Thos, Wm D89;
 Dolly, Milly, Wm. E49; Easter (Hastings) E29; Jean D490;
 Doratha, Isaiah, John S, Martha (..), Martha, Polly D369;
 THOMAS, Thos Jr  D369; Huldah D547;548; James S. E52;
 Eliz, Ephriam, Fanny, Huldah, John, Martha, Milley D490;
 Moses, Sarah (..), Tabitha, THOMAS, Thos Jr, Winney D490;
 John S. D614; Lydia D148; Nancy D548,F224; Neil D580;
 Nealy, Sally (Nealy) D455; Sally (Wilson) F63;
 Richard D547,548; Sarah D547,548; Sary (Hunter) E253;
 Solomon D614; Thomas D103; Thomas R. D614
CATES, Alsey (Horne) E207; Ann D84; Nancy (Andrews) F130;
 Nelly (Laycock) E204; THOMAS, Thos Jr  D84
CAUDLE, Lewis F17
CAUSEY, Wm.  E7
CAVE, Dr. Hudson  E140
CHALMERS, Wm.  E321
CHAMBERS, Eliz, Grace, Hannah, James, Mary, SAMUEL D251;
 Sam Jr, Sarah, William D251; Eliz (Hobbs) D421;
 Ellenor (Lindley) E167; James D424
CHAMBLEE, William E317
CHANCERY ?, Corrinda (Massey)  F83
CHANDLER, David, wife D91
CHANNELLER, Shadrick  D304
CHARLES, George, Michael D424
CHEEK, Alves E240; B. E76; James E240; John E367,404;
 Jenny (Andrew), Patsy (Andrew) E49; Mary (Hobbs) D421;
 MASTING F331; Robert  E306
CHILD, Frances (..), Francis, WILSON D277;
 FRANCES (...), James, Samuel, Sam Jr E271;
 FRANCIS, Martha (..), Samuel  E70;
 James D136,352,E71,76,195; Samuel E240
CHILDERS, Joshua  D477

CHIZENHALL, Anne (primrose) E368,F114; Delancy D564,
  Eliz (Wood) E291; Mary (Wood) D564,E291;
CHRISTIAN, Harrison E74;        CHRISTON, Thomas  page 220
CHRISTMAS, CHARLES, Nathaniel, Richard  D322; Elizabeth E25;
  Henrietta, Jas, John, Mary G, Nancy, RICHARD, William  E300
CHRISTOPHER, Eliz, Eliza, Frances, James, Jane, JOHN F56;
  John Jr, Matty, Nancy, Polly (..), Polly, Sidney Smith  F56
CLANCY, GEORGE SR, Jack, Jenny, Polly, Rebecca (..), D396;
  Thomas, Wm  D396; James, Phebe (Thompson) E195;
  Nancy (Palmer) E358; Thomas D404,407,E25,71,81,192,229,245,/
CLAPP, Abraham, Betsey (Albright) E231;          E271,358.
  Barbara (..), BARNEY, his wife, Ceatty ?, Christian, David,
  Emanuel, George, Isaac, John, Nelly, Peggy, Penny, Polly, Sal-
  ly F229; Barbara, Caty, John, JUDY, Sophia  E99;
  Catherine (Foust) E382; Eliz (Foust) D239; EMANUEL  F327;
  John E382,F176; Peggy (Eulis), Tobias  F242
CLARK, Ann (..), Grace, JAMES, Jas W, Sarah, Stephen  F191;
  Benton  page 220; James D160,E236,343, F193; Jesse  D219;
  John, John N, Letty (Anderson) D458; Nancy, WILLIAM E192;
  Peter S, Susanna (..) E372; Polly (Lindsey) D483; Rob't E375;
  Quinton Esther (Lindley) E167; Sarah (Ward) E18; Susan F213;
  Silas Green  E27; Susey (Baker) E256; Thomas  D160;
  William  D219; E127,192,347
CLARKE, James  D410; Thomas  D380
CLAY, M.G.  D432
CLAYTOR, Rachel (Cabe)  F248; Samuel S.  F163,248
CLEMENTS, Anderson  D593; A.W.  F80
CLENDENNIN, Ann (2), Fanny, Fisher, James, Jenny, John (2),
  Joseph, Mary (..), Polly, Rebecca, WILLIAM; Wm Jr, Younger  D25
  Ann (..), FISHER, Fisher Je, James, Joseph, Sarah, Thomas,
  William, unborn child  D452; Benj, Catherine, Mary (Roney) E143
  Caroline, Fisher, George, Hanar S, Jean (..), Letitia ?,
  Nancy Ann, Sarah M, WILLIAM, Wm Jr  F179; Charles 219-220;
  Frances (Armstrong) F271; ISABELL F394; James D66;
  Isabel (..), James, WILLIAM G, children E363; John D243,E228;
  Joseph D220,237,382; William D66,612,page 219; Wm J. E145
CLENNY, Margaret (Carson), William D61
CLIFTON, Amy, Catron (..), Emily, James K, John J, JOSIAH,
  Mahala, unborn child  E155
CLINTON, Eliz, Geo W, John Linnington, Mary Ann, Nancy,
  Samuel H, Sarah  E20; ELIZABETH, Jesse, John, Samuel  F213
CLOUD, Daniel E52;
  DANIEL, Dan Jr, David, Joel, John, Margaret, Martha; Nancy (..)
  Samuel  D327; Daniel (3), David, Joel, John, Martha, Mary,
  NANCY (..), Nancy (2), Samuel, Sarah E411; Martha  E339;
  Joel  D599; Rebecca (Thompson) E505; Sarah (Jackson) D581
COBBLE, Adam, John  D93
COBLE, Anthony D286,E33; Austin  E42; Daniel E42,F59; David D59;
  Barbara, Cath, David, Eliz, Eve, George, HENRY, Henry Jr,
  Mary, Peggy, Peter, Sally, wife E125;
  Barbary, Caty, DAVID, David Jr, Eli, Eliz, George, John,
  Marg't, Mary, Nancy, Sally  E151;
  Barbary, Benj, Cath (..); Eliz, JOHN, John Jr, Phillip,F240;
  Sarah F240; Cath, David, Eliz, GEORGE, John, Mary, Peter, Wil-
  liam D432; Cath (..), Cath, Daniel, David, George, Henry,
  JOHN, Mary, Milly, Peggy, Peter, Samuel D447; George  D220;
  Christopher, David, Philepena (Troxler) D507; John D331,E18,90
  MARTIN, F331; Sophia (Lineberry) D346, Molly (Shaddy) D331

COCKE, William  D48
COCKRAN, Polly (Dilhu), RICHARD  D141
COGGIN, George T, Nancy (Armstrong)  F76
COLE, Anthony  E35; Eliz (Herndon)  D70; Isaiah F198;
   Jane  F227; John  D282; Lois (Wilson) E180;
   Nancy (White)  F195; Polly E408; Susannah (Scarlett) D510
COLLAR (COLLIER ?), Mary (Shelton) D71
COLLIER, Ann (Pearson, Edward, Eliza (Pearson) E273;     D523
   Chas H. D515; CHARLES, children, Patty (..) D265; Herbert /
COLLINS, Bradley, James, Jenny (Ray),Martha Ann  F11;
   Bradley E22; Enoch, Joseph D406; Isabell (Hastings) D339;
   John, Polly  E193
COLTHER see COULTHER
COMB, Eliz (Watson) D381,E263; John D327,381
COMMINS, John Sr  D197
COMPTON, Alfred D429; Alley  D566; Erasmus D462,566;
   Eliz (Christopher) F56; John E48,F170,191, Thomas D462
CONNALY, Thomas  D120
CONNER, Polly  D228
COOK, Archibald, David, JOHN, Robert, Sarah (..)  D278;
   Cornelius  F17; FRANCES F396; Hannah (Thomas) E387;
   Henry D342,364; J. D109; John D203,364,E382, John P. F171;
   JOHN SR, Sarah  F184; Maderson  E392; Rachel (Pyle) E40;
   Roland D553; Thomas D75; William  D184,E122
COOLEY, Charles  F174
COOPER, Absolom, Catrenah (Armstrong) D267; Betsy  E300
COPELAND, Abner F265
COPLEY, Claricey (..), Ilai F274; Dolly, Iseley, John E30;
   Iley, Jenney, JOHN SR, Sarah (..) D581; Mary D213
CORGIN (CARRIGAN ?), H'm  D278
CORN, Tempy (Jeffrass), Willy  F87
CORNODLE (KERNODLE ?), George, Lucy or Susy (Huffhines) E15
COTNER, Aaron, Grace, Louis, Peter, ROSANNAH  E107;
   Christiner (Huffhines) E15; Thomas D205
COTRELL, Thomas D480,E17
COUCH, Ann, Hardin, Isaac, Jacob, Rachel, Samuel, Susannah,
   THOMAS, Thos Jr, page 221; Edward D500; John E377;
   John, children Susannah (Carlton) E422; Mary F195:
   Samuel F1,5,195; THOMAS, William  F265
COULTER, Allen, Anderson, Asa, Ashley, Bartlett, Charles,
   Eliza, Fanning, Fanny, HENSON, Henson Jr, Jane, Lizzy,
   Milly, Mily ?, Sherly ?, Thomas  E280; Henson D120,374
COURTNEY, Hester Frances, JOSEPH  E25; William D136
COX, Charles F8; Caroline, Charles, Eliz, Isabella F115;
   Marg't, Nancy, THOMAS G. F115; Jeremiah, Patience (W) D529
COZART, Anthony  D253; Dicey (Carrington) F190;
   Charlotte, David, Edy B, Hiram B, JAMES, Jemima, D163a;
   Lively B, Sarah (..), Sarah, William  D163a;
   Don, Holly (Carrington), Polly (Carrington) E241; Wm. F190
CRABTREE, Abraham D510; Arch. D339;
   Abram (2), Anne, Caty (..); Eliz, George, Harriet, Hetty,
   Jacob, James, John, Martha, Nancy, Peggy, Samuel, Susannah,
   THOMAS, Thos Jr, William (2) pages 220-1;
   Abram, Charlotte, Clement, Eliz, Fanny, JAMES, John, Polly,
   Richard, Sally  E382; John E303,377;

232

CRABTREE, Amelia, Ab'm, James, Samuel, WILLIAM D334;
  RICHARD F433; Thomas D339;E287; Thos. Johnson 377
CRAIG, Abraham, Alex, David, Eliz (2), Isaac, JOHN, James,
  Mary (..), Peggy, Polly (2), Sally, Samuel; Nancy D496;
  Ab'm, Andrew, Peggy Ann D498; ABRAM, James, Jane (..) D552;
  Alex E512,F165; Ann, Ellen (..), JAMES SR, James A, John M,
  Wm. I. E146; David E91,F165; D.W. F142; Eliz (Murray) D598;
  David, Isaac, JAMES, Marg't, Nancy, Rebecca (..), Rebecca,
  William D603; Eliz, Isaac, Peggy, Samuel E65; James N. F142;
  James A. E256,267,300,426,508, F144,210; Jno D502; John D549;
  Martha (Blackwood),Mary (Blackwood) E229;
  MARY, Peggy, Polly, Samuel, Wm E103; Mary, Patsy, Peggy F89;
  Nancy F142; Nelly (Turner) D527; Susanna (White) F195
CRAWFORD, Clarissa (Shaw) F1; Eliz, HUGH, Jenny, Samuel D85;
  George F210; Harriett (Walker) E289,F170; John D206,E371;
  Hannah, JAMES, daughters,Jas Jr, John, Margaret (..) D326;
  Samuel, William D326; Mary (Walker) E109; Philip E289;
  Samuel D250,271,367,590,E141,331;
CRESWELL, Alex, Easter, JOHN, John Jr, Margaret, William D306
CRISWELL, Jane (..), WILLIAM, Wm Brown, unborn child E233;
CRESWELL, John D462; William D494,E84
CRISP, Eliz (Hardee) E57
CROOM, William D205
CROTCKETT ?, Marstain D564
CRUTCHER, Martin D478
CRUTCHFIELD, Anderson, Benj, JAMES, Jas Jr, John, Mary (..),
  mother, Stephen or Stapleton, Thomas, William D206;
  Ann (McPherson) D517; Benj, Enoch, James, John, NANCY (..),
  Nancy F273; Fanny (Pickard) D351; John D371517;
  Miriam F163; Sally (Moore) E371; William D187
CULBERHOUSE, Frances (Primrose) E368;F114
CULBERSON, ANNA ELIZ.(..), Anna Eliz, Rhoda D482
CURREY, JAMES, 3 daughters, wife, Jas Jr, John D137
CURRIE, Anderson, Ann, Asenath (Armstrong), Eliz, John E347;
  Ezekiel B. D339; Thomas E347
CURRY, Julia Ann F144; Patsy (Thompson) E425; William E425
CURTIS, Samuel E36

DALE, Deborah (..), ISAAC, Margaret D555
DANIEL, Christopher D471,614; JOHN, Susanna (..) E422
DANIELS, James D243
DANIELY, James E40      DANLEY; Mary (Truet) E191
DANNELLEY, James, JOHN SR, John, Margaret, Nancy (..),
  Priscilla, Rosanna, Sarah E311
DARBY, John D545
DARROCH, Duncan D229
DASK ?, Mary (McPherson) E428
DAUGHERTY, James D190; Sally E408
DAVIS, Ann (Cain), Edward, Wm. Cain E324;
  Anderson, Eliz (..), Eliz, Frances, James, JOHN, John Jr,
  Mary, Nancy, Robert, Sally, William, Wyatt E92;
  Archibald, Dellila, Fanny, Mary, Miles, John Rich'd E239;
  RICHARD, Sarah, Thos Capper, Winifred E239; Charles D529;
  Eliz (..), JAMES, Jas Jr E140; James D114,222,471;
  John E428; JONATHAN, wife, children E47; Kesiah F104;

DAVIS, Kiziah  D253; Miriam  F163; Polly (Strayhorn) F165;
  REBECCA F373; Richard D471; Robert  E67,353; Samuel  D33;
  Sally (Canterial)  D127
DAWES ?, James D79
DEBRULER, ANNA  F474; Wesley #195
DELEY, Isbel (..), Isbel, Resey, William  D105
DENEAL, Polly  E375
DENNING, DAVID, David Jr, Isabella D222; Jean (Boyle) D441,484
DICKEY, Aby, Eliz, Isaac N, Phebe  E332; David  E236;
  Charity (Faucett) E510; George, Mary (Garrison) E275;
  Hannah H. F191; James E237; Phebe (Hall) E255;
  Cathron (..), Hannah, Hester, James, Rachel, SAMUEL, D122;
  Sam Jr, Susannah, William D122; E.M., Franklin  E343;
  Margaret (2), Mary (..), Mary, Zachariah  E343
DICKS, Nathan D47,E167; William  E167
DICKSON, Alex  F143; Eliz (Herndon) D515; Eliz (Wilson) F63;
  Alex C, Caroline, JOSEPH, Mary Ann, Mary M, Julia Newell,
  Robert Wm (") E319; J. E56; Joseph E292; Sarah D226;
  Stewart, Thomas  D199; William  E316;
DIKSON, Adam    see DIXON
DILLIARD, Caroline, Eliza, LYDIA (..), Martha, Mary Jane,
  "other children", Willis E250; Penny, Willis F19; W.I. E76
DIXON, A.M. D457; Benj E60; Eliz (Stanford) F152;
  Hannah, James, John, Jos, Marg't, Martha, Mary, Nancy E335;
  Sally (..), Sally, STEWART, Thomas, William  E335;
  J. D75,235; James D100; Jesse, Joseph  E130;
  Mary (Lindley) E167; Sarah (Booth) D79; Thomas  F181
DOAN, Ephriam  D584
DOBYNA, Jonah  E381
DOCKERY, Caty (..), John, ROBERT  E106; John D381
DODD, James, Mariah  F249
DOLLAR, Cynthia, JONATHAN, Jon Jr, Milly, Sally  E330;
  Eliz F110; Eliz (..), HENRY, Mildred, P.., William  F167;
  James E20,173,294; Jonathan  E20; Lucy D254; Mary  F213;
  Rebecca (Guess) E294; REBECCA, Susan F268; Wm. D104,454
DONNERLY, Jane (Thomas) E139
DORCH, Young E302, his will F315;  see DORTCH
DORKRY, Eliz (Watson) F137
DORSET, Drucilla (Forrester), Wm D23        see DOSSETT
DORTCH, Emeline, Lucy, Polly, Sally  D514
DOSSETT, Nancy (Cate) D304; Phebe D535;      see DORSET
DOUGLASS, David, Henderson, James, JOHN, Marg't (..), Wm D481;
  Eliz (Bradford) E14; James D596; John D46,F172; Sam M. F172;
  Adam, George, Hannah, JOHN, John Jr, Mary (..), Rosanna D224
DUKE, Bedy, Dicey, Green, John, Polly, Reny, WILLIAM SR, F139
  Betsy, her children, HARDEMAN, John  F35; James D211;
  John F276; Washington F213; William F139; W.J. E315
DUNCAN, Chas N, Eliz, Lucy, PRISCILLA  E343; Robert D379
DUNN, Ann D533; DAVID, Drury, Nathaniel D256; Francis D136;
  Elinor, Rachel (Wilson) D67; John E37; Peggy (Nelson) E426
DUNNAGAN, Asby D406; Amelia, Dice (..), Mary, SHERID  D22;
  Sherid Jr, William  D22; Mrs. Sarah D538; William  E26
DUNNIVAN, John  D304
DURHAM, Ann (Cates) D84; Ann (Latta) F121; Arch. D84,560,E215;
  Archibald, Frances, Isaac, John, Mark, Nancy, Susannah F34;
  Thomas, Wm L, Wm Jr F34; Ezra, John E78; Isaac E112,309;
  Aron, Eliz, Ezra, Iley, John, Lucy ?, Lysias, Rebecca D103;

DURHAM, Susey ?; Thomas Jr, William  D103; Mark  D486;
   Arthur, David, Dudley, LYSEAS, Mary Jane, Susannah L.  F3;
   Tabitha, Tarleton  F3; SARAH F.  F422; Sarah (Reeves)  D605;
   Susanna  D369; Susannah (Faucette)  E163;
   Thomas  D421,E421,F178; William  D84
DURNING, Nicholas  D151
DUSKIN, William  E424,512

EASON, Margaret (Roney)  E143
ECCLES, Eliz, Jennet (..), JOHN, Martha, Mary, Sarah, Wm  D567
ECTOR, Hugh, Jas, Jos, Marg't, Keziah, SAMUEL, wife, Thos D314;
   JAMES  F348; James, Jas Jr  D105, Samuel D105,122;
   WIlliam D105,314,E10,his will F416
EDMISTEN, Sam'l  D503
EDWARDS, Allen, Cathery, Eliz, Isaac, JOHN SR, John (2) D520;
   Lucy (..), Lucy, Nancy, Richard, Roda, Stokes, Young  D520;
   David, Henry, JOHN, John Jr, Mary (..), Sell, Sus., Wm. D56;
   Eliz (Andrew), Her children E49; HENRY SR, Henry, John  E112;
   HENRY SR  F466; Robert  F92; Sarah, her children D383;
   Sarah (Fulton), Thomas D430, Thomas, Wesley, William  F224
EFLAND, Catherine (Pickard)  D351; David E382
ELKINS, Eliz (Strain)  E219,221
ELLETT, Samuel  F43
ELLICE, Patsy (Leigh)  D593              see ELLIS
ELLIOTT, Abr'm E417; JAMES, wife, Wm.  D292; Stephen  E417
ELLIS, Matthew  D592                     see ELLICE
ENLEP, John  E7
EPPERSON, Francis  F202
ESKRIDGE, Samuel  E70
ESTES, ELIZABETH  F249
ETHERIDGE, Polly (Glenn)  D475
EUBANK, Edward  E174
EULICE, Actum ?, Barbara, Catherine, Eliz (..), Eliz, Eve D346;
   Henry, John, Marg't, Mary, Molly, PHILIP, Susanna  D346;
   Allen, Cath, George, HENRY, John, Nancy, Peggy, Peter, F242;
   Reney F242; ELI F304; JOHN F322
EVANS, Asa, Eliz (..), HENRY, unborn child D427;
   Betsey, Catey, Marg't (..). Samuel, Susanna, WILLIAM, Wm D33;
   Caroline, Catherine, Mary Jane  F249;
   Eliz (Hutchins) E13; Job  E107

FADDIS, JOHN SR, Nancy (..), Nancy E201; Thomas J. D585,E153,201
FADYEN ?, Jno A.M.  F277
FAN, Jane (Coulter)  F280
FARLOW, Ruth (Lindley)  E167
FARRAR, John, children, wife  E290
FARTHING, Abner, Hargis, Joanna (..), Nancy Watkins F25
   Reuben, Thomas, William  F25; Ann (Holloway), Hargis  E355;
   Reuben  D380,E355; Stephen, William  F52
FAUCETT, Bracken, Charity, Clarissa, Emeline, Martha (..), E510
   Martha, Ralph, RALPH SR, Robert, Sarah, William  E510;
   Chesley F. E213,331,350,F23,94;  Claricy (King) E420;
   David, ELIZABETH (..), James, Joseph E235; Edward  E213;
   Edward, Frances, GEORGE, daughter, Martha (..), Ray  E141;
   Henry, James, John, ROBERT, Rob Jr, William  E137;
   JAMES, daughters, Lucy, Margaret, Mary , Rachel, Robert D309;
   Susannah (..) D309; James, John, Temperence (Palmer) E358;

FAUCETT, Eliz, Nancy, Jinney, Rebecca (..), RICHARD   E163
    Thos Samuel, Sam  E163; John, Parthena (Armstrong) F271;
    John A. E311; JOHN, children, Mary (..), Samuel  D179;
    Owbert D57; Ralph  E109,D413,F200; Rob't D306,556,E257,420;
    ROBERT H. E332; Thomas  D603,F174,198; William  D413,E67,415
FAUSSETT, Eleanor; Eli, George, James, Lucia, Lydia (..) D465
    Margaret, Polly, Ralph, Robert, WILLIAM SR D465;
FAUSETT, George D428; Robert Sr. D208; Robert E331,371,F23
FAWSETT, Thomas  F47          FAUCETT, Thomas  D172
FEAR, Lodwick  D445                                    see FOSSETT
FENN or FINN, MARY  F296
FENNELL, Betsy, Cath. W, JOSEPH, Nancy, Patience F, Patsy;
    Sally F.  F10
FERGUSON, Polly (Laws) D512; Mary (Moore) D383
FERRELL, Anderson E319,F31; Mary Ann (Dickson) E319
    Joseph, Polly D328 (this may be TERRILL)
FINDLEY, Alex D573, F191
    Anne (..), ARCHIBALD, Brice Andrew, Mineau ?, E311;
    Caty (Riley), Jacob  D365; Nathan E420,F43
FINLEY, A.T. F126, Alex page 220; Hugh, James D458
FITCH, Barbara, Empson, James, John, Mary, Susannah E365
    THOMAS, Thomas Jr, William  E365; Thomas E223
FLINT, Thomas  D468,E74,368,F114
FLINTOM, Alsa (Pratt) D446
FLINTHOM, Alsey (..), Clement, Eliz, James, JOHN, Sally  E88
FLINTOFF, Jane, John T, Mary (..), WILLIAM, Wm R. E125, Mary /
FLORENCE, Eliz (Byrd) E180,202,237                          E512
FOGLEMAN, Caty (Shaddy), George, Geo A, Rachel (Shaddy) D331
    David, Geo. D612; GEORGE F380; John, Mary (Albright) D491;
    Mathea D342; Samuel D93; WILLIAM  F428
FONVILLE, Asa, Brice, Edna, Fanna, FREDERICK, wife, Hannah,
    James, John, Mary, Sarah, Washington, William  E350
FOREST, H. D289; James E211,262; John E211; Silus D137
FORGASON, Andrew E345  see FERGUSON
FORREST, James D40,438
FORRESTER, BENJAMIN, Ben Jr, Betsy, Drucilla, Edmund, Ila  D23
    Jemimah, Josiah, Milly, Nancy, Sarah (..)  D23
FORSYTH, Anna, Barnet, Gilla, James, John, Margaret, D560
    Mary (..), WILLIAM  D560
FORSYTHE, Barnett D246; James D246,338,375;
    Harriet) Yeargin) D338,E76; William D30,246
FOSSETT, Agness (McCrory) D367; Edward D248; Robert D62,248
FOSTER, Eliz (King) E420; GEORGE F404; John F97; Sam P. F244
FOUST, Barbara (..), Barbara, Catherine, GEORGE, Geo Jr  E382
    Henry, John (2), Peter, Sally, William  E382; Daniel D73;
    Caroline R, HENRY, Robert M, Wm. M. F53; John F104;
    DANIEL, Dan Jr, Peter, Sarah (..) E124; Mary (Rogers) F217;
    Daniel, Elinor (Thompson) F134;
    Daniel, Eliz, John, Mary (..), PETER, Peter Jr, Sarah  D239;
    George, Maria D. (Holt), Geo Jr E42; Jacob, Sophia (C) E99;
    Susannah (Hornaday) E501; WILLIAM  F308
FOWLER, S.W.  F83,93
FRANKLIN, Betsy (Hancock) D487
FREE, Priscilla ? (Ward) E417    see TREE
FREELAND, Eliz F262; James, John, Polly  E65;
    JAMES, Jas Jr, Jean, John, Joseph, Mary, Susan, Thomas,
    Thos Jr  D199; John, Martha, THOMAS, his brothers  E341;

FREELAND, John J, JOSEPH, wife, Mary, Sally, Thomas, Wm  E409;
   John D552,E52; JOHN, his children, J.J., Nancy (..), Thos F200;
   Johnston, Joseph  F262; JOSEPH F406; Miriam  F163;
   SAMUEL, Seely (..), children D82
FREEMAN, Betsey, Christian, George, John, Nancy, Polly, Sally,
   Sarah (..), WILLIAM, Wm Jr  D43; Eliz (Marshill), Samuel D533;
   R. E501; Richard, SARAH  F82
FRESHWATER, Adaline, Catherine (Trolinger) F181; Sarah E267;
   Betsey, Chloe, David, Luraney, Polley, Sally (..), Sally D301;
   Susannah, Thadeus, W.A.  D301; Wm. A. D85; William  D85
FRIDDLE, Casper, Caty, GEORGE, Henry, John, Martin J, Mary (..),
   Peggy, Purley  D158
FULLERTON, Barenton, BENJAMIN, Eliz, Laney, Polly ?  E366
FULTON, David, Jesse, Robert, Samuel, SUSANNAH D506; Rob D404;
   Esther, JAMES, Jas Jr, Jane, Marg't, Mary, Sarah  D430;
FERGUSON, Mary (..) E302            see FORGASON
FURGASON, John E121,302; Nancy E113
FUTRAL, Matthew  E411

GALBRAITH, John  D85
GANDLEY, JOHN, Mary (..)  D61
GANT, Ann (..), Hannah; Isam, James, JOHN, John Jr, Keziah,
   Mary, Sarah, William, Zacharia D30; John D286;
   Betsy (Trolinger), Jonathan  F181; Margaret (Minnis) E394;
   ISHAM, his children, James, Sally (.:), William  D183
GARRARD, Carter N, Daniel, Eliz, Jacob, John, MILDRED, Samuel;
   Susy, Wm. D477; Eliz (Primrose) E368,F114; Nancy (Leigh) D593;
   Jas, Margaret (Fulton) D430; Jas, SAMUEL, Susan, Tyre E159;
   JAMES, Jas Jr, Sherwood H, Wm, Wilson  F258;
GARRETSON, Mary (Graham)  F94
GARRISON, Eleanor, GARRETT, George, Jehu, John, Levi, Mary (..),
   Rebecca E186; George D443,481; Jacob D481; Nancy (Hurdle) E16
   GEORGE, Hall, Lidia, Marg't (..), Marg't, Susanna, E11
   Wm. H., Zimree E11;  Savana  D122 see others below
GARRAT, Barbara (Albright, John E231
GARRETT, John E89; Nancy (Leigh) E292
GARROT, Averet, Caty (..) D158; Betsy (..), Stephen, ch. E243
GARROTT, Henry E73
GASKILL, Drusilla, ELIZABETH, Mary, Susan  F210
GATES, Catherine (Smith) E160; JOHN F452
GATTIS, Alex  D500,E98,221,F89; Eliz (Leigh) E92;
   Alex, Isaac, Jinnet, JOHN, Martha, Samuel, Sarah, Thos, Wm D269
   ALEXANDER, Alex Jr, Eliz, James, Jane, John, Margaret F153
   Rosanna (.:), Samuel, Thomas, William F153; Isaac D71;
   James E409,F174; Rebecca (..), WILLIAM, his children F212;
   Sarah (Blackwood) E229; Thomas  D500,F89; William E105,382
GEE , John  D374; Robert  D501
GEAR, Tabitha (Durham)  F3;     GEER or GREER, Jacob  D206
GARRISON, Brise F, ELENOR, George, John, Levi  F236; Rachel E275;
   Granderson, Henry, JACOB, Margaret, Mary, Nancy (..)  E275
GEORGE, David D439,E86,F93; Ezekiel, Matilda (Herndon) F220;
   Redding  D606; Sally (Boothe) E86;
GIBENS, Catherine (Deley), James  D105
GIBSON, Andrew D199,424; Jas. D610; Jean (Freeland) D199;
   Joseph D424,E15,33,F262; Moses F262; Rachel (Ray)  D231

GIFFORD, Margrate (Wells) D140; Rosannah E107
GIL, John D379      GILL, Thomas D324,801,F8
GILAM, Edmond D129   GILLAM, Robert E510
GILLIAM, Burwell, Charles; David, EDMUND, Edmund Jr, Eliz D489
  Mary, Sarah (..), Sarah, Susannah D489; David E272;
  James S. D84,F172
GLASS, Anne F143; Betsy (..) E143,300;
  Catherine, Mary D575; Richard E300;
  Stephen D577,E80,143,300, his will F362
GLEN and GLENN, David, Fery ?, James, John, Nanny (..), D262
  Nancy, Robert, Sally, WORHAM D262; James, William F268;
  Feriby, George W, James, JEREMIAH, Kitty Horton D475;
  Lucy, Nancy, Patsey (..), Permelia, Polly, Thos A., Wm D475;
  Jane E25,193; Luvico ? F274; Polly (Southerland) D530;
  Robert E25; Sukey (Wood) E291; Susannah (Southerland) D530
  Tyree D478,535
GOAT ?, Richard D180  see GOTT
GOOCH, I. E25; Pomphrett D539; Thomas W. F58,214
GOODWIN, Meriah (..), Samuel D94
GORDAN, Caroline E298
GORMAN, Polly (Herndon ?) D515
GOTT, Catherine (..), Richard D601      see GOAT
GREGSON, Robert D540
GRAHAM see GRAHAMS, Ann, Charity, Eliz, Fanny, George D259
  James, Jenny, JOHN, John Jr, Mary (..), Mary, Rob, Thos D259
  Catherine (Boswell), George E223; George D481,F94;
  James D481,E365,F94; John D211,F94; MARY (..), Mary (2) F94
  Robert D189,E28; William D189      see GRAYHAM
GRAHAMS, Eliz (Thompson) D568; Jas E371;
  Eliz, George, James, John D53; Robert E124; Thomas E350
GRAVES, A. F130; Ariana D520;
  Barbara, Betsy, Bostian, Daniel, David, Elias, Furby (..),
  Nelly ?, JACOB, John, Sarah D575; Calvin C. F204;
  BETSY B, Betsy C, Elijah, Elijah Calvin, Henry, Jesse Dixon,
  Ralph Lewis, Selina F. E309; E. E47,F127,132;
  Elijah D520,560; Jacob D158; Sebastian E90
GRAY, Andrew, S.C.M. ?, Wm J. F76; Betsy (Jeffries) D543;
  James, Mary (Riley) D365
GRAYHAM, Eliz, Ellick D254
GREEN, Daniel D91, his will F455; Edney (Leathers), Wm F253;
  John, Mary E. E300; Polly (Nealy) D456; Robert D401;
  Samuel D228; Rev. Wm M. E107
GREESON, DAVID, Elias, Mary (..), Peter, Polly, Samuel D610;
  Jacob E365
GRESHAM, David D192; Eliz (Rhodes), Nanny (Rhodes) D293;
  GEORGE, Nancy, Sarah (...) E20; Robert E270
GRICE, Thomas Wm. D42
GRIFFIN, Mathew (This may be Mathew Griffin Stovall) D91
  Peggy, Jas, THOMAS, Thos Jr F178: Sarah (Horn) D368;
  Thomas D424
GRIMES, ANN F447; Ann, Chas, Eliz, James, Lydia, PHEBE D52
  Phebe, Rebekeh D52; Anna, Eliz, Lydia, PHEBE, Rebecca E370;
  John D231,351,377; Lydia F157
GROVE, Sally (Sheppard) E24; Mrs. Wm. B. F137,249
GUESS, Eliz (Rhodes) E351; Eliz, Frances, Jas, John, Jos E294
  Marg't, Mary, Moses, Nancy, Rebecca, Sarah, Thomas E294
  Moses D256,E35,F337; Thos E351; WILLIAM E294, Wm D104;
  Wilson E294

GUINN, Eliz, Joseph, Mary Jane, THOMAS page 220;
  Moses D398; Rebekka (Robertson) D46      see GWINN
GUTHRIE, Elenor E416; Ann, Eliz (..), Eliz, JAMES, Jas (2) D40
  Jean, Margaret, Martha, Mary, Robert (2) D40
GUYE, Eliz (..), VINES, his children E385
GWINN, Moses D366; Wm Baker D379


HACKNEY, John F198
HADDOCK, Margaret (Dale) D555
HADLEY, Jonathan D346,447; Lydia (Hobson) F84;
  Mary (Newlin) D162; Ruth (Marshill) D533; Sarah (Lindley) E167
HAILEY, Andrew, Ezekiel E51; Ezekiel E231; JAMES F378
HALL, Alsy C, Henry, Lucy D494; Alex G, E86,149;
  Jinny, Polly, WILLIAM SR E149; Ann (Graham) D259;
  ANDERSON F290; And., Jehu, Junah, MARY, mother, Wm. E157;
  And.,ELIZABETH (..), Eliz, Jeremiah, Joannah, John, E255;
  Mary, Nancy, Phebe, Samuel C, Sarah, Wm: E255; Durham F253;
  Betsey, DAVID, Delila, Eliz (..), Estey, Rebecca, D233;
  Fanny D53; Gatsy (Truet) E191; Isaac D143; J. D141;
  John D53,73,211; Junia D567,E224,332; Jenny D221; Robert D28;
  Sarah, Shelton D221; Sally E52,D233; Sarah (Wortham) D538;
  Thomas D233,E160; Samuel D73; Thomas D233; William D535,E81;
  WILLIAM W.  E86; Wm Sr  E86
HAMILTON, Albert E213; Archibald D540; John F16;
  James, John, JOSEPH, Martha (..), William D540; Nancy E64;
  Nancy (Bird) D468; William E213,F94
HAMMETON, Elizabeth D197
HANDLY, Mary F104
HAMPTON, Alves, Duran, John, Nolan, Nolan Sr D553
  John D75, John, Noah, Nolen F57
HANCOCK; Betsey, Clarissa (..), JAMES, Jas Jr, John, Nathan D478
  Polly; Robert, Roger, Stanley, Stephen, William D478;
  Betsy, Fletcher, Nancy (..), Polly W, ROGER, Susannah, D531;
  Henrietta, NATHAN, Polly, Robert, Roger D480; Wesley D531
HANES, Dessey (Carrington), Edward E241
HANEY, Henderson, Nancy D494
HANKS, Jinnet (Armstrcng) D267; John D267,393,E297; Rev J. E137
HANNAH, Elizabeth D148
HARDEE, DAVID, Eliz, John, Martha Carlton, Polly, Sally E57;
  Eliza; Frances W, Henrietta, Luiza, Luvina D, Martha C.,
  Polly, Sally, Whitmell H, William, WINNEY E299;
  Thomas, Winney (..), William E57
HARDEN, Betsey, Jean, John, Mary, Peggy, Rebekah, Sarah,
  SARAH (..) D418; John D558                    D235
HARDIN, Betsy, JOHN, John Jr, Peggy, Polly, Sally, Sarah (..)/
HARGIS, Ann 220; Betsy (McKee) E32; Lucindy (McDade) E229;
  Dennis, Drucilla Ann (Shaw), Joseph B.S.,Maria B. E277;
  Thos V. E277; Thomas 221; Willaim D119
HARGRAVE, Jesse F68
HARLOW, Joseph D220
HARRIS , Arlas F256, ARLAS F390;
  Archer, Bulia, Casserna (..), Edney, Harrison, Marcus E259
  Nathaniel; ROBERT, Tempy, William E259;
  Charlotte, Hannah (..), STERLING D387;
  Delia, EDWARD, Ed Jr, Eliz, Mary (..), Mary, Nathaniel D36
  Sterling, Willie D36; DICEY (..), Dicey, Edna, Eliz, E386

HARRIS, Lucy, Mary, Narcissa Ann, Nath, Rufust, Temperence,
   William (2), E386; Edward, Mary F76;
   Ephriam, Elzy, Rebecca D436; Hannah (Whitted) D136,468;
   James S. E17; Nancy (Nealy) D455; POLLY F256;
   Nathaniel D592,F51,202, his will F430; Roberd D547;
   S. D491; Sterling D454; William D186
HART, Betsy, David, Gilbert, JAMES, Jas Jr, Jane, John,
   Miriam, Samuel, William F29; David F165;
   Fin, Rebecca,Susanna, THOMAS E222; Frances (Moore) D471,F142
   Gilbert D600; James D600,E287; James D87,
   John D87,308,371,E339; Joseph D29; Morgan
   Nancy (Moore) F142; Sarah D87
HARVEY, Absolom E224,332,F172; D.H. E458; Eli D47;
   Agness (..), Anthony, Eliz, Isaac, Mary, NATHAN E416;
   Edith, ISAAC, Martha (..), Nathan, William D63;
   Eliz (Hall) E255; Grace, Hannah, MOSES, his children E306;
   Jonathan D211,E275,367; Margaret D458;
HARWARD, Agatha (..) E355
HARWOOD, William D136
HASTINGS, Eliz, Ester, HENRY, Henry Jr, Isbell, James, John,
   Joseph, Margaret, Mary, William D339; Robert F134;
   Easter, Hannah, Henry, JAMES, Jas Jr, Joseph, Margaret E29;
   Nancy, Sarah, Thomas E29; Sally (ODaniel) Thos D377,E208
HATCH, ALEXANDER F456; Geo B, Sally V, Wm E303; Sale D67
HATCHETT, William D156,562
HATHCOCK, David D543
HATRICK, Robert D46
HATWOOD, Jean, John, Nancy (..), THOMAS, Thos Jr D501
HAUGHTON, Kennedy D530
HAY, Susan Jane (Sheppard) E24
HAYS, DARKIS D261
HAYWOOD, John E24
HEARTT, Harrison Bain, Harrul W, Henry J, Julian, Thos E127
HEATH, Thomas D205
HELTON, Abraham, Jas, PETER, daughters, P.Jr, Susannah D93
HENDERSON, Mrs. Ann, Richard D352; Gilley D439;
   Dicey, Eliz, Eliza C, Frances (..), James, JOHN, John Jr,
   Martha, Pleasant, Polly, Sarah, Thomas F80; J. E321;
   Maurice E321; P. D471; R. E140; Richard D276; Thomas E353
HENLEY, Rebecca E167
HENSLEE, R. F19; Richard E422
HENSLEY, Rachel (Canterial) D127
HERMAN, Jno D320
HERNDON genealogy E86, see last page of book
   Aquilla, Coslett M, Eliz, JAMES, Jas Jr, Maturine C, Nancy,
   Mary M (..), Terminia F31; Amelia (Rhodes) D293;
   Clary, DAVID, Edmond, Eliz, Frances, George, Larkin, Martha,
   Martin Pierce, Rachel, Rebecca D373;
   Coslett M, Mary M (Dickson), Maturine C. E319;
   Delilah, Edmond, Eliz, Esther, George, James, Lewis, Mary,
   Maryann, Reuben, Ruth, SARAH, Sarah, Zachariah D70;
   Elias, Eliz, Gustin, Madison, Martha, Mary (Hopson), Mary,
   Reaney, Matilda, Stanford, William F220;
   Eliz, Jas Jr, Macharine C, Nancy, Polly, POMPHRETT, Sally,
   Teresa N. D515; Eliz, MARGARET, William F379;
   George, Jos, LEWIS, Lewis Jr, Polly (..), Polly, Willis D518

HERNDON, John  D535; Hannah (Hutchins); Nelly (Hutchins) Ell;
   Lewis, Lewis Jr, Mary (Boothe), Mary, George, Jos B, E86;
   Rebecca (Rhodes), Wm. D293; Waller  D120; William R. E250;
   Willis E86; Zachariah  D535
HERVEY  see  HARVEY
HESTER, Benjamin  F35; Elijah  F14,119
HEVY ?, John  D461
HICKMAN, Wiatt  D572
HICKS, Eliz (Tatom ?)  D94; James D562,F72; John D562,F184;
   Frances, James, Jane, JOHN, John Jr, Thomas M. E285;
HILL, Eli  D136; Hannah (Anderson) E10; John  F276;
   Rebecca (Hornaday)  E501; Wm. B.  E147
HILLYARD, Dancy, LUCY, Lucy, Martha, Mary  E39
HINCHEY, David D389; Vicey (Horne) E207; William  E41,125
HINSHAW, Mary (Marshill), J.  D533
HOBBS, Caty (Clapp), John  E99;
   David, Eliz, Esther (..), Harbard, James, John, Jonathan,
   Mary, Susannah, Thomas (2), WILLIAM SR, William  D421
HOBSON, CHARLES, Lydia, Peninah, Zernah (..)  E90;
   Emily, Lydia, Pernina, ZERNAH  F84
HODGE, Agness (..), George, JOHN, John Jr (2), Joseph, Robert,
   Samuel, William  D320; Ann (Lindsay)  D483; Joseph D395;
   Robert  D395; Sally (Lindsay)  D483; William  D544
HOGAN, David  D50; Thomas $253,409; William D34,50; W.F. E409
HOGG, Eliz, Jean  D352; James, John, Thomas  D94;
   JAMES, his children, Jean, Mary Eliz, Robert  D146
HOLDEN, Berry  E112; Eliz (Whitted) D136,468; Isaac  D468;
   Eliz (..), Eliz, Harriett, ISAAC, Is Jr, Mary, Sally  D585;
   Thos W. D585; Thos D224; Thos W. E88,193,213,226,265,F11
HOLDER, Abram, Aron, Daniel, Dannel, Elijah, JOHN, John Jr D55;
   Mary (..), William D55; Nancy (Ivey) E215;
   Chesley, Daniel, Elijah, Hosea, John, Lydia, Mourning (..),
   Nancy, Polly, WILLIAM, Wm Jr  E74
HOLEMAN, Charles D521; James E188,F63,158;
   Lucretia (Horner) F202; Richard D521,E188
HOLIDAY, Thomas Sr  D555
HOLLADAY, Hannah (Newlin)  D162
HOLLAND, Mary (Turner) D527
HOLLEN, Nelly (Thomas) E387
HOLLOWAY, Bennehan ?, David, James, John, Lydia (..), Lucy,
   Milly, Lydia Caroline, Polly, Samuel, Sarah, THOMAS SR E355;
   Thomas, Wm, Williamson  E355; James, Patsy (Leathers) F253;
   John E67,F110; Thomas, Thos Sr D380; Thos Jr E67; Thos 220
   William  D380,E67
HOLMAN, Chas D456
HOLMES, Ann, Catherine (..), Hannah, Henry, Jane, JOHN E307;
   Arch'd D377, John E382; Jos, Mary, Nicholas, Sarah, Wm E307
HOLT, Alfred A. E396; Arch M, Eliza, Emily, ISAAC, Is Jr E42;
   Maria D, Mary (..), Thomas S. E42; Edwin F60,277;
   Caty (Albright), Jeremiah, Michael, Rachel  D280;
   Edwin M (2), Jane, MICHAEL, Nancy, Wm R. F126; Is. D575;
   Eliz, Hezekiah, JOHN, Milly, Nelly, Wm. E55; Isaac D203,507;
   Israel E387; James E332; Jane (Rogers), Milton S. F217;
   Jacob, Jane, Mary S, PHILEMON, Sarah (..), Wilkins  E381;
   Jean D235; Jeremiah  E15,231,261,382; Joshua  D141;

HOLT, Lewis  D558; Martha Ann (Mebane) F144; W.R. D610;
  Michael D158,286,331,476,491,579,E396,F60,229,277;
  Michael M.F204; Michael Wm F53; N, Nancy (Eulis) F242;
  Sally (Foust) E382; Samuel  E232; Sally, Thomas  E231;
  William D194,235,286,300,558,E231,232,F53; WILLIAM F306
HOOKER, NATHAN F398
HOOPER, Helen D146; James, Thos, Wm. D352; Wm. Esq. E363
HOPKINS, Bashaba, ELEANOR, Gilbert, Mary F51; Chuza D477;
  Cuza, Martha (D), Sally (Ray) F11; Gemima (Barbee) E410;
  ELZY, his children, Sarah (..) F260; G. F57;
  Harriet, James, Rebecca F157; Jane (Ray) E316;
  Margaret (Woods) D556; Rachel D163a; Samuel  D265
HOPSON, Harriett (..), Rebecca, Rosanna, Sally, Wiley F261
  WILLIAM, Wm.H.H. F261; Rebekah (Brewer) E220; Wm. D103
HORN & HORNE, Alfred E150; Abel, Agnes (..), Edith, D368
  John Tapley, Nancy Ann, Sarah, Thos A, WILLIAM, Wm W. D368;
  Alford, Alsey, Betsey, John, JOSHUA SR, Joshua, Milly E207
  Mikey (..), Polly, Vicey, William  E207; Ann (Couch) 221;
  Archibald D615; CATHERINE, Eliza, John, Nancy Cath. F227
  Norflet Anderson, Wm. Page F227; James E270; Jas B. D615;
  Michel (Rhodes) D293; Susannah (Couch) 221; Thomas A. E385;
  Thomas, Littleberry D300; William  D68
HORNADAY, Alfred, Anna, Balam, Christopher, Hester, Jemima,
  Lewis, Mary (..), Mary Ann, Rebecca, Ruth Elinor, Sally,
  WILLIAM F28; Dinah (..), Ezekiel, Hester, John, LEWIS,
  Lewis Jr, Polly, Rebecca, Ruth, Simon (2), Susannah, Wil-
  liam  E501; Isaiah E107; Lewis D555; Ruth (Piggott) D529
HORNER, Eliz (Smith) E160; Eliz D601; Jeff F139; John E265;
  Eliz, Jefferson, John, Mary, Lucretia, Sarah (..), THOMAS SR,
  William  F202; Olive (Linch) D392; William E302
HORNIDAY, CHRISTOPHER, Chris Jr, Daniel, Isaiah, John,
  Priscilah, Samuel, Solomon  F104
HORTON, Anthony W, Cath. H. (Shaw), Neal H. E277;
  Eliz, HENRY, Hugh, Sarah  D213; Horton E2
HOUSE, Betsey, Nancy (Trice), Polly D114; may be HORNE
HOWARD,  Eliz (..), Henrietta, James, John, Richard, D577
  THOMAS SR, Thomas  D577 Betsy D577; Thomas E296;
  ELIZABETH, Eliz Christmas, Henrietta, Richard E80;
HUBBARD (HUBBERT), Mary (Thomas E139; Nancy (Thomas) E387
HUDGINS, Willoughby  E317
HUDSON, Isaac  D256; Tabitha (Boothe) E86
HUFFIND, John, Rachel (..) F2
HUFFHINES, Betsy, Caty, Christiner, DANIEL, Jacob, John, Geo,
  Lucretia (..), Mary, Susy ?, Sally  E15;
  Eliz (Tickle) E33; Mary (Tickle) E19
HUFFMAN, Catherine, DANIEL, Eliz (..), John, Lydia, Rachel,
  Polly ?, Sally, Susan F222; Eliz (Troxler), Peter D507;
  Molly (Eulice) D346;
HUGGINS, JACOB, Jacob Jr, Mary (..) D395; Jacob D566
HUGHES, Anderson, Ann, Eliza, Franklin, Jane, John, Jos.F,
  JOSEPH D, Paisley, Rice ?, Sarah (..), Samuel, Sidney,
  Thomas  F193; Andrew D223; Chas D334; Jas D. D398;
  J.D. E36,343,366; John D314,507,E105; Joseph D107;
  Joseph D. E299; William, his wife  D130
HUGHS, Andrew, Eliz, JOHN SR, John, Samuel, Thomas E379;
  Sarah (Clark) F191

Name of testator is in capitals

HUNT, Barbary E107; Mary (Cate) D304
HUNTER, Aron D602; Alex, ANDREW, Christa, Eliza, Eliz,
   Frances, Harriet, Jane, Nancy, Sary, Thomas, Susannah E253;
   Frances, James, Jean, Marget, Nancey (..), ROBERT, D76
   Robert Jr, Samuel D76; Sintha (Lloyd),her children F38
HUNTINGTON, Mary (Palmer), Roswell, William E358
HURBIN ?, Sarah (Gilliam) D489
HURDLE; Benj F197,236; Christian, Hardy, James D261;
   Benj, George, HARVEY, Henry, Jacob, James, Josiah, Milly E164
   Nancy, Rachel, Sarah, Thomas E164; George E94,F160;
   Hardy D43,215,278,301; Henry E186,213;275;James D596,E345;
   Josiah E191; Margaret (Garrison) E275; Obediah F1,267
HURLEY, Mary (Rhodes) F6
HUSKE, Ann Alves D146; John D146,352
HUSKIN, Joseph F68
HUTCHESON, James D101,130,271,E94; Ross D101
HUTCHERSON, JAMES, Patience, Sarah (..) F160
HUTCHINGS, Thomas D427
HUTCHINS, Eliz, Hannah, MOSES, Nelly, Peggy, Thomas E13;
   James D293; John E321,418; JOHN, Polly E56;
   Lewis E243,368,F58,114; Sarah (Rhodes) F6
HYMER, Samuel E107

INGOLD, Adam D447; Adam, PETER, his wife, Wm,"other heirs" E89
ISLEY, Boston E395,F4; Christian E395
ISELEY, EDWIN F346; George D575; GEORGE F419;
   Jane (Carmichael) D559; John E118; Malachi D575;
   Rachel (Phillips) F4
IZZLE, William D452
IVEY, Andrew, JOHN, John Jr, Joseph, Mourning (...), Nancy,
   Patterson, Sally, William E215

JACKSON, A.G.,Benoni, Eliz, ISAAC, Jacob, James, Levi, Ruth,
   Sarah D581; Abner, Eliz, Jacob, JAMES, Jas Jr, Mary, Ruth,
   Susanna, William E22; Alfred, BENJAMIN, Bieb ?, Charity,
   Edy, John, Letty (..), Love, Malehu, Nancy, Polly, Ruth E122;
   Anderson, George, JAMES SR, James, Nancy (Riggs) E193;
   Anderson, James (2), Martha Ann (Ray), Polly (Ray) Ell;
   Benjamin D237; Benoni, ISAAC JR, Isaac, Jacob, James, Levi,
   Mary D412; Benoni, Isaac Sr D411;
   Benoni, Brice, Eliz, ISAAC SR, James, Jno, Mary (..) E117;
   Mary, Ruth E117; Charlotte (Crabtree) James E282;
   Betsy, Catherine, Jacob, James, Margaret; Ruth (2) E193;
   Eliz (Armstrong) D267; Isaac D57,166,267,E37;
   James, Jas Jr D556; RACHEL F413
JACOBS, , Rachel D148;
JAMES, Abner F4; Deborah (Lindley) E167;
   Eliz (..), George, JESSE, his grandchildren, Riley F110
   Russell, Thos, Wm F110; Eliz (..), THOMAS , children E268;
   Jane (Thompson), John E396; Thomas E35
JAMISON, Ellen (Ray) D608; Jane D38; Wm. B. D608,E107
JARROT, Mealey (Veazey) F14
JEFFRASS, Addison, Andrew, Betsy, Charles, DRURY, Eaton, Hugh,
   Henry, Partha, Peggy, Polly, Stephen, Sylla, Sylvia (..),
   Tempy F87

JEFRES, Cato, James, LUCY (..), Lucy, Milly, Samuel E257;
JEFFREIS, Betsy, JACOB, Jane (..), John, Katie, Mourning D543;
   Reuben D543
JEFFREYS, Isaac E344; LUCY (..), PETER D244
JENKINS, Ann (..), Jonathan D150, Charles, John D257;
   Joseph, Reany (Herndon) F220; Nancy (Owens) D257;
   Sarah (Linch) D392; William E353
JESSE, John, Mary (Armstrong) D267
JIMMASON, John D221
JOB, Jonathan F72
JOHNS, Eliz (..), Eliz, Henry, JOHN, Kitty, Patsy, Thomas,
   Susannah D42
JOHNSON, Anna, Calvin, Herman, JOSHUA, Lydia, Mary, Sarah (..),
   Susannah F68; Elenor (Robertson) D46; Ruth (McPherson) D517
JOHNSTON, Abigail E70; Avery, JACOB E20; Charles D. E103;
   C.W. E41,512,F174,200; Charles W. E99,F89,153;
   Charles, James, Jean (McCown), John, John Jr, Thos. page 220;
   Daniel D574; David, Isabel (..), JOHN, his daughters D549
   John Jr, Margaret D549; Elenor (Rogers), James, John F217;
   Fanny, ISABEL (..), James, Jane E393; James D25,E363,F62;
   George D269,552,568,611,E99,F155; George J. E103;
   Jennet (Thompson) D568; John D25; Mary D259;
   Mary (McCulloch) D503; Thomas M. E41
JOLLEY, Susannah (Durham) F34;
JONES, AQUILLA SR F309; Christian (Alston), Solomon D450,542;
   AQUILLA, Aquilla Jr, James, John, Mary D119;
   Catherine (..), Eliz, Frances, ISAAC, John Orange E261
   Samuel, Sam Stockard E261; Delia, FRANCIS F198; Ed. D94,276;
   Ed. Sr, Henry W, Martha Ann, Nancy (..), NICHOLAS, Polly E216
   Rebecca, Washington, Willis Simpson, Wm E216; George F9;
   Edward, Nancy (Barbee),Willis E321, George W. F190,276;
   Eliz (Eulice), Eleanor (Lineberry) D346; Isaac D137;
   Jenny (Ray) D231; John E371,F227; JOHN F340;
   Johnson, Margaret, MARY F187; Margaret (Marshill) D533;
   Margaret (Moore) E371; Moses D213; Nancy (Loyd) E342;
   Patsey D425; Samuel E394; Susannah Ludlo D553; Rosanna E408;
   Thos F112; Tignal E87; Westward A. D545,E87; Wm F. E394
JORDAN, Charles, George E237; Jacob, John, Mary, Levina E275;
   George, Jacob, JONATHAN, Mary (..), Nancy, Polly, ch E94;
   Sarah D70
JUSTUS, Allan, Anna (..), Davy, STEPHEN F52;

KECK, Barbara, Caty, Daniel, David, Eliz (..), Eliz, George,
   HENRY, Henry Jr, John, Mary, Sally, William D579;
KEEK, GEORGE, Geo Alex, Polly (..), "other children" F72
KEELING,Benj, Betsy, Ceney, Dolly (..), Dolly, Gregory Perry,
   James (2), John, Rachel, Thomas, WILLIAM, Wm Jr E37; Wm. D42
KEGGS, Mary (Piggott) D529
KELL, Allen, Anna (..), Charlotte, Sally, WILLIAM E382;
   Eliz, Robert, THOMAS, Thos Jr, William E58;
   JOHN, John Jr, Rebeckah (..), Thomas, Wm, children D28
KELLY, Anne E245; Betsy, John, MARY, Nancy E213;
   Betsy, Charity, Dolly, JOHN, John Jr, Kesiah, Mary (..) E115
   James ? Sr D514; John sr D178,208; John F208; Nancy E115;
   Nancy (Fennell) F10; Mary (Berry) D408;

KEMRUCE ?, Frederick E42
KENNION, Paul, Marie (Shaw) E277
KERR, David White, Margaret Graham, Samuel E508;
   Eliza Jane, EUPHENCE B.,son, Samuel, Susan  F50;
   James D446,E344; Margaret F409
KIMBRO, Eliz, George, John, Powel F242; Frederick D522;
   Margaret (Eulice), Susanna (Eulice) D346; Caty (Byrd) E178;
KIMBROUGH, Catherine (Byrd) E202; James D480,530,535
KIME ?, Sally (Clap) F229                                    F89
KING, Anderson, David D464; Ann (Kirkland) Jinney, Jos, Marg't /
   ARMOUR SR, Armour, Elender, Garrison, Henry, Jennison ? F235
   Margret, Mary, Nancy, Rachel (..), Rachel, Sam, Sarah F235;
   BAXTER, Charles, Dolley, Eleanor (..), Eliz, Hannah, John D34;
   Mary, Nancy, Nathaniel D34; Benj, Claricy, Eliz, Nancy E420
   Rebecca, ROBERT, Sally E420;
   Betsey, Biddy, CHARLES, Chas Jr, Eliz (..), Edw'd D282
   Nathaniel, Shurley, William D282; Calvin, Jeremiah, Julius,
   JOHN, John Jr, wife, Thomas (2) D152; Charles E404;
   Dicey, Eliz (..), Marsha ? Ann, THOMAS, Thomas Jr E315;
   Eliz, Fanny, John, Marshall, Peggy, Pleasant, Sarah (..) D571
   Senea, WILLIAM, Wm D. D571; Elizabeth E275,F202;
   ELIZABETH (..), Hezekiah, John (2), Levina E385;
   Fanny (Brewer) E27; George E275; James D211;
   Fanny; NATHANIEL, Nath Jr, N.I., Polly, Sally (..), E61;
   Sally, Thomas, William E61; JOHN D186,286; N.I. E321,402;
   Mary (Barbee) E410; Nancy (Wood) E291; Samuel F45;
   Nathaniel, Sarah (Gattis) D269; Vicy E64
KINNEY, Frederic  D331; Susannah E107
KIRBY, Elizabeth D154; Isaac E155; James F198
KIRK, James D371; John L., John L.F. D423;
   James, John, Josiah, LEWIS, Rebecca, Sarah (..), Wm D289;
   Sarah D423; Thomas D375
KIRKLAND, Alex, John, Margaret (..), Martha, Mary, Phebe, E388
   Susan, WILLIAM E388; Ann, Betsy, Eliz, Isabel, James F89
   Jinney, John, Johnston, JOSEPH SR, Joseph (2), Peggy F89
   Samuel, William (2) F89; John Umstead E182; John U. F29,245;
   Joseph D269;E103,183; Margaret (..), WILLIAM D318;
   William D94,291,371,387,697,E98,99,103,182
KIRKPATRICK, Caroline, Eliz, Frances, HANNAH (..), Hannah F112
   Joseph, Nancy, Paisley, Samuel, Sarah Jane F112; Nancy E237

LACKEY, Robert E139,156,311
LACEY or LACY, Frances (Durham) F34; Philemon F52
LAFFATEE, Vance D559
LAGREE, Christopher, Edward, Isaiah, Jemimah, John, Lixiah,
   Patsy, Polly, William  F104
LANDERS, Jno D373,462; John D566,592
LANE ? or LOVE ?, Geo. D205
LAPSLIE, Eliz; JAMES D588; James D294,398,458,537, E10
LASHLEY, Alex, Betsy; Elijah, Fanny, Hannah (..), Hannah E50
   Jean, Nicy, Rachel, THOMAS, Thomas Jr E50
LASLEY, Margaret (Hastings) E29; Nancy F215; Thos D351,F54
LASSITER, R.W. F47

245

LATTA, Amelia, Ann, Arena, Elenor, Eliz (..), Eliz, Fanny,
James, Jas C, Jane, John W, Jos H, Mary, Rachel, THOS. F121;
Ashahel M, Caleb H, Eliz (Wilson),Jackson, Solomon E188;
Caroline L, Eliz I, James, John Cabe, JOSEPH, Mary P. E66
Nancy A, Sarah (..), Thomas E66; Hannah E355;
James, JOHN, John Jr (2), Joseph, Maria, Thomas E67;
James D304,309,392,475,485,E355,F258; Jas Jr D44; Js Sr F110
James, Nancy (Allen) D178; John D52,E58; John Jr D104,434;
Jane (Scarlett, Mary (Scarlett), Sally (Scarlett) D510;
JOHN, John Jr (2), Mariah, wife D525; John J. D564;
Joseph D586,594; Joseph H. E29;
Mary (Jackson), Susanna (Jackson) E22; Thomas E163
LAWS, Alsey, Charles, David, Eliz, Frances (..), Frances D512
George, James, Jinney, Jonathan, Margaret, Nancy, D512
Polly, Rebecca, Sally WILLIAM D512; Eliz, Leonard, Wm. E302;
Ezekiel E107,D454; GEORGE, Geo Jr, Leonard, Sarah (..) D454
Thomas, William D454;  James E296
LAYCOCK, Delilah, Disey, Eliz, Easter, JOSEPH  or THOMAS Sr ?,
Joseph, Nelly, Rosea (..), Sally, William E204
LAYNE, John D215
LEA, Andrew F186; Gabriel B. E54,84,178,F23,186, E53;
Maria, Martha, Mary Ann, Joel B, Wm M. E53; John, Martha /
LEACHMAN ?, Susannah (Boswell) E223                      F186
LEATHERS, Ann E159; Fanny E355; Fielding E87,159,257;
Edney, Eliz (..), Eliz, JAMES, John, Kintchen, Patsey F253
Moses, Sally, William F253; James E315,507; John E355;
J.B. E231,F260; James B, John B, Parthenia (Armstrong) F76;
Moses, Polly (Duke) F139; Wm D545; WILLIAM, wife, ch. E87
LEIGH, Aleus ?, Betsy, Caty, Dianna, Ewel, Jack B, Jane D593
JOHN, Lear, Nancy, Patsy, Richard, Richardson, Sam. D593
Sullivan, Susannah, Thomas, William D593; Anne, Jack B. E92;
Anna, BETSY, Nancy, Sullivan, Thomas, Wm E292;
Gabriel B. Leigh E95; Nancy (Carlton) E422; Richard E111;
R.S. E273; Sullivan E111,F31;
Richard, Susan, WILLIAM, father, wife (..) George F93
LEMMONS, Jacob D615
LESTER, Patsy (Fennell) F10
LEWIS, Agnes (..), Charles, Frankey, Parsons, WILLIAM  D539;
Eliz, Fielding, Frances, Henry, Jane (:.), John, Mary D151
Robert, THOMAS, William D151; Fielding, Nancy (Wood) D564;
FIELDING, John C, Mary, Nancy (..), Nancy, married ch. F401;
John F4,146; Polly (Hutchins),Wm. E56; William D510,E173
LEWTER, Sally (Fennell) F10; Wm. H. E155
LINCH, Aron, Eliz, JAMES, Jas Jr, Jean (..) D130;
Cleaton, Darling, Gillee, Jackson, JOHN SR, John D392
Olive, Rachel, Sarah D392; Hannah & Susannah (Dickie) D122
LINDLEY, Aaron, Phebe (McPherson) D517;
Catherine, Deborah ("), Ellender, Gubelma, Hannah E167
JONATHAN, Jon Jr, Martha (..), Mary, Owen, Quinton Esther ,
Ruth, Sarah, Thomas, Wm, Zaccheus E167; Gracy, James D170;
Grace (Chambers), Hannah (Chambers) D251; James D509;
JONATHAN D317; Owen D170,172,251; Rachel (Thompson) E505;
Thomas D239; William D317a
LINDSEY, Ann, ELI, Eunice, James, Jane (..), John, Josiah B.,
Martin Luther, Polly, Robert, Sally D483; Patsey D384;
I.B.Bethiah, Jas C. F191; James D26,E375,F354, page 220;
Martha (Brewer) F224

246

LINEBERRY, Cath (Eulice), Eleanor, Geo, Sophia, William D346;
LINER, John D203 This is actually the will of JOHN LINN
LINES, Herbert E17
LINGO, Eliz (Owens) D257
LINN, James, JOHN, John Jr, Margaret, Mary, Nancy, Sarah D203;
   JAMES, Mary (..), their children E7; Mary (Eulice) D346
LINK, John D601; Silas M. E259,268,351,355,412,F110,167,258;
   JOHN, his children his wife, Silas, William E185
LIPSCOMB, Wm. F253
LLOYD, Atlas J, Cornelia A, Delilah (..), Eliz, Frances F38
   Lorren O, Sidney S, Sintha, Sophrinia C, THOMAS, Thos M F38;
   Eliza D30; James D30,E421; Mary E421; Polly (Thrift) E334;
   Thomas E215; Winnie (Weaver) F168;    see LOYD
LOCKHART, Billy, David, Isaac, John K, Peggy, Sally  E115;
   John, Sally E213;
LOFTIN, Betsey, Catherine, Eliz (..), JOSEPH, Leonard D205
   Vineter ?, William D205
LONG, Alphonso, JOHN SR, John, Mary W, Nancy, Polly, E400
   Rachel, Rebecca, Sally  E400; Fanny (McAdams, Wm. E161;
   Anderson, ANN, Charles, Eliza, George, James, Mary, E212
   Nancy, Thomas E212; Hezekiah F206; James E183; Jojn D496;
   Anderson, Boathenia ?, Charles, George, James, JOHN E65
   Nancy, Peggy (..), Thomas, William  E65;
   Jane (McCauly) F23; Jno F68; John Jr E122,417,125;
   Margaret (Blackwood) E229; Mary (Latta) F121;
   Osmond F. F115,116,245,249
LOVE, .. F1; Dilly Ann, HIRAM, John, James, Mary, Rob, Wm D458;
   Nancy D256; Snelson E510,F244
LOVER ?, Jas F235
LOVIN ?, Arthur ?        LOVINS, Anth. D130
LOW, LOWE, Caty (Huffhines), David E15; John, Nelly (Clapp) F229
   Lewis F240; Ludwick D610; Sally (Huffhines) E15; Western F171
LOYD, FREDERICK, Lacey, Mary (..) D142; Frederick jr, John D142
   Eliz, Green, Hannah (..), John, Mary, Nancy, Pleasant E342
   Rebecca, Sarah, Thomas, WILLIAM Sr, Wm E342; Lacy D501;
   Jane (Hunter), Nancy (Hunter) E253        see LLOYD
LUE, John, Penny (Clap) F229; Peggy (Friddle), Michael D158
LYNCH, DANIEL, Logan, Polly (..), Sarah Ann E265; Lemuel F94;
   Jesse, Moses, THOMAS D438; Thomas E178,211,319,F170,188
LYNN, James D515; Sarah (Trice) E422,F48; Wm E56,330. see LINN

MABREY, Randolph C. F210          MABURY ?, Nancy F245
MACQ...?, Samuel D93
MADDEN, Edith (Harvey) D63; Samuel D526,E175
MAJOR, John, William  D75
MAKINS, William F97
MALLORY, James E418
MALONE, David E410; Ellis E82, Emmely E410
MANGUM, Charity A. F35; Charity (Cain) E324; Elisha D91;
   Ellison G. F139; Eliz. E386; J.H. E248; P.H. E241;
   Martha, REEVES, his children, William F214; Presley H. E319;
   Reny (Duke), W.G. F139; Willie P. E258,324,F35,92
MANN, NATHAN  F215
MARAS, Sukey (Nicholson) D612
MARCOM, MARCUM, Amelia, Benj, Celia, Edmond, Eliz, Henderson M,
   Isaiah, Nancy, Nathan, Patsey, Polly, THOMAS, Thos Jr,Wm F17;

MARCOM, MARCUM, Aaron, Anna (..), Cintha, John, Polly E205
  RICHARD, Spencer, Wilie, Wm, Willis E205;
  Caroline (Dickson), Joseph, Mary E319; Eliz (Trice) E422,F48
  Isaiah D160,593,E122,410; Jane (Pearson) E273; John F220;
  Margaret (Carlton) E422; Willis F220
MARIS, Aaron E167; Thomas E167; William D572,E36  see MARAS
MARLET, George F8
MARSHALL, Ann, Eliz (..),Eliz, Mary (..), Rachel, WILLIAM E60
  Dinah E501; Jacob D239; John D140,475,612; Thomas D553;
  Temperance D553, William Jr E60
MARSHILL, Anna, Eliz, Grancis, JACOB, Jacob Jr, John D533
  Marg't (..), Margaret, Mary, Ruth, Ruth (..), William D533;
  Jacob, John, John Jr D595; Joseph E120; Eobert E121
MARTIN, Eliz, George, HENRY, Jane, Nancy, Peggy, Polly D431
  Rebecca, Robert, Sarah (..), Sally D431; George E365;
  John, D26; Nancy D261
MASON, Addison, Berry, Eliz, Joseph, Mary (Herndon) F220
  John, Leroy, Nancy F220; Betsey, Marg't, Nancy, Nelly D500
MASSEY, Abner D233; ABNER, Armon, Christilly, Corinda F83
  Hardy, John, Joel, Kellister, Lavinia, Louisa, Miriam F83
  Valinia ?, William F83; James D509; L., Sarah E421;
  Rachel (Pearson) E273;
MAULDER, Eliz (Borland) D602
MAURY ?, Major Abraham D23
MAY, Barbary (..), Barbary, Catherine, DANIEL, Dan Jr E36
  David, Jacob, Mary, William E36; John D124; Pleasant E363
McAdams, Egness, Eliz, James, REBECCA, Rebecca Jr D250;
McADAMS, Fanny, ISAAC, Jane, Peggy (..), Rebecca, Wiley E161;
McADAMS, Ann (..), Armstrong, Catey, Mary, Peggy, TINNIN E9;
  Benj, Catherine, Sally (Roney) E143; James D271;
  Catherine, Joseph, Peggy F271; Joannah (Hall) E255;
  Margaret (Murray) D598; Sarah (Hall) E255; Wm. D257
McBROOM, Andrew D236,269
McCADDAMS, Absalom; JAMES, Jas Jr, Jos'h, Rebeckah D187;
  Caty (..), David, Eliz, Franky, HUGH, Hugh Jr, Isaac D248
  James, John, Joseph, Mary, Nancy, Tinnin, William D248;
  Catherine, Fanny (..), Hugh, James, Margaret, Martha E318
  Nancy, Samuel, WILLIAM, Wm Jr (") E318; ROBERT F293;
  Samuel D540;
McCAIN, Elizabeth D412
McCALLISTER, Margaret (Robinson) D184
McCAMEY, Catherine (Troxler), James D507
McCANLESS, David, James, JEAN, John, William D197; John D48
McCAULEY, McCAWLEY, A. E511; ANDREW, Jane, Johnson, Mary F23;
  ANDREW, And. J, Hannah, John W, Martha, Robert, Sarah F186;
  Archibald, CHARLES, Crawford, Eliza, Henry, James E183
  John, Johnston, Matthew, Mary (..), Mary Jane, Sarah E183;
  Benjamin, Catred (..), Charles, James ("), John, Matthew E97
  WILLIAM, Wm Jr (2) E97; William (2) E183; Charles E180;
  Chas, Elender, Eliz, George, Jane, John, Martha (..) D611
  Martha, Mathew (2), William D611; Chas J.F.,Ellen Jane E283
  James, JOHN, Lucinda, Marthy E, Mary, Mathew (2), E283
  Nancy F. (2), Orella D, Verlina Ann, William E283;
  CHARLES, Eliz (..), George, Matthew (2), E404; Hunter E290;
  Eliz (Wilson) E180; Grandison, Hamilton, Sarah (Bradford) /
                                           E14;

McCAULEY, McCAWLEY, JAMES W. F383;Jane (Blackwood) E229;
John D120,598,E61,146,219,251,F174; Margaret (Blackwood) F174;
JOHN, Mary R. (..), Robert W. E53; MARTHA F319;
Matthew E41; Matty (Walker) D336; Robert D465; Thomas E213;
William D50,560,E180,212,321,F383
McCLARY, Andrew D127
McCLENNIN, Rebecca D317a
McCLUER, Ann, E.D., Eliz, HENRY, Henry Jr, James, John D156
Mary (..), Mary, Sarah, Susannah, William D156
McCLUSKEY, James D458; William D483
McCULLOCK, John Sr  D42  see McCULLOCK
McCOLLUM, Henry E404,F38; James F136; Jane (McCauley) E97;
Levi E195,311,F137
McCORD, James D380
McCOWN, Agness, GENET (..), Jean 219,220; Moses D581,E20,35
McCOY, Sarah (Herndon) D70
McCRACKEN, Abigail, Alex, Joseph, Martha, Priscilla (..), E339
Robert, Samuel, Stephen, THOMAS SR, Thomas E339;
JEREMIAH, John (2), Sarah (2) D66; John D508; John W. E222;
John, SAMUEL, Thomas F8; John, Susan (..), THOMAS, Thos F264;
Rhoda (Culberson) D482; Samuel D451,E269,F124; SARAH D138;
S.M. E106; Thomas D174,E222,F8
McCRAY, Ann, GEORGE, George Jr, James, John, Margaret D211
Sarah (..), Sarah, Susannah D211; Mary Ann (Roney) F164;
George, Patience (Hutcherson) F160; Jas F235;
McCRORY, Agness, Andrew, David, Jane, JOHN, John Jr, Rob. D367;
DAVID, James, Mary Jane F62; James D460,465; John D160;
DAVID, David Jr, John, Thomas, William  E415; Wm. F152
McCULLEY, Hardy, John, Miles, Milly, Sarah (Hurdle), Sarah,
William E164; LETTICE E213; Margaret E211,
Moore, ROBERT, his children, Sally, William  D574;
McCULLOCK, ANDREW SR. D344; Andrew, Deborah, Eliz, George D503
John, JOSEPH, Jos Jr, Mary, Thomas, William  D503;
Eliz, John D156; JOHN, children, Joseph, Patience J. F143;
MARGARET F343
McDADE, Edward d406; EDWARD, John, Lucindy, Peggy Jane E229;
Henderson C, James B, JOHN, John A, Levina (..), F208
H.C.; J.A. E229; John D219,483,583,E505; Patterson H. F208;
John, John Sr, Lucinda, MARGARET J. F96
McDANIEL, Alez, Elenor, Eli, Eliz, James, Jean, JOHN, J. Jr E62
Margaret (..), Margaret, Susannah E62; Charity (Wells) D140;
ELI, Eliz (..), James, John, Joshua, Peggy, Sally, Susy D241;
Eliz, Henry, Jane, Jesse, Peggy, SAMUEL, Sally, father  F256;
I or J. C. F193; Jane or Jeane (O'Daniel) D377,E208;
Joseph; Nelly (Capps) E308; Margaret (Wilkerson F7; Wm F256;
Martha, MELCHI, Wm E209; Nancy (Watson) E263; Sarah (P) D561
McFARLAINE, Eliz (Horton), Henry, James, John, Larcan D213
Thomas, William D213
McFARLING, Thonton D495
McGEE, J.W. E418
McGINNIS, Judy F245
McJEAN, John F50
McKEE, Aliz, Cath (..), JOHN, John Jr, Mary, Robert D160;
Anne, Betsy, David, Dolly (..), Dolly, James, Rankin E32
Victory, WILLIAM, Wm Jr  E32; Jon R. E408; J. D468,E287;

McKEE, Lydia (Ray) E175,248; Polly, Robert D67;
  Rankin D414,E175,248
McKERRALL, William E271; Wilson E287
McKINZIE, Alex  D318
McKISSICK, Thompson, William D148
McLEAN, David E402
McLEMORE, JOHN C D371
McMANAMY, James, William  D40
McMULLEN, Alex D163a; Ann, James, Jane, John, Marg't D64
  Mary, Rachel, Rebecca, SAMUEL, Sam Jr, Sarah, Thos, wife D64
  John D38,190,166,461,559; Winnfred D213
McMUNN, Eliz, Ginny, JAMES, his wife, William page 220;
  MARY, Sarah  D573
McNEIL, George D318
McPHERSON, Ann, Betty (..); Christian (..); Daniel, Enoch,
  Edith, Hannah (..), John, Margaret, Mary, Mary (..), Othiel,
  Panay (..), Phebe, Ruth, WILLIAM, Wm Jr (2), D517;
  Eli, ENOCH, Enoch Jr, James, John, Mary, Oren, Phebe E428
  Sarah (..), Sarah, William, Wright E428; John E501
McQUISTON & McCUISTON, John E75; Susan E412
McVEY, Catherine (Lindley) E167
MEACHUM, Mary D384
MEBANE; Alexander D112,155,E335; Alex, Allen, David D201
  Eliz, George, JAMES, Jas Jr, Jenny, Nancy, Nathaniel D201
  Polly, Peggy, Robert, wife, William D201;
  Alex, Anderson, Betsey, DAVID, David Jr, Eliz (..), F144
  Fanny, George A, Jane, Martha Ann, Sidney, Wiley F144;
  David D176,324,347,E91; Geo A. E233; George E373; Wm. E233;
  David, James, Rebecca (..), WILLIAM, Wm Brown D101;
  Giles F62; J.A. D429,561,E9; James Jr. D218,155,F249;
  James D176,336,498,506,552,561,E9,247,415; James Sr. D112;
  Samuel D544; Mrs. Susan F249; Wm.M. F53; W., W.B. D30;
MEDLEY (MEDLIN): Jane (Rhodes) E351
MEGOMERY ?, Mary D458    see MONTGOMERY
MELLETT, Nancy (Craig)  D603    see MOLETT
MELVIN; Catherine (..), Elias, Eliz, JAMES, James Jr. E395
  John, Louis, Mary, Matilda, Nancy  E395
MENDENHALL, Geo C. E417                                    F198;
MERRITT, Susanna (Barbee) E321; Thomas D412; Wm. D412,E161,/
  Wm. Henry D412,E321; W.H. F168; WILLIAM H. F458
MICKLE, A. F29,249
MILES or MILER; James D263; JAMES, Nancy (..) F41; Wm. E385
MILLER, George, JAMES, his wife, Jane, Jesse, John, Lydia,
  Polly, Rachel; Rebeckah, Susan, William D594;
  George, Jesse, John, Lydia, Polly, Rebecca, RACHEL (..) E52;
  Geo, John, Polly, Rebeckah E178; James D308,414; Wm E52;
  JESSE, Jesse Jr, Margaret (..), "5 other children" F46;
  John Thompson  219; Jesse, Rebecca (..), William E227;
  Margaret (Tickle) E19
MILIKEN, MILLIKEN, Charles, Haberson, Jane (..), Jesse D390
  John, ROBERT, Rob Jr, William D390; Jesse D341;
  Elias, George, JAMES, Jas Jr, Jesse, Rachel (..) D167
MILLIGAN, Christian (Turner) D527
MILLAN, Rachel D28
MINNIS, Allen, Ashburn, James, Jane, JOHN, Lavinia E394
  Margaret, William  E394; James D423,424,E209

250          Name of testator is in capitals

MINOR, Dolly (Brewer) E27;  WILLIAM D303
MITCHELL, Betsy (Mebane) F144; David D40;Ephriam  F162;
   Caroline (..), James, Lucy, Martha, Robert, SALLY E418;
   David, EPHRIAM ; Efram Jr; Happy, Henry, James, Noah, D181
   Patsey, Randall, Shadrick, William, wife  D181; John D327;
   PERRY, Polly (..) E48; Robert E10; Rob. L. D465,403,543
MOFFITT, Libir ? E90
MOIZE, Allen, Eliz, Frances, Frederic, HENRY; John, Keziah E258
   Lucy (..), Nancy E258; Frederick D564,E204,243,291, page 220;
   John F35; Orford or Oxford F51,139
MOLETT, Isaac  E140       see MELLETT
MONKE, Andrew, John, Mary, WILLIS E51
MONTGOMERY; Alex (2), David, Eady (..), Hugh, James (2), John,
   Jonathan, Nancy, WILLIAM, Wm Jr. D434;
   Alex, Hamilton, HUGH, Hugh Jr, James, Lydia, Rebecca (..),
   William E226; Alex, Hamilton, Hugh, James, Lydia, REBECCA F22;
   Barbary, Cornelia, Daniel A, Harriet, James B, SARAH, Wm F233;
   Daniel A. F181,222; Hugh D525,556,E370; James F157;
   Jonathan D547; Rebecca (Grimes) E370; Sarah (Albright) F176;
   William D547,E7,101,F176       see MEGOMERY
MOON ?, James, Srephen E417
MOOR, Eliz (Ward), Rebecca (Ward) E296; Mary D443
MOORE, Abraham D48; Absalom, David (2), Isabel (..), James F,
   Kesiah, ROBERT, Rob Jr (2), Thomas, William (2), E224;
   ALFRED, Augusta, Caroline, Emma, Sarah L. E503;
   Anderson, DIANNA, Elennor; James, Mary, Thomas E344;
   Andrew, Diana (..), Diana, Elinor, Eliz, James, Jeney D563
   Marthey, Mary, Mathew, Robert, Sarah, THOMAS, Thos Jr. D563;
   Alston;John E57; Ast. E37,F96;  Ashahel D236;
   Betsey, Frances, JOHN, Lewis, Mary, Nancy (..), Nancy D471,
   Sally, Sampson, Susannah, Thomas  D471;
   Carter, Celia, JOSEPH, Jos Jr, Peyton P, Patsey, Susan E247,
   Wm. Stanford E247; Catherine (Robinson) D184; Elizabeth D107;
   Mary (Robinson), Michael Robinson D184;
   Eliz, James, John, Margaret, ROBERT, Sally E371; Hannah F186;
   Eliza, Philip E324; Henry, James, John D49; Capt. Jas. D29;
   Isabella (Denning) D222; James D36,E308,F65;
   James, JOHN, Mary (..) D26; JAMES, John, Robert E388,402;
   John D79,114,316;E372; John L. E239; J.L., Nancy E239;
   John, JOSEPH, Mary, Sampson D383; Joseph D248; NANCY (..) F142;
   Martha (Cole) D490; Mary (Pearson) E273; Nancy  E402;
   Patsey E388; Peyton P. F152; Stephen F115;
   Sampson D79,308,316,349,518,600,606,E66,86,02,140;
   William D94,167,322,384,390
MORELAND, FRANCIS, Joseph, Nancy (..), William D75
MORGAN, Amelia D614, Anny D55; Hardy D 14;JAMES A. D291;
   Hardy D614,E152; James A, Lemuel, James Ruffin, Mary Emeline,
   SARAH, Sally, Thomas  E152; Iddith (McPherson) D517;
   James Allen, John, Lemuel, Solomon D216; John D205;
   Mark D517; PAUL D411; Sarah D614
MORING, Henry F10; John L. F10; John E155
MORPHIS, Alexander D550
MORRAS, HENRY, Henry Jr, John, Richard, Thomas, wife D50
MORRIS, John page 220
MORRISON, Catherine, Deborah, Hannah, James, Jean, Mary, Ruth,
   ROBERT, Robert Jr, William D229;  Enoch  E28

MORROW, Elbridge, Eliza A, Eliz M, George W, Josiah , Julee N,
Mary Jane, ROBERT, his wife, Rob Jr; Sidney M, Vincent F269;
Eliz, James, Jane (2), John, Margat, Sara (..), WILLIAM D189
Geo. W. E220. James D326; Jinnet (Gattis) D269; JOHN F303;
John, Marthy E. (McCauley) E283; Margaret (Creswell) D306;
John, Rachel (Thompson) F134; Martha (Dixon) E335;
Robert E53; Sarah (Vin nt) E84; Wesley E233;
William D189,269,E371
MORTON, Benj F, Henry, Jacob, Martha, Mary; Sarah (..), WM F72
MOSER, Barbara (..), Bostian, Levy, Martin, PETER F162;
William F242;   MOSIER ?, Jacob D109
MOTLEY ?, Luvinia  E410
MULHOLLAN, Hugh  D371;
Hugh, John, MARTHA (..), Samuel, Thomas  E378
MULLAN, Almon  D33
MULLCHEY, J. E402
MURDOCK, A.C. F46; Andrew D25,199,552;                D498;
ANDREW, And Jr, Betsey, James, Margaret (..), Rob., Thos. /
Ann, Caty, David, ELIZABETH (..), Eliz (2), James (2), D399
John (2), Mary (2), Robert, William D399; David E411;
James D197,E32; Nancy (Craig) D496;  Robert D101
MURPHEY, Archibald D. D90,113,111,277,418,451,E143,396,F240;
A.D. E42,143,300,382; Arch'd E300; Hannah (Scott) F107;
MARTIN F432,D414; Victor M.   E143,261,300; Wm. D. E42
MURRAY, A. D183; Andrew E82; Eli  E48;
Ann, Eliz, JAMES, Jas Jr, Jonathan, Ruth, Sarah (..) D175;
Andrew, Eli, John, Margaret (..), Margaret, Robert D143
Walter, WILLIAM, Wm Jr D143; Eliz, JAMES, Jas Jr, Jas M,
Jennet (..), John, Margaret, Mary, Rachel, Walter, D597;
James D336,367,533; John D29,292; Joseph D533,612;
Margaret (Baker) E256; Mary (Pickett), Martha (Pickett) D561;
Thomas D567; Walter D494; William D597,E141,82; Wm Sr.D597
MYRICK, James E282

NASH, F. E271; William D505;  Mrs. Peggy  F249
NEAL, Eliza, Henry, James Monroe, John, Riley E150, Henry D468;
HENRY, his children Lydia (..), Martha E113; James D517
NEALEY, Eliz, Green, Hannah, Isaac, JOHN, John Jr, Mary (..),
Nancy, Nelly, Polly, Rachel, Sally, Thomas D455
NEASE, Anson, GEORGE, George Jr, Jacob, Molly (..), Polly,
Sally, Sampson F60; Martin, Nelly D575;
NEECE, Elias, LETTY, Milly, other daughters F21
NEEL, Polly (Horne) E207
NELSON, Alf. E394,426; Alfred, DAVID, Jennett (..), E91
Margaret, Mary, Paisley; Samuel, William E91;
Alfred, David, Isabella, James, Jane (..), JOHN, John Jr E21
Margaret, Paisley, Sam, Wm. E21; Betsey, David, George E426
Ginney, Ibby, Peggy, SAMUEL, Sam Jr E426; James E36;
John, Samuel D201; Miriam F163; Wm. E229
NEVILL, Benj, Cyntha Aris, Eliz (..), Eliz, Goodman, Goodwick,
Jesse Jr, JESSE, Samuel Parke, Selah, Solomon D263;
Goodman D502,E180,313,377; Solomon D502; Wiley Wtitsell D263
NEVILLS, Jessey E303
NEWLIN, Deborah D73,E167;D401;
Deborah (..), Hannah, JAMES, Jonathan, John, Mary D401
Nathaniel (2), Ruth, Sarah, Thos, Wm. D401;

NEWLIN, Edith, Eli, Hannah, Jas, JOHN, John Jr, Joshua  D162;
   Mary (2), Nathaniel D162; James D63,229;
   John, D73,317,486,E13,124,167,306,416,F82;
   Nathaniel D449,E120,315,F155; Olive E120; Thomas D482
NEWLON, James, John E400
NEWTON, Eliz, GEORGE, Geo Jr, Henry, Isaac, James John D44
   Lette, Mary (..), Robert, Sarah, William D44;
   George D22; Isaac D412
NICHOLS, Alvis E265,F46; ALVIS, his children, Polly (..) F257;
   Amos, Baldwin, Jannah, JONATHAN, Jon Jr, John (2), D170;
   Amos, Rachel (Riggs) E193; Delilah (Boothe) E86;
   Hannah (..), THOMAS, his brothers & sisters E153;
   Jonathan, Jon Jr. D226; Margaret (Craig) D603; Richard E175;
   Nancy (Wilson) F63; Richeson E297,316; Richardson E248;
   Sarah (Cloud) E411; Wm. Sr. F22
NICKOLS, Delila (Ray) E11
NICHOLSON, ARCHIBALD, Caty, Delilah, Dilcy, Nancy, Sukey D612;
   James D595,E11; Sarah (Albright) D595
NOBEL, John, John Jr, Martha, Mary, Robert  F23
NOBLE, John D306
NOE, Daniel, George, JOHN, Mary, Nelly, Sally, Solomon F277
NORWOOD, Eliz. D352; Eliza, Hellen, James H, Jane, John W,
   Joseph, Robina (..), Walter, WILLIAM, Wm Jr. F116; James E392;
   J.H. E392; J.W. E358; John W. F245,249; Robina D146,352;
   William D94,318,352,E195,F86
NUGENT, Jacob D517
NUNN, Charlotte (..) E76;
   DAVID H, Edith, Eliz (..), Hugh, Ilai, Sally D407
NUTT, James D359,E51

OAKLEY, Amelia (..), Barton, Martha, Nancy F276;
   Bedy (Duke), Vincent  F139
OCKELREAS, David E19
O'DANIEL, Eliz (Brewer) E27;          Susannah E78;
   Green, Henry (2), James, Jesse, JOHN, John Jr, Peggy E78;
   Henry D127,E209,369,371,388,402,F175,178,336:
   Henry Jr, HENRY, Jeane, Jesse, John, John Jr, Joshua E208
   Margaret, Margery (..), Sally, Samuel, Susanna, Wm (2), E208;
   HENRY, James, Jane, John, Joshua, Peggy, Sally, Samuel D377
   Susannah D377; Jesse E371,369,388,402,F178; JESSE F175;
   JOHN E369; John, Lavina, Margaret, WILLIAM F227; Wm. F175
ODEAN, Susannah (Edwards) D56
ODIAN ? ODUM ?, Thomas D374
ODONAL (O'DONNELL), Agness (McCown), Henry, James, Jean,
   John, John Jr, Susiana, William  page 219
O'FARNHILL (O'FARRILL ?), BARNABAS B, Nancy (..)  E245
O'KELLY, Franklin E161; William D565;
   LESLIE, his children, Nancy (..), Franklin  E75
OLDHAM, Betsey  E220; Eliz (Brewer), Thomas F224;
   George, John, William  D523
OWEN, Ownley, Samuel D150
OWENS, Relitha, Eliz, John, Lear, Nancy, ONLY, Petigrew ?,
   Samuel Sarah (..), Thomas  D257

PAINE, John, Wm. E307          PANE, D.D.  F212  see PAYNE
PAISLEY, GEORGE, his wife, John, Jos, Luisa, Mary Ann F262;
   Lemuel E236; William D438
PALMER, Agnes, Eliz, James, MARTIN, Mary, Nancy, Sarah E358
   Temperance, William  E358; James D544;
   James N, John C, MARY A, Nathaniel  F47;
   Nathaniel J. E411; William  D327,396
PALSON ?, James D114
PANNILL, Samuel, William  E39
PARIS, James F134
PARISH, Abram E47; Agnes (Palmer) Henry G. E358;
   J. E300; Joel D322                    see PARRISH
PARKER, Anzalette M, Jane (..), WILLIAM H. E380;
   David E216; DAVID F462; Drady E386; Mary (Horner) F202;
   Jesse P., Mary Ann (Armstrong) F76; Susannah (Smith) E160
PARKS, A. F198; Solomon D113
PARRISH, David, Polly (Carrington), James F190   see PARISH
PARRY, Abner  E140
PARTIN, Eve (Springer ?) E90; James D194;
   Bennett, Charles, Jane (..), John, Lennard, Lewis D120
   WILLIAM, Wm Jr  D120
PASMORE, David, William  D292
PARTICK, Wm. C. E95
PATTERSON, Amelia H, Caroline (2), David, Ferdenon M, E353
   James N, Jane, John T, MANN, Mann Jr, Martha, Mary (..) E353
   Mary A, Nancy M, Robert, Sarah M, William  E353;
   Chesley Page D216,293,427; C.P. D192,E13,148;
   Chesley M or W, E265; D. D606,E122,400; David E18;F104;
   DAVID F386; Eliz (Walker) E107; Isaac D432,606,E18,59;
   Jas. D375; James N. E239,F48,195,227,265;
   Mann. D192,389,471,E321; Mann, his daughters, Milly E76;
   Page D75,114; Sarah E13; Thos B. D399; William  E125
PATTISHALL, Delilah (Rhodes), Penny (Rhodes) F6;
   Molly (Rhodes) D293
PATTON, Alex, James, Robert D176;
   Andrew, Eliz, JOHN, Margaret  F16; James E373,393;
   Alex, Eleanor (..), Eleanor, George, Isabel, JAMES F45
   James Jr, Jane, Johnston, Margaret, Mary, Nancy F45
   Samuel, William F45; MARGARET  F365; Samuel D138;
   Mary (..), Polly, Robert, Rob Jr. D138; SAMUEL SR. F283
PAUL, James E94; Margaret (Pratt) D446; Thos. P. E347,F264;
   William E366
PAYNES, Mary D127     see PAINE
PEACOCK, Eliz (Palmer), Richard  E358
PEARSON, Ann, Eliza, Green, Jane, Joel, John M, Mary (..),
   Mary, PARIS, Rachel, Sarah, Stephen, Thomas, William  E273;
   Eliz (henderson) F80; Henry E422; Nancy (Trice), Wm. F48
PEELER, PEELOR, Benjamin D124; Anthony Redwine, Benj  E35
   Cader, Catherine, Eliz (..), Michael Sherman, Pleasant E35
   SAMUEL, Sarah, Thornberry E35
PENDERGRASS, Fanny (Coulter), Milly (Coulter) E280; John D374
PENDERGRAST, Thos.  F215
PENNINGTON, LEVI, Margaret (..)  D450
PERKINS, David  E94; Thomas H.  D86

PERRY, Dicey (Henderson), Sarah (Henderson) F80; Matildy F52;
  Peggy (Pickett) D192; Patsy (..), Persullas, PETER F, sons,
  Samuel, William F155; William F175
PETIGREW, Lear (Owens), Lavinia (Owens) D257
PETTIGREW, CHARLES F350
PETTY, Delila (Thrift) D344
PHILLIPS, ANN, Benj, Hannah, Lucretia, Polly, Rachel F4;
  F.B. E113,201; James D387,505,E2,71,F371;
  Susanna (Garrison) E11; Zachariah D424
PICKARD; Alex, Catherine, Daniel, Elisha, Fanny, Henry D351
  Isaac, James, Jesse, JOHN, John Jr, John H, Michael D351
  Peggy (..), Rebecca, Richard, Sally, Thomas D351;
  Alfred E209,F178; Elijah E335,F261; Elizah E54;
  James, Peggy (..), Thomas F178; John, John H. D231;
  Peggy (O'Daniel), Susannah (O'Daniel) D377,E208; Wm. F196
PICKET, PICKETT, Cressy D611; Catherine (Roney) E143;
  Eliz (..), Eliz, India, Jesse, Joseph, Mark, Peggy D192
  Thomas, WILLIAM D192; George D456; HENRY, Indy (..),D254;
  James E247,332; Jesse D254; Mary (Walker), Walter D336
  Catherine (..), Eliz W, JOHN, John Quincy, Julia Ann F188
  Samuel F188; Edward, Eliz (..), Eliza, Emily, Joseph E54
  Lucretia, Patsy, Polly, WILLIAM, Wm Jr. E54;
  EDWARD, James, John, Margaret, Mary, Martha, Sarah D561
  Walker, William D561; John, Samuel, Sarah (Walker) E64;
  John, John Q, Juliann, Lucretia, Vicey, William E211;
  JOSEPH, Nancy (..) E30; Mark E148,422; Mathew D450,542;
  Nancy (Wilkerson) F7; Ruth (Jackson) E117;
  Sally (Alston) D440,542; William D136,540 see RICKETTS
PICKHARD, Jane (Morrow) see PICKARD above
PICKLE, Rachel (Nealy) D455
PIERCE, Jesse, Margaret (McPherson) D517
PIGGOTT, BENJAMIN, Benj Jr (3), Eliz, Hannah, Jeremiah D529
  John, Joshua, Mary (2), Patience, Ruth D529; Jer. F28
PIKE, Abigail, Hannah, John, Mary, Nancy, Priscilla, WM E203;
  Alfred, Joel, John Jr, SAMUEL, Susanna (..), William E59;
  John Jr, Wm D140; Susanna (Ward) E18; Stephen, Wm. E417
PIPER, Elenor E386; Jno D446; Thomas F248; Wm. E355
PITTS, John D206
PLEASANT, Stephen Sr. F52
PLUMMER, Nancy (Hall) E255
PLUMMET, John D451
POE, Mary (Loyd) E342; Hasten, Rebean C. E253; R.C. F3,34
POOL, Isaac, JOHN SR, John, Samuel, Sarah F58; John F401
POPE, John F82
POTEET, John page 220
POTTER, Frances E, Thomas E418
POTTS, Ann (Blackwood), Anderson E229
POWEL, POWELL, Barbara (Albright), Elias D280;
  Barbara (Clapp), children, John E99; Thomas D375;
  JOHN, Josiah, Margaret, Mary, Oliver, Thomas D80
POWERS, Mary (..), Richard E300
PRATER, Catherine (Perry), William R. F164
PRATHER, John, Mary (Harden) D418

PRATT, Alsa, Caty, George, Margaret, MARY  D446;
   Caroline Mildred  E418; LOFTIN K  F297; Sally (Moore) F142;
   W.N.  F274; W.S ?, E330
PRENDERGAST, Tho.  E385  see PENDERGRASS
PRICE, MARTHA  E377
PRICHARD, Edmond, Milly (..), Nancy, Nelson, Rodah E313
   WILLIAM, Wilson  E313
PRITCHETT, Millicent (Wilson) E180  now spelled PRITCHARD
PRIMROSE, Aga, Ann, Eliz, Grances, George, James, John,
   Mary, Pegga, Rachel, TEMPERENCE, Thos, Wm. E368 and F114;
PROCTOR, Joseph F401; Patsy D412; Richard D447,522
PROSPER ?, Christilly (Massey) F83
PURIFY, George W. C168
PYLE, Cobb, Garrett, Henry, Isaac, JAMES, John, Joseph E40
   Mary, Moses, Rachel, Rebecca, Sarah (..), William  E40
   Eliz (..), JAMES, children, Sally, William  D562;
   Mary, Rebecca F236; James, William  D125; John E428,F197;
   Joseph (2), SAMUEL, Sam Jr D73; Sarah  E157


QUAKENBUSH, Henry  D482


RAILEY, Eliz (Chambers), John  D251,
RAINEY, Ann P, Mary A, MARY, Permelia E, William W. D590;
   B.A. D300; Benjamin D101; Isaac D67; James E150,207;
   Benjamin, Ben. Abel, Isaac, John, Milly, Nancy (..) D286,295
   Nancy, Sally D286,295; Susannah F227; Wm. D175,199;
   Young E. E207                          see RANEY
RANDLES, Elizabeth D412    REYNOLDS ?
RANEY, Cathrin, DAVID, David Jr, James, Jenney, John D68
   Margaret, Mary, Siney or Liney, Susannah  D68;
   David (2), Mary (..), WILLIAM, Wm Jr. D379; Isaac D40;
   John D67, Mary (Trolinger) F181; Nancy (Leigh) E92
RAINS, Rains D584
RASBERRY, John, Sarah (Palmer) E358
RAY, Abijah  D243; Alex, DAVID, David Jr, Henry; Hugh D235
   James, Jenny, John, Mary, Nelly, Rachel, wife, William D235;
   Ann, HANNAH, Lydia, Matthew D509; Benton F260,253;
   Betsy (..), David, Henry E50; Bogan, Charles, Jane E316
   James (2), John (2), Rebecca, Sally, Thomas, WILLIAM E351
   Wm Jr (2) E316; Charles, DAVID, children, wife E297;
   Peggy Jane, Sally (..), Susannah  E297; David D94,119,208,
   David D184,317a; David L, Eliz B, Griffin L, Mary E, E232
   PETER L. E232; DAVID, Ellen, George, Griffin, Jane (..),
   Peggy Jane, Peter, Petronilla, Robert, Tyree, William D607;
   David, JOHN SR, John, Joseph, Lydia, Margaret, Sally (..),
   Sally, Susan, Susy (..) E175;
   David, George, James, John, Joseph, Lydia, Peggy Jane,
   Sally (..), Sally, SUSANNAH  E248; Elinor Ann (Shaw) E277;
   Delilah, GEORGE, Jenny, John, Matheran, Michael D414
   Polly, Sally, wife  D414; Eliz, JAMES SR, James E408;
   Delilah, Jenny, MARTHA, Martha Ann, Michael, Polly, F11
   Eliz, James, Nancy (..), WILLIAM D366; Sally F11;
   Emily (Holt) E42; George D308; Henry F227;  James D317a;
   James, John, Robert, Wm. E382; John D267,306,F260, E66;
   James, Jinnett (Robinson), Martha (Robinson), Jane D184;

RAY, Jane (Bradford), Margaret (Bradford) Robert, Wm. E14;
    John, Joseph, Susannah (Wilkinson) D410; Joseph D526;
    Mary (..), Mary Ann (Woods), Rebecca, Thomas  E26;
    Mathew D550; Michael  E193; Peter L. E55,118;
    Thomas D226,406; William  E42
REACH (or BEACH ?), Rosy (Boothe), Mary  E86
READE, R.R.  D414
READING, Eliz, John, Martha, Mary (..), Mary, Stephen  D591
    THOMAS, Thos Jr. D591
REAVIS, Thomas  D262
REDDEN, John, Nancy (Redmond) E317; Martha (McCaddams) E318;
    Robert E236                      Robert REDING E248
REDDING, Catherine E237; John Jr E343; Milley (Horne) E207;
REDMON; REDMOND, John D581,591, page 220; Milly  F110;
    Eliz, JOHN SR, John, Margaret (..), Nancy, Sally  E317
REDUM ?, William  D458
REED, FREDERICK, Penny (..) D606;
    George, Mary (Deley ?), Wm Deley  D105
REEVES, Frederick, GEORGE, Geo Jr, James, John, Nancy  D605
    Sarah D605; Geo W, John C, Martha E, SALLY LEWIS, Willis E147;
    James D501,E97,F136; John E202; JOHN, Thomas E319;
    Thomas E14,84,109,202,438,E202,362,509,F269
RENCHER, Anne D61; Eliz (Barbee) E410; John G. D61,124,614
REVEL, Hezekias  D411
REYNOLDS, Celia (Moore) E247; Eliz (Jackson) E117; Isaac D229;
    Joel  E86; Winlock ? E60        see RANDLES
REW, Susan (Roberts) F119
RHEW, Sally (Ray) E316; SIMPSON F395
RHINEHART, Adam  D47
RHODES, Anderson  F195; Aquilla D389,581,E20, page 221;
    Alementor (..), HEZEKIAH, Mary Linnington, Wesley, Wm D494;
    Amelia, Benj. Baker, Eliz, Franky, Hannah, John (2) D293;
    Mary (..), Michel, Molly, Nanny, Rebecca, WILLIAM, Wm. D293;
    Artemesia, Belinda, Eliz, Hannah, James, Jane, Noah E351
    Polly, Sally (..), THOMAS SR, Thos, Wesley, Wiley  E351;
    Benjamin D151,427,E150, Page 221;
    Benj, Betsy, JOHN, John Sr, Patsy (..), Patsy, Pleasant E68
    Polly, Sally  E68; Delilah (Herndon) D70,E327;
    Caroline Jane, Claudius Jasper, Cozby Ann, DELILAH (H) F6
    Delilah, Dicey, George W, Laury Jane, Mary, Milley, Penney F6
    Sarah, William, Wm's children, Zachariah F6; James E268;
    John D427,151,E150; John C. E353; Lewis D80; Mary E330;
    Mary (Fulton) D430; Patsy D389; Pleasant E207;
    Rebecca, Sarah  F110; Sally (Leathers), her children F253;
    Sarah M. (Patterson) E353; Thomas D430; Wm. Jr D75;
    Wm. D192,427; WILLIAM, wife, children E329; Zachariah F253
RICE, Eliz (..), JESSE D111; Jesse D110
RICH, Franky (Troxler), Henry  E101
RICKETTS, Mary, Rebecca (..), Rhoda, Richard, William  D520;
    Nelly (Ray) D231
RIGGINS, Edward D265; John D439; Mary (Gant) D30
RIGGS, Eliz (Murdock) D399; George Sr, Margaret, Nancy E193
    Hannah (Nichols), Hannah, Irven, John, Nancy  D190;
    James D236,E58; his will F389; Jno D28,221;
    MARGARET, D221,F445; Rachel  E193

RIGSBY, Arche, Edy, Eliz (Picket), Jesse, Tempy  D192;
  Eliz (..) E148; Eliz E319; Holley D120; Jesse D120,E148
RILEY, Caty, JACOB, Jacob Jr, John, Mary, Peter, Susanna D365;
  Copeland, Judson, Polly, Samuel, Warden, WILLIAM, Wm Jr F238
  Edward E380; Eliz (Whitekar); Mary (Whitekar) 220;
  Eliz, Helen (Watson), Rachel, Washington  D381;
  Helen (W) E263; John D594, E66,317; Samuel  F137;
  Sanders,Warren  E20
RINGSTAFF, Wm. B. E235      RINSTAFF, Elia  E13
RIPPER, Eleanor E139
RIPPEY, Keziah (Gant), Tho. D30;
RIPPY, Edward, James, Jenny, Jesse, John, Joseph, Matthew D508
  Mary F271; Thomas D508
RIVERS, Jones  E122
ROACH, David  D289,E209,F224; James E240; Milly (Cate) D490
ROARK, James D38
ROBARDS, Delia (Andrews)  F130
ROBART, Nancy, Stephen  D181
ROBBS, ALEXANDER  D215
ROBERSON, DAVID  F467; James E140; Wm. B. E32; see ROBERTSON
ROBERTS, Abner, Charles, Ephriam, Winnifred  D186;
  ABNER, Abner Jr, Caroline; Eliz, Elizey Ann, Jesse F119
  Mark, Moses, Sarah, Susan, Thomas, Vinney, Winny F119;
  Beershaba (..), Clary, Calvin H, George, James, Jemima D462
  Lidda, Mary, Margan, Peggy, Rebeckah, VINSON, Zephaniah D462
  Charles, David, Elisha, Jacob, John, Mahala, Richard  E414
  Wesley, WILLIAM, Wm Jr, Willis, Winnifred E414; David E250;
  Ellis, JAMES, his wife & children, James Jr, Lewis, Wm D592;
  James C. E386; James T. F22;  Sarah, WILLIS  D436
  James, Jesse, Loviney, Menday ?, Polly, Sarah (..) D436;
  JOHN, John Wesley, Mary, William  E315;
  Mary (Herndon), Ruth (Herndon) D70; Nancy (Moize) E258;
  Paschall, William  F52; Wm Sr. D512; W.E. D542; Wm. J. F57
ROBERTSON, Andrew (2); Elenor (2), Hugh, JOHN, John Jr  D46
  Margaret (2), Molly, Rebeckka, wife, Zachrias  D46;
  Cynthia Aris (Nevill) D263; Lizy  F52;
  James, John, Joseph, Michael, Sally (..) E248;
  Thomas, Susannah (..) D243; William D167,E353
ROBINSON, Elisha, Jane, James, William D109; Alex  F63;
  Alex, Charles, Catherine, David; James (2), Jane (Ray) D184
  John (2), Joseph, Jinnett, Mary, Margaret, Martha D184
  MICHAEL, Michael Jr, Nancy, William  D184; Michael  D317a;
  Alex, NANCY F158; James, Margaret (Ray) E175;
  Nancy (Wood) D521; Sally (Ray) E175; Wm. R. D408
ROBSON, William E125,512
ROGERS, Ann, ELENOR (..), Elenor, James, Jane (2), John F217
  Mary, Sally, William  F217; Celia Ann, Idelet, NATHAN D445
  Nancy (..) D445; ELIZABETH (..), grandchildren E267
  Idelett, Theopilus, William  E267; LESEY, Laban, Nathan D180
  JAMES, Jas Jr, Jean, John, Polly, wife, William (2) D194;
  WILLIAM F414; Wm. M. F204
ROLAND, Polly (Wilson) F63
RONEY, Andrew; BENJAMIN, Ben Jr, Catherine (..), Cath. E143
  Eliz, James, John, Margaret, Mary, Nancy, Sally E143;
  Catherine, John, Mary Ann, POLLY  F164;
  Margaret (Pickett) D560   see RANEY

ROSE, Eli  D447; Eve (Eulice) D346
ROSS, Andrew F101; Enos, F76;
ROSSER, James E334,421, his will F392; Nancy (Thrift) E334
ROUNDTREE, HARVEY  F402; Sally (Wilson) F63; Thomas D184;
    Nancy (Robinson) D184
ROUNTREE, Charles Jr, J. D416; CHARLES, his children, D467
    Jno, Joseph, Nancy (..), Thomas D467; J. D408;
    Jilsey ? (Thompson) E262; THOMAS, Victory (..) D580;
    John, Joseph, THOMAS, wife, Thomas Jr D148
ROWARK, Elisha  D373     see ROARK
ROWAN, Eliza M. (Holt), Thomas E42
RUFFIN, Thomas  D312,318,608,E76,137,382,388,F217; Will E382
RUMBLEY, Aron, Edward, Eliz (..), James, JOHN, John S. F197
    Rachel, Thomas, William F197; Joseph  D82
RUMLEY, Priscilla (Dannelley) E311
RUSH, Samuel  D553
RUSSELL, Alex, Eliz (Craig)  D496; Alex, John C. D359;
    Alex Jr, ALEXANDER, David, Eliz (..), Jane, John Craig D550;
    Polly, Rob. Paistly, William, Wright  D550 ; James W. D451;
    John, Rachel (Thompson) D568
RYALS, Polly (Walker) D523


SAMPSON, Samuel  F72
SANDERS, Franky, Henry, Joseph, LETTY E150; Jno  D40
SAUNDERS, JOHN, Lydia, Nancy  D412
SAWYER, ELIZABETH F, Mary C. D592
SCARBOROUGH, Jane (McCrory)  D367
SCARLETT, Allen, Delilah, Henderson, JOHN, Mariah, Nancy E412
    Page, Scyntha (..)  E412; Cyntha (Allen) D178;
    Cynthia, Eliz, James, Jane, John, Mary, Rachel, Sally D510
    Sally (..), Susannah  D510; John D602; Stephen  F16;
    Eliz (Laycock), Delilah (Laycock), Sally (Laycock)  E204;
    Thomas  D87
SCHERER  see SHEARER
SCOGGINS, John  D55; Sally D262
SCOTT, Alex, Eliz, Faney, Jennet, John, Mary (..), Mary D271
    Thomas, WILLIAM, Wm Mitchell D271; J. D141,194, Jas M. E164;
    Fanny, Hannah, Henderson, Jane, John, Nancy (..), F107
    Nancy, SAMUEL F107; Jane (Christopher)  F56; Samuel D508;
    John  D203,E2,71,245,373,F54; Mary (Alston), Robert  D542;
    Thomas  E42,48,308,D418,445,577
SCULLEN ?, John  E49
SEARS, Leonard  D439
SEAWELL, Mrs. Mary  F249
SELLARS, Willis  E141
SELPH, Hannah (Blackwood)  E229
SHADDY, Caty, Eliz (..), Daughter, Jacob, JOHN, John Jr  D331
    Molly, Rachel D331;
SHANAON, James  D40
SHARP, Aaron  E382; Eli  F21; Isaac D522,F21
SHATTERLY, Andrew  D346
SHAW, Betsy (King), Charles, Louisa, Wm Franklin  D282;
    Betsey, Fanny, James Jr, JAMES, Joseph, Levi, Samuel D100
    William (2) D100; Catherine H, Drusilla Ann, Elinor E277
    Fantitina J, JOSEPH, Jos B, Jos John, Maria, Neal H E277
    Rebecca E. E277; Clarissa, Elinor, Jane, JOHN, John W. F1
    Joseph W, Kitty, Verlinda D, William V. F1; John W. E289,F267;

SHAW, Nancy (Walker) E289,F170; Wiley D458,483,588;
  William D206,544,F187; Wm. M. E96; Willie E57,159
SHEAREN, A. E400,417; Andrew E121
SHEARER, Frederick, Peggy (Clap) F229     SHERER, Jacob E89
SHELBY, John, Mary (..) E421
SHELTON, Buckner, Cath (..), Edmund, Eliz, Frederick D71
  James, Jeremiah, John, Mary, Rhoda, THOMAS, Thos Jr D71
SHEPHEARD, Wm. D235      SHEPHERD, Thos R. F83
SHEPPARD, Eliz D154; Betsy, Egbert, Henry James, Mary E24
  Margaret L; Sally, Susan Jane, WILLIAM, Wm Jr  E24;
  Caty, Eliz, Henry, James, Mary, WILLIAM, daughters  E111;
  Egbert D537; William D498,537
SHERIDAN ?, John  E60
SHIELDES, Sally (Hardee) E298
SHOARMAN, Benjamin D82
SHOFNER, SHOFFNER, Daniel D447; Frederic D575; FREDERICK F279;
  Magdalane, MICHAEL, Michael Jr, Peter, sons  D342
SHORB, Jacob  D90
SHUGART, HANNAH, Isaac, Nathan, Rachel, Wm. D449; Isaac D482
SHUTT, HENRY, Eliz (..), children  D312; Henry  D277
SILER, Jeremiah, Leah (..)  E417
SIMMONS, Caleb  D53
SIMPSON, Benj. D301,464; Granville E381; Marg't (Garrison) E11
  Joseph F13
SIMS, Herbert  D362
SLAUGHTER, Lida  D553
SMART, Mary  E300
SMITH, ADAM, daughters, Eliz (..), sons D59;
  Agnes, Catherine, Dice, Eliz, Jinney, John, Leonard E160
  Mary, Sarah, STEPHEN MESSER, Susannah (:.), Sus., Wm. E160;
  Alex E175; Barbary, Hannah (..), Nancy, PETER, Polly D364;
  C.C. E378,F8; Charles, John, Nancy, Patheny, Sarah D322;
  David, GEORGE, his wife, Geo Jr, Joseph, Nancy, Sally F132;
  General Daniel  D23; Daniel, LEONARD, Mary (..) E121;
  Delia (Jones), Francis J, James S, Mary R, James Sidney F198;
  Elender, Ferze, John (3), Joseph, Polly, Rob't, WILLIAM D566;
  EVE, Peter  D522; Farmer E263; George D501,E367;
  Hannah (Hastings), Nance (Hastings) E29; Isham  E392;
  Hosea, Patsey (Moore) E388; James E573; Jediah E372;
  J.S. D527,E54,289,410; James L. E23; John E297; Jos. F208;
  Lucy (Faucett) D309; Martha (McDaniel) E209;
  Milly (Rhodes) F6; Nancy (Carmichael) D559; Polly E345;
  Reuben D119,498,520,E80; Simpson D113; Susannah D322,364;
  Sukey F132; Tabitha (Cate) D490;
  William D440,309,527,E99,209,371,F126,132,229, page 220
SMOTHERS, Rosanna (Dannelley) E311; Susannah (Gilliam) D489
SNEED, James F115; J.P. E201,277
SNIPES, Dempsey, ELIZABETH (..), Eliz, Martha, Oren E421
  Robert, Thomas, Willis E421; Eliz (Thrift) D344,E334;
  Manly F3; Margaret (Brewer) F224; Martha (..), OSBOURN F171;
  Thomas D289,486,560,E220; W.S. E220
SOMERS, Jacob E350
SORRELL, Polly (Marcum)  E205
SOUTHARD, John  E48
SOUTHWARD, Carter, Charles, Gilliam, James, JOHN, John Jr F65
  Macklen, Polly, Sally, Tempey F65

SOUTHERLAND, Fendal E507; MORDECAI D535; Polly (Cain) E324;
    Eliz, Frances, MORDECAI, Polly, Ransom, Samuel D530
    Susannah, William D530; Wm. R. E324
SPARROW, Dicey F470; John E280
SPOON, Catherine (Eulis), Daniel F242     SPOONE, Peter E121
SPRINGER, ADAM, David, Eve, George, Mary E90
SQUIRES, John F1,8; Sarah D600; Thomas D600,F8
STAFFORD, Frederick F84; Polly (Hornaday) E501
STAG, James F213
STALCOP; Eliz (Gilliam) D489; Eliz (..), Eliz, JOHN D125
    Lydda, Nancy, Rachel, Susannah, Solomon, Thomas D125
STANFORD, A. D384; Adeline, Ariana, Lawrence, Mary Mebane D486
    RICHARD, his wife D486; Alex, JAMES, James Jr, Jinny F152
    Peggy, Robert F152; Richard D289,F178,261
STARK, Eliz, Phebe, Ruthy, the widow D261
STARR, Adam D93
STEEL, Andrew, Joseph, Peggy D498; Henry, ... (Shaddy) D331;
    Hiram F21; John D206; Rebecca (Pickard) D3511; Thomas D70,75
STEM ? or STERN ?, Mary E368,F114
STEPHENS, Betsey (Nelson) E426
STEVENS, JANE F425
STEWART, Anna, Charles, Eliz (..), James, John, SAMUEL, E145;
    Calvin B, John C, Polly (Christopher) F56; Samuel Jr (2) E145;
    Edward, Mary (McPherson) D517
STOCKARD, John D451,509,E62,307,F179
STONE, Eliz (Boothe) E86
STONOR, Eve E107
STOUT, Henry E501; John D47; Joseph D239; Mary (Borland) D602;
    Mary (Capps) E308; Peter E130; Samuel E308; Solomon E60
STOVALL, Ann (..), Anna, BARTHOLOMEW, Bathew, daughter, D91
    Frederick, George, Henery, Jane, Nancy, Phebe, Thomas D91
    Susanna, William, Wily D91
STOWERS, Polly (Henderson) F80
STRADER, Adam F240; Michael E379
STRAIN, Alex D120,E512; Alex, David, Eliz, James, JOHN E99
    Marian (..), Mary, Samuel, Sarah E99;David D338;
    Alex, David, John, MIRIAM (..), Miriam, Samuel D, Wm D. F163;
    Alex, David, Eliz, James, Jane, Mary, MIRIAM, Sam, Wm. E219;
    DAVID, Eliz, Jane (..), John, Sarah, William E402;
    Eliz, James, Maryan (..), Mary, Samuel, SARAH E221;
    John D87; Mary (Burns) E512
STRAYHORN, Aaron, James (3), John, Maleacy A, Polly, Rachel E406
    RACHEL (..), Samuel, Thompson, William, Willie E406;
    Aaron, WILLIAM, his children E424; Bryant E99,219,221,410;
    ELIZABETH, James (2), John, Polly, Rachel (2), S. E410
    Thompson, William E410; Eliz, Jane, Mary (..), Mary E221;
    Jane, Mary, John E219; Mary (Strain) E99,219;
    Bryant, David, Jane, JOHN, Patsy, Polly F165; David E512;
    David; GILBERT, Gilbert Jr, James, John (2), William D87;
    David, Eliz, Gilbert (2), JAMES Sr, Jas, John (2) E287
    Polly; Rachel (..), Wm. E287; James, Sally, SAMUEL D600;
    James, Sarah F29; Jinney (Kirkland) F89;
    Mary E.M., Samuel, Sam Jr, Thomas, Wm. F. F142;
    Mary (Blackwood) F174; Nancy M. (Patterson) E353;

STRAYHORN, Nancy (Thompson), Rachel  E505;
  Sally (Borland) D602; Samuel D603,E99,163
STREET, Charlotte (Harris), John  D387; Elinor (Shaw) F1;
  John D317a,E76; Joseph Sr, William D129;
  Margaret (Carmichael) D559
STRONG, Joel D390
STROTHER, Martin  D59
STROWD, B.  E334,F34,38,178; Bryant D303,344,E404;
  Celia (Atwater), Lois (Atwater) E292; Henry D303;
  John D300,303; Polly F224; William D30,344
STUBBINS, Nancy F273; Chas ? D172; Joseph D424
STRUDWICK, E. F260; Ed. E185; Edmund E227; Mrs. Martha E137;
  Edmund, MARTHA, Samuel, Wm. F. D154; W.L.  D94
SUIT, John Jr. D553
SULIVAN, Craven, Eliz, Nancy Catherine, Thomas, William E223
SUMMERS, JOSHUA  F314
SUTHERLAND, Mary A, WILLIAM  F9   see SOUTHERLAND
SWEANEY, TIRZA   F276
SWINDLE, Casan, Christopher  D218; SWINDELL, Christ'r D143
SWING, Philipenia (Albright) E231
SYKES, Fanny (Cate, Winney (Cate) D490; James D180;
  John D369,E134; Nancy (Moore), Wm. E402, Thomas F216


TAIT, Anthony, Catherine (..), SIMPSON D129     see TATE
Tapley, Mason D286;     see TARPLEY
TAPP, ABNER, daughter, Elethe, Eliz, Frances (..), D272
  Richard, Susannah D272; Richard E425,F261,273;
  Rebecca (Hopson), Rosanna (Hopson)  F261; Vincent E380,F261
TARPLEY, Abraim, Dolly, Eliz (..), Eliz, Henry, James E118
  MASON; Milly, Nancy, Sarah, William  E118; Mason E55;
  Henry, Peggy (Trolinger) F181;  William E231
TAPSCOTT, John F13
TATE, Abner, Alse, Eliz, JAMES, Jas Jr, Jesse D460   see TAIT
  Joel, Margaret (..) (2), Marg't, Robert, Susannah D460;
  ABNER, Alsa, Jesse F101; Alice, Eliz, Griffith, James E105
  Jenet, JOSEPH, Jos Jr, Mary (..), Polly, Robert, Wm. E105;
  Alfred, James, Joseph, Margaret, Mary, Rachel (:.) E153
  Robert, WILLIAM E153; Ann, Ginny, Joseph, Luiza F100
  Samuel, THOMAS F100; Anthony, Hannah (..), Polly D461
  Anthony, Isabel, Sally E224; ZEPHANIAH  D461;
  Barbary (Tickle) E19; Celia, Elsy, Susannah D506;
  David, George, JAMES, Sam'l N. F8; Miriam F163;
  Eliz (Armstrong), Henrietta (Armstrong), John F271:
  James D53,259,E21,91,378;F8; Joseph E511,F271;
  Robert D143; Samuel E141,415,F144; Sam'l N. E378,F8,265
TATOM, A. D309; Abner, Abel, ABSOLOM, Barnet, Eliz D94
  Harrietta, John, William  D94
TAYLOR, Ann, JAMES, John, Thomas  D333;
  Ann, JOHN, daughters, Joseph, sons, Thomas  D380;
  Caty (Pratt) D446; Eliz (Tate) E105; f. E68; George W. F13;
  Harrison, Henderson, Jula Betsy, Nancy, WILLIAM F33;
  J. D312,387, page 221; Jane (Minnis) E394; Jane (Wilson) F63
  John D404,his will F388; John Jr. D276,277,585;
  Robert D602,E375; Thos E. E251; Thos H. E280; William E272
TERRILL, Joseph D43,328; Sally (..) D328

TERRIS ?, H. E380
TERRY, Hezekiah E408,F42
THOMAS, Caty, EDWARD, Eliz (..), Eliz, Hannah, Jenney E387
  Nancy, Neamia, Richard  E387; Caty, Jane, JESSE, Mary E139
  Nehemiah, Thomas  E139; Cath (McCaddams) E318;
  Eliz (..), JOHN, Micajah  D550; Eliz, GEORGE, Josiah E511
  Mary, William E511; Elender (Thompson) D568; George E272;
  Henry E231; Sarah (Cook) F184;
THOMPSON, A. D203; Abel, Edith, Eliz, Enoch, JOSEPH E269;
  Lydia, Sarah, Thomas E269; Abel, James, JOSHUA, Patsy E425
  Polly (..), Ruth, W.H. E425; Alfred E363; Anderson E415,396;
  ANTHONY, Ant. Jr, Dilly, Jane, Letty, Marmaduke, Michael E396
  Nancy, Polly, William  E396; Anna (Marshill) D533;
  Ann, James, Jilsey ?, John, Joseph, Lawrence, Nicholas E262
  Rebecca, SARAH, Thomas  E262; Archelaus M. D427;
  Ann, Elender, Eliz, James, Jinnet (..), Jinnet, JOHN D568
  John Jr, Rachel, Robert, Thos, Wm. D568;
  Anne, Jane, Nance, Peggy (O'Daniel) Thomas E78;
  Betsy, John B, Patsy, Ralph, Rebeckah (..), Rebeckah D599
  Richard, Robert, Sally, SAMUEL, Sam Jr, Thomas D599;
  David, Eliz (..), Nancy, Rachel, Rebecca, Solomon  E505
  Edith (Nunn), Richard D407; Edward F236; SAMUEL, Wm. E505;
  EDWIN G, Eliza (..), Geo Sidney, James N. F106;
  Elender, Elinor, Eliz (..), Eliz, Jinnett, John (2) F134
  JOSEPH, Jos Jr (2), Lavina (..), Lavina, Rachel, Rob. F134
  Mrs Eliz F249; ELIZABETH F412; Samuel (2), Thomas F134;
  Eliz (..), JAMES, his children, John, Levi, Sarah  D335;
  Ellen, Fanny, Hannah, ISBELL, Richard F86;
  Eliz (..), John, THOMAS, his children, William  F102;
  Ester (Hastings) D339; Frances, Hannah, Isabell (..) E195
  James, Nelly, Phebe, Richard, SAMUEL, Sam Jr. E195;
  Hannah, John; MARY, Nelly, Robert, Thomas  E228;
  HENRY, Nelly, Priscilla (..), Sally, Susan  E71;
  James E50,page 220; Jas H. F273; JAMES SR. F294;
  Jane (Johnston) E393, Jane (Mebane) F144; Jesse F4;
  John Esq. D25,76; D201,251,326,E90,203,406,F16,84,144,357;
  Joseph D170,174,E120,145; Joshua D127; Mary D412;
  Martha Carlton (Hardee) E57,298; Martha Winnefred E57;
  Mary (Jackson) her children E117; Micajah E107;
  Patterson, E363; Richard D533, E62,180; Robert E145;
  Rebecca (Wood) D521; Samuel D114,334, 521 his will D127;
  Sarah D53; Susannah (Whitted) D136,468; Theopilus D384;
  Thomas E120;page 220; W. E80; W.F. D83;
  William E90,203,209,303,501,F28,84,134,261
THOMSON, Henry E280; Jno  D317
THORNBURY, David  D59
THRAILKILL, Wm. D379
THRIFT, David, Delia, Drury, Eliz, Frances, ISHAM, Ish Jr D344
  Levicy, Mary (..), Nancy, Peggy, Perry, Polly, Sally  D344
  Susannah, William D344;
  Eliz, Isham, MARY (..), Nancy, Polly  E334
THROWER, Susanna  E111
TICKLE, Betsy (Huffhines) E15; Barbary, Cath, David, JOHN E19
  John Jr, Margaret, Mary (..), Mary, Sally  E19; Elisha E39;
  Conrad, Eliz, Henry, John, Mary PETER, Peter Jr E33;
  Eliz (Coble), George F240

TILLEY, Eliz (..), John, LAZARUS, Thomas  F92;
  Eliz (Moize), Keziah (Moize)  E258
TINNEN, C.E.? F188;
  Catlett C,  David, Eleanor, Jennet, Margaret, Mary, ROBERT,
  Robert Jr (2), Thomas  E375; James E382; Rob. D244,248,F7
TINNING, ELIZABETH  d53
TOMISON, Charlotte (Cozart ?), James D163a
TOWEL, Jesse, John  D64        TOWELL, Danell D229
TRACY, Barbara (Eulice)  D346
TREE, Druscilla (Ward)  E18  see FREE
TREWETT, James E285; Thomas Sr, Thos Jr  E275; TRUET, Levi E385
TRUET or TREWIT, Eleanor, Eliz, Gatsey ?, John, Levi, Mary,
  Nancy (..), Nancy, Spencer, WILLIS, Willis Jr  E191
TRICE, Amelia, Frances, Henry, Henry Sr, Page, Sarah, Sus. E422
  Chesley P, Henry D, Henry Sr, Zachariah  E329;
  Amelia, Chesley P, Eliz, Frances, HENRY, Henry D, Nanny F48;
  Edward, Nancy, Sally, Sarey (..), THOMAS, Wm. D114; Sarah F48
  Eliz E355; Fanny (Davis) E239; Henry D293; James D160;
  Frances, James, Penny, WILLIAM SR, Wm, Zachariah  E19;
  Jesse D36; Maryan (Herndon) D70; Noah F379;
  Patsy (Strayhorn) F165; Sarah (Pearson) E273; -
  Susan (Leigh) F93; William D160,F6,379; Wm Rhodes D192
TRIMBLE, Eliz D436; John D208,197; Marget, Sarah D197
TRIP, Aron, Eliz (Andrews) F130
TRIPP, Eliz, Eunice, John Wilson, Martha, Millicent E180
  Nancy (Wilson) Polly, Wm Blumer  E180; Jonathan D571
TROLINGER, Benjamin F181; Catheriner (Tickle) E19;
  Betsy, Catherine, HENRY SR, Henry, Jacob, John, Joseph F181
  Mary, Moses, Peggy, Polly (..)  F181; John E256,335,F107,161;
  Eliz (Roney), John  E143; Joseph J. F222
TROTMAN, Polly (Freeman)  D43
TROUSDALE, Catred (McCauley), William E98
TROXLER, Adeline, B., Franky, daughters, GEORGE, John E301;
  BARNEY; Barney Jr, Catherine, David, Eliz (..), Eliz D507
  George, Jacob, Mary, Philipena, Powell  D507;
  David  El; John C.  F72
TUDOR, William  E137
TULBYLOVE, Haritta (..), her children  D94
TURLEY, Eliz (Whitsel)  E7
TURNER; Ann, Christian, David, Hannah, JAMES, Jas Jr  D527
  John, Jane, Mary (..), Mary, Nelly, Sarah  D527; E. D592;
  Eliza, Mary  F249; Frances (Southerland)  D530; Israel E265;
  Henry, James, Martha (Neal)  Ell3; James D550,E81,F268;
  John F249; Josiah F256; Mrs. Josiah F248; Moses H. F185;
  Mrs. ... (Cockran) D141; Peggy (Hutchins) El3;
  Rosanna F224; Sally F245; Simon E70; S?.L. F137; Wm. E269
TURRENTINE, Absolom E370; Abs., Daniel, Deborah, Lydia D38
  James, John, Martha, Mary (..), Mary, SAMUEL, Sam Jr D38
  Sarah, Susannah D38; Abs., Ann (..), Daniel, Mary F266;
  SAMUEL, Sam W. F266; Arch, Alex, Samuel  E81;
  Daniel  D100; David D138; Nelly (Nealy), Samuel Sr  D455;
  Samuel  D107,404,436,E370,F42
TYRELL, Thomas  F160    see TERRILL

UMSTEAD, David, Elisha, JACOB, his mother, brothers, sisters,
 John D495; Elisha D512;E414; Ezekiel D547; Jacob D547;
 Jemima D512; JOHN D289,318,429,450,600, his will E182;
 Richard D547
UNDERWOOD, John  E139; Rachel (Wells) D140

VALLENTINE, Rhoda  D55
VANN, Lorenzo J. F31
VEAZEY, Edward, EZEKIEL, Frances (..), John C, Leonard  F14
 Mealey, Thersday, other children, William  F14;
 Mark, William  D512
VESTAL, Ruth  D162
VICKERS, David  F48, page 220; Eliz (Guinn) 220; Ryley D254
VINCENT, Betsey, James, JOHN B, Polly, William  E95;
 Eliz, James, John, Polly, Sarah, THOMAS, Thos Jr, Wm E84;
 Thomas  D306; Verlinda D. (Shaw)  F1

WADDELL, Francis Nash  E503,F238; Hugh E182,319,F178,238
WADDELTON, Anne  E369
WADLINGTON, Thos.   D84
WAGGONER, Barbary, Catherine, Daniel, Eliz, Hannah E367
 Margaret (..), Marg't, Mary, Nancy, PETER, Peter Jr  E367
 Eliz H. E381; Jacob  E160; Rosanna E367; George  D186
WAGNER, Elizabeth R. F184
WALCOT, Richard  D75
WALKER, Aaron D395; AARON, Empson, Freeman, Harriett E289
 James, John, Levi, Nancy, Sarah (..) E289;  Abner  D465;
 Adam D, Hannah (..), Hannah M, JOHN, Mary  F172;
 Alex, Connerly, James, Jinney, John, Mary, Peggy (..) E109
 PHILIP SR, Philip  E109; ALEXANDER, Conoly, James, John E331
 Margaret (..), Philip, William  E331; Andrew, James D336
 JOHN, John Jr (2), Mary, Peter (2), William  D336;
 Andrew, Eliz (..), PETER, Peter Jr, Sarah, William  E64;
 Andrew, ELIZABETH  E211; Ashford  E95;
 Benj, Betsy, Emily, JOHN, Judy (..), Letty, Lucy  D523
 Nelly, Polly, Rebeckah D523; Connally D127,E345,F1;
 CONNALLY, Eliz (..), Jane, Mary, Phillip, Samuel, Wm F267;
 Deborah (McCulloch), Wm. D503; Eliz (Crawford) D85;
 Eliza  F1; Empson  F56; Fanny (Graham), Jenny (Graham) D259;
 Eliz (2), Ellenor (..), George W, Jane, John, Peggy E107
 Polly, Philip, ROBERT, Robert Jr, Sally, William  E107;
 Empson, Freeman, Harriett, Levi, Nancy, SARAH F170;
 Fanny (Mebane) F144; Fanny, John  D53; Harriet (Wilson) F63;
 James D111,186,213,362,454,477,E315,F1; Jane (Shaw) F1;
 Jinney (Armstrong) F271; Job, John, Rachel (Garrison) E275;
 JOHN F288; Peter D368,E262; Philip D413,E420;
 Polly (Faussett) D465; Rachel (Murray) D598; Rachel F1;
 Rebecca (King) E420; Robert E26,67; Sarah D468,E237
WALL, MARGARET  F301        WALLS, Peggy, William  D224
WALLACE, Owen, Sally (Wood) D564   see WALLIS
WALLER, Allen  F57; Jinney (Laws) D512
WALLIS, Nancy (King), Peter  E420  see WALLACE
WARD, Anthony, Asther, Druscilla, James, Sarah, SUSANNA (..),
 Susanna, Stephen, Thomas, William  E18

WARD, Antony, James, STEPHEN, his wife, Stephen Jr E417
   Susannah, Thomas, William E417; EDWARD J. F286;
   Bethany, Charity (..), Edwin, Eliz, James, John E296
   JOSEPH; Josiah, Luisa, Marvil, Mary, Patsy, Nancy E296
   Ransom, Rebecca, Robertson, Willism E296; John D87,566;
   Eliza (Christopher), Frances (Christopher), James F56;
   Stephen E59; Wm Sr F186
WARE, Gilly (..), SAMUEL, daughter, son E265
WARREN, Adeline (Troxler), Briscoe E101;
   Anney, Henry, Mary Webb E159; David E294,351;
   Esther (Fulton), James, Jane (Fulton), William D430;
   John E204,277; Mary (Guess) E294; Polly (Rhodes) E351
WATKINS, James, Margaret (Faussett) D465; William E40
WATSON, A. E29, An. E294; A.N. F43; Anderson Fl;
   Andrew D339,D421,424; Eliz (Hastings) D339;
   Alex, ANDREW, Eliz, James M, Juliana, Julius, Margaret (..),
   Nancy (..), Tempy T, Wilson F137; Andrew, Eliz, Helen D381
   JAMES SR, James, John, Marg't (..), Nancy, Rebec, Rob D381;
   Andrew, Eliz, Helen, Jas R, James, John, MARGARET (..) E263
   Margaret, Nancy, Rebecca, Robert E263; Bennett D25;
   Betsy (Howard) D577; David, Eliz, JAMES SR, James (2) D49
   John, Jonathan, Peggy, Rosanna (..) D49;
   Eliz Ann, Milly F213; Feriby (Glenn) D475; Lot G. D477;
   James Sr D38; J. D430,431; Margaret F23
WATTS, Thomas D. E23,25,245,283
WAUGH, Permelia F245
WAY, Benjamin E417,F417
WAYNICK, LUDWICK, Margaret (..), children E48
WEAVER, Eliz E372; Eliz C, George, Isham S, John H. F168
   Mary C, Samuel, Sarah (..), THOMAS, Thos S, Wm G. F168
   Sally (Brewer), Thomas E303,F52; Winnie E. F168
WEBB, Ann Alves D352; Eliz E267; H. F116,249;
   J. D183,312,600; J. Jr. F249; Dr. James D352;
   James D247,362,365;457,505,550,552,608,E2,23,24,34,76,87,113
   James E182,192,201,227,241,257,E71,363,F86; John E267
WEEDON, Joshua D267; Sarah (Faucett) E510
WEEKS, Joseph D421
WELBORN, Edward, JOHN, Lewis, Mary (..), Richard, Robert,
   Thomas, Zachariah D553; MARY F57
WELDON, James E95
WELLS, Asther (Ward) E18; Benj, Eliza (Hardee) E298;
   Charity, Eliz, Isaac, Jesse, John, JOSEPH, Jos Jr D140
   Margrate, Mary, Nathan, Rachel, William D140; James D146;
   Miles E57; Polly (Hardee) E57,298; Nathan, Stephen E417;
   Ruth (Hornaday) E501;
WELSH, George D42
WESSON, Austin E20
WEST, Lydia, her sons D509
WHAIT, Daniel, Mary (Tickle) E33; WHEAT ?, James M. E277
WHATLEY, Hannah (Rhodes) D293
WHEELER, America, Rachel (Primrose) E368,F114;
   Eliz (Piggott), Benjamin D529
WHEELEY, BENJAMIN, Ben Jr, Dorothy (..), Dorothy E174
   Phillip, Susannah, other children E174
WHIDBEE, BENJAMIN, children, Joseph, Sally (..) D558

WHITAKER, Ann, Burton, David, Isaac, John, Lucy (..), Nancy,
   Polly, Thomas, WILLIAM, Wm Jr E270; Jacob E30;
   Lucy (Holloway) E355; Robert D76; Susannah E355
WHITEKAR, ABRAHAM, Abr'm Jr, Eliz, Hannah, Isaac, Jacob 220
   James, Joana, Martha (..), Mary, William 220;
WHITE, Ann (..), David, James, John, Joseph, Samuel D544
   STEPHEN, Stephen Jr  D544; Betsy (..), DAVID, Fanny  E508;
   David D107,176,F184; Eliz (Duncan) E243; James E373;F54;
   John F164; Joseph E422; JOSEPH A. F312; Samuel E508;
   JOSEPH, Jos Jr, Nancy (..), Nancy, Susanna, Thomas  F195;
   Joseph Jr, Nancy, Rachel (Couch), Susannah, Thomas 221;
   Robert S. F62; Samuel E100; Stephen  F160; Thomas F274;
   William H. E256                         see WHYTE
WHITFIELD, James D184; Wm. D42
WHITSEL, ADAM, Adam Jr, Barbara, Caty, Christian, Daniel, E7
   daughters, Eliz, Henry, Jacob, John, Ludowick, Mary  E7;
   ADAM, Eliz, Margaret (..), Nancy, Polly E1; Hiram  F233
WHITSETT, Austin, James  F50; Jean (Harden) D418; Moses E161
WHITTED, Anna, JEHU, Anna, Lebi, Susanna (..), Wm, Wm Jr D132;
   Anne, Attelia (..), Eliza I., James, Jehu, Levi, Mary T. E2
   Nancy (..), WILLIAM SR, Wm Henry, Wm Nash  E2;
   Attelia (..); JAMES, Nash, unborn child  D505;
   Eliz, Hannah, Levi, Mary, Susannah, WILLIAM SR, Wm (2) D468;
   Mrs. Attelia, Eliza, Mary F249; Henry F46,157;
   Eliza Jane, Frances (..), James, Termesia M, Wm Nash  E76;
   WILLIAM HENRY E76; James, Wm. D247; John D335,425;
   MARY (..); Eliza Q, Henry, Mary Q, Nash, Termisea, Wm. E34;
   Levi D387,E23,31,193,F11, his will F439; Robert E31,F269;
   Thomas D317,326,425,498,F132; W. E113         see WITTED
WHITTEN ?, John  D82
WHITTENTON, Mary (Pyle) E40
WHYTE, Lucy (..), Joseph, Rebecca Ann, Thomas, WILLIAM E251
WICKS, Janny, Lilla, Rebecca F178
WILBON, John  D257    WILBOURN, John D150   see WELBORN
WILFONG, Mrs. Elizabeth  E229
WILKERSON, ANN (.:), David, Eliz, Frances, Francis, James E7
   John, Margaret, Nancy, Polly; William  E7; Daniel D333,F26;
   Harris F25,58,214,253; James, Nancy (Boswell)  E223;
   John D57,333,F26; Rebecca (Williams) D57
WILKINS, George  D90; Mary (Dixon) E335
WILKINSON, Ann, Caty (..), JAMES, Jas Jr, John, Mary, D410;
   Ann (:.), David, WILLIAM D451; Susannah, William  D526;
   David, FRANCIS, children, John, William  D174;
   DANIEL, Daughters, Eliz (..), John, Sam, Thos, Wm. F124;
   Eliz W. (Pickett) F188; Francis, John D62; John, Rob. D586;
   JOHN, Rachel, Rebecca (..), Daniel  D398; Lemuel F191;
   WILLIAM F349
WILLCOX, Mary (Busick)  D228
WILLIAMS, A. E302; ANDREW, Annis, Matildy, Phebe (..) E507
   Ann, Hester, James, John, Martha, Rachel (..), Rachel D57
   Rebeckah, RICHARD  D57; Betsy (Fennell) F10; Sally E507;
   David F224, his will F469; Hetty D412, her will F427;
   Hester, James, MARTHA, Nancy D166; James D317a,594;
   Patsey (Marcum) F17; Rebecca (Loyd) E342; Wm B. E205

WILLIS, Augustine D109; P. D344; Thos. G.  E209
WILLOCKS, Nancy, Rebecka  D322
WILLOTT, Mary (..), William  D94
WILSON, WILLSON, Anderson  E370; Anderson, Caleb, Chas. E188
    Eliz, Fanny, Jane (..), Nancy; Robert, THOMAS  E188;
    ANN; Caleb, Eliz, James, John, Thomas  D586;
    Ann, Eliz, Eunice (..), JOHN, Lois, Martha, Millicent E180
    Nancy, Rhoda  E180; Ann, Jane (Wood), Thomas  D521;
    Archelaus, Dicey, Drady, George, Henrietta (..), Hyram E81
    JAMES, Jas Jr, Jane, John D, Nancy, Samuel, William E81;
    Caleb  E370,F159; Charles E404,F266; Edward D201;
    Charles, Eliz (..), Eliz, Felix, Harriet, Jane, John F63
    Nancy, Polly, Sally, SAMUEL  F63;
    CHARLES, Rachel, Sally D67;
    EDWARD; Ed. Jr, Hugh, Nancy, Polly, Rachel (..), D347
    Rachel, William (2) D347; Ed., MATHIAS, Rachel, Wm (2) D324;
    Eliz, JAMES, his father & mother, Maryann  D537;
    Eliz (Wortham) D538,E174; Emelia (Faucett) E510;
    George D38; James D293,267; JANE  F453; John D336,E174;
    JOHN, his children, Nancy (..) D362; John W. F43;
    Martha (Faucett) E510; Margaret (Armstrong) D267;
    John, Sarah (..), Sarah, STEPHEN D104; Martha E370,F266;
    Margaret (Robertson)  D46; Mathew D206; Mary D48;
    Nancy D184; Nancy (Wortham)  D538; Samuel D546,E174;
    Thomas  D52,398,456
WINSTON, Patrick H.  E137
WIRICK, Barbary (Cable), Sarah (Cable)  F240
WITHERSPOON, I. or J. D407
WITHEY ?, John  E106
WITTED, Eleanor  D381        see WHITTED
WOLF, Ann  D509; Ann, Barbara, John, Mary, Peter, WILLIAM,
    William Jr. D237
WOMACK, Eliza, Jacob P, Mary Jane, Nancy (Faddis) E201
WOMBLE, James  E385
WOOD, ANNE (..), Jane, John, Nancy, Rebecca, Sally D521;
    Alex N. F112; Anne (McKee) E32; Demsey D475;
    Betty, JAMES, Nancy, Polly, Sally, Willie  D564;
    Dempsey, Eliz, Henry, James, JOSEPH, Jos Jr, Mary E291
    Nancy, Polly, Solomon, Sukey  E291; Elizabeth D228;
    ELIHU, Elihu Jr, Elinor (..), Hugh, Joseph, Lucy  D208
    Margaret, Mary, Rebecka, William D208;
    Eliz (..), Hardy, Isaac, Kezzia; Levin; Mary, SABUT D220
    Sabut Jr D220; Eliz (..), Henry, James, SOLOMON  E231;
    HARDY  F285; Levin  F59; Nancy (Glenn) D475
WOODS, Alex M. F187; Adeline, ELI, Eliz Brown, Ellen F42
    John Washington, Lucy Ann, Margaret R. (..), F42        E226;
    Margaret Ray F42; Alfred, Eli, John, Lydia (Montgomery)
    Anne, Asenath, Elenor (..), John S, WILLIAM  E236;
    Ann (..), David, JOHN, John Jr, Samuel, Thomas, Wm. D393;
    David D607; ELENOR F157; Eli, Elinor, Hugh (2), Jos. D556
    Lucy, Margaret, WILLIAM  D556; Harris D23; Hugh E380;
    Eli, Eliz, John, Joseph, MARY (..), Mary Ann, Mary Mecca,
    Peggy, Sarah, Susannah (2), Timothy  E26; James D23,221;
    Jemima (Forrester) D23; Joseph D23,456; Jos. A. D546;
    Levin  D432,E59; Levina, Matilda F187;  MARY D514;

WOODS, Jane E245; John F22, his will F334; Lydia (Montgomery) F22
  Margaret (Faucett(, Mathew, Nathan D308; Wm. H. E212;
  Polly (Holloway) E555; Samuel E149,306; William  D434,483;
WOODY, Charity, Ellenor, Hannah, Hugh, JAMES, Jane, John E28
  Mary (..), Mary, Rebecca, Ruth, Sarah, Sam, Susanna  E28;
  James, John, Samuel, Sarah (Thompson), Joshua  D335;
  JOSEPH, "all my children", Joshua, Robert, Sarah (..) D425;
  Joseph Jr D425; Thomas  E311
WORLD or WOREL ?, Elder William, his children  F52
WORKMAN, John E134,F273; Wm. E134
WORSHAM, Edward D22
WORTHAM, Alfred, Charles, Eliz, EDWARD, James, John, D538
  Mary (..), Nancy, Sarah, Samuel, William  D538; Edward F76;
  Charles, Mary (Faucett)  D309; Elizabeth, MARY  E174
WRIGHTSEL, Adam  E338; Michael  E151
WYATE, James, John  E385
WYATT, ELIZABETH (..), Frederick, Joshua  D464

YANCEY, Chas R. E88,280; Joel C. E99,396
YARBOROUGH, David D468,E24,195,388; Henry E192;
  Samuel  E96,159,302,324
YATES, Mary, Wm. E86
YEARGIN, Bartlett D375; Bartlett, Harriet, SARAH E76;
  Bartlett, BENJAMIN, Charlotte, Harriett, Mark M. D338;
  Jarratt D216; MARK M. D375; Sarah (..) D338;
  Susannah (Moore) F142
YOUNG,  Charlotte H. (Yeargin) D338; John D244,339,387;
  JOHN, Nancy (..), children E23; Mrs. Mary  E300; Nancy D468
YOUNGER, Edith (Horn) D368;
  HENRY, John, Richard,Robert A, Sarah (..)  D376;
  John, John E, Richard, Robert, SARAH (..)  E371;
  Joseph, Susanna (Fitch)  E365; Robert A. E143,164,191

---

MARRIAGES mentioned in these wills which do not appear in the
collected marriage bonds of Orange County. Indexed by brides.

| bride | groom | date of will | testator |
|---|---|---|---|
| Albright, Philipenia | ....... Swing | Oct 1830 | J. Albright |
| Alston, Christian | Solomon Jones | Jun 1818 | Lemuel Alston |
| "      , Mary | Robett Scott | "    " | D542 |
| Boswell, Susannah | .... Leachman | Jan 1826 | Edward Boswell |
| Carmichael, Jane | .... Iseley | Feb 1816 | Thos Carmichael |
| "        , Nancy | .... Smith | "    " | D559 |
| Cozart, Charlotte | Jas Tomison | Feb 1805 | James Cozart |
| Dale, Margaret | .... Haddock | Oct 1815 | Isaac Dale |
| Deley, Catherine | James Gibens | Aug 1794 | Wm. Deley |
| "     , Mary | George Reed | "    " | D105 |
| Dickie, Hannah | .... Linch | Jan 1804 | Samuel Dickie |
| "      , Hester | .... Cantrill | "    " | "      " |
| "      , Rachel | .... Burd | "    " | D122 |
| Their sister Susannah Dickie m in Orange Moses Linch. | | | |
| Edwards, Rebecca | Richard Ricketts | Dec 1817 | John Edwards |

MARRIAGES not in the collected bonds.

| bride | groom | date of will, testator |
|---|---|---|
| Edwards, Mary | .... Odean | Apr 1796 John Edwards |
| " , Susannah | .... Campbell | " " D56 |
| Eulice, Barbara | .... Tracy | Jul 1812 Philip Eulice |
| Foust, Elizabeth | .... Clap | Sep 1808 Peter Foust |
| Friddle, Caty | Averot Garrott | Nov 1800 Geo. Friddle |
| " , Peggy | Michael Lue | " " D158 |
| Forrester, Jemima | Harris Woods | Nov 1800 B. Forrester |
| Gant, Hannah | .... Boist | Dec 1800 John Gant |
| " ; Keziah | .... Rippy | " " " " |
| " , Mary | .... Riggins | " " D30 |
| Harvey, Edith | .... Madden | Jul 1800 Isaac Harvey |
| Hastings, Marg't | .... Adams | May 1812 H'y Hastings |
| Horn, Edith | .... Younger | pr. 1813 Wm. Horn |
| Lindley, Hannah | .... Braxton | Sep 1824 Jon Lindley |
| " , Quinton Esther | ..... Clark | " " E167 |
| McAdams, Eliz | .... Blair | Oct 1808 Reb McAdams |
| McPherson, Ann | John Crutchfield | Mar 1813 William |
| " , Iddith | Mark Morgan | " " McPherson |
| " , Margaret | Jesse Pierce | " " D517 |
| " , Mary | Thomas Braxton | " " " |
| " , " | Edward Stewart | " " " |
| " ; Phebe | Aaron Lindley | " " " |
| " , Ruth | ..... Johnson | " " " |
| Newlin, Hannah | .... Holloday | Aug 1805 John Newlin |
| " , Mary | ..... Hadley | " " D162 |
| Owens, Elizabeth | ..... Lingo | Nov 1809 Only Owens |
| Primrose, Eliz. | ..... Garrard | Oct 1835 Temperance |
| " ; Frances | ..... Culberhouse | " " Primrose |
| " , Rachel | America Wheeler | " " E368 |

Their sister Ann Primrose m in Orange 1824 Sam Chisenhall.

| Rhodes; Mary | ..... Pattishall | Sep 1802 Wm. Rhodes |
|---|---|---|
| " , Eliz. | ..... Gresham | " " D293 |
| " ; Frances | ..... Barbee | " " " |
| " , Hannah | ..... Whatley | " " " |
| " , Nancy | ..... Gresham | " " " |

Marriages of 3 other Rhodes daughters are recorded in Orange.

| Robertson, Elenor | ..... Johnson | Jun 1800 John |
|---|---|---|
| " , Margaret | ..... Wilson | " " Robertson |
| " , Rebekka | ..... Guin | " " D46 |
| Rountree, Rachel | .... Jacobs | Sep 1803 T. Rountree |
| Shaddy, Caty | Geo A. Fogleman | Feb 1809 John Shaddy |
| " ; Molly | John Coble | " " D331 |
| " , Rachel | George Fogleman | " " " |
| " , ...... | Henry Steel | " " " |
| Sheldon, Mary | ..... Collier ? | Apr 1802 Thos Shelton |
| Stovall, ..... | David Chandler | Dec 1802 Bart. Stovall |
| Trice, Sally | Joseph Barbee | Aug 1801 Thomas Trice |
| Troxler, Philipena | /David Coble | Mar 1814 Barney Troxler |
| Ward, Asther | ..... Wells | Mar 1817 Susanna Ward |
| " , Druscilla | .... Free ? Tree ? | " " " " |
| " , Sarah | ..... Clark | " " E18 |
| " , Susannah | ..... Pike | " " " |
| Wells, Margrate | ..... Gifford | Feb 1804 Joseph Wells |
| " , Mary | ..... Jamison | " " " |
| " , Rachel | ..... Underwood | " " D 140 |
| Wilson, Rachel | ..... Dunn | Apr 1802 Chas. Wilson |
| Woods, Susanna | James Faucett | Oct 1820 Mary Woods |

*************************************************************

ABSTRACTS OF ORANGE COUNTY, NORTH CAROLINA, WILLS  1800-1850

Page      Testator (All additions are indexed, unless so stated.)

17 D105 WM DELEY - son: "John Deley the 200 acres whereon he lives
(Samuel Ector to make the deed) Not indexed

27 D169 JOHN ANDERSON - add- daughter: Lettice

31 D192 WM PICKETT-add-"Daughter Nancy Bryant and her husband
Williamson Bryant"     not indexed

32 D192 3rd line should read "Joseph Pickett & Jesse Pickett ..."

33 D203 Testator is LINN, not Liner.

43 D277 WILSON CHILD - William Bruce should be Wilson Bruce.

49 D334 WM CRABTREE- add- daughter Nancy     not indexed

50 D336 JOHN WALKER-add- "son William Walker 450 acres ..."etc..

   D339 HENRY HASTINGS - "grandson Thomas Crabtree" is son-in-law.

61 D418 SARAH HARDEN - dau: Jean Whitsett, 200 acres in Caswell.

64 D434 WM MONTGOMERY - add- son: William

65 D JOHN BOYLE - strike married from "My three married daus ...
The married daughters are in the line below this.

73 D491 LUDWICK ALBRIGHT - add- married daughters "Mary Fogleman,
deceased wife of John, Elizabeth Albright
wife of John"
75 D500 Testator is NANCY MASON , not Moore.

30 D522 The Testator is EVE (x) SMITH.

32 D538 Testator is EDWARD WORTHAM, not Wilson.

‹5 D550 ALEX. RUSSELL - add- daughter: Polly
son: William "my land warrant for 800 acres now in the
hands of I.G.McLemore of Tennessee."

86 D555 ISAAC DALE - wife's name is Deborah.

103 E26 MARY WOODS - add- grandson: Joseph Woods

107 E42 ISAAC HOLT - Thomas Rowan's wife is Eliza M, not Emily.

108 E49 WM ANDREW, SR - add- "grandchildren Milly, William & Dolly
Cate, 5 shillings each."

   E51 WILLIS MONK - add - Witnesses: Andrew Hailey, James Nutt.

109 E55 JOHN HOLT - wife's name is Nelly, not Molly.

Corrections to ORANGE COUNTY, N.C. WILLS 1800-1850    Page 2

Page    Testator.All corrections are indexed unless so stated.

110 E59 Testator is SAMUEL PIKE, not Pyle.

112 E67 JOHN LATTA - Executors are Thomas & James Latta, not John.

    E71 HENRY THOMPSON - Witness is J.H.Bland, not Hand.

118 E101 GEORGE TROXLER - add - wife: Peggy Troxler. Not indexed.

    E103 MARY CRAIG - grandchildren are "William, Peggy, Polly &
              Patsy, children of ..." Patsy not indexed.

124 E137 ROBERT FAUCETT - add - "friend Duncan Cameron"

125 E143 BENJAMIN RONEY - add- son: Benjamin Roney

129 E162 ISAAC McCADAMS - Exec. is brother in law, not son in law.

    E167 JONATHAN LINDLEY-add- "To sister Deborah Newlin, $100."

135 E207 JOSHUA HORNE, SR-add- sons: Alford, William, 5 shillings
                        daughter is Vicey

136 E213 LETTICE McCULLEY - Executor is "friend Hardy Hurdle".

148 E277 JOSEPH SHAW - add - grandson: Joseph B.S.Hargis.
    E280 HENSON COULTER, SR - add - son: Henson Coulter.

153 E303 WM BREWER - add - daughter: Sally Weaver

165 E375 ROBERT TINNEN - add - "My four daughters , Margaret,
                        Jennet, Elenor and Mary."

171 E407 RACHEL STRAYHORN - add - son: James Strayhorn

174 E420 ROBERT KING - "To heirs of my daughter Elizabeth Foster."

178 F1  JOHN SHAW - add - granddaughter: Eliza Walker

189 F76  JOSEPH ARMSTRONG - add -    Witness: Enos Ross.

208 F229 BARNEY CLAPP - add - son Christian,"deceased son John".

214 F273 NANCY CRUTCHFIELD - add - son: Benjamin Crutchfield.

Also add to the INDEX, HILLYARD, John, Wm. E39

www.ingramcontent.com/pod-product-compliance
Lightning Source LLC
Chambersburg PA
CBHW060129280326
41932CB00012B/1462